Microsoft Official Academic Course
MICROSOFT ACCESS 2013

WILEY

Editor	Bryan Gambrel
Publisher	Don Fowley
Director of Sales	Mitchell Beaton
Technical Editor	Joyce Nielsen
Executive Marketing Manager	Chris Ruel
Assistant Marketing Manager	Debbie Martin
Editorial Program Assistant	Allison Winkle
Senior Content Manager	Kevin Holm
Senior Production Editor	Jill Spikereit
Creative Director	Harry Nolan
Cover Designer	Tom Nery
Product Designer	Jennifer Welter
Content Editor	Wendy Ashenberg

This book was set in Garamond by Aptara®, Inc. and printed and bound by Courier/Kendallville. The covers were printed by Courier/Kendallville.

ISBN 978-0-470-13310-1

Printed in the United States of America

10 9 8 7 6 5 4 3 2 1

Foreword from the Publisher

Wiley's publishing vision for the Microsoft Official Academic Course series is to provide students and instructors with the skills and knowledge they need to use Microsoft technology effectively in all aspects of their personal and professional lives. Quality instruction is required to help both educators and students get the most from Microsoft's software tools and to become more productive. Thus our mission is to make our instructional programs trusted educational companions for life.

To accomplish this mission, Wiley and Microsoft have partnered to develop the highest quality educational programs for Information Workers, IT Professionals, and Developers. Materials created by this partnership carry the brand name "Microsoft Official Academic Course," assuring instructors and students alike that the content of these textbooks is fully endorsed by Microsoft, and that they provide the highest quality information and instruction on Microsoft products. The Microsoft Official Academic Course textbooks are "Official" in still one more way—they are the officially sanctioned courseware for Microsoft IT Academy members.

The Microsoft Official Academic Course series focuses on workforce development. These programs are aimed at those students seeking to enter the workforce, change jobs, or embark on new careers as information workers, IT professionals, and developers. Microsoft Official Academic Course programs address their needs by emphasizing authentic workplace scenarios with an abundance of projects, exercises, cases, and assessments.

The Microsoft Official Academic Courses are mapped to Microsoft's extensive research and job-task analysis, the same research and analysis used to create the Microsoft Office Specialist (MOS) exams. The textbooks focus on real skills for real jobs. As students work through the projects and exercises in the textbooks they enhance their level of knowledge and their ability to apply the latest Microsoft technology to everyday tasks. These students also gain resume-building credentials that can assist them in finding a job, keeping their current job, or in furthering their education.

The concept of life-long learning is today an utmost necessity. Job roles, and even whole job categories, are changing so quickly that none of us can stay competitive and productive without continuously updating our skills and capabilities. The Microsoft Official Academic Course offerings, and their focus on Microsoft certification exam preparation, provide a means for people to acquire and effectively update their skills and knowledge. Wiley supports students in this endeavor through the development and distribution of these courses as Microsoft's official academic publisher.

Joe Heider
Senior Vice President, Wiley Global Education

Illustrated Book Tour

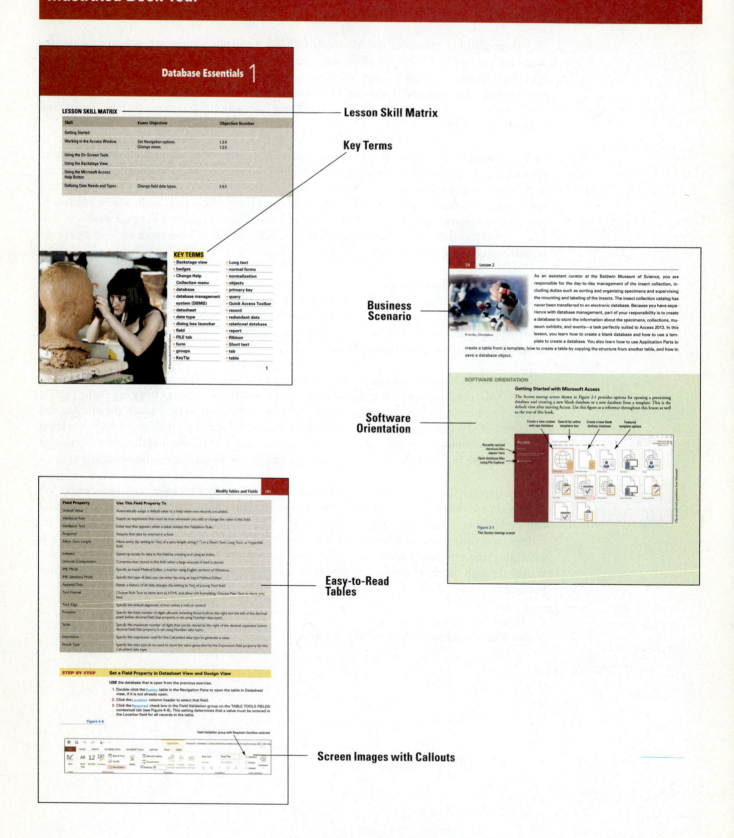

Lesson Skill Matrix

Key Terms

Business Scenario

Software Orientation

Easy-to-Read Tables

Screen Images with Callouts

Illustrated Book Tour

Workplace Ready Scenarios

Bottom Line

Another Way Reader Aids

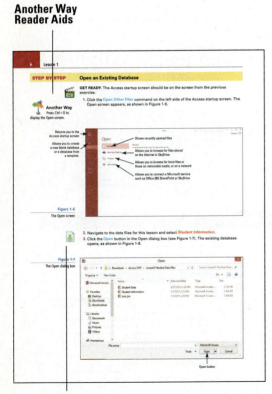

Data Files Icon

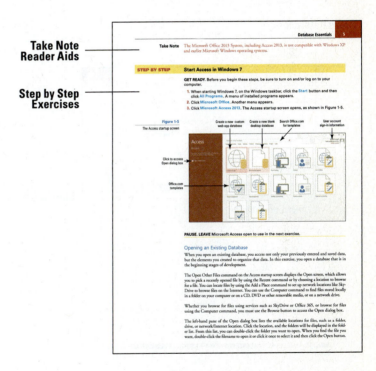

Take Note Reader Aids

Step by Step Exercises

Illustrated Book Tour

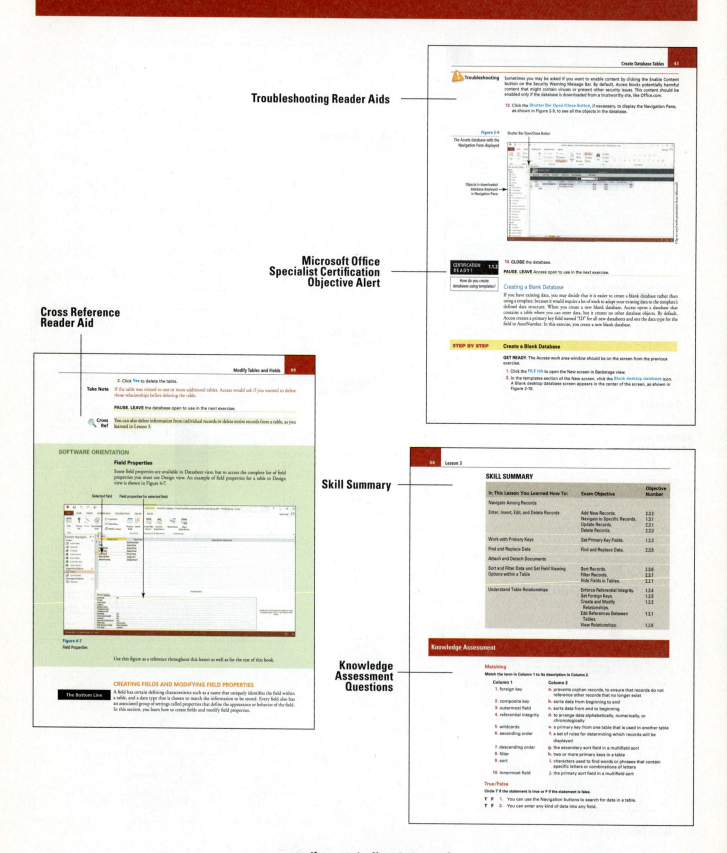

Troubleshooting Reader Aids

Microsoft Office Specialist Certification Objective Alert

Cross Reference Reader Aid

Skill Summary

Knowledge Assessment Questions

www.wiley.com/college/microsoft

or call the MOAC Toll-Free Number: 1+(888) 764-7001 (U.S. & Canada only)

Illustrated Book Tour

Competency Assessment

Proficiency Assessment

Circling Back Exercises

Mastery Assessment Projects

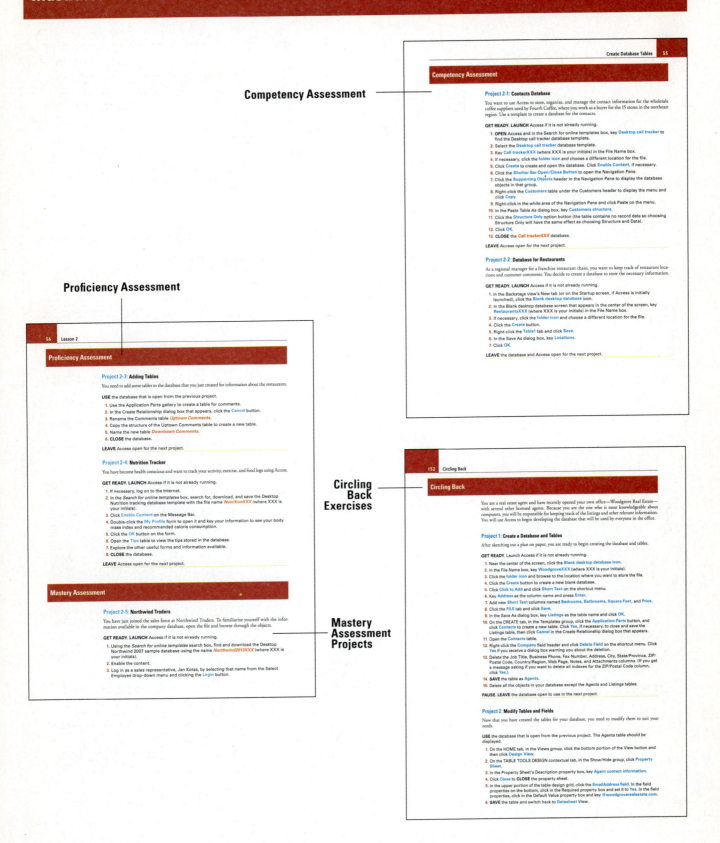

Competency Assessment

Project 2-1: Contacts Database

You want to use Access to store, organize, and manage the contact information for the wholesale coffee suppliers used by Fourth Coffee, where you work as a buyer for the 15 stores in the northeast region. Use a template to create a database for the contacts.

GET READY. LAUNCH Access if it is not already running.

1. OPEN Access and in the Search for online templates box, key Desktop call tracker to find the Desktop call tracker database template.
2. Select the Desktop call tracker database template.
3. Key Call trackerXXX (where XXX is your initials) in the File Name box.
4. If necessary, click the folder icon and choose a different location for the file.
5. Click Create to create and open the database. Click Enable Content, if necessary.
6. Click the Shutter Bar Open/Close Button to open the Navigation Pane.
7. Click the Supporting Objects header in the Navigation Pane to display the database objects in that group.
8. Right-click the Customers table under the Customers header to display the menu and click Copy.
9. Right-click in the white area of the Navigation Pane and click Paste on the menu.
10. In the Paste Table As dialog box, key Customers structure.
11. Click the Structure Only option button (the table contains no record data so choosing Structure Only will have the same effect as choosing Structure and Data).
12. Click OK.
13. CLOSE the Call trackerXXX database.

LEAVE Access open for the next project.

Project 2-2: Database for Restaurants

As a regional manager for a franchise restaurant chain, you want to keep track of restaurant locations and customer comments. You decide to create a database to store the necessary information.

GET READY. LAUNCH Access if it is not already running.

1. In the Backstage view's New tab (or on the Startup screen, if Access is initially launched), click the Blank desktop database icon.
2. In the Blank desktop database screen that appears in the center of the screen, key RestaurantsXXX (where XXX is your initials) in the File Name box.
3. If necessary, click the folder icon and choose a different location for the file.
4. Click the Create button.
5. Right-click the Table1 tab and click Save.
6. In the Save As dialog box, key Locations.
7. Click OK.

LEAVE the database and Access open for the next project.

Proficiency Assessment

Project 2-3: Adding Tables

You need to add some tables to the database that you just created for information about the restaurants.

USE the database that is open from the previous project.

1. Use the Application Parts gallery to create a table for comments.
2. In the Create Relationship dialog box that appears, click the Cancel button.
3. Rename the Comments table Uptown Comments.
4. Copy the structure of the Uptown Comments table to create a new table.
5. Name the new table Downtown Comments.
6. CLOSE the database.

LEAVE Access open for the next project.

Project 2-4: Nutrition Tracker

You have become health conscious and want to track your activity, exercise, and food logs using Access.

GET READY. LAUNCH Access if it is not already running.

1. If necessary, log on to the Internet.
2. In the Search for online templates box, search for, download, and save the Desktop Nutrition tracking database template with the file name NutritionXXX (where XXX is your initials).
3. Click Enable Content on the Message Bar.
4. Double-click the My Profile form to open it and key your information to see your body mass index and recommended calorie consumption.
5. Click the OK button on the form.
6. Open the Tips table to view the tips stored in the database.
7. Explore the other useful forms and information available.
8. CLOSE the database.

LEAVE Access open for the next project.

Mastery Assessment

Project 2-5: Northwind Traders

You have just joined the sales force at Northwind Traders. To familiarize yourself with the information available in the company database, open the file and browse through the objects.

GET READY. LAUNCH Access if it is not already running.

1. Using the Search for online templates search box, find and download the Desktop Northwind 2007 sample database using the name Northwind2013XXX (where XXX is your initials).
2. Enable the content.
3. Log in as a sales representative, Jan Kotas, by selecting that name from the Select Employee drop-down menu and clicking the Login button.

Circling Back

You are a real estate agent and have recently opened your own office—Woodgrove Real Estate—with several other licensed agents. Because you are the one who is most knowledgeable about computers, you will be responsible for keeping track of the listings and other relevant information. You will use Access to begin developing the database that will be used by everyone in the office.

Project 1: Create a Database and Tables

After sketching out a plan on paper, you are ready to begin creating the database and tables.

GET READY. Launch Access if it is not already running.

1. Near the center of the screen, click the Blank desktop database icon.
2. In the File Name box, key WoodgroveXXX (where XXX is your initials).
3. Click the folder icon and browse to the location where you want to store the file.
4. Click the Create button to create a new blank database.
5. Click Click to Add and click Short Text on the shortcut menu.
6. Key Address as the column name and press Enter.
7. Add new Short Text columns named Bedrooms, Bathrooms, Square Feet, and Price.
8. Click the FILE tab and click Save.
9. In the Save As dialog box, key Listings as the table name and click OK.
10. On the CREATE tab, in the Templates group, click the Application Parts button, and click Contacts to create a new table. Click Yes, if necessary, to close and save the Listings table, then click Cancel in the Create Relationship dialog box that appears.
11. Open the Contacts table.
12. Right-click the Company field header and click Delete Field on the shortcut menu. Click Yes if you receive a dialog box warning you about the deletion.
13. Delete the Job Title, Business Phone, Fax Number, Address, City, State/Province, ZIP/Postal Code, Country/Region, Web Page, Notes, and Attachments columns. (If you get a message asking if you want to delete all indexes for the ZIP/Postal Code column, click Yes.)
14. SAVE the table as Agents.
15. Delete all the objects in your database except the Agents and Listings tables.

PAUSE. LEAVE the database open to use in the next project.

Project 2: Modify Tables and Fields

Now that you have created the tables for your database, you need to modify them to suit your needs.

USE the database that is open from the previous project. The Agents table should be displayed.

1. On the HOME tab, in the Views group, click the bottom portion of the View button and then click Design View.
2. On the TABLE TOOLS DESIGN contextual tab, in the Show/Hide group, click Property Sheet.
3. In the Property Sheet's Description property box, key Agent contact information.
4. Click Close to CLOSE the property sheet.
5. In the upper portion of the table design grid, click the EmailAddress field. In the field properties on the bottom, click in the Required property box and set it to Yes. In the field properties, click in the Default Value property box and key @woodgroverealestate.com.
6. SAVE the table and switch back to Datasheet View.

Preface

Welcome to the Microsoft Official Academic Course (MOAC) program for Microsoft Access 2013. MOAC represents the collaboration between Microsoft Learning and John Wiley & Sons, Inc. publishing company. Microsoft and Wiley teamed up to produce a series of textbooks that deliver compelling and innovative teaching solutions to instructors and superior learning experiences for students. Infused and informed by in-depth knowledge from the creators of Microsoft Office and Windows, and crafted by a publisher known worldwide for the pedagogical quality of its products, these textbooks maximize skills transfer in minimum time. Students are challenged to reach their potential by using their new technical skills as highly productive members of the workforce.

Because this knowledgebase comes directly from Microsoft, architect of the Office 2013 system and creator of the Microsoft Office Specialist (MOS) exams (www.microsoft.com/learning/mcp/mcts), you are sure to receive the topical coverage that is most relevant to students' personal and professional success. Microsoft's direct participation not only assures you that MOAC textbook content is accurate and current; it also means that students will receive the best instruction possible to enable their success on certification exams and in the workplace.

THE MICROSOFT OFFICIAL ACADEMIC COURSE PROGRAM

The Microsoft Official Academic Course series is a complete program for instructors and institutions to prepare and deliver great courses on Microsoft software technologies. With MOAC, we recognize that, because of the rapid pace of change in the technology and curriculum developed by Microsoft, there is an ongoing set of needs beyond classroom instruction tools for an instructor to be ready to teach the course. The MOAC program endeavors to provide solutions for all these needs in a systematic manner in order to ensure a successful and rewarding course experience for both instructor and student—technical and curriculum training for instructor readiness with new software releases; the software itself for student use at home for building hands-on skills, assessment, and validation of skill development; and a great set of tools for delivering instruction in the classroom and lab. All are important to the smooth delivery of an interesting course on Microsoft software, and all are provided with the MOAC program. We think about the model below as a gauge for ensuring that we completely support you in your goal of teaching a great course. As you evaluate your instructional materials options, you may wish to use the model for comparison purposes with available products.

PEDAGOGICAL FEATURES

The MOAC courseware for *Microsoft Access 2013* are designed to cover all the learning objectives for that MOS exam, which is referred to as its "objective domain." The Microsoft Office Specialist (MOS) exam objectives are highlighted throughout the textbooks. Many pedagogical features have been developed specifically for *Microsoft Official Academic Course* programs. Unique features of our task-based approach include a Lesson Skills Matrix that correlates skills taught in each lesson to the MOS objectives; Certification, and three levels of increasingly rigorous lesson-ending activities: Competency, Proficiency, and Mastery Assessment.

Presenting the extensive procedural information and technical concepts woven throughout the textbook raises challenges for the student and instructor alike. The Illustrated Book Tour that follows provides a guide to the rich features contributing to *Microsoft Official Academic Course* program's pedagogical plan. Following is a list of key features in each lesson designed to prepare students for success on the certification exams and in the workplace:

- Each lesson begins with a **Lesson Skill Matrix**. More than a standard list of learning objectives, the skill matrix correlates each software skill covered in the lesson to the specific MOS exam objective domain.

- Each lesson features a real-world **Business Case** scenario that places the software skills and knowledge to be acquired in a real-world setting.

- Every lesson opens with a **Software Orientation**. This feature provides an overview of the software features students will be working with in the lesson. The orientation will detail the general properties of the software or specific features, such as a ribbon or dialog box; and it includes a large, labeled screen image.

- Concise and frequent **Step-by-Step** instructions teach students new features and provide an opportunity for hands-on practice. Numbered steps give detailed, step-by-step instructions to help students learn software skills. The steps also show results and screen images to match what students should see on their computer screens.

- **Illustrations**: Screen images provide visual feedback as students work through the exercises. The images reinforce key concepts, provide visual clues about the steps, and allow students to check their progress.

- **Key Terms:** Important technical vocabulary is listed at the beginning of the lesson. When these terms are used later in the lesson, they appear in bold italic type with yellow highlighter and are defined. The Glossary contains all of the key terms and their definitions.

- Engaging point-of-use **Reader aids**, located throughout the lessons, tell students why this topic is relevant (*The Bottom Line*), provide students with helpful hints (*Take Note*), or show alternate ways to accomplish tasks (*Another Way*), or point out things to watch out for or avoid (*Troubleshooting*). Reader aids also provide additional relevant or background information that adds value to the lesson.

- **Certification Ready?** features throughout the text signal students where a specific certification objective is covered. They provide students with a chance to check their understanding of that particular MOS exam objective and, if necessary, review the section of the lesson where it is covered. MOAC provides complete preparation for MOS certification.

- **Workplace Ready.** These new features preview how the Microsoft Office 2013 system applications are used in real-world situations.

- Each lesson ends with a **Skill Summary** recapping the topics and MOS exam skills covered in the lesson.

- **Knowledge Assessment:** Provides a total of 20 questions from a mix of True/False, Fill-in-the-Blank, Matching or Multiple Choice testing students on concepts learned in the lesson.

- **Competency, Proficiency, and Mastery Assessment:** provide three progressively more challenging lesson-ending activities.

- **Circling Back:** These integrated projects provide students with an opportunity to renew and practice skills learned in previous lessons.

- **Online files:** The student companion website contains the data files needed for each lesson. These files are indicated by the file download icon in the margin of the textbook.

Conventions and Features Used in This Book

This book uses particular fonts, symbols, and heading conventions to highlight important information or to call your attention to special steps. For more information about the features in each lesson, refer to the Illustrated Book Tour section.

Convention	Meaning
The Bottom Line	This feature provides a brief summary of the material to be covered in the section that follows.
CLOSE	Words in all capital letters indicate instructions for opening, saving, or closing files or programs. They also point out items you should check or actions you should take.
CERTIFICATION READY?	This feature signals the point in the text where a specific certification objective is covered. It provides you with a chance to check your understanding of that particular MOS objective and, if necessary, review the section of the lesson where it is covered.
Take Note	Reader aids appear in shaded boxes found in your text. Take Note provides helpful hints related to particular tasks or topics.
Another Way	Another Way provides an alternative procedure for accomplishing a particular task.
Cross Ref	These notes provide pointers to information discussed elsewhere in the textbook or describe interesting features that are not directly addressed in the current topic or exercise.
ALT + Tab	A plus sign (+) between two key names means that you must press both keys at the same time. Keys that you are instructed to press in an exercise will appear in the font shown here.
A **shared printer** can be used by many individuals on a network.	Key terms appear in bold italic.
Key My Name is	Any text you are asked to key appears in color.
Click OK	Any button on the screen you are supposed to click on or select will also appear in color.
	The names of data files will appear in bold, italic and red for easy identification. These data files are available for download from the Student Companion Site (www.Wiley.com/college/Microsoft).
	Step-by-step tutorial videos are available for many of the activities throughout this course. For information on how to access these videos, see the Student Companion Site (www.Wiley.com/college/Microsoft).
OPEN *BudgetWorksheet1*	The names of data files will appear in bold, italic and red for easy identification.

Instructor Support Program

The *Microsoft Official Academic Course* programs are accompanied by a rich array of resources that incorporate the extensive textbook visuals to form a pedagogically cohesive package. These resources provide all the materials instructors need to deploy and deliver their courses. Resources available online for download include:

- The **Instructor's Guide** contains Solutions to all the textbook exercises as well as chapter summaries and lecture notes. The Instructor's Guide and Syllabi for various term lengths are available from the Instructor's Book Companion site (www.wiley.com/college/microsoft).

- The **Solution Files** for all the projects in the book are available online from our Instructor's Book Companion site (www.wiley.com/college/microsoft).

- The **Test Bank** contains hundreds of questions organized by lesson in multiple-choice, true-false, short answer, and essay formats and is available to download from the Instructor's Book Companion site (www.wiley.com/college/microsoft). A complete answer key is provided.

    This title's test bank is available for use in Respondus' easy-to-use software. You can download the test bank for free using your Respondus, Respondus LE, or StudyMate Author software.

    Respondus is a powerful tool for creating and managing exams that can be printed to paper or published directly to Blackboard, WebCT, Desire2Learn, eCollege, ANGEL and other eLearning systems.

- **Test Bank Projects.** Two projects for each lesson are provided on the Instructor's Book Companion Site as well as solution files suitable for grading with OfficeGrader. These projects cover topics from within one specific lesson.

- **Comprehensive Projects:** Two comprehensive projects are provided on the Instructor's Book Companion Site for each Circling Back These projects cover topics from all lessons in the book up to that point. Solution files suitable for grading with OfficeGrader are also provided.

- **Capstone Projects:** Two capstone projects are provided with the final Circling Back on the Instructor's Book Companion Site. These projects are suitable for a final exam or final project for the course. These projects cover a range of topics from throughout the entire book. Solution files suitable for grading with OfficeGrader are also provided.

- **PowerPoint Presentations and Images**. A complete set of PowerPoint presentations is available on the Instructor's Book Companion site (www.wiley.com/college/microsoft) to enhance classroom presentations. Tailored to the text's topical coverage and Skills Matrix, these presentations are designed to convey key Microsoft .NET Framework concepts addressed in the text.

    All figures from the text are on the Instructor's Book Companion site (www.wiley.com/college/microsoft). You can incorporate them into your PowerPoint presentations, or create your own overhead transparencies and handouts.

    By using these visuals in class discussions, you can help focus students' attention on key elements of Windows Server and help them understand how to use it effectively in the workplace.

- **Office Grader** automated grading system allows you to easily grade student data files in Word, Excel, PowerPoint or Access format, against solution files. Save tens or hundreds of hours each semester with automated grading. More information on OfficeGrader is available from the Instructor's Book Companion site (www.wiley.com/college/microsoft).

- The **Student Data Files** are available online on both the Instructor's Book Companion Site and for students on the Student Book Companion Site.

- Wiley **Faculty Network:** When it comes to improving the classroom experience, there is no better source of ideas and inspiration than your fellow colleagues. The Wiley Faculty Network connects teachers with technology, facilitates the exchange of best practices, and helps to enhance instructional efficiency and effectiveness. Faculty Network activities include technology training and tutorials, virtual seminars, peer-to-peer exchanges of experiences and ideas, personal consulting, and sharing of resources. For details visit www.WhereFacultyConnect.com.

IMPORTANT WEB ADDRESSES AND PHONE NUMBERS

To locate the Wiley Higher Education Rep in your area, go to the following Web address and click on the *"Contact Us"* link at the top of the page.

www.wiley.com/college

Or Call the MOAC Toll Free Number: 1 + (888) 764-7001 (U.S. & Canada only).

To learn more about becoming a Microsoft Certified Professional and exam availability, visit **www.microsoft.com/learning/mcp.**

DREAMSPARK PREMIUM

Free 3-Year Membership available to Qualified Adopters

DreamSpark Premium is designed to provide the easiest and most inexpensive way for schools to make the latest Microsoft developer tools, products, and technologies available in labs, classrooms, and on student PCs. Dream-Spark Premium is an annual membership program for departments teaching Science, Technology, Engineering, and Mathematics (STEM) courses. The membership provides a complete solution to keep academic labs, faculty, and students on the leading edge of technology.

Software available through the DreamSpark Premium program is provided at no charge to adopting departments through the Wiley and Microsoft publishing partnership.

Contact your Wiley rep for details.

Visit Microsoft.com for more information.

BOOK COMPANION WEBSITE (WWW.WILEY.COM/COLLEGE/MICROSOFT)

The students' book companion site for the MOAC series includes any resources, exercise files, and web links that will be used in conjunction with this course.

WILEY E-TEXT: POWERED BY VITALSOURCE

When you choose a Wiley E-Text you not only save money; you benefit from being able to access course materials and content anytime, anywhere through a user experience that makes learning rewarding.

With the Wiley E-Text you will be able to easily:
- Search
- Take notes
- Highlight key materials
- Have all your work in one place for more efficient studying

In addition, the Wiley E-Text is fully portable. Students can access it online and download to their computer for off line access and access read and study on their device of preference—computer, tablet, or smartphone.

WHY MOS CERTIFICATION?

Microsoft Office Specialist (MOS) 2013 is a valuable credential that recognizes the desktop computing skills needed to use the full features and functionality of the Microsoft Office 2013 suite.

In the worldwide job market, Microsoft Office Specialist is the primary tool companies use to validate the proficiency of their employees in the latest productivity tools and technology, helping them select job candidates based on globally recognized standards for verifying skills. The results of an independent research study show that businesses with certified employees are more productive compared to non-certified employees and that certified employees bring immediate value to their jobs.

In academia, as in the business world, institutions upgrading to Office 2013 may seek ways to protect and maximize their technology investment. By offering certification, they validate that decision—because powerful Office 2013 applications such as Word, Excel and PowerPoint can be effectively used to demonstrate increases in academic preparedness and workforce readiness.

Individuals seek certification to increase their own personal sense of accomplishment and to create advancement opportunities by establishing a leadership position in their school or department, thereby differentiating their skill sets in a competitive college admissions and job market.

PREPARING TO TAKE THE MICROSOFT OFFICE SPECIALIST (MOS) EXAM

The Microsoft Office Specialist credential has been upgraded to validate skills with the Microsoft Office 2013 system. The MOS certifications target information workers and cover the most popular business applications such as Word 2013, Excel 2013, PowerPoint 2013, Outlook 2013 and Access 2013.

By becoming certified, you demonstrate to employers that you have achieved a predictable level of skill in the use of a particular Office application. Employers often require certification either as a condition of employment or as a condition of advancement within the company or other organization. The certification examinations are sponsored by Microsoft but administered through exam delivery partners like Certiport.

To learn more about becoming a Microsoft Office Specialist and exam availability, visit http://www.microsoft.com/learning/en/us/mos-certification.aspx.

Preparing to Take an Exam

Unless you are a very experienced user, you will need to use a test preparation course to prepare to complete the test correctly and within the time allowed. The *Microsoft Official Academic Course* series is designed to prepare you with a strong knowledge of all exam topics, and with some additional review and practice on your own. You should feel confident in your ability to pass the appropriate exam.

After you decide which exam to take, review the list of objectives for the exam. This list can be found in the MOS Objectives Appendix at the back of this book. You can also easily identify tasks that are included in the objective list by locating the Lesson Skill Matrix at the start of each lesson and the Certification Ready sidebars in the margin of the lessons in this book.

To take the MOS test, visit http://www.microsoft.com/learning/en/us/mos-certification.aspx to locate your nearest testing center. Then call the testing center directly to schedule your test. The amount of advance notice you should provide will vary for different testing centers, and it typically depends on the number of computers available at the testing center, the number of other testers who have already been scheduled for the day on which you want to take the test, and the number of times per week that the testing center offers MOS testing. In general, you should call to schedule your test at least two weeks prior to the date on which you want to take the test.

When you arrive at the testing center, you might be asked for proof of identity. A driver's license or passport is an acceptable form of identification. If you do not have either of these items of documentation, call your testing center and ask what alternative forms of identification will be accepted. If you are retaking a test, bring your MOS identification number, which will have been given to you when you previously took the test. If you have not prepaid or if your organization has not already arranged to make payment for you, you will need to pay the test-taking fee when you arrive.

Test Format

MOS exams are Exams are primarily performance-based and conducted in a "live," or simulated, environment. Exam candidates taking exams for MOS 2007 or 2010 are asked to perform a series of tasks to clearly demonstrate their skills. For example, a Word exam might ask a user to balance newspaper column lengths or keep text together in columns. The new MOS 2013 exam format presents a short project the candidate must complete, using the specifications provided. This creates a real-world testing experience for candidates. All MOS exams must be completed in 90 minutes or less.

Student Data Files

All of the practice files that you will use as you perform the exercises in the book are available for download on our student companion site. By using the practice files, you will not waste time creating the samples used in the lessons, and you can concentrate on learning how to use Microsoft Office 2013. With the files and the step-by-step instructions in the lessons, you will learn by doing, which is an easy and effective way to acquire and remember new skills.

COPYING THE PRACTICE FILES

Your instructor might already have copied the practice files before you arrive in class. However, your instructor might ask you to copy the practice files on your own at the start of class. Also, if you want to work through any of the exercises in this book on your own at home or at your place of business after class, you may want to copy the practice files.

1. **OPEN** Internet Explorer.
2. In Internet Explorer, go to the student companion site: www.wiley.com
3. Search for your book title in the upper right hand corner
4. On the Search Results page, locate your book and click on the Visit the Companion Sites link.
5. Select Student Companion Site from the pop-up box.
6. From the menu, select the arrow next to Browse By Resource and select Student Data Files from the menu.
7. A new screen will appear.
8. On the Student Data Files page, you can select to download files for just one lesson or for all lessons. Click on the file of your choice.
9. On the File Download dialog box, select Save As to save the data files to your external drive (often called a ZIP drive or a USB drive or a thumb drive) or a local drive.
10. In the Save As dialog box, select a local drive in the left-hand panel that you'd like to save your files to; again, this should be an external drive or a local drive. Remember the drive name that you saved it to.

Acknowledgments

We would like to thank the many instructors and reviewers who pored over the Microsoft Official Academic Course series design, outlines and manuscript, providing invaluable feedback in the service of quality instructional materials.

Erik Amerikaner, *Oak Park Unified*

Connie Aragon, *Seattle Central Community College*

Sue Bajt, *Harper College*

Gregory Ballinger, *Miami-Dade College*

Catherine Bradfield, *DeVry University*

DeAnnia Clements, *Wiregrass Georgia Technical College*

Mary Corcoran, *Bellevue College*

Andrea Cluff, *Freemont High School*

Caroline de Gruchy, *Conestoga College*

Janis DeHaven, *Central Community College*

Rob Durrance, *East Lee County High School*

Janet Flusche, *Frenship High School*

Greg Gardiner, *SIAST*

Debi Griggs, *Bellevue College*

Phil Hanney, *Orem Junior High School*

Portia Hatfield, *Tennessee Technology Center-Jacksboro*

Dee Hobson, *Richland College*

Terri Holly, *Indian River State College*

Kim Hopkins, *Weatherford College*

Sandra Jolley, *Tarrant County College*

Keith Hoell, *Briarcliffe College*

Joe LaMontagne, *Davenport University*

Tanya MacNeil, *American InterContinental University*

Donna Madsen, *Kirkwood Community College*

Lynn Mancini, *Delaware Technical Community College*

Edward Martin, *Kingsborough Community College-City University of New York*

Lisa Mears, *Palm Beach State College*

Denise Merrell, *Jefferson Community and Technical College*

Diane Mickey, *Northern Virginia Community College*

Robert Mike, *Alaska Career College*

Cynthia Miller, *Harper College*

Sandra Miller, *Wenatchee Valley College*

Mustafa Muflehi, *The Sheffield College*

Aditi Mukherjee, *University of Florida—Gainesville*

Linda Nutter, *Peninsula College*

Diana Pack, *Big Sandy Community & Technical College*

Bettye Parham, *Daytona State College*

Tatyana Pashnyak, *Bainbridge State College*

Kari Phillips, *Davis Applied Technical College*

www.wiley.com/college/microsoft

or call the MOAC Toll-Free Number: 1+(888) 764-7001 (U.S. & Canada only)

Michelle Poertner, *Northwestern Michigan College*
Barbara Purvis, *Centura College*
Dave Rotherham, *Sheffield Hallam University*
Theresa Savarese, *San Diego City College*
Janet Sebesy, *Cuyahoga Community College-Western*
Lourdes Sevilla, *Southwestern College*
Elizabeth Snow, *Southwest Florida College*
Denise Spence, *Dunbar High School*
Amy Stolte, *Lincoln Land Community College*
Linda Silva, *El Paso Community College*
Dorothy Weiner, *Manchester Community College*

We would also like to thank the team at Microsoft Learning Xperiences (LeX), including Alison Cunard, Tim Sneath, Zubair Murtaza, Keith Loeber, Rob Linsky, Anne Hamilton, Wendy Johnson, Julia Stasio, and Josh Barnhill for their encouragement and support in making the Microsoft Official Academic Course programs the finest academic materials for mastering the newest Microsoft technologies for both students and instructors. Finally we would like to thank Jeff Riley and his team at Box Twelve Communications, Laura Town and her team at WilliamsTown Communications, Debbie Collins and Sandy DuBose for their editorial and technical assistance.

We would like to thank the following instructors for their contributions to particular titles in the series as well:

ACCESS 2013

Catherine Bradfield, *DeVry University*
Mary Corcoran, *Bellevue College*
Cynthia Miller, *Harper College*
Aditi Mukherjee, *University of Florida—Gainesville*
Elizabeth Snow, *Southwest Florida College*

EXCEL 2013

Catherine Bradfield, *DeVry University*
DeAnnia Clements, *Wiregrass Georgia Technical College*
Dee Hobson, *Richland College*
Sandra Jolley, *Tarrant County College*
Joe Lamontagne, *Davenport University*
Edward Martin, *Kingsborough Community College-City University of New York*
Aditi Mukherjee, *University of Florida—Gainesville*
Linda Nutter, *Peninsula College*
Dave Rotherham, *Sheffield Hallam University*

POWERPOINT 2013

Mary Corcoran, *Bellevue College*
Rob Durrance, *East Lee County High School*
Phil Hanney, *Orem Junior High School*
Terri Holly, *Indian River State College*

Kim Hopkins, *Weatherford College*

Tatyana Pashnyak, *Bainbridge State College*

Michelle Poertner, *Northwestern Michigan College*

Theresa Savarese, *San Diego City College*

WORD 2013

Erik Amerikaner, *Oak Park Unified*

Sue Bajt, *Harper College*

Gregory Ballinger, *Miami-Dade College*

Andrea Cluff, *Freemont High School*

Caroline de Gruchy, *Conestoga College*

Donna Madsen, *Kirkwood Community College*

Lynn Mancini, *Delaware Technical Community College*

Denise Merrell, *Jefferson Community and Technical College*

Diane Mickey, *Northern Virginia Community College*

Robert Mike, *Alaska Career College*

Bettye Parham, *Daytona State College*

Barbara Purvis, *Centura College*

Janet Sebesy, *Cuyahoga Community College-Western*

Dorothy Weiner, *Manchester Community College*

Author Credits

KEITH HOELL

Keith Hoell is a professor and Director of Online Education at Briarcliffe College in Long Island, New York. An experienced technology and academic professional, he has served as an instructor, dean, and technology consultant for several schools. He has a broad range of experience in various areas of technology, including database management, network administration, web design, and programming. He also served on the Microsoft Official Academic Curriculum (MOAC) Advisory Board, and continues to contribute to the development of other MOAC textbooks. Besides his interest in technology, he is an avid runner, having run in several marathons including New York and Boston.

Brief Contents

LESSON 1: DATABASE ESSENTIALS   1

LESSON 2: CREATE DATABASE TABLES   37

LESSON 3: WORK WITH TABLES AND DATABASE RECORDS   58

LESSON 4: MODIFY TABLES AND FIELDS   93

LESSON 5: CREATE FORMS   125

CIRCLING BACK   152

LESSON 6: CREATE REPORTS   157

LESSON 7: CREATE AND MODIFY QUERIES   179

LESSON 8: USE CONTROLS IN REPORTS AND FORMS   211

LESSON 9: ADVANCED TABLES   263

LESSON 10: ADVANCED FORMS   283

CIRCLING BACK   307

LESSON 11: ADVANCED REPORTS   312

LESSON 12: ADVANCED QUERIES   339

LESSON 13: DISPLAY AND SHARE DATA   389

LESSON 14: IMPORT AND EXPORT DATA   415

LESSON 15: DATABASE TOOLS   450

CIRCLING BACK   480

APPENDIX   485

GLOSSARY   490

INDEX   493

Contents

Lesson 1: Database Essentials

LESSON SKILL MATRIX 1
Key Terms **1**
Getting Started **3**
   Starting Access **3**
   Opening an Existing Database **5**
Working in the Access Window **8**
   Using the Navigation Pane **9**
   Using Object Tabs **14**
   Changing Views **16**
Using the On-Screen Tools **18**
   Using the Ribbon **18**
   Using the Quick Access Toolbar **20**
   Using KeyTips **21**
Using the Backstage View **23**
   Using the Backstage View **23**
Using the Microsoft Access Help Button **24**
   Using the Help Button and Change Help Collection Menu **24**
Defining Data Needs and Types **27**
   Review Database Fields **27**
   Defining and Modifying Data Types for Fields **28**
   Defining Database Tables **31**

Summary Skills Matrix 33
■ Knowledge Assessment **33**
■ Competency Assessment **34**
■ Proficiency Assessment **35**
■ Mastery Assessment **36**

© baranozdemir/iStockphoto

www.wiley.com/college/microsoft
or call the MOAC Toll-Free Number: 1+(888) 764-7001 (U.S. & Canada only)

Lesson 2: Create Database Tables

LESSON SKILL MATRIX 37

Key Terms **37**

Creating a Database **39**
　Using a Template to Create a Database **39**
　Creating a Blank Database **43**

Creating a Table **46**
　Using the Application Parts Gallery and Quick Start **46**
　Creating a Table from Another Table **48**

Saving a Database Object **51**
　Saving a Table **51**

Skill Summary 53

■ Knowledge Assessment **53**
■ Competency Assessment **55**
■ Proficiency Assessment **56**
■ Mastery Assessment **56**

© nicolas_/iStockphoto

Lesson 3: Work with Tables and Database Records

LESSON SKILL MATRIX 58

Key Terms **58**

Navigating Among Records **59**
　Navigating Using the Keyboard **59**
　Using Navigation Buttons **60**

Entering, Inserting, Editing, and Deleting Records **62**
　Entering, Editing, and Deleting Records **62**

Working with Primary Keys **65**
　Defining a Primary Key **65**
　Defining and Modifying a Multifield Primary Key **66**

Finding and Replacing Data **67**
　Finding and Replacing Data **68**

Attaching and Detaching Documents **69**
　Attaching and Detaching Documents **69**

Sorting and Filtering Data and Setting Field Viewing Options Within a Table **71**
　Sorting Data within a Table **72**
　Filtering Data within a Table **74**

© leezsnow/iStockphoto

Removing a Filter **78**
Freezing/Unfreezing and Hiding/Unhiding Fields **79**
Understanding Table Relationships **82**
Defining Table Relationships **82**
Modifying Table Relationships **84**
Viewing and Printing Table Relationships **86**

Skill Summary 88

■ Knowledge Assessment **88**
■ Competency Assessment **89**
■ Proficiency Assessment **90**
■ Mastery Assessment **91**

Lesson 4: Modify Tables and Fields

LESSON SKILL MATRIX 93
Key Terms **93**
Modifying a Database Table **94**
Modifying Table Properties **94**
Renaming a Table **96**
Deleting a Table **98**
Creating Fields and Modifying Field Properties **99**
Setting Field Properties **100**
Defining Input Masks **102**
Allowing Zero-Length Strings in a Field **105**
Setting Data Validation Rules **106**
Entering Captions **108**
Creating Fields **109**
Deleting a Field **113**
Creating Multivalued Lookup Fields **115**

Skill Summary 119

■ Knowledge Assessment **120**
■ Competency Assessment **121**
■ Proficiency Assessment **122**
■ Mastery Assessment **123**

© groveb/iStockphoto

Lesson 5: Create Forms

LESSON SKILL MATRIX **125**

Key Terms **125**

Creating Forms **126**

Creating a Simple Form and Deleting a Form **127**

Creating a Form in Design View **128**

Creating a Form in Layout View **132**

Using the Form Wizard **134**

Applying a Theme **136**

Sorting and Filtering Data Within a Form **138**

Sorting Data within a Form **138**

Filtering Data within a Form **141**

Using Filter by Form **143**

Skill Summary **146**

■ Knowledge Assessment **147**

■ Competency Assessment **147**

■ Proficiency Assessment **149**

■ Mastery Assessment **150**

Circling Back **152**

© 4FR/iStockphoto

Lesson 6: Create Reports

LESSON SKILL MATRIX **157**

Key Terms **157**

Creating Reports **158**

Creating a Simple Report and Deleting a Report **158**

Using the Report Wizard **160**

Creating a Report in Design View **164**

Applying a Theme **167**

Applying a Theme **167**

Working with Reports **169**

Sorting Data within a Report **169**

Filtering Data within a Report **171**

Finding Data within a Report **173**

Skill Summary **174**

■ Knowledge Assessment **175**

■ Competency Assessment **175**

■ Proficiency Assessment **176**

■ Mastery Assessment **178**

© Gorfer/iStockphoto

Lesson 7: Create and Modify Queries

LESSON SKILL MATRIX 179
Key Terms **179**
Creating a Query **180**
  Creating a Query from a Table and Deleting a Query **181**
  Creating a Find Duplicates Query **183**
  Creating a Query from Multiple Tables **186**
  Finding Unmatched Records **189**
Modifying a Query **193**
  Adding a Table to a Query **193**
  Removing a Table from a Query **194**
  Adding Criteria to a Query **195**
Sorting and Filtering Data Within a Query **200**
  Sorting Data within a Query **200**
  Filtering Data within a Query **204**

Skill Summary 206
■ Knowledge Assessment **206**
■ Competency Assessment **208**
■ Proficiency Assessment **209**
■ Mastery Assessment **210**

© seanrmcdermid/iStockphoto

Lesson 8: Use Controls in Reports and Forms

LESSON SKILL MATRIX 211
Key Terms **211**
Adding Bound and Unbound Controls **213**
  Adding Unbound Controls **213**
  Adding Bound Controls **216**
  Adding Calculated Controls **221**
  Adding Controls Using a Wizard **224**
  Adding Button Controls Using the Wizard **227**
Defining Control Tab Order **231**
Formatting Controls **234**
  Formatting Controls **234**
  Formatting Controls on a Form **236**
  Creating Conditional Formatting on Controls **238**

© artedetimo/iStockphoto

Arranging Control Layout **240**

    Add, Move, and Remove a Control **243**

    Arranging and Anchoring Controls **246**

Arranging Control Alignment, Size, and Position **249**

Adjusting Page Margins and Changing Page Orientation for Forms and Reports **252**

Skill Summary 256

- Knowledge Assessment **256**
- Competency Assessment **257**
- Proficiency Assessment **259**
- Mastery Assessment **261**

Lesson 9: Advanced Tables

LESSON SKILL MATRIX 263

Key Terms **263**

Creating a Custom Table **264**

    Creating a Custom Table **264**

    Inserting and Deleting Rows **268**

Using the Table Analyzer **268**

    Using the Table Analyzer **269**

Summarizing Table Data **275**

    Summarizing Table Data **275**

Skill Summary 278

- Knowledge Assessment **278**
- Competency Assessment **279**
- Proficiency Assessment **280**
- Mastery Assessment **281**

© Deejpilot/iStockphoto

Lesson 10: Advanced Forms

LESSON SKILL MATRIX 283

Key Terms **283**

Creating Advanced Forms **286**
   Creating a Multi-Item Form **286**
   Creating a Split Form **287**
   Creating a Subform **291**

Using Application Parts to Create Blank Forms **295**

Creating a Navigation Form **299**

Skill Summary 301

- Knowledge Assessment **302**
- Competency Assessment **303**
- Proficiency Assessment **304**
- Mastery Assessment **305**

Circling Back **307**

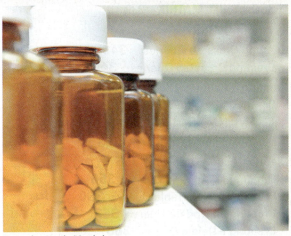
© gemphotography/iStockphoto

Lesson 11: Advanced Reports

LESSON SKILL MATRIX 312

Key Terms **312**

Defining Groups **313**
   Using the Report Wizard **313**
   Adding Group Headers and Footers **317**
   Changing Grouping Options **319**

Creating Aggregate Fields **322**
   Creating Aggregate Fields **322**

Creating a Subform on a Report **324**

Creating the Print Layout **326**
   Using Print Preview to Create a Print Layout **326**

Using the Label Wizard **330**
   Creating Labels Using the Label Wizard **330**

Skill Summary 335

- Knowledge Assessment **335**
- Competency Assessment **336**
- Proficiency Assessment **337**
- Mastery Assessment **338**

© joebrandt/iStockphoto

Lesson 12: Advanced Queries

LESSON SKILL MATRIX   **339**

Key Terms   **339**

Creating Crosstab Queries   **340**
    Creating Crosstab Queries   **340**

Creating a Subquery   **345**
    Creating a Subquery   **346**

Saving a Filter as a Query   **353**
    Saving a Filter as a Query   **353**

Creating Action Queries   **356**
    Creating an Append Query   **356**
    Creating a Make Table Query   **360**
    Creating an Update Query   **362**
    Creating a Delete Query   **366**

Understanding Advanced Query Modification   **370**
    Creating a Join   **370**
    Creating a Calculated Query Field   **373**
    Creating Aggregated Queries   **378**

Skill Summary   **383**
- Knowledge Assessment   **384**
- Competency Assessment   **385**
- Proficiency Assessment   **386**
- Mastery Assessment   **387**

© GgWink/iStockphoto

Lesson 13: Display and Share Data

LESSON SKILL MATRIX   **389**

Key Terms   **389**

Creating a Chart Using the Chart Wizard   **390**
    Creating a Chart Using the Chart Wizard   **390**

Formatting a Chart   **395**
    Changing Chart Options   **396**
    Changing Format Options   **400**
    Refreshing Data in a Chart   **402**

Changing Chart Types   **403**
    Changing Chart Types   **403**

Saving a Database Object as Another File Type   **406**
    Using the Save Object as Command   **406**

Printing a Database Object   **408**

© dan_prat/iStockphoto

Skill Summary   410

- Knowledge Assessment   **410**
- Competency Assessment   **411**
- Proficiency Assessment   **412**
- Mastery Assessment   **413**

Lesson 14: Import and Export Data

LESSON SKILL MATRIX   415

Key Terms   **415**

Importing Data   **416**
   Importing Data from a Specific Source   **416**
   Linking to an External Data Source   **423**

Saving and Running Import Specifications   **428**
   Saving Specifications   **428**
   Running Import Specifications   **432**

Exporting Data   **435**
   Exporting from a Table to Excel   **435**
   Exporting from a Query to Word   **437**

Saving and Running Export Specifications   **439**
   Saving Export Specifications   **440**
   Running Export Specifications   **442**

Skill Summary   444

- Knowledge Assessment   **444**
- Competency Assessment   **446**
- Proficiency Assessment   **447**
- Mastery Assessment   **448**

© AfricaImages/iStockphoto

Lesson 15: Database Tools

LESSON SKILL MATRIX   450

Key Terms   **450**

Maintaining a Database   **451**
   Backing Up a Database   **451**
   Saving as a Previous Version   **453**
   Compacting and Repairing a Database   **455**

Saving a Database as a Template   **457**

Merging Databases   **461**

Setting Database Properties   **463**

Encrypting a Database   **465**
   Encrypting and Decrypting a Database   **465**

www.wiley.com/college/microsoft
or call the MOAC Toll-Free Number: 1+(888) 764-7001 (U.S. & Canada only)

Configuring Database Options   468
   Configuring Database Options   468
Using Database Tools   471
   Identifying Object Dependencies   471
   Using the Database Documenter   472
   Splitting a Database   474

Skill Summary   476

- Knowledge Assessment   477
- Competency Assessment   477
- Proficiency Assessment   478
- Mastery Assessment   479

Circling Back   480

APPENDIX A   485
GLOSSARY   490
INDEX   493

© JanMika/iStockphoto

LESSON SKILL MATRIX

Skill	Exam Objective	Objective Number
Getting Started		
Working in the Access Window	Set Navigation options. Change views.	1.3.4 1.3.5
Using the On-Screen Tools		
Using the Backstage View		
Using the Microsoft Access Help Button		
Defining Data Needs and Types	Change field data types.	2.4.5

© baranozdemir/iStockphoto

KEY TERMS

- Backstage view
- badges
- Change Help Collection menu
- database
- database management system (DBMS)
- datasheet
- data type
- dialog box launcher
- field
- FILE tab
- form
- groups
- KeyTip

- Long text
- normal forms
- normalization
- objects
- primary key
- query
- Quick Access Toolbar
- record
- redundant data
- relational database
- report
- Ribbon
- Short text
- tab
- table

© baranozdemir/iStockphoto

The School of Fine Art in Poughkeepsie, New York, is the brainchild of two professional artists—Shaun Beasley, a printmaker, and Jane Clayton, a sculptor. Last year, the new private high school opened with an enrollment of 12 students and with Jane and Shaun as the only full-time instructors. All academic and business records were maintained manually by the founders. This year, however, you were hired as an executive assistant to help them manage an increasing amount of information. Enrollment is climbing, new full-time faculty members are being hired, and the school is receiving scholarship funds from local patrons. With the help of an Access database, you will organize the school's academic and business data. In this lesson, you will learn basic database concepts and how to define data needs and types.

SOFTWARE ORIENTATION

Microsoft Access' Opening Screen

Before you begin working in Microsoft Access 2013, you need to be familiar with the primary user interface. In the next section, you will be asked to open a new blank desktop database in Access. When you do so, a screen appears that is similar to the one shown in Figure 1-1.

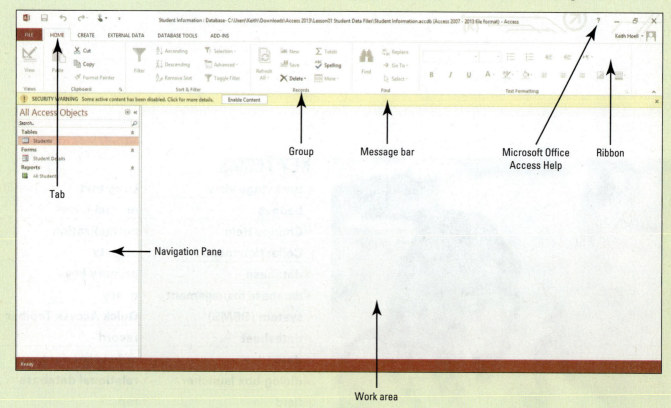

Figure 1-1

Opening screen for new blank Access database

When you create a blank database in Microsoft Access, the opening screen provides you with a workspace in which to build a database. Understanding the screen elements helps orient you to important tools and information. The elements and features of your screen may vary if default settings have been changed or if other preferences have been set. Use this figure as a reference throughout this lesson as well as the rest of this book.

GETTING STARTED

The Bottom Line

A **database** is a tool for collecting and organizing information. For example, as a database, a phone book organizes a large amount of data—names, addresses, and phone numbers—so you can access it by name in alphabetic order. Even a grocery list is a simple type of database. A computerized **database management system (DBMS)**, such as Microsoft Office Access, enables you to easily collect large volumes of data organized into categories of related information. This type of database allows you to store, organize, and manage your data, no matter how complex it is, and then retrieve and present it in various formats and reports. Organizing data by using a DBMS gives you the power to manipulate, view and report the data in ways that other applications like spreadsheets and word processing documents cannot. For example, a spreadsheet application like Microsoft Excel has its own unique purpose to store, analyze and report data using tools unique to it; however, Access is the better choice to perform various management functions on data such as asking it complex questions and creating structures to input and report it using standardized business structures which you'll learn throughout this book. As with any program, however, the first tasks are the most basic. This section shows you how to start Access and open an existing database.

Starting Access

Access 2013 runs on either the Windows 7 or Windows 8 operating system, and the steps to start Access differ depending on the version of Windows you have installed on your system.

You'll see that when you start Access, a start screen with several options related to creating a database appears. The Access startup screen allows you to create a new custom web app database, a blank desktop database, a database from a template, or open a recent database (if you have already created one). You can also access Office.com for featured content and more information about the Microsoft Office 2013 system and Access 2013.

New to the Office 2013 System is the ability to sign into an Office application using your Microsoft or Organizational account. A Microsoft account can be easily created when you sign up for a Microsoft web service such as SkyDrive, Xbox LIVE, Outlook.com, or other Microsoft service. An Organizational account is an account that your workplace or school would use to connect you to a Microsoft service. Once you sign in, your sign-in information will appear in the upper-right corner of each of the Office 2013 applications. This account information will include your name, e-mail address and user icon. You also have the ability to switch to a different user account using the Switch Account command beside your user icon. Microsoft enables you to sign into Office to make it easier for you to access and share your documents from virtually anywhere. You can open and save your documents using Microsoft SkyDrive, a free cloud-based file sharing service that can be accessed from any Internet-connected computer. Signing into Office also allows access to your personalized application settings and themes, and will even remind you where you left off in your document.

In this exercise, you learn to start Access from both a Windows 8 and Windows 7 system.

Take Note

A web app database is a new type of database introduced in Access 2013 that you can share with others as a Microsoft SharePoint app (an application on a network-based service that allows for collaboration) in a web browser or through Microsoft Office 365 (a subscription-based version of Microsoft Office provided on the web).

STEP BY STEP | **Start Access in Windows 8**

GET READY. Before you begin these steps, be sure to turn on and/or log on to your computer.

1. When starting Windows 8, if the Windows 8 Start screen doesn't appear, press the **Windows key** on the keyboard to display it. Your screen should look similar to Figure 1-2.

Figure 1-2

Windows 8 Start screen

2. If necessary, scroll to the Access 2013 tile, as shown in Figure 1-3.

Figure 1-3

Access 2013 tile

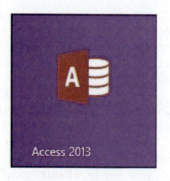

3. Click the Access 2013 tile. The Access startup screen opens, as shown in Figure 1-4.

Figure 1-4

The Access startup screen

Create a new custom web app database

Create a new blank desktop database

Search Office.com for templates

User account sign-in information

Click to access Open dialog box

Office.com templates

Another Way

On the Start screen, you can type the first few letters of the application you want to open and you will be presented with context-sensitive matches. You can then click on the appropriate application name to open it.

PAUSE. LEAVE Microsoft Access open to use in the next exercise.

Take Note   The Microsoft Office 2013 System, including Access 2013, is not compatible with Windows XP and earlier Microsoft Windows operating systems.

Start Access in Windows 7

GET READY. Before you begin these steps, be sure to turn on and/or log on to your computer.

1. When starting Windows 7, on the Windows taskbar, click the Start button and then click All Programs. A menu of installed programs appears.
2. Click Microsoft Office. Another menu appears.
3. Click Microsoft Access 2013. The Access startup screen opens, as shown in Figure 1-5.

Figure 1-5

The Access startup screen

Create a new custom web app database

Create a new blank desktop database

Search Office.com for templates

User account sign-in information

Click to access Open dialog box

Office.com templates

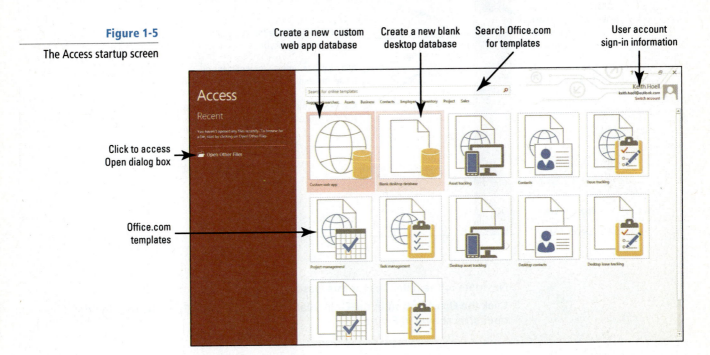

PAUSE. LEAVE Microsoft Access open to use in the next exercise.

Opening an Existing Database

When you open an existing database, you access not only your previously entered and saved data, but the elements you created to organize that data. In this exercise, you open a database that is in the beginning stages of development.

The Open Other Files command on the Access startup screen displays the Open screen, which allows you to pick a recently opened file by using the Recent command or by choosing a location to browse for a file. You can locate files by using the Add a Place command to set up network locations like Sky-Drive to browse files on the Internet. You can use the Computer command to find files stored locally in a folder on your computer or on a CD, DVD or other removable media, or on a network drive.

Whether you browse for files using services such as SkyDrive or Office 365, or browse for files using the Computer command, you must use the Browse button to access the Open dialog box.

The left-hand pane of the Open dialog box lists the available locations for files, such as a folder, drive, or network/Internet location. Click the location, and the folders will be displayed in the fold-er list. From this list, you can double-click the folder you want to open. When you find the file you want, double-click the filename to open it or click it once to select it and then click the Open button.

Open an Existing Database

GET READY. The Access startup screen should be on the screen from the previous exercise.

1. Click the **Open Other Files** command on the left side of the Access startup screen. The Open screen appears, as shown in Figure 1-6.

Another Way
Press Ctrl+O to display the Open screen.

Returns you to the Access startup screen →

Allows you to create a new blank database or a database from a template

Shows recently opened files

Allows you to browse for files stored on the Internet in SkyDrive

Allows you to browse for local files or those on removable media, or on a network

Allows you to connect a Microsoft service such as Office 365 SharePoint or SkyDrive

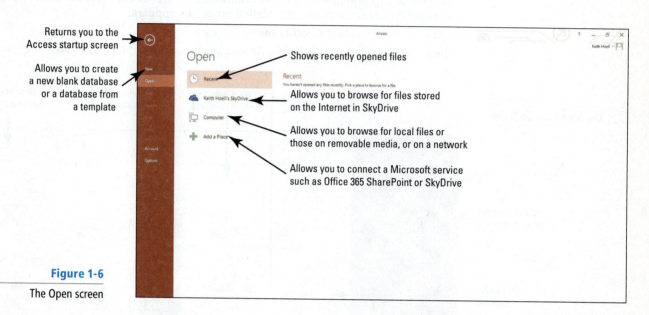

Figure 1-6

The Open screen

2. Navigate to the data files for this lesson and select *Student Information*.
3. Click the **Open** button in the Open dialog box (see Figure 1-7). The existing database opens, as shown in Figure 1-8.

Figure 1-7

The Open dialog box

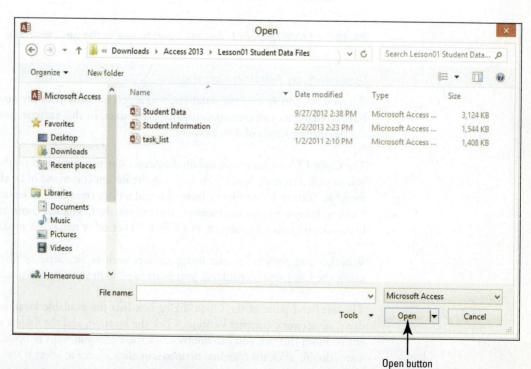

Open button

Take Note   Your figures might look slightly different depending upon which folder you have stored your files.

Figure 1-8

The existing database open
in Access

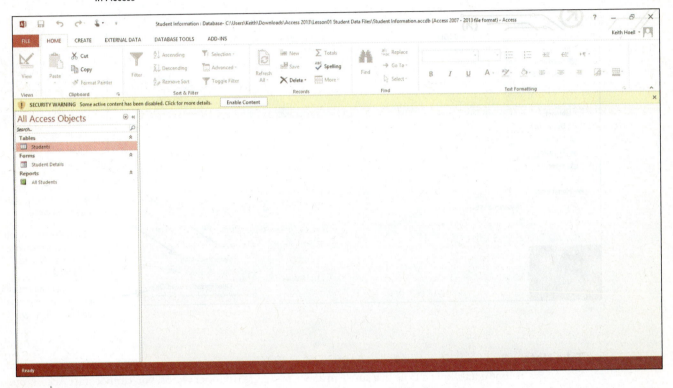

 **Troubleshooting**   As part of the Microsoft Access 2013 security model, when you open a database outside of a trusted location or the database contains active content (content that can be misused by an unscrupulous person to cause harm to your computer), a Message Bar appears, warning you that certain content has been disabled. If you know you can trust the database, click Enable Content.

Take Note   Since you know you can trust the databases downloaded from the book companion website, click Enable Content on the Message Bar for all databases in this book.

PAUSE. LEAVE the database open to use in the next exercise.

Clicking the Open button opens the database for shared access in a multi-user environment so that you and other users can read and write to the database. If you click the down arrow next to the Open button, as shown in Figure 1-9, other options are available on the menu:

- **Open:** Opens with default access.
- **Open Read-Only:** Opens with only viewing ability and not editing ability. Others can still read and write.
- **Open Exclusive:** Opens so that the database is only available to you. Others will receive a message that the file is already in use.
- **Open Exclusive Read-Only:** Opens with only viewing ability and not editing ability. Others can only view and not edit the database.

Figure 1-9

Open button menu

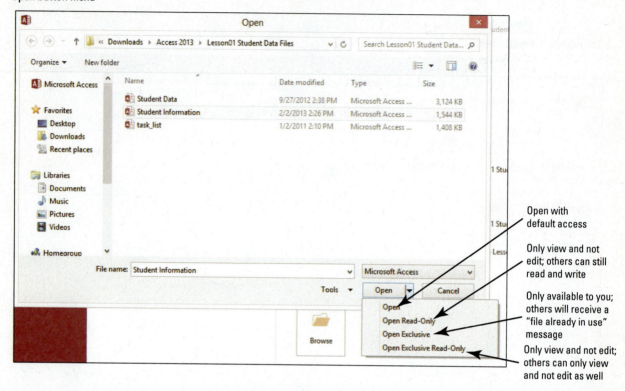

Take Note   Each time you start Access 2013, you open a new instance or copy of Access. You can open only one database at a time in a single instance of Access. In other words, you cannot start Access, open one database, and then open another database-not without first closing the first database. However, you can open multiple databases at the same time by double-clicking another database's icon. For example, to open two Access databases, start Access, open the first Access database, and then open a second Access database by double-clicking its database icon in Windows 8's File Explorer (referred to as Windows Explorer in previous versions of Windows).

WORKING IN THE ACCESS WINDOW

The Bottom Line   The Access 2013 Window user interface was designed to help you find the commands you need quickly so that you can successfully perform your tasks. You will immediately begin using the Navigation Pane and exploring the Ribbon. Also in this lesson, you will practice using other on-screen tools and features, such as the Backstage view and Access Help.

SOFTWARE ORIENTATION

Navigation Pane

By default, the Navigation Pane, shown in Figure 1-10, appears on the left side of the Access screen each time you create or open a database.

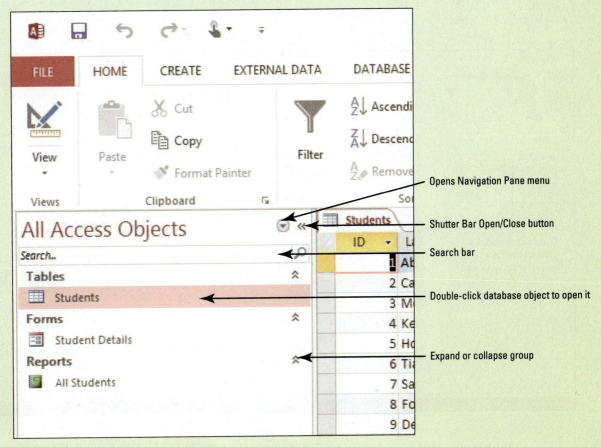

Figure 1-10
Navigation Pane

The Navigation Pane enables you to open, copy, and delete tables and other database **objects**. It also lists all the objects in your database, including: **tables** (the most basic database object that stores data in categories), **queries** (allow you to search and retrieve the data you have stored), **forms** (control data entry and data views and provide visual cues that make data easier to work with) and **reports** (present your information in ways that are most useful to you). You learn more about managing database objects (such as forms, queries, and reports) in later lessons of this book. For now, just familiarize yourself with the Navigation Pane. Use this figure as a reference throughout this lesson as well as the rest of this book.

Using the Navigation Pane

Before you can create a database, you need to understand its most basic elements. This section introduces you to some of the elements in a database that help you organize data and navigate using the Navigation Pane, object tabs, and different views.

Use the Navigation Pane

USE the database from the previous exercise.

1. In the Navigation Pane, double-click **Students** to display the table in the Access work area, as shown in Figure 1-11.

Figure 1-11

A table open in the Access work area

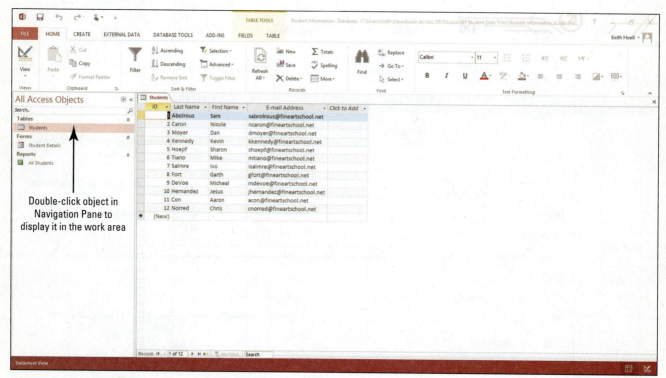

Double-click object in Navigation Pane to display it in the work area

Take Note   The Navigation Pane replaces an older tool, referred to as the Database window, which appeared in versions prior to Access 2007.

2. Click the **down arrow** next to All Access Objects at the top of the Navigation Pane to display the menu, as shown in Figure 1-12.

Figure 1-12

The Navigation Pane menu

Figure 1-12

The Navigation Pane menu

Categories

Groups that relate to
the selected category

3. Click **Tables and Related Views**. The default group in this category is All Tables, which appears in the menu at the top of the Navigation Pane. Notice the Students table and all other objects related to it are displayed under the Students header.

4. Click the **down arrow** next to All Tables at the top of the Navigation Pane to display the menu again, and click **Object Type** to return to the original view.

5. Right-click in the white area of the Navigation Pane to display a shortcut menu. Click **View By** and then choose **Details**, as shown in Figure 1-13.

Figure 1-13

The Navigation Pane
shortcut menu

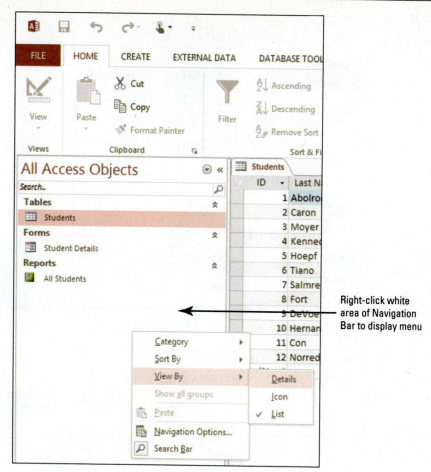

Right-click white
area of Navigation
Bar to display menu

6. The database objects are displayed with details. Click the right side of the Navigation Pane and drag to make it wider so all the information can be read, as shown in Figure 1-14.

7. If the search bar does not appear at the top of the Navigation Pane, right-click the **All Access Objects** header of the Navigation Pane. On the shortcut menu, click **Search Bar**. A search bar is now displayed at the top of the Navigation Pane. You can toggle the search bar display by clicking the Search Bar option.

Figure 1-14

Widening the Navigation Pane

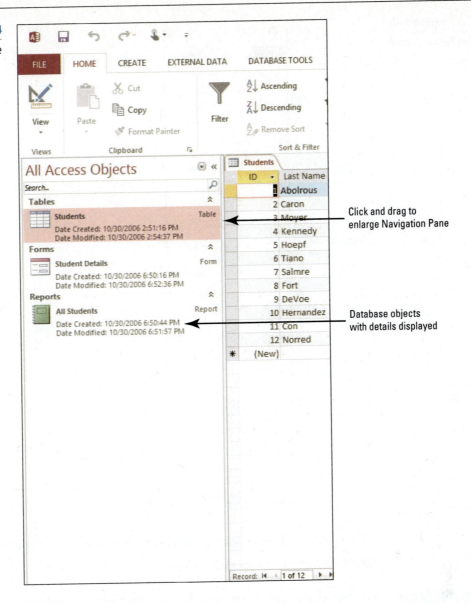

Click and drag to
enlarge Navigation Pane

Database objects
with details displayed

8. Display the Navigation Pane shortcut menu, click **View By**, and then click **List** to display the database objects in a list again.

9. Click the **Shutter Bar Open/Close Button** to collapse the Navigation Pane. Notice it is not entirely hidden, as shown in Figure 1-15.

Figure 1-15

The Navigation Pane collapsed

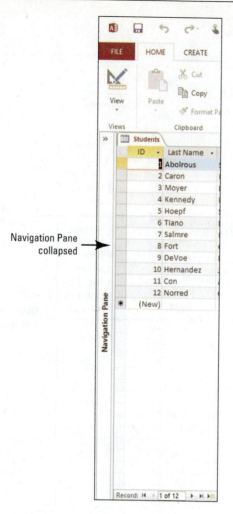

Navigation Pane collapsed

10. Click the **Shutter Bar Open/Close Button** to expand the Navigation Pane again.

PAUSE. LEAVE the database open to use in the next exercise.

CERTIFICATION READY?	1.3.4
How do you set navigation options?	

The Navigation Pane divides your database objects into categories, and those categories contain groups. The default category is Object Type, which groups database objects by their type-tables, forms, reports, and so on. You can change the category to Tables and Related Views, which groups the objects in a database by the tables to which they are related. You can also change the category to one of several other views as shown in Figure 1-12.

Using Object Tabs

When you create a database in Access, all the objects in that database—including forms, tables, reports, queries—are displayed in a single window separated by tabs. Tabs help keep open objects visible and accessible. To move among the open objects, click a tab. To close a tab, click its Close button. You can also right-click a tab to display the shortcut menu, which you can use to save, close, close all, or switch views. In this exercise, you practice opening and displaying object tabs.

STEP BY STEP   **Use Object Tabs**

USE the database you used in the previous exercise.

1. In the Navigation Pane, double-click **Student Details**. A new object tab opens to display the form, as shown in Figure 1-16.

Figure 1-16

A tab showing a form

Object tabs

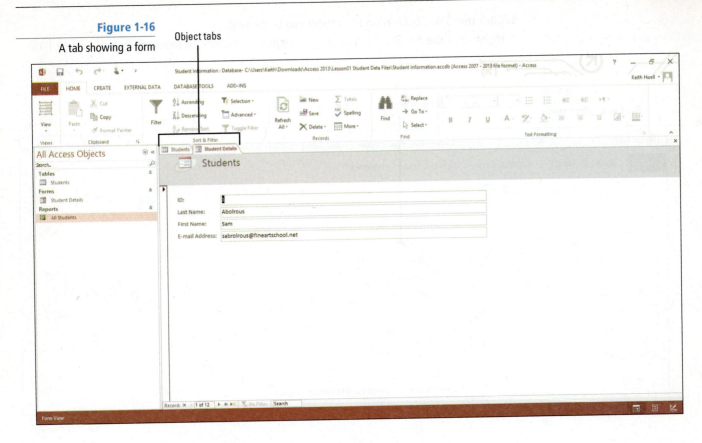

2. In the Navigation Pane, double-click **All Students**. A new object tab opens to display the report, as shown in Figure 1-17.

Figure 1-17

A tab showing a report

Close button on the report tab

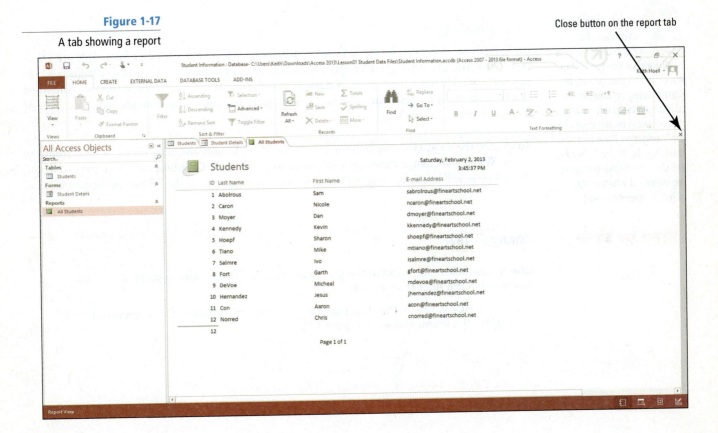

3. Click the **Close** button on the report tab to close it.

4. Right-click the **Student Details** tab to display the shortcut menu shown in Figure 1-18.

Figure 1-18

The tab shortcut menu

Right-click tab to display shortcut menu

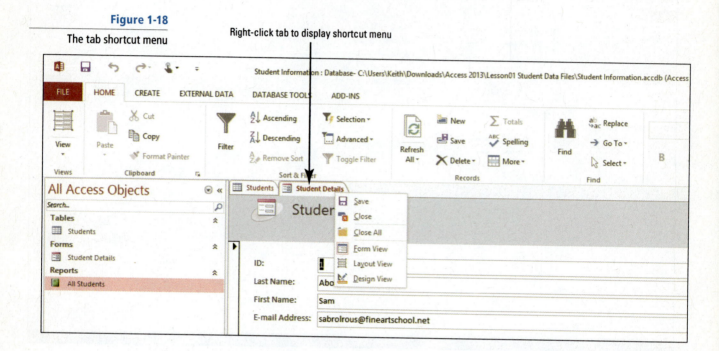

5. Click **Close** to close the form.

PAUSE. LEAVE the database open to use in the next exercise.

Another Way
You can also change an open object's view by clicking on the top half of the object's View button, by right-clicking on an open object's window tab, or by right-clicking on the object in the Navigation Pane and choosing the desired view from the shortcut menu that appears regardless of whether the object is open or closed.

Changing Views

Each database object can be viewed several different ways. The main views for a table are Datasheet View and Design View. Datasheet View can be used to perform most table design tasks, so you will probably use it most often. A **datasheet** is the visual representation of the data contained in a table or of the results returned by a query. A query is simply a question you can ask a table or another query.

To change the view, click the bottom half of the View button and then choose a view from the menu. When you change views, the commands available on the **Ribbon** change context to match the tasks you will be performing in that view. You learn more about the Ribbon in the next section.

STEP BY STEP   **Change Views**

USE the database you used in the previous exercise. The Students table should be displayed in the Access work area.

1. On the HOME tab, in the Views group, click the **down arrow** on the View button to display the menu shown in Figure 1-19.

Figure 1-19

The View menu for a table

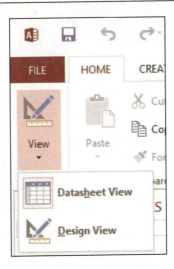

2. Click **Design View**. The table is displayed in Design View, as shown in Figure 1-20. Notice that the DESIGN tab is now displayed on the Ribbon.

Figure 1-20

The table shown in Design View

Contextual design commands

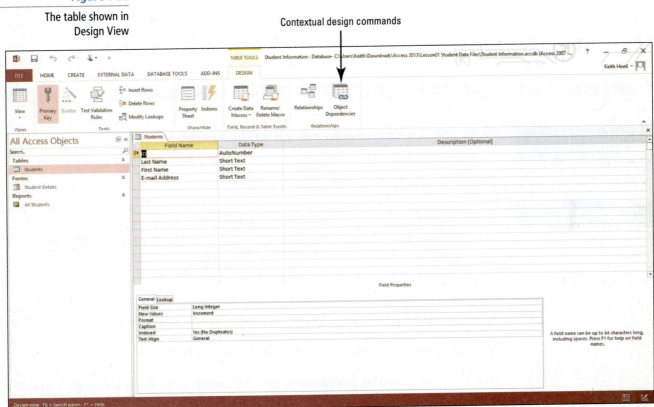

3. On the DESIGN tab, in the Views group, click the **down arrow** on the View button, and then click **Datasheet View**.

4. On the Ribbon, under the TABLE TOOLS tab, click the **FIELDS** tab to display the contextual commands for that view, as shown in Figure 1-21.

Figure 1-21

The table shown in
Datasheet View

Contextual datasheet commands on Fields tab

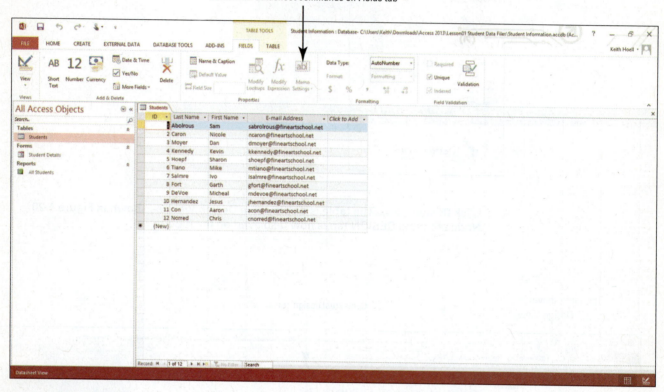

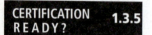

CERTIFICATION READY?   1.3.5

How do you change views?

The Bottom Line

PAUSE. LEAVE the database open to use in the next exercise.

USING THE ON-SCREEN TOOLS

Access has many tools to help with your database needs. In this section, you explore the Ribbon, which displays **groups** of common commands arranged by tabs. You'll also learn about other on-screen tools to help you get your work done faster, such as the **Quick Access Toolbar** and KeyTips.

Using the Ribbon

The Ribbon is located across the top of the screen and contains tabs and groups of commands. It is divided into several tabs, which organize tasks according to similar commands you'd like to perform on a database. The Ribbon is contextual, which means it offers you commands related to the object that you are working on or the task that you are performing.

Some groups have a **dialog box launcher**, which is a small arrow in the lower-right corner of the group that you click to launch a dialog box or task pane that displays additional options or information. Some commands on the Ribbon have small arrows pointing down. These arrows indicate that a menu is available that lists more options from which you can choose.

In the next exercise you practice using the Ribbon.

Use the Ribbon

USE the database you used in the previous exercise.

1. Click the **HOME** tab to make it active. As shown in Figure 1-22, the Ribbon is divided into groups of commands. Notice the dialog box launcher in the lower-right corner of the Clipboard group.

Figure 1-22

The Ribbon and dialog box launcher

Dialog box launcher

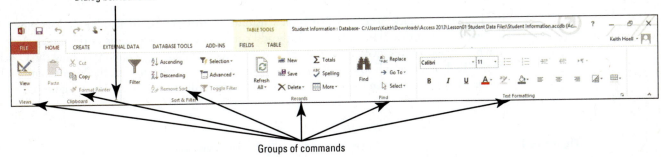

Groups of commands

2. Click the **CREATE** tab to make it the active tab. Notice that the groups of commands change.

3. Click **External Data** and then **Database Tools** to see the commands available on those tabs.

4. Click the **HOME** tab.

5. Click the **ID** column header in the table to select the ID column.

6. Click the **dialog box launcher** in the lower-right corner of the Text Formatting group. The Datasheet Formatting dialog box appears, as shown in Figure 1-23.

Figure 1-23

The Datasheet Formatting dialog box

Datasheet Formatting ? ×

Cell Effect
- ⦿ Flat
- ◯ Raised
- ◯ Sunken

Gridlines Shown
- ☑ Horizontal
- ☑ Vertical

OK

Cancel

Background Color:

Alternate Background Color: Gridline Color:

Sample:

Border and Line Styles

Datasheet Border   ∨   Solid   ∨

Direction
- ⦿ Left-to-right
- ◯ Right-to-left

7. Click **Cancel** to close the dialog box.

8. Double-click the **HOME** tab. Notice the groups are hidden to give you more screen space to work with your database.

9. Double-click **HOME** again to display the groups.

PAUSE. LEAVE the database open to use in the next exercise.

Take Note You can customize the Ribbon to have greater control over the commands that appear on it by turning off tabs and groups you rarely use, moving and/or duplicating groups from one tab to another, creating custom groups, and even creating custom tabs.

Using the Quick Access Toolbar

The Quick Access Toolbar located by default at the top-left corner of the Access screen contains the commands that you use most often, such as Save, Undo, and Redo. The Touch/Mouse Mode command also exists on this toolbar, which allows you to select either touch or mouse mode. Selecting touch mode creates more space between the commands on the Ribbon which helps optimize menu access on touch-enabled devices. Mouse mode is the traditional mode optimized for mouse use.

Located on the Quick Access Toolbar is the Customize Quick Access Toolbar button that presents you with a menu that allows you to quickly add commonly used commands to the Quick Access Toolbar, as shown in Figure 1-24. You can use this menu to choose an option to show the Quick Access Toolbar above or below the Ribbon; you can also use this menu to click the More Commands button to open the Customize screen in the Access Options dialog box, as shown in Figure 1-25.

Figure 1-24

The Customize Quick Access Toolbar menu

Customize Quick Access Toolbar button and menu

Figure 1-25

The Access Options dialog box

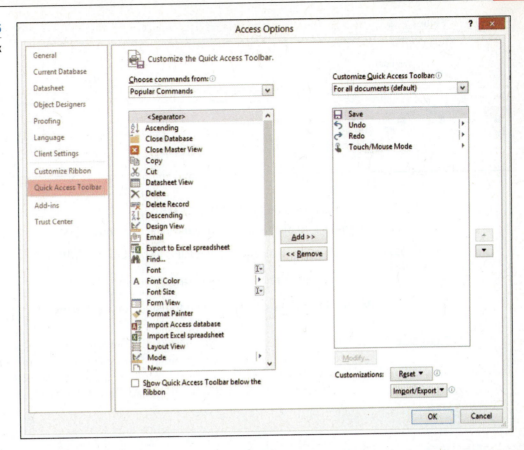

Use this dialog box to add buttons for commands that you use most often, so they are always just one click away.

In this exercise, you use the Customize Quick Access Toolbar menu to place the toolbar below the Ribbon.

STEP BY STEP | **Use the Customize Quick Access Toolbar Menu**

USE the database you used in the previous exercise.

1. On the Quick Access Toolbar, click the **Customize Quick Access Toolbar** button. A menu appears.

2. Click **Show Below the Ribbon**. The toolbar is moved.

3. Click the **Customize Quick Access Toolbar** button again. Click **Show Above the Ribbon**.

PAUSE. LEAVE the database open to use in the next exercise.

Using KeyTips

When you press the ALT key, small letters and numbers called **KeyTips** appear on the Ribbon in small square labels, called **badges**. To execute a command using KeyTips, press the ALT key then press the KeyTip or sequence of KeyTips that corresponds to the command you want to use. Every command on the Ribbon has a KeyTip. You learn to display KeyTips in the next exercise.

STEP BY STEP | **Use KeyTips**

USE the database you used in the previous exercise.

1. Press **ALT**. Letters and numbers appear on the Ribbon to let you know which key to use to access commands or tabs. See Figure 1-26.

Figure 1-26

Using KeyTips

KeyTips

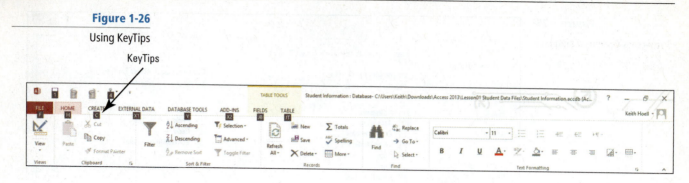

2. Press **C** to activate the CREATE tab.

3. Press **P** to display the Application Parts menu.

Cross Ref   You learn more about Application Parts in Lessons 2 and 10.

4. Press **ALT** to remove the KeyTips.

PAUSE. LEAVE the database open to use in the next exercise.

Take Note   Shortcut keys are keys or combinations of keys pressed together to perform a command. Shortcut keys provide a quick way to execute commands without having to move your hands off the keyboard and reach for a mouse. Keyboard shortcuts from previous versions of Access that begin with CTRL are the same. However, those that begin with ALT are different and require the use of KeyTips.

SOFTWARE ORIENTATION

Introducing the Backstage View

In Office 2010, Microsoft introduced the Backstage view. The **Backstage view** displays when you click the FILE tab and contains access to many of the commands that were on the File menu in versions prior to Microsoft Access 2010. The Backstage view enables you to access various screens that let you perform various tasks including creating a new database, creating a database from a template, opening an existing database, modifying user account settings and application options, and performing database maintenance tasks as seen in Figure 1-27.

Default screen. Provides info, such as file location of open database, and provides access to maintenance tools and database properties

Click to access New screen to create new databases from templates and new custom web app and desktop databases

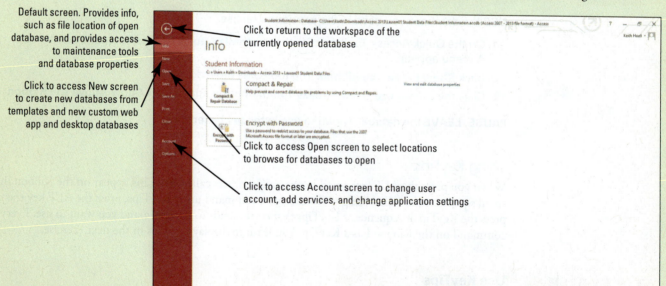

Click to return to the workspace of the currently opened database

Click to access Open screen to select locations to browse for databases to open

Click to access Account screen to change user account, add services, and change application settings

Figure 1-27
Backstage view

USING THE BACKSTAGE VIEW

The **FILE tab** on the Ribbon accesses the Backstage view—a menu of options and commands that allows you to access various screens to perform common tasks with your database files—such as opening, saving, printing, closing, and changing user account settings and options. It also contains additional commands for managing your database.

Using the Backstage View

The FILE tab opens the Backstage view (Figure 1-27), a menu of basic options and commands for opening, saving, and printing files, as well as more advanced options. You can click several options and commands to view related screens containing various options and commands used to create and manage your database. The Back button returns you to the Access database workspace.

The following is an overview of the options in the Backstage view:

- **Info:** Default view. Use this option to view the current database file path and view and edit database properties. Compact and repair the database and encrypt the database with a password to restrict access.
- **New:** Use this option to create a new database from scratch or from available templates.
- **Open:** Use this option to open an existing database and view a list of recently accessed databases.
- **Save:** Use this option to return to the open database window where objects can be saved.
- **Save As:** Use this option to save the current database object (such as a table, query, form, or report) as a new object or save the database in another format that is compatible with earlier versions of Access. You can save the database to a document management server for sharing or you can package the database and apply a digital signature. You can also back up the database.
- **Print:** Use this option to quick-print straight to the printer, open a dialog box from which to choose print options, or preview your document before printing.
- **Close:** Use this option to close the open database but keep the Access application open.
- **Account:** Use this option to view and modify user account settings. Change application background and theme. Add a service and activate Access with a product key.
- **Options:** Use this option to customize language settings, display settings, and other settings.

You practice using the Backstage view in the next exercise.

STEP BY STEP **Use the Backstage View**

USE the database you used in the previous exercise.

1. Click the FILE tab. Backstage view opens, displaying a menu of options down the left side of the window and information about the currently opened database, as shown in Figure 1-28.

Figure 1-28

Using the Backstage view

Back button to return to the database workspace

New option used to create new databases

Save As option used to view Save As commands

2. Click the **New** option to view the options and commands available.

3. Click the **Save As** option to view more options and commands.

4. Click the **Back button** to exit the menu and return to the Access workspace.

PAUSE. LEAVE the database open to use in the next exercise.

USING THE MICROSOFT ACCESS HELP BUTTON

The Bottom Line

If you have questions, Microsoft Access Help has answers. In fact, you can choose to use the help topics on your computer that were installed with Office or, if you are connected to the Internet, you can choose to use the help that is available online. Either way, you can key in search words and/or click on links to browse help topics to get your answers. In this exercise, you use the Help button to access the Help information installed on your computer with Access 2013.

Using the Help Button and Change Help Collection Menu

The **Change Help Collection menu** in the lower-right corner of the Access Help heading lets you choose between the help topics that are available online and the help topics installed in your computer offline. If you are usually connected to the Internet, you might prefer to set the Change Help Collection to Access Help from Office.com so you can get the most thorough and updated help available. But there may be times when you can't or don't want to be online; in those instances you can choose Access Help from your computer so you can get help topics that are offline, which consists of more basic help on the functions of buttons appearing on the Office Ribbon. In the next exercise, you practice using Access Help and the Change Help Collection menu.

STEP BY STEP **Use the Help Button and Change Help Collection Menu**

Take Note   When you rest the mouse pointer over a command on the Ribbon, a ScreenTip displays the name of the command. Access 2013 also has Enhanced ScreenTips, which provide you with more information about the command.

USE the database you used in the previous exercise.

1. Click the **Microsoft Access Help** button, as shown in Figure 1-29. The Access Help dialog box appears, as shown in Figure 1-30. Notice the Search box and Search button. Also notice the Change Help Collection button; after selecting it, an option is set to Access Help from Office.com to search online for help topics. If the Change Help Collection is set to Access Help from your computer, the screen will look different.

Figure 1-29

The Microsoft Access Help button

Microsoft Access Help button

Figure 1-30

The Access Help dialog box when connected to Office.com

Change Help Collection button

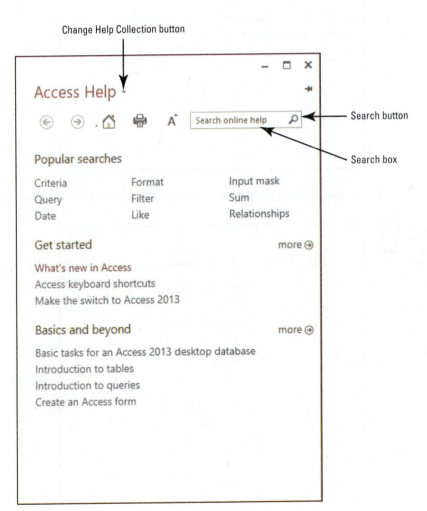

Search button

Search box

2. Click the **Change Help Collection** button. A menu appears, as shown in Figure 1-31.

Figure 1-31

The Change Help
Collection menu

Figure 1-31

The Change Help
Collection menu

3. Click **Access Help from your computer**. Basic Help appears, as shown in Figure 1-32.

Figure 1-32

The Access Help dialog box
when offline

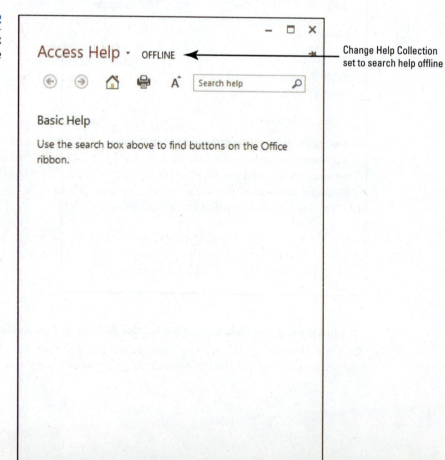

4. In the Search help text box, key **font** and then click the **Search** button. A list of possible locations on the Ribbon where fonts can be manipulated appears.

5. In the search results that appear, click the **Font is under Home/Text Formatting** link. Help on this topic appears.

6. Click the **Keep Help on Top** button ⊡. The Access Help dialog box is now pinned to the front of the window so it is always on top and easily referred and not hidden even if another screen element is clicked.

7. Click the **Back** button ⊛. The search results for font appear again.

8. Click the **Home** button ⌂. The home page of Access Help appears.

9. Click the **Change Help Collection** button.

10. Click **Access Help from Office.com** to reset the help Collection.

11. Click the **Close** button to close Access Help.

12. Choose **FILE** and then click **Close** to **CLOSE** the database without closing Access.

STOP. Leave Access open for the next exercise.

Another Way
The Access Help button is positioned in some dialog boxes for quick access to context-related help. Click it wherever you see it to launch Access Help. You can also launch Access Help by pressing the F1 function key on your keyboard.

The Bottom Line

DEFINING DATA NEEDS AND TYPES

To create a database that achieves your goals and provides you with up-to-date, accurate information you need to spend time planning and designing it.

When planning a database, the first step is to consider the purpose of your database. You need to design the database so that it accommodates all your data-processing and reporting needs. You should gather and organize all the information that you want to include, starting with any existing forms or lists, and think about the reports and mailings you might want to create using the data.

Once you have decided how the information will be used, the next step is to categorize the information by dividing it into subjects such as Products or Orders, which become the tables in your database. Each table should only contain information that relates to that subject. If you find yourself adding extra information, create a new table.

In a database table, data is stored in rows and columns—similar in appearance to a spreadsheet. Each row in a table is called a **record**. Each column in a table is called a **field**. For example, if a table is named "Student List," each record (row) contains information about a different student and each field (column) contains a different type of information about a student, such as last name or email address.

Once you have decided to create a Student List table, you need to determine what information you want to store in the table—such as Age, Birthdate, or Tuition. Organize each piece of information into the smallest useful part—for example, use First Name and Last Name instead of just Name if you want to sort, search, calculate, or report using either a first name or a last name (or both). These pieces of information will eventually become your fields (columns), and each record (row) will then contain complete information about each student.

For each table, you will choose a primary key. A **primary key** is a column that uniquely identifies each row, such as Student ID Number. In the case of our Student List table, the primary key (Student ID Number) uniquely identifies each student.

Review Database Fields

Reviewing preexisting database fields can give you an idea of the type of information that you can store in a database. In this exercise, you open a database that is further along in the process of being developed and view the fields in a form to see what a more advanced database looks like.

STEP BY STEP   **Review Database Fields**

OPEN the *Student Data* database from the data files for this lesson.

1. On the Student List form, click the **ID** for record 5 to display the Student Details dialog box for Sharon Hoepf, as shown in Figure 1-33.

Figure 1-33

The Student Details dialog box

2. Click the **Guardian Information** tab and then the **Emergency Information** tab. Each field on each tab is an example of the type of information that could be contained in a database table.

3. Click **Close** to close the Student Details dialog box.

PAUSE. LEAVE the database open to use in the next exercise.

Cross Ref   You learn more about defining and modifying a primary key in Lesson 3.

Defining and Modifying Data Types for Fields

When designing the database, you set a **data type** for each field (column) that you create to match the information it will store. A data type controls the type of data a field will contain—whether it is text, number, date/time, or some other type of data. When defining table fields, it is important to define them as specifically as possible. For example, if you are using a number, you should determine whether you need to use the Currency data type, the Calculated data type, or the Number data type. Or, if you need to store large amounts of text, you may need to use the Long Text data type instead of the Short Text data type. Sometimes you may also need to modify data types for preexisting fields. In this exercise, you practice reviewing and modifying data types.

When you create a new field in a table and then enter data in it, Access 2013 automatically tries to detect the appropriate data type for the new column. For example, if you key a price, such as $10, Access recognizes the data as a price and sets the data type for the field to Currency. If Access doesn't have enough information from what you enter to detect the data type, the data type is set to Short Text.

There are two data types new to Access 2013: Short Text and Long Text. The Short Text data type replaces the Text data type used in previous versions of Access; the Long Text data type replaces the Memo data type. The **Short Text** data type is used to store up to 255 characters of data in a field and is a good data type for a field that stores small amounts of text, such as names, cities, and states. To store data greater than 255 characters, you can use the Long Text data type. The **Long Text** data type can display up to 64,000 characters on the screen, but can store about one gigabyte of text. This data type can be used for a field that contains large amounts of text, like customer comments.

Take Note   The Short Text data type and the Long Text data type each has unique properties and size limits, depending on whether you're using them in a desktop database or an Access web app.

STEP BY STEP   **Review and Modify Data Types for Fields**

USE the database you used in the previous exercise.

1. Close the Student List form.
2. In the Navigation Pane, in the Students group, double-click the **Students** table to open it.
3. Click the **Date of Birth** field header.
4. On the Ribbon, click the **FIELDS** tab. Notice in the Formatting group that the Data Type is Date/Time.
5. In the Format box, click the **down arrow** to display the menu of formatting options for that type, as shown in Figure 1-34.

Figure 1-34

Format options for the Date/Time data type

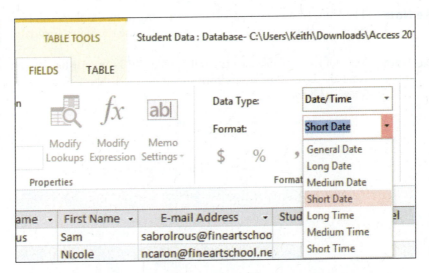

6. Click the **Last Name** header. Notice that the Data Type is Short Text and that no formatting options are available for that data type.
7. Scroll to the right and click the **Address** header.
8. In the Data Type box, click the **down arrow** and then click **Short Text** to change the data type.

Take Note   Be aware that changing a data type might cut off some or all of the data in a field; in some cases, it might remove the data entirely.

9. Scroll to the far right and click the **Click to Add** Click to Add ⌄ column header. In the Data Type drop-down list that appears, click **Yes/No**. Notice the name of the column header, Field1, is highlighted.

10. Rename the field by keying **Additional Contact Info on File?**.

11. On the Ribbon, in the Formatting group, click the **down arrow** in the Format box to display the menu of formatting options for the Yes/No data type, as shown in Figure 1-35.

Figure 1-35

The formatting options for Yes/No data type

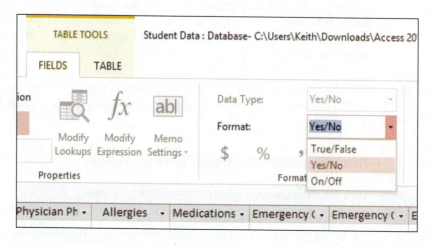

12. Click outside the menu to close it.

PAUSE. LEAVE the database open to use in the next exercise.

CERTIFICATION READY?   2.4.5

How do you change field data types?

Access provides 11 data types, each with its own purpose. Table 1-1 describes the types of data that each field can store.

Take Note   The Number data type should be used only if the numbers will be used in mathematical calculations. For numbers such as phone numbers, use the Short Text data type.

Take Note   Some of the available data types in Access 2013 can only be chosen in table Design View and not from the Data Type drop down menu on the Ribbon. You will learn more about table Design View in Lesson 9.

Table 1-1

Types of data stored in fields

Data Type	Example	Description
Short Text (formerly Text data type in versions prior to Access 2013)	Last Name: D'Amato Street: 1234 Landau Ave.	The most common data type for fields. Can store up to 255 characters of text, and numbers (or a combination of both).
Long Text (formerly Memo data type in versions prior to Access 2013)	Comments: Student will make monthly payments on the 15th of each month of $247.	Stores large amounts of text—up to 1 gigabyte (GB) —but only the first 64,000 characters of text, and numbers (or a combination of both) will be visible on the screen.
Number	Age: 19 Grade: 95.5	Stores numeric data that can be used in mathematical calculations.
Date/Time	Birthday: September 5th, 1972	Stores date and/or time data.
Currency	Registration Fee: $50.00	Stores monetary data with precision to four decimal places. Use this data type to store financial data and when you don't want Access to round values.
AutoNumber	Student ID: 56	Unique values created by Access when you create a new record. Tables often contain an AutoNumber field used as the primary key.
Yes/No	Insurance: Yes	Stores Boolean (true or false) data. Access uses 1 for all Yes values and 0 for all No values.
OLE Object	Photo	Stores images, documents, graphs, and other objects from Office and Windows-based programs.
Hyperlink	Web addresses	Stores links to websites, sites or files on an intranet or Local Area Network (LAN), and sites or files on your computer.
Attachment	Any supported type of file	You can attach images, spreadsheet files, documents, charts, and other types of supported files (up to 2 GB per record) to the records in your database, much like you attach files to email messages.
Calculated	FullName: John Derenzo	Stores an expression based on two or more fields within the same table. Example using concatenation operator (&): First: John Last: Derenzo FullName stored as: [First]&" "&[Last]

Defining Database Tables

Tables are the most basic organizational element of a database. Not only is it important to plan the tables so they will hold the type of data you need, it's important to plan how the tables and information will be connected. In this exercise, you view a visual representation of the relationship between two tables.

In a simple database, you might only have only one table. Most databases, however, will have more than just one table. The tables you include in a database will be based on the data available. For example, a database of students might have a table for contact information, a table for grades, and a table for tuition and fees.

In database applications like Access, you can create a relational database. A **relational database** stores information in separate tables and these tables are connected or linked by a defined relationship that ties the data together.

Define Database Tables

USE the database you used in the previous exercise.

1. On the DATABASE TOOLS tab, in the Relationships group, click **Relationships** to display a visual representation of the relationship between the Students and Guardians tables, as shown in Figure 1-36.

Figure 1-36

A relationship between tables

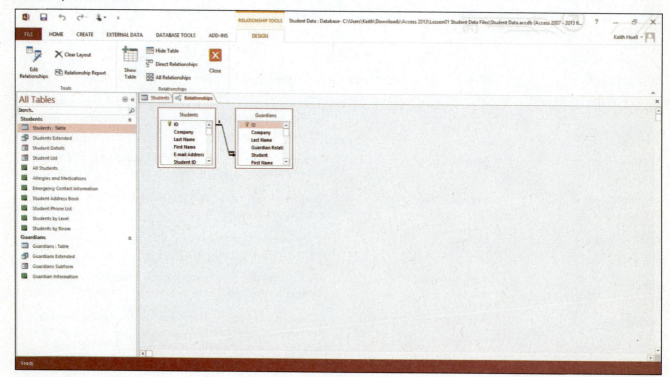

2. **CLOSE** the Relationships tab.
3. **CLOSE** the Students tab.

STOP. CLOSE the database.

 Cross Ref   You learn more about table relationships in Lesson 3.

An important principle to consider when planning a database is to try to record each piece of information only once. Duplicate information, or **redundant data**, wastes space and increases the likelihood of errors. Relationships among database tables help ensure consistency and reduce repetitive data entry.

As you create each table, keep in mind how the data in the tables are related to each other. Enter test data and then add fields to tables or create new tables as necessary to refine the database. The last step is to apply data normalization rules to see if your tables are structured correctly and make adjustments as needed. **Normalization** is the process of applying rules to your database design to ensure that you have divided your information items into the appropriate tables.

Database design principles include standards and guidelines that can be used to determine if your database is structured correctly. These are referred to as **normal forms**. There are five normal forms, but typically only the first three are applied, because that is usually all that is required. The following is a summary of the first three normal forms:

- **First Normal Form (1NF):** This form divides each field according to its smallest meaningful value, removes repeating groups of data, and creates a separate table for each set of related data.
- **Second Normal Form (2NF):** With this form, each non-key column should be fully dependent on the entire primary key. Create new tables for data that applies to more than one record in a table and add a related field to the table.
- **Third Normal Form (3NF):** Use this form to remove fields that do not relate to, nor provide a fact about, the primary key.

Before normalizing a database and defining fields for the efficient storage of data in tables, it's important to know where your data will come from. Data can be brought into an Access database in a number of ways, including linking and importing. When defining tables, you have to decide whether data should be linked to or imported from external sources. When you import data, Access creates a copy of the data or objects in the destination database without altering the source. Linking lets you connect to data from another source without importing it, so that you can view and modify the latest data in both the source and destination databases without creating and maintaining two copies of the same data thereby reducing redundant data. Any changes you make to the data in the source are reflected in the linked table in the destination database, and vice versa.

 Cross Ref You learn more about importing data and linking to an external data source in Lesson 14.

SUMMARY SKILLS MATRIX

In This Lesson You Learned How To:	Exam Objective	Objective Number
Get Started		
Work in the Access Window	Set Navigation options. Change views.	1.3.4 1.3.5
Use the On-Screen Tools		
Use the Backstage View		
Use the Microsoft Access Help Button		
Define Data Needs and Types	Change field data types.	2.4.5

Knowledge Assessment

Matching

Match the term in Column 1 to its description in Column 2.

Column 1	Column 2
1. record	**a.** most basic database object; stores data in categories
2. field	**b.** database object that presents information in a format that is easy to read and print
3. redundant data	**c.** duplicate information in a database
4. primary key	**d.** row in a database table
5. database	**e.** database object that asks a table a question

6. table	**f.** column in a database that uniquely identifies each row
7. query	**g.** database object that simplifies the process of entering, editing, and displaying data
8. report	**h.** column in a database table
9. form	**i.** kind of information a field contains
10. data type	**j.** tool for collecting and organizing information

True/False

Circle T if the statement is true or F if the statement is false.

T F 1. Any list you make for a specific purpose—even a grocery list—can be considered a simple database.

T F 2. By default, the Navigation Pane appears on the right side of the Access screen each time you create or open a database.

T F 3. Forms, queries, and reports are examples of database objects.

T F 4. The dialog box launcher contains the commands that you use most often, such as Save, Undo, and Redo.

T F 5. When you press the Shift key, small letters and numbers called KeyTips appear on the Ribbon.

T F 6. The Change Help Collection menu lets you choose between the help topics that are available online and the help topics installed in your computer offline.

T F 7. In a database table, data is stored in rows and columns—similar in appearance to a spreadsheet.

T F 8. Each field in a table must be designated for a particular data type.

T F 9. An important principle to consider when planning a database is to try to record each piece of information as many times as possible for easy access.

T F 10. Normalization is the process of applying rules to your database design to ensure that you have organized your information items into the appropriate tables and columns within tables.

Competency Assessment

Project 1-1: Personalizing Access

When working in Access or another Microsoft Office application, it is useful to personalize your copy of the software. Personalizing your software helps credit you as the creator of the Access database or other Office application.

GET READY. LAUNCH Access if it is not already running.

1. Click the **FILE** tab.
2. Click the **Options** command to display the Access Options dialog box.

Take Note Throughout this lesson you will see information that appears in black text within brackets, such as [Press **Enter**], or **your e-mail address**. The information contained in the brackets is intended to be directions for you rather than something you actually type word-for-word. It will instruct you to perform an action or substitute text. Do **not** type the actual text that appears within brackets.

3. In the *Personalize your copy of Microsoft Office* section of the dialog box, key [**your name**] in the User name box and key [**your initials**] in the Initials box.
4. Click **OK** to close the dialog box.

LEAVE Access open for the next project.

Project 1-2: Using the Navigation Pane

As a busy editor at Lucerne Publishing, you use Access to organize and manage your task list.

GET READY. LAUNCH Access if it is not already running.

1. **OPEN** *Task_List* from the data files for this lesson.
2. To display the Navigation Pane, click the **Shutter Bar Open/Close Button**.
3. Click the **Contacts** group header in the Navigation Pane to display those database objects.
4. Click the **Supporting Objects** group header to display those database objects.
5. In the Supporting Objects group, double-click **Tasks** to open that table.
6. In the Tasks group, double-click **Tasks by Assigned To** to open that report and view data taken from the Tasks table.
7. In the Navigation Pane, click the **Tasks Navigation** header to display the menu and then click **Object Type**.
8. **CLOSE** the database.

LEAVE Access open for the next project.

Proficiency Assessment

Project 1-3: Understanding Database Creation

You work at Margie's Travel, a full-service travel agency that specializes in providing services to senior citizens. You plan to create a database of tours, cruises, adventure activities, group travel, and vacation packages geared toward seniors, but first you want to learn more about ways you can begin creating a database.

GET READY. LAUNCH Access if it is not already running.

1. **OPEN** Access Help.
2. Search for "Basic tasks for an Access 2013 desktop database."
3. Read the article titled "Basic tasks for an Access 2013 desktop database" to understand the paths you can take to create an Access desktop database.
4. **OPEN** a new Word document.
5. List the two general ways you can create a new Access desktop database with a short description of each. List the benefits of choosing each way.
6. **SAVE** the document as *database_creation* and then **CLOSE** the file.

LEAVE Access open for the next project.

Project 1-4: Planning Table Fields

You are a volunteer for the Tech Terrace Neighborhood Association that holds an annual March Madness 5K Run. In the past, all data has been kept on paper, but you decide it would be more efficient to create a database. Decide what fields would make sense for a table holding data about the runners.

GET READY.

1. Think about what fields would be useful in a database table that contains information about the runners in an annual 5K road race.
2. **OPEN** a new Word document.

3. In the document, key a list of the names of at least six possible field names.
4. **SAVE** the document as *race_fields* and keep the file open.

LEAVE Access open for the next project.

Mastery Assessment

Project 1-5: Planning Data Types for Fields

Now that you have decided what fields to use in a database table containing information about runners in an annual 5K road race, you need to determine what data type should be used for each field.

USE the document you used in the previous project.

1. Beneath the name of each possible field name for the table about runners in the annual 5K road race, key the data type that would be used with a short explanation of why you chose that type.
2. **SAVE** the document as *data_type* and then **CLOSE** the file.

CLOSE Word. **LEAVE** Access open for the next project.

Project 1-6: What's New in Microsoft Access 2013

Your supervisor at Margie's Travel has suggested that you research what's new in Access 2013 before you begin to create a database.

GET READY. LAUNCH Access if it is not already running.

1. **OPEN** the Backstage View and access the Help menu.
2. Use Access Help to locate the article "What's New in Access 2013."
3. Read the overview.

CLOSE Access.

Create Database Tables 2

LESSON SKILL MATRIX

Skill	Exam Objective	Objective Number
Creating a Database	Create databases using templates	1.1.2
	Create new databases	1.1.1
Creating a Table	Create tables from templates and application parts	2.1.5
	Create new tables	2.1.1
	Create reports with application parts	5.1.2
Saving a Database Object		

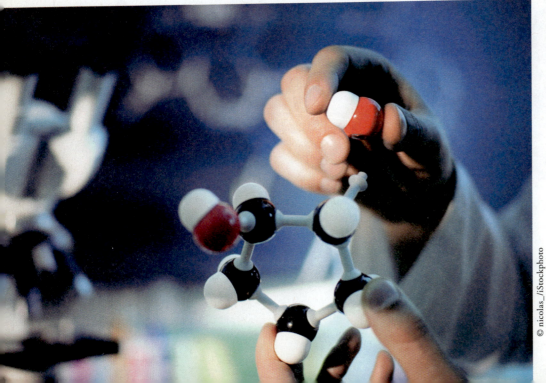

KEY TERMS

- Application Parts
- Quick Start
- template

© nicolas_/iStockphoto

37

© nicolas_/iStockphoto

As an assistant curator at the Baldwin Museum of Science, you are responsible for the day-to-day management of the insect collection, including duties such as sorting and organizing specimens and supervising the mounting and labeling of the insects. The insect collection catalog has never been transferred to an electronic database. Because you have experience with database management, part of your responsibility is to create a database to store the information about the specimens, collections, museum exhibits, and events—a task perfectly suited to Access 2013. In this lesson, you learn how to create a blank database and how to use a template to create a database. You also learn how to use Application Parts to create a table from a template, how to create a table by copying the structure from another table, and how to save a database object.

SOFTWARE ORIENTATION

Getting Started with Microsoft Access

The Access startup screen shown in Figure 2-1 provides options for opening a preexisting database and creating a new blank database or a new database from a template. This is the default view after starting Access. Use this figure as a reference throughout this lesson as well as the rest of this book.

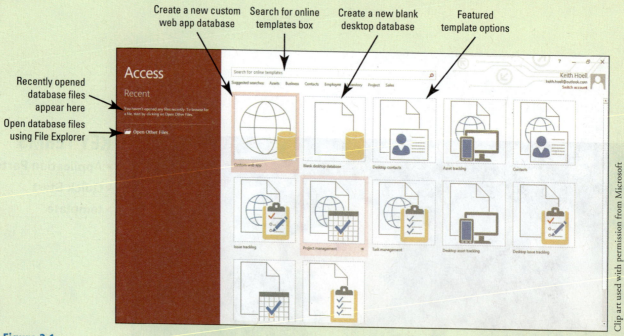

Figure 2-1

The Access startup screen

Clip art used with permission from Microsoft

CREATING A DATABASE

The Bottom Line

In Access 2013, the process of creating a new database is easier than ever. You can create a database using one of the many available **templates** (ready-to-use databases that contain all of the tables, queries, forms, and reports needed for performing specific tasks) or by creating a new blank database.

Using a Template to Create a Database

Access offers a variety of templates to help get you started. Some templates are immediately available for your use because they are built into Access while others can be easily downloaded from Office.com. Built-in and Office.com templates are available that can be used to track issues, manage contacts, or keep a record of expenses. Some templates contain a few sample records to help demonstrate their use. You can use templates as-is or you can customize them to better suit your purposes. In this exercise, you use one of the many available templates to create a database.

STEP BY STEP | **Use a Template to Create a Database**

GET READY. Before you begin these steps, be sure that you are logged on to the Internet. **LAUNCH** Microsoft Access to display the startup screen.

1. On the top center of the startup screen window, in the *Search for online templates* search box, key **personal** and then press **Enter**.
2. In the list of Personal templates that appears in the middle of the startup screen results pane, click **Desktop home inventory**. A preview screen of the selected template appears in the center of the startup screen, as shown in Figure 2-2. Close the Desktop home inventory template preview screen.

Figure 2-2

The Desktop home inventory template preview screen

Information about selected template displayed

Clip art used with permission from Microsoft

3. In the *Search for online templates* search box, key **education** and then press **Enter**.
4. In the list of Education templates that appears, click **Desktop faculty**. Your screen should look similar to Figure 2-3. Close the Desktop faculty template preview screen.

Figure 2-3

The Desktop faculty template preview screen

5. In the *Search for online templates* search box, key in **assets** and then press **Enter**.

6. In the Assets template results list shown in Figure 2.4, click the **Desktop asset tracking** database. The Desktop asset tracking template preview screen appears.

Figure 2-4

Assets templates

Assets template results list

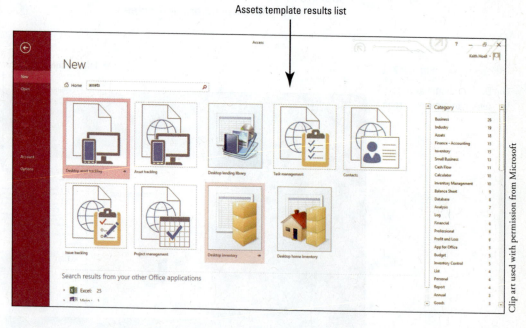

7. In the Desktop asset tracking template preview screen, click in the **File Name** box and replace the default file by keying **AssetsXXX** (where XXX is your initials), as shown in Figure 2-5.

Figure 2-5

The File Name box and
folder icon

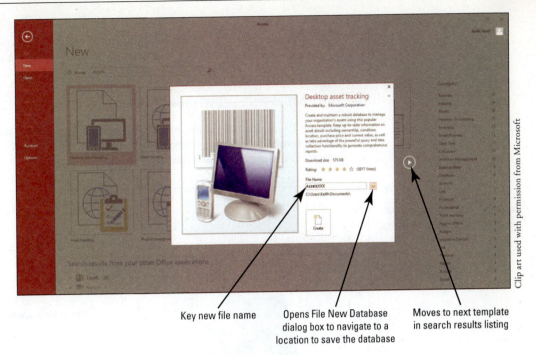

Key new file name   Opens File New Database   Moves to next template
dialog box to navigate to a   in search results listing
location to save the database

*If you do not add an extension to your database file name, Access does it for you—for example,
AccessXXX.accdb.*

8. Click the **folder icon** to the right of the File Name box. The File New Database dialog
box appears, as shown in Figure 2-6.

Figure 2-6

The File New Database
dialog box

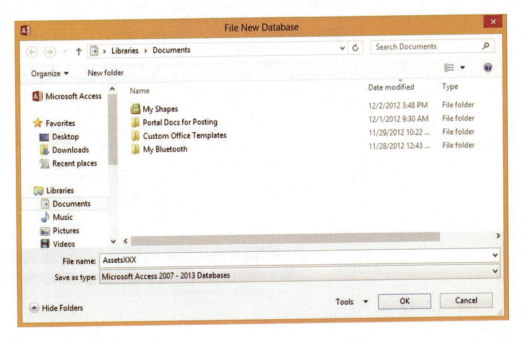

9. Navigate to the location where you want to save the file and then click **OK**.

Take Note You should save your files in a separate directory from where your data files are stored. This will ensure that you don't overwrite the original data files with your updated files. Check with your instructor to see if she wants you to save your work on a flash drive or in a particular network directory.

Take Note Unless you choose a different folder, Access uses the following default location in Windows Server 2008/2012, Windows 7, and Windows 8 to store your databases: c:\Users\user name\Documents

10. Click the **Create** button at the bottom of the preview pane. The preview pane indicates that the template is being downloaded, as shown in Figure 2-7. When the download is complete, the preview pane closes.

Figure 2-7

The preview pane indicating that the template is downloading

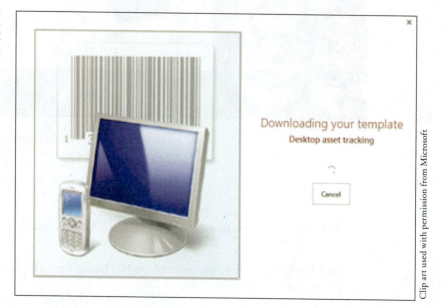

Clip art used with permission from Microsoft

11. Access creates and then opens the AssetsXXX database, as shown in Figure 2-8. Because this database was downloaded from Office.com (a trusted source), click **Enable Content** on the Message Bar. Getting Started and Access Help windows may appear, which contain helpful videos and links about using the Asset tracking database. Close these windows, if necessary, to return to the AssetsXXX database with the Asset List form active. Click to place the insertion point in the first cell of the Item field and then key **Canon EOS Rebel T3i**.

Figure 2-8

The Assets template database

Access 2007–2013 file format indication on title bar specifies database format is of the latest specification   Message Bar

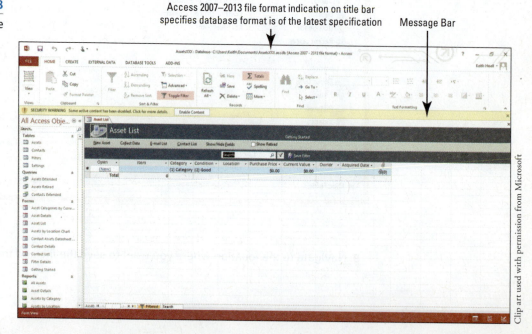

Clip art used with permission from Microsoft

Troubleshooting   Sometimes you may be asked if you want to enable content by clicking the Enable Content button on the Security Warning Message Bar. By default, Access blocks potentially harmful content that might contain viruses or present other security issues. This content should be enabled only if the database is downloaded from a trustworthy site, like Office.com.

12. Click the **Shutter Bar Open/Close Button**, if necessary, to display the Navigation Pane, as shown in Figure 2-9, to see all the objects in the database.

Figure 2-9

The Assets database with the Navigation Pane displayed

Shutter Bar Open/Close Button

Objects in downloaded database displayed in Navigation Pane

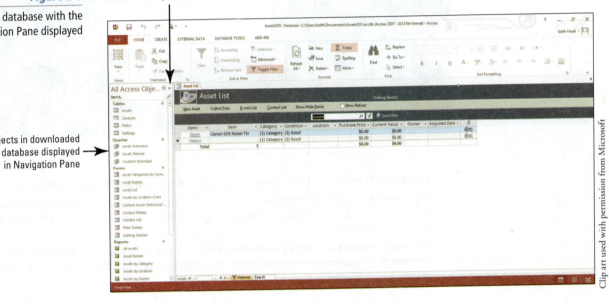

Clip art used with permission from Microsoft

13. **CLOSE** the database.

PAUSE. LEAVE Access open to use in the next exercise.

CERTIFICATION READY?   1.1.2

How do you create databases using templates?

Creating a Blank Database

If you have existing data, you may decide that it is easier to create a blank database rather than using a template, because it would require a lot of work to adapt your existing data to the template's defined data structure. When you create a new blank database, Access opens a database that contains a table where you can enter data, but it creates no other database objects. By default, Access creates a primary key field named "ID" for all new datasheets and sets the data type for the field to AutoNumber. In this exercise, you create a new blank database.

STEP BY STEP   **Create a Blank Database**

GET READY. The Access work area window should be on the screen from the previous exercise.

1. Click the **FILE tab** to open the New screen in Backstage view.
2. In the templates section of the New screen, click the **Blank desktop database** icon. A Blank desktop database screen appears in the center of the screen, as shown in Figure 2-10.

Figure 2-10

A Blank desktop database screen

Blank desktop database screen

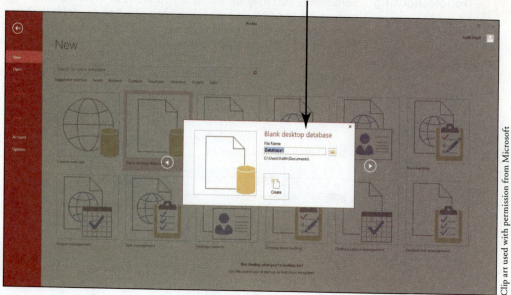

3. In the File Name box, key **BlankDatabaseXXX** (where XXX is your initials).

4. If you want to save the file in a location other than the one shown beneath the File Name box, click the **folder icon** to the right of the File Name box and browse to a different location.

5. Click the **Create** button to create the blank database in your chosen location. Access creates the database and then opens an empty table named Table1 in Datasheet view, as shown in Figure 2-11.

Figure 2-11

A new blank database

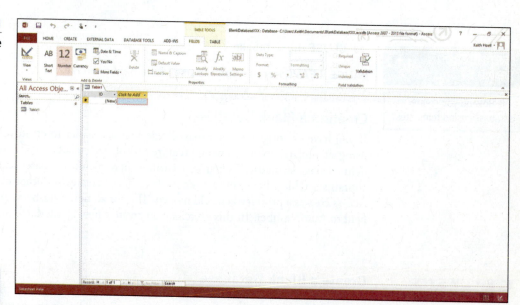

CERTIFICATION
READY?   1.1.1

How do you create new databases?

PAUSE. LEAVE the database open to use in the next exercise.

Take Note   The New screen appears in the Backstage view after you click on the FILE tab when no database is open. When a database is open, the FILE tab takes you to the Info screen in the Backstage view.

Cross Ref   You learn more about defining and modifying a primary key in Lesson 3.

With the insertion point placed in the first empty cell of your new, blank database, you can begin keying to add data. Entering data in Datasheet view is very similar to entering data into an Excel worksheet, except that data must be entered in related rows and columns, starting at the upper-left corner of the datasheet.

The table is structured through rows and columns, which become meaningful as you enter appropriate data. Any time you add a new column to the table, Access defines a new field for that column's data. You do not need to format your data by including blank rows or columns, as you might do in an Excel worksheet, because that just wastes space in your table. The table merely contains your data. All visual presentation of that data will be done in the forms and reports that you design later.

Take Note   A database has to be saved first before any objects like tables, queries, forms or reports can be added to it. For example, you cannot create a table first and then create the database to hold it.

Cross Ref   You learn more about creating forms and reports in Lessons 5 and 6.

SOFTWARE ORIENTATION

Templates Group and Application Parts

The Templates group on the CREATE tab contains the Application Parts gallery that you can use to insert predefined templates consisting of objects like tables, forms, and reports into a pre-existing database. Use as a reference throughout this lesson as well as the rest of this book.

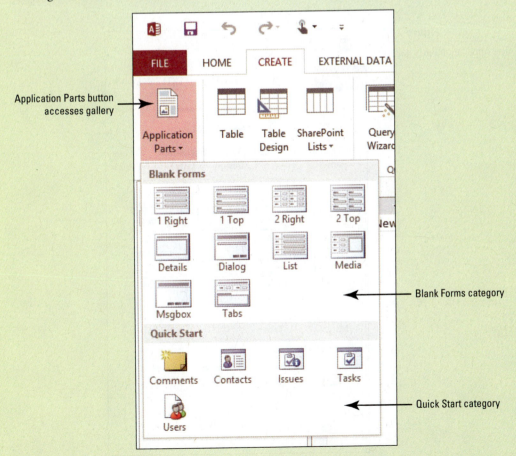

Figure 2-12

Application Parts gallery

CREATING A TABLE

It is easy to create a new table by using the Application Parts gallery and Quick Start. **Application Parts** were introduced in Access 2010 and consist of predefined templates that you can add to an existing database to help extend its functionality. Another way to create a table is to copy the structure of an existing table and then paste it into the database. You can copy a database object and paste it into the same database or into a different database that is open in another instance of Access.

Cross Ref

You learn more about creating forms using the Application Parts gallery in Lesson 10.

Using the Application Parts Gallery and Quick Start

Application parts vary from a single table to a collection of database objects like tables, forms, and reports. The Application Parts gallery consists of two categories, Blank Forms and Quick Start. The Blank Forms category contains a collection of form parts that allows you to add predefined forms to a database. The **Quick Start** category of these templates contains a collection of predefined objects arranged by parts for tracking things such as comments, contacts, and issues. In this exercise, you will quickly create a table using the Application Parts gallery and Quick Start.

STEP BY STEP   **Create a Table Using the Application Parts Gallery and Quick Start**

USE the database that is open from the previous exercise.

1. On the CREATE tab, in the Templates group, click the **Application Parts** button to display the gallery shown in Figure 2-13.

Figure 2-13

The Application Parts gallery

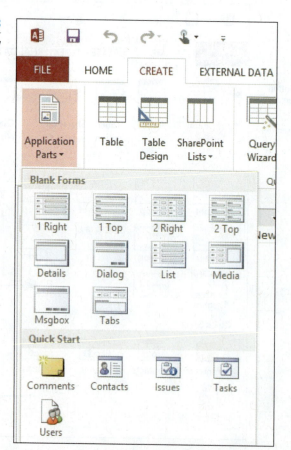

2. In the Quick Start section of the gallery, click **Comments**. When prompted to close all open objects before instantiating this application part, click **Yes** on the Microsoft Access dialog box that appears. Notice the Comments table appears as a new object in the Navigation Pane.

3. Click the **Enable Content** button on the Message Bar to trust the database.

4. In the Navigation Pane, double-click **Comments** to display the newly created table with fields for comments, as shown in Figure 2-14. Close the Comments table by clicking the Comments table Close button.

Figure 2-14

New Comments table for comments

New table object named Comments in Navigation Pane

Comments table tab

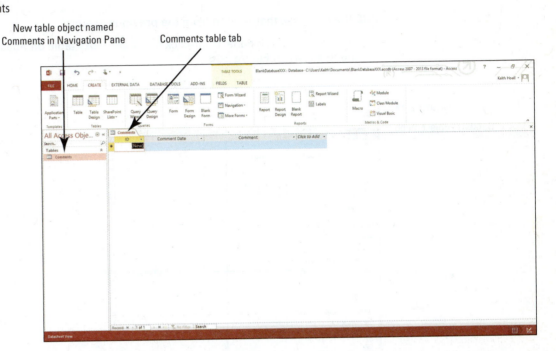

5. On the Application Parts menu, click **Contacts**. In the Create Relationship dialog box that appears, select the **There is no relationship** option button then click **Create**. A new table is created along with supporting forms and report objects, as shown in Figure 2-15.

Figure 2-15

New table, forms, and reports for contacts

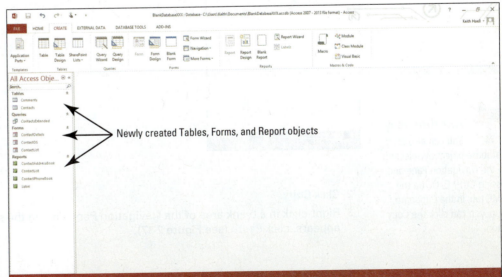

Newly created Tables, Forms, and Report objects

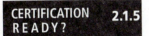

CERTIFICATION READY?   2.1.5

How do you create tables from templates and application parts?

CERTIFICATION READY?   2.1.1

How do you create new tables?

PAUSE. LEAVE the database open to use in the next exercise.

Cross Ref   You learn how to create a custom table in Lesson 9.

You learn how to create a custom table in Lesson 9.

CERTIFICATION READY?   **5.1.2**

How do you create reports with application parts?

Creating a Table from Another Table

Another way to create a table is to copy the structure of an existing table using the Copy and Paste commands. In this exercise, you copy the structure of an existing table to create a new table.

STEP BY STEP   **Create a Table from Another Table**

USE the database that is open from the previous exercise.

1. On the Navigation Pane, right-click the **Comments** table database object to display the menu shown in Figure 2-16.

Figure 2-16

Database object menu

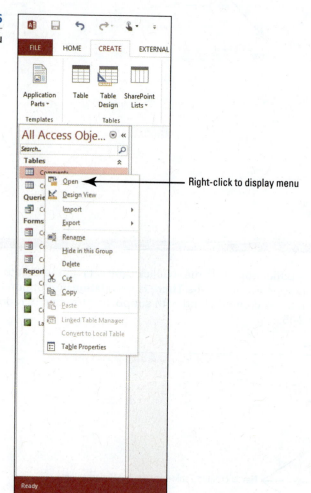

Right-click to display menu

Another Way

You can also copy a database object by selecting it in the Navigation Pane and pressing Ctrl+C. Or, on the HOME tab, in the Clipboard group, you can click the Copy button.

2. Click **Copy**.

3. Right-click in a blank area of the Navigation Pane and, in the shortcut menu that appears, click **Paste** (see Figure 2-17).

Figure 2-17

Database object menu

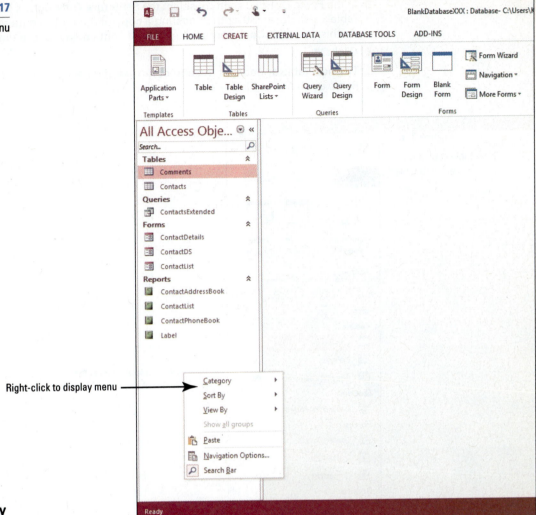

Right-click to display menu →

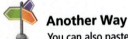

Another Way
You can also paste a database object by selecting the destination location in the Navigation Pane and pressing Ctrl+V. Or on the HOME tab, in the Clipboard group, you can click the Paste button.

4. The Paste Table As dialog box appears, as shown in Figure 2-18. Notice the default name, Copy Of Comments, in the Table Name box.

Figure 2-18

Paste Table As dialog box

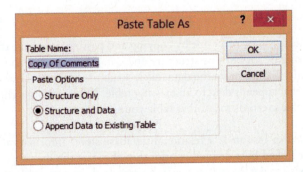

5. In the Paste Options section, select the **Structure Only** option button, to paste only the table's structure, rather than pasting a copy of the table's data along with its structure (in this case, the Comments table doesn't contain any record data).
6. Click **OK**.
7. The new table appears at the end of the list of database table objects in the Navigation Pane, as shown in Figure 2-19.

Figure 2-19

New table copied from existing table

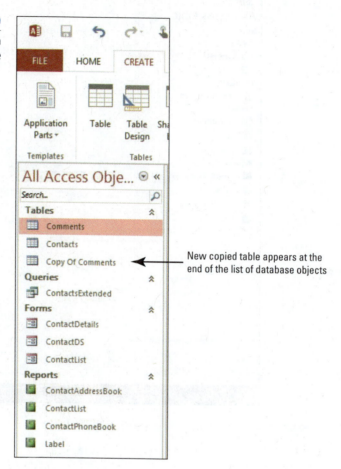

New copied table appears at the end of the list of database objects

8. Double-click **Copy Of Comments** to open the new table. Notice that the structure of the new table is the same as the table from which it was copied.

PAUSE. CLOSE the database.

LEAVE Access open for the next project.

When you create a copy of a table by copying and pasting, you have the option of re-creating just the table's structure, or both its structure and data. To paste just the structure of the table, click Structure Only. To also paste the data, click Structure and Data. Access also provides you with a third option that appends data to an existing table. If this option is chosen, Access will attempt to append the table's records to another table you specify.

As you learned in Lesson 1, a relational database stores information in separate tables that are connected or linked by a defined relationship that ties the data together. When you add a new table to an existing database, that new table stands alone until you relate it to your existing tables. For example, say you need to track orders placed by a distributor. To do that, you add a table named Distributor Contacts to a sales database. To take advantage of the power that a relational database can provide—to search for the orders placed by a given contact, for example— you must create a relationship between the new table and any tables that contain the order data.

Cross Ref   You learn more about defining table relationships in Lesson 3.

SAVING A DATABASE OBJECT

The Bottom Line

Access automatically saves data that you have entered any time you add an Application Part like a Quick Start template, move to a new record, close an object or database, or quit the application. But you will need to save the design of a table, or any other database object, after it is created. Additionally, using the Save Object As command in the Backstage view, you can create a duplicate of a database object (like a table, query, or report) by specifying an alternate name, or even save objects in other formats such as the Adobe Portable Document Format (PDF) or XML Paper Specification (XPS) which helps you share data with others who may not have Access installed. Lastly, you can even save some objects as other compatible object types. For example, you can save a table as a new report which will, by default, include all table fields.

Saving a Table

When you save a new table for the first time, give it a name that describes the information it contains. You can use up to 64 characters (letters or numbers), including spaces. For example, you might name a table Orders 2014, Clients, Tasks, Inventory Parts, or Comments. In this exercise, you save a database table and then use the Save Object As command to create a duplicate of the same table.

STEP BY STEP   Save a Table

GET READY. The blank Access screen should be displayed from the previous exercise.

1. From the FILE tab, click the **New** command, then click the **Blank desktop database** icon; a Blank desktop database screen appears in the center of the screen.

2. In the Blank desktop database screen's File Name box, the default name should be *Database1*. If not, replace the default name by keying **Database1**.

3. If you want to save the file in a location other than the one shown beneath the File Name box, click the **folder icon** and browse to a different location.

4. Click the **Create** button. A new blank database appears with the default table labeled Table1 displayed, as shown in Figure 2-20.

Figure 2-20

New blank database with default table

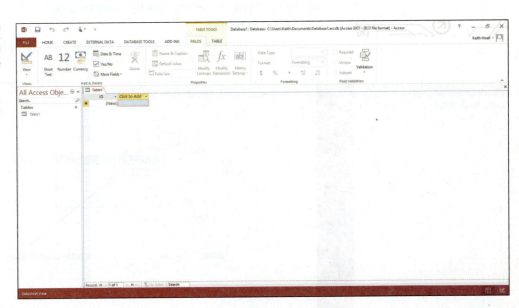

5. Click to place the insertion point in the cell under the Click to Add field and key **Sample Data**.

6. Right-click on the **Table1** tab to display the shortcut menu, as shown in Figure 2-21.

Figure 2-21

Shortcut menu

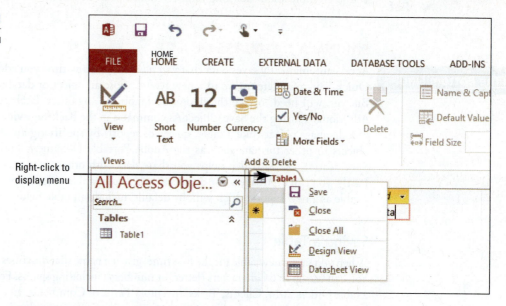

Right-click to
display menu

7. Click **Save**. The Save As dialog box appears, as shown in Figure 2-22.

Figure 2-22

Save As dialog box

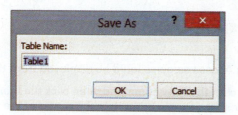

8. In the Table Name box, key **Sample Table**.

9. Click **OK** to close the dialog box and return to the table, which now is labeled Sample Table.

10. Click the **FILE** tab to display the Backstage view.

11. Click **Save As** to display the Save As screen.

12. Under the File Types heading, click the **Save Object As** command.

13. Click the **Save As** button.

14. In the Save As dialog box that appears, key **Backup of Sample Table** in the area under "Save 'Sample Table' to:" as shown in Figure 2-23.

Figure 2-23

Save As dialog box on Save
As screen

Save Object
As command

Save As button

New table name in Save As dialog box

Another Way
You can also save a table by pressing Ctrl+S. You do not need to save new data that you enter. Access automatically saves a record when you move to a different record or close the object or database.

Access also automatically saves changes to your data whenever you quit the program. However, if you have made changes to the design of any database objects since you last saved them, Access asks whether you want to save these changes before quitting.

15. Click OK.
16. Notice the new table object named Backup of Sample Table in the Navigation Pane.
17. The Backup of Sample Table should now be open. Notice the table contains the same row you created in the Sample Table table.
18. **CLOSE** Backup of Sample Table.
19. **CLOSE** the database.

CLOSE Access.

SKILL SUMMARY

In This Lesson You Learned How To:	Exam Objective	Objective Number
Create a Database	Create databases using templates	1.1.2
	Create new databases	1.1.1
Create a Table	Create tables from templates and application parts	2.1.5
	Create new tables	2.1.1
	Create reports with application parts	5.1.2
Save a Database Object		

Knowledge Assessment

Fill in the Blank
Complete the following sentences by writing the correct word or words in the blanks provided.

1. You can create a database using one of the many templates available or by creating a new _____ database.
2. By default, Access creates a(n) _____ field named "ID" for all new datasheets.
3. Entering data in Datasheet view is very similar to entering data in a(n) _____.
4. The _____ contains predefined templates included in two categories, Blank Forms and Quick Start.
5. One way to create a table is to copy the _____ of an existing table and paste it into the database.
6. When you add a new table to an existing database, that new table stands alone until you _____ it to your existing tables.
7. You can use up to _____ characters (letters or numbers), including spaces, to name a database object.
8. Several options for creating a database are provided on the _____ screen in Backstage view or the _____ screen when Access is initially launched.
9. The _____ category in the Application Parts gallery contains a collection of predefined database objects for tracking comments, contacts, and issues.
10. A table is structured through rows and _____, which become meaningful when you enter data into it.

Multiple Choice

Select the best response for the following statements.

1. In Access, a template is
   a. a database to manage contacts.
   b. where a database is stored.
   c. two tables linked together.
   d. a ready-to-use database.

2. When you create a new blank desktop database, Access opens a database that contains
   a. one of each type of database object.
   b. a table.
   c. sample data.
   d. a template.

3. To save a database file in a location other than the default, click the
   a. folder icon.
   b. blank database icon.
   c. file name button.
   d. Help button.

4. The table structure is created when you
   a. format the data.
   b. enter data.
   c. query the data.
   d. create forms.

5. The Templates group commands are located on which tab?
   a. Home
   b. Create
   c. Database Tools
   d. Datasheet

6. To copy a table, you must first select it in
   a. the Clipboard.
   b. Microsoft Office Online.
   c. the Navigation Pane.
   d. Datasheet view.

7. When you paste a table, which dialog box is displayed?
   a. Table Structure
   b. Copy Table
   c. Paste Data
   d. Paste Table As

8. After you have created a table or other database object, you should
   a. save it with a descriptive name.
   b. copy it to create a backup.
   c. link it to an external data source.
   d. insert a blank column at the end.

9. When you quit the program, Access automatically
   a. creates a link between all tables.
   b. leaves the Navigation Pane open.
   c. saves the data.
   d. renames the file.

10. Which is *not* a way to create a new database table?
    a. Use Quick Start.
    b. Choose Create on the Table menu.
    c. Copy the structure of another table.
    d. Create a new blank desktop database.

Competency Assessment

Project 2-1: Contacts Database

You want to use Access to store, organize, and manage the contact information for the wholesale coffee suppliers used by Fourth Coffee, where you work as a buyer for the 15 stores in the northeast region. Use a template to create a database for the contacts.

GET READY. LAUNCH Access if it is not already running.

1. **OPEN** Access and in the Search for online templates box, key **Desktop call tracker** to find the Desktop call tracker database template.
2. Select the **Desktop call tracker** database template.
3. Key **Call trackerXXX** (where XXX is your initials) in the File Name box.
4. If necessary, click the **folder icon** and choose a different location for the file.
5. Click **Create** to create and open the database. Click **Enable Content**, if necessary.
6. Click the **Shutter Bar Open/Close Button** to open the Navigation Pane.
7. Click the **Supporting Objects** header in the Navigation Pane to display the database objects in that group.
8. Right-click the **Customers** table under the Customers header to display the menu and click **Copy**.
9. Right-click in the white area of the Navigation Pane and click Paste on the menu.
10. In the Paste Table As dialog box, key **Customers structure**.
11. Click the **Structure Only** option button (the table contains no record data so choosing Structure Only will have the same effect as choosing Structure and Data).
12. Click **OK**.
13. **CLOSE** the *Call trackerXXX* database.

LEAVE Access open for the next project.

Project 2-2: Database for Restaurants

As a regional manager for a franchise restaurant chain, you want to keep track of restaurant locations and customer comments. You decide to create a database to store the necessary information.

GET READY. LAUNCH Access if it is not already running.

1. In the Backstage view's New tab (or on the Startup screen, if Access is initially launched), click the **Blank desktop database** icon.
2. In the Blank desktop database screen that appears in the center of the screen, key **RestaurantsXXX** (where XXX is your initials) in the File Name box.
3. If necessary, click the **folder icon** and choose a different location for the file.
4. Click the **Create** button.
5. Right-click the **Table1** tab and click **Save**.
6. In the Save As dialog box, key **Locations**.
7. Click **OK**.

LEAVE the database and Access open for the next project.

Project 2-3: Adding Tables

You need to add some tables to the database that you just created for information about the restaurants.

USE the database that is open from the previous project.

1. Use the Application Parts gallery to create a table for comments.
2. In the Create Relationship dialog box that appears, click the **Cancel** button.
3. Rename the Comments table *Uptown Comments*.
4. Copy the structure of the Uptown Comments table to create a new table.
5. Name the new table *Downtown Comments*.
6. **CLOSE** the database.

LEAVE Access open for the next project.

Project 2-4: Nutrition Tracker

You have become health conscious and want to track your activity, exercise, and food logs using Access.

GET READY. LAUNCH Access if it is not already running.

1. If necessary, log on to the Internet.
2. In the *Search for online templates* box, search for, download, and save the Desktop Nutrition tracking database template with the file name *NutritionXXX* (where XXX is your initials).
3. Click **Enable Content** on the Message Bar.
4. Double-click the **My Profile** form to open it and key your information to see your body mass index and recommended calorie consumption.
5. Click the **OK** button on the form.
6. Open the **Tips** table to view the tips stored in the database.
7. Explore the other useful forms and information available.
8. **CLOSE** the database.

LEAVE Access open for the next project.

Project 2-5: Northwind Traders

You have just joined the sales force at Northwind Traders. To familiarize yourself with the information available in the company database, open the file and browse through the objects.

GET READY. LAUNCH Access if it is not already running.

1. Using the *Search for online templates* search box, find and download the Desktop Northwind 2007 sample database using the name *Northwind2013XXX* (where XXX is your initials).
2. Enable the content.
3. Log in as a sales representative, Jan Kotas, by selecting that name from the Select Employee drop-down menu and clicking the **Login** button.

4. Open the Navigation Pane and open each group to view all the objects that are part of the database.

5. **CLOSE** the database.

LEAVE Access open for the next project.

Project 2-6: Customer Service Database

Southridge Video has a large membership of customers that rent new release and film library movies, as well as video games. As the store manager, customer complaints are directed to you. Create an Access database for the purpose of tracking customer service issues.

GET READY. LAUNCH Access if it is not already running.

1. Choose an Application Parts template to create a database called *SouthridgeXXX* (where XXX is your initials) that will store information about customer service issues.

2. **CLOSE** the database.

LEAVE Access open for the next project.

LESSON SKILL MATRIX

Skill	Exam Objective	Objective Number
Navigating Among Records		
Entering, Inserting, Editing, and Deleting Records	Add New Records.	2.3.2
	Navigate to Specific Records.	1.3.1
	Update Records.	2.3.1
	Delete Records.	2.3.3
Working with Primary Keys	Set Primary Key Fields.	1.2.3
Finding and Replacing Data	Find and Replace Data.	2.3.5
Attaching and Detaching Documents		
Sorting and Filtering Data and Setting Field Viewing Options within a Table	Sort Records.	2.3.6
	Filter Records.	2.3.7
	Hide Fields in Tables.	2.2.1
Understanding Table Relationships	Enforce Referential Integrity.	1.2.4
	Set Foreign Keys.	1.2.5
	Create and Modify Relationships.	1.2.2
	Edit References Between Tables.	1.2.1
	View Relationships.	1.2.6

KEY TERMS

- ascending
- composite key
- descending
- filter
- foreign key
- innermost field
- outermost field
- referential integrity
- sort
- wildcard

© leezsnow/iStockphoto

© leezsnow/iStockphoto

Fourth Coffee is a national chain of coffee shops. A new store recently opened in your neighborhood. You were able to get a part-time job working in the office, helping the office manager organize data on the computer. In addition to being a traditional neighborhood coffee shop, the store has also started selling coffees to companies for use at their business sites. It is your job to manage the inventory, customers, and order tables in Access. In this lesson, you learn to navigate among records; enter, edit, and delete records; find and replace data; sort and filter data; attach and detach documents; and define, modify, and print table relationships.

NAVIGATING AMONG RECORDS

The Bottom Line

Database tables can be very large, and contain useful information that can be manipulated in different ways. When a table contains many records and fields, it is important to be able to navigate among them.

Navigating Using the Keyboard

Access users who prefer using the keyboard to navigate records can press keys and key combinations to move among records in Datasheet view. In Datasheet view, you can navigate among records using the up, down, left, and right arrow keys to move to the field you want. You can also use the Tab key to move from field to field in a record and from the last field in a record to the first field of the next record. If you prefer to use the mouse, you can move among records by clicking the navigation buttons, which you will do in a later exercise. However, in this exercise, you use the keyboard to navigate among records.

STEP BY STEP   **Use the Keyboard to Navigate among Records**

GET READY. Before you begin these steps, be sure to turn on and/or log on to your computer and start Access.

1. **OPEN** *Fourth Coffee* from the data files for this lesson.
2. Click the **FILE** tab, then click the **Save As** option on the left side of the Backstage view.
3. Click the **Save As** command. The Save As dialog box appears. Key **FourthCoffeeXXX** (where XXX is your initials) in the File name box. Find the location where you will save the solution files for this lesson and click **Save**.

Troubleshooting   If you are asked to enable the content, click the Enable Content button on the Security Warning Message Bar. By default, Access blocks potentially harmful content that might contain viruses or present other security issues. This content should only be enabled if the database is downloaded from a trustworthy site, like Office.com.

4. In the Navigation Pane, double-click **Coffee Inventory: Table** to open the table.
5. Notice that the first cell of the first record is selected.
6. Press the **Down Arrow** key to move down to the next row. Notice that the first cell is selected.
7. Press the **Right Arrow** key to move to the Product Name field.
8. Press the **Tab** key to move to the next cell.
9. Press the **Tab** key to move to the next cell.
10. Press the **Tab** key to move to the next row.
11. Press **Ctrl+Down Arrow** to move to the first field of the last record.

PAUSE. LEAVE the database open to use in the next exercise.

Table 3-1 lists keys and key combinations for moving among records.

Table 3-1

Keyboard Commands for
Navigating Records

Commands	Results
Tab or Right Arrow	Moves cursor to the next field
End	Moves cursor to the last field in the current record
Shift + Tab or Left Arrow	Moves cursor to the previous field
Home	Moves cursor to the first field in the current record
Down Arrow	Moves cursor to the current field in the next record
Ctrl + Down Arrow	Moves cursor to the current field in the last record
Ctrl + End	Moves cursor to the last field in the last record
Up Arrow	Moves cursor to the current field in the previous record
Ctrl + Up Arrow	Moves cursor to the current field in the first record
Ctrl + Home	Moves cursor to the first field in the first record

Using Navigation Buttons

Access users who prefer to use the mouse can move among records by clicking the navigation buttons. In this exercise, you use the mouse to navigate among records.

The record navigation buttons are displayed at the bottom of the screen in Datasheet view. Click the First record, Previous record, Next record, Last record, and New (blank) Record buttons to go to those records. Key a record number into the Current Record box and press Enter to go to that record. Key data into the Search box to find a match in the table. The Filter Indicator shows whether a filter has been applied to the table, which will be covered later in this lesson.

STEP BY STEP   **Use Navigation Buttons**

USE the database open from the previous exercise.

1. Click the **First record** button (see Figure 3-1). The selection moves to the first record.

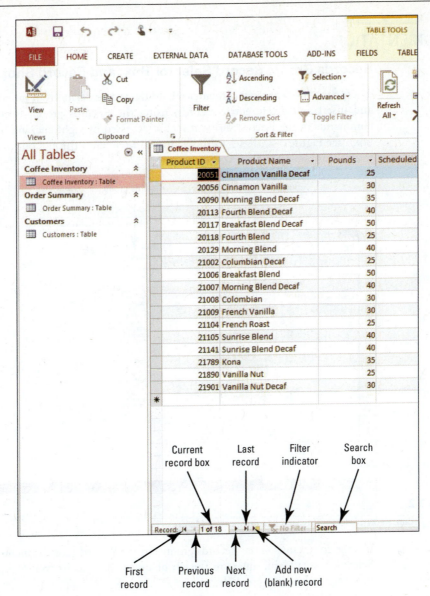

Figure 3-1

Record navigation buttons

2. Click the **Next record** button. The selection moves to the next record.

3. Select and then delete the number **2** in the Current Record box. Key **5** and press **Enter**. The selection moves to the fifth record.

4. Click the **Search** box to position the insertion point. Key **sunrise** into the Search box. Notice that the selection moves to the first occurrence of the word Sunrise.

5. Press **Enter**. The selection moves to the next occurrence of the word Sunrise.

6. Click the **New (blank) record** button. The insertion point moves to the first column and last row of the table.

PAUSE. LEAVE the database open to use in the next exercise.

SOFTWARE ORIENTATION

Records Group, Record Selector Box, and Record Shortcut Menu

There are a few ways you can enter record data, delete data from individual fields of records, and insert and delete entire records, using the Records group, Record Selector box, and commands in the Record shortcut menu (accessed by right-clicking on the Record Selector box) (see Figure 3-2). Refer to this figure as a reference throughout this lesson as well as the rest of this book.

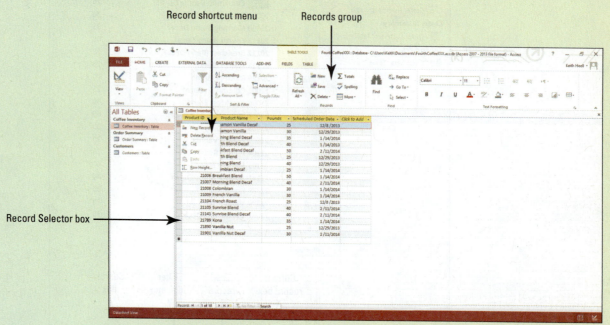

Figure 3-2

Records Group, Record Selector Box, and Record Shortcut Menu

Use the commands in the Records group and the Record shortcut menu, as well as the Record Selector box (a blank square to the left of a record), to assist you in entering record data and inserting and deleting records.

ENTERING, INSERTING, EDITING, AND DELETING RECORDS

The Bottom Line

Keeping a database up-to-date and useful is an ongoing process. You can easily enter data by positioning the insertion point in the table cell where you want to add data and begin keying. To insert a new record, select any record in the table and click the New button on the HOME tab in the Records group. You can also click the Record Selector box, then right-click the selected record and select New Record from the shortcut menu. A new record is added to the end of the table. Select existing data to edit or delete it.

Entering, Editing, and Deleting Records

To enter new data, in Datasheet view, position the insertion point in the first empty cell of a record and begin keying the data. After you enter data and move to a new field, Access automatically saves the data in the table. Each field in a table is formatted with a specific data type, so you must enter that kind of data in the field. If you do not, you will get an error message. To delete information from an individual field of a record, highlight the field data and press the Delete key or click the Delete button on the HOME tab in the Records group. If you change your mind after you delete information from a field, you can undo the action by clicking the Undo button on the Quick Access Toolbar. In this exercise, you enter a new record as well as edit and delete existing records.

You can delete an entire record or several records at once from a database. Just select the row or rows using the Record Selector box, and then press the Delete key or click the Delete button on the HOME tab in the Records group. You can also right-click and select Delete Record from the shortcut menu. After you delete a record, you cannot undo it.

STEP BY STEP   **Enter, Edit, and Delete Records**

USE the database you used in the previous exercise.

1. The insertion point should be positioned in the first field of the new, blank row at the bottom of the datasheet (see Figure 3-3). Notice the asterisk in the Record Selector box, which indicates that this is a new record, ready for data.

Figure 3-3

Blank Record in Datasheet View

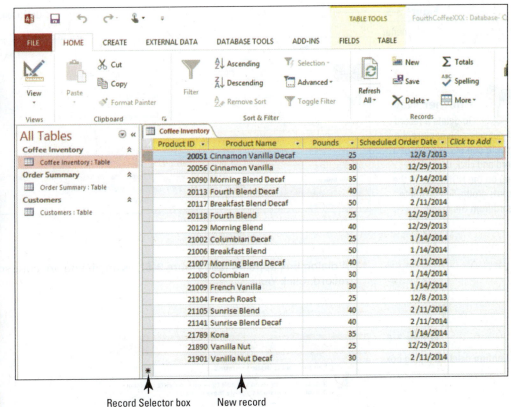

Record Selector box   New record

CERTIFICATION READY?   2.3.2

How do you add new records?

CERTIFICATION READY?   1.3.1

How do you navigate to specific records?

CERTIFICATION READY?   2.3.1

How do you update records?

CERTIFICATION READY?   2.3.3

How do you delete records?

2. Key **21905** and press **Tab**. Notice that the asterisk has changed to a pencil icon (see Figure 3-4), indicating that the record is being edited.

Figure 3-4

Entering data into a record

Pencil icon in Record Selector box indicates that the record is being edited

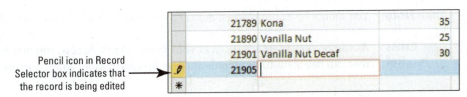

Another Way
An easy way to select an entire record is to click the Record Selector box. If you need to select other records above or below it, you can drag the mouse up or down to include those in the selection.

3. Key **Hazelnut** and press **Tab**.

4. Key **30** and press **Tab**.

5. Key **02112014** and press **Enter**.

6. Highlight **sunrise** in the Search box and key **Kona** to locate the Kona record.

7. Click **Kona** in the record to position the blinking insertion point there. Delete **Kona** and key **Hawaiian** and press **Tab**.

8. Click the **Undo** button on the Quick Access Toolbar. Notice Hawaiian disappears and Kona reappears.

9. Press **Tab**. Key **01142013** and press **Tab**.

10. Click the **Record Selector** box to the left of the Product ID field of the first record, 20051.

11. On the HOME tab, in the Records group, click the **Delete button drop-down arrow**. Select **Delete Record** from the menu (see Figure 3-5).

Figure 3-5

Delete menu

Another Way
To delete a record without selecting it, place the cursor in one of the fields of a record and click the Delete menu on the HOME tab in the Records group. Select Delete Record from the menu.

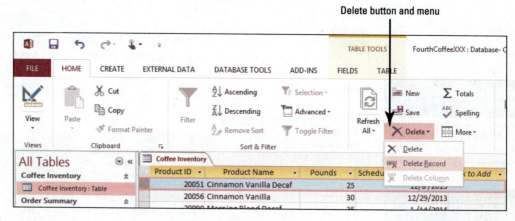

Delete button and menu

12. A dialog box appears (see Figure 3-6), asking if you are sure you want to delete the record. Click **Yes**.

Figure 3-6

Confirm deletion dialog box

13. Notice that the Undo button on the Quick Access Toolbar is not available because you cannot undo a record deletion. **CLOSE** the table.

PAUSE. LEAVE the database open to use in the next exercise.

Take Note   You should be cautious when deleting record data. You cannot undo the deletion of a record.

Cross Ref   As you become more advanced in your knowledge of Access, you may want to create a delete query that can delete multiple records at once. You learn more about queries in Lesson 7.

WORKING WITH PRIMARY KEYS

The Bottom Line

As you learned in Lesson 1, a primary key is a column that uniquely identifies a record or row in a table. Customer IDs, serial numbers, or product IDs usually make good primary keys. Each table should have a primary key, and some tables might have two or more. When you divide information into separate tables, the primary keys help Access bring the information back together again.

Defining a Primary Key

CERTIFICATION READY? 1.2.3

How do you set primary key fields?

You can define a primary key for a field in Design view by selecting the row that contains the field for which you want to assign a primary key and clicking the Primary Key button on the DESIGN tab in the Tools group on the Ribbon. When you create a new database, Access creates a primary key field named "ID" by default and sets the data type for the field to AutoNumber. If you do not have a field in an existing database that you think will make a good primary key, you can use a field with the AutoNumber data type. It does not contain factual information (such as a telephone number) about a record, and it is not likely to change. In this exercise, you define a primary key.

Once a primary key is defined, you can use it in other tables to refer back to the table with the primary key. When a primary key from one table is used in another table, it is called the **foreign key**. The foreign key is used to reference the data from the primary key to help avoid redundancy.

You can modify a primary key by deleting it from one field and adding it to another field. To remove a primary key in Design view, select the row and click the Primary Key button on the DESIGN tab in the Tools group on the Ribbon to remove it.

STEP BY STEP   **Define a Primary Key**

USE the database you used in the previous exercise.

1. In the Navigation Pane, double-click Order Summary: Table to open the table.
2. On the HOME tab, in the Views group, click the bottom half of the View button, and from the menu that appears, select Design View.
3. Click the Row Selector box beside the Order ID row to select the row.
4. On the DESIGN tab, in the Tools group, click the Primary Key button. The Primary Key button is highlighted. A key icon appears on the Order ID row to designate the field as a primary key (see Figure 3-7).

Figure 3-7

Primary Key

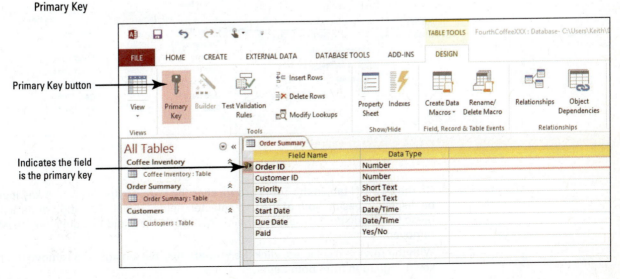

Primary Key button

Indicates the field is the primary key

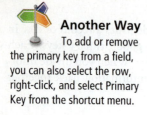

Another Way
To add or remove the primary key from a field, you can also select the row, right-click, and select Primary Key from the shortcut menu.

PAUSE. LEAVE the table open to use in the next exercise.

Defining and Modifying a Multifield Primary Key

In some cases, you may want to use two or more fields that, together, provide the primary key of a table. In Design view, select the rows you want to designate as primary keys and click the Primary Key button. To remove multiple primary keys, select the rows and click the Primary Key button. In this exercise, you practice defining and modifying a multifield primary key.

Two or more primary keys in a table are called the **composite key**. Composite keys are useful in unique situations when a combination of data from two fields needs to provide a unique identifier in a table. For example, area code field data and phone number field data can be combined to create a unique combination of numbers that cannot be duplicated. Separate, neither the area code data nor the phone number data is unique and can be duplicated; however, together they form a unique set of numbers that cannot be duplicated. Likewise, a business can repeat both order identification number field data and customer identification number field data for multiple customers; however, these numbers become unique when combined resulting in a composite key for each customer.

STEP BY STEP **Define and Modify a Multifield Primary Key**

USE the database open from the previous exercise.

1. Press and hold the **CTRL** key.

2. Click the **Row Selector** box beside the Paid row. Continue to hold down the **CTRL** key, and then click the **Order ID Row Selector** box. Both fields should be selected (see Figure 3-8). If not, continue to hold the **CTRL** key, and then click the **Paid Row Selector** box again.

Figure 3-8

Primary Key row and another row selected

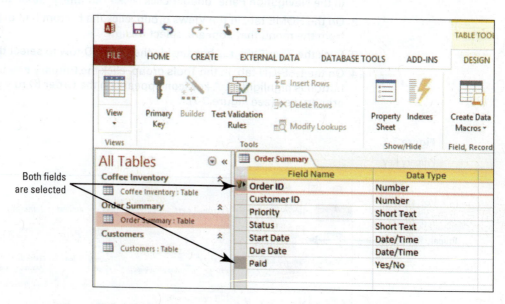

3. On the DESIGN tab, in the Tools group, click the **Primary Key** button. A key icon should be displayed beside both of the two selected fields. The combination of data from these two fields *do not* make a sensible composite key, and this designation will be removed.

4. With the rows still selected, click the **Primary Key** button again to remove the primary key designation from both fields.

5. Click on any field name to remove the selection.

6. Click the Row Selector box beside the Order ID row. Press and hold the CTRL key, and then click the Row Selector box beside the Customer ID row. Both fields should be selected.

7. On the DESIGN tab, in the Tools group, click the Primary Key button. Both rows should have a key displayed beside them. The resulting composite key is more valid.

8. Click the Save button on the Quick Access Toolbar.

9. CLOSE the table.

PAUSE. LEAVE the database open to use in the next exercise.

Workplace *Ready*

CREATING PRACTICAL COMPOSITE KEYS TO UNIQUELY DEFINE DATA

Occasionally, your table may not have one field that can be used as a unique identifier for each record. This may be the case if you never initially designed your table with good database design principles in mind and never chose a primary key. Instead of creating a new field to serve as a primary key and then entering the data for each record which can be a very time consuming process—you can instead combine two or more fields in your table to create a multifield primary key, or composite key. Another reason you may want to use a composite key is if you want to choose a unique identifier that is more inherently meaningful instead of using a random unique number to serve as a primary key.

For example, you may have preexisting fields in an orders table named Order_ID (a number that can be repeated for orders) and Customer_ID (a number that can be repeated for customers). Each of these fields cannot serve as a standalone primary key since the record data for each repeats. However, when the data in each field is combined into a composite key, it is highly unlikely that this combination of data will be duplicated. You can even include a third or additional fields to create the composite key and further ensure uniqueness.

It will be up to you to determine what makes practical sense for your database. Keep in mind that composite keys can further complicate your database design. For example, all child tables related to the parent table with the composite key must contain the same composite key fields as the parent. However, using composite keys may make sense in cases where you may need to quickly add a primary key where one never existed or may need a composite key that contains more meaningful data.

FINDING AND REPLACING DATA

The Bottom Line

A big advantage of using a computer database rather than paper and pencil for recordkeeping is the ability to quickly search for and/or replace data. These features may be accessed from the Find and Replace dialog box. The Find and Replace commands in Access work very much like those in Word or other Office applications you might have used. You can use the Find command to search for specific text in a table or to move quickly to a particular word or number in the table. The Replace command can be used to automatically replace a word or number with another.

In the Find and Replace dialog box, key the text or numbers that you want to search for into the Find What box and click Find Next to locate the record containing the data. If you want to replace the data, key the new data into the Replace With box and click Replace or Replace All.

Take Note When replacing data, it is usually a good practice to click Replace instead of Replace All so that you can confirm each replacement to make sure that it is correct.

Finding and Replacing Data

The Find and Replace dialog box searches only one table at a time; it does not search the entire database. The Look In menu allows you to choose to search by field or to search the entire table. By default, Access searches the field that was selected when you opened the Find and Replace dialog box. If you want to search a different field, select the field while the dialog box is open; you do not have to close it first. In this exercise, you find and replace table data.

Remember these points when finding and replacing data in Access 2013:

- In the Match menu, you can specify where you want Access to look in a field. Select Any Part of Field for the broadest search.

- Sometimes, Access selects the Search Fields As Formatted check box. When it does, do not clear the check box, or your search probably will not return any results.

- Click the Match Case box to search for text with the same uppercase and/or lowercase capitalization of text.

- You can use **wildcard** characters such as a question mark or asterisk to find words or phrases that contain specific letters or combinations of letters. Key a question mark (?) to represent a single character—for example, keying *b?t* will find *bat*, *bet*, *bit*, and *but*. Key an asterisk (*) to represent a string of characters—for example, *m*t* will find *mat*, *moment*, or even *medium format*.

- If you key a wildcard character in the Replace With box, Access will insert that character just as you keyed it.

STEP BY STEP   **Find and Replace Data**

USE the database open from the previous exercise.

1. **OPEN** the **Customers** table.

2. On the HOME tab, in the Find group, click the **Find** button. The Find and Replace dialog box appears with the Find tab displayed.

3. Click the **Replace** tab in the Find and Replace dialog box.

4. Key **Elm** into the Find What box.

5. Key **Little Elm** into the Replace With box.

6. Click the **down arrow** beside the Look in menu, and then select **Current document**, so that the entire table will be searched instead of just the Customer ID field.

7. Click the **down arrow** beside the Match menu and select **Any Part of Field** if it already is not selected to broaden the search (see Figure 3-9).

Figure 3-9

Find and Replace dialog box

Find and Replace	? ✕
Find Replace	
Find What: Elm ▾	Find Next
Replace With: Little Elm ▾	Cancel
Look In: Current document ▾	Replace
Match: Any Part of Field ▾	Replace All
Search: All ▾	
☐ Match Case ☑ Search Fields As Formatted	

CERTIFICATION
R E A D Y ?   2.3.5

How do you find and
replace data?

Another Way
To open the Find
tab in the Find and Replace
dialog box using the keyboard,
press Ctrl+F. To open the
Replace tab, press Ctrl+H.

8. Click the **Find Next** button. Access searches the table, finds, and selects the word *Elm*.

9. Click the **Replace** button. Access replaces *Elm* with *Little Elm*.

10. Click the **Find Next** button. Access finds *Elm* in the new text that was just inserted.

11. Click **Find Next** again. Access displays a message saying that no more occurrences of the word have been found. Click **OK**.

12. Click **Cancel** to close the Find and Replace dialog box.

13. Press the **down arrow** to remove the selection and allow Access to save the change.

14. **CLOSE** the table.

PAUSE. LEAVE the database open to use in the next exercise.

Take Note   If you want to use the Find and Replace dialog box to search for characters that are used as wild-cards, such as a question mark, you must enclose that character in brackets, for example [?]. Follow this rule when searching for all wildcard characters except exclamation points (!) and closing brackets (]) where you would simply search for these without any surrounding brackets.

ATTACHING AND DETACHING DOCUMENTS

The Bottom Line

Access 2013 allows you to attach documents, such as Word documents or photo files, to records in a database. For example, the human resources department of a large company could keep a photo, a resume, and employee evaluation documents with each employee record. These attached files can also be easily detached, if necessary. The Attachments dialog box allows you to manage the documents attached to records.

Take Note   You cannot attach files to databases created in versions of Access prior to Access 2007. You cannot share attachments with a database created in these prior versions of Access.

Attaching and Detaching Documents

Before you can start attaching documents, you must create a field in a table and format it with the Attachment data type. You can add the field in Datasheet view or in Design view. Access displays a paper clip icon in the header row and in every record in the field along with a number in paren-theses indicating the number of attached files in the field. In this exercise, you create a new field and format it with the Attachment data type, then remove the attachment from your database records.

Another Way
You can also
right-click in the Attachments
field to display a shortcut menu.
Select Manage Attachments
from the menu to display the
Attachments dialog box.

Double-click the record in the Attachments field to display the Attachments dialog box where you can add, remove, open, or save multiple attachments, such as images, documents, and spread-sheets, for a single record. You can save attached files to your hard disk or network drive so that you can save changes to documents there before saving them to the database.

Take Note   You can attach a maximum total of 2 gigabytes of data, but each individual file cannot exceed 256 megabytes in size.

If the program that was used to create the attached file is installed on your computer, you can open and edit the file using that program. For example, if you open a Word resume that is attached to a record, the Word program starts and you view the document in Word. If you do not have the program that was used to create a file, Access prompts you to choose a program you do have to view the file.

STEP BY STEP   **Attach and Detach Documents**

USE the database open from the previous exercise.

1. **OPEN** the Order Summary table.
2. Click the **header** row of the Due Date field to select it.
3. In the Add & Delete group on the TABLE TOOLS FIELDS contextual tab, click the **More Fields** button. The More Fields menu appears.
4. Click **Attachment** under Basic Types (see Figure 3-10). The Attachment field is inserted in the table.

Figure 3-10

More Fields menu

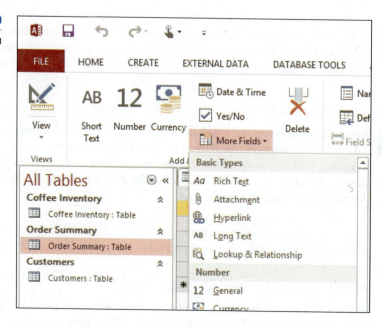

5. Double-click the first row of the Attachments field. The Attachments dialog box appears.

6. Click the **Add** button. Navigate to the data files for this lesson and select *invoice100.docx*. Click **Open**. The document appears in the Attachments dialog box (see Figure 3-11).

Figure 3-11

Attachments dialog box

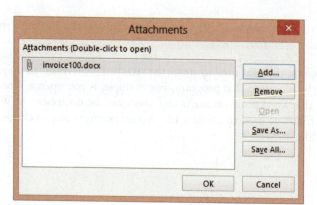

7. Click **OK**. The number of attachments in the first record changes to 1 (see Figure 3-12).

Figure 3-12

Attachments field displaying the number of attachments

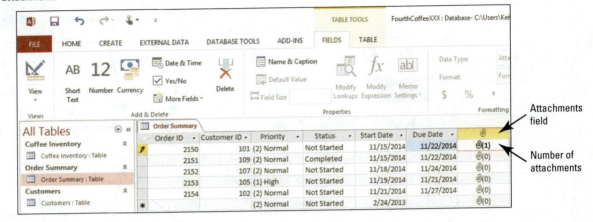

8. Double-click the **attachment number** in the Attachment field. The Attachments dialog box appears.

9. Click the **Open** button. The attachment, an invoice document, opens in Microsoft Word.

10. Click the **Close** button to close the invoice document.

11. Click the **Access** button on the taskbar, if necessary, to return to Access.

12. In the Attachments dialog box, click the **Remove** button, and click **OK**. The attachment is removed from the record.

13. **CLOSE** the Order Summary table.

PAUSE. LEAVE the database open to use in the next exercise.

Take Note   Once a field has been set to the Attachment data type, it cannot be converted to another data type.

 Cross Ref   The Add & Delete group and the More Fields menu will be covered in greater detail in Lesson 4.

SORTING AND FILTERING DATA AND SETTING FIELD VIEWING OPTIONS WITHIN A TABLE

The Bottom Line

It is often helpful to display data in order, display similar records, or hide and freeze certain fields without affecting the preexisting data. Sorting allows you to order records. For example, an office contact list that displays employees in alphabetical order by last name would help the user find information for a particular employee quickly. If you wanted to view only the records of employees in a particular department, you could create a filter to display only those records. You could also hide or freeze certain fields. For example, in a table that has several fields, you can hide or freeze fields to help you concentrate on certain data.

SOFTWARE ORIENTATION

Sort & Filter Group

The Sort & Filter group is located on the HOME tab in the Ribbon (see Figure 3-13). Use the Sort & Filter group of commands to sort and filter records in tables.

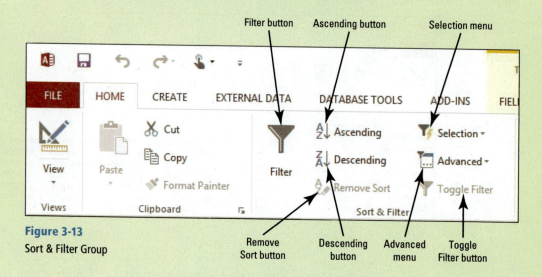

Figure 3-13

Sort & Filter Group

Sorting Data within a Table

To **sort** data means to arrange it alphabetically, numerically, or chronologically. Sorting within a table displays all the records in the table in the order that you select. You can easily sort by one or more fields to achieve the order that you want. Access can sort text, numbers, or dates in ascending or descending order. **Ascending** order sorts data from beginning to end, such as from A to Z, 1 to 10, and January to December. **Descending** order sorts data from the end to the beginning, such as from Z to A, 10 to 1, and December to January. In this exercise, you sort data using multiple fields and then remove the sort.

To sort text, numbers, dates, or other data types in a column, you first need to select the column. Then click the Ascending or Descending button in the Sort & Filter group of the HOME tab. You can also right-click a selected column and choose a Sort command from the shortcut menu. The available sort commands in the shortcut menu vary depending on the type of data in the column (see Table 3-2).

Table 3-2

Sort Commands on the shortcut menu

Type of Data	Sort Commands on the Shortcut Menu
Number, Currency, or AutoNumber	A→Z Sort Smallest to Largest Z→A Sort Largest to Smallest
Text, Memo, or Hyperlink	A→Z Sort A to Z Z→A Sort Z to A
Yes/No	A→Z Sort Selected to Cleared Z→A Sort Cleared to Selected
Date/Time	A→Z Sort Oldest to Newest Z→A Sort Newest to Oldest

You can also sort records on multiple fields. When you are using multiple fields, determine in which order you want them to be sorted. The primary sort field is called the **outermost field**. A secondary sort field is called an **innermost field**. For example, if you want to sort a contact list so that each employee's last name is sorted primarily and first name is sorted secondarily, Last Name would be the outermost field and First Name would be the innermost field. In your completed sort, Smith, Lauren, would be listed before Smith, Mark, in an A to Z (ascending) sort. When designating the sort order, however, you select the innermost field first and choose the type of sort you want from the shortcut menu. Then select the outermost field and select the type of sort that you want.

After you sort one or more columns, Access inserts sort arrows in the header row to show that the field is sorted. These sort commands remain with the table until you remove them. When you want to remove a sort order, click the Remove Sort button from the Sort & Filter group on the HOME tab. This removes the sorting commands from all the fields in the table. In a table with more than one sorted field, you cannot remove just one sort.

STEP BY STEP   **Sort Data within a Table**

USE the database you used in the previous exercise.

1. **OPEN** the Customers table.
2. Click the header row of the Customer ID field to select it.
3. Right-click in the field to display the shortcut menu (see Figure 3-14). Select Sort Largest to Smallest.

Figure 3-14

Shortcut menu

- A↓ Sort Smallest to Largest
- Z↓ Sort Largest to Smallest
- Copy
- Paste
- Field Width
- Hide Fields
- Unhide Fields
- Freeze Fields
- Unfreeze All Fields
- Find...
- Insert Field
- Modify Lookups
- fx Modify Expression
- Rename Field
- Delete Field

4. The data is sorted and an arrow is inserted in the header row (see Figure 3-15), indicating that the data is displayed in sort order.

Figure 3-15

Sorted column

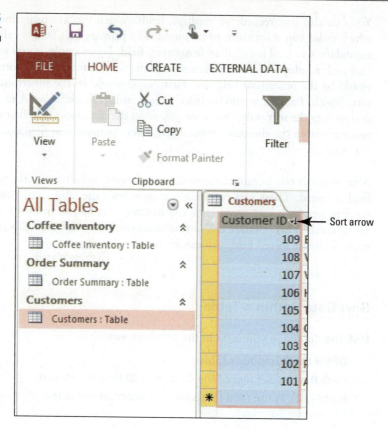

5. On the HOME tab, in the Sort & Filter group, click the **Remove Sort** button. The sort is removed from the Customer ID field.

6. Select the **First Name** field. On the HOME tab, in the Sort & Filter group, click the **Ascending** button. The data in the First Name field is sorted in ascending order.

7. Select the **Last Name** field. On the HOME tab, in the Sort & Filter group, click the **Ascending** button. The data in the Last Name field is sorted in ascending order.

8. On the HOME tab, in the Sort & Filter group, click the **Remove Sort** button. The sort is removed from both the First Name and Last Name fields.

9. Close the **table**. If a dialog box appears asking if you want to save changes to the table, click **No**.

CERTIFICATION READY? 2.3.6

How do you sort records?

PAUSE. LEAVE the database open to use in the next exercise.

Filtering Data within a Table

A **filter** is a set of rules for determining which records will be displayed. When you apply a filter, Access displays only the records that meet your filter criteria; the other records are hidden from view. Once the filtered records are displayed, you can edit and navigate the records just as you would without a filter applied. Filters remain in effect until you close the object. You can switch between views, and the filter settings will stay in effect. To make the filter available the next time you open the object, save the object before closing it. You can then reapply the filter the next time you open the object by clicking the Toggle Filter button in the Sort & Filter group on the Ribbon. In this exercise, you practice creating filters in several different ways.

STEP BY STEP   **Apply a Filter**

USE the database you used in the previous exercise.

1. **OPEN** the Coffee Inventory table.
2. Select the **Product Name** field. On the HOME tab, in the Sort & Filter group, click the **Filter** button. A menu appears.
3. Point to **Text Filters**. A second menu appears. Select **Contains** (see Figure 3-16).

Figure 3-16

Filter menu with Contains selected

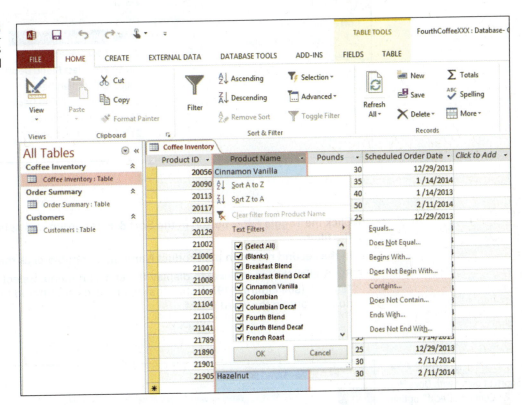

4. The Custom Filter dialog box appears. Key **Decaf** (see Figure 3-17), and click **OK**. Access filters the database to display only the records containing the word Decaf. A filter icon is displayed in the header row of the field (see Figure 3-18).

Figure 3-17

Custom filter dialog box

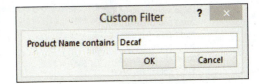

Figure 3-18

Filtered records

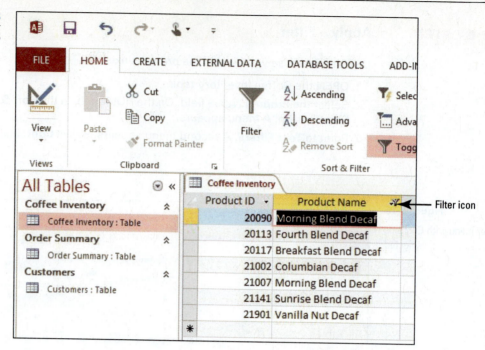

Filter icon →

5. Click the **Toggle Filter** button in the Sort & Filter group to display the records without the filter.

6. In the second record in the Product Name field, double-click the word **Decaf** to select it.

7. Right-click the word **Decaf** to display the shortcut menu. Select **Does Not Contain "Decaf"** (see Figure 3-19). Notice that the records are filtered to show only those that do not contain the word Decaf.

Figure 3-19

Shortcut menu with Does Not Contain "Decaf" option selected

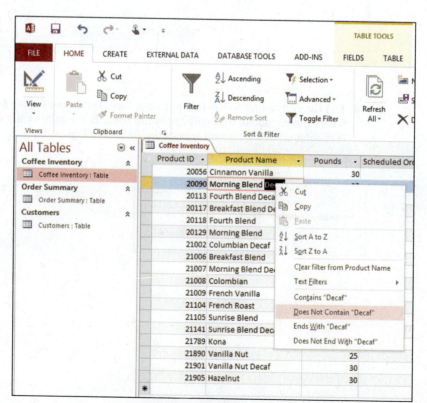

8. Click in the **Pounds** field of the first record.

9. On the HOME tab, in the Sort & Filter group, click the **Filter** button.

10. Click the check boxes to remove the check marks beside **(Blanks)**, **30**, **35**, **40**, and **50** (see Figure 3-20). Only the check mark beside 25 should remain.

Figure 3-20

Filter menu selected to show only 25 in the Pounds column

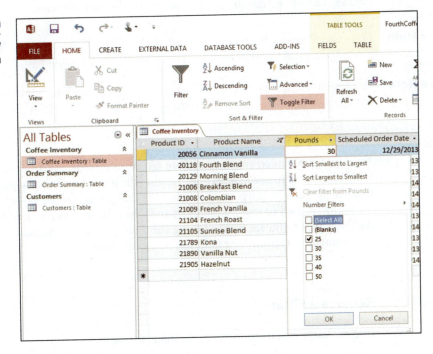

11. Click **OK**. Access filters the records to show only those containing the number 25 in the Pounds field.

12. Click the **Toggle Filter** button.

13. In the second row of the Scheduled Order Date field, highlight **1/14/2014** by clicking and dragging the mouse. Notice a '#' appears after the '1' in the month part of the selected date. This is a placeholder character that is part of the input mask field property for this field.

 Cross Ref   You learn more about input masks and how they help conform data to various formats in Lesson 4.

14. On the HOME tab, in the Sort & Filter group, click the **Selection** button. A menu appears (see Figure 3-21).

Figure 3-21

Selection button and menu

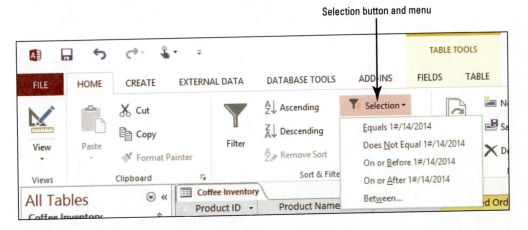

15. Select **On or After 1/14/2014.** The data is filtered to show only those records with content in the Scheduled Order Date field that matches the filter selection.

16. In the seventh row of the Pounds field, select **30.**

17. On the HOME tab, in the Sort & Filter group, click the **Selection** button. Select **Less Than or Equal to 30.** The records are filtered accordingly.

PAUSE. LEAVE the database open to use in the next exercise.

CERTIFICATION READY? **2.3.7**

How do you filter records?

Take Note Only one filter can be applied per column. When you apply a filter to a column that is already filtered, the previous filter is removed and the new filter is applied.

Take Note You cannot apply a case-specific filter. For example, filtering a table for "Decaf" will find all occurrences of the word "decaf" including "Decaf", "decaf", "deCaf" etc.

Removing a Filter

After applying a filter, you may need to return to records not displayed by the filter. The Toggle Filter button lets you switch between viewing the filtered records and viewing the table without the filter. Note that the purpose of this button changes accordingly—when the records are filtered the button is used to remove the filter, and when the filter is removed the button is used to apply the filter. When you are finished using the filter, you can permanently remove it. In this exercise, you permanently remove the filter you previously applied.

STEP BY STEP **Remove a Filter**

USE the table you used in the previous exercise.

1. Select the **Pounds** field. On the HOME tab, in the Sort & Filter group, click the **Filter** button. A menu appears.

2. Select **Clear filter from Pounds** (see Figure 3-22).

Figure 3-22

Removing filter from the Pounds column

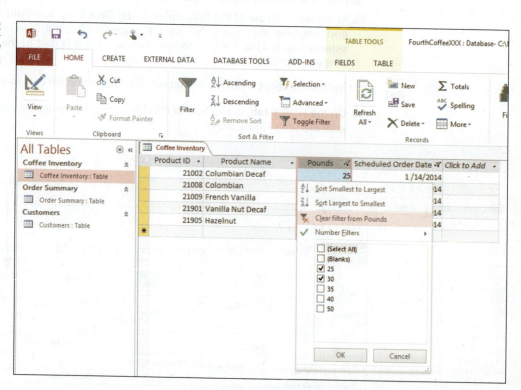

3. On the HOME tab, in the Sort & Filter group, click the **Advanced** button. A menu appears.

4. Select **Clear All Filters** from the menu (see Figure 3-23).

Figure 3-23

Advanced button and menu

Advanced Filter Options button

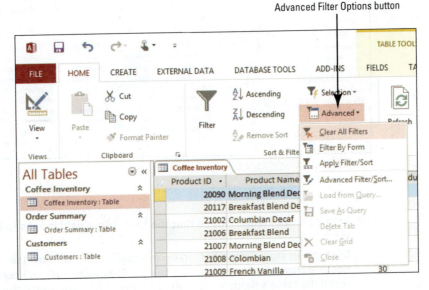

5. **SAVE** and **CLOSE** the table.

PAUSE. LEAVE the database open to use in the next exercise.

Freezing/Unfreezing and Hiding/Unhiding Fields

Sometimes you may need to change the view of a table's data to more efficiently find the information you are looking for. For example, it may be helpful to freeze First Name and Last Name fields so you can keep them fixed on the screen and then horizontally scroll and view other pertinent fields, like E-mail or Telephone Number, to get a better view of your data. You can also hide those fields that may distract you from getting a better view of the data. For example, if you are interested in viewing just a person's name and telephone number, you may decide to hide all fields except First Name, Last Name, and Phone Number. In this exercise, you practice freezing and unfreezing fields, as well as hiding and unhiding them.

STEP BY STEP   **Freeze/Unfreeze and Hide/Unhide Fields**

USE the database you used in the previous exercise.

1. **OPEN** the Customers table.

2. Select the **Last Name** field. On the HOME tab, in the Records group, click the **More** button. A menu appears (see Figure 3-24).

Figure 3-24

More button menu

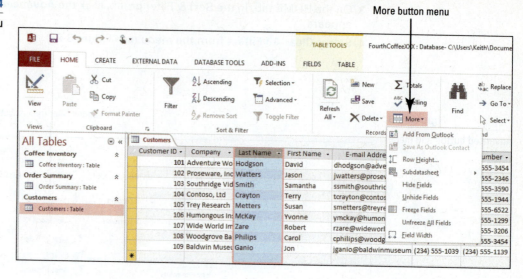

3. Select **Freeze Fields**. Notice that the Last Name field moves to the first field position in the table.

4. Click the **Restore Down** button on the application window (see Figure 3-25). The Restore Down button now becomes the Maximize button. Press the **Right Arrow** key to scroll the table's fields to the left, and stop when you reach the ZIP/Postal Code field. Notice that the Last Name field stays fixed as the other fields scroll.

Figure 3-25

Restore Down button

Restore Down button

5. Click the **More** button again and select **Unfreeze All Fields**. Notice how the Last Name field remains in the table's first field position. Press the **Right Arrow** key several times until the Last Name field scrolls off from view. Notice how the Last Name field moved with the other fields when the Right Arrow key was pressed several times.

Take Note   Fields can be rearranged in Datasheet view by clicking on the field name headers and dragging them to where you want to move them.

6. Click the **Maximize** button on the application window.

7. Select the **Customer ID** field. Click the **More** button and select **Hide Fields**. Notice the Customer ID field is now hidden from view (see Figure 3-26).

Figure 3-26

Figure 3-26

Hidden Customer ID field

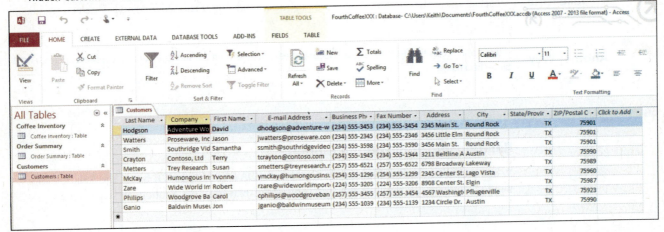

8. Click the **More** button and select **Unhide Fields**. The Unhide Columns dialog box should appear as shown in Figure 3-27. Notice the check mark is missing from the Customer ID check box, signifying that it is hidden.

Figure 3-27

Unhide Columns dialog box

Customer ID checkbox is unselected

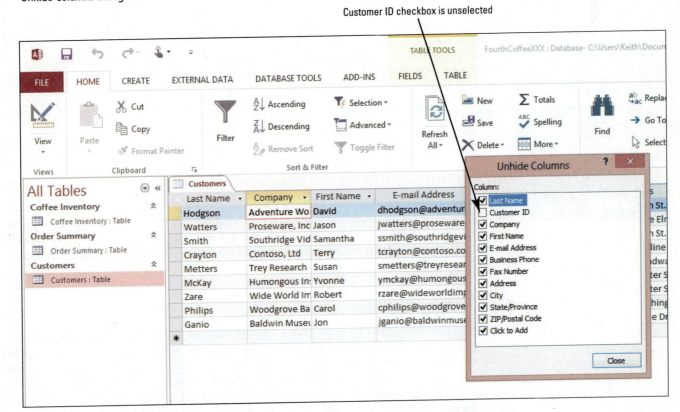

9. Deselect the check boxes next to all the other field representations except Last Name and Business Phone, and then click the **Close** button in the Unhide Columns dialog box. Notice the only fields now displayed in Datasheet view are the Last Name and Business Phone fields.

10. **CLOSE** the Customers table without saving the changes to the layout.

PAUSE. LEAVE the database open to use in the next exercise.

CERTIFICATION READY? 2.2.1

How do you hide fields in tables?

Take Note   You can save your table so it retains your formatting the next time you open it.

Take Note   To select more than one field to freeze or hide, hold down the Shift key while selecting adjacent fields.

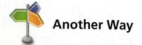   **Another Way**   You can also access the Hide/Unhide and Freeze/Unfreeze options from the shortcut menu that appears after you right-click a field name.

SOFTWARE ORIENTATION

Relationship Tools on the Ribbon

When you click the Relationships button on the DATABASE TOOLS tab, the Relationships window appears and the Relationship Tools are displayed in the Ribbon (see Figure 3-28).

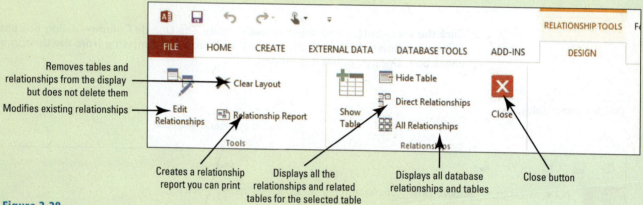

Figure 3-28
Use the Relationship Tools to define and modify table relationships

UNDERSTANDING TABLE RELATIONSHIPS

The Bottom Line   As you have already learned, most databases have more than one table. Creating relationships among these tables allows Access to bring that information back together again through objects such as reports and queries so that you can display information from several tables at once. It is much easier to create effective reports and queries when you start out with well defined table relationships.

Defining Table Relationships

In relational database applications like Access, you can store information in separate tables that are connected by a defined relationship that ties the data together. You define a table relationship in the Relationships window. To create that relationship, you place common fields in tables and define the relationships between the tables. Common fields used in different tables do not have to have the same names, but they usually do. They must have the same data type, though. In this exercise, you use a table that already has a primary key field to create a relationship with another table.

You can create three types of relationships in Access tables: one-to-one, one-to-many, and many-to-many.

In a one-to-one relationship, both tables have a common field with the same data. Each record in the first table can only have one matching record in the second table, and each record in the second table can have only one matching record in the first table. This type of relationship is not common, because information related in this way is usually stored in the same table.

A one-to-many relationship is more common, because each record in the first table can have many records in the second table. For example, in a Customers table and an Orders table, one customer could have many orders. The Customer ID would be the primary key in the Customers table (the one) and the foreign key in the Orders table (the many).

In a third type of relationship, called a many-to-many relationship, many records in the first table can have many records in the second table.

STEP BY STEP   ## Define Table Relationships

USE the database you used in the previous exercise.

1. On the DATABASE TOOLS tab in the Relationships group, click the **Relationships** button. The Relationships view appears with the Customers table represented.

2. Click the **Show Table** button. The Show Table dialog box appears (see Figure 3-29).

Show Table button   Show Table dialog box

Figure 3-29

Show Table button and dialog box

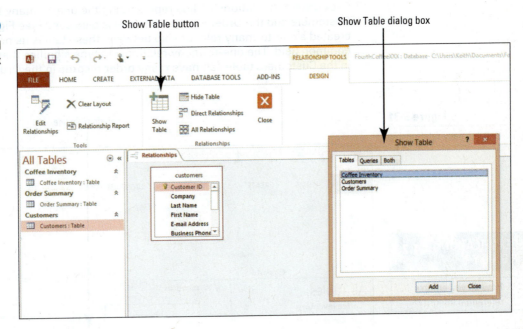

3. Select **Order Summary** and click **Add**.

4. Click **Close**. The Customer table and Order Summary table are represented in Relationships view.

5. Click the **Customer ID** primary key field in the Customers table, and then drag it to the Customer ID field of the **Order Summary** table and release the **mouse button**. The Customer ID field represents the common field between the two tables. The Customer ID field of the Order Summary table is now set as the foreign key. The Edit Relationships dialog box appears (see Figure 3-30).

Figure 3-30

Edit Relationships dialog box

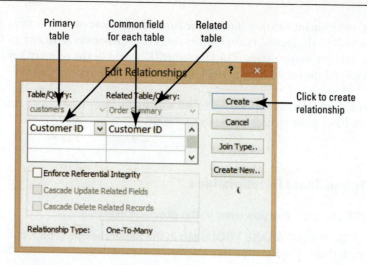

Figure 3-30

Edit Relationships dialog box

6. Select the **Enforce Referential Integrity** check box. Then select the **Cascade Update Related Fields** and **Cascade Delete Related Records** check boxes.

7. Click **Create**. A relationship line representing the one-to-many table relationship of the Customers and the Order Summary tables is displayed (see Figure 3-31). You just created a one-to-many relationship between these tables using Customer ID, the common field. The one-to-many relationship type signifies that each customer record in the Customers table can have many order records in the Order Summary table.

Figure 3-31

One-to-many relationship

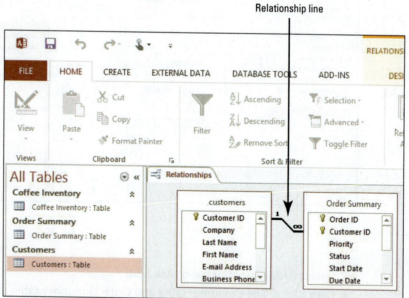

PAUSE. LEAVE the database open to use in the next exercise.

Modifying Table Relationships

A table relationship is represented by the line that connects the tables in the Relationships window. To modify the relationship, you can double-click the line to display the Edit Relationships dialog box or delete the line to delete the relationship. The Edit Relationships dialog box allows you to change a table relationship. You can change the tables on either side of the relationship or the fields on either side. You can also perform actions like enforcing referential integrity and choosing cascade options. In this exercise, you delete the relationship you previously created, and then recreate and edit the relationship to enforce referential integrity.

Referential integrity is an option that you can select in the Edit Relationships dialog box to prevent orphan records. An orphan record is a record in one table that references records in another table that no longer exist. For example, when referential integrity is enforced, Access will not permit a Customer ID value as the foreign key in the Order Summary table that does not have a matching Customer ID value as the primary key in the Customers table. In this way, referential integrity ensures your tables contain logically related data. If an operation that violates referential integrity is performed once this option is selected, Access will display a dialog box with a message stating that referential integrity is being violated and therefore will not permit the operation. You can also choose one or both types of cascade options—cascade update related fields or cascade delete related records—in the Edit Relationships dialog box once referential integrity has been selected. For example, if the cascade update related fields option is selected, Access will update the Customer ID value in the Order Summary table if the Customer ID value in the Customers table is updated. This ability to update related fields automatically ensures consistent Customer ID values in the related tables. Similarly, if the cascade delete related records option is selected, Access will delete all Customer ID records from the Order Summary table if the related Customer ID record is deleted from the Customers table, therefore preventing orphaned records. When you enforce referential integrity between tables, the line connecting the tables becomes thicker. The number 1 is also displayed on the line on the one side of the relationship and an infinity symbol (∞) appears on the other side, to represent the "many" field values that can be included in this side of the relationship.

To remove a table relationship, you must delete the relationship line. You can select the line by pointing to it and clicking it. When the relationship line is selected, it appears thicker. Press the Delete key to delete the line and remove the relationship or right-click the line to display the shortcut menu.

STEP BY STEP   **Modify Table Relationships**

USE the database you used in the previous exercise.

1. Right-click the center section of the relationship line connecting the two tables. A shortcut menu appears (see Figure 3-32).

Figure 3-32

Edit/Delete shortcut menu

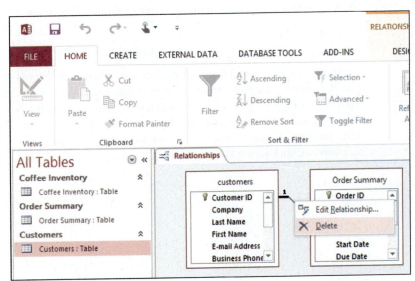

2. Select Delete. A message appears asking if you are sure you want to delete the relationship. Click Yes. The line disappears.

3. Select the **Customer ID** field in the first table. Drag the mouse to the Customer ID field in the second table and release the mouse button. The Edit Relationships dialog box appears.

4. Click the **Create** button. A line appears, creating the relationship.

5. Double-click the center section of the relationship line. The Edit Relationships dialog box appears again, listing the tables and the Customer ID fields on each side.

6. Click the **Enforce Referential Integrity** box and click **OK**. The line appears thicker, with the number 1 beside the first table and the infinity symbol (∞) beside the second (see Figure 3-33).

Figure 3-33

Relationship displaying enforced referential integrity

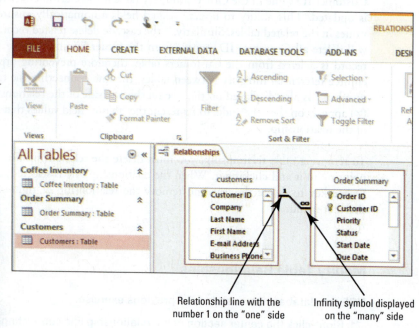

Relationship line with the number 1 on the "one" side

Infinity symbol displayed on the "many" side

CERTIFICATION READY? 1.2.2

How do you create and modify relationships?

CERTIFICATION READY? 1.2.1

How do you edit references between tables?

PAUSE. LEAVE the database open to use in the next exercise.

Viewing and Printing Table Relationships

You may want to print a table relationship to save for your records or to discuss with a colleague. The Relationship Report command makes this easy. When you choose to print the relationship report, the PRINT PREVIEW tab will appear with options for viewing and printing the report. After you make any changes to the layout of the report, click the Print button to start printing. After printing the report, you can choose to save it. In this exercise, you view and print table relationships without saving the relationship report.

STEP BY STEP   **Print Table Relationships**

USE the database you used in the previous exercise.

1. In the Tools group of the RELATIONSHIP TOOLS DESIGN tab, click the **Relationship Report** button. The report is created and the PRINT PREVIEW tab appears (see Figure 3-34).

Figure 3-34

Print preview of Relationship Report

Page Size group: Controls margins and page size

Page Layout group: Controls page orientation and printing options

Zoom group: Controls viewing options

Data group: Controls all aspects of data exporting

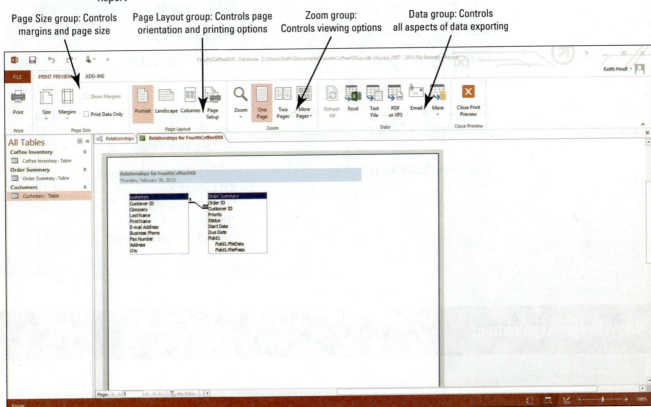

2. Click the **Print** button. The Print dialog box appears, allowing you to select the printer you want to use.

3. Click **OK** to keep the default settings, and then print the report.

4. Click the **Close** button to close the Relationships for FourthCoffee tab. A message appears asking if you want to save changes to the report. Click **No**.

5. **CLOSE** the Relationships tab.

STOP. CLOSE the database.

CERTIFICATION READY?   **1.2.6**

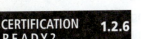

How do you view relationships?

SKILL SUMMARY

In This Lesson You Learned How To:	Exam Objective	Objective Number
Navigate Among Records		
Enter, Insert, Edit, and Delete Records	Add New Records.	2.3.2
	Navigate to Specific Records.	1.3.1
	Update Records.	2.3.1
	Delete Records.	2.3.3
Work with Primary Keys	Set Primary Key Fields.	1.2.3
Find and Replace Data	Find and Replace Data.	2.3.5
Attach and Detach Documents		
Sort and Filter Data and Set Field Viewing Options within a Table	Sort Records.	2.3.6
	Filter Records.	2.3.7
	Hide Fields in Tables.	2.2.1
Understand Table Relationships	Enforce Referential Integrity.	1.2.4
	Set Foreign Keys.	1.2.5
	Create and Modify Relationships.	1.2.2
	Edit References Between Tables.	1.2.1
	View Relationships.	1.2.6

Knowledge Assessment

Matching

Match the term in Column 1 to its description in Column 2.

Column 1	Column 2
1. foreign key	**a.** prevents orphan records, to ensure that records do not reference other records that no longer exist
2. composite key	**b.** sorts data from beginning to end
3. outermost field	**c.** sorts data from end to beginning
4. referential integrity	**d.** to arrange data alphabetically, numerically, or chronologically
5. wildcards	**e.** a primary key from one table that is used in another table
6. ascending order	**f.** a set of rules for determining which records will be displayed
7. descending order	**g.** the secondary sort field in a multifield sort
8. filter	**h.** two or more primary keys in a table
9. sort	**i.** characters used to find words or phrases that contain specific letters or combinations of letters
10. innermost field	**j.** the primary sort field in a multifield sort

True/False

Circle T if the statement is true or F if the statement is false.

T F 1. You can use the Navigation buttons to search for data in a table.

T F 2. You can enter any kind of data into any field.

T F   3. After you enter data and move to a new field, Access automatically saves the data for you in the table.

T F   4. After you delete a record, you can click the Undo button to bring it back.

T F   5. The Find and Replace dialog box searches all the tables in a database at one time.

T F   6. An AutoNumber field will usually make a good primary key.

T F   7. Before you can attach a document, there must be a field in a table formatted with the Attachment data type.

T F   8. The outermost field is the primary sort field in a multifield sort.

T F   9. The Toggle Filter button lets you permanently remove a filter and switches you back to the original view.

T F 10. In a one-to-many relationship, each record in the first table can have many records in the second table.

Competency Assessment

Project 3-1: **Charity Event Contacts List**

You are working as an intern for Woodgrove Bank. Part of your job is helping your supervisor organize a charity event. Use an Access table to create a contacts list that your supervisor will use to make calls to local businesses requesting sponsorships and donations for the event.

GET READY. LAUNCH Access if it is not already running.

1. **OPEN** the *Charity Event* database.
2. **SAVE** the database as *CharityEventXXX* (where *XXX* is your initials).
3. **OPEN** the Contacts table.
4. Enter the records shown in the following table: (Note: Do not type the hyphens when entering the Business Phone data)

ID	Company	Last Name	First Name	Business Phone
17	Trey Research	Tiano	Mike	469-555-0182
18	Fourth Coffee	Culp	Scott	469-555-0141
19	Wingtip Toys	Baker	Mary	972-555-0167
20	Margie's Travel	Nash	Mike	972-555-0189

5. Click the bottom half of the **View** button and choose **Design** View.
6. Select the **ID** row. On the DESIGN tab, in the Tools group, click the **Primary Key** button.
7. Save the **design** of the table, and then return to **Datasheet** view.
8. On the HOME tab, in the Find group, click the **Find** button. The Find and Replace dialog box appears. Key **0177** into the Find What box.
9. Select **Current document** from the Look In menu, and then select **Any Part of Field** in the Match menu.
10. Click the **Replace** tab. Key **0175** into the Replace With box.
11. Click **Find Next** and then click **Replace**.
12. Click **Cancel** to close the dialog box.
13. Select the **Lucerne Publishing** record.
14. On the HOME tab, in the Records group, click the **Delete** button. Click **Yes** to delete the record.
15. **CLOSE** the database.

LEAVE Access open for the next project.

Project 3-2: Angels Project Wish List

The four kindergarten classes at the School of Fine Art have adopted one boy and one girl "angel" from the community. Children from the classes may purchase holiday gifts for their angels. As an office assistant at the school, you are working with the Angel Project staff to organize information about each angel.

GET READY. LAUNCH Access if it is not already running.

1. **OPEN** *Angels* from the data files for this lesson.
2. **SAVE** the database as *AngelsXXX*, where *XXX* is your initials.
3. **OPEN** the List table.
4. Select the **Gender** field. On the HOME tab, in the Sort & Filter group, click the **Ascending** button.
5. Select the **Age** field. On the HOME tab, in the Sort & Filter group, click the **Descending** button.
6. On the HOME tab, in the Sort & Filter group, click the **Remove Sort** button.
7. In the Gender field, select the **M** in the first record.
8. On the HOME tab, in the Sort & Filter group, click the **Selection** button and select **Equals "M"**.
9. On the HOME tab, in the Sort & Filter group, click the **Toggle Filter** button.
10. Select the **Wants** field. On the HOME tab, in the Sort & Filter group, click the **Filter** button. Select **Text Filters** from the menu, select **Contains** from the next menu, and key **Bike** in the Custom Filter dialog box and press **Enter**.
11. On the HOME tab, in the Sort & Filter group, click the **Advanced** button, and then select **Clear All Filters** from the menu.
12. **SAVE** and **CLOSE** the table.

LEAVE Access open for the next project.

Proficiency Assessment

Project 3-3: Angel Project Contact Information

GET READY. LAUNCH Access if it is not already running.

1. The Angels database should be open on your screen.
2. **OPEN** the **Contact Information** table.
3. Enter the following new records:

ID	Last Name	First Name	Parent's Name	Address	City	State	Zip Code	Home Phone
15	Wright	Steven	Kevin	2309 Monroe Ct	Marietta	GA	34006	770-555-0142
16	Cook	Cathan	Patrick	1268 Oak Dr	Marietta	GA	34006	770-555-0128

4. Switch to Design view. Remove the primary key from the Home Phone field and define the **ID field** as the primary key.
5. **SAVE** the design and return to Datasheet view.
6. Select the **ID** field and sort it in ascending order.
7. On the DATABASE TOOLS tab, in the Relationships group, click the **Relationships** button.

8. Create a one-to-one relationship between the ID field of the List table and the ID field of the Contact Information table.

9. **SAVE** the Relationships view and close it.

10. **CLOSE** the database.

LEAVE Access open for the next project.

Project 3-4: Wingtip Toys Inventory Table

Wingtip Toys, a small manufacturer of wooden toys, has kept most of its records on paper for the last 20 years. The business has recently expanded, and you have been hired to help the company transfer its entire inventory and other administrative data to Office 2013. Edit the table to include all the latest handwritten data you have found.

GET READY. LAUNCH Access if it is not already running.

1. **OPEN** the *Wingtip Toys* database and save it as *WingtipXXX*, where *XXX* is your initials.

2. **OPEN** the Inventory table.

3. On the HOME tab, in the Find group, click the **Replace** button to display the Find and Replace dialog box. Change the following prices:

    Find all **14.99** and replace with **29.99**.

    Find all **16.99** and replace with **34.99**.

    Find all **15.99** and replace with **30.99**.

    Find all **24.99** and replace with **34.99**.

4. Delete the following records from the database:

    ID = **13**

    ID = **19**

    ID = **16**

5. Edit the following records:

    ID = **30**, change the number of items in stock to **3**

    ID = **28**, change the number of items in stock to **6**

    ID = **6**, change the number of items in stock to **4**

6. Select the **In Stock** field, and then create a filter to display all the records with a value less than or equal to 10 in the field.

7. Remove the filter.

8. **CLOSE** the table.

9. **CLOSE** the database.

LEAVE Access open for the next project.

Mastery Assessment

Project 3-5: Soccer Roster

As coach of your son's soccer team, you have created a database in which to store information about the team. Enter, edit, and delete records to update it.

GET READY. LAUNCH Access if it is not already running.

1. **OPEN** the *Soccer* database from the data files for this lesson.

2. **SAVE** the database as *SoccerXXX*, where *XXX* is your initials.

3. **OPEN** the Roster table.

4. Enter the following record for a new player:

   Eric Parkinson, 806-555-0170, uniform number 9

5. One player has quit the team, Russell King. Replace his data with this data for the following new player:

   George Jiang, 806-555-0123, uniform number 4

6. In the Size field, enter **XS** for each player, except for uniform numbers 4, 6, and 7, which should be size **S**.

7. Create an Attachment field and attach the Word document *medicalalert.docx* to the record for Garrett Young.

8. Define the Uniform # field as the primary key.

9. **SAVE** the table design and **CLOSE** the database.

LEAVE Access open for the next project.

Project 3-6: Donations Table

Donations are starting to come in for Woodgrove Bank's charity event. Track the donation commitments received.

GET READY. LAUNCH Access if it is not already running.

1. **OPEN** the *CharityEventXXX* database you created in Project 3-1.

2. **OPEN** the Donations table.

3. Create a filter to display the items in the Needs field without Commitments from a company.

4. Remove the filter.

5. Use Find and Replace to find each occurrence of the word Company in the Needs field and replace it with the word Volunteer.

6. Create a relationship between the ID field in the Contacts table and the Committed Company ID in the Donations table.

7. Print the relationship.

8. **CLOSE** the relationship without saving.

9. **CLOSE** the tables.

10. **CLOSE** the database.

CLOSE Access.

Modify Tables and Fields 4

LESSON SKILL MATRIX

Skill	Exam Objective	Objective Number
Modifying a Database Table	Add table descriptions.	2.2.4
	Rename tables.	2.2.5
Creating Fields and Modifying Field Properties	Set default values.	2.4.7
	Change field sizes.	2.4.4
	Use input masks.	2.4.8
	Add validation rules to fields.	2.4.2
	Change field captions.	2.4.3
	Add fields to tables.	2.4.1
	Delete fields.	2.4.9

© groveb/iStockphoto

KEY TERMS

- input mask
- multivalued lookup field
- properties
- Quick Start field
- validation rule
- validation text
- zero-length string

© groveb/iStockphoto

Erin's Travel is a full-service travel agency that specializes in sports-event travel packages. The company offers both individual and group travel packages to many of the leading sports events throughout the country. The travel packages can be customized to include plane tickets, event tickets, event transportation, hotel accommodations, official event souvenirs, and on-site staff assistance. As an assistant event coordinator, you are responsible for gathering information about a variety of events; you use Access to store the necessary data. In this lesson, you learn how to modify table properties, rename a table, delete a table, modify field properties, and create and modify fields—including multivalue and attachment fields.

MODIFYING A DATABASE TABLE

The Bottom Line

After a table has been created, you may need to modify it. You can make many changes to a table—or other database object—using its property sheet. You can also rename or delete a table, but keep in mind that such a change could possibly break the functionality of the database, because in a relational database the various components work together.

Modifying Table Properties

You can set **properties** that control the appearance or behavior characteristics for an entire table in the table's property sheet. Sometimes it is necessary to describe the purpose of a table by modifying the table's Description property since others who view your table may require more information about its purpose. Other table properties are more advanced and used less often. In this exercise, you modify the description property for a table.

STEP BY STEP   **Modify Table Properties**

GET READY. Before you begin these steps, be sure to launch Microsoft Access.

1. **OPEN** the *Events* database from the data files for this lesson.
2. **SAVE** the database as *EventsXXX* (where *XXX* is your initials).
3. In the Navigation Pane, double-click **Events** to open that table.
4. On the HOME tab, in the Views group, click the bottom half of the **View** button, and then click **Design View** from the menu that appears.
5. On the DESIGN tab, in the Show/Hide group, click **Property Sheet**. The Property Sheet pane appears on the right of the Access window (see Figure 4-1).

Figure 4-1
Property Sheet pane displayed

Property sheet pane

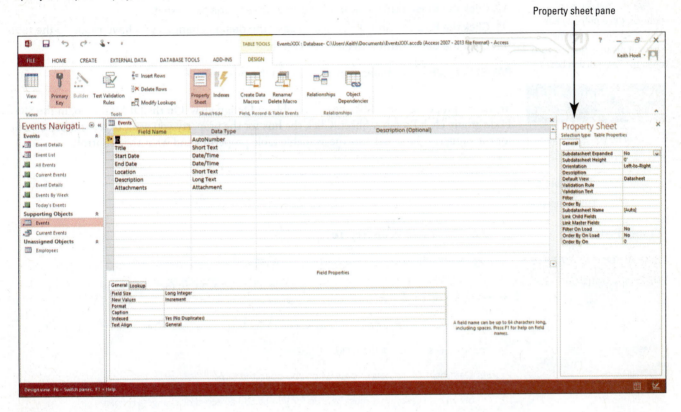

Another Way
You can also press
Alt+Enter to display the property
sheet for an object.

6. Place the insertion point in the property box for Description.

7. Press **Shift+F2** to open the Zoom dialog box (see Figure 4-2) to provide more space.

Figure 4-2
Zoom dialog box

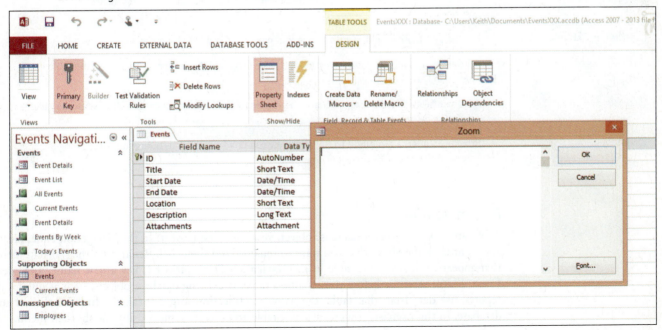

Another Way
You can also right-click in a property box and select Zoom from the shortcut menu that appears to open the Zoom dialog box.

CERTIFICATION READY?   2.2.4

How do you add table descriptions?

8. Key **Most popular events for 2014**.
9. Click **OK**.
10. Click the **Close** button on the Property Sheet pane to close it.
11. Click the **FILE** tab and click **Save** to save the design changes you have made to the table.
12. Click the **Close** button to close the table.

PAUSE. LEAVE the database open to use in the next exercise.

To set the properties for a table, open the table in Design view. On the DESIGN tab, in the Show/Hide group, click Property Sheet. Click the box for the property you want to set and key a setting for the property. Table 4-1 lists the available table properties and what they control.

Table 4-1

Table Properties

Table Property	Use This Table Property To
Subdatasheet Expanded	Specify whether to expand all subdatasheets when you open the table.
Subdatasheet Height	Specify whether to expand to show all available subdatasheet rows (default) when opened or to set the height of the subdatasheet window to show when opened.
Orientation	Set the view orientation, according to whether your language is read left-to-right or right-to-left.
Description	Provide a description of the table.
Default View	Set Datasheet as the default view when you open the table.
Validation Rule	Supply an expression that must be true for you to add a record or change a record.
Validation Text	Enter text that appears when a record violates the Validation Rule expression.
Filter	Define criteria to display only matching rows in Datasheet view.
Order By	Select one or more fields to specify the default sort order of rows in Datasheet view.
Subdatasheet Name	Specify whether a subdatasheet should appear in Datasheet view, and, if so, which table or query should supply the rows in the subdatasheet.
Link Child Fields	List the fields in the table or query used for the subdatasheet that match this table's primary key field(s).
Link Master Fields	List the primary key field(s) in this table that match the child fields for the subdatasheet.
Filter On Load	Automatically apply the filter criteria in the Filter property (by setting to Yes) when the table is opened in Datasheet view.
Order By On Load	Automatically apply the sort criteria in the Order By property (by setting to Yes) when the table is opened in Datasheet view.
Order By On	Provide an alternate method to the Order By On Load property by automatically applying the sort criteria in the Order By property when set to −1 (Yes).

Renaming a Table

To rename a table or other database object, you must first close it. In the Navigation Pane, locate and right-click the object that you want to rename, and then click Rename on the shortcut menu that appears. Or, select the table in the Navigation Pane, press F2, key a new name, and press Enter. Think carefully before you rename a table. If existing database objects, such as queries or reports, use data from that table, the name modification might break the functionality of the database. In this exercise, you create a new table and then rename it using the shortcut menu.

Rename a Table

USE the database that is open from the previous exercise.

1. On the CREATE tab, in the Templates group, click the **Application Parts** button and click **Comments** to create a new table.

2. In the Create Relationship dialog box that appears, select **There is no relationship** and then click **Create**.

3. Open the Comments table and right-click **Comments in the Navigation Pane** to display the shortcut menu shown in Figure 4-3. Select **Rename** and a dialog box appears that states *You can't rename the database object 'Comments' while it's open* (see Figure 4-4). Close the dialog box.

Figure 4-3

Rename command on table
shortcut menu

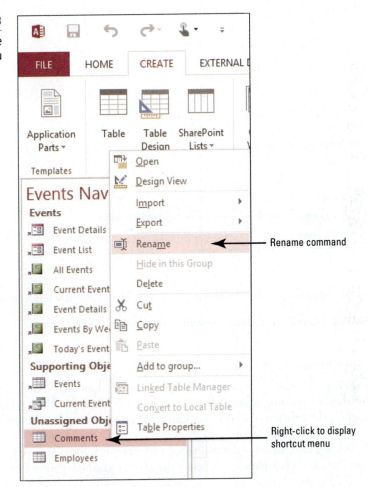

Figure 4-4

Cannot rename table
dialog box

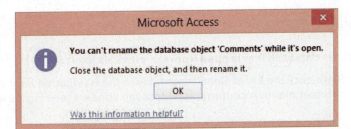

4. Close the Comments table.

5. Right-click **Comments** in the Navigation Pane to display the shortcut menu.

6. Click **Rename**. The table name is now selected for renaming (see Figure 4-5).

Figure 4-5

Table name selected for renaming

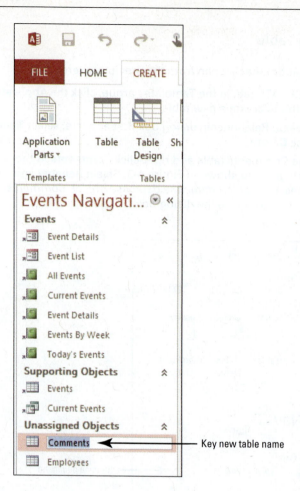

Key new table name

7. Key **Event Comments** and press **Enter**. The table has been renamed.

PAUSE. LEAVE the database open to use in the next exercise.

Deleting a Table

Deleting an entire table is not a complex process; however, remember that when you delete an entire table you might break the functionality of your database. Although you will be asked to confirm the deletion of a table, you can always undo the action. In this exercise, you delete a table.

To delete a table or other database object like a report, form, or query, right-click it in the Navigation Pane and click Delete. Or, select the table in the Navigation Pane and press Delete.

STEP BY STEP   **Delete a Table**

USE the database that is open from the previous exercise.

1. Right-click the **Event Comments** table in the Navigation Pane and click **Delete** on the shortcut menu. A confirmation message appears (see Figure 4-6).

Figure 4-6

Delete table confirmation message

2. Click **Yes** to delete the table.

Take Note   If the table was related to one or more additional tables, Access would ask if you wanted to delete those relationships before deleting the table.

PAUSE. LEAVE the database open to use in the next exercise.

Cross Ref   You can also delete information from individual records or delete entire records from a table, as you learned in Lesson 3.

SOFTWARE ORIENTATION

Field Properties

Some field properties are available in Datasheet view, but to access the complete list of field properties you must use Design view. An example of field properties for a table in Design view is shown in Figure 4-7.

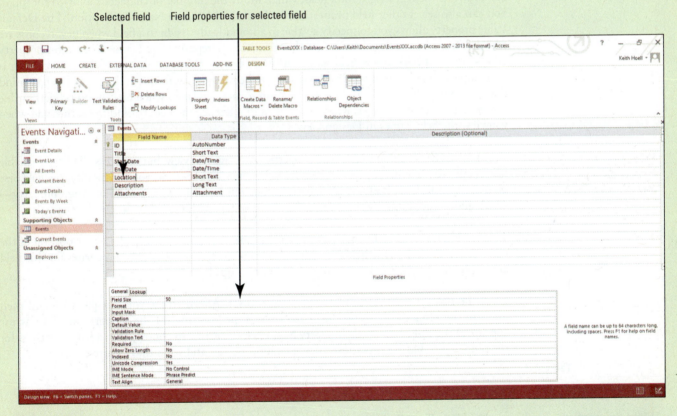

Figure 4-7
Field Properties

Use this figure as a reference throughout this lesson as well as for the rest of this book.

CREATING FIELDS AND MODIFYING FIELD PROPERTIES

The Bottom Line   A field has certain defining characteristics such as a name that uniquely identifies the field within a table, and a data type that is chosen to match the information to be stored. Every field also has an associated group of settings called properties that define the appearance or behavior of the field. In this section, you learn how to create fields and modify field properties.

Access uses the field property settings when you view and edit data. For example, the Format, Input Mask, and Caption properties affect how your information appears in table and query datasheets. In addition, any controls on new forms and reports that are based on the fields in the table inherit these same property settings by default.

Setting Field Properties

You can control the appearance of information, prevent incorrect entries, specify default values, speed up searching and sorting, and control other appearance or behavior characteristics by setting or modifying field properties. For example, you can format numbers to make them easier to read, or you can define a validation rule that must be satisfied for information to be entered in a field. In this exercise, you set the Required field property in Datasheet view and both the Default Value and Field Size field properties in Design view.

To set a field property in Datasheet view, open the table in Datasheet view. Click in the field for which you want to set the property. In the Field Validation group on the TABLE TOOLS FIELDS contextual tab, select the Unique check box to require the values in the field to be unique for all the records in the table. Or, select the Required check box to make this a required field, where all instances of this field must contain a value. In the Properties group, select the Field Size property box to define the text length for a field, which limits the number of characters allowed for input. You can also select other field properties like Default Value, and Name & Caption. The Default Value property allows you to specify a value to automatically assign to a field when new records are added. This is useful if you have data that consistently repeats. The Name & Caption property allows you to specify a new field name and the associated caption for that field. The caption is what appears as column names in tables, and as labels in queries, forms, and reports. Keep in mind that Access will show field names as the column names and labels when no caption property value is specified. The field name is what Access uses to reference the field behind the scenes and when you view the field names in Design view.

You can set a few of the available field properties in Datasheet view, but to access all of the available field properties, you must open the table in Design view. For example, you can modify the Field Size property in both Datasheet and Design views, but you can only modify the Text Align property—which allows you to specify the default alignment of text within a field—in Design view.

To set field properties in Design view, open the table in Design view. In the upper portion of the table design grid, click the field for which you want to set properties. The properties for this field are displayed in the lower portion of the table design grid.

Click the box for the field property you want to set. Alternatively, you can press F6 and then move to the property by using the arrow keys. Type a setting for the property or, if an arrow appears at the right side of the property box, click the arrow to choose from a list of settings for the property. Table 4-2 lists the available field properties and what they control.

Table 4-2

Available Field Properties

Field Property	Use This Field Property To
Field Size	Set the maximum size for data stored as a Short Text, Number, or AutoNumber data type.
Format	Customize the way the field appears when displayed or printed.
Decimal Places	Specify the number of decimal places to use when displaying numbers.
New Values	Set whether an AutoNumber field is incremented or assigned a random number.
Input Mask	Display editing characters to guide data entry.
Caption	Set the text displayed by default as the column name in tables and labels for forms, reports, and queries.

Field Property	Use This Field Property To
Default Value	Automatically assign a default value to a field when new records are added.
Validation Rule	Supply an expression that must be true whenever you add or change the value in this field.
Validation Text	Enter text that appears when a value violates the Validation Rule.
Required	Require that data be entered in a field.
Allow Zero Length	Allow entry (by setting to Yes) of a zero-length string ("") in a Short Text, Long Text, or Hyperlink field.
Indexed	Speed up access to data in this field by creating and using an index.
Unicode Compression	Compress text stored in this field when a large amount of text is stored.
IME Mode	Specify an Input Method Editor, a tool for using English versions of Windows.
IME Sentence Mode	Specify the type of data you can enter by using an Input Method Editor.
Append Only	Retain a history of all data changes (by setting to Yes) of a Long Text field.
Text Format	Choose Rich Text to store text as HTML and allow rich formatting. Choose Plain Text to store only text.
Text Align	Specify the default alignment of text within a field or control.
Precision	Specify the total number of digits allowed, including those both to the right and the left of the decimal point (when decimal Field Size property is set using Number data type).
Scale	Specify the maximum number of digits that can be stored to the right of the decimal separator (when decimal Field Size property is set using Number data type).
Expression	Specify the expression used for the Calculated data type to generate a value.
Result Type	Specify the data type to be used to store the value generated by the Expression field property for the Calculated data type.

STEP BY STEP | **Set a Field Property in Datasheet View and Design View**

USE the database that is open from the previous exercise.

1. Double-click the **Events** table in the Navigation Pane to open the table in Datasheet view, if it is not already open.
2. Click the **Location** column header to select that field.
3. Click the **Required** check box in the Field Validation group on the TABLE TOOLS FIELDS contextual tab (see Figure 4-8). This setting determines that a value must be entered in the Location field for all records in the table.

Figure 4-8

Field Validation group with Required checkbox selected

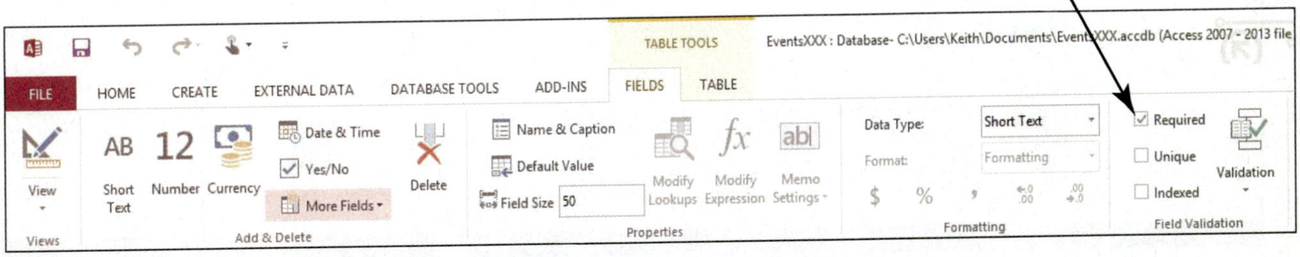

CERTIFICATION READY? 2.4.7

How do you set default values?

CERTIFICATION READY? 2.4.4

How do you change field sizes?

4. On the HOME tab, in the Views group, click the bottom half of the View button and click Design View.

5. In the Field Name column in the middle portion of the table design grid, click in the Location cell.

6. In the Default Value row in the lower portion of the table design grid, click in the property box and key To Be Announced to specify a value that will be automatically entered in this field for new records.

7. In the Field Name column in the upper portion of the table design grid, click in the Title cell.

8. In the Field Size row in the lower portion of the table design grid, select 150 in the property box and key 175 to change the maximum number of characters you can enter in the Title field.

PAUSE. LEAVE the database open to use in the next exercise.

Defining Input Masks

You use an **input mask** whenever you want users to enter data in a specific way. An input mask can require users to enter dates in a specific format, for example, DD-MM-YYYY, or telephone numbers that follow the conventions for a specific country or region. An input mask is helpful because it can prevent users from entering invalid data (such as a phone number in a date field). In addition, input masks can ensure that users enter data in a consistent way. In this exercise, you specify that the dates in the Start Date field be entered in Medium Date format, following the required pattern, *28-Aug-73*.

You can add input masks to table fields by running the Input Mask Wizard or by manually entering masks in the Input Mask field property.

STEP BY STEP **Define Input Masks for Fields**

USE the database that is open from the previous exercise.

1. In the Field Name column in the upper portion of the table design grid, click in the Start Date cell.

2. Click the Input Mask property box in the lower portion of the table design grid to display the Input Mask Wizard button (...) on the far right of the cell (see Figure 4-9).

Figure 4-9

Input Mask Wizard button

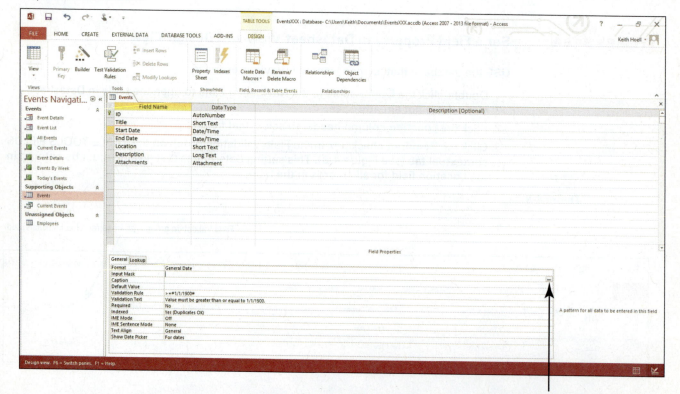

Click to open Input Mask Wizard

3. Click the **Input Mask Wizard** button. A message box appears asking if you want to save the table now.

4. Click **Yes** to close the message box and display the Input Mask Wizard (see Figure 4-10).

Figure 4-10

Input Mask Wizard

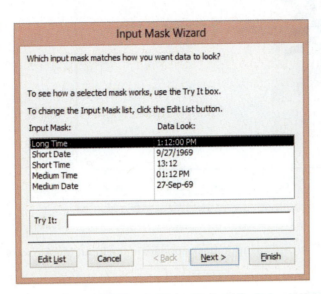

5. Click **Medium Date**, to select the DD-MON-YR date format, and then click **Next >**. The next screen in the Input Mask Wizard appears (see Figure 4-11).

Figure 4-11

Input Mask Wizard, next screen

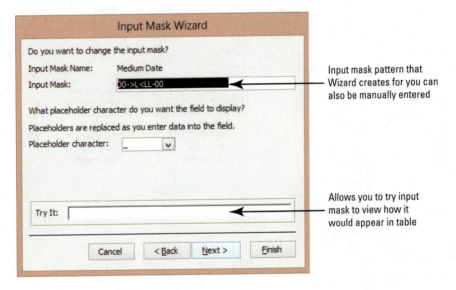

6. Click **Next** to accept the default settings in this screen and display the final Input Mask Wizard screen (see Figure 4-12).

Figure 4-12

Input Mask Wizard,
final screen

7. Click **Finish**. The input mask appears in the Input Mask row (see Figure 4-13).

Figure 4-13

Input Mask row

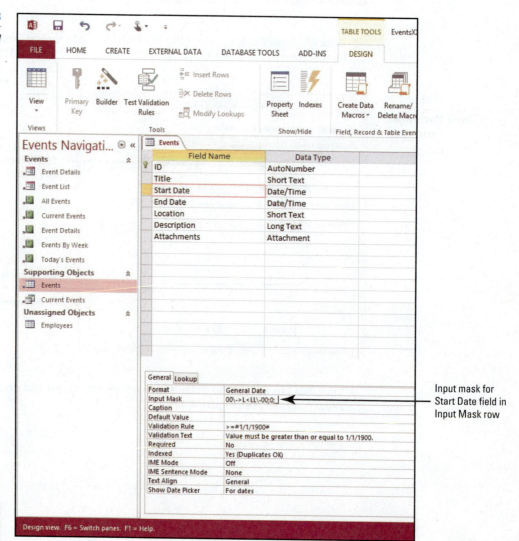

Input mask for
Start Date field in
Input Mask row

PAUSE. LEAVE the database open to use in the next exercise.

Workplace *Ready* _____

USING INPUT MASKS TO STANDARDIZE BUSINESS DATA

When designing a database to be used in the workplace, it is good practice to use input masks for a variety of reasons. Input masks require users to enter data in a specific way to help ensure data consistency. They also help users enter data into the correct field using the correct format. For example, people use different formats to enter a date. Europeans typically enter dates starting with the day, followed by the month, and then year; conversely, Americans typically enter dates beginning with the month, followed by the day, and then year. Input masks help standardize the input of data—like dates—by forcing users to enter the data in a prescribed format. Input masks also help speed the input of data since, for example, users do not need to type the slashes or dashes between date elements.

Access provides you with built-in input masks for commonly used formats. These formats differ between short text and date/time data types. If you set a field to the short text data type, the input mask wizard provides you with a variety of built-in input masks, including those for a phone number, social security number, and even one for a password. The date/time data type input mask wizard provides you with a variety of formats such as entering dates in conventional American or European formats, or retaining a seconds element for time data.

However, what if you needed the flexibility to create an input mask to enter data in formats unique to your business, like those used for customer or order numbers? Access gives you the flexibility to create your own input mask formats using a variety of special characters that define input masks.

Performing a search for "input masks" in Access Help will lead you to information on the characters that define input masks, and how you can use them to create your own input masks that will help conform the data to the particular format your business uses. Once your custom input mask is created, you can be confident users are entering data in a format your business intended, and you will have taken an extra step to help ensure the validity of your data.

Allowing Zero-Length Strings in a Field

When the Allow Zero Length field property is set to Yes, you can enter zero-length strings in a field. A **zero-length string** contains no characters; you use the string to indicate that you know no value exists for a particular field. This recognition of a nonexistent value actually represents a string. You enter a zero-length string by typing two double quotation marks with no space between them (""). In this exercise, you modify the Allow Zero Length property for the Description field.

STEP BY STEP   **Allow Zero Length**

USE the database that is open from the previous exercise.

1. In the Field Name column in the upper portion of the table design grid, click in the **Description** cell.

2. Click the **Allow Zero Length** property box in the lower portion of the table design grid to display the down arrow on the far right of the cell.

3. Click the **down arrow** to display the menu (see Figure 4-14).

Figure 4-14

Zero Length property menu

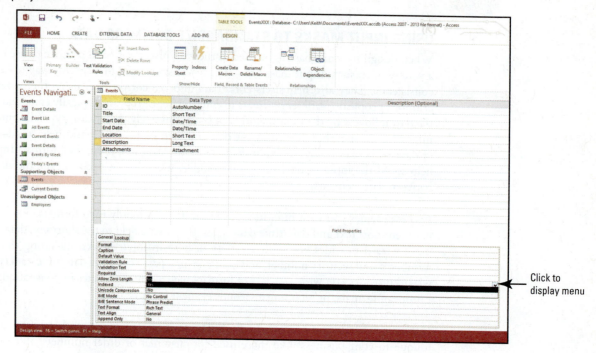

Click to display menu

4. Click **Yes.**

PAUSE. LEAVE the database open to use in the next exercise.

Setting Data Validation Rules

Validation rules help to ensure that your database users enter the proper types or amounts of data. A **validation rule** is an expression that limits the values that can be entered in the field. The maximum length for the Validation Rule property is 2,048 characters. For example, if the field contains a date, you can require that the date entered in the field be later than June 4, 1977. **Validation text** specifies the text in the error message that appears when a user violates a validation rule. For example, the error message could say "Please enter a date that is later than June 4, 1977." The maximum length for the Validation Text property is 255 characters. In this exercise, you modify the Validation Rule and Validation Text properties for the End Date field.

Data can be validated in several ways, and you will often use multiple methods to define a validation rule. Each of the following can be used to ensure that your users enter data properly:

- **Data types:** When you design a database table, you define a data type for each field in the table, and that data type restricts what users can enter. For example, a Date/Time field accepts only dates and times, a Currency field accepts only monetary values, and so on.

- **Field sizes:** Field sizes provide another way to validate text. For example, if you create a field that stores first names, you can set it to accept a maximum of 15 characters. This can prevent a malicious user from pasting large amounts of text into the field. It could also prevent an inexperienced user from mistakenly entering a first, middle, and last name in a field designed only to hold a first name.

- **Table properties:** Table properties provide very specific types of validation. For example, you can use the Order By property to select one or more fields to specify the default sort order of rows in Datasheet view.

- **Field properties:** You can also use field properties, such as the Validation Rule property to require specific values, and the Validation Text property to alert your users to any mistakes. For example, entering a rule such as >1 and <100 in the Validation Rule property forces users to enter values between 1 and 100. Entering text such as "Enter values between 1 and 100" in the Validation Text property tells users when they have made a mistake and how to fix the error.

Another Way

As you already learned in this lesson, you can also use the Input Mask property to validate data by forcing users to enter values in a specific way.

STEP BY STEP   **Set Data Validation Rules**

USE the database that is open from the previous exercise.

1. In the Field Name column in the upper portion of the table design grid, click the **End Date** cell.

2. Click the **Validation Rule** property box in the lower portion of the table design grid to display the Expression Builder button (…) on the far right of the cell (see Figure 4-15).

Figure 4-15

Expression Builder button

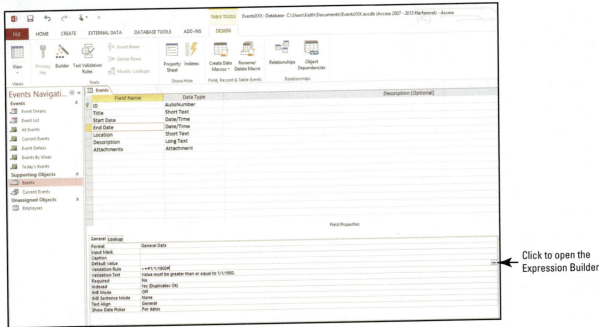

Click to open the Expression Builder

3. Click the **Expression Builder** button to display the Expression Builder dialog box (see Figure 4-16).

Figure 4-16

Expression Builder dialog box

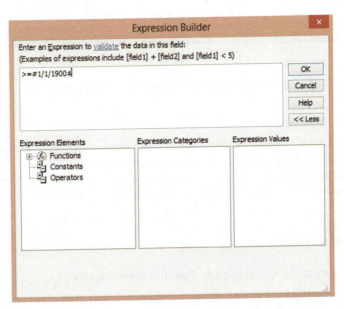

4. Select the number **1900** and replace it by keying **2014**.

5. Click **OK**.

6. Click the **Validation Text** property box in the lower portion of the table design grid.

7. Select the number **1900** and replace it by keying **2014**. The property boxes should look like those shown in Figure 4-17.

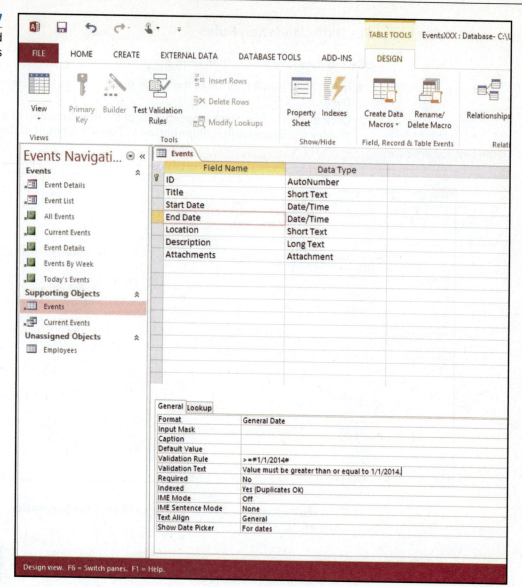

PAUSE. LEAVE the database open to use in the next exercise.

Entering Captions

The Caption property field specifies the text displayed by default as column names in tables and in labels for forms, reports, and queries. The maximum length for the Caption property is 255 characters. If you do not specify a caption to be displayed, the field name is used as the label. In this exercise, you set the Caption property for the Location field.

STEP BY STEP   **Enter Captions**

USE the database that is open from the previous exercise.

1. In the Field Name column in the upper portion of the table design grid, click the **Location** cell.

2. Click the **Caption** property box in the lower portion of the table design grid.

3. Key **Venue**. The caption property has now been set to *Venue* and will display as a column name in table Datasheet view, as well as labels for forms, reports, and queries.

PAUSE. LEAVE the database open to use in the next exercise.

SOFTWARE ORIENTATION

Add & Delete Group

When creating fields in table Datasheet view, you use the Add & Delete group on the TABLE TOOLS FIELDS contextual tab, which is shown in Figure 4-18. You can use these commands to add fields with associated data types, add Quick Start fields, insert lookup columns, and delete columns.

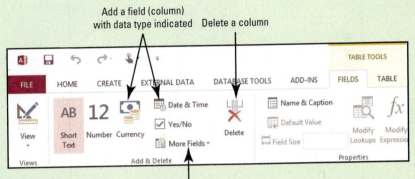

Figure 4-18

Add & Delete group

Use this figure as a reference throughout this lesson as well as the rest of this book.

Creating Fields

Fields can be created in different ways. You can add fields to a table in Design view, or add fields in Datasheet view using the Click to Add column or Add & Delete group. Sometimes it is easier to choose from a predefined list of fields than to manually create a field. Access includes a quick and easy way for you to add fields to a table using the Add & Delete group on the TABLE TOOLS FIELDS contextual tab, which includes a collection of fields with associated data types and built-in Quick Start fields that can save you considerable time. In this exercise, you add fields to a table by using both the Click to Add column and the Add & Delete group.

The last column in a table in Datasheet view has a Click to Add column, which you can use to add a field simply by clicking on the Click to Add column header and choosing a data type from the menu that appears. Rename the field by right-clicking the column header, choosing Rename Field from the menu, and keying a new name. You can also key information directly in a column. Access will try to automatically determine the field data type by the data entered.

A **Quick Start field** is a predefined set of characteristics and properties that describes a field, including a field name, a data type, and a number of other field properties. Quick Start fields allow you to quickly add commonly used single fields or several related ones. For example, using Quick Start fields, you can choose from a variety of fields including "Status" to quickly add a field named Status with built-in options like Not Started, In Progress, and so on, or you can choose the "Address" Quick Start to quickly include related fields like City, State, and Zip Code.

To create a new field in table Datasheet view, you can simply choose from commonly used fields in the Add & Delete group, or click the More Fields button to access a menu with a greater variety of field types. To create a new field using Quick Start, click the More Fields button and then choose a Quick Start from the menu (see Figure 4-19).

Figure 4-19

More Fields button menu

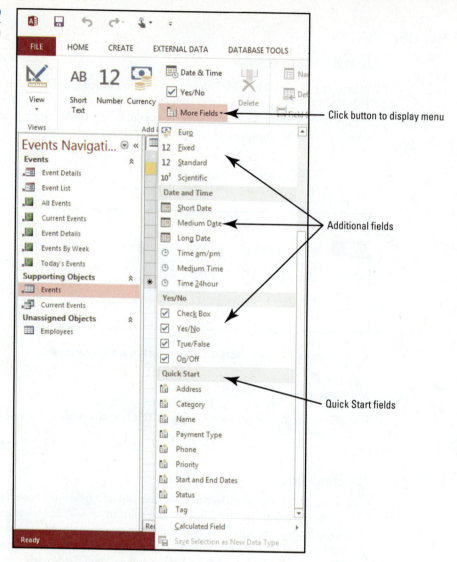

STEP BY STEP   Create Fields

USE the database that is open from the previous exercise.

1. On the HOME tab, in the Views group, click the bottom half of the **View** button and click **Datasheet View**. Save the table, if required. If you get a message about data integrity, click **Yes**.

Take Note   Whenever you add or modify field validation rules for fields that contain data, the data may violate these new rules. You can allow Access to test the data against the rules and inform you if there are any violations.

2. Scroll to the right of the Events table to display the last column and click the **Click to Add** header. Click **Yes/No** from the menu of available data types that appear (see Figure 4-20). You are going to add a new field with the Yes/No data type in which you can indicate whether or not events will have on-site staff.

Figure 4-20

Click to Add column

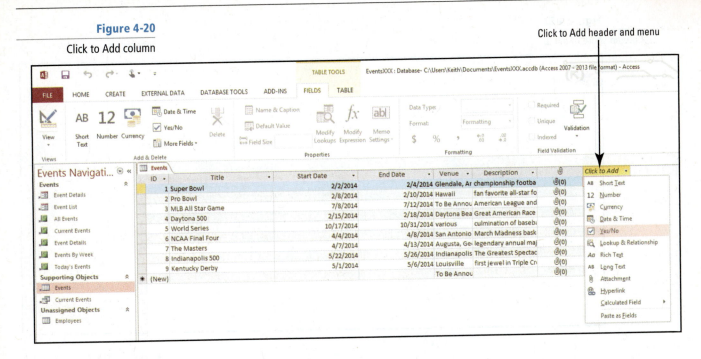

Click to Add header and menu

3. A new field named Field1 is added, and the Click to Add column becomes the last column in the table (see Figure 4-21).

Figure 4-21

New field created

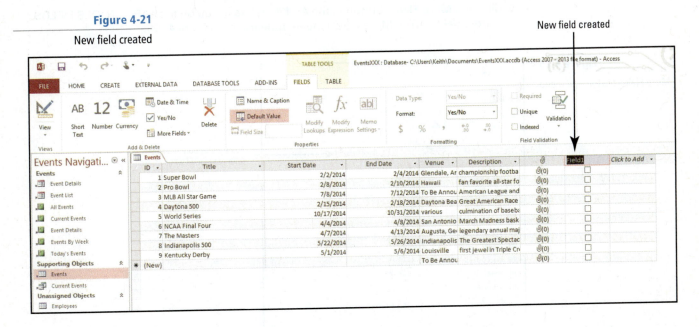

New field created

4. Right-click the Field1 column header to display the shortcut menu and click Rename Field (see Figure 4-22).

Figure 4-22

Column shortcut menu

Right-click to display menu

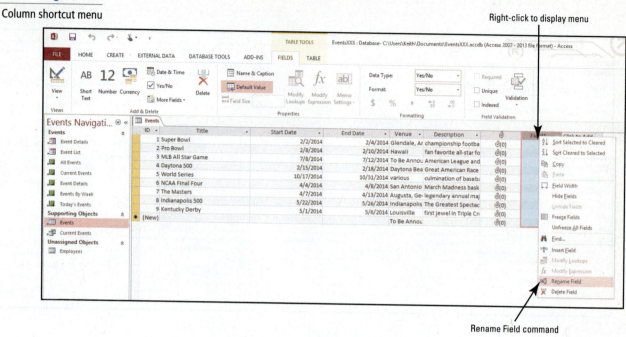

Rename Field command

5. Key **On-site staff?** as the column name.
6. Click the **More Fields** button in the Add & Delete group on the TABLE TOOLS FIELDS contextual tab. The More Fields menu appears (see Figure 4-23).

Figure 4-23

More Fields button and menu

More Fields button displays menu with categories when clicked

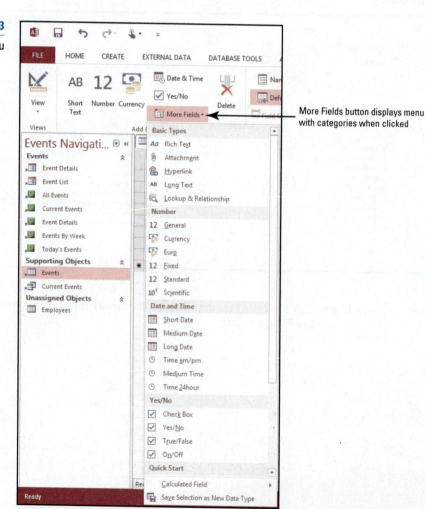

7. In the Quick Start category, click **Status**. A new Quick Start field named Status, in which you now have options to indicate the status of an event, appears to the left of the On-site staff? field (see Figure 4-24).

Figure 4-24

Status field created

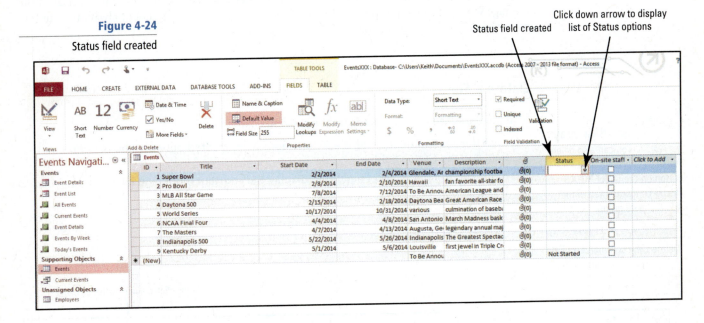

8. Click the **Status field drop-down box** button to view the available options, and click **Not Started** (see Figure 4-25).

Figure 4-25

Status field drop-down box options

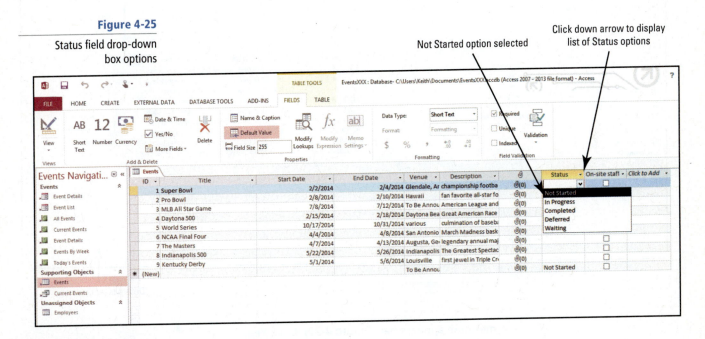

PAUSE. LEAVE the database open to use in the next exercise.

CERTIFICATION
READY?   2.4.1

How do you add fields to tables?

Deleting a Field

Before you delete a column from a datasheet, remember that doing so deletes all the data in the column and that the action cannot be undone. For that reason, you should back up the table before you delete the column. Before you can delete a primary key or a lookup field, you must first delete the relationships for those fields. In this exercise, you learn how to use the shortcut commands to delete two fields from an Access 2013 table.

To delete a field in Datasheet view, select the column, right-click, and then click Delete Field from the shortcut menu. Or, on the TABLE TOOLS FIELDS contextual tab in the Add & Delete group, click the Delete button. You will see a confirmation message asking if you are sure you want to delete the column and all the data. Sometimes you may see an additional confirmation message warning you about potential issues when deleting fields. You should always be cautious when deleting fields from a table.

STEP BY STEP   **Delete a Field**

USE the database that is open from the previous exercise.

Another Way
You can also delete a field by clicking the Delete button on the TABLE TOOLS FIELDS contextual tab in the Add & Delete group.

1. Click the **column header for the Attachment field**, located between the *Description* field and the *Status* field.

2. Right-click on the **column header** to display the shortcut menu and click **Delete Field** (see Figure 4-26).

Figure 4-26

Delete Field command on field shortcut menu

Right-click column to display menu

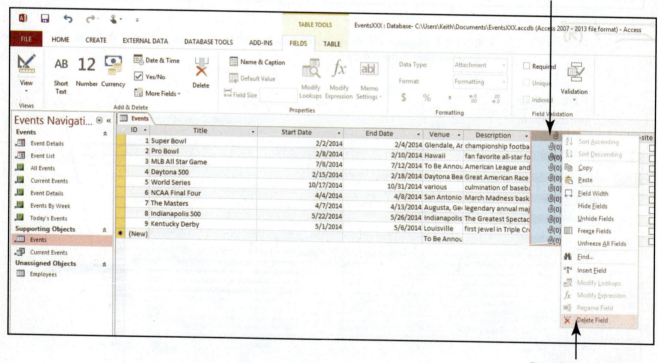

Delete Field command

3. A message appears (see Figure 4-27). Click **Yes**.

Figure 4-27

Delete field message

4. A confirmation message appears (see Figure 4-28). Click **Yes**. The field is deleted.

Figure 4-28

Delete field confirmation message

CERTIFICATION READY? 2.4.9

How do you delete fields?

5. Click the **column header** for the Status field.
6. Right-click in the **column** to display the shortcut menu then click **Delete Field**. In the message box that appears, click **Yes** to delete the Status field.

PAUSE. LEAVE the database open to use in the next exercise.

Another Way
You can also delete a field in Design view by selecting the field (row) that you want to delete and clicking Delete Rows on the TABLE TOOLS DESIGN contextual tab, in the Tools group.

Creating Multivalued Lookup Fields

In Office Access 2013, it is possible to create a **multivalued lookup field** that lets you select more than one choice from a list, without having to create a more advanced database design. You can create a field that holds multiple values, such as a list of employees that you have assigned to a particular event. Use the Lookup Wizard to create multivalued fields. The Lookup Wizard guides you through the process of creating a field or lookup column that can "look up" data that exists in one or more tables to automate the complexity of manually relating tables. In this exercise, you create a multivalued lookup field using the Lookup Wizard in Datasheet view.

Use a multivalued lookup field when you want to store multiple selections from a list of choices that are relatively small. This is useful if you want to limit the choices a user can select to store in a table field to prevent erroneous data from being entered. For example, you can create a multivalued lookup field to assign only those employees who work in your department to a specific task. Limiting the choices a user can make to enter into a field helps protect the validity of your data.

Take Note You can also create lookup columns that allow for a single selection of a value.

STEP BY STEP **Create a Multivalued Lookup Field**

USE the database that is open from the previous exercise.

1. Place the insertion point in the first cell of the table. Click the **More Fields** button in the Add & Delete group on the TABLE TOOLS FIELDS contextual tab, then click the **Lookup & Relationship** button. The Lookup Wizard appears (see Figure 4-29).

Figure 4-29

Lookup Wizard

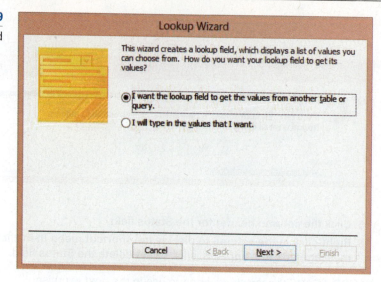

2. Click **Next** > to accept the default setting (*I want the lookup field to get the values from another table or query*) and display the next screen in the Lookup Wizard (see Figure 4-30). Notice you have a choice of two tables to provide the values for the lookup field you are creating. The first table, Employees, should already be selected for you.

Figure 4-30

Lookup Wizard, second screen

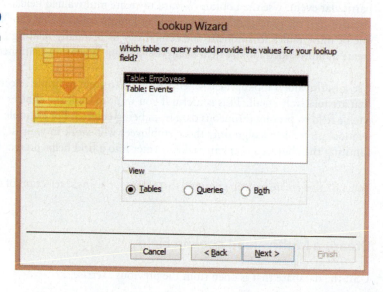

3. Click **Next** > to accept the default settings and display the next screen in the Lookup Wizard (see Figure 4-31). The Available Fields scroll box contains all the fields of the Employees table, two of which you will select since they contain the values you want to eventually look up.

Figure 4-31

Lookup Wizard, third screen

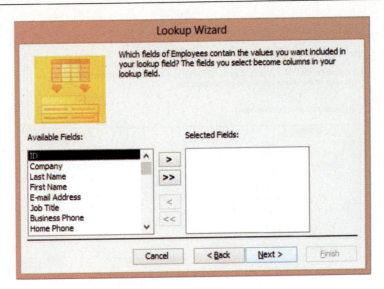

4. In the Available Fields list, select **Last Name**, then click the > button to move it to the Selected Fields box.

5. In the Available Fields list, select **First Name**, then click the > button to move it to the Selected Fields box.

6. Click **Next** > to accept your settings and display the next screen in the Lookup Wizard.

7. Click the **down arrow** in the first box and click **Last Name** (see Figure 4-32). This will sort the Lookup column in alphabetical order by Last Name.

Figure 4-32

Lookup Wizard, fourth screen

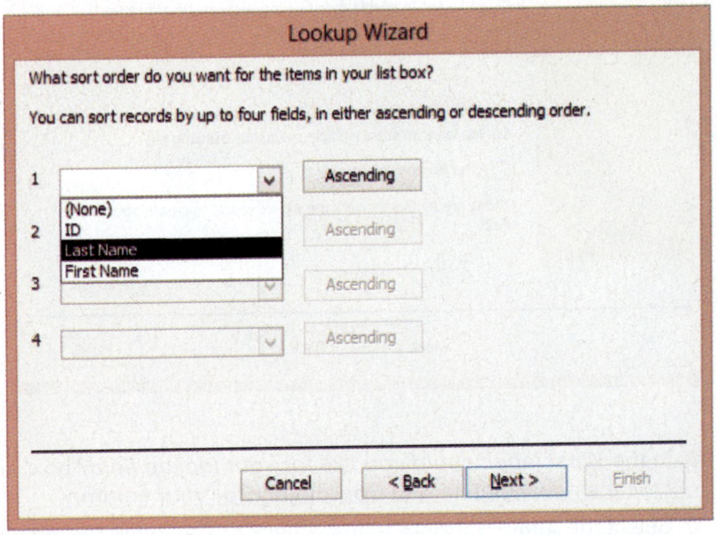

8. Click **Next** > to accept your selection and to display the next screen in the Lookup Wizard (see Figure 4-33).

Figure 4-33

Lookup Wizard, fifth screen

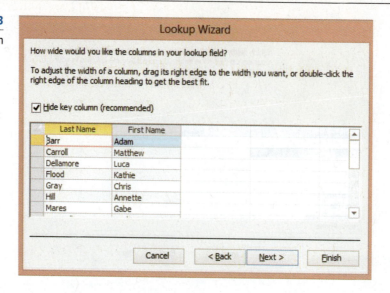

Figure 4-33

Lookup Wizard, fifth screen

9. Click **Next >** to accept the default selection and to hide the primary key column to ensure only relevant and meaningful data displays in the lookup column later. The final screen of the Lookup Wizard displays (see Figure 4-34).

Figure 4-34

Lookup Wizard, final screen

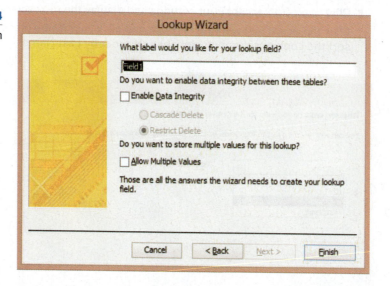

Another Way

You can also modify the Allow Multiple Values property in the Lookup Field Properties sheet in table Design view.

10. In the *What label would you like for your lookup field?* box, key **Coordinator**. This will create a new label named Coordinator for your column.

11. Select the **Allow Multiple Values** check box to allow for the multiple selections of values.

12. Click the **Finish** button. A new column named Coordinator appears after the ID field. Click the **down arrow** in the first cell to display the list of names (see Figure 4-35).

Figure 4-35

Lookup column list

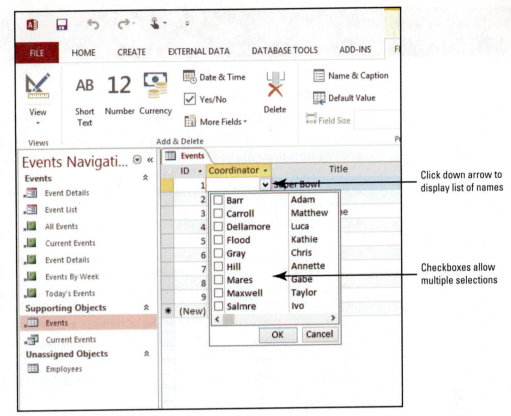

Figure 4-35

Lookup column list

Click down arrow to display list of names

Checkboxes allow multiple selections

13. Click **Flood/Kathie** and **Mares/Gabe** on the list and then click **OK** to choose those multiple values for the field.

STOP. CLOSE the database.

SKILL SUMMARY

In This Lesson You Learned How To:	Exam Objective	Objective Number
Modify a Database Table	Add table descriptions.	2.2.4
	Rename tables.	2.2.5
Create Fields and Modify Field Properties	Set default values.	2.4.7
	Change field sizes.	2.4.4
	Use input masks.	2.4.8
	Add validation rules to fields.	2.4.2
	Change field captions.	2.4.3
	Add fields to tables.	2.4.1
	Delete fields.	2.4.9

Knowledge Assessment

Fill in the Blank

Complete the following sentences by writing the correct word or words in the blanks provided.

1. _____ or _____ a table could possibly break the functionality of the database.

2. If you want more space to enter or edit a setting in the property box, press Shift+F2 to display the _____ dialog box.

3. A(n) _____ contains no characters, and you use it to indicate that you know no value exists for a field.

4. _____ specifies the text in the error message that appears when users violate a validation rule.

5. The _____ property field specifies the text displayed by default as column names in tables and in labels for forms, reports, and queries.

6. When creating fields, use the commands in the _____ group on the TABLE TOOLS FIELDS contextual tab.

7. A(n) _____ is a predefined set of characteristics and properties that describes a field.

8. Creating multivalued lookup fields can be accomplished by using the _____ Wizard.

9. The _____ Quick Start includes fields for City, State, and Zip.

10. You should always consider _____ a table before deleting a column.

Multiple Choice

Select the best response for the following statements or questions.

1. To rename a table or other database object, first
   a. save it.
   b. close it.
   c. edit it.
   d. open it.

2. If you delete a database table,
   a. you cannot undo the action.
   b. click Undo to restore the table.
   c. it is still available in the Navigation Pane.
   d. the data is transferred to the Clipboard.

3. A complete list of field properties is available in
   a. the Navigation Pane.
   b. Datasheet view.
   c. Design view.
   d. all of the above.

4. Which of the following is *not* a field property?
   a. Column Template
   b. Field Size
   c. Caption
   d. Allow Zero Length

5. Which field property requires users to enter data in a specific format?
   a. Validation Text
   b. Default Value
   c. Required
   d. Input Mask

6. The Default Value property can be used for which field?
   a. Short Text.
   b. Number.
   c. Currency.
   d. All of the above.

7. Which of the following is *not* a way to validate data?
    a. Data type
    b. Field sizes
    c. Filtering
    d. Field properties

8. The Caption field property is used for which field type?
    a. Short Text
    b. Attachment
    c. Date/Time
    d. All of the above

9. Which type of field allows you to select more than one choice from a list?
    a. Attachment
    b. Multivalued
    c. Caption
    d. Validation

10. To delete a field in Datasheet view, select the column, right-click, and then click Delete Field from the
    a. Quick Access toolbar.
    b. Lookup Wizard.
    c. Shortcut menu.
    d. HOME tab.

Competency Assessment

Project 4-1: Home Inventory

You decide to use Access to create a home inventory database for insurance purposes. To include all the information you want, you need to add several fields to the existing table.

GET READY. LAUNCH Access if it is not already running.

1. **OPEN** the *Home inventory* database from the data files for this lesson.
2. **SAVE** the database as *Home inventoryXXX* (where *XXX* is your initials).
3. In the Navigation Pane, double-click the **Assets** table to open it.
4. Horizontally scroll to the end of the table and click in the **cell** below the Click to Add header.
5. On the TABLE TOOLS FIELDS contextual tab, in the Add & Delete group, click the **More Fields** button and click **Yes/No** in the Yes/No category. A column named Field1 is created.
6. On the TABLE TOOLS FIELDS contextual tab, in the Properties group, click the **Name & Caption** button.
7. Key **Insured** to rename the Field1 column. Click **OK** to close the dialog box.
8. Click in the **cell** below the Click to Add header.
9. On the TABLE TOOLS FIELDS contextual tab, in the Add & Delete group, click the **More Fields** button and click **Attachment** in the Basic Types category to create an attachment field.
10. **CLOSE** the database.

LEAVE Access open for the next project.

Project 4-2: Customer Service

You are employed in the customer service department at City Power & Light. Each call that is received is recorded in an Access database. Because you know how to modify tables and fields, your supervisor asks you to add a lookup column to the Calls table to record the customer service representative who receives the call.

GET READY. LAUNCH Access if it is not already running.

1. **OPEN** *Customer service* from the data files for this lesson.
2. **SAVE** the database as *Customer serviceXXX* (where *XXX* is your initials).
3. In the Navigation Pane, double-click the **Calls** table to open it. Place the insertion point in the first cell of the table, if necessary.
4. On the TABLE TOOLS FIELDS contextual tab, in the Add & Delete group, click the **More Fields** button, and then click the **Lookup & Relationship** button. The Lookup Wizard appears.
5. Click **Next >** to display the next screen in the Lookup Wizard.
6. Select **Table: Employees** and click **Next >**.
7. In the Available Fields list, select **First Name**, then click the **>** button to move it to the Selected Fields box.
8. In the Available Fields list, select **Last Name**, then click the **>** button to move it to the Selected Fields box.
9. Click **Next >** to display the next screen in the Lookup Wizard.
10. Click the **down arrow** in the first box and click **Last Name**.
11. Click **Next >** to display the next screen in the Lookup Wizard.
12. Click **Next >** again to display the final screen in the Lookup Wizard.
13. In the *What label would you like for your lookup field?* box, key **Service Rep**.
14. Click the **Finish** button. A new column named Service Rep appears as the second column of the table.
15. Click the **down arrow** and choose **Clair/Hector** from the list.

LEAVE the database open for the next project.

Proficiency Assessment

Project 4-3: Modify Field Properties

Your supervisor at City Power & Light asks you to make some modifications to the field properties in the Calls table of the customer service database.

USE the database that is open from the previous project.

1. Switch to Design View.
2. Display the Lookup field properties for the **Service Rep** field.
3. Change the Allow Multiple Values property to **Yes** and confirm the change.
4. Display the General field properties for the Call Time field.
5. Change the Validation Rule property so that the value must be **greater than 1/1/2000**.
6. Change the Validation Text property to say **Please enter a value that is later than 1/1/2000**.
7. Display the General field properties for the Caller field.
8. Change the Field Size property to **60**.
9. Display the General field properties for the Notes field.
10. Change the Allow Zero Length property to **Yes**.
11. Set the Default Value property by keying **Comments:**.

12. Save the table. If a data integrity message appears, click **No**.
13. **CLOSE** the database.

LEAVE Access open for the next project.

Project 4-4: Modify Database Tables

You work as the operations manager at Alpine Ski House and decide to increase your efficiency by using Access to plan the annual race events. You have started to create a database to manage the events sponsored by the company but need to modify the tables.

GET READY. LAUNCH Access if it is not already running.

1. **OPEN** *Alpine* from the data files for this lesson.
2. **SAVE** the database as *AlpineXXX* (where *XXX* is your initials).
3. Delete the Nordic Events table and confirm the action.
4. Rename the World Cup table to **Championships**.
5. Open the **Events** table and switch to **Design view**.
6. Display the property sheet.
7. In the Description property box, key **Annual events**.
8. Save the table.
9. **CLOSE** the database.

LEAVE Access open for the next project.

Mastery Assessment

Project 4-5: Changing List Items

You are the owner of Fourth Coffee, a growing company that is converting all of its data from spreadsheets to Access. You directed an intern to create a database with tables to be used to track inventory. You want to make some modifications to these database tables before you enter information in the database.

GET READY. LAUNCH Access if it is not already running.

1. **OPEN** *Fourth Coffee* from the data files for this lesson.
2. **SAVE** the database as *Fourth CoffeeXXX* (where *XXX* is your initials).
3. Open the Coffee Beans table and create a **new Lookup field** as the last field in the table that uses the Country field in the Countries table. Specify an **ascending sort order** for the records in this field.
4. Rename the field **Origin**.
5. In Datasheet view, change the name and caption of the Current Value field to **Market Value**.
6. In Datasheet view, change the name and caption of the Acquired Date field to **Acquisition Date**.
7. Create a Yes/No field as the last field in the table named *Stocked* with a caption named **In Stock?**
8. In Design view, create an input mask for all fields that use the Date/Time data type. Choose **Medium Date** as the input mask and accept all default values.
9. **SAVE** the table.
10. **CLOSE** the database.

LEAVE Access open for the next project.

Project 4-6: Lending Library

You have an extensive personal library that friends and family frequently ask to share. To keep track of all your books, you decide to use Access to create a lending library database.

GET READY. LAUNCH Access if it is not already running.

1. **OPEN** *Lending library* from the data files for this lesson.
2. **SAVE** the database as *Lending libraryXXX* (where *XXX* is your initials).
3. Delete the Manufacturer, Model, and Retired Date fields from the Assets table.
4. Create a new field in the Assets table with the Yes/No datatype and change its name and caption to Rare?
5. In the Assets table, change the Field Size property of the Item field to 100.
6. Rename the Assets table to Books.
7. Save and close the table.
8. In the Contacts table, create a new Lookup field named Borrower Status that looks up data from the Status field of the Borrower table.
9. Save and close the table.
10. **CLOSE** the database.

CLOSE Access.

LESSON SKILL MATRIX

Skill	Exam Objective	Objective Number
Creating Forms	Create new forms.	4.1.1
	Save forms.	4.1.3
	Delete forms.	4.1.4
	Create databases using wizards.	1.1.4
	Apply themes.	4.3.4
Sorting and Filtering Data within a Form	Sort Records.	4.3.3

KEY TERMS

- Blank Form tool
- common filters
- filter
- filter by form
- Form Design button
- Form tool
- Form Wizard
- Themes

© 4FR/iStockphoto

You are the owner of the Graphic Art Institute, a small fine-arts gallery dedicated to presenting challenging and contemporary visual arts and educational programs. The current exhibition is successfully underway; you are now calling for submissions for the next exhibition—a juried art show featuring photographic work from the local region. The competition is open to all regional artists who use photographic processes in their work. This particular event will be open to digital submissions. As each submission is received, you will enter the artist and image information into an Access database for easy retrieval. In this lesson, you learn how to create forms using a variety of methods; how to apply a Theme to a form; and how to sort and filter data within a form.

SOFTWARE ORIENTATION

Forms Group

The Forms group (see Figure 5-1) is located on the CREATE tab in the Ribbon and can be used to create a variety of forms.

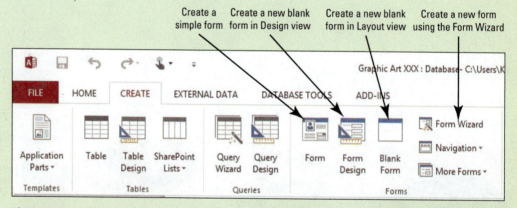

Create a simple form   Create a new blank form in Design view   Create a new blank form in Layout view   Create a new form using the Form Wizard

Figure 5-1

Forms group

Use this figure as a reference throughout this lesson as well as the rest of this book.

CREATING FORMS

The Bottom Line

A form is a database object that you can use to enter, edit, or display data from a table or query. Forms can be used to control access to data by limiting which fields or rows of data are displayed to users. For example, certain users might need to see only certain fields in a table. Providing those users with a form that contains just those fields makes it easier for them to use the database. Think of forms as windows through which people see and reach your database in a more visually attractive and efficient way.

You can create forms in several different ways, depending on how much control you want over the form's design. Forms that include all fields in a table can be quickly created through a single mouse-click by using the Form tool, or you can control the number of fields you'd like to include on the form as well as the layout of the form by using the Form Wizard. You have the most flexibility with the amount and placement of fields on the form by using Layout or Design view, with

Design view giving you the greatest control over field placement and properties. You can quickly apply a chosen theme to the form to modify its color and font scheme using the Themes command. Finally, you can delete any form by simply using the Delete command. In this section, you practice creating forms using a variety of these skills. You also delete a pre-existing form.

Creating a Simple Form and Deleting a Form

You can use the **Form tool** to create a form with a single mouse-click. When you use this tool, all the fields from the underlying data source are placed on the form. Access creates the form and displays it in Layout view. You can begin using the new form immediately, or you can modify it in Layout view or Design view to better suit your needs. You can also delete a form to remove it permanently from the database. In this exercise, you create a simple form by using the Form tool and delete a form by using the Delete command.

To use the Form tool to create a simple form, first click in the Navigation Pane on the table that contains the data you want to see on the form. On the CREATE tab, in the Forms group, click Form.

To save a form design, click the FILE tab and click Save. Key a name in the Form Name box and click OK. After you save your form design, you can run the form as often as you want. The design stays the same, but you see current data every time you view the form. If your needs change, you can modify the form design or create a new form that is based on the original. You can also permanently delete the form or any preexisting forms from the database by using the Delete command in the Records group of the HOME tab. You can delete a form if you erroneously created it or simply want to unclutter the database.

STEP BY STEP	Create a Simple Form and Delete a Form

GET READY. Before you begin these steps, be sure to **LAUNCH** Microsoft Access.

1. **OPEN** the *Graphic Art* database from the data files for this lesson.
2. **SAVE** the database as *Graphic ArtXXX* (where *XXX* is your initials).
3. In the Navigation Pane, click the **Photo Exhibit** table. This is the table for which you will create a form.
4. On the CREATE tab, in the Forms group, click the **Form** button. Access creates the form and displays it in Layout view (see Figure 5-2). Your form may be slightly different.

Figure 5-2

Simple form

Close 'Photo Exhibit' button

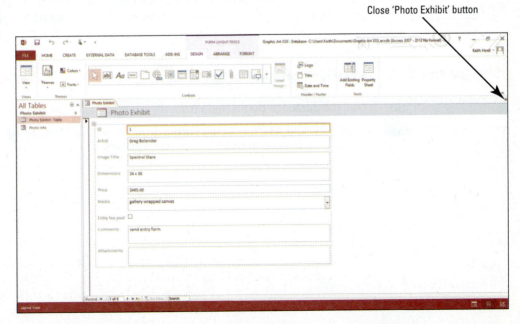

5. Click the **FILE** tab and click **Save**. The Save As dialog box appears (see Figure 5-3).

Figure 5-3

Save As dialog box

Take Note   You can use the record navigation buttons at the bottom of a form to navigate among the form's records, just as you used them to navigate among records in a table in Lesson 3.

6. Click **OK** to accept the Photo Exhibit form name suggested by Access. The form name appears in the Navigation Pane.

7. Click the **Close** button on Photo Exhibit to close the form.

8. In the Navigation Pane, click the **Photo Info** form. This is a form that you no longer need.

9. In the Records group, click the **Delete** button arrow and then click the **Delete** command on the menu that appears.

10. Click **Yes** on the dialog box asking you if you want to permanently delete the Photo Info form. The form is now permanently deleted from the database.

PAUSE. LEAVE the database open to use in the next exercise.

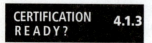

Another Way

You can also delete a form or any other object by right-clicking it in the Navigation Pane and choosing Delete from the shortcut menu that appears.

CERTIFICATION READY?   4.1.1

How do you create new forms?

CERTIFICATION READY?   4.1.3

How do you save forms?

CERTIFICATION READY?   4.1.4

How do you delete forms?

Creating a Form in Design View

When you click the **Form Design button**, a new blank form is created in Design view. Design view gives you a more detailed view of the structure of your form than Layout view. The form is not actually running when it is shown in Design view, so you cannot see the underlying data while you are making design changes. In this exercise, you create a new blank form in Design view and manually add fields to it.

You can fine-tune your form's design by working in Design view. To switch to Design view, right-click the form name in the Navigation Pane and then click Design view. You can also use the View button on the HOME tab of the Ribbon. You can add new controls—used to enter, edit, and find information—and fields to the form by adding them to the design grid. Plus, the property sheet gives you access to a large number of properties that you can set to customize your form.

STEP BY STEP   **Create a Form in Design View**

USE the database that is open from the previous exercise.

1. On the CREATE tab, in the Forms group, click the **Form Design** button. A new blank form is created in Design view (see Figure 5-4).

Figure 5-4

New blank form in Design view

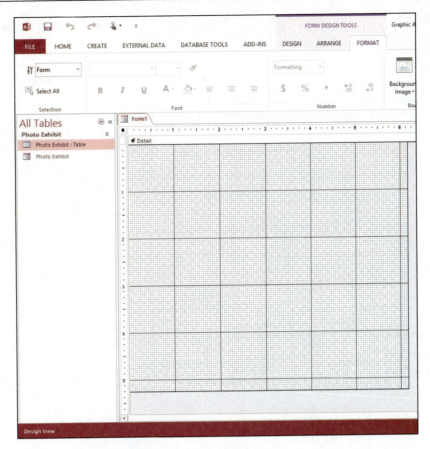

2. On the FORM DESIGN TOOLS Design contextual tab, in the Tools group, click the **Add Existing Fields** button. The Field List pane appears (see Figure 5-5).

Figure 5-5

Field List pane

Field List pane

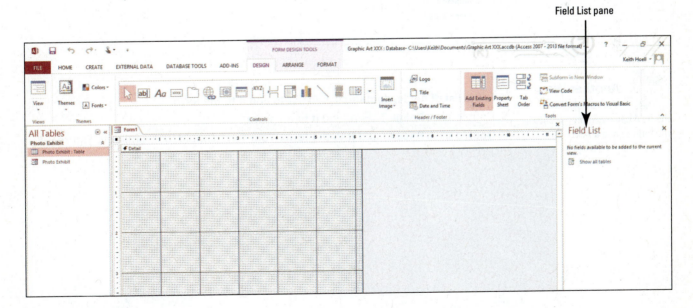

Another Way
You can also display the Field List pane by pressing Alt+F8.

3. Click the **Show all tables** link, then the **expand button** to the left of the table name (see Figure 5-6). The available fields display from the Photo Exhibit table (see Figure 5-7).

Figure 5-6

Field List pane with
expand button

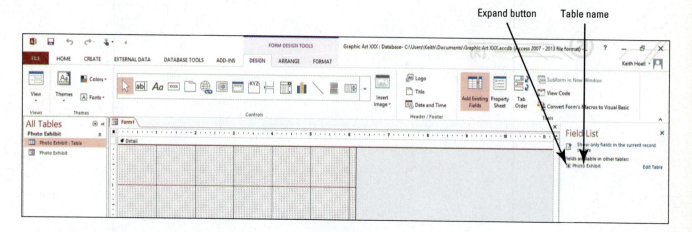

Figure 5-7

Field List pane with
available fields

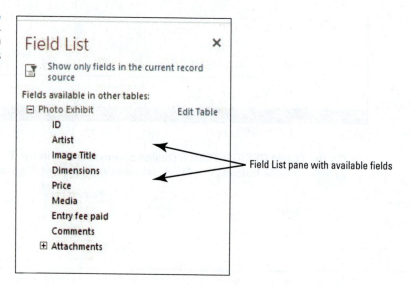

Field List pane with available fields

Another Way
You can also click
the field name and drag it onto
the form to add a field.

4. In the list of fields, double-click **Artist** to add it to the form.

5. Double-click **Image Title** to add it to the form.

6. Double-click **Price** to add it to the form. Your form should look similar to Figure 5-8.

Figure 5-8

Fields inserted in Design view

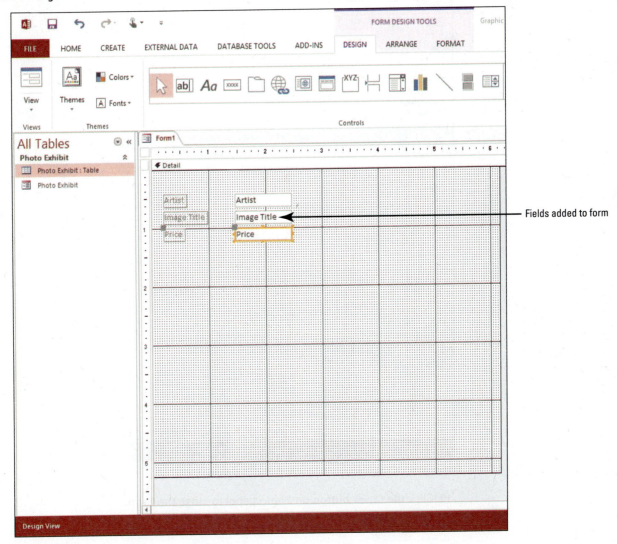

7. Click the **FILE** tab and click **Save**.

8. In the Save As dialog box, key **Photo Label**, and click **OK**.

9. On the Design menu, in the Views group, click the lower half of the **View** button and click **Form View** to display the form in Form view (see Figure 5-9).

Figure 5-9

Form view

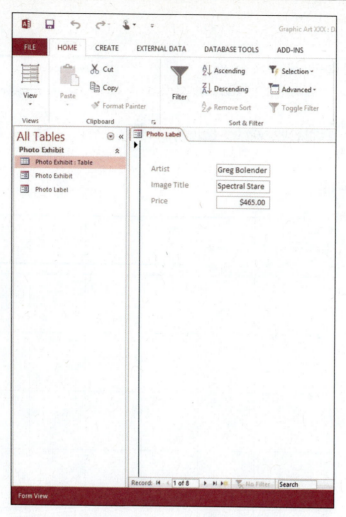

10. Click the Close button on Photo Label to close the form.

PAUSE. LEAVE the database open to use in the next exercise.

Cross Ref   You learn how to use the commands in the Controls group and a greater variety of form design tools in Lessons 8 and 10.

Creating a Form in Layout View

If other form-building tools do not fit your needs, you can use the Blank Form tool to create a form. The **Blank Form tool** creates a new form in Layout view. This can be a very quick way to build a form, especially if you plan to put only a few fields on your form. Click the Blank Form button to quickly create a new blank form in Layout view; you can make design changes to the form while viewing the underlying data. In this exercise, you use the Blank Form tool to create a form in Layout view.

On the CREATE tab, in the Forms group, click the Blank Form button. Access opens a blank form in Layout view and displays the Field List pane. To add a field to the form, double-click it or drag it onto the form. In Layout view, you can make design changes to the form while it is displaying data.

STEP BY STEP   Create a Form in Layout View

USE the database that is open from the previous exercise.

1. On the CREATE tab, in the Forms group, click the **Blank Form** button. A new blank form is created in Layout view.

2. Click the **Show all tables** link in the Field List pane to show the Photo Exhibit table name, if necessary.

3. If necessary, click the **expand button** ⊞ next to the Photo Exhibit table name to show a list of fields related to the table and double-click **Image Title** to add it to the form. Your screen should look like Figure 5-10.

Figure 5-10

Image Title field added to new blank form

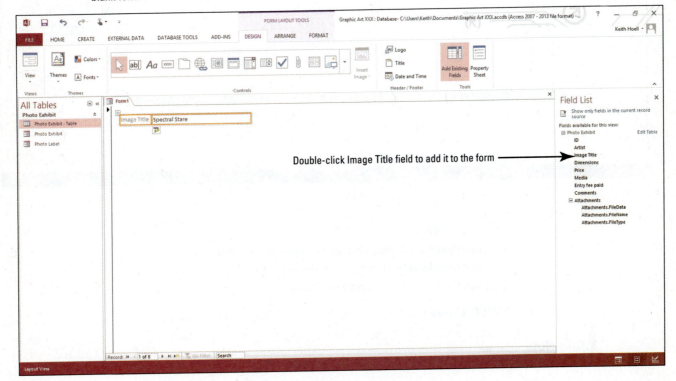

Double-click Image Title field to add it to the form

4. Double-click **Dimensions** to add it to the form.

5. Double-click **Media** to add it to the form. Your form should look similar to Figure 5-11.

Figure 5-11

Fields inserted in Layout view

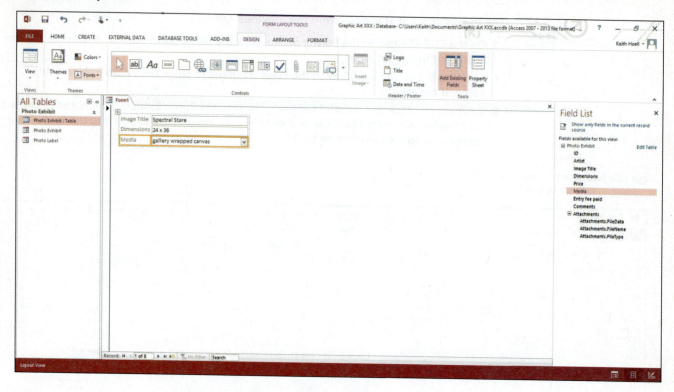

6. Click the **FILE** tab and click **Save**.

7. In the Save As dialog box, key **Image Info**, and click **OK**.

8. Click the **Close** button to close the Field List.

9. Click the **Close** button on Image Info to close the form.

PAUSE. LEAVE the database open to use in the next exercise.

Take Note To add more than one field at a time after adding at least one other field, press Ctrl and click several fields; then, drag them all onto the form at once.

Using the Form Wizard

Another method of building a form is to use the **Form Wizard** tool. The Form Wizard allows you to select the fields that will appear on the form, choose the form layout (which determines the positioning of controls, objects, and data on a form), and also choose a predefined style, if desired. In this exercise, you use the Form Wizard to create a datasheet form. A datasheet form looks very similar to the table upon which it is based and provides a way to enter data using columns and rows.

STEP BY STEP   **Use the Form Wizard**

USE the database that is open from the previous exercise.

1. On the CREATE tab, in the Forms group, click the **Form Wizard** button (see Figure 5-12).

Figure 5-12

Form Wizard button in Forms group

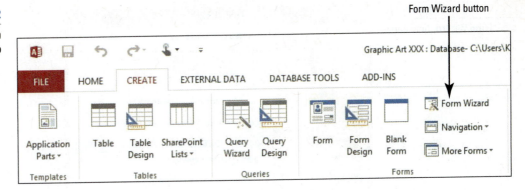

Form Wizard button

2. The Form Wizard appears (see Figure 5-13).

Figure 5-13

Form Wizard

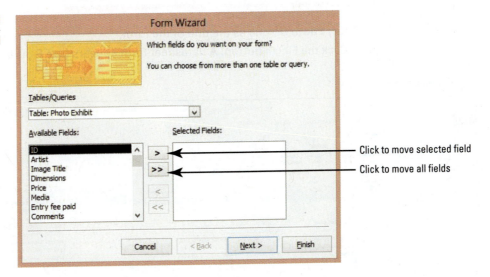

Click to move selected field

Click to move all fields

3. Click the **>>** button to move all the fields from the Available Fields box to the Selected Fields box.

4. Click the **Next >** button to move to the next page in the Form Wizard (see Figure 5-14).

Figure 5-14

Form Wizard, page 2

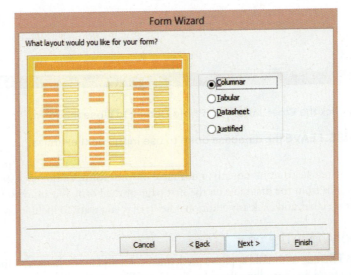

5. Click **Datasheet** as the layout for the form. Form layouts help determine the positioning of controls, objects, and data on a form.

6. Click the **Next >** button to move to the final page in the Form Wizard (see Figure 5-15).

Figure 5-15

Form Wizard, final page

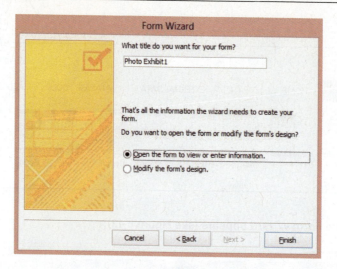

7. Key **Photo Details** as the title of the form.
8. Click the **Finish** button. A datasheet form appears (see Figure 5-16).

Figure 5-16

Datasheet form

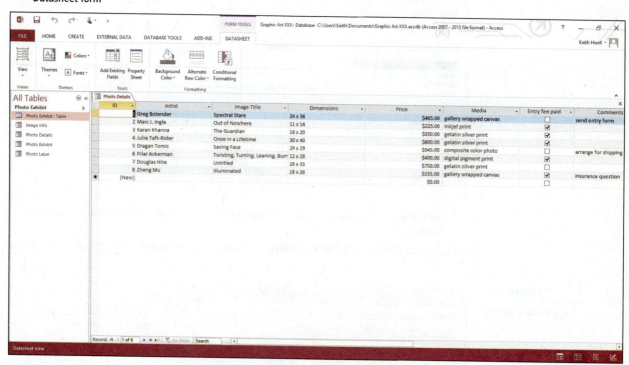

9. Click the **Close** button on Photo Details to close the form.

PAUSE. LEAVE the database open to use in the next exercise.

Take Note   To include fields from more than one table on your form, do not click Next or Finish after you select the fields from the first table on the first page of the Form Wizard. Instead, repeat the steps to select another table, and click any additional fields that you want to include on the form before continuing.

CERTIFICATION
READY?   1.1.4

How do you create databases using wizards?

Applying a Theme

The **Themes** command applies a predefined color and font scheme to a form or report. A theme modifies a form by controlling the color and fonts of its text. In this exercise, you apply a Theme to a form.

Take Note   Access certification exam objective 1.1.4, "How do you create databases using wizards," is met by using any number of wizards used to create database objects including other wizards you'll learn about in later lessons.

To apply a theme, first switch to Layout view. On the FORM LAYOUT TOOLS Design contextual tab, in the Themes group, click the Themes button to view a gallery of theme styles from which to choose. You can point to each option to see the name of that format and a live preview before it is applied to the form.

STEP BY STEP **Apply a Theme**

USE the database that is open from the previous exercise.

1. Double-click the **Image Info** form in the Navigation Pane to open it.
2. On the HOME tab, in the Views group, click the lower half of the **View** button, and click **Layout View** on the View menu.
3. On the FORM LAYOUT TOOLS Design contextual tab, in the Themes group, click the **Themes** button (see Figure 5-17).

Figure 5-17

Themes button

Themes button accesses Themes gallery

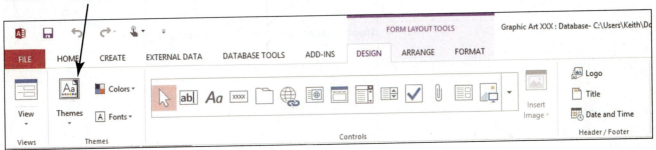

4. A gallery of themes appears (see Figure 5-18).

Figure 5-18

Themes gallery

5. Click the **Integral theme** (first row, third column) to apply it to the form. Notice how the form's text has changed (see Figure 5-19).

Figure 5-19

Form in Layout view with Integral theme applied

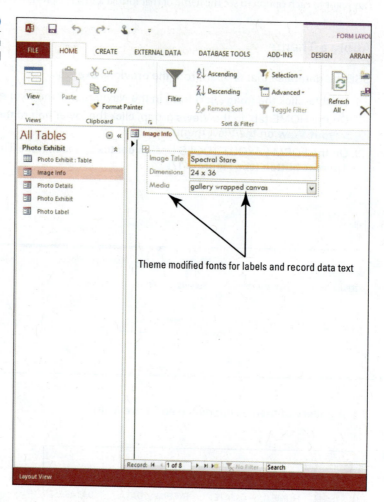

Theme modified fonts for labels and record data text

6. Click the **Close** button on Image Info to close the form.

PAUSE. LEAVE the database open to use in the next exercise.

SORTING AND FILTERING DATA WITHIN A FORM

The Bottom Line

Sorting data in a form can help make it much more effective and easy to use. Sorting helps users review and locate the records they want without having to browse the data. To find one or more specific records in a form, you can use a filter. A **filter** limits a view of data to specific records without requiring you to alter the design of the form. You also can use a tool called filter by form to filter on several fields in a form or to find a specific record.

Sorting Data within a Form

Data can be sorted in the Form view of a form. The order that is chosen when a form is designed becomes that object's default sort order. But when viewing the form, users can sort the records in whatever way is most useful. You can sort the records in a form on one or more fields. In this exercise, you sort data in a form in ascending order.

STEP BY STEP | Sort Data within a Form

USE the database that is open from the previous exercise.

1. Double-click the **Photo Label** form in the Navigation Pane to open it in Form view.

2. Right-click the **Price** field to display the shortcut menu (see Figure 5-20).

Figure 5-20

Price field shortcut menu

Right-click to display shortcut menu

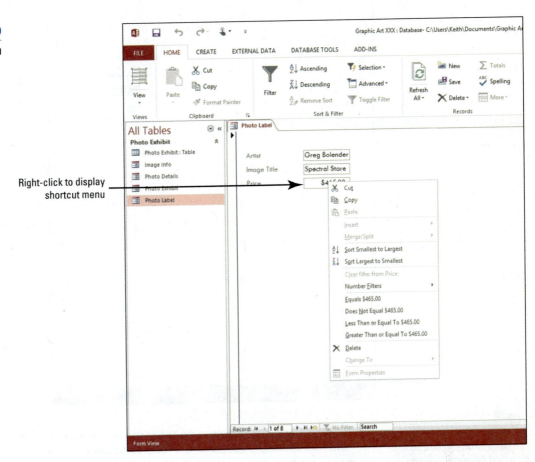

3. Click **Sort Smallest to Largest**. The form is sorted by price from smallest to largest. The record with the smallest price is displayed first (see Figure 5-21).

Figure 5-21

Form sorted by price

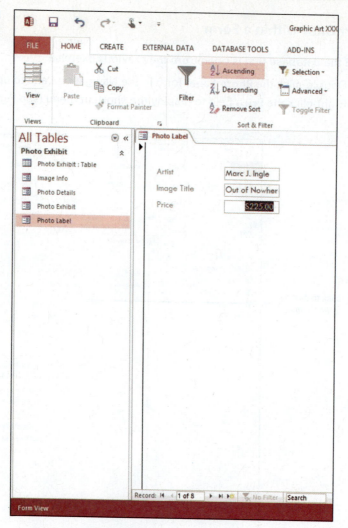

Another Way
You can also sort on a field by selecting it and clicking the Ascending or Descending button on the HOME tab in the Sort & Filter group.

4. Click the **Next record** button on the record navigator at the bottom of the form. Continue clicking through all the records to see the records in order according to price.

5. On the HOME tab, in the Sort & Filter group, click the **Remove Sort** button. The records have resorted back to their original order.

6. Click the **Close** button on Photo Label to close the form.

PAUSE. LEAVE the database open to use in the next exercise.

Take Note   You cannot sort on a field that contains attachments. When sorting on a field with the Yes/No data type, a value of "Yes," "True," or "On" is considered "Selected," and when sorted in ascending order will appear at the top of the list; a value of "No," "False," or "Off" is considered "Cleared," and when sorted in ascending order will appear at the bottom of the list.

You must identify the fields on which you want to sort. To sort on two or more fields, identify the fields that will act as the innermost and outermost sort fields. Right-click anywhere in the column corresponding to the innermost field, and click one of the sort commands. The commands vary based on the type of data that is in the selected field. Repeat the process for each sort field, ending with the outermost sort field. The records are rearranged to match the sort order.

Cross Ref   You already learned how to sort data within a table in Lesson 3. Sorting in a form is very similar.

The last-applied sort order is automatically saved with the form. If you want it automatically applied the next time you open the form, make sure the Order By On Load property of the form is set to Yes. Remember that you cannot remove a sort order from just a single field. To remove sorting from all sort fields, on the HOME tab, in the Sort & Filter group, click Remove Sort.

Filtering Data within a Form

Common filters are built into every view that displays data. The filters available depend on the type and values of the field. When you apply the filter, only records that contain the values that you are interested in are included in the view. The rest are hidden until you remove the filter. In this exercise, you filter form data using common filters.

Filters are easy to apply and remove. Filter settings remain in effect until you close the form, even if you switch to another view. If you save the form while the filter is applied, it will be available the next time you open the form. To permanently remove a filter, on the HOME tab, in the Sort & Filter group, click the Advanced button and click Clear All Filters.

STEP BY STEP | **Filter Data with Common Filters**

USE the database that is open from the previous exercise.

1. Double-click the **Photo Exhibit** form in the Navigation Pane to open it in Form view.
2. Right-click the **Media** field to display the shortcut menu and click **Text Filters** (see Figure 5-22).

Figure 5-22

Media field text filters

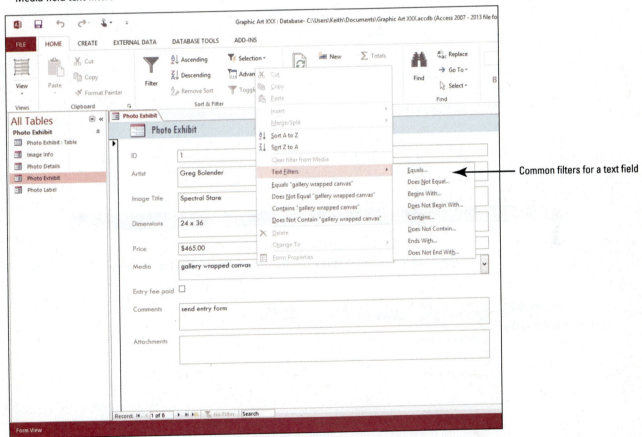

Common filters for a text field

3. Click **Contains...** to display the Custom Filter dialog box (see Figure 5-23).

Figure 5-23

Custom Filter dialog box

4. In the *Media contains* box, key **print**, and click **OK**.

5. Click the **Next record** button on the record navigator at the bottom of the form. Continue clicking to see the five records that contain the word "print" in the Media field.

6. Right-click the **Price** field to display the shortcut menu and click **Number Filters** (see Figure 5-24).

Figure 5-24

Price field number filters

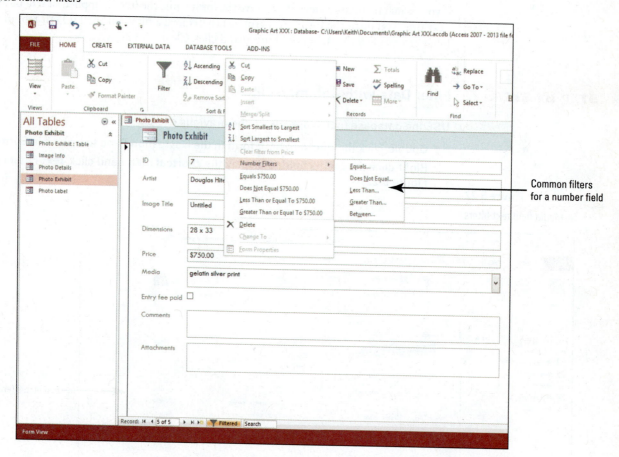

Common filters for a number field

7. Click **Less Than...** to display the Custom Filter dialog box shown in Figure 5-25.

Figure 5-25

Custom Filter dialog box

8. In the *Price is less than or equal to* box, key **500**, and click **OK**.

9. Click the **Next record** button on the record navigator at the bottom of the form. Continue clicking to see the three photos that use print media and are less than $500.

10. On the HOME tab, in the Sort & Filter group, click the **Advanced Filter Options** button to display the menu shown in Figure 5-26.

Figure 5-26

Advanced Filter Options
button menu

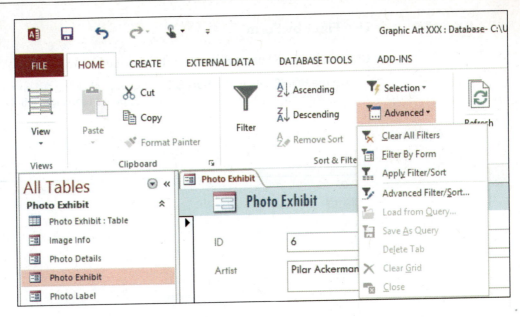

11. Click **Clear All Filters**.

PAUSE. LEAVE the database open to use in the next exercise.

 Cross Ref You already learned how to filter data within a table in Lesson 3. Filtering in a form using common filters is very similar.

Using Filter by Form

Although only a single filter can be in effect for any one field at any one time, you can specify a different filter for each field that is present in the view. In addition to the ready-to-use filters for each data type, you can also filter a form by completing an action called filter by form. **Filter by form** is useful when you want to filter several fields in a form or if you are trying to find a specific record. Access creates a blank form that is similar to the original form; you then complete as many of the fields as you want. When you are finished, Access finds the records that contain the specified values. In this exercise, you filter by form.

To use filter by form, open the form in Form view and make sure the view is not already filtered by verifying that either the Unfiltered icon [Unfiltered] or the dimmed No Filter icon [No Filter] is present on the record selector bar. On the HOME tab, in the Sort & Filter group, click Advanced, and then click Filter By Form. Click the down arrow in a field to display the available values.

Enter the first set of values on the Look for tab, and then click the Or tab and enter the next set of values. Each time you click the Or tab, Access creates another Or tab; so you can continue to add additional filter values. Click the Toggle Filter button to apply the filter. The filter returns any record that contains all of the values specified on the Look for tab, or all of the values specified on the first Or tab, or all of the values specified on the second Or tab, and so on.

STEP BY STEP   Use Filter by Form

USE the database that is open from the previous exercise.

1. On the HOME tab, in the Sort & Filter group, click the **Advanced Filter Options** button and click **Filter By Form**. A form filter appears (see Figure 5-27).

Figure 5-27

Form filter

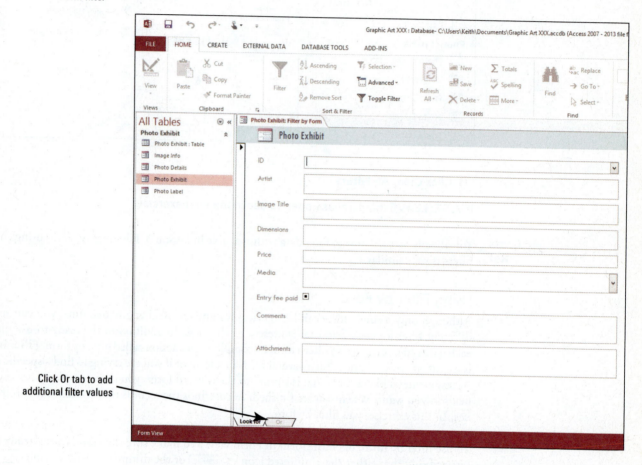

Click Or tab to add additional filter values

2. Place the insertion point in the Dimensions box, and click the **down arrow** on the right to display the list of options shown in Figure 5-28.

Figure 5-28

Form filter field options

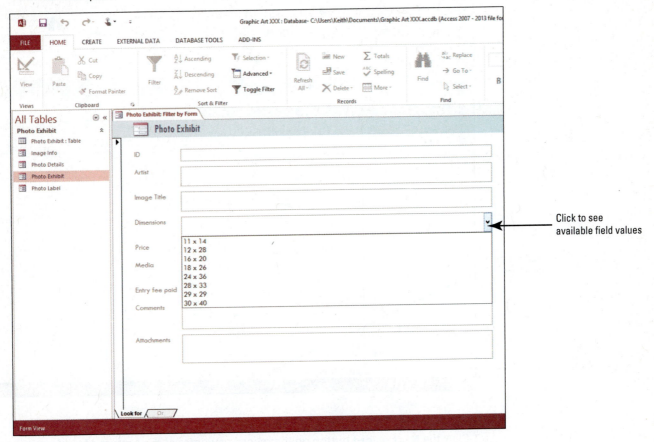

3. Click **30 X 40**.
4. Click the **Or** tab at the bottom of the form.
5. Place the insertion point in the Dimensions box, click the **down arrow**, and then click **12 X 28**.
6. On the HOME tab, in the Sort & Filter group, click the **Toggle Filter** button to apply the filter. The records containing either the dimensions **30 X 40** or **12 X 28** are displayed (see Figure 5-29).

Figure 5-29

Form filter results

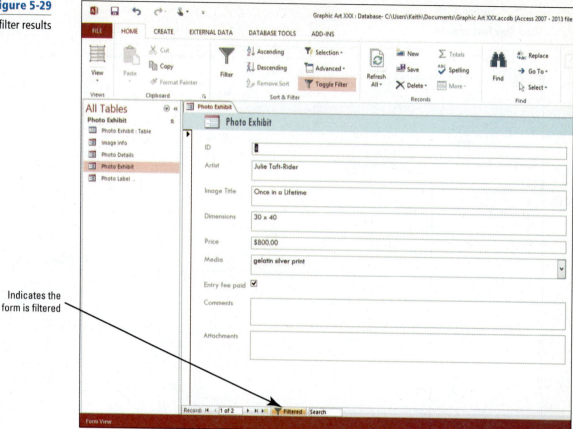

Indicates the
form is filtered

7. Click the **Next record** button on the record navigator at the bottom of the form to see the second record in the form filter results.

8. On the HOME tab, in the Sort & Filter group, click the **Toggle Filter** button again to remove the filter.

9. On the HOME tab, in the Sort & Filter group, click the **Advanced** button and click **Clear All Filters**.

10. Click the **FILE** tab and click **Close**.

STOP. LEAVE Access open for use in the projects.

Take Note   If you want a field value to operate as a filter that is independent of other field values, you must enter that value on the Look for tab and each Or tab. In other words, the Look for tab and each Or tab represents an alternate set of filter values.

CERTIFICATION READY?   4.3.3

How do you sort records within a form?

SKILL SUMMARY

In This Lesson You Learned How To:	Exam Objective	Objective Number
Create Forms	Create new forms.	4.1.1
	Save forms.	4.1.3
	Delete forms.	4.1.4
	Create databases using wizards.	1.1.4
	Apply themes.	4.3.4
Sort and Filter Data within a Form	Sort Records.	4.3.3

Knowledge Assessment

Matching

Match the term in Column 1 to its description in Column 2.

Column 1

1. Form Wizard

2. Form Design button

3. Theme command

4. Blank Form button

5. form

6. filter by form

7. sorting

8. Form tool

9. common filters

10. filter

Column 2

a. useful when you want to filter on several fields in a form or if you are trying to find a specific record

b. creates a simple form with a single mouse-click

c. applies a predefined combination of colors and fonts that you select for a form or report

d. quickly creates a new blank form in Design view

e. allows you to select fields for the form, choose the form layout, and also choose a predefined style

f. limits a view of data to specific records without requiring you to alter the design of the form

g. built into every view that displays data

h. database object that you can use to enter, edit, or display data from a table or a query

i. helps users review and locate records without having to browse the data

j. quickly creates a new blank form in Layout view

True/False

Circle T if the statement is true or F if the statement is false.

T F 1. The Forms group is located on the HOME tab of the Ribbon.

T F 2. Forms can be used to control access to data, such as which fields or rows of data are displayed.

T F 3. After you save your form design, you can run the form as often as you want.

T F 4. Layout view gives you a more detailed view of the structure of your form than Design view.

T F 5. Using the Blank Form tool is a very quick way to build a form, especially if you plan to put only a few fields on your form.

T F 6. To access the Theme options, first switch to Form view.

T F 7. You cannot remove a sort order from just a single field.

T F 8. The filters available depend on the field's data type and values.

T F 9. To delete a form click on the Remove button in the Forms group.

T F 10. When using the Form Wizard, you can only include fields from one table.

Competency Assessment

Project 5-1: Form Wizard

As a travel agent at Erin's Travel, you need an easy way to input data about events into the database. You decide to use the Form Wizard to create a datasheet form that has a preformatted style.

GET READY. LAUNCH Access if it is not already running.

1. **OPEN** *Travel Events* from the data files for this lesson.
2. **SAVE** the database as *Travel Events XXX* (where *XXX* is your initials).
3. On the CREATE tab, in the Forms group, click the Form Wizard button.
4. Click the >> button to move all the fields from the Available Fields box to the Selected Fields box.
5. Click the Next > button to move to the next page in the Form Wizard.
6. Click Datasheet as the layout for the form.
7. Click the Next > button to move to the final page in the Form Wizard.
8. Key Event Details as the title of the form.
9. Click the Finish button to create a datasheet form.
10. On the HOME tab, in the Views group, click the lower half of the View button, and click Form View.
11. Click the Close button on Event Details to close the form.
12. **CLOSE** the database.

LEAVE Access open for the next project.

Project 5-2: Used Games Forms

You are the manager at Southridge Video. To expand the store, you have recently started taking used games in trade. You store information about each title in an Access database. You decide to create some forms to help you use the database more efficiently.

GET READY. LAUNCH Access if it is not already running.

1. **OPEN** *Games inventory* from the data files for this lesson.
2. **SAVE** the database as *Games inventory XXX* (where *XXX* is your initials).
3. In the Navigation Pane, double-click Games: Table to open the table.
4. On the CREATE tab, in the Forms group, click the Form button to create a simple form and display it in Layout view.
5. Click the FILE tab and click Save.
6. In the Save As dialog box, click OK to accept the Games form name suggested by Access.
7. Click the Close button for Games to close the form.
8. On the CREATE tab, in the Forms group, click the Form Design button to create a new blank form in Design view.
9. On the FORM DESIGN TOOLS Design contextual tab, in the Tools group, click the Add Existing Fields button to display the Field List pane.
10. Click the Show all tables link in the Field List pane, if necessary.
11. Click the expand button next to Games to list the available fields, if necessary.
12. Double-click Title to add it to the form.
13. Double-click Rating to add it to the form.
14. Double-click Platform to add it to the form.
15. Click the FILE tab and click Save.
16. In the Save As dialog box, key Game Rating, and click OK.
17. Click the Close button to close the Field List.
18. On the DESIGN contextual tab, in the Views group, click the lower half of the View button and click Form View to display the form in Form view.
19. Click the Close button for Game Rating to close the form.

LEAVE the database open for the next project.

Proficiency Assessment

Project 5-3: **Sort and Filter Games**

A customer comes into Southridge Video and asks about game publishers and the availability of a particular game. Sort and filter data in the forms you created to get the information that you need.

USE the database that is open from the previous project.

1. In the Navigation Pane, double-click the **Games** form to open it.
2. Right-click the **Publisher** field to display the shortcut menu.
3. Click **Sort A to Z** to sort the form by publisher name in alphabetic order.
4. Navigate to record 3, titled Marvel: Ultimate Alliance.
5. Right-click the **Title** field and click **Contains "Marvel: Ultimate Alliance."**
6. Click the **Next record** button on the record navigator at the bottom of the form to see all the versions of the game with that name.
7. On the HOME tab, in the Sort & Filter group, click the **Remove Sort** button.
8. **CLOSE** the database.

LEAVE Access open for the next project.

Project 5-4: **Toy Inventory**

Your brother owns Wingtip Toys and recently started keeping a list of the store inventory in an Access database. He wants to add a form to the database and asks for your help. Add a simple form, and then show him how to sort and apply filters.

GET READY. LAUNCH Access if it is not already running.

1. **OPEN** *Toy inventory* from the data files for this lesson.
2. **SAVE** the database as *Toy inventory XXX* (where *XXX* is your initials).
3. **OPEN** **Inventory: Table**.
4. Use the Form tool to create a simple form.
5. Format the form using the **Organic** theme option (last row, first column).
6. Save the form as **Inventory**.
7. Sort the form's In Stock field from **Largest to Smallest**.
8. Sort the Description field from **A to Z**.
9. Run a filter that finds all the records where the Price field is **between $50 and $100**.
10. Clear all sorts and filters.
11. Create a **filter by form** to find all the records that have two items in stock.
12. **CLOSE** the form and close the database.

LEAVE Access open for the next project.

Mastery Assessment

Project 5-5: Coffee of the Month

Fourth Coffee has started a "Coffee of the Month" club. Each month features a new coffee type chosen for its unique blend. Information about the monthly club selections is stored in an Access database; you will create forms so that you can retrieve the data in a useful way.

GET READY. LAUNCH Access if it is not already running.

1. **OPEN** the *Coffee Selections* database from the data files for this lesson.
2. **SAVE** the database as *Coffee Selections XXX* (where *XXX* is your initials).
3. Create a simple form that contains all the fields in the Coffee Inventory table and save it with the default name of Coffee Inventory.
4. Use the Form Design button to create a form named **Coffee of the Month** that uses the Organic theme and looks like the one shown in Figure 5-30 when displayed in Form view.

Figure 5-30

Coffee of the Month form

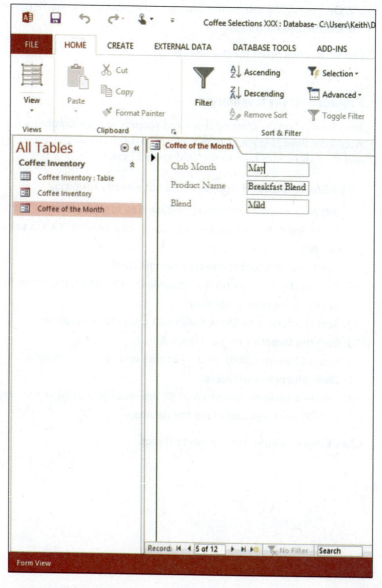

5. **CLOSE** the database.

LEAVE Access open for the next project.

Project 5-6: **Personal Contacts**

Your address book is becoming outdated, and you decide to transfer all the current information about friends and family to an Access database. Input the data and then create forms to manage it efficiently.

GET READY. LAUNCH Access if it is not already running.

1. **OPEN** *Personal Contacts* from the data files for this lesson.
2. **SAVE** the database as *Personal Contacts XXX* (where *XXX* is your initials).
3. Input as much contact information as you have about at least five friends or family members.
4. Create at least two forms that help you input, sort, or filter the data in a useful way. Use Themes to improve the look of the forms.
5. **CLOSE** the database.

STOP. CLOSE Access.

Circling Back

You are a real estate agent and have recently opened your own office—Woodgrove Real Estate—with several other licensed agents. Because you are the one who is most knowledgeable about computers, you will be responsible for keeping track of the listings and other relevant information. You will use Access to begin developing the database that will be used by everyone in the office.

Project 1: Create a Database and Tables

After sketching out a plan on paper, you are ready to begin creating the database and tables.

GET READY. Launch Access if it is not already running.

1. Near the center of the screen, click the **Blank desktop database icon**.
2. In the File Name box, key **WoodgroveXXX** (where XXX is your initials).
3. Click the **folder icon** and browse to the location where you want to store the file.
4. Click the **Create** button to create a new blank database.
5. Click **Click to Add** and click **Short Text** on the shortcut menu.
6. Key **Address** as the column name and press **Enter**.
7. Add new **Short Text** columns named **Bedrooms**, **Bathrooms**, **Square Feet**, and **Price**.
8. Click the **FILE** tab and click **Save**.
9. In the Save As dialog box, key **Listings** as the table name and click **OK**.
10. On the CREATE tab, in the Templates group, click the **Application Parts** button, and click **Contacts** to create a new table. Click **Yes**, if necessary, to close and save the Listings table, then click **Cancel** in the Create Relationship dialog box that appears.
11. Open the **Contacts** table.
12. Right-click the **Company** field header and click **Delete Field** on the shortcut menu. Click **Yes** if you receive a dialog box warning you about the deletion.
13. Delete the Job Title, Business Phone, Fax Number, Address, City, State/Province, ZIP/Postal Code, Country/Region, Web Page, Notes, and Attachments columns. (If you get a message asking if you want to delete all indexes for the ZIP/Postal Code column, click **Yes**.)
14. **SAVE** the table as **Agents**.
15. Delete all the objects in your database except the Agents and Listings tables.

PAUSE. LEAVE the database open to use in the next project.

Project 2: Modify Tables and Fields

Now that you have created the tables for your database, you need to modify them to suit your needs.

USE the database that is open from the previous project. The Agents table should be displayed.

1. On the HOME tab, in the Views group, click the bottom portion of the View button and then click **Design View**.
2. On the TABLE TOOLS DESIGN contextual tab, in the Show/Hide group, click **Property Sheet**.
3. In the Property Sheet's Description property box, key **Agent contact information**.
4. Click **Close** to **CLOSE** the property sheet.
5. In the upper portion of the table design grid, click the **EmailAddress field**. In the field properties on the bottom, click in the Required property box and set it to **Yes**. In the field properties, click in the Default Value property box and key **@woodgroverealestate.com**.
6. **SAVE** the table and switch back to **Datasheet** View.

7. **OPEN** the **Listings** table. Place the insertion point in the **Price** column.

8. On the TABLE TOOLS FIELDS contextual tab, in the Formatting group, click the **down arrow** in the Data Type box and click **Number**.

9. In the Format box, click the **down arrow** and choose **Currency**.

10. Change the data type/format on the Bedrooms, Bathrooms, and Square Feet fields to **Number**/**General Number**.

11. Click the **Click to Add** column. Choose **Attachment** as the data type to create an attachment column.

12. **SAVE** the table.

PAUSE. LEAVE the database open for the next project.

Project 3: Create Forms and Enter Data

Now it is time to enter data into your database. First you create a form to make this task easier.

USE the database that is open from the previous project. The Listings table should be displayed.

1. On the CREATE tab, in the Forms group, click the **More Forms** button.

2. Click **Datasheet** to create a datasheet form.

3. Click the **FILE** tab and click **Save**.

4. In the Save As dialog box, key **Listings** as the form name and click **OK**.

5. Use the form to enter data into the Listings table, as shown in Figure 1.

Figure 1

Listings data

ID	Address	Bedrooms	Bathrooms	Square Feet	Price	📎
1	214 Main Street	4	2	3150	$352,800.00	(0)
2	3328 Broadway	3	2	2125	$265,625.00	(0)
3	89 Ridge Road	3	1	1550	$201,500.00	(0)
4	677 West Avenue	3	3	2892	$303,660.00	(0)
5	40 Upper Grant	5	3	4984	$697,760.00	(0)
6	2002 Sundown Lane	2	2	1880	$253,800.00	(0)
7	2828 Green Briar	2	1	1060	$185,500.00	(0)
8	685 South Grand	4	3	3535	$530,250.00	(0)
9	13811 Crown Bluff	3	2	2248	$319,216.00	(0)
10	1505 Pinehurst	4	3	2670	$435,210.00	(0)
*	(New)					(0)

6. Display the **Agents** table.

7. On the CREATE tab, in the Forms group, click the **Form** button.

8. **SAVE** the form as **Agents**.

9. Switch to Form View and use the form to enter the data shown in Figure 2.

Figure 2

Agents data, record 1

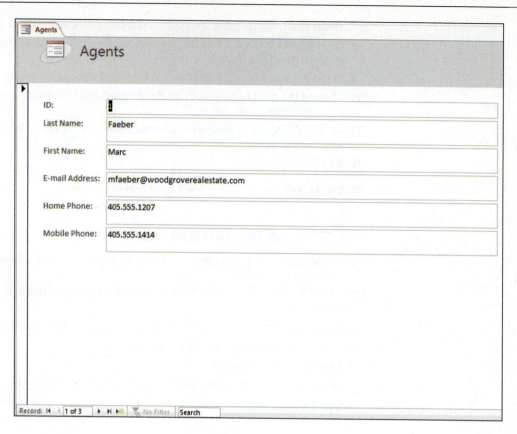

10. Click the **Next record** button on the record navigator.
11. Enter the data shown in Figure 3 as the second record.

Figure 3

Agents data, record 2

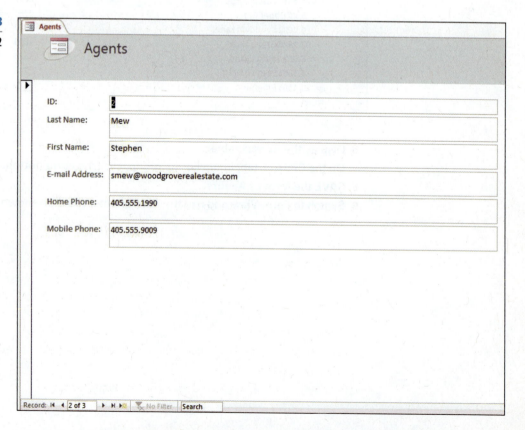

12. Enter the data shown in Figure 4 as the third record.

Figure 4

Agents data, record 3

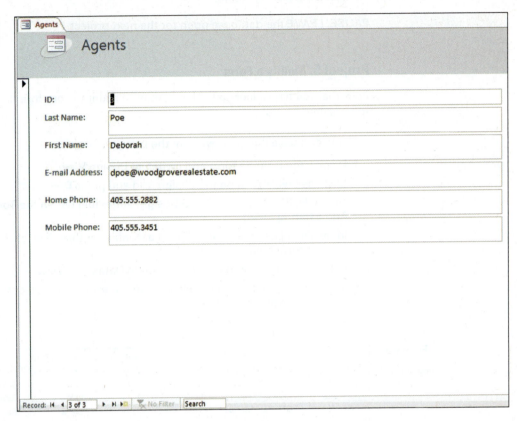

13. CLOSE the Agents form and the Listings form.

PAUSE. LEAVE the database open for the next project.

Project 4: Add Attachments and Create a Lookup Field

You have begun to use the database and realize it would be helpful for the Listings table to include the listing agent. Create a lookup field with this information and attach photos for some of the houses.

USE the database that is open from the previous project.

1. In the Listings table, double-click the **Attachment** field for the fourth record (677 West Avenue).

2. In the Attachments dialog box, click **Add**.

 3. Navigate to the data files for this lesson, select **677_West_Avenue**, and click **Open**.

4. In the Attachments dialog box, click **OK**.

5. Attach the photo named **2002_Sundown_Lane** to the sixth record.

6. In the Listings table, place the insertion point in the cell under the Click to Add column.

7. On the TABLE TOOLS FIELDS contextual tab in the Add & Delete group, click the **More Fields** button. Click the **Lookup & Relationship** command.

8. Click **Next>** twice.

9. Click **LastName** and then click the **>** button to move it to the Selected Fields box.

10. Click **Next>** three times.

11. Key **Listing Agent** as the title for your lookup column.

12. Click **Finish**.

13. SAVE the Listings table.

PAUSE. LEAVE the database open for the next project.

Project 5: Modify a Form

Now that you have a lookup field, you want to add it to your form and use it to enter additional information.

USE the database that is open from the previous project.

1. Display the Listings form and switch to Design View.
2. Click the **Field1** field on the design grid and press **Delete**.
3. On the FORM DESIGN TOOLS Design contextual tab, in the Tools group, click **Add Existing Fields**.
4. In the Field List pane, under Fields available for this view, click **Listing Agent** and drag it to the form below the Price field.
5. **CLOSE** the Field List pane and switch to Datasheet View.
6. In the Listing Agent column click the **down arrow** and select the last name for each record, as shown in Figure 5.

Figure 5

Listing agents

ID	Address	Bedrooms	Bathrooms	Square Feet	Price	Listing Agent
1	214 Main Street	4	2	3150	$352,800.00	Faeber
2	3328 Broadway	3	2	2125	$265,625.00	Faeber
3	89 Ridge Road	3	1	1550	$201,500.00	Poe
4	677 West Avenue	3	3	2892	$303,660.00	Mew
5	40 Upper Grant	5	3	4984	$697,760.00	Faeber
6	2002 Sundown Lane	2	2	1880	$253,800.00	Poe
7	2828 Green Briar	2	1	1060	$185,500.00	Poe
8	685 South Grand	4	3	3535	$530,250.00	Faeber
9	13811 Crown Bluff	3	2	2248	$319,216.00	Mew
10	1505 Pinehurst	4	3	2670	$435,210.00	Faeber
* (New)						

7. CLOSE the form.

STOP. CLOSE the database.

Create Reports 6

LESSON SKILL MATRIX

Skill	Exam Objective	Objective Number
Creating Reports	Create new reports.	5.1.1
	Delete reports.	5.1.3
	Create reports in Design view.	5.1.2
Applying a Theme	Apply themes.	5.3.10
Working with Reports	Sort data.	5.2.2
	Change sort order.	5.3.6

© Gorfer/iStockphoto

KEY TERMS

- record source
- report

157

© Gorfer/iStockphoto

Alpine Ski House is a small mountain lodge that features cross-country skiing in the winter and hiking in the summer. As an administrative assistant for Alpine Ski House, you take care of many of the administrative duties for the innkeepers, including reservations, billing, and record keeping. You have recently started using Access to keep track of customers and reservations at the lodge. In this lesson, you learn three different ways to create reports for the lodge, how to apply auto formats to reports, and how to sort and filter report data.

SOFTWARE ORIENTATION

Reports Group

The Reports group is located on the CREATE tab in the Ribbon, as shown in Figure 6-1.

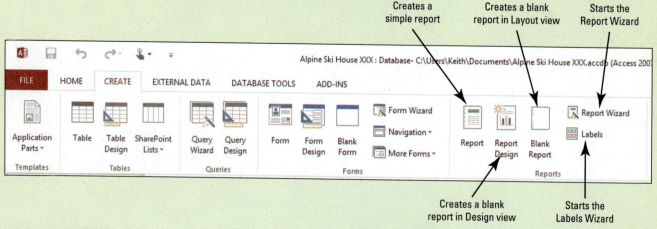

Figure 6-1

Reports group

Use the Reports group of commands to create reports.

CREATING REPORTS

The Bottom Line

A **report** is a database object that is used to organize and display data pulled from tables and queries. You can create a report using the Report button, the Report Wizard button, Report Design button, and Blank Report button, depending on the amount of customization desired. You can also create labels using the Labels button. After creating a report, you can instantly apply a Theme to create a professional look. You can also sort and filter data in a report to display the records to suit your needs.

Creating a Simple Report and Deleting a Report

You can use Access 2013 to create simple or complex reports. When creating a complex report, you might spend quite a bit of time choosing which fields you want to include from various tables or queries. That is fine when you need such a report, but when you need a simple display of all the fields in a table or query, you can use the Report button to create a simple report. You can also delete a report to remove it permanently from the database. In this exercise, you use the Report button to create a simple report and delete a report by using the Delete command.

Reports are commonly used as formatted hard copies of table or query data. You can modify a report's design, but you cannot add or edit data in a report. The purpose of a report is to allow users to view data, not edit it. For example, a supervisor might ask you to create a sales report that is filtered to show only one region's sales. The supervisor does not need to edit the data, just view it.

A report's **record source** is the table or query that provides the data used to generate a report. Before you can create a report, you need to define the record source by clicking in the Navigation Pane on the table or query on which you want to base the report. Then, click the Report button and a report is automatically generated based on the table or query you selected.

You can modify a report's design, print, or save and close a report. You should save a report's design if you are likely to use it again. To save a report, click the Save button on the FILE tab or in the Quick Access Toolbar. If you click the Close button without saving, Access will display a dialog box asking if you want to save it. Once it is saved, the report is listed in the Navigation Pane. You can open it and modify it in the future or create a new report based on the original. The next time you run the report, the design will be the same, but the data will be different if the data in the table or query has been updated.

You can also permanently delete a report from the database by using the Delete command in the Records group on the HOME tab. You can delete a report if you erroneously created it or simply want to unclutter the database by removing pre-existing reports you no longer use.

STEP BY STEP   Create and Delete a Report

GET READY. Before you begin these steps, be sure to turn on and/or log on to your computer and start Access.

1. **OPEN** *AlpineSkiHouse* from the data files for this lesson.
2. **SAVE** the database as *AlpineSkiHouseXXX* (where *XXX* is your initials).
3. In the Navigation Pane, click the **Rooms** table to select it. This is your record source.
4. On the CREATE tab, in the Reports group, click the **Report** button. The report appears in Layout view (see Figure 6-2). Notice the Report Layout tools that appear in the Ribbon.

Figure 6-2

Simple report

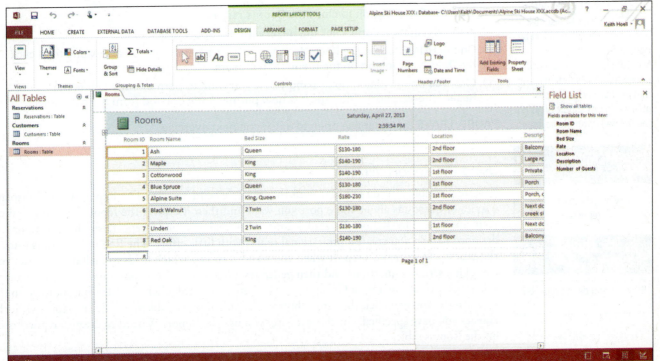

5. Click the Room ID header to select it. Position the pointer over the right border until you see a double-sided arrow. Click and drag to the left, resizing the column to remove excess white space.

6. Resize the other columns until your screen looks similar to Figure 6-3.

Figure 6-3

Report with resized columns

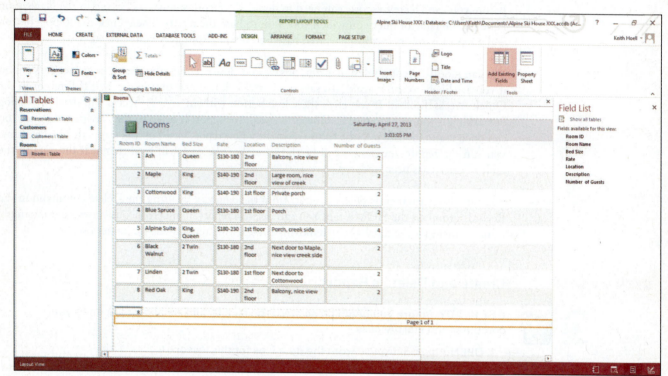

7. Click the **Save** button on the Quick Access Toolbar. The Save As dialog box appears with Rooms in the Report Name box. Click **OK**. Notice that the Rooms report is listed in the Navigation Pane.

8. Click the **Close** button to close the Rooms report.

9. In the Navigation Pane, click the **Reservations** report to select it.

10. On the HOME tab, in the Records group, click the **Delete** button arrow and then click the **Delete** command on the menu that appears.

11. Click **Yes** on the dialog box asking you if you want to permanently delete the Reservations report. The report is now permanently deleted from the database.

PAUSE. LEAVE the database open to use in the next exercise.

Another Way
You can also delete a report or any other object by right-clicking it in the Navigation Pane and choosing Delete from the shortcut menu that appears, or clicking the object and just simply pressing the Delete key on the keyboard.

CERTIFICATION READY? 5.1.1

How do you create new reports?

CERTIFICATION READY? 5.1.3

How do you delete reports?

Using the Report Wizard

You are probably already familiar with the way a "wizard" works. The Report Wizard displays a series of questions about the report you want and then it creates the report for you based on your answers. The Report Wizard knows what makes a good report, so the questions are designed to help you create a professional report with little effort. The Report Wizard is usually the easiest way to create a report when you want to choose which fields to include. It guides you through a series of questions and then generates a report based on your answers. If you want to skip steps such as Sorting or Grouping in the Report Wizard, click the Next button to go to the next screen. You can click the Finish button anytime it is available to create the report with the choices you have specified. In this exercise, you use the Report Wizard to create a report based on the Rooms table.

The Report Wizard allows you to include fields from more than one table or query. You can click the double right arrow button (>>) to include all the fields in the report or click the single right arrow button (>) to move them one at a time. Likewise, you can click the double left arrow button (<<) to move all the fields out of the report or the single left arrow button (<) to move them one at a time.

You can specify group levels, such as grouping all of the first-floor rooms together and all of the second-floor rooms together if creating a room report. You can also choose up to four fields on which to sort data in ascending or descending order. On the layout screen, you can choose from various layouts such as stepped, block, or outline, all of which indent fields and records in different ways to make the report clearer to read. You can also choose to display the report in portrait or landscape orientation. Access provides a wide variety of design styles from which to choose. On the last screen of the Report Wizard, you can key a name for the report and choose to preview or modify the report.

 Cross Ref You learn more about grouping in Lesson 11.

STEP BY STEP **Use the Report Wizard**

USE the database you used in the previous exercise.

1. On the CREATE tab, in the Reports group, click the **Report Wizard** button. The first screen of the Report Wizard appears.

2. Select the Rooms table in the Tables/Queries menu.

3. Click the >> button to move all the fields into the Selected Fields list.

4. Click the **Room ID** field to select it and click the < button to move it back to the Available Fields list (see Figure 6-4). Click the **Next >** button.

Figure 6-4

The Report Wizard Fields screen

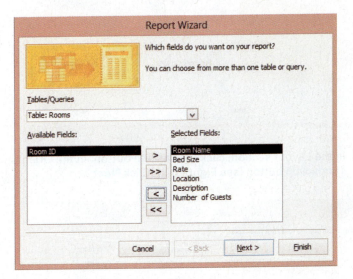

5. Click the **Location** field to select it and click the > button to add it as a grouping level (see Figure 6-5).

Figure 6-5

The Report Wizard
Grouping screen

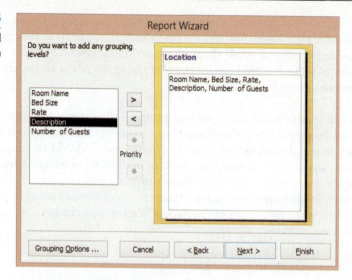

6. Click the **Next >** button.
7. Select **Room Name** from the fields menu to sort in ascending order (see Figure 6-6), and click the **Next >** button.

Figure 6-6

The Report Wizard Sort screen

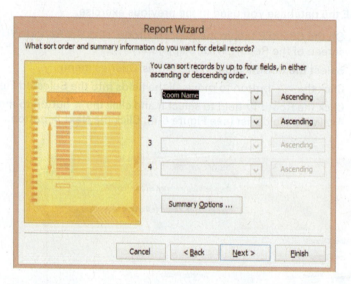

8. In the Layout section, click the **Outline** button. In the Orientation section, click the **Landscape** button (see Figure 6-7). Click **Next >**.

Figure 6-7

The Report Wizard
Layout screen

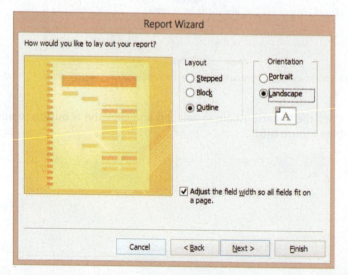

9. Key **Rooms Wizard** as the title of the report (see Figure 6-8).

Figure 6-8

Figure 6-8

The Report Wizard Title screen

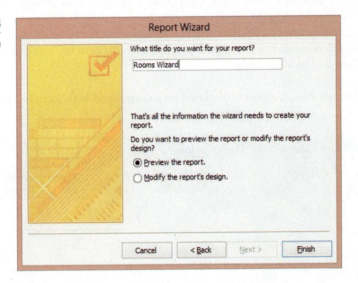

10. Click **Finish**. The Rooms Wizard report appears on the screen (see Figure 6-9).

Figure 6-9

The Report Wizard report

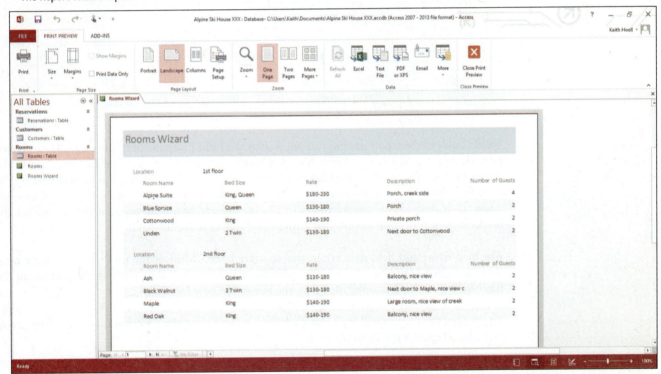

11. **CLOSE** the report. Notice that the new report is listed in the Navigation Pane.

PAUSE. LEAVE the database open to use in the next exercise.

Creating a Report in Design View

When you want a customized report, you can create it in Design view, which offers you many options for creating the report exactly the way you want it. Design view gives you the most options for creating a report, because it shows you the underlying structure of the report. It also provides you with more design tools and capabilities. In this exercise, you create a report in Design view by adding and moving fields.

In Design view, a report is displayed on a design grid with sections. Table 6-1 lists the sections.

Table 6-1

Design view sections

Section Name	Description
Report header	This section is printed once at the beginning of every report. This is a good place to include a logo, a date, or information that might normally appear on a cover page.
Page header	This section is printed at the top of every page of a report, so it would be a good place to include the report title.
<Group> header	This section is printed at the beginning of a group. (The name of the grouping field replaces <Group>.) It is a good place to include the group name.
Detail	This section includes the body of the report. It is printed once for every row in a record source.
<Group> footer	This section is only printed at the end of a group that contains summary information for the group. (The name of the grouping field replaces <Group>.)
Page footer	This section is printed at the bottom of every page of a report, so it would be a good place to include information such as a page number.
Report footer	This section is printed once at the end of every report. It is a good place for report totals.

To add fields to the report design, you can display the Field List pane (if it is not already displayed) by clicking the Add Existing Fields button. Double-click a field in the Field List to add it to the design grid, or you can drag the field to a location on the grid. If you need to move a field on the grid, click the field to select it and then position the pointer on the border until you see a four-sided arrow, then drag to the new location. To change the size of a field, position the pointer on the border until it turns into a two-sided arrow, then drag to resize the field.

The field name and field data are in two separate boxes. Most of the time you will move both boxes together; however, to move one box separately from the other, position the pointer on the box border's selection handle, then drag the box to the new location.

To see what your report will look like, click the bottom half of the View button in the Views group and select Report View from the menu.

STEP BY STEP **Create a Report in Design View**

USE the database you used in the previous exercise.

1. If necessary, click the **Rooms** table in the Navigation Pane to select it.
2. On the CREATE tab, in the Reports group, click the **Report Design** button. A new blank report is displayed in Design view (see Figure 6-10).

Figure 6-10

New blank report in
Design view

View button   Page Header section   Detail section   Add Existing Fields button   Field List pane

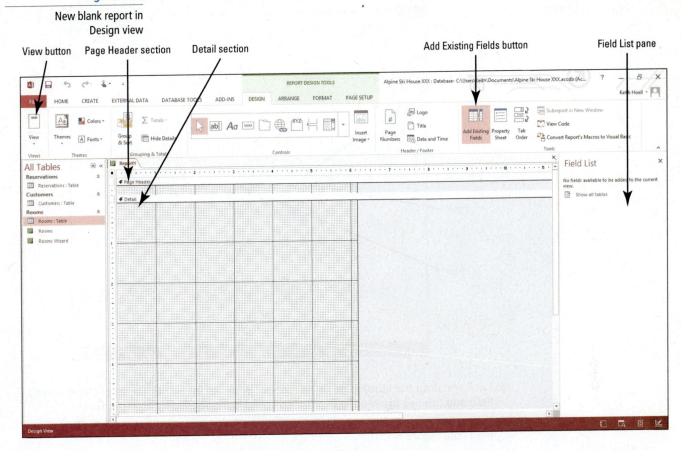

Figure 6-10

New blank report in
Design view

3. If the Field List pane is not already displayed, on the DESIGN tab, in the Tools group, click the **Add Existing Fields** button. The Show All Tables link appears.

4. Click the **Show all tables link** then the **plus (+)** box beside Rooms to display the fields in the table (see Figure 6-11).

Figure 6-11

Field List pane

5. Double-click **Room ID**. The field is inserted onto the design grid.

6. Double-click **Room Name**, **Bed Size**, and **Rate**.

7. Click the **Close** button on the Field List pane.

8. Click the **Bed Size** label. The border around the label changes to orange, indicating that it is selected. Position the insertion point over the top of the border (see Figure 6-12) until the pointer changes to a four-sided arrow.

Figure 6-12

Bed Size label selected

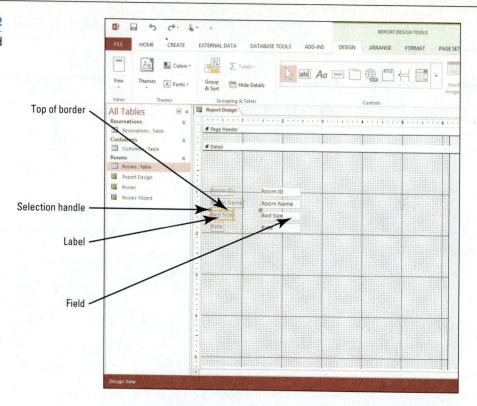

Top of border

Selection handle

Label

Field

9. Click and drag the label to position it about one-half inch to the right of the Room ID field and release the mouse button. The field is moved along with the label.

10. In the same manner, move the **Rate** label and field to position it below the Bed Size field (see Figure 6-13).

Figure 6-13

Moved fields

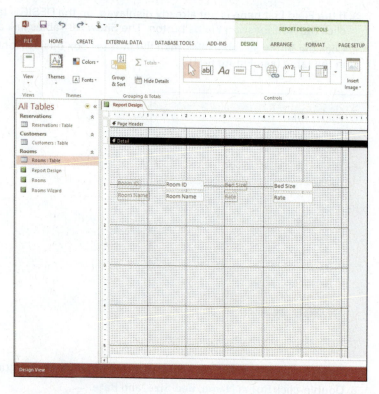

11. Click the **Room ID** field to select it. Position the mouse pointer on the square handle in the middle of the right-side border. Click and drag the field to the left to decrease the size by about one-quarter inch.

12. On the Ribbon, in the Views group, click the bottom half of the **View** button and select **Report View** from the menu. The report is shown in Report view. Scroll down to see all the records.

13. Click the **Save** button on the Quick Access Toolbar.

14. Key **Report Design** in the Report Name box, and click **OK**.

15. **CLOSE** the report.

PAUSE. LEAVE the database open to use in the next exercise.

CERTIFICATION READY?   5.1.2

How do you create a report in Design view?

Take Note   You can add more than one field to a report design at once only after at least one other field has been added. Hold down the Ctrl key and click the fields you want, and then drag the selected fields onto the report.

Cross Ref   In Lesson 8, you learn how to add more functionality to a report by adding controls in Design view.

APPLYING A THEME

The Bottom Line

A theme applies a set of predefined fonts, colors, and design to a report. You can apply a theme to any report in Layout view or Design view. The Themes gallery displays a variety of designs. After you click the design you want, it is applied to the report. This instant formatting can quickly give your report the professional look you want.

Applying a Theme

To apply a theme, on the REPORT LAYOUT TOOLS Design contextual tab, in the Themes group, click the Themes button to display the Themes gallery. You can select a design from the list displayed or browse for saved themes. You can also customize and then save a theme based on the current report. You can click the Colors button and choose a color scheme from the menu to update the currently applied theme's colors, and even create new theme colors. You can also click the Fonts button and choose a font scheme to update the currently applied theme's fonts and create new theme fonts. In this exercise, you apply a theme to the Rooms report and modify the fonts.

STEP BY STEP   **Apply a Theme**

USE the database open from the previous exercise.

1. **OPEN** the **Rooms** report.

2. On the Ribbon, in the Views group, click the bottom half of the **View** button. Select **Layout View** from the menu.

3. On the REPORT LAYOUT TOOLS Design contextual tab, in the Themes group, click the **Themes** button. The Themes gallery of predefined report themes appears.

4. In the Office section and the first row, third column, click the **Integral** design (see Figure 6-14). The format is applied to the report.

Figure 6-14

The Themes gallery with
Integral theme chosen

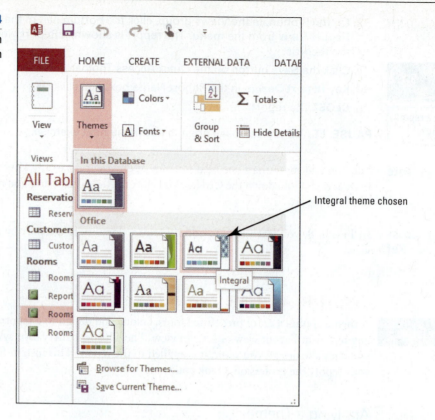

Integral theme chosen

5. In the Themes group, click the **Fonts** button. Select **Cambria** from the menu (see Figure 6-15). The new Font theme is applied.

Figure 6-15

The Fonts menu with Cambria
font chosen

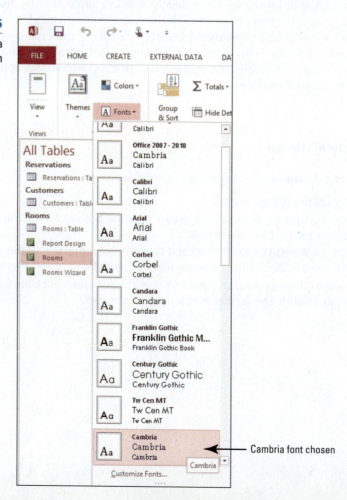

Cambria font chosen

6. **SAVE** the report.

PAUSE. LEAVE the report open to use in the next exercise.

WORKING WITH REPORTS

Reports help group and summarize data in different ways. However, after a report is created, you can use Layout view as well as Report view to help locate data. For example, you can use Layout view to easily sort field data one at a time, or perform more complex sorts using the Group, Sort, and Total pane. You can also use Layout view to filter data and view only those records based on the criteria you specify, and use Report view or Layout view to find data based on any term you specify.

Sorting Data within a Report

Sorting organizes data into a particular sequence, such as alphabetic order or from smallest to largest numbers. For example, you can sort a customer list in alphabetic order by last name or by customer ID number. You can sort data by clicking the buttons on the Ribbon, right-clicking and choosing commands from the shortcut menu, or by using the Group, Sort, and Total pane. In this exercise, you sort data within a report by using the Ribbon, the shortcut menu, and the Group, Sort, and Total pane.

Sorting data in a report is similar to sorting in a table. In Layout view, select the field you want to sort and click the Ascending or Descending button on the HOME tab, in the Sort & Filter group. Click the Remove Sort button to remove the sort order. You can sort as many fields as you like one at a time.

 Cross Ref   Lesson 3 has more information about sorting in a table.

You can also easily sort data by right-clicking in a field and choosing the type of sort you want from the shortcut menu. The sort commands in the shortcut menu vary depending on the type of data in the field. For text, you will choose Sort A to Z or Sort Z to A; for numbers, you will choose Sort Smallest to Largest or Sort Largest to Smallest; and for dates, you will choose Sort Oldest to Newest or Sort Newest to Oldest.

 Cross Ref   Lesson 5 has more information about sorting in a form.

The Group, Sort, and Total pane gives you more sorting options. You can use the pane to specify the sort order or to view the results of sorting using the shortcut menu. To specify a sort, click the Add a Sort button and select a field from the pop-up menu. Click the drop-down menu to specify the type of sort you want. Click the More Options button to display additional commands for creating detailed sorts. Click the Less Options button to return to the basic sorting options.

To delete a sort in the Group, Sort, and Total pane, click the Delete button at the end of the sort line.

 Cross Ref   Lesson 7 has more information about sorting in a query.

STEP BY STEP   **Sort Data within a Report**

USE the report open from the previous exercise.

1. On the HOME tab in the Views group, click the bottom half of the **View** button. Select **Layout View** from the menu.
2. Click the **Room Name** header.
3. On the HOME tab, in the Sort & Filter group, click the **Ascending** button. The column is sorted in ascending alphabetic order.
4. On the HOME tab, in the Sort & Filter group, click the **Remove Sort** button. The Sort is removed.

5. Right-click the **Room Name** header. The shortcut menu appears.

6. Select **Sort Z to A** (see Figure 6-16). The column is sorted.

Figure 6-16

Shortcut menu

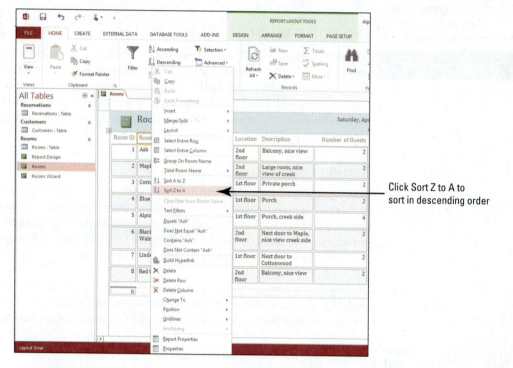

Click Sort Z to A to
sort in descending order

7. On the HOME tab, in the Sort & Filter group, click the **Remove Sort** button. The Sort is cleared.

8. On the REPORT LAYOUT TOOLS Design contextual tab, in the Grouping & Totals group, click the **Group & Sort** button. The *Group, Sort, and Total* pane appears at the bottom of the screen (see Figure 6-17).

Figure 6-17

Group, Sort, and Total pane

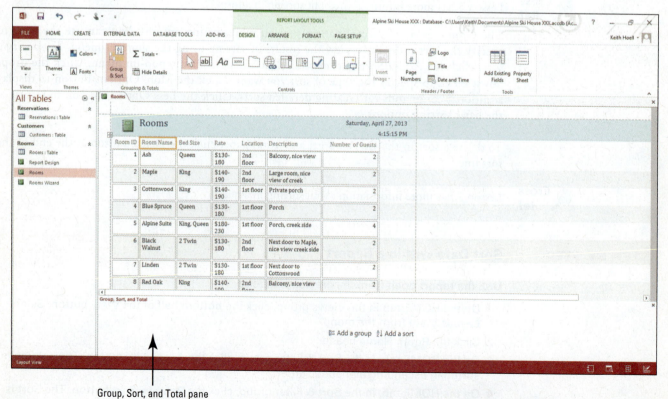

Group, Sort, and Total pane

9. Click the **Add a sort** button in the *Group, Sort, and Total* pane.
10. Click the **Room Name** field in the fields list. Notice that the field was sorted in ascending order by default and a line was added describing the sort.
11. Click the **down arrow** beside *with A on top* and select **with Z on top** from the menu (see Figure 6-18). The field is sorted in descending order.

Figure 6-18

Sort displayed in the Group, Sort, and Total pane

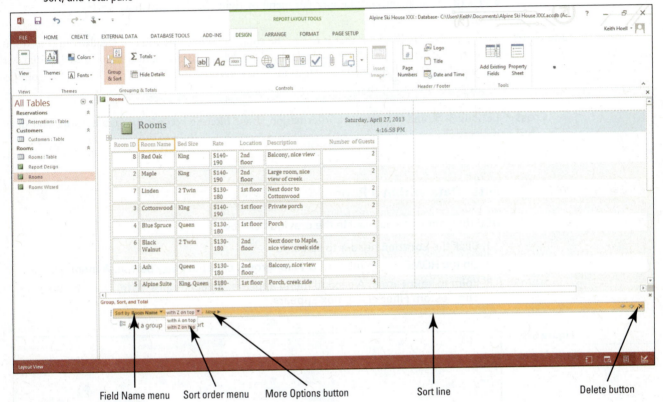

Field Name menu   Sort order menu   More Options button   Sort line   Delete button

12. Click the **More Options** button in the Sort line. Notice the options available for customizing a sort.
13. Click the **Delete** button. The sort is cleared.
14. In the Grouping & Totals group on the Ribbon, click the **Group & Sort** button. The *Group, Total, and Sort* pane is removed.
15. **SAVE** the report.

PAUSE. LEAVE the database open to use in the next exercise.

Filtering Data within a Report

A filter displays only data that meet the criteria you have specified and hides the rest. It does not modify the table data or the design of the report. After you remove a filter, all the records are displayed again. Filtering data in Layout view of a report is very similar to filtering data in a table. You can apply common filters using the commands in the Sort & Filter group or by right-clicking a field and choosing a filter from the shortcut menu. The filters available on the shortcut menu vary depending on the type of data in the field. Only one filter can be applied to a field at a time. However, you can specify a different filter for each field. In this exercise, you filter a report using a custom filter, and filter by selection.

You can toggle between filtered and unfiltered views using the Toggle Filter button. To remove a filter from a field, right-click in the field and select the Clear filter from field name command. To remove all filters permanently, select the Clear All Filters command on the Advanced menu in the Sort & Filter group.

Take Note   If you save a report (or other object) while a filter is applied, it will be available the next time that you open the report. If you want to open the report and see the filter already applied, set the Filter On Load property setting to Yes.

You can also filter by selection in a report. If you want to view only the reservations for 12/13/14, select that date in the Check-in field and click the Selection button. That date will appear in the menu, so that you can choose Equals 12/13/14, Does Not Equal 12/13/14, and so on. You can also access these commands on the shortcut menu by right-clicking the value.

Take Note   If you need to apply a filter that is not in the common filters list, you can write an advanced filter using the Advanced Filter/Sort command on the Advanced menu. You need to be familiar with writing expressions, which are similar to formulas, and be familiar with the criteria that you specify when designing a query.

 Cross Ref   Lessons 3, 5, and 7 have more information about filtering records in a table, form, and query, respectively.

STEP BY STEP   **Filter Data within a Report**

USE the database you used in the previous exercise.

1. Click the **Location** header to select it.
2. On the HOME tab, in the Sort & Filter group, click the **Filter** button. A menu appears.
3. Point to **Text Filters**. A second menu appears. Select **Begins With...** (see Figure 6-19). The Custom Filter dialog box appears.

Figure 6-19

Shortcut menu

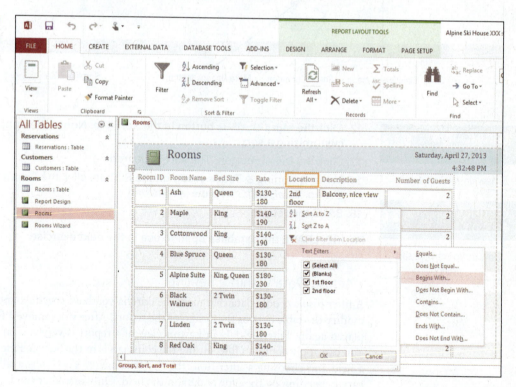

4. Key **1** into the Custom Filter dialog box and click **OK**. The data is filtered to show only the rooms on the first floor.
5. Click the **Toggle Filter** button on the Ribbon. The report returns to its unfiltered state.
6. In the Bed Size field, click **King** in the second row.
7. On the HOME tab, in the Sort & Filter group, click the **Selection** button. Select **Equals "King"** from the menu. The data is filtered to show only the rooms with King-sized beds.

8. Right-click the **Bed Size** header. A shortcut menu appears. Notice that the Equals "King" filter and the other filters from the Selection menu are also available in the shortcut menu (see Figure 6-20).

Figure 6-20

Shortcut menu

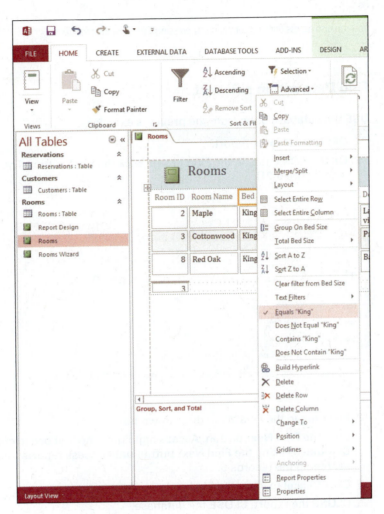

9. Select **Clear filter from Bed Size** from the menu. The filter is cleared.

10. **CLOSE** the report.

PAUSE. LEAVE the database open to use in the next exercise.

Finding Data within a Report

When you want to quickly locate records in a report, you can use the Find command, which searches all the records of the report for any term you specify. Sometimes, you may need to quickly find records within a report while in Report view or Report Layout view. To accomplish this, you can use the Find command in the Find group on the HOME tab. In this exercise, you locate data in Report view by using the Find command.

Cross Ref

Lesson 3 has more information about the Find command.

The Find command was overviewed for tables in Lesson 3. Like the Find command in table data-sheet view, once clicked, the Find dialog box appears where you can enter search criteria, set options for where you would like Access to look for the data, and set data matching and other search options. You can quickly locate records that match your search term and view multiple occurrences; however, remember that you cannot modify record data from within a report, so you cannot replace the record data that is found.

Take Note   You cannot use the Find command when you are in Report Design view.

Take Note   You can also use the Find command in tables, forms, and queries.

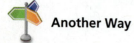

Another Way   You can also access the Find command by pressing Ctrl+F on the keyboard.

STEP BY STEP   **Find Data within a Report**

USE the database open from the previous exercise.

1. **OPEN** the Rooms report.
2. On the HOME tab, in the Find group, click the **Find** button. The Find dialog box appears (see Figure 6-21).

Figure 6-21

Find dialog box

3. Key King in the Find What drop-down box.
4. Click the **Find Next** button. Access highlights the first occurrence of 'King' in the report. Continue clicking the Find Next button until Access reports that it has finished searching the records 6.
5. Click Cancel to close the Find dialog box.
6. **CLOSE** the report. **CLOSE** the database.

STOP. CLOSE Access.

SKILL SUMMARY

In This Lesson You Learned How To:	Exam Objective	Objective Number
Create Reports	Create new reports.	5.1.1
	Delete reports.	5.1.3
	Create reports in Design view.	5.1.2
Apply a Theme	Apply themes.	5.3.10
Work with Reports	Sort data.	5.2.2
	Change sort order.	5.3.6

Knowledge Assessment

Matching

Match the term in Column 1 to its description in Column 2.

Column 1	Column 2
1. report	**a.** organizes data in a particular order
2. record source	**b.** displays data that meets the criteria you have specified and hides the rest
3. Report Wizard	**c.** a list of available fields for adding to a report
4. Field List pane	**d.** a database object that is used to organize and display data from tables and queries
5. Detail	**e.** locates data in an open object like a table, query, or report
6. theme	**f.** the table or query that provides the data used to generate a report
7. Sort	**g.** the way a report is displayed in Design view
8. Filter	**h.** guides you through a series of questions and then generates a report based on your answers
9. design grid	**i.** the section of a report that includes the body of the report
10. Find command	**j.** a predefined format that you can apply to any report in Layout view

True/False

Circle T if the statement is true or F if the statement is false.

T F   1. A simple report contains all the records in a table or query.

T F   2. You can edit the data in a report.

T F   3. Click the Report button to define a record source.

T F   4. In the Report Wizard, you can skip steps such as Sorting or Grouping by clicking the Next button.

T F   5. You can drag a field from the Field List pane to the design grid to add it to the report.

T F   6. Layout view gives you the most options for creating a report, because it shows you the underlying structure of the report.

T F   7. In Report Design view, you can click on the top of the border of a label to move both the field and its label.

T F   8. You can save a filter with a report.

T F   9. You can use the Group, Sort, and Total pane to specify sort order or view the results of sorting using the shortcut menu.

T F   10. The Toggle Filter button removes a filter permanently.

Competency Assessment

Project 6-1: Soccer Team Report

You need a copy of the soccer team's roster that you can print and take with you to work. Create a simple report and apply a theme.

GET READY. LAUNCH Access if it is not already running.

1. **OPEN** the *SoccerTeam* database.
2. **SAVE** the database as *SoccerTeamXXX* (where *XXX* is your initials).
3. Click the Roster table to select it.
4. On the CREATE tab, in the Reports group, click the Report button. A new report is created.
5. Resize each field so that all fields fit on one page.
6. On the REPORT LAYOUT TOOLS Design contextual tab, in the Themes group, click the Themes button.
7. In the Office category, select the format in the second row, third column, named Retrospect.
8. Click the Save button on the Quick Access Toolbar. The Save As dialog box appears with the name Roster in it. Click OK to accept that name for the report.
9. **CLOSE** the report.
10. **CLOSE** the database.

LEAVE Access open for the next project.

Project 6-2: Fourth Coffee Inventory Report

In your job at Fourth Coffee, you are responsible for maintaining the coffee inventory. Create a report to view the inventory and prepare for the next order.

GET READY. LAUNCH Access if it is not already running.

1. **OPEN** *Coffee* from the data files for this lesson.
2. **SAVE** the database as *CoffeeXXX* (where *XXX* is your initials).
3. Click the Coffee Inventory Table in the *Navigation Pane* to select it.
4. On the CREATE tab, in the Reports group, click the Report Wizard button. The first Report Wizard screen appears.
5. Click >> to move all the fields to the Selected Fields list and click Next.
6. On the grouping screen, click the Scheduled Order Date field, click the >, and click Next.
7. On the sorting screen, click the active down arrow on the menu, select Pounds, and click Next.
8. Keep the defaults as is on the layout screen and click Next.
9. Click Finish. The report is created.
10. **CLOSE** the report.
11. In the Navigation Pane, double-click the Coffee Inventory report you just created to open it.
12. Switch to Layout view and resize the label columns and field boxes so all text and data appear completely in them.
13. **SAVE** and **CLOSE** the report.
14. **CLOSE** the database.

LEAVE Access open for the next project.

Proficiency Assessment

Project 6-3: Alpine Ski House Reservations Report

Every week is different at the Alpine Ski House. Sometimes the lodge is full of guests, and sometimes only a few rooms are occupied. Create a report to show the innkeepers what to expect in the coming weeks.

GET READY. LAUNCH Access if it is not already running.

1. **OPEN** the *AlpineHouse* database.
2. **SAVE** it as *AlpineHouseXXX* (where *XXX* is your initials).
3. Use the Report Wizard to create a report using the Room, Check-in Date, and Check-out Date fields from the Reservations table.
4. Group the report by Room and sort it in **ascending order** by Check-in Date.
5. Use **stepped** layout and **portrait** orientation.
6. Keep the default report name as **Reservations**, and finish the wizard.
7. Switch to Layout view.
8. Apply the **Organic** theme.
9. **SAVE** and **CLOSE** the report.
10. **CLOSE** the database.

LEAVE Access open for the next project.

Project 6-4: Wingtip Toys Design View Report

The manufacturing department at Wingtip Toys needs summary information about each toy in inventory. Create a report in Design view that will display the requested information.

GET READY. LAUNCH Access if it is not already running.

1. **OPEN** *WingtipToys* and **SAVE** it as *WingtipToysXXX* (where *XXX* is your initials).
2. Click the **Inventory** table in the Navigation Pane to select it.
3. On the CREATE tab, in the Reports group, click the **Report Design** button.
4. On the DESIGN tab, in the Tools group, click the **Add Existing Fields** button, if necessary, to display the Field List pane.
5. Add and position the fields from the Inventory table onto the design grid (see Figure 6-22). Adjust the Description field width as shown.

Figure 6-22

Wingtip Toys report in Design view

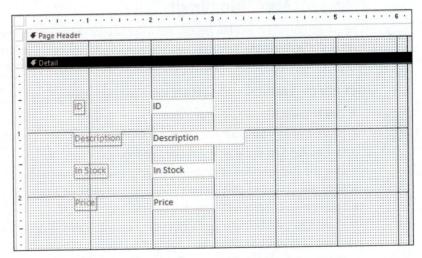

6. **SAVE** the report as **Toy Summary**.
7. **CLOSE** the report.

LEAVE the database open for the next project.

Mastery Assessment

Project 6-5: Filter, Sort, and Find Records in a Wingtip Toys Report

A large order was recently filled, and now the inventory at Wingtip Toys is quite low on some items. Create a report that displays this information.

The *WingtipToysXXX* database should be open.

GET READY. LAUNCH Access if it is not already running.

1. Define the Inventory table as the record source for a new report.
2. Create a simple report.
3. Apply the Ion Boardroom theme to the new report.
4. Sort the report in ascending order by the Description field.
5. Click the first row of the In Stock field, which contains the number 10.
6. Filter by selection to display the toys with 10 or fewer items in stock.
7. Click the In Stock field header and sort the field in ascending order.
8. Clear all sorts.
9. Clear all filters.
10. Find and cycle through all occurrences of the word, Car.
11. SAVE the report as Inventory.
12. CLOSE the report.
13. CLOSE the database.

LEAVE Access open for the next project.

Project 6-6: Angel Project Report

The school Angel Project has begun. Information for the boy angels needs to be distributed to the boys in the kindergarten classes, and the girl angels' information needs to be distributed to the girls. Create a report with filters that display the boy and girl information separately.

GET READY. LAUNCH Access if it is not already running.

1. **OPEN** the *AngelProject* database.
2. **SAVE** the database as *AngelProjectXXX* (where *XXX* is your initials).
3. Define the List table as the record source for a new report.
4. Use the Report Wizard to create a report with all the fields.
5. Skip the grouping and sorting screens, and choose a tabular, portrait layout.
6. Name the report *Angel Needs and Wants*.
7. Switch to Layout view and adjust field widths as necessary so that all data fits on the screen and on one page, and apply the Organic theme.
8. Display the *Group, Sort, and Total* pane.
9. Sort the report in ascending order by Age.
10. Create a filter to show only the information for the males.
11. Toggle the filter and create a new filter to show only the information for the females.
12. **SAVE** and **CLOSE** the report.
13. **CLOSE** the database.

CLOSE Access.

LESSON SKILL MATRIX

Skill	Exam Objective	Objective Number
Creating a Query	Save queries	3.1.6
	Run queries	3.1.1
	Rename queries	3.2.1
	Delete queries	3.1.7
	Create multi-table queries	3.1.5
Modifying a Query	Hide fields	3.2.4
	Create parameter queries	3.1.3
Sorting and Filtering Data within a Query	Sort data within queries	3.2.5

© seanrmcdermid/iStockphoto

KEY TERMS

- field list
- null value
- parameter query
- query criterion
- select query

© seanrmcdermid/iStockphoto

You work for Northwind Traders, a mountain climbing apparel company dedicated to producing high-quality and technically innovative products. The company has a program called industry friends that offers discount purchasing privileges for employees and other outdoor professionals and friends who qualify. As operations coordinator, you are responsible for approving applications for the program and entering related information into the database. You often need to pull specific data from the database. In this lesson, you learn how to create queries from a single table, including a simple query and a find duplicates query, and how to create queries from multiple tables, including a find unmatched query; how to modify a query by adding a table, removing a table, and adding criteria to a query; how to sort and filter data within a query; and how to rename and delete a query.

SOFTWARE ORIENTATION

Queries Group

The Queries group (Figure 7-1) on the CREATE tab contains the commands used to create queries. The Query Wizard button launches the Query Wizard, which helps you create a simple query, a crosstab query, a find duplicates query, or a find unmatched query. The Query Design button creates a new, blank query in Design view. Use this figure as a reference throughout this lesson as well as the rest of this book.

Launches the   Creates a new blank
Query Wizard   query in Design View

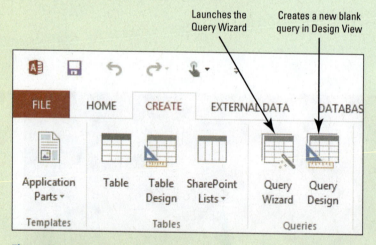

Figure 7-1
Queries group

CREATING A QUERY

The Bottom Line

A query is a set of instructions used for working with data. Creating a query is like asking the database a question. Running a query performs these instructions and provides the answers. The results that a query returns can be sorted, grouped, or filtered. There are several different types of queries. Basic queries can be used to extract useful information from one or more tables in the database, while more advanced queries can be used to manipulate data in tables (e.g., create, copy, modify, delete or find duplicate or unmatched table data). A **select query** is the most basic type of Access query. It creates subsets of data that you can use to answer specific questions or to supply data to other database objects such as forms and reports. The data is displayed in Datasheet view without being changed. A query is a powerful and versatile database tool. Queries differ from sort or filter commands because they can be saved for future use and can utilize data from multiple tables or other queries.

Cross Ref

You learn more about advanced queries that can manipulate table data in Lesson 12.

Creating a Query from a Table and Deleting a Query

A query can get its data from one or more tables, from existing queries, or from a combination of the two. The tables or queries from which a query gets its data are referred to as its record source. When one table provides the information that you need, you can create a simple select query using the Query Wizard. You can also use a query to find records with duplicate field values in a single table. You can delete a query to remove it permanently from the database and rename a query if you want to modify the previous name. In this exercise, you create a simple select query that searches the data in a single table and rename the query. You also delete a pre-existing query using the Delete command.

To create a simple select query, click the Query Wizard button in the Queries group on the CREATE tab. Click Simple Query Wizard and then click OK. Specify the table you want to use as the record source and the fields that you want to show. Name the query and click Finish. When you close the query, it is automatically saved.

To run a query after it has been created, simply double-click it in the Navigation Pane to open it in Datasheet view and see the results.

You can also permanently delete a query from the database by using the Delete command in the Records group on the HOME tab. You can delete a query if you erroneously created it or simply want to unclutter the database by removing preexisting queries you no longer use.

Finally, you can rename a query by right-clicking on it in the Navigation Pane, choosing the Rename command from the shortcut menu that appears, and keying in the new name.

STEP BY STEP   **Create a Simple Query**

GET READY. Before you begin these steps, be sure to **LAUNCH** Microsoft Access.

1. **OPEN** the *Northwind* file from the data files for this lesson.
2. **SAVE** the database as *NorthwindXXX* (where *XXX* is your initials).
3. On the CREATE tab, in the Queries group, click the **Query Wizard** button. The New Query dialog box appears, as shown in Figure 7-2.

Figure 7-2

New Query dialog box

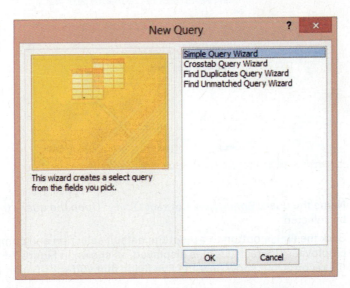

4. Click **Simple Query Wizard** and then click **OK**. The Simple Query Wizard appears, as shown in Figure 7-3.

Figure 7-3

Simple Query Wizard, screen 1

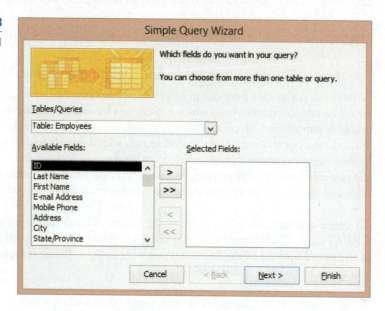

5. In the Tables/Queries drop-down list, **Table: Employees** should be selected by default. If it is not, select it.

6. Under Available Fields, double-click **Last Name**, **First Name**, **E-mail Address**, **Mobile Phone**, and **Position** to move them to the Selected Fields box.

Take Note   To remove a field from the Selected Fields box, double-click the field. This moves it back to the Available Fields box.

7. Click the **Next >** button. The second screen in the Simple Query Wizard appears, as shown in Figure 7-4.

Figure 7-4

Simple Query Wizard, screen 2

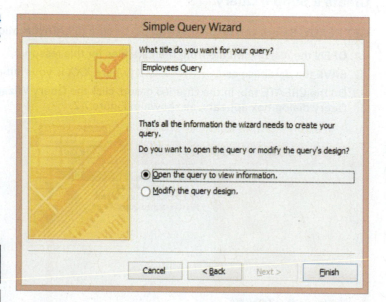

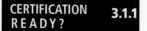

CERTIFICATION READY?   3.1.6

How do you save queries?

CERTIFICATION READY?   3.1.1

How do you run queries?

8. Name the query **Employees Contact Query**. *Open the query to view information* should be selected.

9. Click the **Finish** button to accept the default selection and complete the query. The Employees Contact Query is displayed, as shown in Figure 7-5. The results show all of the records, but show only the five fields that you specified in the Query Wizard.

Figure 7-5

Simple select query

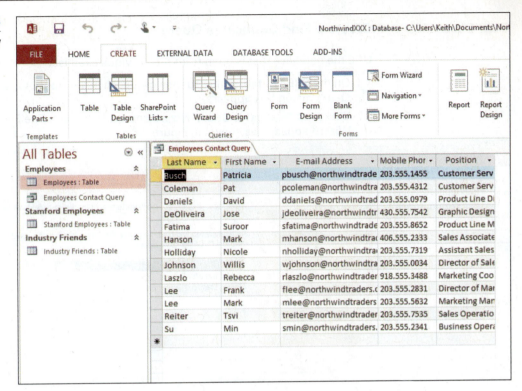

Figure 7-5

Simple select query

Another Way
You can also delete a query or any other object by right-clicking it in the Navigation Pane and choosing Delete from the shortcut menu that appears, or clicking the object and just simply pressing the Delete key on the keyboard.

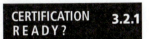

CERTIFICATION READY? **3.2.1**

How do you rename queries?

CERTIFICATION READY? **3.1.7**

How do you delete queries?

---

10. Click the **Close** button on the Employees Contact Query window to close the query.

11. In the Navigation Pane, double-click the **Employees Contact Query** to run it. The query results are displayed in Datasheet view.

12. Click the **Close** button on the Employees Contact Query window to close the query.

13. In the Navigation Pane, right-click the **Employees Contact Query** to select it.

14. On the shortcut menu that appears, click the **Rename** command.

15. In the query name box, key **Employees Contact Info Query** to rename it and press **Enter**. The query has been renamed.

16. In the Navigation Pane, click the **Marketing Employees** query to select it.

17. On the HOME tab, in the Records group, click the **Delete** button arrow and then click the **Delete** command on the menu that appears.

18. Click **Yes** on the dialog box asking you if you want to permanently delete the Marketing Employees query. The query is now permanently deleted from the database.

PAUSE. LEAVE Access open to use in the next exercise.

Creating a Find Duplicates Query

As a general rule, duplicate data should be eliminated from a database whenever possible to minimize redundancy and increase accuracy. The first step in this process is finding duplicate data. Two or more records are considered duplicates only when all the fields in your query results contain the same values. If the values in even a single field differ, each record is unique. In this exercise, you use the Find Duplicates Query Wizard to find duplicate records.

You can also use the Find Duplicates Query Wizard to find records that contain *some* matching field values. You should include the field or fields that identify each record uniquely, typically the primary key. The query returns matching records where the values in the specified fields match character for character.

Create a Find Duplicates Query

USE the database that is open from the previous exercise.

1. On the CREATE tab, in the Queries group, click the Query Wizard button. The New Query dialog box appears.

2. Click Find Duplicates Query Wizard and then click OK. The Find Duplicates Query Wizard appears, as shown in Figure 7-6.

Figure 7-6

Find Duplicates Query Wizard, screen 1

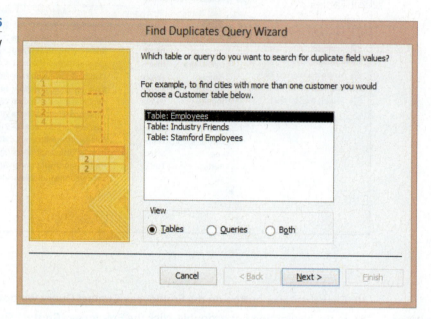

3. Click Table: Industry Friends and then click Next >. The next screen in the Find Duplicates Query Wizard appears, as shown in Figure 7-7.

Figure 7-7

Find Duplicates Query Wizard, screen 2

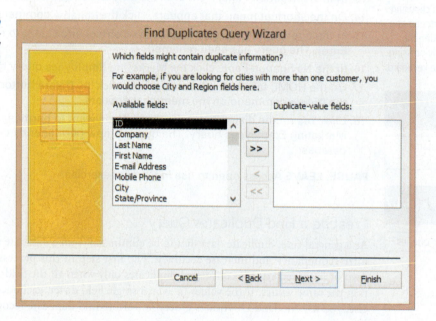

4. Double-click Last Name, First Name, and E-mail Address to move them to the Duplicate-value fields box. These are the fields that you think may include duplicate information.

5. Click **Next >** to display the next screen in the Find Duplicates Query Wizard, shown in Figure 7-8. This screen asks if you want to show other fields of the duplicate record besides just the ones with the duplicate data.

Figure 7-8

Find Duplicates Query
Wizard, screen 3

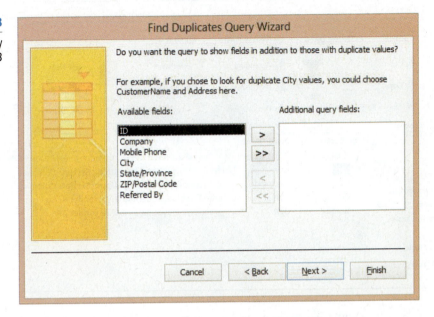

6. Double-click **Company** and **Referred By** to move them to the Additional query fields box.
7. Click **Next >** to display the final screen in the Find Duplicates Query Wizard, shown in Figure 7-9.

Figure 7-9

Find Duplicates Query Wizard,
final screen

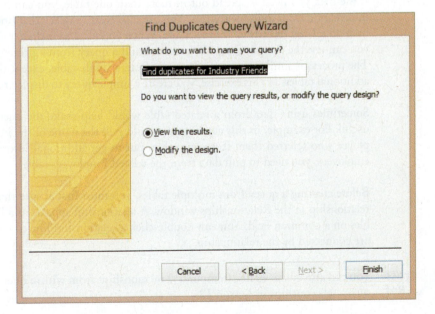

8. Name the query **Duplicates for Industry Friends** and click **Finish**. The query showing duplicate records in the table is displayed, as shown in Figure 7-10.

Figure 7-10

Duplicates for Industry Friends query

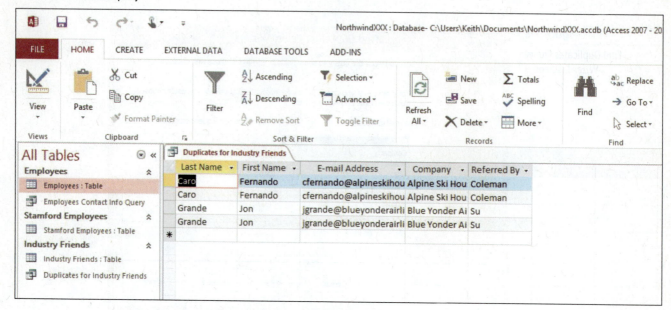

9. Click the **Close** button on the Duplicates for Industry Friends tab to close the query.

PAUSE. LEAVE Access open to use in the next exercise.

Creating a Query from Multiple Tables

If the data you need is spread out in more than one table, you can build a query that combines information from multiple sources. You can also create a query that finds records in one table that have no related records in another table. When you need to include multiple tables in your query, you can use the Simple Query Wizard to build a query from a primary table and a related table. The process is similar to creating a query from a single table, except that you include fields from additional tables. In this exercise, you create a simple query to display related data from two tables.

Sometimes using data from a related table would help make the query results clearer and more useful. For example, in this activity, you could pull the name of the industry friends and the employee who referred them from one table. But to get additional information about the referring employees, you need to pull data from the related Employees table.

Before creating a query from multiple tables, you must first ensure that the tables have a defined relationship in the Relationships window. A relationship appears as a line connecting the two tables on a common field. You can double-click a relationship line to see which fields in the tables are connected by the relationship.

 Cross Ref
You can also create ad hoc (temporary) relationships from within queries. You learn about ad hoc query relationships in Lesson 12.

STEP BY STEP **Create a Query from Multiple Tables**

USE the database that is open from the previous exercise.

1. In the Navigation Pane, double-click **Employees: Table** to open the table.

2. On the DATABASE TOOLS tab, in the Relationships group, click the **Relationships** button to display the table relationship, as shown in Figure 7-11. The Employees table has a defined relationship with the Industry Friends table as indicated by the relationship line connecting the two tables.

Figure 7-11

Relationships for
Employees table

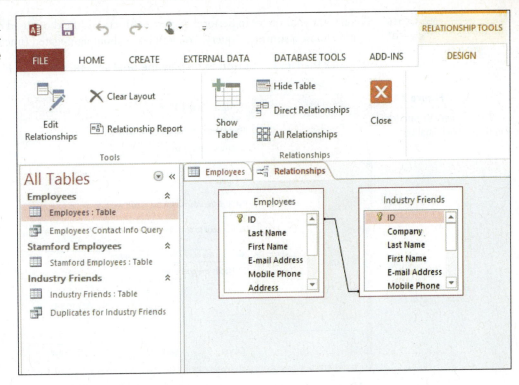

3. Click the **Close** button in the Relationships group on the Ribbon to close the Relationships window and click the **Close** button on the Employees tab to close the Employees table.

4. On the CREATE tab, in the Queries group, click the **Query Wizard** button to display the New Query dialog box.

5. Click **Simple Query Wizard** and then click **OK** to display the Simple Query Wizard.

6. In the Tables/Queries drop-down list, click **Table: Industry Friends**.

7. Under Available Fields, double-click **Last Name**, **First Name**, and **Referred By** to move them to the Selected Fields box.

8. In the Tables/Queries drop-down list, click **Table: Employees**.

9. Under Available Fields, double-click **Position** and then **E-mail Address** to move them to the Selected Fields box.

10. Click the **Next >** button to display the next screen, as shown in Figure 7-12. The *Detail* option should be selected by default.

Figure 7-12

Simple Query Wizard for
multiple tables

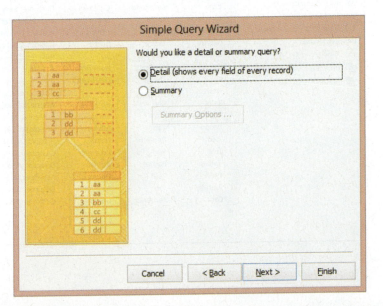

Cross Ref   If you want your query to perform aggregate functions like those used to sum or average data, you would choose a summary query. You will learn about aggregated functions in Lesson 12.

11. Click the **Next >** button to display the final screen, shown in Figure 7-13.

Figure 7-13

Simple Query Wizard for multiple tables, final screen

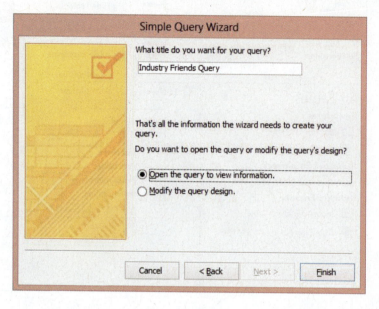

12. Click the **Finish** button to accept the default settings in this screen and display the query, shown in Figure 7-14. This query shows the name, position, and e-mail address of the employee who referred each industry friend.

Figure 7-14

Industry Friends query

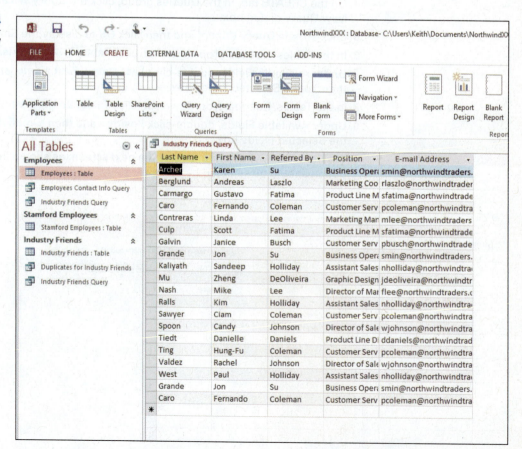

13. Click the **Close** button on the Industry Friends Query tab to close the query.

PAUSE. LEAVE the database open to use in the next exercise.

 Cross Ref   You learned about defining and modifying table relationships in Lesson 3.

Finding Unmatched Records

To view only the records in one table that do not have a matching record in another table, you can create a Find Unmatched query. On the CREATE tab, in the Queries group, click Query Wizard, and then click Find Unmatched Query Wizard to start the wizard. In this exercise, you run a Find Unmatched query to display the employees who do not live in Stamford.

STEP BY STEP   **Find Unmatched Records**

USE the database that is open from the previous exercise.

1. On the CREATE tab, in the Queries group, click the **Query Wizard** button. The New Query dialog box appears.

2. Click **Find Unmatched Query Wizard** and then click **OK**. The Find Unmatched Query Wizard appears, as shown in Figure 7-15.

Figure 7-15

Find Unmatched Query Wizard, screen 1

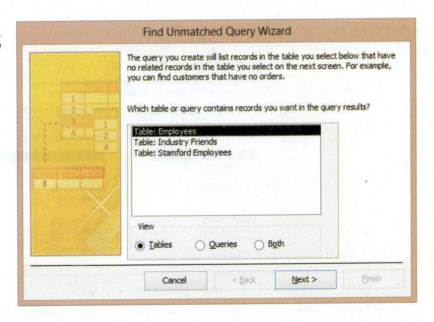

3. Table: Employees is the default selection in this screen. This table will contain the records you'll want to display. Click the **Next >** button to display the next screen in the Find Unmatched Query Wizard, shown in Figure 7-16.

Figure 7-16

Find Unmatched Query
Wizard, screen 2

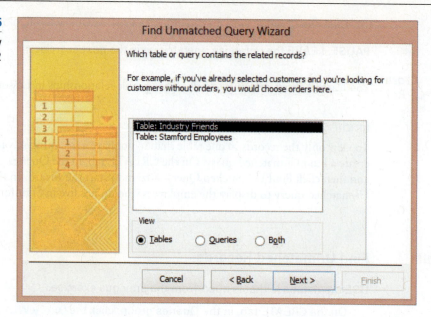

Figure 7-16

Find Unmatched Query
Wizard, screen 2

4. Select **Table: Stamford Employees** to select the table that is related to the Employees table and contains the records you *don't* want to display. Click the **Next >** button to display the next screen in the Find Unmatched Query Wizard, shown in Figure 7-17.

Figure 7-17

Find Unmatched Query
Wizard, screen 3

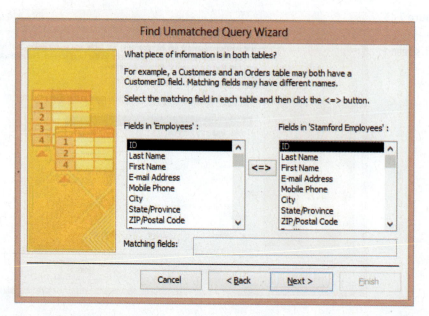

5. Click **E-mail Address** in the Fields in "Employees" list. Click **E-mail Address** in the Fields in "Stamford Employees" list. Click the **<=>** button to display them in the Matching fields box. These fields contain data that is in both tables.

6. Click the **Next >** button to display the next screen in the Find Unmatched Query Wizard, shown in Figure 7-18.

Figure 7-18

Find Unmatched Query
Wizard, screen 4

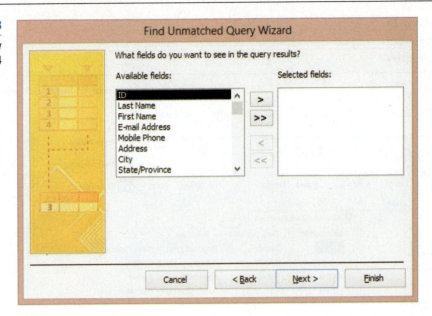

7. In the Available fields box, double-click **Last Name**, **First Name**, **Position**, and **City** to move them to the Selected fields box.

8. Click the **Next >** button to display the final screen in the Find Unmatched Query Wizard, shown in Figure 7-19.

Figure 7-19

Find Unmatched Query
Wizard, final screen

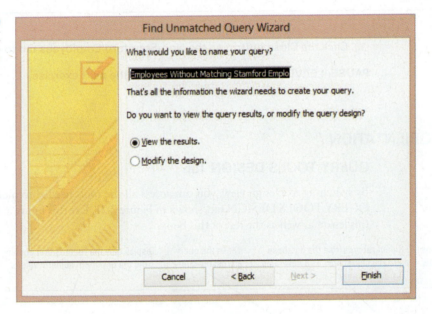

9. Click in the text box at the top of this screen and key **Non-Stamford Employees** to name your query, then click the **Finish** button. The query is displayed, as shown in Figure 7-20.

Figure 7-20

Non-Stamford
Employees query

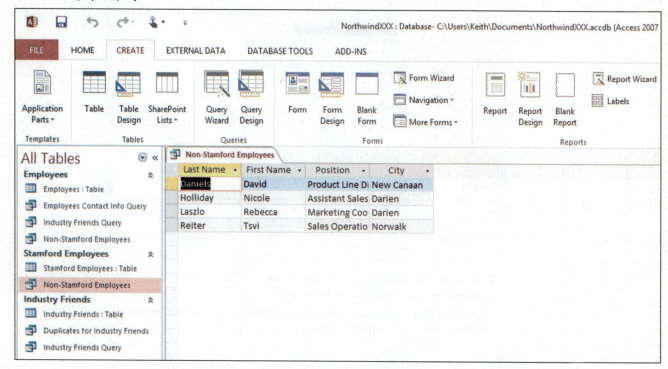

10. Click the **Close** button on the Non-Stamford Employees tab to close the query.

PAUSE. LEAVE the database open to use in the next exercise.

SOFTWARE ORIENTATION

QUERY TOOLS DESIGN Tab

By switching to Design view, you can access all the tools needed to modify your query on the QUERY TOOLS DESIGN tab, shown in Figure 7-21. Use this figure as a reference throughout this lesson as well as the rest of this book.

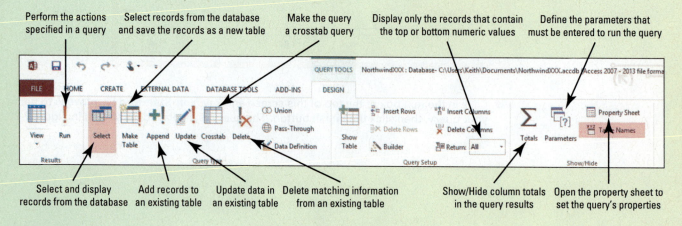

Figure 7-21

QUERY TOOLS DESIGN tab

MODIFYING A QUERY

The Bottom Line

A query can be modified in Design view, regardless of how it was created. You can add or remove a table, add or remove fields, or add criteria to refine query results.

Another Way
You can also add a table to a query by clicking and dragging the table from the Navigation Pane to the Query Design window.

Adding a Table to a Query

To add a table to a query, you must be in Design view. Run the query and click Design View on the lower half of the View button. On the **QUERY TOOLS DESIGN** tab, in the Query Setup group, click the Show Table button to display the Show Table dialog box. There is a tab that contains the tables in the database, a tab with the queries, and a tab that displays both. Select the object you want to add to the query and click the Add button. If you add a second copy of a table to the query, it is indicated by a "1" in the title. In this exercise, you add additional tables to a query using the Show Table dialog box.

STEP BY STEP   **Add a Table to a Query**

USE the database that is open from the previous exercise.

1. Double-click the **Industry Friends Query** in the Navigation Pane to open it.
2. On the HOME tab, in the Views group, click the lower half of the **View** button and then click **Design View**. The query appears in Design view, as shown in Figure 7-22.

Figure 7-22

Query in Design view

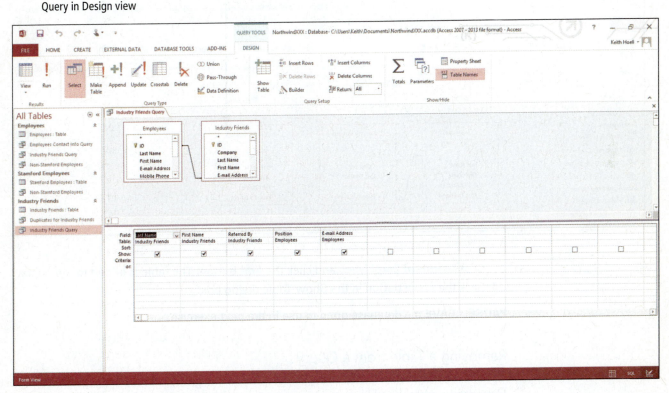

3. On the QUERY TOOLS DESIGN tab, in the Query Setup group, click the **Show Table** button to display the Show Table dialog box, shown in Figure 7-23.

Figure 7-23

Show Table dialog box

4. Click **Industry Friends** and click the **Add** button. A second copy of the Industry Friends table is added to the query, as indicated by the "1" in the title, as shown in Figure 7-24.

Figure 7-24

Second copy of table in a query

The "1" indicates a second copy of the table has been added to the query

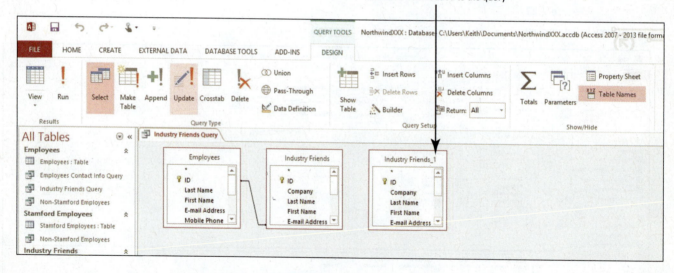

5. Click **Stamford Employees** and click the **Add** button. The table is added to the query.
6. Click the **Close** button in the Show Table dialog box.

PAUSE. LEAVE the database open to use in the next exercise.

Removing a Table from a Query

To remove a table from a query, first open the query in Design view. In the upper portion of Query Design view, select the table you want to remove by clicking anywhere in its field list—a **field list** is a window that lists all the fields in the underlying record source or database object—then press the Delete key. The table is removed from the query, but it is not deleted from the database. In this exercise, you remove a table from a query.

Remove a Table from a Query

USE the database that is open from the previous exercise.

1. Click anywhere in the **Industry Friends_1** field list.
2. [Press the **Delete** key] to remove the table.
3. Click anywhere in the **Stamford Employees** field list.
4. [Press the **Delete** key] to remove the table.
5. Click the **Close** button on the Industry Friends Query tab to close the query. If a message asks you if you want to save the changes, click **Yes**.

PAUSE. LEAVE the database open to use in the next exercise.

Adding Criteria to a Query

Not all queries must include criteria, but if you are not interested in seeing all the records that are stored in the underlying record source, you can add criteria to a query when designing it. A **query criterion** is a rule that identifies the records you want to include in the query result. A criterion is similar to a formula. Some criteria are simple and use basic operators and constants. Others are complex and use functions, special operators, and include field references. Criteria can look very different from each other, depending on the data type of the field to which they apply and your specific requirements. You can also run a **parameter query**, in which the user interactively specifies one or more criteria values. This is not a separate query; it extends the flexibility of another type of query, such as a select query, by prompting the user for a parameter value when it is run. In this exercise, you add criteria to queries to display certain records, use the Show check box, and create and run a parameter query which will prompt the user for a city name and display matching records.

To specify one or more criteria to restrict the records returned in the query results, open the query in Design view. Select the field and type the condition that you want to specify in the Criteria row. To see the results, switch to Datasheet view. The results will show each field, including the one where the criterion was specified.

Sometimes, you may want to show only certain fields (while hiding others) from the records that match the criterion to get a more concise view of the resulting data. In this case, deselect the Show row check box above the Criteria row for those fields you don't want to display in the results. The fields that you choose not to show, except the field with the criterion, will be hidden from the results after you switch to Datasheet view.

Add Criteria to a Query

USE the database that is open from the previous exercise.

1. In the Navigation Pane, double-click the **Employees Contact Info Query** to open it.
2. On the HOME tab, in the Views group, click the lower half of the **View** button and click **Design View**.
3. In the Criteria row of the Position field, key **Like "*Manager"** as shown in Figure 7-25 to display all records that end with the string "Manager" in the Position field (e.g., Assistant Manager, Sales Manager, Product Manager, etc.).

Figure 7-25

Query criterion

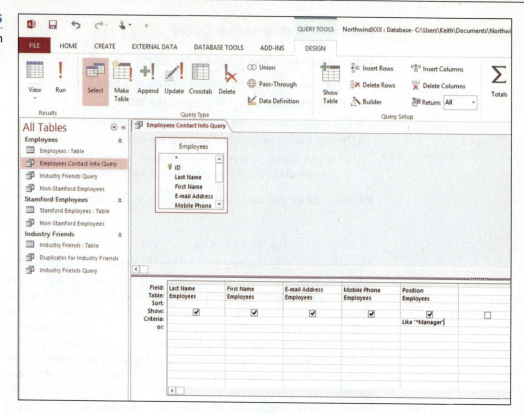

4. On the QUERY TOOLS DESIGN tab, in the Results group, click the lower half of the **View** button and click **Datasheet View**. The query results display all records that end with the string "Manager" in the Position field, as shown in Figure 7-26. (You may have to increase the width of the Position field to completely view the data within it.)

Figure 7-26

Results with query criteria applied

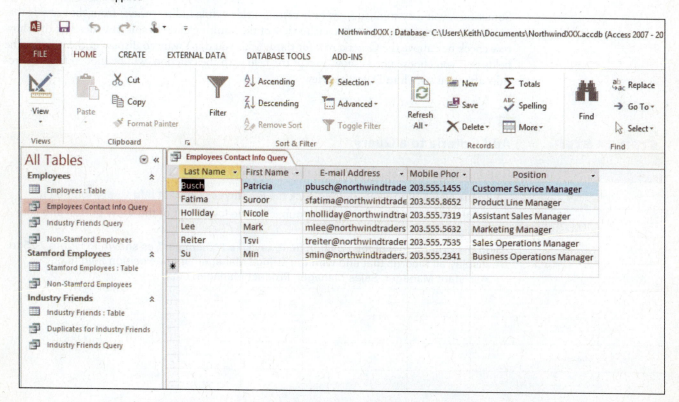

5. On the HOME tab, in the Views group, click the lower half of the **View** button and click **Design View**.

6. In the Show row, under the First Name field, click the **Show** check box to deselect it, as shown in Figure 7-27. The First Name field data will not appear in the query results.

Figure 7-27

Show check box deselected
for First Name field

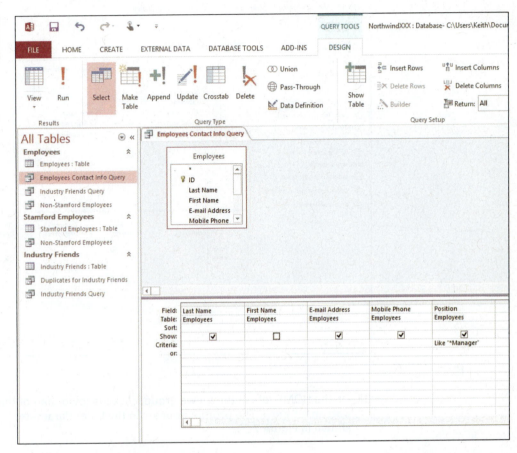

7. On the HOME tab, in the Views group, click the lower half of the **View** button and click **Datasheet View**. Notice that the First Name field doesn't appear.

8. Click the **Close** button on the Employees Contact Info Query tab to close the query. When prompted to save, click **Yes**.

9. In the Navigation Pane, double-click the **Non-Stamford Employees Query** to open it.

10. On the HOME tab, in the Views group, click the lower half of the **View** button and click **Design View**.

11. In the Criteria row of the City field, key **[City?]** as shown in Figure 7-28. This will create the parameter and require you to enter a city name when the query is run.

Figure 7-28

Parameter query criteria

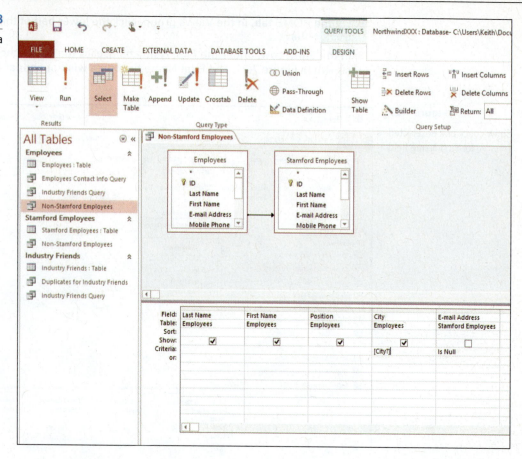

12. On the HOME tab, in the Views group, click the lower half of the **View** button and click **Datasheet View**. The prompt appears in the Enter Parameter Value dialog box, as shown in Figure 7-29.

Figure 7-29

Enter Parameter Value dialog box

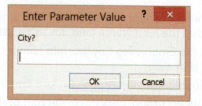

13. Key **Darien** in the City? box.

14. Click **OK**. The records for non-Stamford employees who live in Darien are displayed in the results, as shown in Figure 7-30.

Figure 7-30

Parameter query result

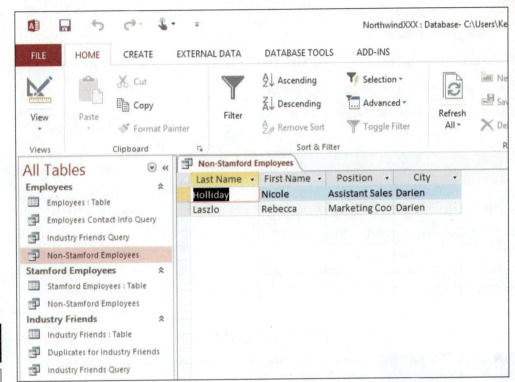

15. Click the **Close** button on the Non-Stamford Employees tab to close the query. When prompted to save, click **Yes**.

PAUSE. LEAVE the database open to use in the next exercise.

Table 7-1 shows some sample criteria and explains how they work. Table 7-2 shows the query results that are returned when a specific criterion is used.

Table 7-1

Criteria examples

Criteria	Description
>25 and <50	This criterion applies to a Number field, such as Inventory. It includes only those records where the Inventory field contains a value greater than 25 and less than 50.
DateDiff ("yyyy", [BirthDate], Date()) > 21	This criterion applies to a Date/Time field, such as BirthDate. Only records where the number of years between a person's birth date and today's date is greater than 21 are included in the query result.
Is Null	This criterion can be applied to any type of field to show records where the field value is null. (A **null value** is a marker that a value does not exist for a field and is differentiated from a value that has been missed being entered by a user.)

Query result examples

To Include Records That...	Use This Criterion	Query Result
Exactly match a value, such as Manager	"Manager"	Returns records where the given field is set to Manager.
Do not match a value, such as Chicago	Not "Chicago"	Returns records where the given field is set to a value other than Chicago.
Begin with the specified string, such as B	Like B*	Returns records for the given field where the value starts with "B," such as Boston, Bakersfield, and so on.
Do not begin with the specified string, such as B	Not Like B*	Returns records for the given field where the value starts with a character other than "B."
Contain the specified string, such as Sales	Like "*Sales*"	Returns records for the given field that contain the string "Sales."
Do not contain the specified string, such as Sales	Not Like "*Sales*"	Returns records for the given field that do not contain the string "Sales."

SORTING AND FILTERING DATA WITHIN A QUERY

The Bottom Line

Sorting and filtering data within a query allows you to display only the records you want and/or display records in a particular order.

Sorting Data within a Query

Sorting data in a query can help organize data efficiently and make it easier for users to review and locate the records they want without having to browse the data. Data can be sorted in the Datasheet view of a query. Right-click the field on which you want to sort and click the sort order you want—ascending or descending—from the shortcut menu. The records are rearranged to match the sort order. In this exercise, you sort data using the Datasheet view of a query.

To sort by more than one field, on the **HOME** tab, in the Sort & Filter group, click the Advanced button and click Advanced Filter/Sort to open a tab where you can specify more than one field by which to sort and the sort order.

 Cross Ref You learned about sorting data within a table in Lesson 3, sorting data within a form in Lesson 5, and sorting data within a report in Lesson 6.

STEP BY STEP   **Sort Data within a Query**

USE the database that is open from the previous exercise.

1. In the Navigation Pane, double-click the Industry Friends Query to open it.
2. Right-click the Referred By field to display the shortcut menu shown in Figure 7-31.

Figure 7-31

Shortcut menu

3. Click **Sort A to Z**. The field is sorted in alphabetical order from A to Z, as shown in Figure 7-32.

Figure 7-32

Sorted query

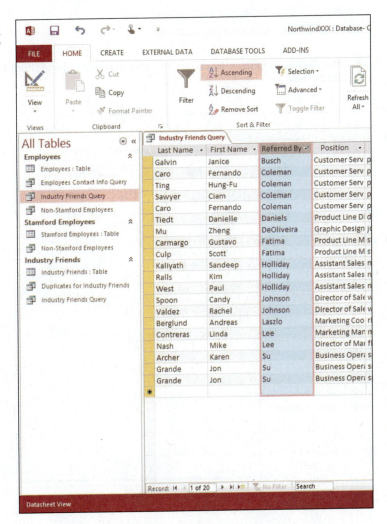

4. On the HOME tab, in the Sort & Filter group, click the **Remove Sort** button. The sort order is removed from the Referred By field.

5. On the HOME tab, in the Sort & Filter group, click the **Advanced** button to display the menu shown in Figure 7-33.

Figure 7-33

Advanced menu

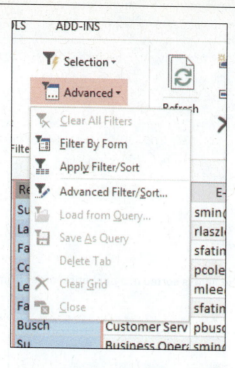

6. Click **Advanced Filter/Sort**. An Industry Friends QueryFilter1 tab appears, as shown in Figure 7-34.

Figure 7-34

Industry Friends
QueryFilter1 tab

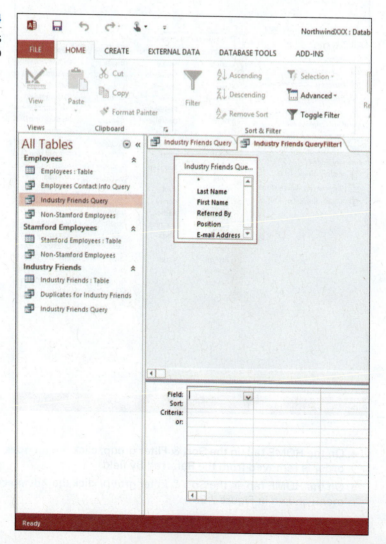

7. Click the **Field cell** in the first column, click the **down arrow**, and click **Referred By** on the drop-down menu.

8. Click the **Sort cell** in the first column, click the **down arrow**, and click **Ascending** on the drop-down menu.

9. Click the **Field cell** in the second column, click the **down arrow**, and click **Last Name** on the drop-down menu.

10. Click the **Sort cell** in the second column, click the **down arrow**, and click **Ascending** on the drop-down menu. Your screen should look similar to Figure 7-35.

Figure 7-35

Advanced sort criteria

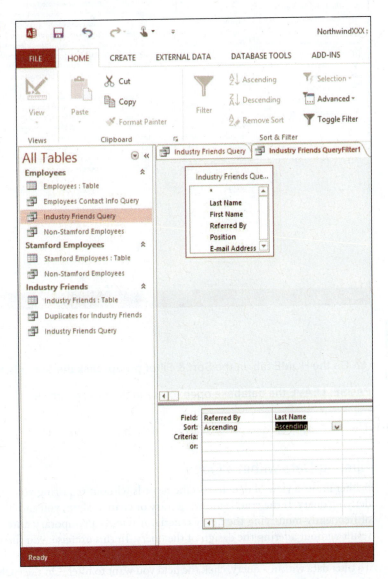

11. On the HOME tab, in the Sort & Filter group, click the **Advanced** button and click **Apply Filter/Sort**. The query is sorted by the Referred By field in ascending order and then by the Last Name field in ascending order, as shown in Figure 7-36.

Figure 7-36

Sorted query

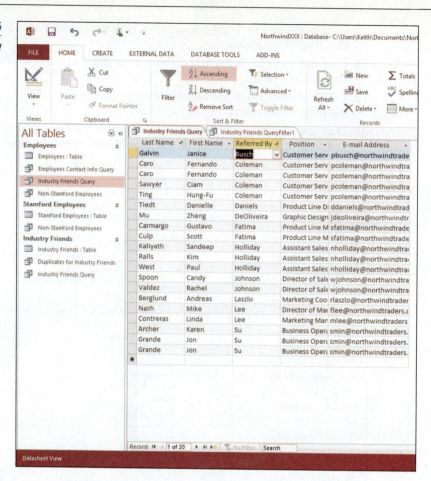

Figure 7-36

Sorted query

CERTIFICATION READY?   3.2.5

How do you sort data within queries?

12. On the HOME tab, in the Sort & Filter group, click the **Remove Sort** button.

PAUSE. LEAVE the database open to use in the next exercise.

Take Note   The same tab is used to perform an advanced filter for the query.

Filtering Data within a Query

A filter limits a view of data to specific records without requiring you to alter the design of the underlying query. If the criteria are temporary or change often, you can filter the query results instead of frequently modifying the query criteria. A filter is a temporary criterion that changes the query result without altering the design of the query. In this exercise, you filter data within a query.

To filter data within a query, click the field you want to filter. On the **HOME** tab, in the Sort & Filter group, click the Filter button. The filters available depend on the type and values of the field. When you apply the filter, only records that contain the values in which you are interested are included in the view. The rest are hidden until you remove the filter by clicking the Toggle Filter button.

Cross Ref   You learned about filtering data within a table in Lesson 3, filtering data within a form in Lesson 5, and filtering data within a report in Lesson 6.

STEP BY STEP   **Filter Data within a Query**

USE the database that is open from the previous exercise. The Industry Friends Query should be open.

1. Click the **Position header** to select the field.

2. On the HOME tab, in the Sort & Filter group, click the **Filter** button. A menu appears on the field, as shown in Figure 7-37.

Figure 7-37

Filter menu

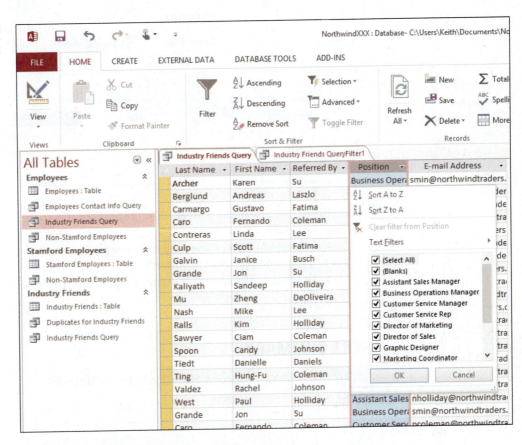

3. On the menu, click **Text Filters** and click **Contains** on the submenu. A Custom Filter dialog box appears, as shown in Figure 7-38.

Figure 7-38

Custom Filter dialog box

4. In the Position contains box, key **Marketing** and click **OK**. The records are filtered to show only those results containing the word "Marketing" in the Position field, as shown in Figure 7-39.

Figure 7-39

Filtered query

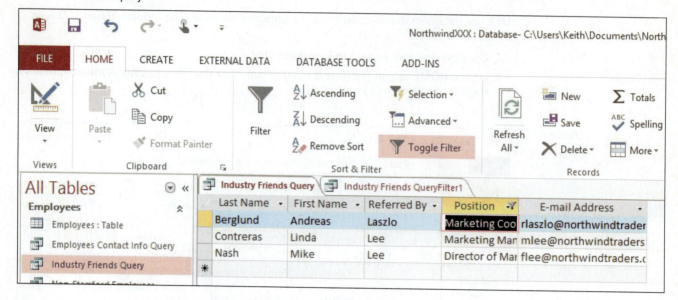

5. On the HOME tab, in the Sort & Filter group, click the **Toggle Filter** button to remove the filter.

6. Click the **Close** button on the Industry Friends Query tab to close the query, and click **Yes** to save changes when prompted.

7. Click the **Close** button on the Industry Friends QueryFilter1 tab to close the query.

CLOSE the database.

SKILL SUMMARY

In This Lesson You Learned How To:	Exam Objective	Objective Number
Create a query	Save queries	3.1.6
	Run queries	3.1.1
	Rename queries	3.2.1
	Delete queries	3.1.7
	Create multi-table queries	3.1.5
Modify a query	Hide fields	3.2.4
	Create parameter queries	3.1.3
Sort and filter data within a query	Sort data within queries	3.2.5

Knowledge Assessment

Fill in the Blank

Complete the following sentences by writing the correct word or words in the blanks provided.

1. The Queries group on the _____ tab contains the commands used to create queries.

2. The _____ button creates a new, blank query in Design view.

3. A(n) _____ is the most basic type of Access query.

4. The tables or queries from which a query gets its data are referred to as its _____.

5. To run a query after it has been created, double-click it in the Navigation Pane to open it in _____ view and see the results.

6. Two or more records are considered _____ only when all the fields in your query results contain the same values.

7. When you need to include multiple tables in your query, use the _____ Wizard to build a query from a primary table and a related table.

8. To view only the records in one table that don't have a matching record in another table, you can create a _____ query.

9. By switching to _____ view, you can access all the tools needed to modify your query.

10. A(n) _____ is a window that lists all the fields in the underlying record source or database object.

Multiple Choice

Select the best response for the following statements or questions.

1. Creating a query is like
   a. sorting the data.
   b. asking the database a question.
   c. creating a new table.
   d. opening an existing database.

2. The results that a query returns can be
   a. sorted.
   b. grouped.
   c. filtered.
   d. all of the above.
   e. none of the above.

3. When one table will provide the information you need, you can create a
   a. record source.
   b. simple select query.
   c. query criterion.
   d. parameter query.

4. Which query cannot be created using the Query Wizard?
   a. Parameter query
   b. Simple query
   c. Find duplicates query
   d. Find unmatched query

5. Queries are different from sort or filter commands because they can be
   a. applied to multiple fields.
   b. saved.
   c. modified.
   d. used on forms.

6. A query can get its data from
   a. one or more tables.
   b. existing queries.
   c. all of the above.
   d. none of the above.

7. To find records that contain matching field values, you can create a query using which wizard?
   a. Find Matching
   b. Matching Fields
   c. Duplicate Records
   d. Find Duplicates

8. Before creating a query from multiple tables, you must first ensure that the tables have
   a. unmatched records.
   b. a defined relationship.
   c. a filter applied.
   d. no related records.

9. To add a table to a query, you must be in what view?
   a. SQL
   b. Datasheet
   c. Normal
   d. Design

10. A rule that identifies the records you want to include in the query result is called a
   a. parameter query.
   b. query criterion.
   c. select query.
   d. field list.

Competency Assessment

Project 7-1: Create a Games Select Query

As the manager at Southridge Video, you have stored information in an Access database about each used game that the store has taken in trade. Now that you know how to create queries, you decide to create a select query to list the title, rating, and category, which are the fields that you most often need to view.

GET READY. LAUNCH Access if it is not already running.

1. **OPEN** *Games* from the data files for this lesson.
2. **SAVE** the database as *GamesXXX* (where *XXX* is your initials).
3. On the CREATE tab, in the Queries group, click the **Query Wizard** button to display the New Query dialog box.
4. Click **Simple Query Wizard** and then click **OK**.
5. In the Tables/Queries drop-down list, Table: Games should be selected.
6. Under Available Fields, double-click **Title**, **Rating**, and **Category** to move them to the Selected Fields box.
7. Click the **Next >** button. The second screen in the Simple Query Wizard appears.
8. Name the query **Games Query**. *Open the query to view information* should be selected.
9. Click the **Finish** button.
10. Click the **Close** button on the Games Query tab to close the query.
11. **LEAVE** the database open for the next project.

LEAVE Access open for the next project.

Project 7-2: Create a Find Duplicates Query

You have taught the night manager at Southridge Video how to enter used game information into the database, but you have not yet developed a reliable system for determining if the game has already been entered. You are concerned there may be duplicate records. Create a Find Duplicates query to determine if there are duplicates.

USE the database that is open from the previous project.

1. On the CREATE tab, in the Queries group, click the **Query Wizard** button.
2. In the New Query dialog box, click **Find Duplicates Query Wizard**, and then click **OK**.
3. Click **Table: Games** and then click **Next >**. The next screen in the Find Duplicates Query Wizard appears.
4. Double-click **Title**, **Platform**, and **Publisher** to move them to the Duplicate-value fields box.
5. Click **Next >** to display the next screen in the Find Duplicates Query Wizard.
6. Double-click **Category** to move it to the Additional query fields box.
7. Click **Next >** to display the final screen in the Find Duplicates Query Wizard.
8. Name the query **Duplicates for Games** and click **Finish** to display the query showing duplicate records in the table.
9. Click the **Close** button on the Duplicates for Games tab to close the query.
10. **CLOSE** the database.

LEAVE Access open for the next project.

Proficiency Assessment

Project 7-3: Create a Query from Multiple Tables

Information about each selection for the Fourth Coffee monthly coffee club is stored in an Access database. Information about regular coffee and decaf coffee is stored in separate tables. In your position as customer service rep, it would be useful to be able to query information from both tables.

GET READY. LAUNCH Access if it is not already running.

1. **OPEN** *Fourth Coffee Club* from the data files for this lesson.
2. **SAVE** the database as *Fourth Coffee ClubXXX* (where *XXX* is your initials).
3. Open the **Regular Coffee: Table**.
4. Open the **Relationships** window to ensure there is a relationship between the regular coffee and decaf coffee tables. Close the Relationships window.
5. Start the Query Wizard and choose **Simple Query Wizard**.
6. In the Tables/Queries drop-down list, click **Table: Regular Coffee**.
7. Move the Name, Country, Month, and Type fields to the Selected Fields box.
8. In the Tables/Queries drop-down list, click **Table: Decaf Coffee**.
9. Move the Name, Country, Month, and Type fields to the Selected Fields box.
10. Click the **Next >** button.
11. Click the **Next >** button and name the query **Coffee Query**.
12. Click the **Finish** button.
13. Review the information in the query and then close it.
14. **LEAVE** the database open for the next project.

LEAVE Access open for the next project.

Project 7-4: Create a Find Unmatched Query

A decaf coffee and a regular coffee should be selected for each month. To determine if there are any records in the decaf coffee table that don't have a matching record in the regular coffee table, you decide to create a Find Unmatched query.

USE the database that is open from the previous project.

1. Start the **Query Wizard** and choose **Find Unmatched Query Wizard**.
2. Table: Decaf Coffee should be selected. Click **Next >**.
3. Table: Regular Coffee should be selected. Click **Next >**.
4. Click **ID** in the Fields in 'Decaf Coffee' list. Click **ID** in the Fields in 'Regular Coffee' list. Click the **<=>** button to display them in the Matching fields box.
5. Click the **Next >** button.
6. Move the Name, Month, and Type fields to the Selected fields box.
7. Click the **Next >** button.
8. Name the query **Unmatched Month** and click the **Finish** button to display the query results.
9. Close the query.
10. **CLOSE** the database.

LEAVE Access open for the next project.

Mastery Assessment

Project 7-5: Create a Query with Criteria

In your job as a travel agent at Erin's Travel, a client has asked you to provide a list of all the travel packages available to sporting events that start in the month of April or May. You will add criteria to a query to get this information from the database.

GET READY. LAUNCH Access if it is not already running.

1. **OPEN** *Sports Events* from the data files for this lesson.
2. Save the database as *Sports EventsXXX* (where *XXX* is your initials).
3. Open the Events query and switch to Design view.
4. Add criteria that will query the database and display all fields for all events that start between 4/1/2014 and 5/31/2014.
5. Use the Show row to hide the Start Date and End Date fields.
6. Run the query.
7. Close the query and **SAVE** the design changes when prompted.
8. **CLOSE** the database.

LEAVE Access open for the next project.

Project 7-6: Create a Parameter Query

Your brother, who owns Wingtip Toys, wants to pull data from his toy inventory and asks for your help in creating a query. He wants to query the database for toys for specific ages when prompted, so you show him how to create a parameter query.

GET READY. LAUNCH Access if it is not already running.

1. **OPEN** *Toys* from the data files for this lesson.
2. **SAVE** the database as *ToysXXX* (where *XXX* is your initials).
3. Create a simple query named **Inventory Query** that contains all the available fields in the Inventory table except the ID field.
4. Create a parameter query on the For Ages field that gives you the prompt shown in Figure 7-40 when the query is run.

Figure 7-40

Enter Parameter Value prompt

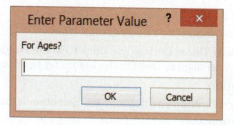

5. Query the database for all toys intended for ages **10–14 years**.
6. Close the query and **SAVE** when prompted.
7. **CLOSE** the database.

CLOSE Access.

Use Controls in Reports and Forms 8

LESSON SKILL MATRIX

Skill	Exam Objective	Objective Number
Adding Bound and Unbound Controls	Add report controls	5.2.5
	Format a Report: Insert images	5.3.8
	Format a Report: Insert page numbers	5.3.9
	Format a Report: Modify existing reports	5.3.11
	Format a Report: Insert headers and footers	5.3.7
	Format a Form: Insert headers and footers	4.3.8
	Format a Form: Insert images	4.3.9
	Set Report Controls: Manage labels	5.2.6
	Set Form Controls: Manage labels	4.2.6
	Remove form controls	4.2.4
	Format a Report: Add calculated fields	5.3.2
	Set form control properties	4.2.5
	Add form controls	4.2.2
	Set Form Controls: Modify data sources	4.2.3
	Move form controls	4.2.1
Defining Control Tab Order	Auto-order forms	4.3.7
	Modify tab order in forms	4.3.1
	Modify existing forms	4.3.10
Formatting Controls	Format a Form: Insert backgrounds	4.3.6
	Format a Report: Add backgrounds	5.3.4
Arranging Control Layout	Format reports into multiple columns	5.3.1
Arranging Control Alignment, Size, and Position		
Adjusting Page Margins and Changing Page Orientation for Forms and Reports	Format a Form: Format print layouts	4.3.2
	Format a Form: Change margins	4.3.5
	Format a Report: Set margins	5.3.3

© arredetimo/iStockphoto

KEY TERMS

- bound control
- calculated control
- conditional formatting
- control
- control layouts
- control tab order
- Control Wizard
- Expression Builder
- stacked layout
- tabular layout
- unbound control

© artedetimo/iStockphoto

Wingtip Toys is a mom-and-pop operation with fewer than 25 employees, many of whom craft the heirloom-style wooden toys that the company has sold successfully for more than 20 years. As the newly-hired marketing coordinator, you are learning every aspect of the business in order to market its products effectively. In this lesson, you will learn to add, format, and arrange controls on forms and reports that you can use to evaluate sales and inventory for the company.

SOFTWARE ORIENTATION

Design and Layout Tools for Reports and Forms

When you view a report in Design view, the Report Design Tools are displayed on the Ribbon. Similarly, when you view a report in Layout view, the Report Layout Tools are displayed on the Ribbon. Both the Report Design Tools and the Report Layout Tools contain a DESIGN contextual tab with groups of tools that are nearly identical, except for 4 additional commands that exist on the REPORT DESIGN TOOLS DESIGN contextual tab: Tab Order, Subreport in New Window, View Code, and Convert Report's Macros to Visual Basic. You can add controls to a report in both Design view and Layout view. The commands in the Controls, Header/Footer and Tools groups on the REPORT DESIGN TOOLS DESIGN contextual tab are shown in Figure 8-1. When you position the mouse pointer over a tool, Access will display the tool's name as a ScreenTip.

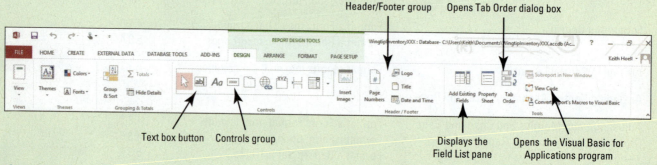

Figure 8-1

REPORT DESIGN TOOLS DESIGN contextual tab

When you view a form in Design view, the Form Design Tools are displayed on the Ribbon. Similarly, and like reports, when you view a form in Layout view, the Form Layout Tools are displayed on the Ribbon. Both the Form Design Tools menu and the Form Layout Tools menu contain a DESIGN contextual tab with nearly identical tools, except for 4 additional commands that exist on the FORM DESIGN TOOLS DESIGN contextual tab: Tab Order, Sub-form in New Window, View Code, and Convert Form's Macros to Visual Basic. Like reports, you can also add controls in form Layout view. The commands in the Controls, Header/Footer and Tools groups on the FORM LAYOUT TOOLS DESIGN contextual tab are shown in Figure 8-2. The procedures for adding controls to a form and a report are similar as well.

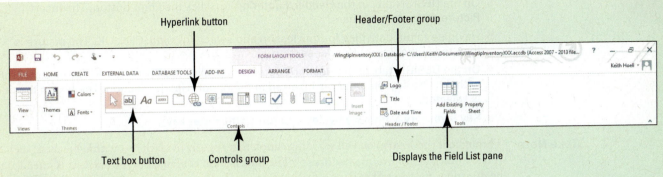

Figure 8-2

FORM LAYOUT TOOLS DESIGN contextual tab

Take Note   Although you'll be using the tools on the REPORT and FORM DESIGN TOOLS DESIGN contextual tabs in this lesson, it is still necessary to understand that the REPORT and FORM LAYOUT TOOLS DESIGN contextual tabs have almost identical tools that can be used in Layout view.

ADDING BOUND AND UNBOUND CONTROLS

The Bottom Line   A **control** is an object that displays data, performs actions, and lets you improve the look and usability of a form or report. Access uses three different types of controls: bound, unbound, and calculated. Controls add functionality to a report or form. For example, you can add a logo control to a report to enhance the look of the report or a list box control to allow users to choose from a list of items. You can insert bound, unbound, and calculated controls using the tools in the Controls and Header/Footer groups. The Use Control Wizards button, located in the Controls group, is helpful when creating some of the more complicated controls.

Adding Unbound Controls

An **unbound control** does not have a data source; it displays information such as lines, shapes, or pictures. Unbound controls are not connected to a field, but they display information that is important for reports and forms, some of which will appear in report and form header and footer sections, such as titles, dates, and page numbers. You can add both bound and unbound controls using the tools in the Controls group, or you can add unbound controls to the header and footer sections of reports and forms by using the Header/Footer group. In this exercise, you will use the tools in the Header/Footer group to add unbound controls to the Report Header section.

Take Note   The process for adding a control to a form and a report using the Header/Footer group is the same. Once shown how to add a control using the Header/Footer group to a report, you can add a similar control to a form in the same manner.

Add Unbound Controls

GET READY. Before you begin these steps, be sure to turn on and/or log on to your computer and **LAUNCH** Access.

1. **OPEN** *WingtipInventory* from the data files for this lesson.
2. **SAVE** the database as *WingtipInventoryXXX* (where *XXX* is your initials).
3. Double-click the **Toy Summary** report in the Navigation Pane.
4. On the HOME tab, in the Views group, click the lower half of the **View** button and select **Design View** from the menu.

5. On the DESIGN tab, in the Header/Footer group, click the Logo button. The Insert Picture dialog box appears.

6. Navigate to the data files for this lesson and select *Toys.jpg*. Click OK. The picture is inserted in the Report Header section.

7. On the DESIGN tab, in the Header/Footer group, click the Title button. The title control with the title Toy Summary is inserted in the Report Header section. The text in the title is selected.

8. Key Inventory Summary by Toy and [press the Enter key].

Take Note   Throughout this lesson you will see information that appears in black text within brackets, such as [Press Enter], or [your e-mail address]. The information contained in the brackets is intended to be directions for you rather than something you actually type word-for-word. It will instruct you to perform an action or substitute text. Do **not** type the actual text that appears within brackets.

9. On the DESIGN contextual tab, in the Header/Footer group, click the Date and Time button. The Date and Time dialog box appears, as shown in Figure 8-3.

Figure 8-3

Date and Time dialog box

10. Click OK to accept the default date and time formats. The Date and Time controls are inserted in the Report Header section of the report, as shown in Figure 8-4.

Figure 8-4

Report Header shown
in Design view

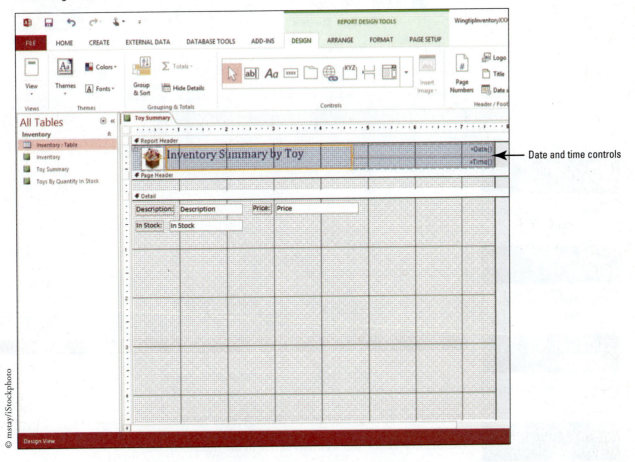

Date and time controls

© mstay/iStockphoto

11. On the DESIGN contextual tab, in the Header/Footer group, click the **Page Numbers** button. The Page Numbers dialog box appears, as shown in Figure 8-5.

Figure 8-5

Page Numbers dialog box

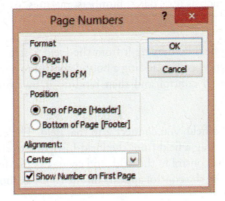

12. In the Position section of the Page Numbers dialog box, select the **Bottom of Page [Footer]** option then click **OK**. If necessary, scroll to the bottom of the report window. The Page number control is inserted in the Page Footer section near the bottom of the report, as shown in Figure 8-6.

Figure 8-6

Report shown with page number control in Design view

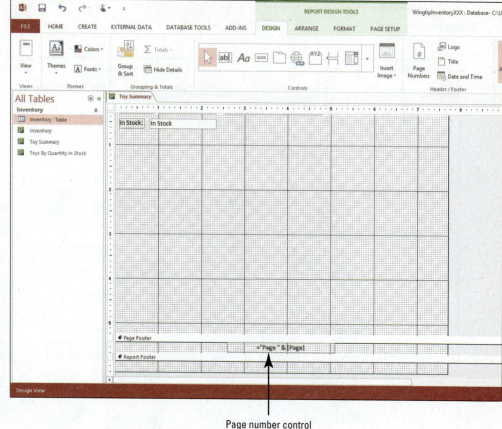

Page number control

13. Click the **Save** button on the Quick Access Toolbar.

PAUSE. LEAVE the report open to use in the next exercise.

Adding Bound Controls

A **bound control** uses a field in a table or query as the data source. Bound controls, such as text boxes, display information such as text, dates, numbers, pictures, or graphs from a field in a table or query.

You can bind a control to a field by moving it from the Field List pane or by using the Property Sheet. In this exercise, you will practice adding a bound control to a report by using the Field List pane and adding an unbound control and then binding it by using the Controls group and Property Sheet, respectively.

When you bind a control to a field, you connect it to that field. The easiest way to create a bound control is to double-click or drag a field from the Field List pane to the report. Access creates the appropriate control, binds the control to the field, and creates a label for the control. The control's label appears on the left, while the control appears on the right, as shown in Figure 8-7.

Figure 8-7

Control label and control

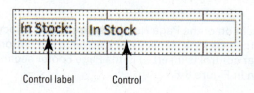

Control label   Control

 **Another Way**
You can also display the Field List pane by pressing ALT+F8.

You can display the Field List pane by clicking the Add Existing Fields button in the Tools group on the DESIGN contextual tab.

Another Way
You can also display the property sheet by clicking the control and pressing F4.

Another way to bind a control to a field is to first add an unbound text box to a report or form using the Controls group. Then, open its Property Sheet either by right-clicking and choosing Properties from the shortcut menu or by clicking the Property Sheet button in the Tools group on the DESIGN contextual tab. On the Property Sheet, in the DATA tab, click the down arrow beside the Control Source property and select the field you want to display in the control. You can then change the default text in the control's label to text that corresponds to the field to which the control is bound simply by clicking on the label and keying in the new name.

Take Note The process for changing a control's default label name for a report or a form is the same. Once shown how to change a label name for a report control, you can change a label name for a form control in the same manner.

Take Note The process for adding or removing a control to and from a form and a report is the same. Once shown how to add/remove a control to/from a report, you can add/remove a similar control to a form in the same manner.

When you click any button in the Controls group (except the Hyperlink and Insert Image buttons) the pointer changes to the move pointer with a plus sign (+). On the design grid, click where you want the upper-left portion of the control to start. Remember that a label will also be inserted, so leave enough space for the label. Click once to create a default-sized control, or click and drag the move pointer to create the size you want.

When you click the Hyperlink and Insert Image buttons in the Controls group, a dialog box appears requesting additional information before these unbound controls are created. For example, the Insert Hyperlink dialog box asks to which file or location you would like to link and the corresponding hyperlink text to display on the form or report. Similarly, the Insert Image button displays a submenu with two selections, one of which allows you to browse your computer for images to add to the report or form and the other of which allows you to view a gallery of images you have already included on your report or form so you may easily add them again.

You can use the Controls group to add other unbound controls like lines and page breaks to forms and reports. For example, you may want to use the line control to visually separate controls on a form to help it look more aesthetically pleasing or use the Insert Page Break control to create a report's title page by separating controls in the Report Header from the rest of the report.

To move a control and its label simultaneously, select the control and position the mouse pointer over the orange selection border until you see a four-sided arrow, then drag it to the new position.

To delete a control from the grid, select it, right-click the control to display the shortcut menu, and choose Delete.

STEP BY STEP **Add a Bound Control to a Report**

USE the database that is open from the previous exercise.

1. On the DESIGN contextual tab, in the Tools group, click the **Add Existing Fields** button. The Field List pane appears. Click the **Show all tables** link. The fields for the Inventory table appear, as shown in Figure 8-8.

Figure 8-8

Field List pane

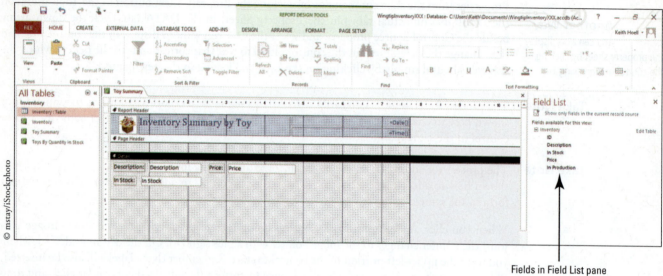

Fields in Field List pane

2. Click the **ID** field and drag it to the right of the Price control, as shown in Figure 8-9.

Figure 8-9

Bound control dragged from the Field List pane

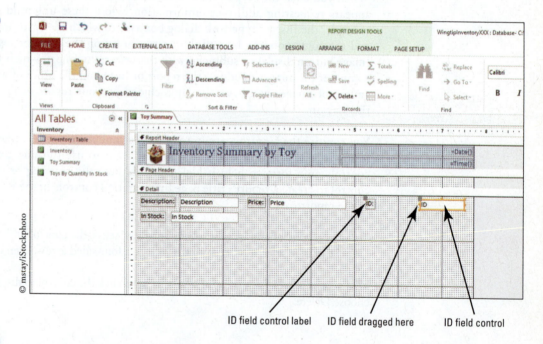

ID field control label   ID field dragged here   ID field control

CERTIFICATION
READY?   **4.2.6**

How do you manage form labels?

3. Drag the **In Production** field to the design grid below the ID control.

4. Click **Close** on the Field List pane.

5. Click the **ID field control** until you see the orange border with selection handles on the borders and corners.

6. Right-click in the control to display the shortcut menu.

7. Select **Delete** from the menu, as shown in Figure 8-10. The control and label are removed from the design grid.

Figure 8-10

Shortcut menu

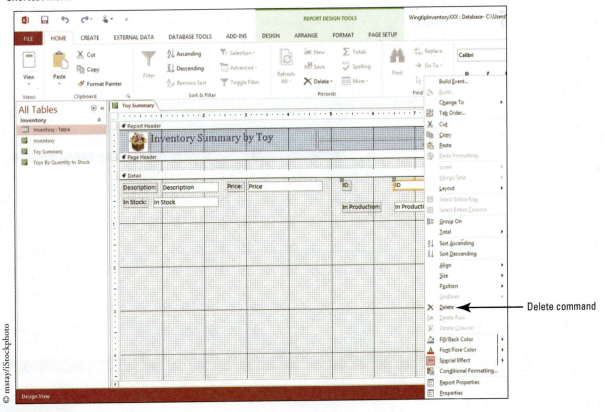

Delete command

CERTIFICATION READY?   4.2.4

How do you remove form controls?

Another Way

You can also use the arrow keys on the keyboard to move a control after it has been selected.

8. Select the **In Production** control, right-click, and select **Delete** from the menu.

9. On the DESIGN contextual tab, in the Controls group, click the **Text Box** button. The mouse pointer changes to the move pointer with a plus sign (+).

10. Position the pointer under the Price control and click to create the text box control as shown in Figure 8-11. If you need to move the control, select it and move the mouse pointer over the selection border until it appears as a four-sided pointer, then click and drag it to the appropriate location. Notice that the word Unbound is shown in the control and the word Text and a number (depending on the number of controls you have created in this session) appear in the label.

Figure 8-11

Unbound control

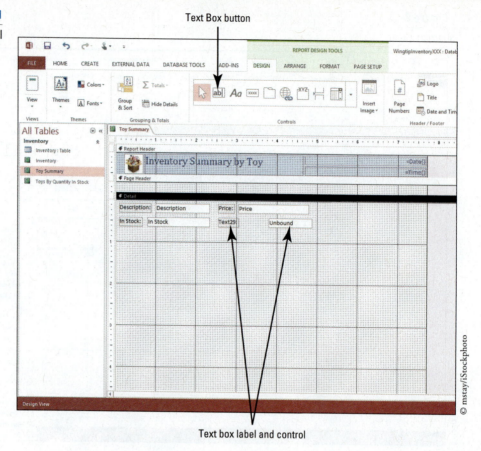

Text box label and control

11. Select the text box control if it isn't already selected.

12. On the DESIGN contextual tab, in the Tools group, click the **Property Sheet** button. The Property Sheet appears.

13. In the DATA tab, click the down arrow on the **Control Source** row and click the **In Production** field, as shown in Figure 8-12. Notice the control now displays the field name In Production, which means that it is now bound to the control.

Figure 8-12

Property Sheet pane

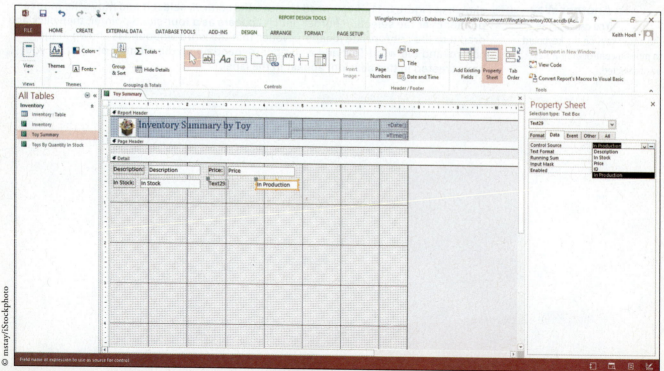

14. Click **Close** on the Property Sheet.

15. Click the **In Production** control label and select the text in the label.

16. Key **In Production:** and then [press **Enter**]. Your screen should look similar to Figure 8-13.

Figure 8-13

Bound control

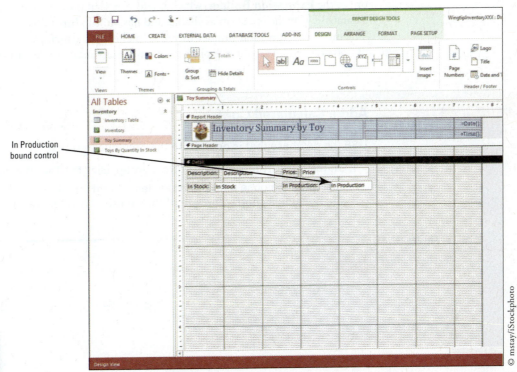

In Production
bound control

**CERTIFICATION
READY?**   **5.2.6**

How do you manage report
labels?

17. Switch to Report view to view your changes. When finished, switch back to Design view.

18. Click the **Save** button on the Quick Access Toolbar.

PAUSE. LEAVE the report open to use in the next exercise.

Take Note   The process for setting report control properties is the same for a form. Once shown how to set a report control property, you can set a form control property in the same manner.

Adding Calculated Controls

A **calculated control** is a control that displays the result of a calculation or expression. Calculated controls can display calculations that are vital to the usefulness of a report or form. For example, when your company needs to know the amount of sales dollars generated by each toy in a product line, you can multiply the number of toys sold by the price and display the value in a report or form. Text boxes are the most popular choice for a calculated control because they can display so many different types of data. However, any control that has a Control Source property can be used as a calculated control. In this exercise, you will use the Expression Builder to add a calculated control to a report.

An expression in Access is like a formula in Excel. An expression consists of the following elements used alone or in combination:

Identifiers: The names or properties of fields or controls

Operators: Such as + (addition), – (subtraction), or * (multiplication)

Functions: Such as SUM or AVG

Constants: Values that do not change, such as numbers that are not calculated

To create a calculated control, you can either key an expression in the Control Source property box or use the **Expression Builder**, which is a feature that provides names of the fields and controls in a database, lists the operators available, and has built-in functions to help you create an expression. The intuitive Expression Builder includes IntelliSense, which presents you with a drop-down box of potential values as you're typing an identifier or function name to create your expression.

STEP BY STEP   **Add a Calculated Control**

USE the database that is open from the previous exercise.

1. On the DESIGN tab, in the Controls group, click the **Text Box** button.
2. Position the mouse pointer on the design grid and drag down and to the right to create and position a control the size of the one shown in Figure 8-14.

Figure 8-14

Text box control

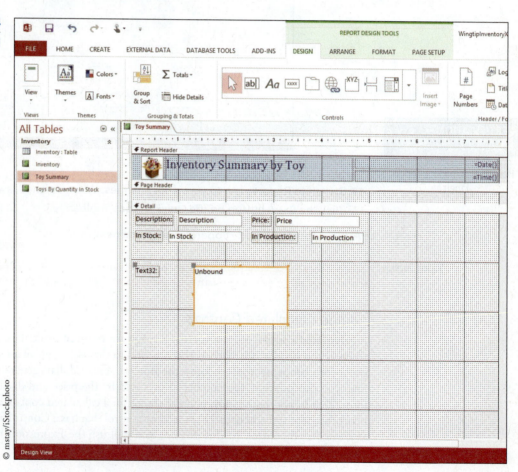

© mstay/iStockphoto

3. With the control selected, right-click it to display the shortcut menu.
4. Select **Properties** from the menu to display the Property Sheet if it isn't already displayed.
5. On the DATA tab, in the Control Source row, click the **Build** button. The Expression Builder dialog box appears.
6. In the Expression Categories list, scroll down and double-click **In Stock**, as shown in Figure 8-15. The In Stock field is inserted in the expression box.

Take Note   All the list items in the Expression Categories on your screen may not match exactly to the figure shown.

Figure 8-15

Expression Builder

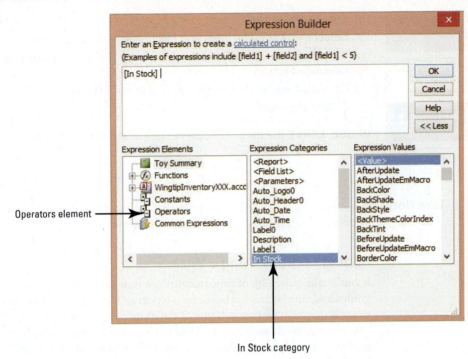

Figure 8-15

Expression Builder

Operators element ——→

In Stock category

7. In the Expression Elements section, click the **Operators** element, then double-click the * **asterisk** value in the Expression Values section to select the multiplication operator.

8. In the Expression Elements section, click the **Toy Summary** element, then find and double-click the **Price** field in the Expression Categories section.

9. Click **OK**. The expression appears in the Control Source row of the Property Sheet as well as in the control box in the Detail section of the report, as shown in Figure 8-16.

Figure 8-16

Expression in Control Source row

Expression in Control Source row of Property Sheet

Expression in control box

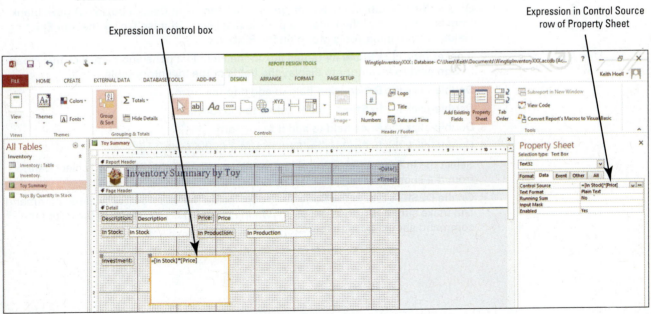

© mstay/iStockphoto

CERTIFICATION READY? 5.3.2

How do you add calculated fields to a report?

CERTIFICATION READY? 4.2.5

How do you set form control properties?

10. Click **Close** on the Property Sheet.
11. Select the text in the label and key **Investment:**.
12. Switch to Report view and scroll through the report records to view the calculated totals.
13. Click the **Save** button on the Quick Access Toolbar.
14. **CLOSE** the report.

PAUSE. LEAVE the database open to use in the next exercise.

Take Note   It is often easiest to add and arrange all the bound controls first, and then add the unbound and calculated controls to complete the design of the report.

Adding Controls Using a Wizard

It could take quite a bit of time to figure out how to set all the properties necessary to create option groups and combo and list boxes for a report or form. To speed up this task, Access 2013 includes wizards that help you create some of the more complicated controls. A **Control Wizard** can help you create controls such as command buttons, list boxes, combo boxes, and option groups. Some of these types of controls can modify underlying table data sources. For example, after you add a combo box to a form, you can use it to select a value to be stored in an underlying table field. In this exercise, you add a combo box to a form using the Control Wizard.

Like other wizards you have used, a Control Wizard asks you questions about how you want the control to look and operate, and then it creates the control based on your answers. The Control Wizard's button is a toggle button that you can click to activate and deactivate wizards on controls that use them.

STEP BY STEP   **Use the Control Wizard**

USE the database that is open from the previous exercise.

1. On the CREATE tab, in the Forms group, click the **Form Design** button. A new, blank form is created, and the Field List pane is displayed. (If it isn't, click the **Add Existing Fields** button in the Tools group on the Ribbon.)
2. If necessary, click **Show all tables** link in the Field List pane and then click the **expand** button next to Inventory to display the fields of the Inventory table.
3. Double-click the **Description** field to add it to the form.
4. Double-click the **In Stock** field to add it to the form.
5. Double-click the **Price** field to add it to the form.
6. Double-click the **In Production** field to add it to the form.
7. Select the **In Production** control that you just added, right-click it and select **Delete** from the shortcut menu.
8. On the DESIGN tab, in the Controls group, locate the **Use Control Wizards** command and make sure it is turned on, as shown in Figure 8-17. The image to the left of the command should be highlighted.

Figure 8-17

Control Wizards command

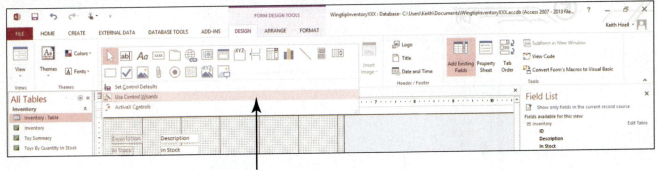

Use Control Wizards command
selected in Controls group

9. On the DESIGN tab, in the Controls group, locate and click the Combo Box button (hover your mouse pointer over each control button to view its ScreenTip until you find the Combo Box button).

10. Position the mouse pointer and drag to draw a rectangle, as shown in Figure 8-18.

Combo box button

Figure 8-18

Drag to draw a custom control

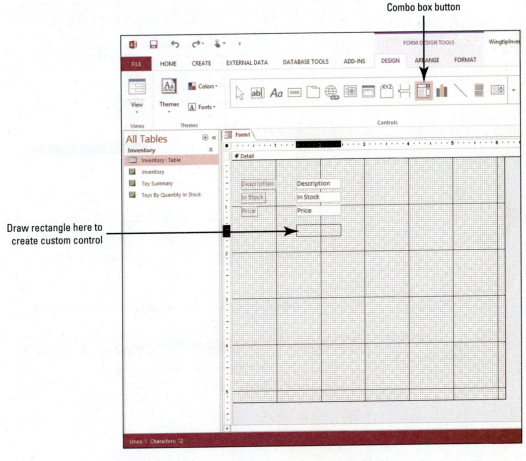

Draw rectangle here to
create custom control

11. When you release the mouse button, the Combo Box Wizard appears. Click the button beside *I will type in the values that I want* and click Next>. In the empty cell below the Col1 header, key Yes. Continue keying values in the column as shown in Figure 8-19 using the down arrow key to move to the next row.

Figure 8-19

Combo Box Wizard

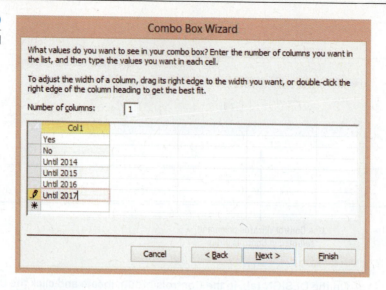

12. Click **Next >**.
13. Click the button beside *Store that value in this field* and click the **down arrow** to display the menu. Select **In Production** from the menu, as shown in Figure 8-20.

Figure 8-20

Combo Box Wizard store
values screen

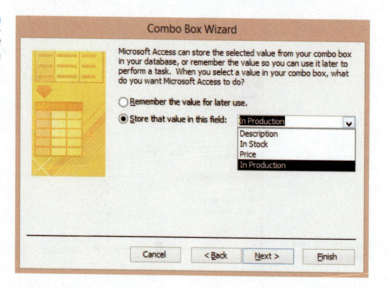

14. Click **Next >**.
15. Key **In Production** in the text box, as shown in Figure 8-21.

Figure 8-21

Combo Box Wizard
label screen

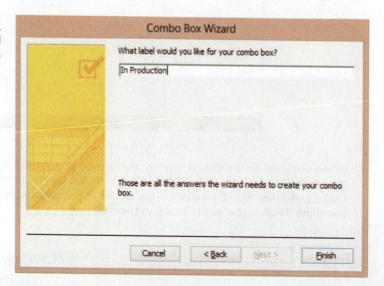

16. Click **Finish**. Your screen should look similar to Figure 8-22.

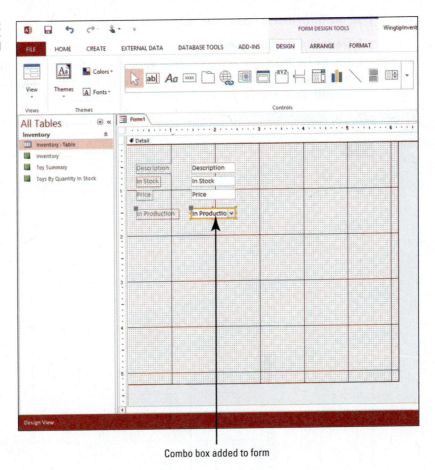

Combo box added to form

Take Note   *A combo box is also known as a drop-down control, because it is a combination of a text box with a list box that is hidden until you select the arrow next to the text box and it drops down.*

17. Switch to Form view, scroll through the records, and modify the In Production field by selecting an item in the combo box for one or more records.

18. Click the **Save** button on the Quick Access Toolbar and **SAVE** the form as **Inventory**.

PAUSE. LEAVE the form open to use in the next exercise.

Adding Button Controls Using the Wizard

You can also use Control Wizards to add Button controls to forms. Button controls can be created by using the Command Button wizard and can be assigned certain tasks that are created by macros. Macros are useful since they add additional functionality to a database by automating a series of tasks to create an action. For example, Button controls can be created on a form to perform many different actions, including moving to the next or previous record, displaying the Print dialog box, or closing the form. The code that enables this functionality is automatically created as a macro by the Command Button wizard. In this exercise, you will create a Button control using the Command Button Wizard and use the View Code button to open the Visual Basic for Applications program.

You can further customize the function of database controls and even objects by viewing and modifying their code using a programming language called Visual Basic for Applications (VBA). You can click the View Code button in the Tools group of the DESIGN tab to open the VBA program. The VBA program is built into Access and provides you with an interface to write and modify code associated with database controls and objects. You can really harness the power of Access 2013 by directly interacting with controls and objects via VBA.

STEP BY STEP   Use the Control Wizard to Add Button Controls

USE the form that is open from the previous exercise.

1. Switch to Design view, if necessary.
2. On the DESIGN tab, in the Controls group, click the **Button** button.
3. Position the mouse pointer on the design grid and drag down and to the right to create a control the size of the one shown in Figure 8-23.

Figure 8-23

Button control

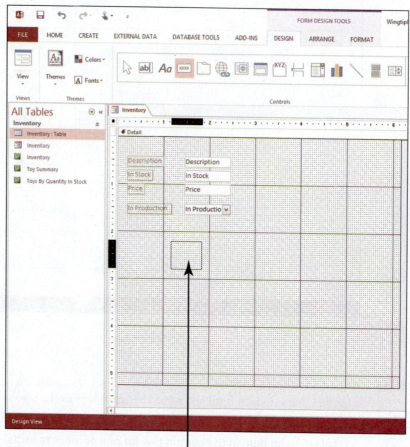

Draw square here to create Button control

4. When you release the mouse button, the Command Button Wizard appears. In the Categories: section, click **Form Operations**, and in the Actions: section click **Close Form**, as shown in Figure 8-24.

Figure 8-24

Command Button Wizard, screen 1

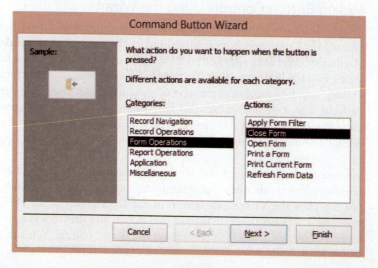

5. Click **Next >**.

6. On the next screen, keep the default settings to have the button contain the Exit Doorway picture displayed in the dialog box, as shown in Figure 8-25.

Figure 8-25

Command Button
Wizard, screen 2

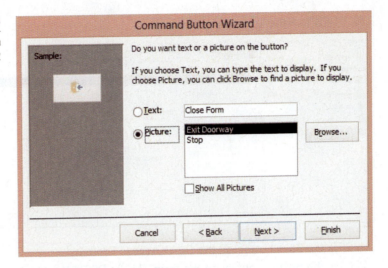

7. Click **Next >**.

8. On the final screen, key **Exit_Inventory_Form** as the default button name, as shown in Figure 8-26, and click **Finish**. (The default button name indicated on your screen may differ depending on how many controls you have previously attempted to include.)

Figure 8-26

Command Button Wizard,
final screen

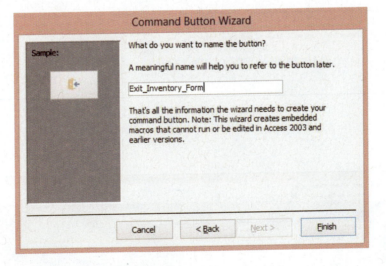

9. Notice that the image on the Button control on the form has changed to the Exit Doorway picture.

10. Click the **In Production** control and move your pointer over the control's border until it appears as a four-sided arrow, then drag the control so it is positioned on the form as shown in Figure 8-27, if necessary.

Figure 8-27

Figure 8-27

Inventory Form in Design view

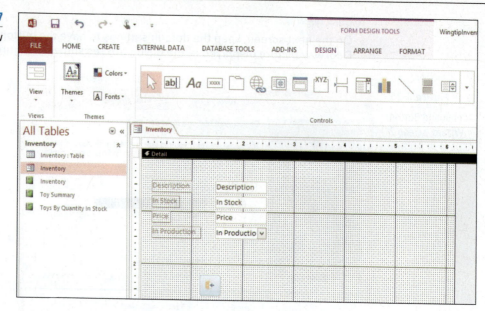

11. Click the **Save** button on the Quick Access Toolbar.

12. Click the **Button** control on the form. On the DESIGN tab, in the Tools group, click the **View Code** button, as shown in Figure 8-28. The Microsoft Visual Basic for Applications window appears, as shown in Figure 8-29. If you're fluent in Visual Basic for Applications (VBA), you can use this window to add VBA code to customize the function of this control.

Figure 8-28

View Code button in Tools group

View Code button

Figure 8-29

Microsoft Visual Basic for Applications window

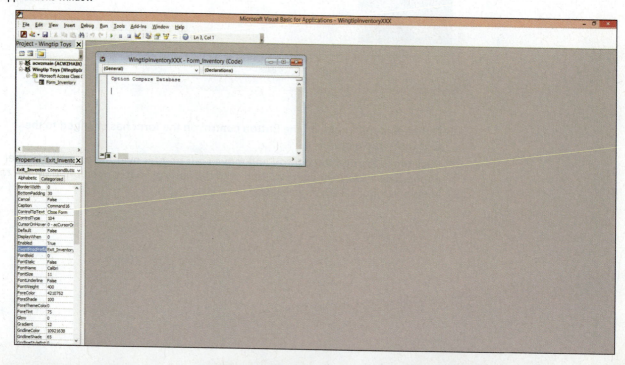

13. Click the **Close** button on the Visual Basic for Applications window to return to Access.
14. Switch to Form view and click the newly created **Close Form** button to close the form. If a dialog box appears asking you if you want to **SAVE** the changes to the form, click **Yes**.

PAUSE. LEAVE the database open to use in the next exercise.

CERTIFICATION READY?   4.2.3

How do you modify data sources?

CERTIFICATION READY?   4.2.1

How do you move form controls?

The Bottom Line

DEFINING CONTROL TAB ORDER

When you are in Form or Report view, pressing the Tab key moves the selection, or focus, to the next field. **Control tab order** refers to the order in which the selection, or focus, moves from field to field in a form or report. When entering data in a form, it is helpful to set the control tab order to a sequence that matches the order of the data you are entering. It's also helpful to set the tab order of a report to a logical field sequence when reviewing report records. In this way, you can efficiently concentrate on meaningful data as you use the change of focus as a guide. In this exercise, you will define form control tab order.

Another Way
You can also right-click the design grid in Design view to access the Tab Order dialog box.

You can change the tab order using the Tab Order dialog box, which is located in the Tools group of both the REPORT DESIGN TOOLS and FORM DESIGN TOOLS DESIGN tabs. The Tab Order dialog box lists each section of the report or form and the tab order of the fields in each section. Click the selection button to the left of each row in the Custom Order list to select the row. You can drag the rows into the tab order you want, from top to bottom. The Auto Order button places the fields in the order that they appear on the form or report, from top to bottom, left to right.

STEP BY STEP   **Define Control Tab Order**

USE the database you used in the previous exercise.

1. Open the **Inventory** form in Form view.
2. [Press the **Tab** key] several times to see the order in which the controls are selected each time you press it. Notice that the tab order begins with the Description field, then moves to the In Stock field, the Price field, the In Production field, and the Close Form button. The tab order then continues to the next record in sequence and through the same fields as before.
3. Switch to Design view.
4. On the DESIGN tab, in the Tools group, click the **Tab Order** button. The Tab Order dialog box appears, displaying the tab order in the Custom Order list, as shown in Figure 8-30. Notice the In Production combo box field is referred to as Combo10 since Access stores this name to use as a coding reference in Visual Basic for Applications. (You may have a different name, depending on how many controls you have had and removed previously on the form.)

Figure 8-30

Tab Order dialog box

Row selector

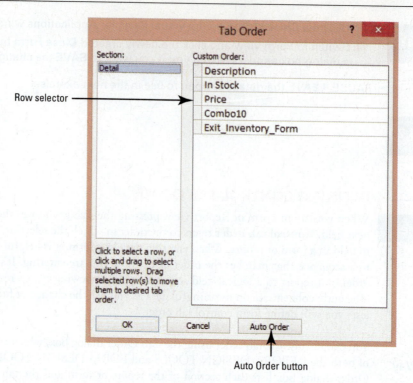

Auto Order button

5. Click the **row selector** to the left of the Combo10 field to select it.

6. Click and hold the **row selector**. The mouse pointer changes to a move pointer with an empty rectangle. Drag up a row and notice the black horizontal line moves with you. Drag up until the black horizontal line is in place at the top of the Description field; release the mouse button. The Combo10 field should be the first item in the list, as shown in Figure 8-31.

Figure 8-31

New order in the Tab Order dialog box

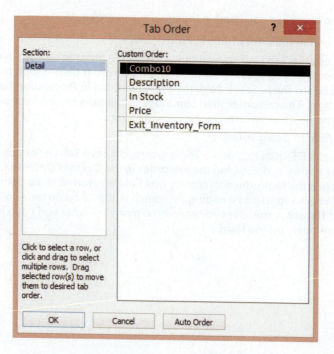

7. Click the **Auto Order** button. The order of the fields automatically resets based on the order that they appear on the form or report.

8. Click the **row selector** to the left of the Combo10 field to select it. Click and hold the **row selector** and drag it up until the black horizontal line is in place above the In Stock field; release the mouse button. The Combo10 field should now be the second item in the list, as shown in Figure 8-32.

Figure 8-32

Final order in the Tab Order
dialog box

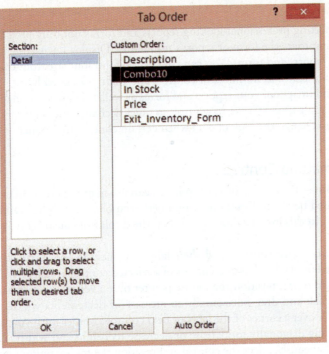

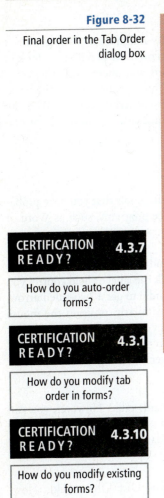

CERTIFICATION READY?   4.3.7

How do you auto-order forms?

CERTIFICATION READY?   4.3.1

How do you modify tab order in forms?

CERTIFICATION READY?   4.3.10

How do you modify existing forms?

9. Click **OK**.
10. **SAVE** the form design.
11. Switch to Form view.
12. [Press the **Tab** key] several times to see the new tab order.
13. **CLOSE** the form.

PAUSE. LEAVE the database open to use in the next exercise.

SOFTWARE ORIENTATION

REPORT DESIGN TOOLS FORMAT Tab

When you are working with reports, the FORMAT tab is located in the Report Design Tools. It contains groups of commands used to format reports, as shown in Figure 8-33. Refer to this figure in the following section and throughout the book.

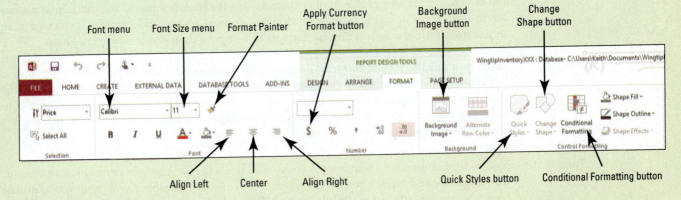

Figure 8-33

FORMAT tab in Report Design Tools

When you are working with forms, the FORMAT tab contains the same groups of commands and is available in the Form Layout Tools. Use these common formatting commands to change the display of controls and their labels in forms and reports.

FORMATTING CONTROLS

The Bottom Line

Formatting professional-looking reports and forms not only projects a high-quality image, but it also improves the form or report's readability. Display formatting allows you to refine the look of your reports and forms. You can change the font, font size, font color, alignment, and other attributes of text and numbers in controls and their associated labels. You can also change the background images of your reports and forms as well as change the shapes of certain controls. You can even apply Quick Styles to controls to quickly change their appearance or use conditional formatting to change the look of data when certain conditions are met.

Formatting Controls

To format the display of a control, you can use many of the formatting tools that you have probably used before to format text, numbers, and objects in other Office programs, such as Word or Excel. In this exercise, you will format the display of controls on a report.

You can resize controls and their labels by clicking the resize handles, which are tiny squares located on the borders and corners of a selected control or label. Click the label or field control you want to resize, position the mouse pointer over a vertical border handle to get a two-sided arrow, and click and drag horizontally to increase or decrease its width. Similarly, position the mouse pointer over a corner of the label or field control's border until you get a diagonal arrow, then click and drag diagonally to increase or decrease its height and width. To move a control and its label simultaneously, select the control and position the mouse pointer over the orange selection border until you see a four-sided arrow, then drag to the new position.

Controls on forms and reports display the format applied to the source table. However, you can change the display formatting for each control and label on a form or report. Your changes will only affect each control and the way the data appears. It does not change how users enter data or how data is stored.

Take Note   You cannot apply visual formats to controls bound to Attachment and OLE Object fields. However, you can change the format of the label associated with the control.

You can format a control in Design view or Layout view using the commands in the Font group. You can change the font as well as the size, color, alignment, and background color of text. You can also add bold, underline, and italics. The Format Painter button copies formats so that you can easily apply the same formatting to another control.

The Background group allows you to insert a background image into your form or report or alternate row colors to help make the form or report more visually appealing.

You can change the format of a number control using the Number group. You can format a number to include dollar signs, increase or decrease decimal places, add commas, percentages, or choose from a list of standard number formats by using the drop-down box in the group.

Lastly, you can also format controls using the commands in the Control Formatting group. You can apply Quick Styles, change the shape of a control, apply shape effects to quickly change the appearance of certain controls like button controls, and change the fill and outline color of controls. You can even use conditional formatting to change the look of the data that appears in a control when certain conditions are met.

Take Note   By default, text does not automatically wrap when it reaches the edge of a control box. It remains on a single line and extends beyond the edges of the control. To enable text wrapping in a form or report, set the height to a non-default size and change the CanGrow and CanShrink properties for the control to Yes. By default, a control's label box will expand to include the entire label.

| STEP BY STEP | Format Controls on a Report |

USE the database that is open from the previous exercise.

1. Open the **Toy Summary** report and switch to Design view.

2. Click the **In Stock** control. Position the mouse pointer over the resize handle on the right border. The mouse pointer changes to a double-sided arrow. Using the horizontal ruler at the top of the report as a guide, drag to the left to resize the control until its right side is at the $1^{6/8}$" mark.

3. In the same manner, reduce the width of the Price control until its right side is at the horizontal ruler's 4" mark.

4. In the same manner, reduce the size of the Investment control until its right side is at the horizontal ruler's $2^{1/2}$" mark and its bottom is at the vertical ruler's $1^{1/2}$" mark.

5. Click the **Description** control to select it.

6. On the FORMAT tab, in the Font group, click the **Bold** button. The Description control displays bold.

7. Click the arrow on the Font Size menu and select **12** from the menu. The font size becomes 12.

8. Click the **In Stock** control to select it.

9. On the FORMAT tab, in the Font group, click the **Center** button. The In Stock text becomes centered in the control box. Your report should look similar to Figure 8-34.

Figure 8-34

Report with display formatting applied

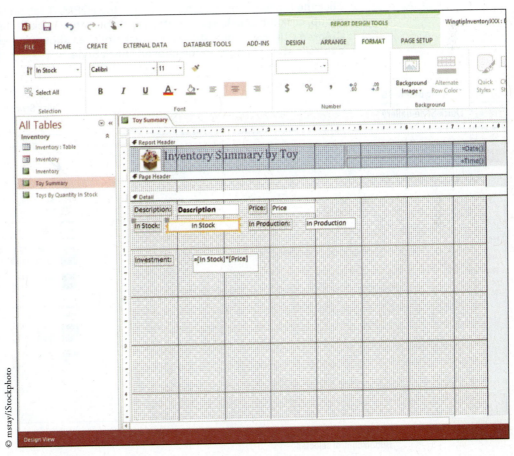

10. Click the **Investment** control that contains the formula you entered in an earlier exercise.

11. On the FORMAT tab, in the Number group, click the **Apply Currency Format** command.

12. Click the **Price** control.

13. On the FORMAT tab, in the Number group, click the **Apply Currency Format** command.

14. **SAVE** the report.

15. Switch to Report view to see the changes you've made. Notice the text formatting changes as well as the currency formats for the Investment and Price fields.

16. **CLOSE** the report.

17. **OPEN** the Toys By Quantity In Stock report in Design view.

18. In the Report Header section, click the Print Report Button control to select it.

19. On the FORMAT tab, in the Control Formatting group, click the Change Shape button to display the menu. Click the Oval option. The Button control's shape changes to an oval.

20. **SAVE** and **CLOSE** the report.

PAUSE. LEAVE the database open to use in the next exercise.

Formatting Controls on a Form

In this exercise, you will learn how to format the display of controls on a form and include a background image.

Format the Controls on a Form

USE the database that is open from the previous exercise.

1. Open the Inventory form if it's not open already, and switch to Design view.

2. Click the Button control on the form. On the FORMAT tab, in the Control Formatting group, click the Quick Styles button to display the Quick Styles gallery. Click the Colored Outline – Aqua, Accent 5 Quick Style, as shown in Figure 8-35. The Button control's style changes to the chosen Quick Style.

Figure 8-35

Quick Style gallery

Quick Styles button and gallery

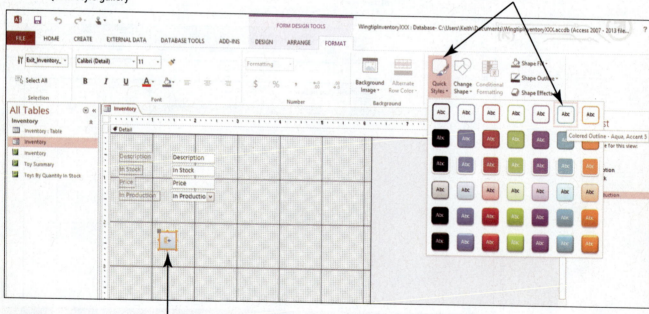

Button control selected

3. Click the Description label to select it.

4. On the FORMAT tab, in the Font group, click the Font Color button and click Black from the Theme Colors menu. The Description label displays in black. Change the font color to black for the In Stock, Price, and In Production labels. Your screen should resemble Figure 8-36.

Figure 8-36

Color of labels changed
to black

Label colors
changed to black

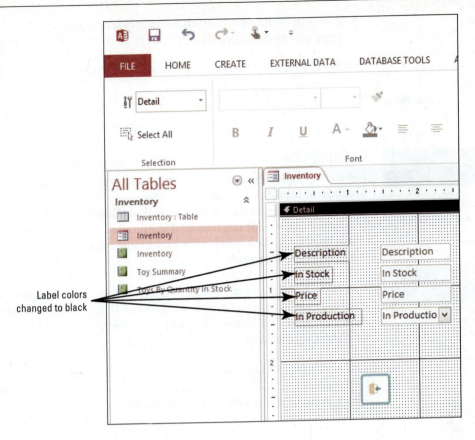

5. On the FORMAT tab, in the Background group, click the **Background Image** button and click the **Browse** command to locate the ***Winter Theme Background.jpg*** image file and click **OK**. Notice the form's background image is now that of the image, as shown in Figure 8-37.

Figure 8-37

Form with background image

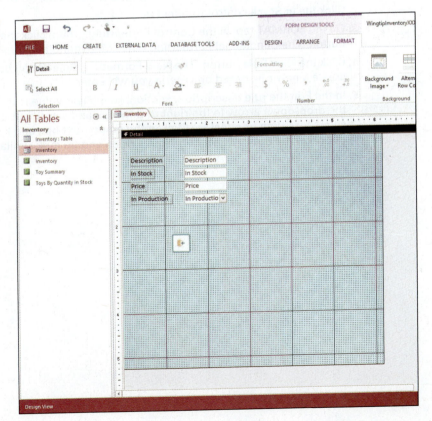

6. Switch to Form view to see the changes you made.

7. SAVE and **CLOSE** the form.

PAUSE. LEAVE the database open to use in the next exercise.

The process for adding a background image to a form or a report is the same. Once shown how to add a background image to a form, you can add a background image to a report in the same manner.

Creating Conditional Formatting on Controls

Sometimes employees need a little help recognizing when inventory is low or when sales are high. Conditional formatting in forms and reports helps alert users to text or numbers that need attention so that important data is not overlooked. **Conditional formatting** changes the appearance of a control or the value in a control when certain conditions are met. You can change the color of text or numbers in the control or the background color. In this exercise, you will create conditional formatting for a report field.

You can create conditional formatting based on a value or expression. For example, when the number of products in an inventory falls below 10 for a single product, you can set the conditional formatting so that Access will display the number in red or with a red background so that you and others will notice the low inventory number.

The easiest way to add conditional formatting to a form or report is by using the Conditional Formatting Rules Manager dialog box, which displays a list of the existing formatting rules, if any. Here you can add new rules and edit or delete existing rules.

STEP BY STEP   **Create Conditional Formatting**

USE the database you used in the previous exercise.

1. Open the **Toy Summary** report, if necessary, and switch to Design view.
2. Click the **In Stock** control to select it.
3. On the FORMAT tab, in the Control Formatting group, click the **Conditional Formatting** button. The Conditional Formatting Rules Manager dialog box appears.
4. Click the **New Rule** button. The New Formatting Rule dialog box appears. You will create a new rule based on criteria you will enter.
5. In the Edit the rule description: section, keep Field Value Is in the first menu. Click the drop-down arrow to the right of *between* and scroll to the bottom of the list to select **less than or equal to**. Click in the empty text box and key **10**. Click the **Bold** button in the Preview: section. Your screen should look similar to Figure 8-38.

Figure 8-38

New Formatting Rule
dialog box

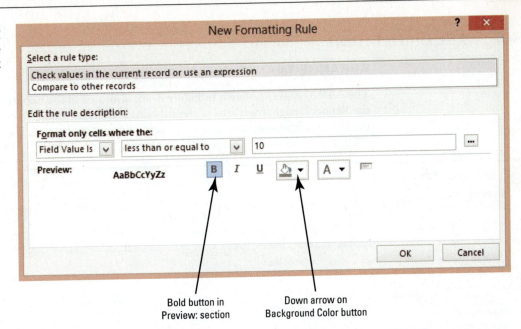

Figure 8-38

New Formatting Rule
dialog box

6. Click the down arrow on the **Background Color** button. A menu of colors appears. Click **Red**.

7. Click the **OK** button. A formatting rule for the In Stock field is added to the dialog box, as shown in Figure 8-39. Now, when the report is viewed in Report view, the value for the In Stock field will appear bold and the control background color will appear red if the formatting rule applies.

Figure 8-39

Formatting rule for the In
Stock field

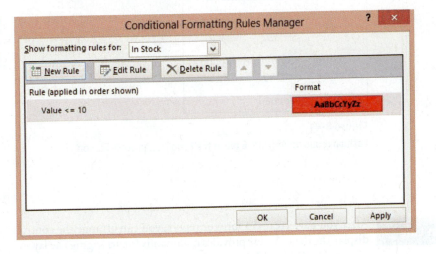

8. Click **OK**.

9. **SAVE** the report.

10. Switch to Report view and scroll through the records to see the conditional formatting at work.

11. **CLOSE** the report.

PAUSE. LEAVE the database open to use in the next exercise.

SOFTWARE ORIENTATION

ARRANGE Tab

The ARRANGE tab, shown in Figure 8-40, is located in the Report Layout Tools as well as the Report Design Tools area of the Ribbon. It contains groups of commands for arranging the layout, alignment, size, and position of controls on a report. Use the commands on the ARRANGE tab to arrange controls on a report.

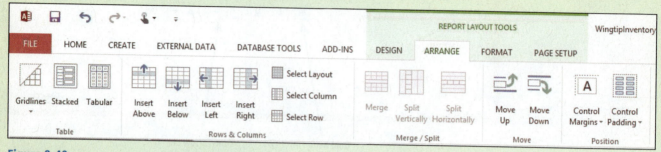

Figure 8-40

ARRANGE tab in the Report Layout Tools Ribbon

Similar to a report, the ARRANGE tab is displayed in both the Form Layout Tools and Form Design Tools area of the Ribbon. The buttons and commands on the ARRANGE tab are the same as the ARRANGE tab for reports, except for the Anchoring button located in the Position group. The Position group, shown in Figure 8-41, contains an Anchoring button that helps position controls on a form when the containing window is resized. Use the commands on the ARRANGE tab to arrange controls on a form.

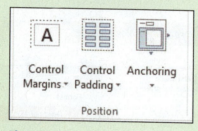

Figure 8-41

Position group on ARRANGE tab in the Form Design Tools Ribbon

ARRANGING CONTROL LAYOUT

The Bottom Line

After you have created a form or report, you can arrange the controls on it to fit the data or to best display the data. Access provides commands for arranging the layout, alignment, position, and size of controls. **Control layouts** align your controls horizontally and vertically to give your report or form a uniform appearance. The two types of control layouts are tabular and stacked. Controls are arranged vertically in a **stacked layout**, with a label on the left and the control on the right. Stacked layouts are contained in one report or form section. In a **tabular layout**, the controls are arranged in rows and columns like a spreadsheet, with labels across the top. Tabular layouts use two sections of a report or form. The labels are displayed in one section and the fields are arranged in the section below. In this exercise, you will arrange controls on a report using control layouts.

You can have more than one layout on a report. For example, you could have a tabular layout to create a row of data for each record, then a stacked layout underneath with more information about the same record.

Access automatically creates tabular control layouts when you create a new report using the Report button or the Blank Report button on the CREATE tab. When you create a new form using the Form button or the Blank Form button, Access creates stacked control layouts.

On an existing blank report, you can create a new control layout by holding down the Shift key and selecting the fields you want to include in the form or report from the Field List pane. On the ARRANGE tab, in the Table group, click the Stacked button or the Tabular button.

You can switch the entire layout of a report or form to the other layout by selecting all the cells in the layout and then clicking the layout button you want, either Stacked or Tabular.

You can also split a control layout into two different layouts. Hold down the Shift key and click the controls you want to move to the new control layout and click the Tabular or Stacked button.

STEP BY STEP **Arrange Control Layout**

USE the database that is open from the previous exercise.

1. Click the **Inventory** table in the Navigation Pane to select it.
2. On the CREATE tab, in the Reports group, click the **Blank Report** button. A new, blank report is created and the Field List pane is displayed. (If it isn't, click the **Add Existing Fields** button in the Tools group on the DESIGN tab.)
3. Double-click the **ID** field to add it to the report.
4. Double-click the **Description** field to add it to the report.
5. Double-click the **In Stock** field to add it to the report.
6. Double-click the **Price** field to add it to the report.
7. [Press and hold the **Shift** key] and click each of the **four controls** to select them all. Make sure you select the controls and not the labels, as shown in Figure 8-42.

Figure 8-42

Selected report controls

Selected controls

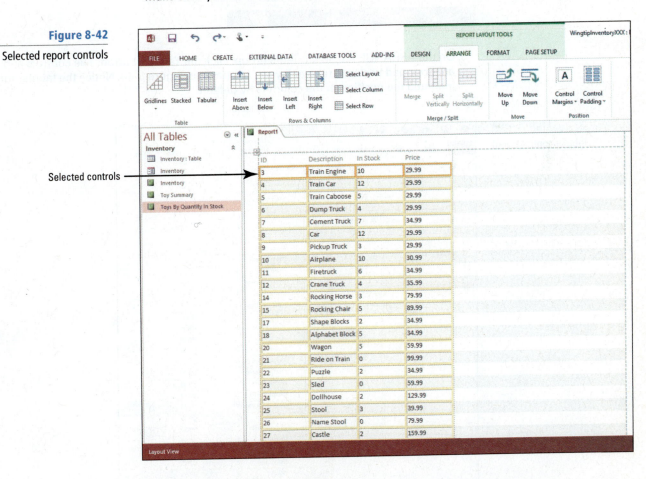

8. On the ARRANGE tab, in the Table group, click the **Stacked** button. The controls and labels are arranged in a 2-column stacked layout, as shown in Figure 8-43.

Figure 8-43

Stacked control layout

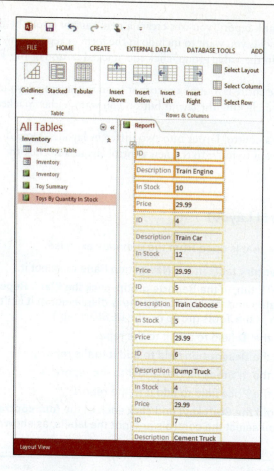

Figure 8-43

Stacked control layout

9. On the ARRANGE tab, in the Table group, click the Tabular button. The controls and labels are arranged back in a tabular layout, as shown in Figure 8-44. Notice the tabular format indented the position of the columns by default.

Figure 8-44

Tabular control layout

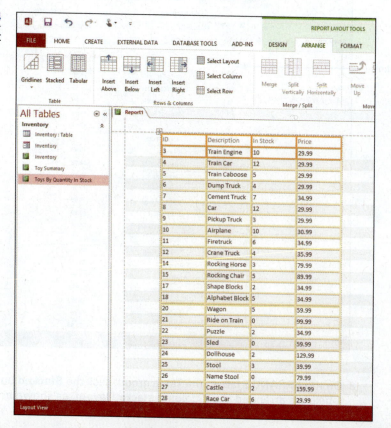

10. On the ARRANGE tab, in the Table group, click the **Stacked** button to switch it back to a stacked layout.

11. **SAVE** the report as **Stacked Report** and leave it open for use in the next exercise.

PAUSE. LEAVE the database open to use in the next exercise.

By using the tools in the various groups on the ARRANGE tab, Access 2013 gives you even greater flexibility over arranging and controlling the cells in control layouts.

By using the tools in the Rows & Columns group, you can add new rows and columns of cells above and below existing cell rows and to the left and right of existing cell columns. By using the tools in the Merge/Split group, you can merge two cells into one, as well as split them vertically and horizontally. The tools in the Move group can be used to reorganize cells by moving them up or down.

You can adjust the location of information displayed in a control in relation to the control's border with the Control Margins button in the Position group. You can choose the None, Narrow, Medium, or Wide setting in the Control Margins menu.

The Control Padding button adjusts the amount of space between a label and its field control. The Control Padding menu contains choices for None, Narrow, Medium, or Wide padding.

The Position group also contains the Anchoring button and menu. The Anchoring button only appears in the Form Layout Tools and Form Design Tools ARRANGE tab in the Position group since the anchoring option is only available for forms and not reports. Anchoring can be used so that control sizes automatically increase or decrease when the Access window size is increased or decreased. You may never have to anchor a control since most of the time you will keep the Access window a consistent size. Anchoring is helpful when you want to control the position of the controls on a form when the Access window is increased. If anchoring is not applied, controls that contain more text than visible within the default size will remain the default size even when the Access window is made larger. When you anchor a field control in a layout, the newly anchored field and all the others grow when the Access window size is increased to display more field data, if applicable. Anchoring is best used on fields that contain a large amount of text like those with the Long Text data type. For example, you can anchor a Notes field control to stretch down and to the right as you increase the size of the Access window. This allows you to see more text within the field control in the larger Access window, including text you'd normally not see if you didn't anchor it. Field controls that are not anchored will remain the default size even if you increased the Access window size, hiding the excess text. Once a control is anchored, all other controls in the layout will behave the same way. You can only have one anchored control in a Stacked or Tabular layout, but many anchored controls with different anchoring options if they're not in a specific layout.

Add, Move, and Remove a Control

When you want to add a new field from the Field List to an existing control layout, just drag the field from the Field List pane to the grid. To add it to the layout, select all the controls in the layout and the new control and click the Stacked or Tabular button to integrate the new field into the control layout. Removing a control from a control layout allows you to place it anywhere on the report or form without affecting the positioning of any other controls. Click the control you want to remove and click Remove Layout from the Table group. The Remove Layout button is only available in the Table group in report or form Design view. In this exercise, you will add and move controls within a layout and remove a control from a layout.

STEP BY STEP   **Add, Move, and Remove a Control from a Layout**

USE the database that is open from the previous exercise.

1. Switch to Report Design view, if necessary.

2. Click the **Show all tables** link in the Field List pane, if necessary, to view all the available fields in the Inventory table.

3. Click the **In Production** field in the Field List pane. Drag it to the grid and place it in any location on the design grid to the right of the four controls. Your screen should look similar to Figure 8-45.

Figure 8-45

Report Design view

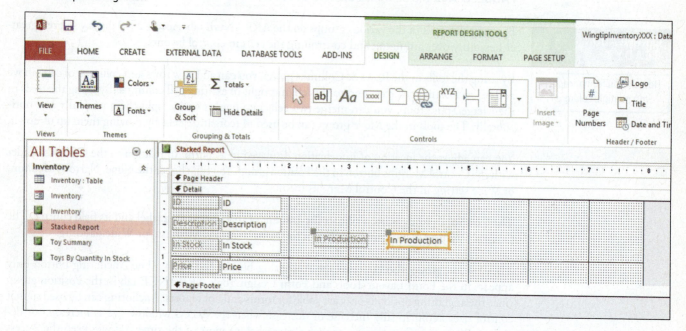

4. [Press and hold the **Shift** key] and select the **ID** field control. Still [holding the **Shift** key], select the **Description**, **In Stock**, and **Price** field controls so that all five are selected.

5. On the ARRANGE tab, in the Table group, click the **Stacked** button. The In Production control is added to the bottom of the stacked layout.

6. With all five controls still selected, click the **Control Margins** button on the ARRANGE tab in the Position group, and select **Narrow** from the menu, as shown in Figure 8-46. The text within the field controls and labels is formatted by the Narrow option.

Figure 8-46

Control Margins button and menu

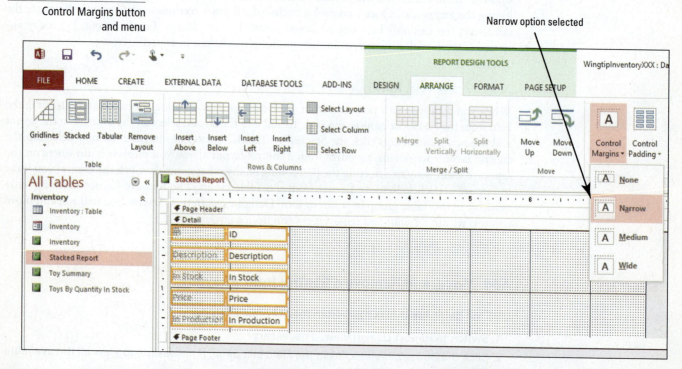

7. On the ARRANGE tab, in the Position group, click the **Control Padding** button and select **Medium** from the menu, as shown in Figure 8-47.

Figure 8-47

Control Padding button
and menu

Medium option selected

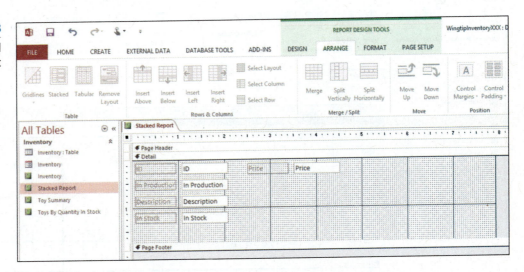

8. Click anywhere on a blank area of the design grid to deselect the field controls, then select the **In Production** field control and click **Select Row** in the Rows & Columns group. Notice the In Production label and field control are both outlined in orange. In the Move group on the Ribbon, click the **Move Up** button three times to move it under the ID label and field control.

9. Click and drag the **ID** control out of the layout. It will not move out of the layout.

10. Click anywhere on a blank area of the design grid to deselect the field controls, then [press and hold the **Shift** key] and select the **Price** label and control.

11. In the Table group on the Ribbon, click the **Remove Layout** button.

12. Click and drag the **Price** field control to the right of the ID field control, as shown in Figure 8-48.

Figure 8-48

Price label and control moved
out of the layout

13. **SAVE** the report and switch to Report view to view your changes.

Take Note   If the In Production text within the label is partially hidden, switch to Design view and select the In Production control and label. On the ARRANGE tab, in the Position group, click the Control Margins button and select None from the menu, then **SAVE** the report.

> 14. **CLOSE** the report.
>
> **PAUSE. LEAVE** the database open to use in the next exercise.

Take Note   To select multiple controls, hold down the Shift key and then click the controls.

Arranging and Anchoring Controls

In this exercise you practice arranging controls within a layout using a variety of arrangement tools.

STEP BY STEP   **Arrange and Anchor Controls within a Layout**

> **USE** the database that is open from the previous exercise.
>
> 1. Click the **Inventory** table in the Navigation Pane to select it.
> 2. On the CREATE tab, in the Forms group, click the **Form** button. A new form containing all the fields from the Inventory table is created in Layout view. Notice the stacked control layout is the default.
> 3. Switch to Design view.
> 4. Click the **ID** control to select it.
> 5. On the ARRANGE tab, in the Merge/Split group, click the **Split Horizontally** button. Click to the right of the ID field control and notice the orange border of the new column created after the split.
> 6. Click the **In Production** field control and drag it to the right of the ID field control to place it next to it. The In Production label and field control is now in the column. Your screen should resemble Figure 8-49. Notice the new additional space automatically created to the right of the other field controls.

Figure 8-49

In Production control next to
ID control

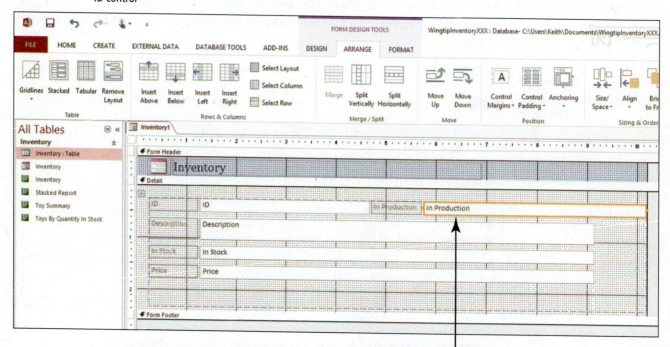

In Production control dragged to this location

Take Note   Access automatically creates a new column of placeholders in a layout when a field control is horizontally split and another field control is dragged into the placeholder created next to the horizontally split field control.

7. Click the **In Stock** field control to select it. [Press and hold the **Shift** key] and select the **In Stock** control label. On the ARRANGE tab, in the Move group, click the **Move Down** button once. The In Stock field control and label move to the bottom of the layout.

8. Click the **Description** field control to select it. [Press and hold the **Shift** key] and click the empty space below the Description field control to select the cell. Both the Description field control and cell below should be outlined in orange. On the ARRANGE tab, in the Merge/Split group, click the **Merge** button. The Description field control and cell have now merged into one, as shown in Figure 8-50.

Figure 8-50

Description field control merged with cell

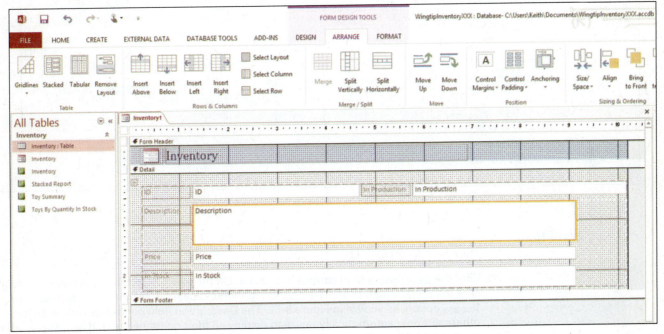

9. Click the **In Stock** field control to select it. On the ARRANGE tab, in the Rows & Columns group, click the **Insert Below** button twice. Two empty cells are added under the In Stock control. The In Stock field control should still be selected.

10. On the ARRANGE tab in the Rows & Columns group, click the **Select Row** button. Both the In Stock label and field control should be selected as well as an empty column created when we dragged the In Production field control to the right of the ID field control.

11. On the ARRANGE tab, in the Move group, click **Move Down** twice to move the In Stock control to the last cell row at the bottom of the layout, as shown in Figure 8-51.

Figure 8-51

In Stock control moved to
bottom of layout

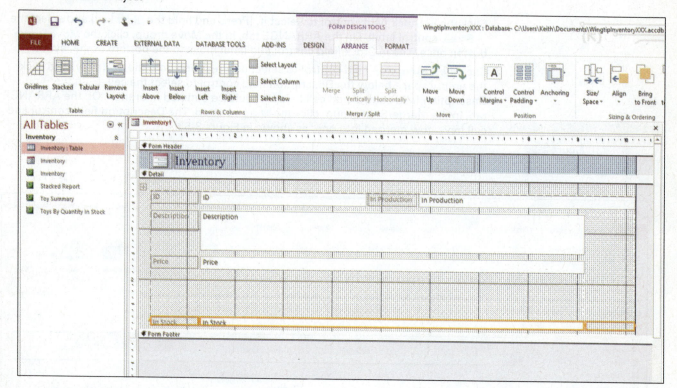

Take Note In Layout view, you can also use the tools on the ARRANGE tab to arrange controls within a layout for both forms and reports.

12. Click the **Description** field control to select it. On the ARRANGE tab in the Position group, click the **Anchoring** button. The Anchoring menu appears. Click the **Stretch Down and Across** option, as shown in Figure 8-52. The Description field control as well as all the others will now automatically resize to display all their contained text, if necessary, when the Access window is made larger.

Figure 8-52

Anchor menu

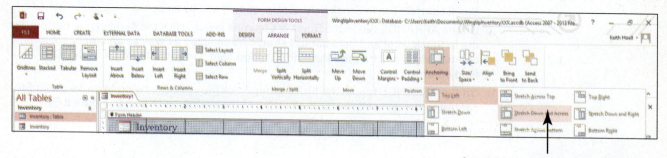

Stretch Down and Across option selected

13. Click the **In Stock** field control and increase its height by positioning the pointer over the top-right corner of the control until a diagonal two-sided arrow appears and then clicking and dragging upward until the text is no longer obstructed.

14. Switch to Form view to display the new arrangement of the controls and resize the Access application window (not the form window) to see the controls stretch and shrink in conjunction with the window size.

15. **SAVE** the form as Modified Inventory Form and **CLOSE** it.

PAUSE. LEAVE the database open to use in the next exercise.

ARRANGING CONTROL ALIGNMENT, SIZE, AND POSITION

The Bottom Line

You can change the alignment, size, or position of controls and associated labels. Aligning, sizing, and positioning commands using the ARRANGE tab gives you more options for improving the look of controls and labels in forms and reports. The Sizing & Ordering group, present on the ARRANGE tab only in report or form Design view, has commands for aligning labels and controls to the grid (the intersecting horizontal and vertical lines and points that appear in Design view) to allow for precise position. For example, you can precisely align a group of controls and related labels using the Align To Grid command to ensure all the labels' upper-left corners align to their nearest grid points. This will help ensure the organization of your controls is consistent throughout. In this exercise, you arrange the alignment, size, and position of controls and labels.

You can align multiple controls and labels at one time so their left, right, top, and bottom borders are perfectly aligned to each other using the align left, right, top, and bottom commands.

Also in the Sizing & Ordering group, you can use the commands to adjust the size of controls and labels to Size to Fit, Size to Grid, Size to Tallest, Size to Widest, Size to Shortest, or Size to Narrowest.

Additionally, you can use the Bring to Front and Send to Back commands to move objects in front or to the back of other objects. Also in the Sizing & Ordering group, you can use the commands to increase or decrease horizontal or vertical spacing using the Equal Horizontal, Equal Vertical, Increase Horizontal, Decrease Horizontal, Increase Vertical, and Decrease Vertical commands.

Finally, the Sizing & Ordering group contains toggle commands for showing or hiding the Grid and the Ruler and enabling or disabling Snap to Grid. This allows you to precisely arrange a label when you move the associated control by enabling Access to automatically align the upper-left corner of a label to its closest grid point. There are also Group and Ungroup commands that allow you to group several controls together so you can move or modify them all at once.

STEP BY STEP | **Arrange Control Alignment, Size, and Position**

USE the database that is open from the previous exercise.

1. On the CREATE tab, in the Forms group, click the Form Design button. A new, blank form is created, and the Field List pane is displayed. (If it isn't displayed, click the Add Existing Fields button in the Tools group on the DESIGN tab.)

2. Double-click the Description field to add it to the form.

3. Double-click the In Stock field to add it to the form.

4. Double-click the Price field to add it to the form.

5. Double-click the In Production field to add it to the form.

6. [Press and hold the Shift key] and click the Description, In Stock, and Price field controls to select them. The In Production field control should already be selected.

7. On the ARRANGE tab, in the Table group, click the Stacked button. The controls and labels are arranged in a stacked layout.

8. Click on a blank space on the design grid then select the In Production field control and label.

9. On the ARRANGE tab, in the Sizing & Ordering group, click the Size/Space button. In the Size category on the menu that appears, click the To Fit button. Notice all the field controls and labels are slightly resized in the layout based on the best fit of the text within the In Production field control and label since the layout forces all fields to conform to this action.

10. Select all the controls in the stacked layout (the labels and controls for the Description, In Stock, Price, and In Production controls).

11. On the ARRANGE tab, in the Table group, click the Remove Layout button.

12. All the controls and labels should still be selected. On the ARRANGE tab, in the Sizing & Ordering group, click the Size/Space button. In the Size category on the menu that appears, click the To Fit button. Notice all the field controls independently change their width to best fit their text since they are no longer part of a layout. Your screen should look similar to Figure 8-53.

Figure 8-53

Form Design view with controls

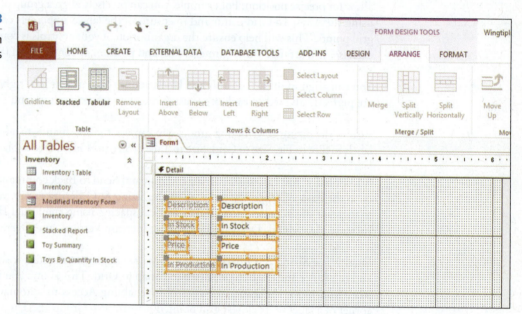

13. With the controls and labels still selected, on the ARRANGE tab, in the Sizing & Ordering group, click the Align button. In the menu that appears, click the Right button. The labels are right-aligned to the controls.

14. Click and drag the ID field from the Field List pane to any blank spot on the design grid above the Description field.

15. Select the ID label and control and in the Sizing & Ordering group, click the Align button. In the menu that appears, click the Right button.

16. [Press and hold the Shift key] and click on both the labels and controls for all the controls. In the Sizing & Ordering group, click the Align button. In the menu that appears, click the Left button. All the controls are left-aligned as a group.

17. In the Sizing & Ordering group, click the Align button. In the menu that appears, click the Right button. All the controls are now right-aligned as a group. Your screen should look similar to Figure 8-54.

Figure 8-54

Form Design view with
right-aligned controls

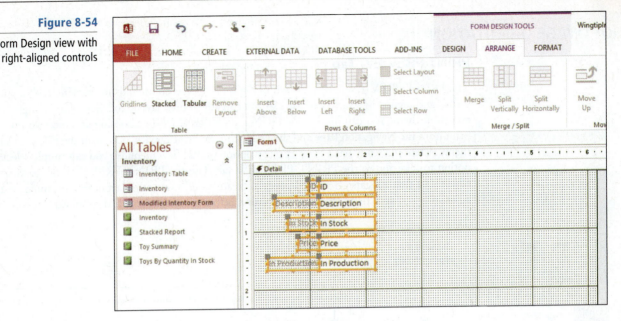

18. Select all the labels and controls, if necessary.
19. On the ARRANGE tab, in the Sizing & Ordering group, click the **Size/Space** button. In the Spacing category on the menu that appears, click the **Equal Vertical** button. Notice that the vertical space between the controls is now equal.
20. Click on a blank space on the design grid.
21. On the ARRANGE tab, in the Sizing & Ordering group, click the **Size/Space** button. In the Grid category on the menu that appears, click the **Grid** button. The design grid disappears.
22. Click the **Grid** button again. The design grid appears.
23. Click on a blank space on the design grid and drag to draw a box around the labels and controls so they are all selected, or [press and hold the **Shift** key] and select each label and control.
24. On the ARRANGE tab, in the Sizing & Ordering group, click the **Align** button. In the menu that appears, click the **To Grid** button. Notice the control and labels slightly move. The upper-left corners of all the labels are now aligned to their nearest grid points.
25. On the ARRANGE tab, in the Sizing & Ordering group, click the **Size/Space** button. In the Grid category on the menu that appears, click the **Ruler** button. The rulers disappear.
26. Click the **Ruler** button again. The rulers reappear.
27. **SAVE** the form as **Arranged Inventory Form** and **CLOSE** it.

PAUSE. LEAVE the database open to use in the next exercise.

SOFTWARE ORIENTATION

PRINT PREVIEW Tab

The PRINT PREVIEW tab, as shown in Figure 8-55, has commands for viewing tables, queries, forms, and reports in a variety of ways so you can adjust their layout and view your changes before you print them. You can display the PRINT PREVIEW tab by choosing an object you want to print from the Navigation Pane and then selecting the Print Preview option on the FILE tab's Print menu. A report already has a Print Preview option on its View menu, so you can simply select that option to take you to the PRINT PREVIEW tab. Use the PRINT PREVIEW tab to view and adjust data that appears on printed pages to create an effective print layout. For example, you can adjust margins and change the page orientation before printing to ensure data appears appropriately.

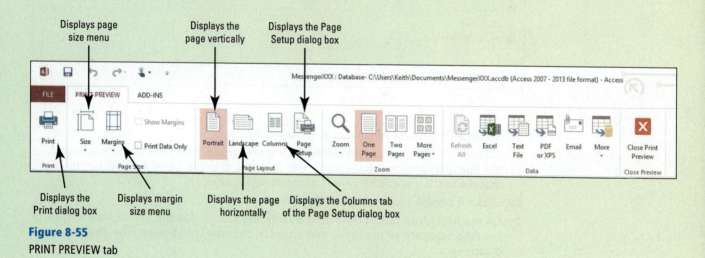

Figure 8-55

PRINT PREVIEW tab

ADJUSTING PAGE MARGINS AND CHANGING PAGE ORIENTATION FOR FORMS AND REPORTS

The Bottom Line

Forms and reports – and all other Access objects – can be printed to easily communicate data to others in a hardcopy format. The PRINT PREVIEW tab provides options that allow you to adjust page margins and/or change orientation to ensure data fits appropriately on a page. When you are satisfied with the page layout, you can click the Print button to send the page to the printer.

It may be easy to understand why you would want to print a report to share data with your colleagues, but Access also gives you the option of printing all other database objects. For example, you may want to print a table to view data in a datasheet format to which you're more accustomed or print a form to share with a graphic design team so it can be aesthetically evaluated and redesigned.

The Page Size group on the PRINT PREVIEW tab contains commands for controlling page size and margins. The Print Data Only checkbox gives you the option of printing only object data without the corresponding structure (like gridlines and borders). The Show Margins checkbox allows you to view an object's margins on the preview of the object to help you better adjust them.

The Page Layout group allows you to change the page orientation of an object, either by choosing the Portrait (vertical) or Landscape (horizontal) options. You can also change the layout of data by converting it into any number of columns by choosing the Columns option. Lastly, the Page Setup option, when clicked, displays a dialog box with many of the same options that appear in the Page Size and Page Layout groups. In this exercise, you use Print Preview to adjust the page margins and change page orientation for forms and reports.

Changes to an object's print layout using Print Preview are automatically retained when you close Print Preview.

 Cross Ref In Lesson 11, you will learn more about the options on the PRINT PREVIEW tab when you create a print layout for a report.

STEP BY STEP **Adjust Page Margins and Change Page Orientation for Forms and Reports**

USE the database that is open from the previous exercise.

1. Click the **Modified Inventory Form** in the Navigation Pane and click the **FILE** tab.

2. On the FILE tab, click the **Print** button to display the Print menu, as shown in Figure 8-56.

Figure 8-56

Print menu

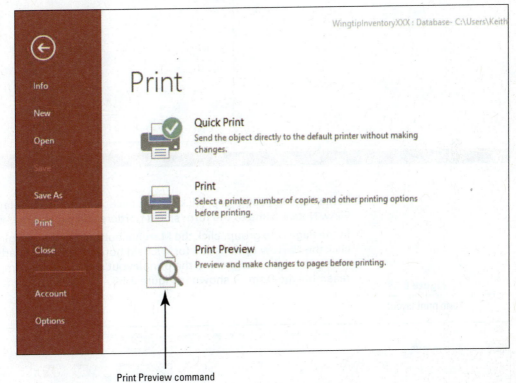

Print Preview command

3. Click the **Print Preview** command. The Print Preview screen appears with a preview of the form, as shown in Figure 8-57. Notice the form's field borders exceed the width of the right margin.

Figure 8-57

Form in Print Preview

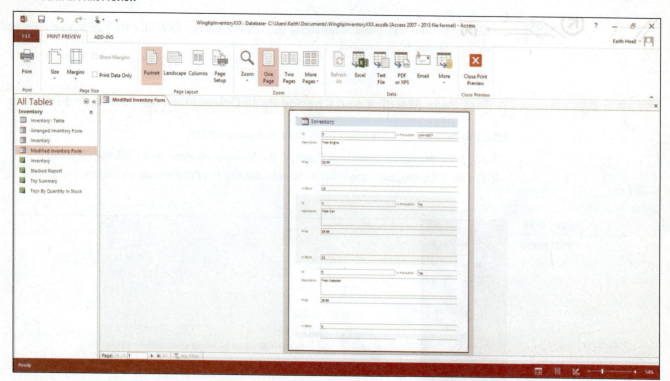

4. In the Page Layout group, click the **Landscape** button to display the form in landscape view. Notice some of the form's field borders still exceed the width of the right margin.

5. In the Page Size group, click the **Margins** button. On the Margins menu that appears, click the **Narrow** option. The form's field borders have been adjusted and are now within the right margin, and the print layout now appears complete. Your screen should resemble the form as shown in Figure 8-58.

Figure 8-58

Form print layout

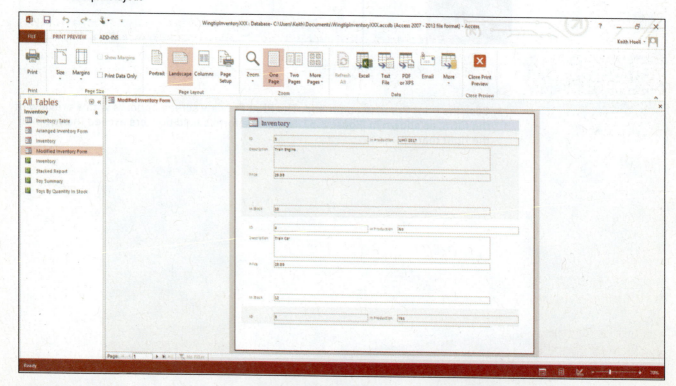

6. In the Close Preview group, click the **Close Print Preview** button to return to the Access database screen.

7. Open the **Toys By Quantity In Stock** report.

8. On the HOME tab, in the Views group, click the lower half of the **View** button and select **Print Preview** from the menu. The report is displayed in Print Preview, as shown in Figure 8-59. Notice the Price field header and data in the last column exceed the width of the right margin.

Figure 8-59

Report in Print Preview

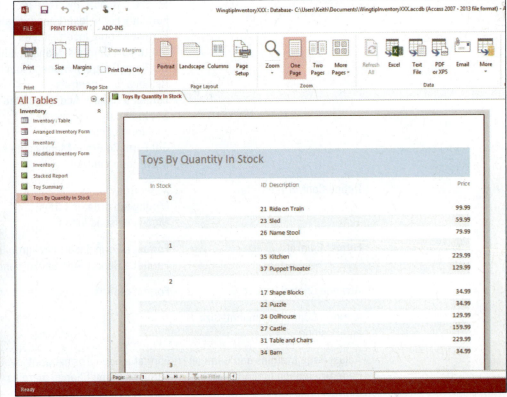

CERTIFICATION READY? 4.3.2

How do you format form print layouts?

CERTIFICATION READY? 4.3.5

How do you change form margins?

CERTIFICATION READY? 5.3.3

How do you set report margins?

9. On the PRINT PREVIEW tab, in the Page Size group, click the **Margins** button and select **Narrow** from the menu that appears. The Price field header and data are now completely visible.

10. On the PRINT PREVIEW tab, click the **Close Print Preview** button to return to Report view.

11. **CLOSE** the report.

CLOSE the database.

SKILL SUMMARY

In This Lesson You Learned How To:	Exam Objective	Objective Number
Add Bound and Unbound Controls	Add report controls	5.2.5
	Format a Report: Insert images	5.3.8
	Format a Report: Insert page numbers	5.3.9
	Format a Report: Modify existing reports	5.3.11
	Format a Report: Insert headers and footers	5.3.7
	Format a Form: Insert headers and footers	4.3.8
	Format a Form: Insert images	4.3.9
	Set Report Controls: Manage labels	5.2.6
	Set Form Controls: Manage labels	4.2.6
	Remove form controls	4.2.4
	Format a Report: Add calculated fields	5.3.2
	Set form control properties	4.2.5
	Add form controls	4.2.2
	Set Form Controls: Modify data sources	4.2.3
	Move form controls	4.2.1
Define Control Tab Order	Auto-order forms	4.3.7
	Modify tab order in forms	4.3.1
	Modify existing forms	4.3.10
Format Controls	Format a Form: Insert backgrounds	4.3.6
	Format a Report: Add backgrounds	5.3.4
Arrange Control Layout	Format reports into multiple columns	5.3.1
Arrange Control Alignment, Size, and Position		
Adjust Page Margins and Change Page Orientation for Forms and Reports	Format a Form: Format print layouts	4.3.2
	Format a Form: Change margins	4.3.5
	Format a Report: Set margins	5.3.3

Knowledge Assessment

Matching

Match the term in Column 1 to its description in Column 2.

Column 1

1. control
2. unbound control
3. bound control
4. calculated control
5. Expression Builder
6. Control Wizards

Column 2

a. a control that displays the result of a calculation or expression

b. help you create controls such as command buttons, list boxes, combo boxes, and option groups

c. a layout in which the controls are arranged in rows and columns, with labels across the top

d. a control that doesn't have a source; it displays information such as lines, shapes, or pictures

e. controls that are arranged vertically with a label on the left and the control on the right

f. layouts that align controls horizontally and vertically to give your report or form a professional appearance

7. conditional formatting

g. an object that displays data, performs actions, and lets you improve the look and usability of a form or report

8. control layouts

h. a control that uses a field in a table or query as the data source

9. tabular layout

i. used to change the appearance of a control or the value in a control when certain conditions are met

10. stacked layout

j. provides the names of the fields and controls in a database, lists the operators available, and has built-in functions to help you create an expression

True/False

Circle T if the statement is true or F if the statement is false.

T F 1. The easiest way to create a bound control is to double-click or drag a field from the Property Sheet to the report.

T F 2. You can bind a control to a field using the Property Sheet.

T F 3. You can turn off Control Wizards.

T F 4. Display formatting can be applied to controls and labels in a form or report.

T F 5. You can specify only one condition for conditional formatting.

T F 6. You can switch an entire control layout of a report or form from one type to the other.

T F 7. Control padding adjusts the amount of space between a label and its field control.

T F 8. The Remove Layout command in the Table group removes a control from a form or report.

T F 9. You can use Print Preview to set the margins for a form or report.

T F 10. Tab order refers to the order of tabs displayed in a dialog box.

Competency Assessment

Project 8-1: Refine the Alpine Ski House Report

You have learned a great deal about reports and forms while working as an administrative assistant at the Alpine Ski House. You want to refine the basic report you created previously so you can display it proudly at the front desk.

GET READY. LAUNCH Access if it is not already running.

1. OPEN the *Alpine* database.

2. SAVE the database as *AlpineXXX* (where *XXX* is your initials).

3. Open the Report Design report.

4. Switch to Design view.

5. Select all four controls in the report.

6. On the ARRANGE tab, in the Table group, click the Tabular button.

7. On the ARRANGE tab, in the Position group, click the Control Margins button, and select Narrow from the menu.

8. On the ARRANGE tab, in the Position group, click the Control Padding button, and select Medium from the menu.

9. On the DESIGN tab, in the Header/Footer group, click the Title button. A title is inserted in the report header.

10. Key Alpine Ski House Rooms Report and [press Enter].

11. On the DESIGN tab, in the Header/Footer group, click the Logo button. Navigate to the data files for this lesson and select *Ski Lodge.jpg*. Click OK.

12. On the FORMAT tab, in the Background group, click the **Background Image** button. Navigate to the data files for this lesson and select *Winter Theme Background.jpg*. Click **OK**.

13. [Press and hold the **Shift** key] and click on **all four controls** (not control labels) to select them.

14. On the FORMAT tab in the Font group, click the **Font Color** menu button. Select the dark blue color called **Dark Blue, Text 2** in the first row and fourth column of the Theme Colors section.

15. Make sure all the controls are still selected. On the ARRANGE tab, in the Table group, click **Remove Layout**.

16. With the controls still selected, click and drag them up together and position them just below the Detail section bar.

17. Scroll down and position the mouse pointer over the top of the Page Footer section bar. Drag the section bar up to position just below the controls. Your screen should look similar to Figure 8-60.

Figure 8-60

Report design

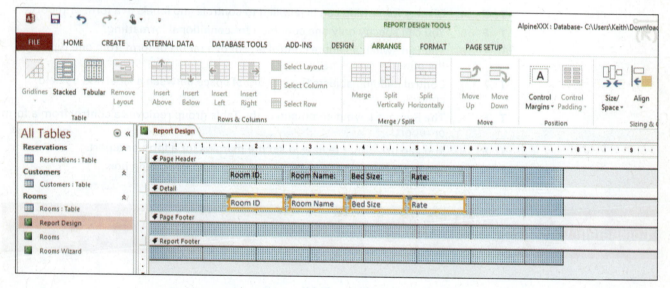

18. **SAVE** the report.

19. Switch to Print Preview.

20. Click the **Landscape** button in the Page Layout group on the PRINT PREVIEW tab.

21. Close Print Preview.

CLOSE the database.

Project 8-2: **Format the Soccer Roster**

Since you have increased your Access skills while working as an assistant coach for a youth soccer team, you decide to improve the soccer roster you created at the beginning of the season. There have been a few changes anyway, so you need an updated version.

GET READY. LAUNCH Access if it is not already running.

1. **OPEN** *SoccerData* from the data files for this lesson.

2. **SAVE** the database as *SoccerDataXXX* (where *XXX* is your initials).

3. **OPEN** the **Roster** report.

4. Switch to Design view.

5. [Press and hold the **Shift** key] and click on all the **labels** in the Page Header section to select them.

6. On the FORMAT tab, in the Font group, click the **Bold** button.

7. Select the title, Roster, and key **Soccer Roster**.

8. On the FORMAT tab, in the Font group, click the drop-down arrow to the right of the **Font** box and select **Arial Black**.

9. On the FORMAT tab, in the Font group, click the **Font Size** menu and select **22**.

10. On the ARRANGE tab, on the Size/Space menu in the Sizing & Ordering group, click the **To Fit** button.

11. [Press and hold the **Shift** key] and click on all the **controls** in the Detail section. On the ARRANGE tab, on the Align menu in the Sizing & Ordering group, click **To Grid**.

12. Delete the report image.

13. On the DESIGN tab, in the Header/Footer group, click the **Logo** button.

14. Navigate to the data files for this lesson and select *Soccer.jpg*. Click the newly created **logo** control and drag the sizing border handles to increase the logo size until the soccer ball image can be seen clearly in the header.

15. **SAVE** the report and view it in Report view.

CLOSE the database.

Proficiency Assessment

Project 8-3: Create the Fourth Coffee Order Summary Form

In your part-time job at Fourth Coffee, you are often involved in taking and filling orders. Create a summary table to help make your job easier.

GET READY. LAUNCH Access if it is not already running.

1. **OPEN** *Coffee Data* from the data files for this lesson.

2. **SAVE** the database as *CoffeeDataXXX* (where *XXX* is your initials).

3. Select the **Order Summary: Table** in the Navigation Pane.

4. Create a simple form using the Form button.

5. Insert a **Date and Time control** in the form header section to include both the date and time with a date format of **00/00/0000**, and default time format.

6. Delete the **Paid** control and create a **Yes/No option** group control using check boxes with **Paid** as the caption. Set the value for Yes as **–1** and the value for No as **0**.

7. Delete the **Attachment** field.

8. Resize and arrange the controls to look similar to the form in Figure 8-61. Remember to remove the control layout formatting so that you can move individual controls.

Figure 8-61

Order Summary form

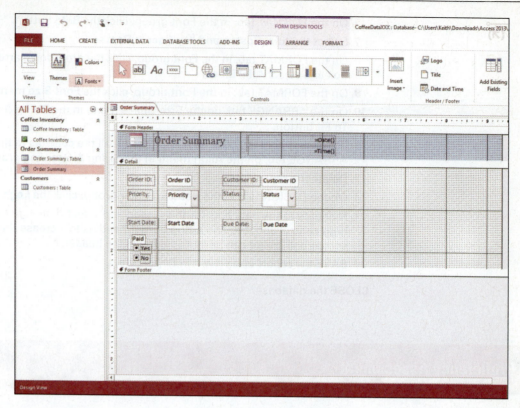

9. **SAVE** the form as Order Summary.
10. Check your work in Form view.
11. **CLOSE** the form.

CLOSE the database.

Project 8-4: Create the Alpine Ski House Reservations Form

While working as an administrative assistant at Alpine Ski House, entering data in the table is becoming cumbersome, so you decide to create a form you can use to enter reservation data.

USE the *AlpineXXX* database, which you saved in a previous exercise.

1. Click the Reservations: Table in the Navigation Pane to select it.
2. Create a new form using Design view.
3. Insert a title control. Change the title to Alpine Ski House Reservations Form.
4. Insert a logo control by navigating to the data files for this lesson and selecting *Ski Lodge.jpg*.
5. Add the following bound controls to the design grid: Customer ID, Room, Rate, Check-In Date, Check-Out Date, and Notes.
6. Select all the controls and apply the Stacked control layout.
7. Position the controls in the upper-left corner of the Detail section, remove the stacked layout and resize the Notes control, as shown in Figure 8-62.

Figure 8-62

Reservations form

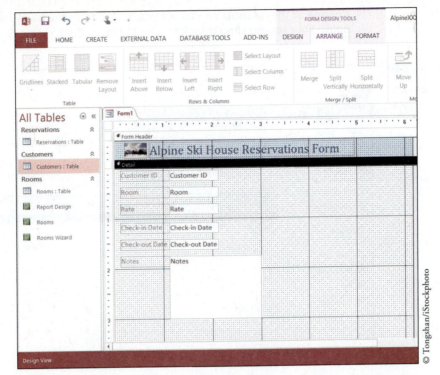

© Tongshan/iStockphoto

8. **SAVE** the form as **Reservations Form** and leave it open for use in the next exercise.

LEAVE the database open for the next project.

Mastery Assessment

Project 8-5: Refine the Alpine Ski House Reservations Form

The reservations form you created is very helpful; however, you need to add more functionality to the form using calculated controls and Control Wizards.

USE the form that is open from the previous exercise.

1. Add an Option group control on the right side of the form. Use the Control Wizard to create the option box for the Credit Card on File field. Using the Option Group Wizard, add two Labels: one for Yes and the other for No. Set the value for Yes to **–1** and the value for No to **0**. Use option buttons, and label the control **Credit Card on File**.
2. Add an unbound text box control below the Credit Card on File field.
3. Open the Property Sheet and click the **Build** button in the Control Source property.
4. Create an expression to subtract the **Check-in Date** from the **Check-out Date**.
5. Key **Number of Nights** as the label. (Note the default label number, such as Text##.)
6. Add an unbound text box control beside the Notes control.
7. Open the Property Sheet and click the **Build** button in the Control Source property.
8. Create an expression to multiply the **Number of Nights** (or Text##) by the **Rate**.
9. Key **Rate Subtotal** as the label.
10. Format the Rate Subtotal field control for **Currency**.

11. Change all the controls and labels you added from the black font color to a red font color. Your screen should look similar to Figure 8-63.

Figure 8-63

Revised Reservations form

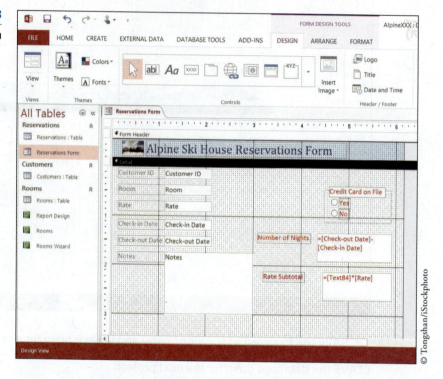

12. SAVE the form and switch to Form view to view your changes.

CLOSE the database.

Project 8-6: Fix the Angel Project Contact Information Form

A volunteer did some work on the Angel Project database while you were on vacation. The Contact Information form has a few problems that you need to fix.

GET READY. LAUNCH Access if it is not already running.

1. OPEN *AngelData* from the data files for this lesson.
2. SAVE the database as *AngelDataXXX* (where *XXX* is your initials).
3. OPEN the Contact Information Form.
4. Change the layout from tabular to stacked.
5. Bind the unbound control to the City field.
6. Modify the control tab order so the order is sequential from top to bottom.
7. SAVE and CLOSE the form.

CLOSE Access.

LESSON SKILL MATRIX

Skill	Exam Objective	Objective Number
Creating a Custom Table	Create new tables	2.1.1
	Configure fields to auto-increment	2.4.6
	Change data formats	2.2.2
Using the Table Analyzer		
Summarizing Table Data	Add total rows	2.2.3

© Decjpilot/iStockphoto

© Deejpilot/iStockphoto

Lucerne Publishing is a large publisher with a variety of products. You have just been hired as sales manager for the business books division. You will be responsible for working with the sales people in your division to increase sales. The previous sales manager used Access 2010 to track sales, so some data is already available. In this lesson, you create a new custom table, use the Table Analyzer to divide one table into two tables, and add a total row to a table.

CREATING A CUSTOM TABLE

The Bottom Line	When a table template doesn't suit your needs, you can create a custom table in Design view. In Design view, you can insert fields, set data types, and perform other advanced table design tasks.

Creating a Custom Table

Creating a table from scratch in Design view gives you maximum flexibility. You can do everything you need to do to create the table in Design view, including adding fields, setting data types, defining field properties, and defining a primary key. As you create a table, you can also easily insert and delete rows in your table design. In this exercise, you create a new blank table and then add fields for the new table in Design view.

Creating a new field for a table in Design view includes keying the name in the Field Name column; choosing a data type from the menu in the Data Type column; and keying a description, if you want, in the Description column. Additionally, you can modify field properties in the Field Properties section of the design grid.

After you have completed your table design, you'll need to save it. If you haven't already defined a primary key, Access will prompt you to do so when you save the table.

STEP BY STEP **Create a Custom Table in Design View**

GET READY. Before you begin these steps, be sure to turn on and/or log on to your computer and **LAUNCH** Access.

1. **OPEN** *Lucerne Publishing* from the data files for this lesson.
2. **SAVE** the database as *Lucerne PublishingXXX* (where *XXX* is your initials).
3. On the CREATE tab, in the Tables group, click the **Table Design** button. A new blank table is created in Design view, as shown in Figure 9-1.

Figure 9-1

Blank table in Design view

New blank table   Field Name column   Data Type column   Description column

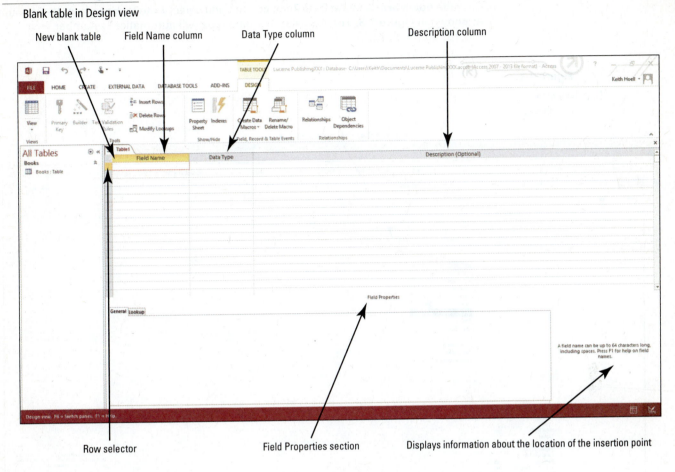

Row selector   Field Properties section   Displays information about the location of the insertion point

4. Key **ID** in the Field Name column, as shown in Figure 9-2.

Figure 9-2

Field Name in Design view

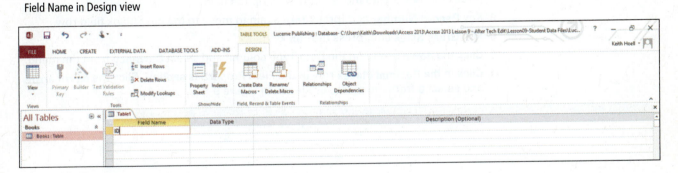

Take Note   Throughout this lesson you will see information that appears in black text within brackets, such as [Press **Enter**], or [**your e-mail address**]. The information contained in the brackets is intended to be directions for you rather than something you actually type word-for-word. It will instruct you to perform an action or substitute text. Do **not** type the actual text that appears within brackets.

5. [Press the **Tab** key] to move to the Data Type column.

6. Click the **down arrow** in the Data Type column and select **AutoNumber** from the menu, as shown in Figure 9-3. The AutoNumber data type will automatically number your records starting at 1.

Figure 9-3

Data Type menu in Design view

AutoNumber data type selected

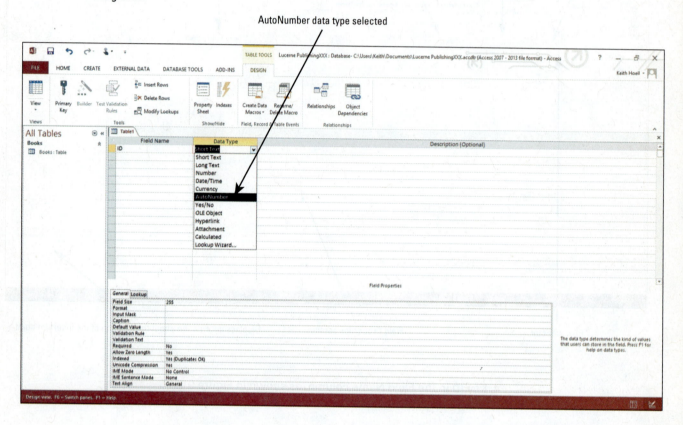

7. [Press the **Tab** key] to move to the Description field.

8. Key **Record Number** and [press **Tab**] again to move to the next blank field row.

9. Key **Gross Sales** and [press the **Tab** key].

10. Click the **down arrow** on the Data Type column and select **Currency** from the menu.

11. Click in the **Decimal Places** row in the Field Properties section. Click the **down arrow** and select **0** from the menu, as shown in Figure 9-4.

Figure 9-4

Field Properties in Design view

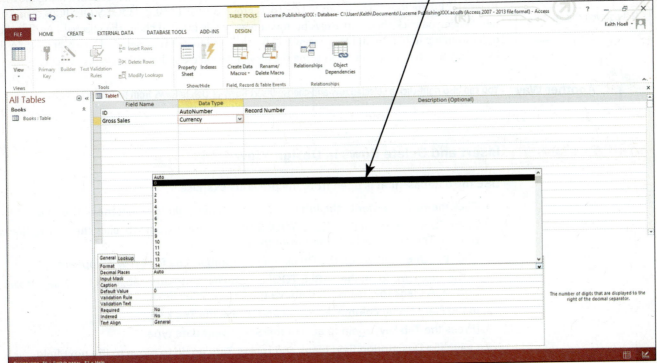

12. Enter the remaining fields, as shown in Figure 9-5, formatting each with the **Currency** data type and **0** decimal places.

Figure 9-5

Custom Table in Design view

Row selector

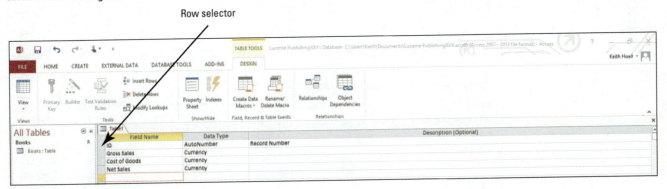

13. Click the **row selector** to the left of the ID field to select the row.
14. On the DESIGN tab, in the Tools group, click the **Primary Key** button.
15. Click the **Save** button on the Quick Access Toolbar. The Save As dialog box appears.
16. Key **Sales** and click **OK**.

PAUSE. LEAVE the database open to use in the next exercise.

CERTIFICATION READY?   2.1.1

How do you create new tables?

CERTIFICATION READY?   2.4.6

How do you configure fields to auto-increment?

Inserting and Deleting Rows

When creating a custom table in Design view, you can insert and delete rows as needed using the Insert Rows and Delete Rows commands in the Tools group on the TABLE TOOLS DESIGN contextual tab. When you click the Insert Rows button, a new row is inserted above the selected row. The field order from top to bottom in Design view will be displayed from left to right in Datasheet view. In this exercise, you insert and delete rows using the new table you created in the previous exercise.

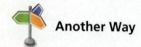

Another Way   You can also right-click a selected row and choose Insert Rows or Delete Rows from the shortcut menu.

STEP BY STEP   **Insert and Delete Rows in Design View**

USE the database that is open from the previous exercise.

1. Click the **row selector** to the left of the Gross Sales field to select the entire row.
2. In the Tools group on the TABLE TOOLS DESIGN contextual tab, click the **Delete Rows** button. The field row is deleted from the table.
3. Click the **Undo** button on the Quick Access Toolbar. The field row reappears.
4. In the Tools group on the TABLE TOOLS DESIGN contextual tab, click the **Insert Rows** button. A blank row is inserted above the Gross Sales field.
5. In the Field Name column, key **Area** and [press the **Tab** key].
6. [Press the **Tab** key] again to accept the **Short Text** data type.
7. Leave the Description field blank and [press **Tab**] again to move to the next field.
8. Click the **Save** button on the Quick Access Toolbar.
9. Switch to Datasheet view and enter the records in the table as shown in Figure 9-6. The ID field will be automatically generated, so just [press **Tab**] to get past it.

Figure 9-6

Sales table

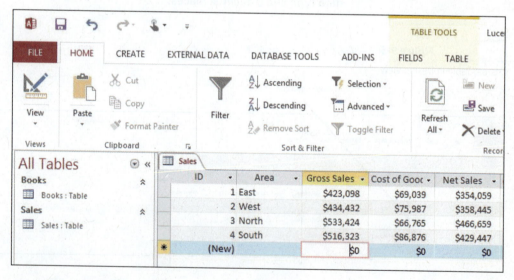

10. **SAVE** and **CLOSE** the table.

PAUSE. LEAVE the database open to use in the next exercise.

USING THE TABLE ANALYZER

The Bottom Line

The **Table Analyzer** is a wizard that performs the normalization process for you by examining a table design and suggesting a way to divide the table for maximum efficiency. The Table Analyzer helps you design efficient tables. The Table Analyzer will suggest primary keys for the new tables or will allow you to determine the primary keys. You can also have the wizard insert a unique identifier field. If it determines that a table has duplicate information, it can split a table into two more efficient tables for you, or you can choose to do it yourself.

Using the Table Analyzer

The Table Analyzer is a wizard that examines a table and asks you a series of questions about the table to determine whether it should be divided into two or more tables. In this exercise, you use the Table Analyzer Wizard to analyze a table in the database.

Well-designed databases do not store the same data in more than one place. Redundant data storage takes more disk space and increases the likelihood for data entry errors. In Lesson 1, you were introduced to the concept of normalization, which is the process of applying rules to a database design to ensure that you have divided your data into the appropriate tables.

In the Books table, contact information for authors has to be entered for each book the author wrote. The Table Analyzer Wizard will determine that a more efficient database would split the table into two tables—one with author contact information and one with book sales data.

 Cross Ref   Lesson 1 contains more information about normalization.

In addition to analyzing the table, the Table Analyzer Wizard will also analyze the redundant data in a table and suggest corrections for records that should match. It will also give you the choice of whether to create a query, which is similar to the original table. Creating the query allows forms and reports that were created with the original table to continue to function properly. The original table may be renamed, but it will not be removed or altered.

 **Troubleshooting**   If you run the Table Analyzer before entering records in the table, you may get a message stating that you need to enter at least two records in the table to get a meaningful analysis.

STEP BY STEP   **Use the Table Analyzer**

USE the database that is open from the previous exercise.

1. Open the **Books** table.
2. Scroll through the table to become familiar with the fields in the table.
3. On the DATABASE TOOLS tab, in the Analyze group, click the **Analyze Table** button. The Table Analyzer Wizard dialog box, screen 1, appears, as shown in Figure 9-7. This first dialog box provides more information about the types of problems the wizard will find. Click the two **Show me an example** buttons to read more about how duplicating information can lead to problems.

Figure 9-7

Table Analyzer Wizard, screen 1

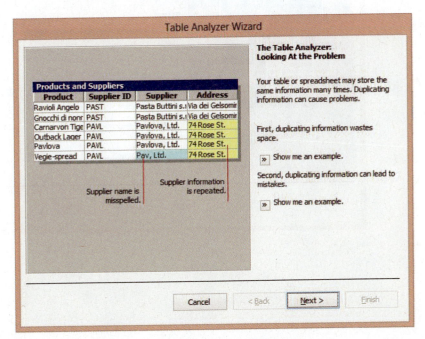

4. Click the **Next >** button. The Table Analyzer Wizard dialog box, screen 2, appears, as shown in Figure 9-8. This dialog box provides more information about what the wizard will do. Click the two **Show me an example** buttons to read more about how splitting the table is helpful.

Figure 9-8

Table Analyzer Wizard, screen 2

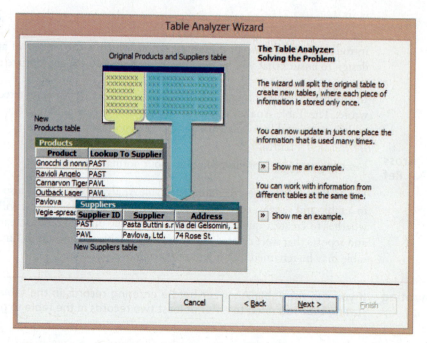

5. Click the **Next >** button. The Table Analyzer Wizard dialog box, screen 3, appears, as shown in Figure 9-9.

Figure 9-9

Table Analyzer Wizard, screen 3

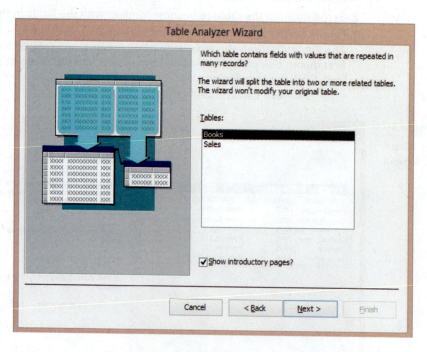

6. The **Books** table should be selected in the list; if it is not, select it. Click the **Next >** button. The Table Analyzer Wizard dialog box, screen 4, appears, as shown in Figure 9-10.

Figure 9-10

Table Analyzer Wizard, screen 4

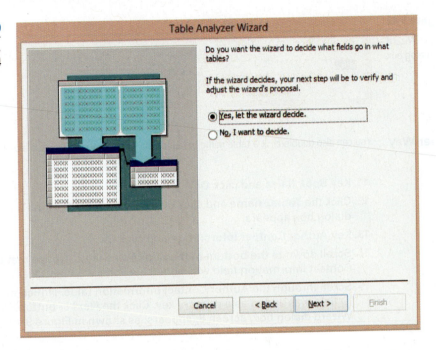

7. The **Yes, let the wizard decide** button should be selected; if it is not, select it. Click the **Next >** button. The Table Analyzer Wizard dialog box, screen 5, appears, as shown in Figure 9-11.

Figure 9-11

Table Analyzer Wizard, screen 5

Table names   Rename Table button   Tips button

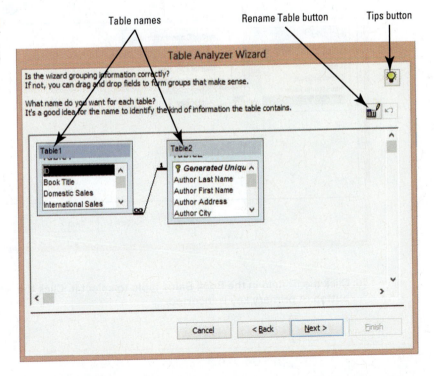

8. Scroll to the bottom of the Table2 box and click the **Year** field to select it. Notice that the wizard has placed it in the wrong table.

9. Drag the selected field to the Table1 box, positioning the horizontal black line below the Book Title field and releasing the mouse button to place the Year field in its new location.

10. Click the **Table1** name to select it. Click the **Rename Table** button. The Table Analyzer Wizard dialog box appears, as shown in Figure 9-12.

Figure 9-12

Table Analyzer Wizard
dialog box

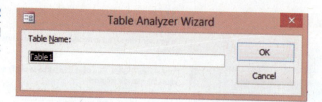

Another Way   You can also double-click a table name to launch the Table Analyzer Wizard dialog box.

11. Key **Book Sales** and click **OK**.

12. Click the **Table2** name and click the **Rename Table** button. The Table Analyzer Wizard dialog box appears.

13. Key **Author Contact Information** and click **OK**.

14. Scroll down to the bottom of the Book Sales table. Notice that the Lookup to Author Contact Information field was added.

15. Scroll through the Author Contact Information table. Notice that the Generated Unique ID field was added as a primary key. Click the **Next >** button. The Table Analyzer Wizard dialog box, screen 6, appears, as shown in Figure 9-13.

Figure 9-13

Table Analyzer Wizard,
screen 6

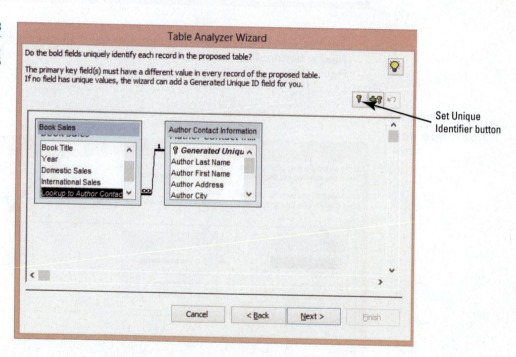

16. Click the **ID** field in the Book Sales table to select it. Click the **Set Unique Identifier** button. A primary key is inserted.

17. Click **Next >**. The Table Analyzer Wizard dialog box, screen 7, appears, as shown in Figure 9-14.

Figure 9-14

Table Analyzer Wizard, screen 7

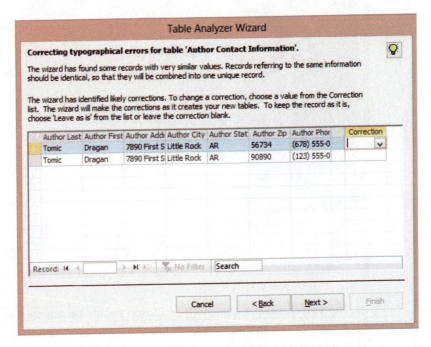

18. Notice that the Table Analyzer Wizard has detected two similar records, one with an incorrect zip code and phone number. Click the **down arrow** in the first row of the Correction field and select **Leave as is**. This is the correct record.

19. Click the **down arrow** on the second row of the Correction field and select the **Tomic** correction from the menu, as shown in Figure 9-15, to replace the incorrect record.

Figure 9-15

Corrections to the new tables

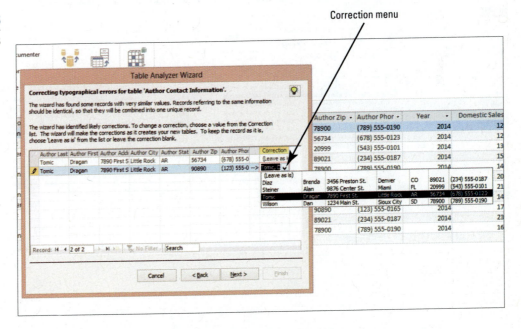

Correction menu

20. Click **Next >**. The final Table Analyzer Wizard dialog box appears, as shown in Figure 9-16.

Figure 9-16

Final Table Analyzer Wizard dialog box

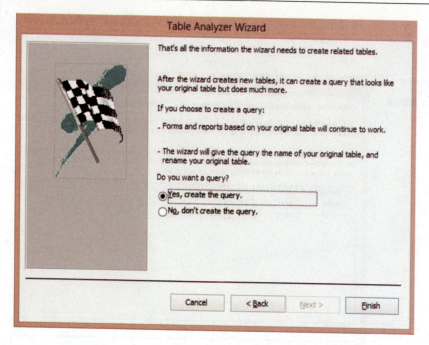

21. The **Yes, create the query** option button should be selected. Click the **Finish** button.

22. A message saying that the new query will be saved as Books_NEW appears. Click **OK**.

23. If Access Help appears on your screen, close it. Your screen should look similar to Figure 9-17.

Figure 9-17

New tables and queries created by the Table Analyzer Wizard

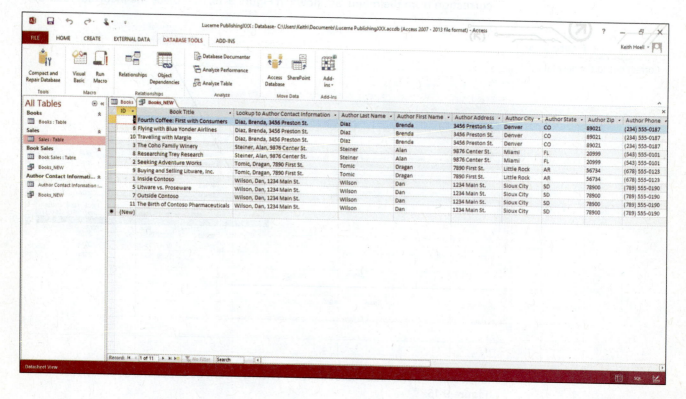

24. **SAVE** and **CLOSE** all tables and queries.

PAUSE. LEAVE the database open to use in the next exercise.

SUMMARIZING TABLE DATA

It is often necessary to count or summarize data in a table, column by column. Tables that contain columns of sales figures or other numbers need to be summed, averaged, or counted to be more useful. The Total row makes these tasks easy.

Summarizing Table Data

Much like the bottom row of a spreadsheet, the Total row is a feature in Access 2013 that makes it easy to sum, average, or count the values in a datasheet column. You can also find maximum or minimum values and use statistical functions such as standard deviation and variance. In this exercise, you summarize table data by inserting a Total row.

Aggregate functions are functions that calculate values across a range of data, such as in a column. You can use these functions in queries or in Visual Basic for Applications (VBA) code. Although you can still use those methods, the Total row saves your time by allowing you to choose one of these functions from a menu, applying it instantly. The **Total row** is a row inserted at the bottom of a table that provides a menu of functions for each column in the row.

Take Note   You can also add a Total row to queries open in Datasheet view and to a split form open in Form view. You cannot add a Total row to a report, but you can use aggregate functions in reports using other methods.

STEP BY STEP   **Insert a Total Row**

USE the database open from the previous exercise.

1. Open the Book Sales table.
2. On the HOME tab, in the Records group, click the Totals button. The Total row appears below the row with the asterisk (*) in the record selector box.
3. Click the down arrow in the Book Title column of the Total row. Select Count from the menu, as shown in Figure 9-18. The number of records in the column is counted, and the number 11 is displayed.

Figure 9-18

Total row

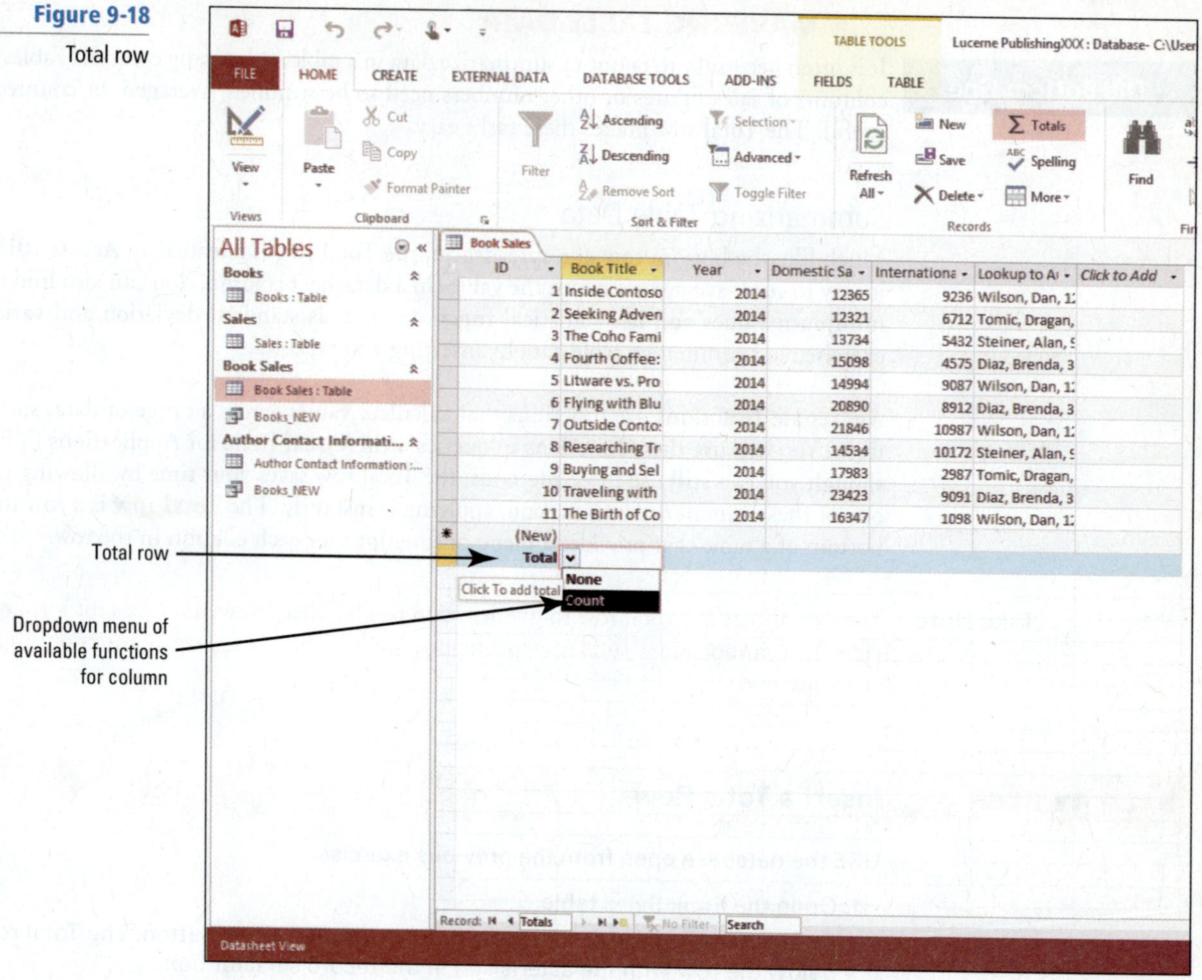

Total row

Dropdown menu of available functions for column

4. Click the **down arrow** in the **Domestic Sales** column of the Total row and select **Sum** from the menu.

5. Click the **down arrow** in the **International Sales** column of the Total row and select **Sum** from the menu. Your screen should look similar to Figure 9-19.

Figure 9-19

Total row in the Book Sales table

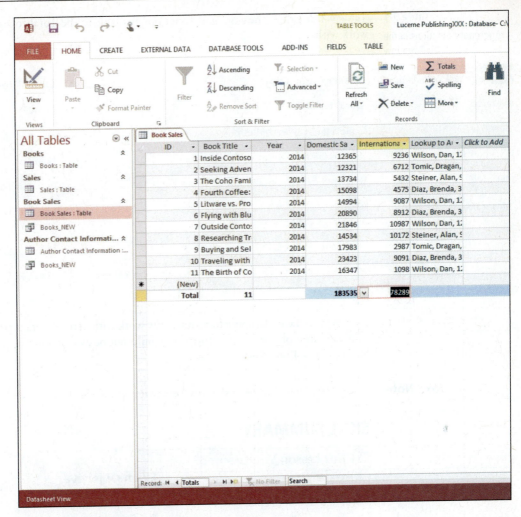

6. Save the table.

7. On the HOME tab, in the Records group, click the **Totals** button. The Total row is hidden.

8. On the HOME tab, in the Records group, click the **Totals** button again. The Total row reappears.

9. Save and close the table.

CLOSE Access.

CERTIFICATION READY? 2.2.3

How do you add total rows?

Table 9-1 describes the aggregate functions available in the Total row and the data types that they work with.

Aggregate Function	Description	Data Types
Average	Calculates the average value for a column	Number, Decimal, Currency, Date/Time
Count	Counts the number of items in a column	All (except multivalued list)
Maximum	Returns the item with the highest value	Number, Decimal, Currency, Date/Time
Minimum	Returns the item with the lowest value	Number, Decimal, Currency, Date/Time
Standard Deviation	Measures how widely values are dispersed from an average value	Number, Decimal, Currency
Sum	Adds items in a column	Number, Decimal, Currency
Variance	Measures the statistical variance of all values in the column	Number, Decimal, Currency

As shown in the table, some functions only work with certain data types. For example, you cannot sum a column of text, so that function would not be available for a column with the data type of Short Text or Long Text.

Take Note   If you want to sort or filter data, Access will exclude the Total row by default.

SKILL SUMMARY

In This Lesson You Learned How To:	Exam Objective	Objective Number
Create a Custom Table	Create new tables	2.1.1
	Configure fields to auto-increment	2.4.6
	Change data formats	2.2.2
Use the Table Analyzer		
Summarize Table Data	Add total rows	2.2.3

Knowledge Assessment

Matching

Match the term in Column 1 to its description in Column 2.

Column 1

1. aggregate function
2. Table Analyzer
3. Total row

4. row selector

5. Insert Rows button

Column 2

a. square to the left of a field in Design view

b. inserts a blank row above a selected row in Design view

c. the process of applying rules to a database design to ensure that you have divided your information into the appropriate tables

d. a wizard that performs the normalization process by examining a table design and suggesting a way to divide the table for maximum efficiency

e. an aggregate function that counts the records in a column

6. Delete Rows button

f. an optional part of Design view where you can enter a field description

7. normalization

g. a data type

8. count

h. function that calculates values across a range of data

9. currency

i. a row inserted at the bottom of a table that provides a menu of functions for each column in the row

10. description

j. deletes a selected field row in Design view

True/False

Circle T if the statement is true or F if the statement is false.

T F 1. If you haven't already defined a primary key, Access will prompt you to do so when you save the table in Design view.

T F 2. Well-designed databases store the same data in more than one place.

T F 3. The row selector is located at the bottom of the table.

T F 4. The Table Analyzer does not remove the original table.

T F 5. The Table Analyzer gives you the choice of whether to create a query.

T F 6. The Table Analyzer does not add new fields.

T F 7. Average is an example of an aggregate function.

T F 8. The Total row is inserted above the asterisk row.

T F 9. Certain functions only work with certain data types.

T F 10. You cannot delete a Total row, but you can hide it.

Competency Assessment

Project 9-1: Summarize the Sales Table

The Sales table you created at Lucerne Publishing seems incomplete. Add a Total row to summarize the data.

USE Lucerne PublishingXXX that you saved in a previous exercise.

1. Open the Sales table.
2. On the HOME tab, in the Records group, click the **Totals** button. The Total row appears.
3. Click the **down arrow** in the Total row of the Gross Sales column. Select **Sum** from the menu.
4. Click the **down arrow** in the Total row of the Cost of Goods column. Select **Sum** from the menu.
5. Click the **down arrow** in the Total row of the Net Sales column. Select **Sum** from the menu.
6. Save and close the table.

CLOSE the database.

Project 9-2: Analyze the Fourth Coffee Customers Table

In your part-time job as an office assistant at Fourth Coffee, you have been taking on most of the database responsibilities. As you learn more and more about Access, you decide to use the Table Analyzer to check a table you created previously to make sure it is efficient.

GET READY. LAUNCH Access if it is not already running.

1. **OPEN** *Fourth Coffee Inventory* from the data files for this lesson.
2. **SAVE** the database as *Fourth Coffee InventoryXXX* (where *XXX* is your initials).
3. Open the Customers table.
4. On the DATABASE TOOLS tab, in the Analyze group, click the Analyze Table button. The Table Analyzer Wizard dialog box appears.
5. Click Next > to display the next Table Analyzer Wizard dialog box.
6. Click Next > to display the next Table Analyzer Wizard dialog box.
7. The Customers table should be selected. Click Next>.
8. The Yes, let the Wizard decide option button should be selected. Click Next>.
9. A message is displayed that says the wizard does not recommend dividing the table. Click OK.
10. Click Cancel to close the Table Analyzer Wizard.
11. **CLOSE** the table.

LEAVE the database open for use in the next project.

Proficiency Assessment

Project 9-3: Design the Fourth Coffee Sales Table

Sales data for Fourth Coffee has just come in for the first quarter. The manager asks you to create a table that displays the sales for each of the five stores in your division. Note: Each store is known by a three-digit number, such as 656.

USE the *Fourth Coffee InventoryXXX* database that you saved in a previous exercise.

1. Create a new table in Design view.
2. Key ID as the first field name and [press the Tab key]. Set the data type to AutoNumber.
3. Key Sales Month as the second field name and [press the Tab key]. Keep the default data type.
4. Enter the remaining field names and data types, as shown in Figure 9-20. Set the primary key as shown.

Figure 9-20

Monthly Sales by Store in Design view

Field Name	Data Type	Description (Optional)
🔑 ID	AutoNumber	
Sales Month	Short Text	
Store	Short Text	
Sales	Currency	

Monthly Sales by Store

5. Save the table as Monthly Sales by Store.
6. Switch to Datasheet view.
7. Enter the data in the table as shown in Figure 9-21.

Figure 9-21

Monthly Sales by Store table

ID	Sales Month	Store	Sales	Click to Add
1	January	651	$88,432.00	
2	February	651	$97,798.00	
3	March	651	$67,890.00	
4	April	651	$59,098.00	
5	January	656	$105,890.00	
6	February	656	$96,789.00	
7	March	656	$96,789.00	
8	April	656	$87,890.00	
9	January	660	$106,098.00	
10	February	660	$77,998.00	
11	March	660	$94,927.00	
12	April	660	$84,123.00	
13	January	662	$90,890.00	
14	February	662	$67,223.00	
15	March	662	$87,010.00	
16	April	662	$74,280.00	
*	(New)			

8. Insert a **Total** row.
9. Count the Sales Month field and sum the Sales field.
10. Save and close the table.

CLOSE the database.

Project 9-4: Summarize the Wingtip Toys Table

As marketing coordinator at Wingtip Toys, you are constantly examining sales data and trying to think of ways to increase sales. Total the inventory table to get a clear picture of the current inventory.

GET READY. LAUNCH Access if it is not already running.

1. **OPEN** *Wingtip Toys Inventory* from the data files for this lesson.
2. **SAVE** the database as *Wingtip Toys InventoryXXX* (where *XXX* is your initials).
3. Open the **Inventory** table.
4. Insert a Total row.
5. Count the Description field, sum the In Stock field, and sum the Price field.
6. **SAVE** and **CLOSE** the table.

LEAVE the database open for use in the next project.

Mastery Assessment

Project 9-5: Design the Wingtip Toys Yearly Sales Table

The owner of Wingtip Toys has given you yearly sales data for each of the company's sales channels. Create a table in which to store and total the data.

USE the *Wingtip Toys InventoryXXX* that you saved in a previous exercise.

1. Create a new table in Design view.
2. Create the table as shown in Figure 9-22.

Figure 9-22

Yearly Sales table in
Design view

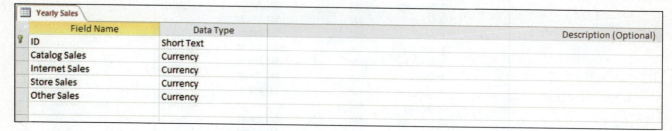

3. Save the table as **Yearly Sales** and switch to Datasheet view to review the table you just created.

4. Switch back to Design view.

5. Insert a blank row above the Catalog Sales field.

6. Key **Yr** as a new field with the Short Text data type.

7. Select the **Yr** field and click the **Primary Key** button to designate the Yr field as the new primary key.

8. Delete the **ID** field.

9. **SAVE** the table and switch to Datasheet view.

10. Enter data in the table as shown in Figure 9-23.

Figure 9-23

Yearly Sales table

Yr	Catalog Sales	Internet Sales	Store Sales	Other Sales	Click to Add
2014	$87,987.00	$109,897.00	$208,767.00	$23,987.00	
2015	$57,984.00	$98,789.00	$197,098.00	$10,761.00	
2016	$61,089.00	$78,907.00	$168,234.00	$9,125.00	
*					

11. **SAVE** the table.

12. Insert a **Total** row.

13. Sum the Catalog Sales, Internet Sales, Store Sales, and Other Sales columns.

14. **SAVE** and **CLOSE** the table.

CLOSE the database.

Project 9-6: Analyze the Alpine Reservations Table

As administrative assistant for Alpine Ski House, you have noticed that one of the tables you use on a regular basis seems large and cumbersome and you have to enter some of the same data again and again. You decide to run the Table Analyzer to see if the table needs to be split.

GET READY. LAUNCH Access if it is not already running.

1. **OPEN** *Alpine Reservations* from the data files for this lesson.

2. **SAVE** the database as *Alpine ReservationsXXX* (where XXX is your initials).

3. Select the **Reservations** table in the Navigation Pane.

4. Run the Table Analyzer, letting the wizard decide how to split the table.

5. Rename Table1 to **Reservation Details** and rename Table2 to **Room Details**.

6. Select the **ID** field in the Reservation Details table and designate it as the primary key.

7. Create the query and finish the wizard.

8. **SAVE** and **CLOSE** the database.

CLOSE Access.

LESSON SKILL MATRIX

Skill	Exam Objective	Objective Number
Creating Advanced Forms		
Using Application Parts to Create Blank Forms	Create forms with Application Parts	4.1.2
Creating a Navigation Form	Use Navigation forms	1.3.3

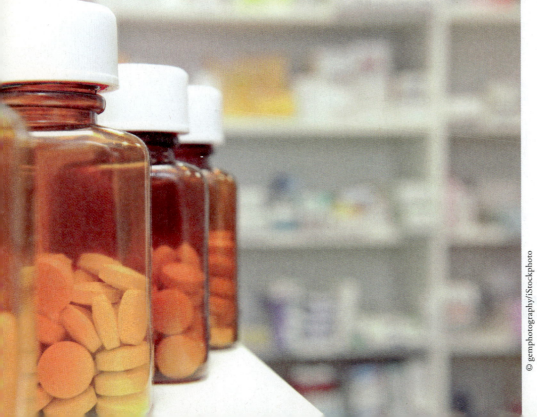

KEY TERMS

- Blank Forms
- hierarchical form
- main form
- Multiple Items tool
- Navigation form
- split form
- subform

© gemphotography/iStockphoto

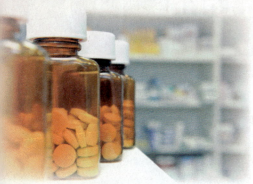

© gemphotography/iStockphoto

As a regional manager for Contoso Pharmaceuticals, you are in charge of overseeing the sales reps in your division. The salespeople you supervise call on doctors to promote Contoso medications and to leave samples. You use Access to put the sales information together and pull data from a variety of sources. In this lesson, you learn how to create a multi-item form, a split form, and a subform.

SOFTWARE ORIENTATION

The Templates Group and the Forms Group

The Application Parts button in the Templates group and the Navigation and More Forms buttons in the Forms group, all located on the CREATE tab, contain menus with commands for creating all types of forms—some of which you have already learned about in Lesson 5. Figures 10-1, 10-2, and 10-3 show the menus and commands you use to create advanced forms. Use these figures as references throughout this lesson as well as the rest of this book.

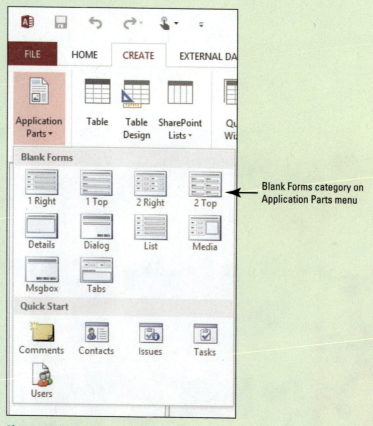

Blank Forms category on Application Parts menu

Figure 10-1

Application Parts button and menu

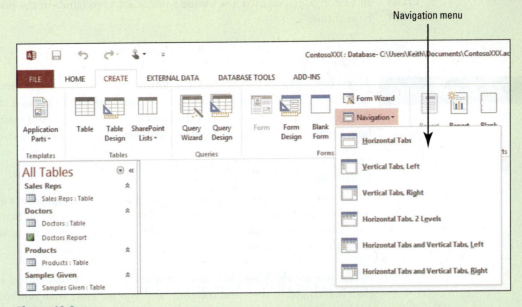

Figure 10-2
Navigation button and menu

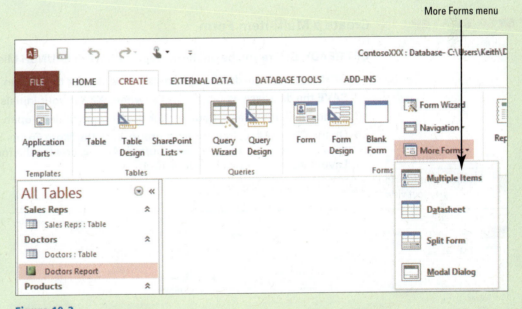

Figure 10-3
More Forms button and menu

Cross Ref In Lesson 5, you learned how to use some of the commands in the Forms group to create several basic forms.

CREATING ADVANCED FORMS

The Bottom Line

Access provides tools to help you create forms quickly—including advanced forms with features that can improve the usability of your database. The **Multiple Items tool** creates a customizable form that displays multiple records. A **split form** gives you two views of your data at the same time—in both Form view and Datasheet view. A **subform** is a form that is inserted into another form.

Creating a Multi-Item Form

When you create a simple form by using the Form tool, Access creates a form that displays a single record at a time. To create a form that displays multiple records but that is more customizable than a datasheet, you can use the Multiple Items tool. In this exercise, you create a Multi-Item form using the Multiple Items tool.

When you use the Multiple Items tool, the form that Access creates resembles a datasheet. The data is arranged in rows and columns, and you see more than one record at a time. However, a Multiple Items form gives you more customization options than a datasheet, such as the ability to add graphical elements, buttons, and other controls.

STEP BY STEP **Create a Multi-Item Form**

GET READY. Before you begin these steps, be sure to **LAUNCH** Microsoft Access.

1. **OPEN** the *Contoso* database from the data files for this lesson.
2. **SAVE** the database as *ContosoXXX* (where *XXX* is your initials).
3. In the Navigation Pane, double-click the **Doctors** table to open it.
4. On the CREATE tab, in the Forms group, click the **More Forms** button. On the menu that appears, click the **Multiple Items** button. Access creates the form and displays it in Layout view, as shown in Figure 10-4.

Figure 10-4

Multiple Items form in Layout view

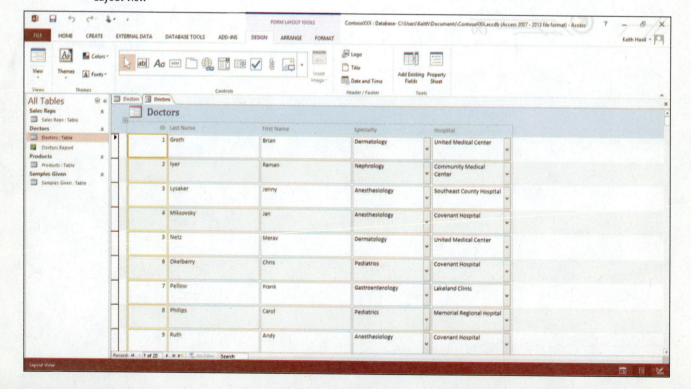

5. Scroll down to view the multiple records on the form.

6. Click the **FILE** tab and click **Save**.

7. In the Save As dialog box, key **Doctors Multiple** and click **OK**.

8. Click the **Close** button on Doctors Multiple to close the form.

9. Click the **Close** button on Doctors to close the table.

10. **LEAVE** the database open.

PAUSE. LEAVE Access open to use in the next exercise.

 Cross Ref   You learned about using controls to format your forms in Lesson 8.

Creating a Split Form

Creating a split form allows you to see two views of your data at the same time—in Form view and in Datasheet view. The two views are connected to the same data source and are completely synchronized with each other. In this exercise, you create a split form.

Working with split forms gives you the benefits of both types of forms in a single form. Selecting a field in the Datasheet view of the form selects the same field in the Form view part of the form. When you add, edit, or delete data in the Datasheet view, the change is reflected in the Form view.

STEP BY STEP   **Create a Split Form**

USE the database that is open from the previous exercise.

1. In the Navigation Pane, double-click the **Sales Reps** table to open it.

2. On the CREATE tab, in the Forms group, click the **More Forms** button. On the menu that appears, click the **Split Form** button. Access creates the form and displays it in Form view and Datasheet view at the same time, as shown in Figure 10-5.

Figure 10-5

Split form

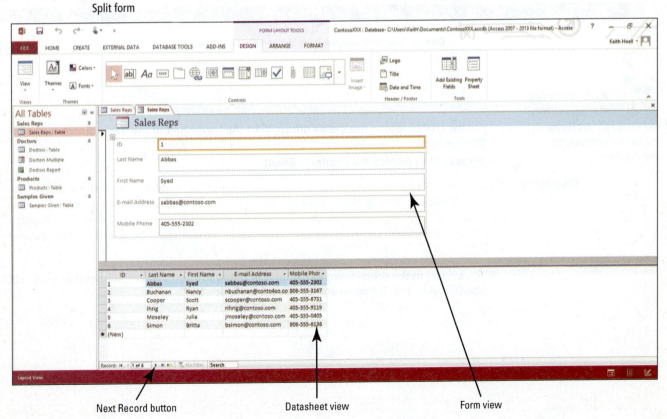

Next Record button   Datasheet view   Form view

3. Click the Next Record navigation button to display the next record in Form view.

4. In the Datasheet view on the bottom, place the insertion point in the Mobile Phone field for Nancy Buchanan. Notice that the same field is selected in the Form view at the top.

5. Change the number for Nancy Buchanan in the Mobile Phone field to 806-555-4489.

6. Click anywhere on the Form view above the datasheet and notice that the mobile phone number has been changed there as well, as shown in Figure 10-6.

Figure 10-6

Editing a split form

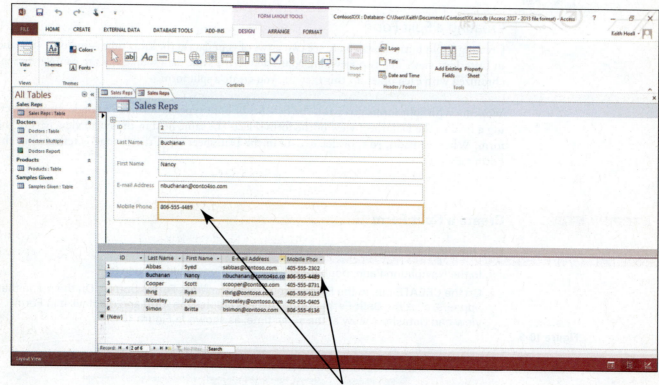

Changes made to the datasheet will also be reflected on the form

Another Way
You can also click the Property Sheet button on the Ribbon to display the Property Sheet.

7. On the HOME tab, in the Views group, click the lower half of the View button and click Design View.

8. [Press F4] to display the Property Sheet.

Take Note   Throughout this lesson you will see information that appears in black text within brackets, such as [Press Enter], or [your e-mail address]. The information contained in the brackets is intended to be directions for you rather than something you actually type word-for-word. It will instruct you to perform an action or substitute text. Do **not** type the actual text that appears within brackets.

9. Click Form in the drop-down list at the top of the Property Sheet, if necessary, and click the FORMAT tab, if necessary, as shown in Figure 10-7.

Figure 10-7

Property Sheet

Press F4 to display the Property Sheet

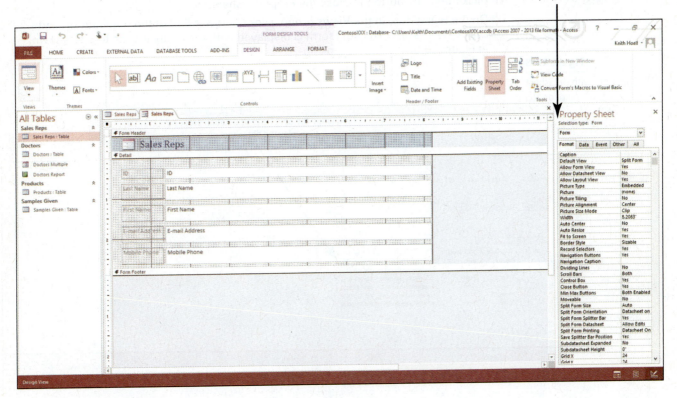

10. Scroll down to the Split Form Orientation property, click the **down arrow**, and click **Datasheet on Top**, as shown in Figure 10-8.

Figure 10-8

Changing a property

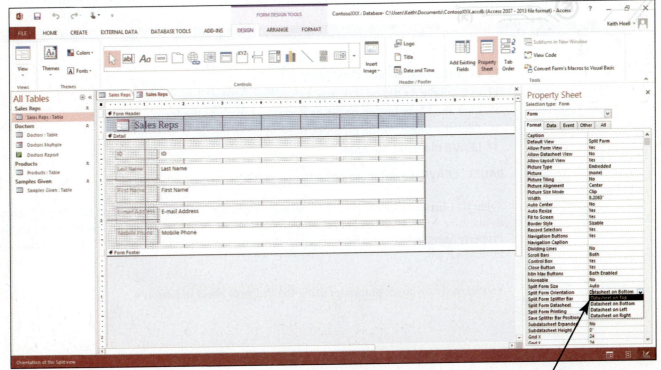

Datasheet on Top property selected

Take Note If all text for the properties is not visible, click the left border of the Property Sheet and drag to widen it.

11. Click the **Close** button to close the Property Sheet.
12. On the HOME tab, in the Views group, click the lower half of the **View** button and click **Layout View**. The split form is displayed with the datasheet on top, as shown in Figure 10-9.

Figure 10-9

Split form with datasheet on top

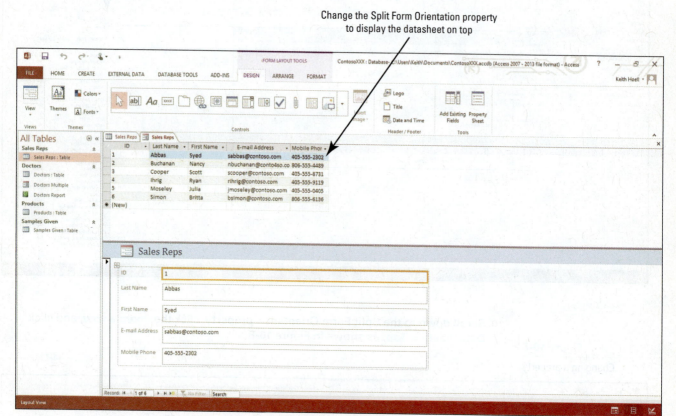

13. Click the **FILE** tab and click **Save**.
14. In the Save As dialog box, key **Sales Reps Split** and click **OK**.
15. Click the **Close** button on Sales Reps Split to close the form.
16. Click the **Close** button on Sales Reps to close the table.
17. **LEAVE** the database open.

PAUSE. LEAVE the database open to use in the next exercise.

Table 10-1 lists some of the properties related to split forms that you can set on the Property Sheet to fine-tune your form. To change form properties, switch to Design view, press F4 to display the Property Sheet, select Form from the drop-down list at the top of the Property Sheet, and click the FORMAT tab.

 Cross Ref You learned how to set properties using the Property Sheet in Lesson 4.

Table 10-1

Properties related to
split forms

Property	View(s) in which you can set the property	Description
Split Form Orientation	Design view	Allows you to define whether the datasheet appears above, below, to the left, or to the right of the form.
Split Form Datasheet	Design view or Layout view	If set to Allow Edits (and the form's record source is updateable), Access allows edits to be made on the datasheet. If set to Read Only, Access prevents edits from being made on the datasheet.
Split Form Splitter Bar	Design view	If set to Yes, Access allows you to resize the form and datasheet by moving the splitter bar that separates the two parts. If set to No, the splitter bar is hidden, and the form and datasheet cannot be resized.
Save Splitter Bar Position	Design view	If set to Yes, the form opens with the splitter bar in the same position in which you last left it. If set to No, the form and datasheet cannot be resized, and the splitter bar is hidden.
Split Form Size	Design view or Layout view	Allows you to specify an exact height or width (depending on whether the form is split vertically or horizontally) for the Form view of the split form. For example, key 1" to set the form to a height or width of 1 inch. Key Auto to set the dimension by other means, such as dragging the splitter bar in Layout view.
Split Form Printing	Design view or Layout view	Allows you to define which portion of the form is printed when you print the form. If set to Form Only, only the form portion is printed. If set to Datasheet Only, only the datasheet portion is printed.

Creating a Subform

A subform is a convenient tool that allows you to view data from more than one table or query on the same form. A subform is a form that is inserted into another form. The primary form is called the **main form**, and the form within the form is called the subform. A form/subform combination is sometimes referred to as a **hierarchical form**, a *master/detail form*, or a *parent/child form*. You can use the Form Wizard to help you create subforms quickly. For best results, all relationships should be established first. This enables Access to automatically create the links between subforms and main forms. In this exercise, you create a subform.

When working with a relational database, you often need to view data from more than one table or query on the same form. For example, you want to see customer data, but you also want to see information about the customer's orders at the same time. Subforms are a convenient tool for doing this.

Subforms are especially effective when you want to show data from tables or queries that have a one-to-many relationship—the main form shows data from the "one" side of the relationship and the subform shows the data from the "many" side of the relationship.

STEP BY STEP   **Create a Subform**

USE the database that is open from the previous exercise.

1. On the CREATE tab, in the Forms group, click Form Wizard.
2. In the first screen on the Form Wizard, click the down arrow in the Tables/Queries box and click Table: Samples Given.
3. In the Available Fields box, double-click the Week Name, Sales Rep, Product, and Quantity fields to move them to the Selected Fields box.
4. Click the down arrow in the Tables/Queries box and click Table: Doctors.

5. In the Available Fields box, double-click the **Last Name**, **First Name**, **Specialty**, and **Hospital** fields to move them to the Selected Fields box. The screen should look like Figure 10-10.

Figure 10-10

Form Wizard, screen 1

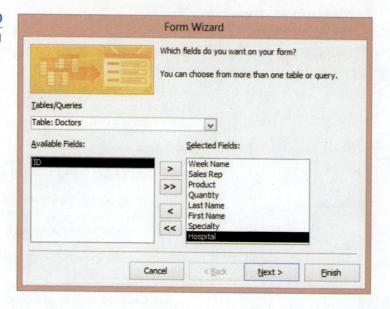

6. Click the **Next >** button.

7. In the *How do you want to view your data?* box, click **by Doctors**. The *Form with subform(s)* option button should be selected, and the Form Wizard should look like Figure 10-11.

Figure 10-11

Form Wizard, screen 2

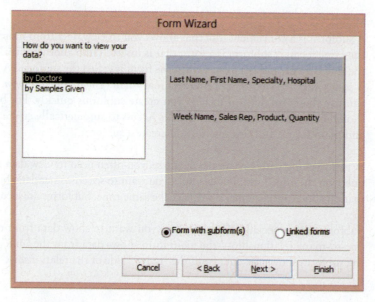

8. Click the **Next >** button.

9. Click the **Tabular** option button to select that as the layout for your subform, as shown in Figure 10-12.

Figure 10-12

Form Wizard, screen 3

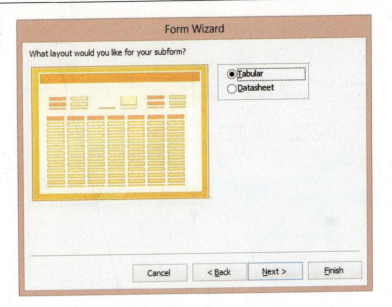

Figure 10-12

Form Wizard, screen 3

10. Click the **Next >** button. Access has suggested titles for the forms, as shown in Figure 10-13. Keep the default selection to open the form.

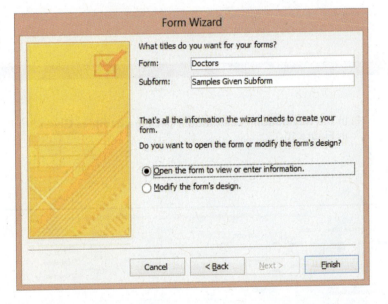

Figure 10-13

Form Wizard, screen 4

11. Click the **Finish** button to create the forms. The Doctors form appears with the Samples Given subform, as shown in Figure 10-14.

Figure 10-14

Doctors form with subform

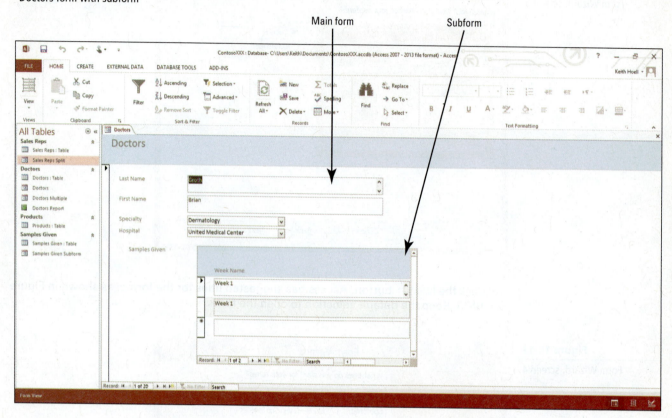

12. In the Navigation Pane, double-click the **Samples Given Subform** to open it, as shown in Figure 10-15.

Figure 10-15

Samples Given subform

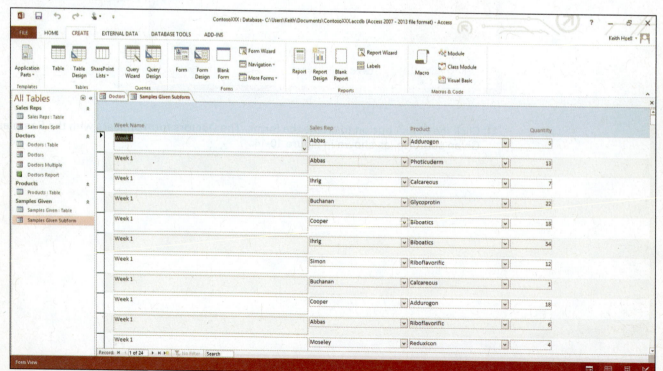

13. Scroll down and to the right, if necessary, to see the data contained in the records and then click the Close button on the Samples Given Subform to close the subform.

14. Click the Close button on the Doctors form to close the form.

15. **LEAVE** the database open.

PAUSE. LEAVE the database open to use in the next exercise.

USING APPLICATION PARTS TO CREATE BLANK FORMS

The Bottom Line

As you learned in Lesson 2, the Application Parts gallery consists of two categories, **Blank Forms** and Quick Start. The Blank Forms category contains a collection of 10 form parts that allow you to add predefined forms to a database. In this exercise, you create an Application Parts Blank Form and populate the form with bound controls using the Field List.

Application Parts Blank Forms are created as unbound forms and provide a prearranged control layout. They can also provide unbound command button controls, depending on what type of Blank Form you choose. These forms can also be easily populated with bound controls by using the Field List.

Application Parts Blank Forms differ from adding a form using the Blank Forms tool since you can add forms that automatically include command buttons that provide additional functionality such as saving a record or closing a form. Using Application Parts Blank Forms, you can also easily add forms that do more than just display data from a record source. Unbound forms can be created to display messages to a user or to provide dialog boxes that prompt the user for an action. These unbound forms can be referenced through code using Visual Basic for Applications (VBA) to help provide a more functional database.

STEP BY STEP **Use Application Parts to Create Blank Forms**

USE the database that is open from the previous exercise.

1. On the CREATE tab, in the Templates group, click the Application Parts button. In the Blank Forms category, hover your mouse over the 1 Right button. A ScreenTip appears informing you of the form's layout.

2. Click the 1 Right button and a new form object named SingleOneColumnRightLabels appears in the Navigation Pane in the Unrelated Objects category, as shown in Figure 10-16.

Figure 10-16

New Blank Form object in Navigation Pane

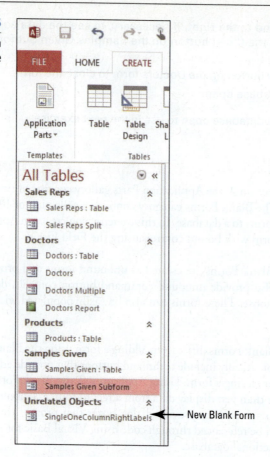

New Blank Form

3. Open the **SingleOneColumnRightLabels** form. The form displays in Form view, as shown in Figure 10-17.

Figure 10-17

Blank Form in Form view

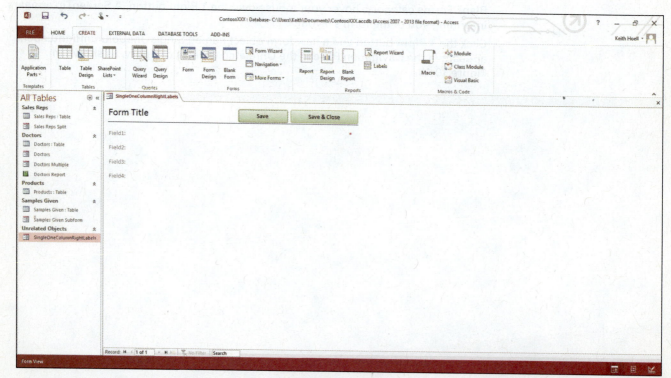

4. Switch to Layout view and [press **Shift**] while clicking on the label control placeholders titled **Field1**, **Field2**, **Field3**, and **Field4** to select them all. [Press the **Delete** key] on the keyboard to delete the label controls. Also delete the label control placeholder that contains the red asterisk, which could be used to denote an important field, like a key field.

5. Click the **Add Existing Fields** button in the Tools group. The Field List pane appears. If necessary, click the **Show all tables** link. Your screen should resemble Figure 10-18.

Figure 10-18

Blank Form in Layout view and Field List pane

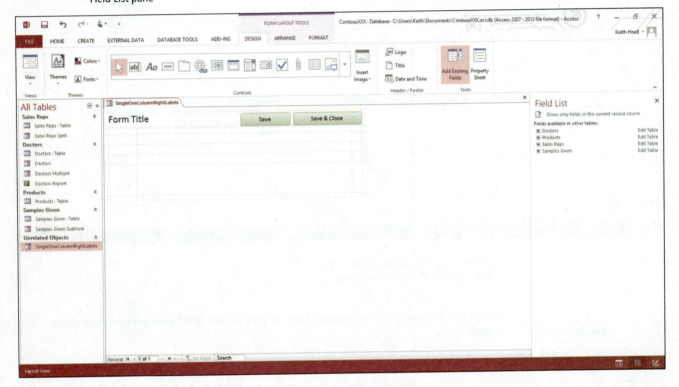

6. In the Field List pane, expand the Doctors table.

7. In the Field List pane, click and drag each **Last Name**, **First Name**, **Specialty**, and **Hospital** field to the form and to the right placeholder of the original locations of the Field1, Field2, Field3, and Field4 label controls that you just deleted. You screen should resemble Figure 10-19.

Figure 10-19

Form with fields from Field
List pane

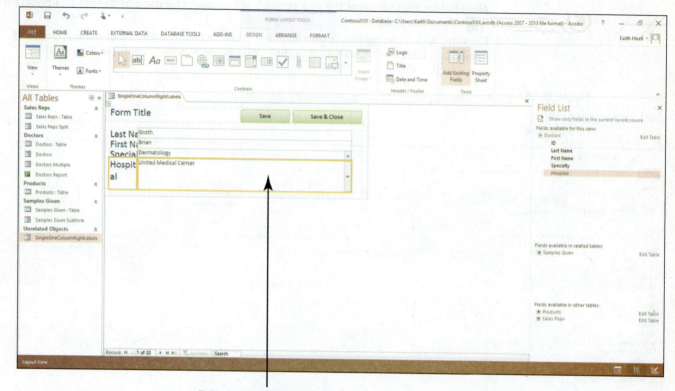

Fields dragged to placeholders on
right side of previously deleted labels

8. Resize the label and field controls that you just added until your screen resembles Figure 10-20.

Figure 10-20

Form with re-sized label and
field control

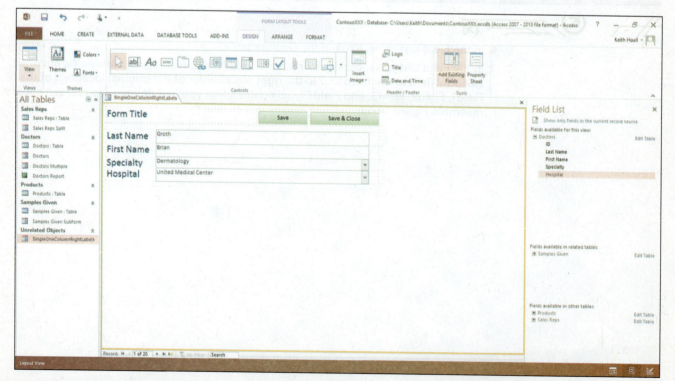

9. Click the Form Title label and delete Form Title. Key Doctors.

10. Switch to Form view and cycle through the records. Click the Save & Close button on the form to close the form. Click Yes in the dialog box prompting you to save design changes to the form.

11. Rename the SingleOneColumnRightLabels form as Doctors Blank Form.

PAUSE. LEAVE the database open to use in the next exercise.

CERTIFICATION READY?   4.1.2

How do you create forms with Application Parts?

CREATING A NAVIGATION FORM

The Bottom Line

The ability to create **Navigation forms** was introduced in Access 2010. A Navigation form includes a set of navigation tabs that you can click to display forms and reports. In this exercise, you create a Navigation form.

As you learned in Lesson 2, you can create databases based on templates. When a database is created using a web database template, a Navigation form is used as the main interface within the database since the Navigation Pane cannot be viewed from within a web browser. However, Navigation forms can also be used from within the Access application window to simplify your interaction with database objects. For example, you can easily click a tab on a Navigation form to view a form to add, view, or edit data. Similarly, you can simply click a button on the Navigation form to work with reports. Navigation forms are created by clicking the Navigation button in the Forms group on the CREATE tab. There are six Navigation form layouts from which to choose. Each layout includes a specific arrangement of tabs that can then be modified in Layout or Design view to access forms and reports. In Layout view, form and report objects can be clicked and dragged from the Navigation Pane to tabs to quickly add functionality to the Navigation form. You can also type a form or report's name as the tab's label and Access will automatically bind the associated form or report to that label. You can also work with Navigation forms using Design view to have the most control over design options, but you lose the ability to quickly add form and report objects just by clicking and dragging them to the tabs or modifying the labels.

Take Note   You can also add fields from multiple tables to your Navigation form using the Field List pane in both Design and Layout views to allow for even greater customization.

STEP BY STEP   **Create a Navigation Form**

USE the database that is open from the previous exercise.

1. On the CREATE tab, in the Forms group, click the Navigation button to display a menu that contains six form layouts.

2. Click the Horizontal Tabs button and a new Navigation form appears in Layout view, as shown in Figure 10-21.

Figure 10-21

Figure 10-21

Navigation form in
Layout view

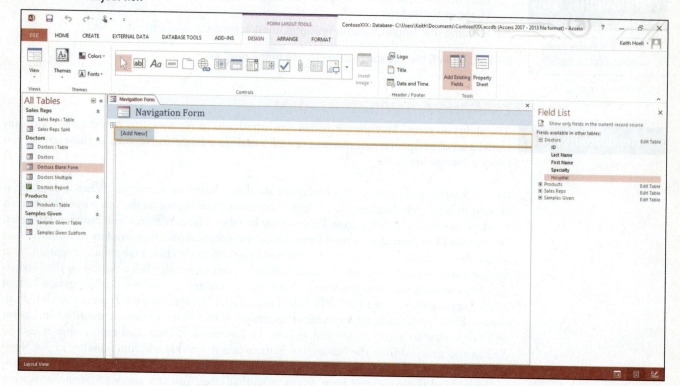

3. Click and drag the **Doctors** form object from the Navigation Pane to the [Add New] tab near the top of the form. The form tab has been renamed Doctors and all the Doctors form's controls appear. A new [Add New] tab appears next to the Doctors tab. Your screen should resemble Figure 10-22.

Figure 10-22

Navigation form displaying
Doctors form

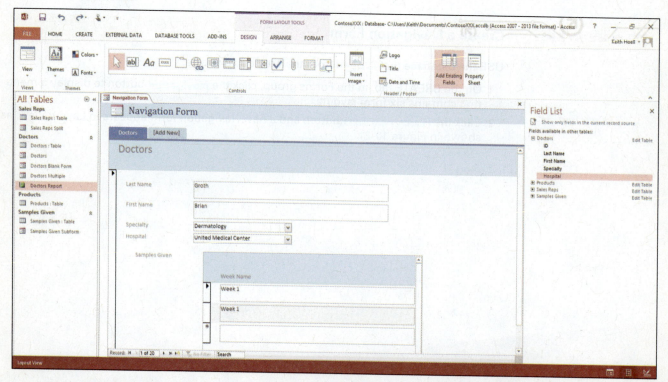

Take Note You cannot drag table objects from the Navigation Pane to the [Add New] tab.

4. Click and drag the Doctors Report object from the Navigation Pane to the [Add New] tab near the top of the form. The form tab has been renamed Doctors Report and all the Doctors report controls appear. A new [Add New] tab appears next to the Doctors Report tab. Your screen should resemble Figure 10-23.

Figure 10-23

Navigation form displaying Doctors report

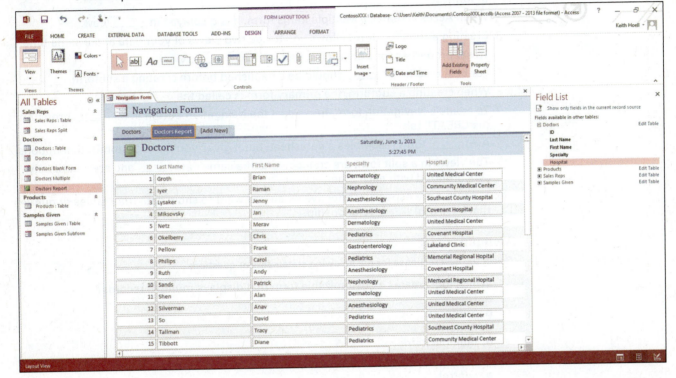

5. Double-click the Doctors tab and key Doctors Form to rename the tab.
6. Switch to Form view and use the form's tabs to switch between the form and report.
7. Click the FILE tab and click Save.
8. In the Save As dialog box, key Doctors Navigation Form and click OK.
9. Click the Close button to close the Doctors Navigation Form.

STOP. CLOSE the database.

CERTIFICATION READY? 1.3.3

How do you use Navigation forms?

SKILL SUMMARY

In This Lesson You Learned How To:	Exam Objective	Objective Number
Create Advanced Forms		
Use Application Parts to Create Blank Forms	Create forms with Application Parts	4.1.2
Create a Navigation Form	Use Navigation forms	1.3.3

Knowledge Assessment

Fill in the Blank

Complete the following sentences by writing the correct word or words in the blanks provided.

1. The Forms group, located on the _____ tab, contains commands for creating all types of forms.

2. When Access creates a Multiple Items form, it is displayed in _____ view.

3. Creating a(n) _____ form allows you to see two views of your data at the same time.

4. To set properties for a split form, first switch to _____ view.

5. For best results, all _____ should be established before creating a subform.

6. When creating a subform, the primary form is called the _____ form.

7. To create a Navigation form, first select the Navigation button in the _____ group on the CREATE tab.

8. A(n) _____ form resembles a datasheet, but it gives you more customization options.

9. The views in a split form are connected to the same data _____ and are completely synchronized with each other.

10. Subforms are especially effective when you want to show data from tables or queries that have a(n) _____ relationship.

Multiple Choice

Select the best response for the following statements or questions.

1. Which tool creates a customizable form that displays multiple records?
   a. Query
   b. Subform
   c. Report
   d. Multiple Items

2. When you use the Multiple Items tool, the form that Access creates resembles a
   a. control.
   b. datasheet.
   c. filter.
   d. query.

3. A split form shows your data in which views?
   a. Form view and Datasheet view
   b. Layout view and Design view
   c. Form view and Design view
   d. Layout view and Datasheet view

4. Which split form property allows you to define whether the datasheet appears above, below, to the left, or to the right of the form?
   a. Split Form Orientation
   b. Split Form Datasheet
   c. Split Form Splitter Bar
   d. Split Form Size

5. Which type of form allows you to view data from more than one table or query on the same form?
   a. Multi-item form
   b. Split form
   c. Subform
   d. Navigation form

6. Which tool would you use to create a subform?
   a. Form Design
   b. Blank Form
   c. Form
   d. Form Wizard

7. A form/subform combination is sometimes referred to as a
   a. hierarchical form.
   b. master/detail form.
   c. parent/child form.
   d. all of the above.

8. Which type of form already has a predefined layout and can automatically contain command buttons?
   a. Multi-item form
   b. Split form
   c. Subform
   d. Application Parts Blank form

9. What type of form can be added to a database to simplify your interaction with objects preventing the need to use the Navigation Pane?
   a. Subform
   b. Blank form
   c. Split form
   d. Navigation form

10. Unbound forms can be easily created that display messages to users using
   a. Application Parts Blank forms.
   b. Navigation forms.
   c. Split forms.
   d. none of the above.

Competency Assessment

Project 10-1: Create a Multi-Item Form

In your job as a travel agent at Margie's Travel, you want to create a form that displays multiple database records but that is more customizable than a datasheet. You use the Multiple Items tool to create the form.

GET READY. LAUNCH Access if it is not already running.

1. **OPEN** the *Margie's Events* database from the data files for this lesson.
2. **SAVE** the database as *Margie's EventsXXX* (where *XXX* is your initials).
3. In the Navigation Pane, double-click the Events table to open it.
4. On the CREATE tab, in the Forms group, click the More Forms button and then click the Multiple Items button on the menu that appears.
5. Scroll down and to the right to view the multiple records on the form.
6. Click the FILE tab and click Save.
7. In the Save As dialog box, key Events Multiple and click OK.
8. Click the Close button to close the Events Multiple form.
9. Click the Close button to close the Events table.
10. **CLOSE** the database.

LEAVE Access open for the next project.

Project 10-2: Create a Split Form

Your brother, who owns Wingtip Toys, wants to see two views of his inventory data at the same time—in Form view and in Datasheet view. He asks you to help him create a split form and to modify it so that the datasheet is on top.

GET READY. LAUNCH Access if it is not already running.

1. **OPEN** *Toy Stock* from the data files for this lesson.
2. **SAVE** the database as *Toy StockXXX* (where *XXX* is your initials).
3. In the Navigation Pane, double-click the **Inventory** table to open it.
4. On the CREATE tab, in the Forms group, click the **More Forms** button and then the **Split Form** button on the menu that appears. This will create the split form and display the Inventory table in Form view and Datasheet view at the same time.
5. On the HOME tab, in the Views group, click the **View** button and click **Design View**.
6. [Press **F4**] to display the Property Sheet.
7. Click **Form** in the drop-down list at the top and click the **FORMAT** tab, if necessary.
8. Scroll down to the Split Form Orientation property, click the **down arrow**, and click **Datasheet on Top**.
9. Click the **Close** button to close the Property Sheet.
10. On the HOME tab, in the Views group, click the **View** button and click **Layout View** to display the split form with the datasheet on top.
11. Click the **FILE** tab and click **Save**.
12. In the Save As dialog box, key **Inventory Split** and click **OK**.
13. Click the **Close** button to close the Inventory Split form.
14. Click the **Close** button to close the Inventory table.
15. **CLOSE** the database.

LEAVE Access open for the next project.

Proficiency Assessment

Project 10-3: Create Forms for the Fourth Coffee Club Database

Information about each selection for the Fourth Coffee monthly coffee club is stored in an Access database. As purchasing manager, you use the database frequently and need to have several types of forms available to work with the data. Create a multi-item form and a split form.

GET READY. LAUNCH Access if it is not already running.

1. **OPEN** *Fourth Coffee Club* from the data files for this lesson.
2. **SAVE** the database as *Fourth Coffee ClubXXX* (where *XXX* is your initials).
3. Create a multi-item form for the Regular Coffee table.
4. Name the form **Regular Coffee Multi** and close it.
5. Create a multi-item form for the Decaf Coffee table.
6. Name the form **Decaf Coffee Multi** and close it.
7. Create a split form for the Regular Coffee table.
8. Name the form **Regular Coffee Split** and close it.
9. Create a split form for the Decaf Coffee table.
10. Name the form **Decaf Coffee Split** and close it.
11. **LEAVE** the database open for the next project.

LEAVE Access open for the next project.

Project 10-4: **Create a Subform**

As purchasing manager for Fourth Coffee, it would be helpful to view order data about coffee by coffee name. Create a subform that shows this data.

GET READY. LAUNCH Access if it is not already running.

1. On the CREATE tab, in the Forms group, click **Form Wizard**.
2. In the first screen on the Form Wizard, select **Table: Regular Coffee** in the Tables/Queries box.
3. Move the Name field to the Selected Fields box.
4. Select **Table: Orders** in the Tables/Queries box.
5. Move the Order Date, Distributor, and Pounds Ordered fields to the Selected Fields box.
6. In the second screen of the Form Wizard, choose to view your data **by Regular Coffee**.
7. In the third screen of the Form Wizard, choose to view your data in **tabular** layout.
8. In the final screen of the Form Wizard, accept the default form names and click **Finish**.
9. Navigate to the fourth record to see information about the orders placed to the distributors for River Road coffee.
10. Close the form.
11. **CLOSE** the database.

LEAVE Access open for the next project.

Mastery Assessment

Project 10-5: **Modify a Split Form**

As the manager at Southridge Video, you created a split form to work with the used game information in the Access database. However, when you open the form, it appears that someone has made changes because the datasheet is on the right and the splitter bar is not visible. Change the form properties back to the way you want them.

GET READY. LAUNCH Access if it is not already running.

1. **OPEN** *Used Games* from the data files for this lesson.
2. **SAVE** the database as *Used GamesXXX* (where *XXX* is initials).
3. Open the split form Games.
4. Switch to Design view and open the form properties.
5. Change the property to make the datasheet appear **on the top**.
6. Change the property to make the splitter bar visible, thus allowing the form and datasheet to be resized.
7. Change the form property so the form will open with the splitter bar in the same position in which you last left it.
8. Change the property to allow edits to be made on the datasheet.
9. Change the property to print only the datasheet portion of the form.
10. Switch to Layout view.
11. **CLOSE** the form and save the changes to the design when prompted.
12. **CLOSE** the database.

LEAVE Access open for the next project.

Project 10-6: Create a Navigation Form

Your son plays on a recreational league basketball team, and you have volunteered to manage the team's database of games, players, and statistics by tracking and updating data. In order to quickly and efficiently update data, you decide to create a Navigation form.

GET READY. LAUNCH Access if it is not already running.

1. **OPEN** *Stats* from the data files for this lesson.
2. **SAVE** the database as *StatsXXX* (where *XXX* is your initials).
3. Use the Stats: Table and the skills you have learned in this lesson to create a Navigation form using the Horizontal Tabs layout.
4. Save the form as Games, Players, Stats Navigation Form and close it.
5. **CLOSE** the database.

CLOSE Access.

Circling Back

Woodgrove Real Estate is growing and adding more listings. Your office has added another real estate agent and has begun listing commercial properties as well as residential ones. The database you created has been a great way to keep track of all the listings and other relevant information. As you learn more about Access, you begin using it for a wider variety of tasks.

Project 1: Create and Format a Report

You want to create a report to display data about each agent's listings. Use the Report Wizard and then switch to Design view to make changes to the format and add a control.

GET READY. Launch Access if it is not already running.

1. **OPEN** the *Real Estate* database from the data files for this lesson.
2. **SAVE** the database as *Real EstateXXX* (where XXX is your initials).
3. On the CREATE tab, in the Reports group, click the **Report Wizard** button.
4. In the Tables/Queries menu, choose **Table: Listings**.
5. Click the double right arrow **>>** button to move all the fields into the Selected Fields list.
6. Click the **ID** field to select it and click the left arrow **<** button to move it back to the Available Fields list.
7. Click the **Next >** button.
8. Click the **Listing Agent** field to select it and click the **>** button to add it as a grouping level.
9. Click the **Next >** button.
10. Select **Price** from the fields menu to sort in ascending order and click the **Next >** button.
11. In the Layout section, click the **Outline** button. In the Orientation section, click the **Landscape** button. Click **Next**.
12. Key **Listings Report** as the title of the report.
13. Click **Finish** to display the Listings Report.
14. On the PRINT PREVIEW tab, in the Close Preview group, click the **Close Print Preview** button to display the report in Design view.
15. In the Listing Agent Header section, click and drag the right border of the *Listing Agent* field to make it smaller.
16. Continue clicking and dragging the borders of the remaining report fields to resize them so your report looks similar to the report displayed in Report View, as shown in Figure 1.

Figure 1

Listings report

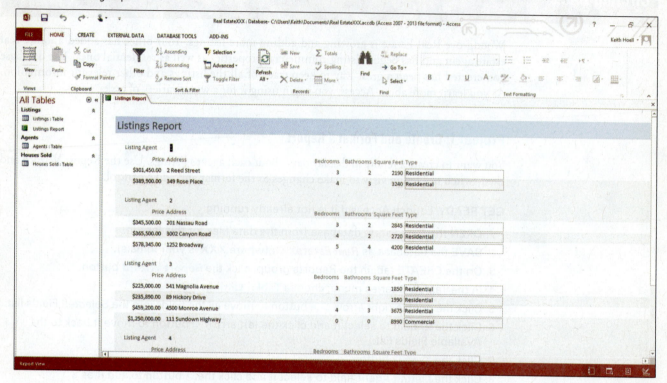

17. Click the **Close** button on the Listings Report to close the report and save the changes when prompted.

PAUSE. LEAVE the database open to use in the next project.

Project 2: Create and Modify Queries

You want to query the database to find all the house sales that closed in June. Create a query using the Query Wizard and then add criteria to get the information you need.

USE the database that is open from the previous project.

1. On the CREATE tab, in the Queries group, click the **Query Wizard** button to display the New Query dialog box.
2. Click **Simple Query Wizard** and then click **OK** to display the Simple Query Wizard.
3. In the Tables/Queries dropdown list, click **Table: Houses Sold**.
4. Under Available Fields, double-click **Listing Agent**, **Address**, **Selling Price**, and **Closing Date** to move them to the Selected Fields box.
5. Click the **Next** > button to display the next screen. Detail query should be selected.
6. Click the **Next** > button to display the final screen.
7. Click the **Finish** button to display the query.
8. On the HOME tab, in the Views group, click the **View** button and click **Design View**.
9. In the Criteria row of the Closing Date field, key **Between #6/1/2014# And #6/30/2014#**.
10. On the DESIGN tab, in the Results group, click the lower half of the **View** button and click **Datasheet View** to display the query results of all records for houses that closed in June.
11. Right-click the **Closing Date** field header and choose **Sort Oldest to Newest** on the menu. Your query should look similar to Figure 2.

Figure 2

Query Results

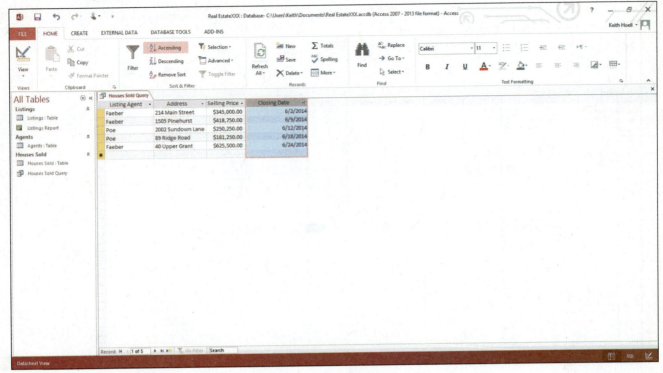

12. Click the **Close** button on the Houses Sold Query to close the query. When prompted to save, click **Yes**.

PAUSE. LEAVE the database open for the next project.

Project 3: Sum Table Data

You want to know the total value of the current listings. Open the table and add a Total row to get this information.

USE the database that is open from the previous project.

1. **OPEN** the **Listings** table.
2. On the HOME tab, in the Records group, click the **Totals** button. The Total row appears below the asterisk (*) row.
3. Click the **down arrow** in the Price column of the Total row. Select **Sum** from the menu. Your screen should look similar to Figure 3.

Figure 3

Totals row

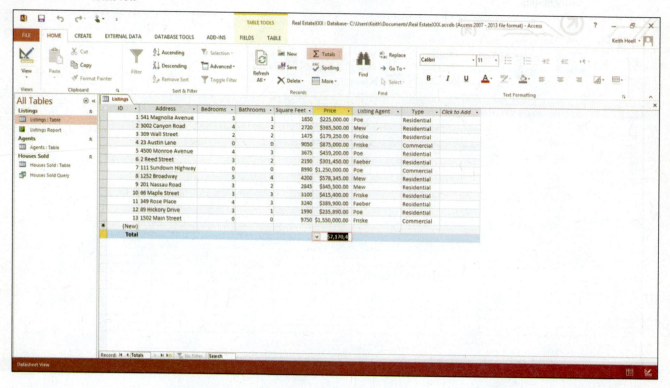

4. On the HOME tab, in the Records group, click the **Totals** button to hide the Total row.

5. On the HOME tab, in the Records group, click the **Totals** button again. The Total row reappears.

6. **SAVE** and **CLOSE** the table.

PAUSE. LEAVE the database open for the next project.

Project 4: Create a Subform

You want to see the real estate agent's contact information along with the listings. Use the Form Wizard to create a subform that will show all the data in the same place.

USE the database that is open from the previous project.

1. On the CREATE tab, in the Forms group, click **Form Wizard**.

2. In the first screen on the Form Wizard, click the **Tables/Queries box** down arrow and click **Table: Agents**.

3. In the Available Fields box, double-click the **Last Name**, **First Name**, and **Mobile Phone** fields to move them to the Selected Fields box.

4. Click the **Tables/Queries box** down arrow and click **Table: Listings**.

5. In the Available Fields box, double-click the **Address**, **Square Feet**, and **Price** fields to move them to the Selected Fields box.

6. Click **Next >**.

7. In the *How do you want to view your data?* box, click **by Agents**. The *Form with subform(s)* option button should be selected.

8. Click **Next >**.

9. Click the **Tabular** option button to select that as the layout for your subform.

10. Click **Next >**.

11. Click the **Finish** button to create the Agents form with the Listings Subform. Your form should look similar to Figure 4.

Figure 4

Subform

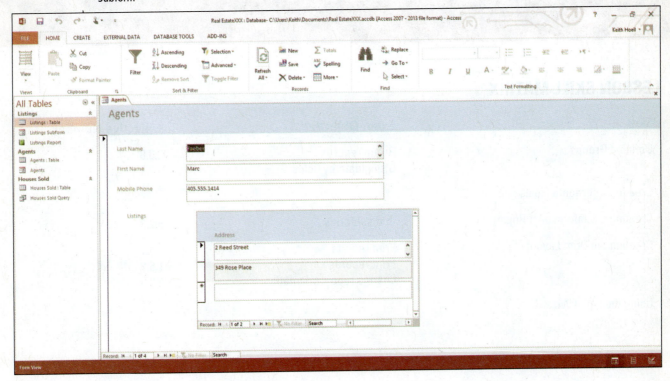

12. In the Navigation Pane, double-click the **Listings subform** to open it.

13. Scroll down to see the data contained in the records and then click the **Close** button on the Listings subform to close the subform.

14. Click the **Close** button on the Agents form to close it.

STOP. CLOSE the database.

11 Advanced Reports

LESSON SKILL MATRIX

Skill	Exam Objective	Objective Number
Defining Groups	Group records	2.3.8
	Group data by fields	5.2.1
Creating Aggregate Fields		
Creating a Subform on a Report	Add subforms	5.2.3
Creating the Print Layout	Print reports	1.5.1
	Print records	1.5.2
	Change report orientation	5.3.5
Using the Label Wizard		

KEY TERMS

- aggregate fields
- group
- group footer
- group header
- grouping fields
- grouping intervals
- grouping levels
- Label Wizard
- Print Preview

© joebrandt/iStockphoto

Consolidated Messenger is a New York City–based company that provides quick and reliable pickup and delivery services to area businesses. The company provides courier service by foot, bike, or truck. The company has a sales force that negotiates contracts with some of its larger corporate clients. As sales manager, you have created a database with tables and reports to keep track of this data. In this lesson, you generate reports that group and sort data, add a subform to a report, create aggregate fields to total data in reports, use Print Preview to adjust reports before printing, and use the Label Wizard to create labels for customer mailings.

DEFINING GROUPS

The Bottom Line

A **group** is a collection of records separated visually with any introductory or summary information displayed with it. Reports can be grouped on fields or expressions. A **grouping field** is a field by which data is grouped. **Grouping levels** are the nested arrangement of the groups in a report. Access creates indented levels to show the groups from highest to lowest priority. You can change a group's level in the Report Wizard by using the priority up and down arrows. Access allows you to specify as many as 10 grouping levels in a report. Groups can be nested so you can easily see the group structure.

When data is arranged in groups, it is often easier to comprehend and it becomes more meaningful. For example, if you want to see the sales performance for each region, it is easier to review this data if each region's sales are grouped together. You can go a step further and specify another group level, such as salesperson. This allows you to group a report by region and by salesperson within each region.

You can specify grouping intervals by using the Grouping Options button. **Grouping intervals** establish the way that records are grouped together. They can be very useful in arranging a large number of records in a group. You can group on the first character of a text field so that all of the records are visually separated alphabetically. You can specify a group interval of a day, week, month, or quarter on a date field. This is useful if you want to view the sales for each week in a report. You can also specify a custom interval.

Using the Report Wizard

You can easily specify groups with the Report Wizard when creating a new report. This is an easy and fast way to create a report with groups. The Report Wizard lets you specify how you would like data to be grouped as you create the report. You can also add grouping to an existing report using the Group, Sort, and Total pane. Grouping options let you further specify how you want the groups to appear in your report. In this exercise, you use the Report Wizard to specify grouping levels and create a report.

STEP BY STEP **Use the Report Wizard**

GET READY. Before you begin these steps, be sure to turn on and/or log on to your computer and **LAUNCH** Access.

1. **OPEN** *Messenger* from the data files for this lesson.
2. **SAVE** the database as *MessengerXXX* (where *XXX* is your initials).
3. Open the **Corporate Sales** table.
4. On the CREATE tab, in the Reports group, click the **Report Wizard** button. The first Report Wizard dialog box appears.
5. Select the **Region (Borough)** field and click the **>** button to move the field to the Selected Fields list.

6. Using the same method, move the Sales Person Last Name, Company Name, and Contract Amount fields from the Available Fields list to the Selected Fields list, as shown in Figure 11-1.

Figure 11-1

First Report Wizard dialog box

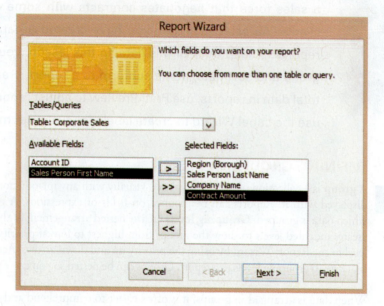

7. Click the Next > button. The second Report Wizard dialog box appears.
8. Select the Region (Borough) field and click the > button to move it to the grouping levels box.
9. Select the Contract Amount field and click the > button to move it to the grouping levels box.
10. Select the Sales Person Last Name field and click the > button to move it to the grouping levels box.
11. Notice that the Sales Person Last Name field is the active field in bold type. Click the Priority up arrow to move the Sales Person Last Name field to the second level of grouping. Your screen should look similar to Figure 11-2.

Figure 11-2

Second Report Wizard dialog box

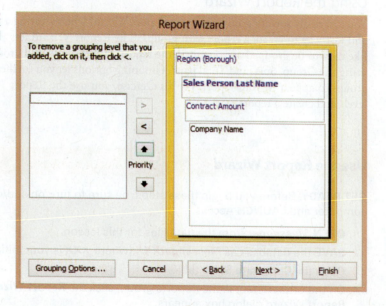

12. Click the **Grouping Options** button at the bottom of the dialog box. The Grouping Intervals dialog box appears, as shown in Figure 11-3.

Figure 11-3

Grouping Intervals dialog box

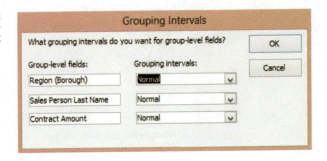

13. Click the **down arrow** on the first Grouping intervals menu to see the choices available. Select **Normal** from the menu and click **OK**.

14. Click the **Next >** button. The third Report Wizard dialog box appears. You can sort in either ascending or descending order and by up to four fields.

15. Click the **down arrow** on the Sort menu and select **Company Name**, as shown in Figure 11-4. You will sort in **ascending** order by Company Name.

Figure 11-4

Third Report Wizard dialog box

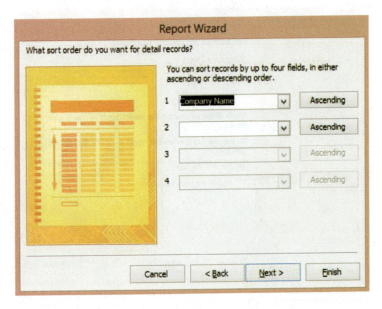

16. Click the **Next >** button. The fourth Report Wizard dialog box appears. You can choose from three different layouts for your report as well as two different orientations.

17. In the Layout section, click the **Block** option button, as shown in Figure 11-5. Keep the default orientation as **Portrait** and keep the selection so all fields fit on one page.

Figure 11-5

Fourth Report Wizard dialog box

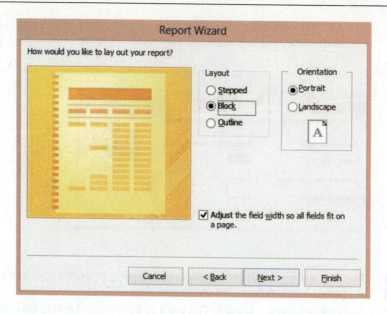

18. Click the **Next >** button. The fifth Report Wizard dialog box appears, as shown in Figure 11-6.

Figure 11-6

Fifth Report Wizard dialog box

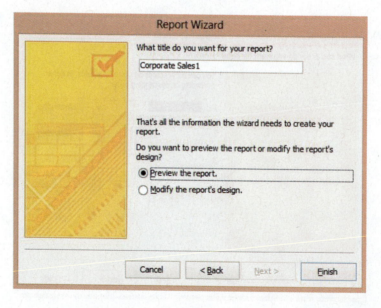

19. Key **Corporate Sales by Region/Salesperson** as the title of your Report, replacing the default title of Corporate Sales1.

20. Click the **Finish** button to accept the settings. The Report Wizard creates the report, shown in Figure 11-7, with the groups you specified.

Figure 11-7

Corporate Sales by Region/
Salesperson report

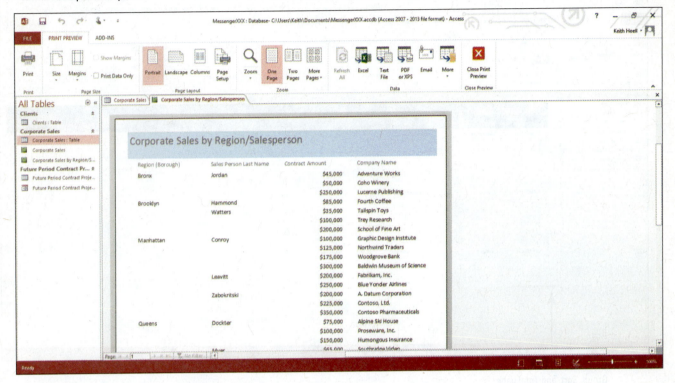

21. CLOSE the report and the table.

PAUSE. LEAVE the database open to use in the next exercise.

Adding Group Headers and Footers

You can add group headers and footers to a report using the Group, Sort, and Total pane. When you select a field from the Group On menu, the group header is added to the report. In this exercise, you add group headers using the Group, Sort, and Total pane.

As you may remember from Lesson 6, a report is organized into sections. You can view sections of a report in Design view. The **group header** is the section of a report where the name of a grouped field is displayed and printed. Group headers take on the name of the group, so instead of seeing a group header named *Group Header* you will see *[Fieldname] Header*.

A **group footer** is the section of the report where the data in the group is summarized. It is optional. If you do not have any summary data, such as a total, you don't need a group footer.

STEP BY STEP   **Use the Group, Sort, and Total Pane**

USE the database that is open from the previous exercise.

1. **OPEN** the **Corporate Sales** report. Notice that the report is not arranged by groups.
2. Switch to Layout view and close the Field List pane if it opens.
3. On the DESIGN tab, in the Grouping & Totals group, click the **Group & Sort** button. The Group, Sort, and Total pane appears at the bottom of the screen, as shown in Figure 11-8.

Figure 11-8

Group, Sort, and Total Pane

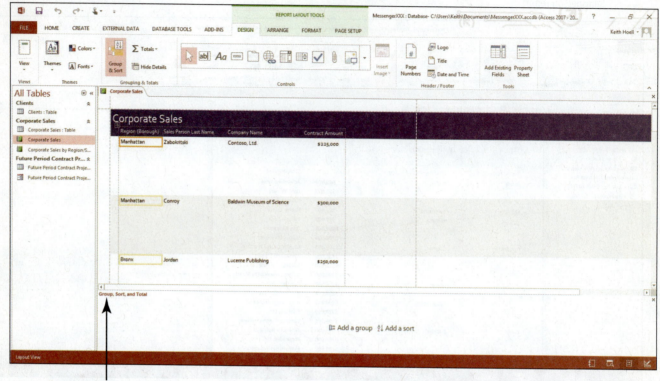

Group, Sort, and Total pane

4. Click the **Add a group** button. Select **Region (Borough)** from the Group On menu, as shown in Figure 11-9. The report is now grouped on the Region (Borough) field.

Figure 11-9

Group On menu

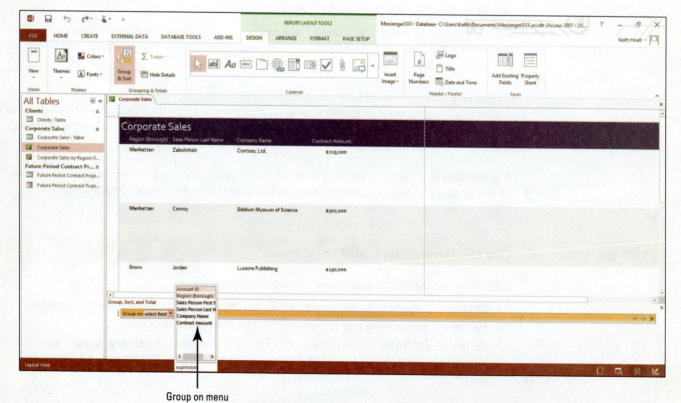

Group on menu

Another Way
You can also right-click a field header in Layout view and select Group On Field Name from the shortcut menu to define a group header.

5. Click the **Add a group** button on the Group, Sort, and Total pane. Select **Sales Person Last Name** from the Group On menu. The report is now also grouped on the Sales Person Last Name field.

6. Switch to Design view. Your screen should look similar to Figure 11-10. Notice that there is a Region (Borough) Header for that group and a Sales Person Last Name header for that group. The Company Name and Contract Amount fields are arranged in the Detail section.

Figure 11-10

Group headers in Design view

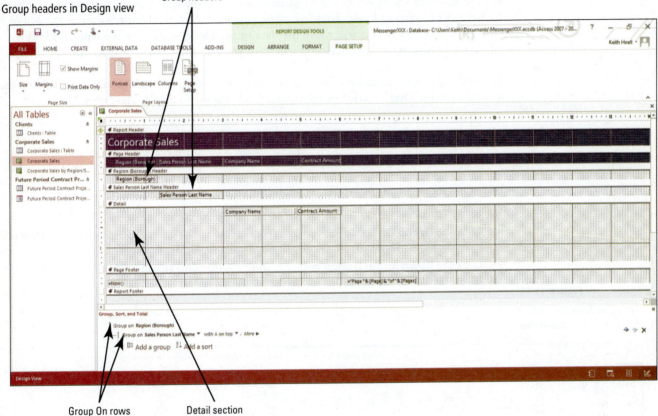

Group headers

Group On rows

Detail section

7. SAVE the report.

PAUSE. LEAVE the database open to use in the next exercise.

Changing Grouping Options

After grouping data, Access gives you options for displaying grouped data. To display the grouping options in the Group, Sort, and Total pane, click More on the group level that you want to change. If you want to hide the grouping options, click Less. In this exercise, you use the Group, Sort, and Total Pane to change group options.

Grouping options include:

- **Sort order:** Choose ascending or descending
- **Group interval:** Change the way records are grouped together
- **Totals:** Add totals to fields

- **Title:** Change the label of a column heading or summary field
- **With/without header:** Add or remove the header section
- **With/without footer:** Add or remove footer section
- **Do not keep group together on one page:** Groups can be broken up by page breaks
- **Keep whole group together on one page:** Minimizes the number of page breaks in a group on one page
- **Keep header and first record together on one page:** Makes sure a group header is not printed by itself at the bottom of a page

You can also click the Move up and Move down arrows at the end of the Group On row to change the priority of grouping levels. To delete a grouping level, click the Delete button at the end of its Group On row and Access will move the data to the Detail section of the report. However, if other controls are in the header, Access will warn you that these could be deleted.

The Hide Details command is a toggle button in the Grouping & Totals group on the Ribbon that hides data in the Detail section of the report. Click it again to display the data.

STEP BY STEP   **Change Grouping Options**

USE the database and report that is open from the previous exercise.

1. Switch to Layout view.
2. Click the **Group On Sales Person Last Name** row in the Group, Sort, and Total pane and then click the **More** button to view the available grouping options.
3. Click the **down arrow** beside *with a header section* and select **without a header section** from the drop-down menu, as shown in Figure 11-11.

Figure 11-11

Group on *Sales Person Last Name* row

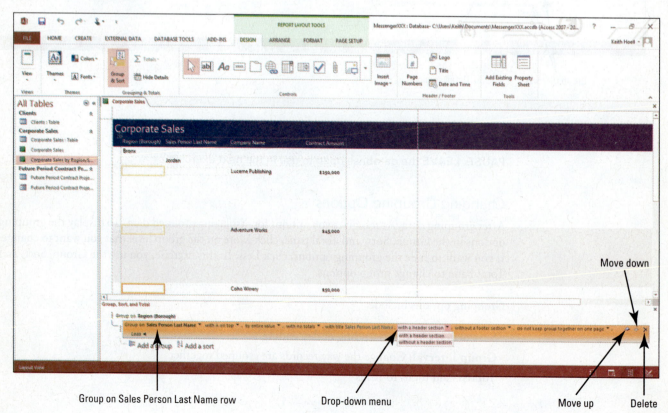

Group on Sales Person Last Name row   Drop-down menu   Move up   Delete

4. Switch to Design view. Notice that the Sales Person Last Name Header has been deleted from the grouping area.

5. Switch to Layout view.

6. Click the **down arrow** beside the *without a header section* (if the *without a header section* option doesn't appear, click the **More** button) and select **with a header section** from the drop-down menu.

7. Click the **Move up** arrow at the end of the Group On Sales Person Last Name row. Notice that the Sales Person Last Name group is now the top level group in the report.

8. Click the **Add a group** button and select **Company Name** from the menu. A new group level is added to the report.

9. On the DESIGN tab, in the Grouping & Totals group, click the **Hide Details** button. The data in the Contract Amount field is hidden.

10. On the DESIGN tab, in the Grouping & Totals group, click the **Hide Details** button. The data in the Contract Amount field is displayed.

11. Click the **More** button in the Group, Sort, and Total pane.

12. Click the **with A on top** down arrow on the Group On Company Name row in the Group, Sort, and Total Pane and select **with Z on top** from the drop-down menu. The sort order is changed from ascending to descending order.

13. Click the **with Z on top** down arrow and select **with A on top**.

14. Click the **Delete** button on the right side of the Group On Company Name row in the Group, Sort, and Total pane. The row is deleted, as is the Company Name header section.

15. Switch to Report view to see the report. Your screen should resemble Figure 11-12.

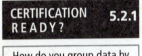

CERTIFICATION READY? 5.2.1

How do you group data by fields?

Figure 11-12

Corporate Sales report

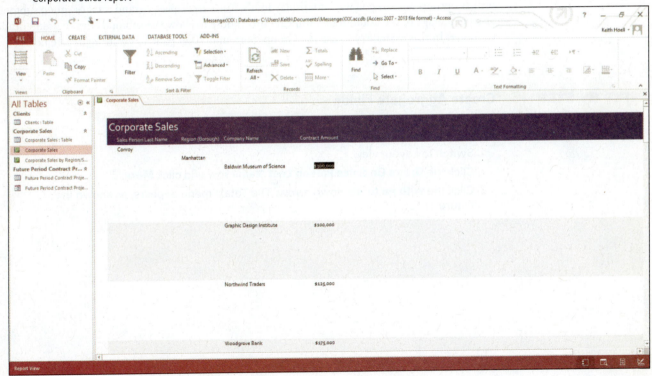

16. **SAVE** the report.

PAUSE. LEAVE the database open to use in the next exercise.

CREATING AGGREGATE FIELDS

Report data often contains numbers, such as sales figures, that need to be totaled. A report that lists sales for each month in a quarter but does not total all the sales for the quarter is incomplete. **Aggregate fields** use functions to provide summary information of such data. You can create an aggregate field by using aggregate functions to calculate data in a field. The aggregate functions you can use are Sum, Average, Count Records, Count Values, Maximum, Minimum, Standard Deviation, or Variance.

Access 2013 provides a Totals command that lets you create an aggregate field that provides not only grand totals, but totals for groups in a report as well. You can also use the Group, Sort, and Total pane to add aggregate functions to fields.

The Totals command is located on the DESIGN tab, in the Grouping & Totals group, but you can also access it on the shortcut menu. In Layout view, just right-click the field you want to total and select Total, which will be followed by the field name, from the shortcut menu. The Totals command adds a calculated control in the report footer where it displays the grand total. If you don't already have group footers in your report, the Totals command adds group footers and calculated controls to calculate the totals for each group.

Cross Ref   Lesson 9 describes the Total row, a way to use aggregate functions to provide a summary of table data.

Creating Aggregate Fields

You have a few more options when using the Group, Sort, and Total pane to create an aggregate field in a report. The Totals menu gives you options for choosing the field and type of function as well as options on how you want to display totals. You can display a grand total or group subtotals as a percentage of the grand total. You can also choose to show the subtotals in the group header or footer. In this exercise, you use the Group, Sort, and Total pane to create aggregate fields.

Create Aggregate Fields

USE the database and report that is open from the previous exercise.

1. Switch to Layout view.
2. Click the **Group On Sales Person Last Name** row and click **More**.
3. Click the **with no totals** down arrow. The Totals menu appears, as shown in Figure 11-13.

Figure 11-13

Totals menu

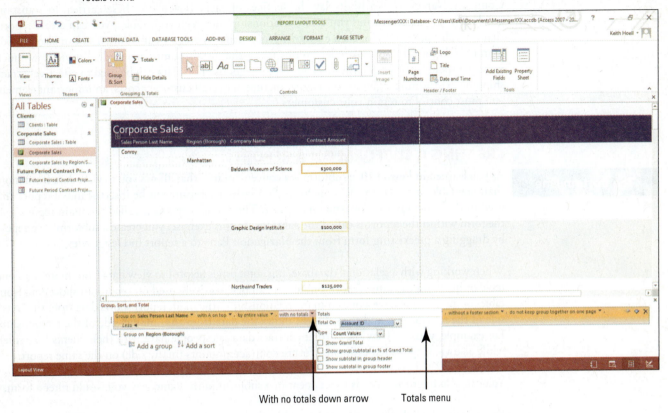

With no totals down arrow   Totals menu

4. Click the **Total On** menu down arrow and select **Contract Amount**.

5. Click the **Type** menu down arrow and select **Sum** if it isn't selected already.

6. Click the **Show Grand Total** box. The menu disappears and the grand total appears in the Contract Amount column at the bottom of the report.

7. Click the **Group On Sales Person Last Name** row again and click **More**, then click the **with Contract Amount totaled** down arrow.

8. Click the **Total On** menu down arrow and select **Contract Amount**, then click the **Show subtotal in group footer** box. The settings are applied, and the subtotals are now shown in each group's footer.

9. Select the **Sales Person Last Name** field header on the report.

10. On the DESIGN tab, in the Grouping & Totals group, click the **Totals** button and select **Count Records** from the menu.

11. Switch to Report view. The total number of records appears at the bottom of the report.

12. **SAVE** the report.

PAUSE. LEAVE the database open to use in the next exercise.

Another Way
You can also right-click a field in Layout view and select Total from the shortcut menu to apply an aggregate function to a field.

Workplace *Ready*

Delivery service companies are used extensively in business. As a result, comparing service and prices can be very important for a company to make sure it is using a reliable and economical delivery service. Also knowing how much money your customers are spending on shipping when purchasing goods from your business can help you make important decisions related to keeping or dropping the carriers you use. Access reports are effective tools for comparing and reporting such data. You can easily create a table of delivery service companies using field names such as Company Name, Service Type, and Service Charge. You can then create a report that groups on Company Names to clearly display the services of each. If you use these carriers to transport goods to your customers and you create relationships between your tables, you can create reports that total shipping costs for each customer group using aggregate functions. You can also provide grand totals for all your customer groups using the Totals command to determine how much money is spent by all your customers on shipping goods. This data can be used to effectively track shipping expenditures, giving you a larger picture of overall customer costs, an important element you must control to retain your customers.

CREATING A SUBFORM ON A REPORT

The Bottom Line

As you learned in Lesson 10, a subform is a convenient tool that allows you to view data from more than one table or query on the same form. Similarly, a subform can be inserted into a report and used in the same way to view data on a report. The primary report is called the main report, and the form within the report is called the subform. In this exercise, you create a subform on a report by dragging a preexisting form from the Navigation Pane to a report in Design view.

When working with a relational database, it is sometimes helpful to view data from more than one table or query on the same report. Subforms can be effectively used on reports to show data from tables or queries that have a one-to-many relationship—the main report shows data from the "one" side of the relationship and the subform shows the data from the "many" side of the relationship. For example, you can view the current contract data salespeople have with their clients (one side), while also viewing related estimated future contract amounts (many side) on the same report.

You can also filter the records that appear in a subform in the same way you would filter a form.

You can use the Subreport Wizard located in the Controls group on the DESIGN tab to create a new subform to add to a report and include which fields you want to appear. The Wizard can also be used to include the fields from a preexisting form to use as a subform in a report or to establish a relationship between a report and a subform.

If you already have a preexisting form in your database, you can simply drag the form object from the Navigation Pane to an appropriate section of the main report in Design view. For best results, all relationships should be established first. This enables Access to automatically create the links between subforms and main reports to effectively show related data.

Take Note   A subreport can be also be added to a report in a similar way and serves a similar function as a subform. The determination to add a subform or subreport to a report depends mainly on what form or report objects you already have in your database and what additional data you want to communicate.

 Cross Ref   For more information about subforms, see Lesson 10.

STEP BY STEP   **Create a Subform on a Report**

USE the database and report that is open from the previous exercise.

1. Switch to Design view.

2. Click and drag the **Future Period Contract Projections** form object from the Navigation Pane to the Report *Detail* section under the *Company Name* and *Contract Amount* controls. Your screen should look similar to Figure 11-14.

Figure 11-14

Report and subform

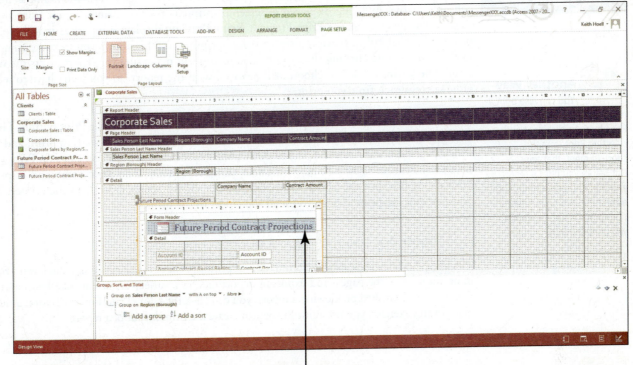

Subform dragged to Report Detail section

CERTIFICATION READY?   **5.2.3**

How do you add subforms?

3. Switch to Report View to view the Report and related subform, and cycle through the two records in the top subform using the record navigation buttons on the subform.

4. **SAVE** the report and **CLOSE** it.

PAUSE. LEAVE the database open to use in the next exercise.

SOFTWARE ORIENTATION

PRINT PREVIEW Tab

The PRINT PREVIEW tab, as shown in Figure 11-15, has commands for viewing a report in a variety of ways, adjusting its layout, and exporting its data into a variety of formats like Excel and Word. You can display the PRINT PREVIEW tab by choosing the Print Preview option on the File tab's Print menu. Use the PRINT PREVIEW tab to view and adjust the page layout before printing.

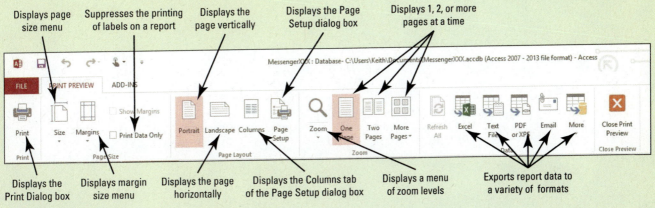

Figure 11-15

PRINT PREVIEW tab

CREATING THE PRINT LAYOUT

Reports are often created so records can be appropriately arranged, formatted, and shared with colleagues either by being displayed onscreen or printed. You can print a report from any view: Report, Layout, Design, or Print Preview. ==Print Preview== displays a report as it will look when printed. It is helpful to preview a report before printing it. This allows you to make adjustments to the layout before clicking the Print button so you can make sure the report prints the way you want. The settings that you choose will be saved with the report, so you won't have to select the same settings each time you print.

When you are confident your report will print correctly, you can click the Print button. The Print dialog box lets you select the printer, choose the number of copies you want to print, and specify which pages you want to print. If you don't need to preview a report, you can skip Print Preview and select Print or Quick Print on the File tab's Print menu. The Print command displays the Print dialog box, but the Quick Print command sends the report directly to the printer. The report's records are printed once you send the report to the printer.

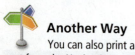

Another Way
You can also print a report from the Navigation Pane by right-clicking it and selecting Print from the shortcut menu that appears. But before you print a report, you should check settings such as margins and page orientation to make sure the report will print correctly.

Using Print Preview to Create a Print Layout

The PRINT PREVIEW tab has commands for printing, changing the page size and layout, zooming in or out to view the pages, and exporting report data to a variety of formats like Excel and Word. When you are finished previewing a report, you can click the Close Print Preview button to leave the view. In this exercise, you use Print Preview to create the print layout of a report.

STEP BY STEP **Create the Print Layout**

USE the database that is open from the previous exercise.

1. Right-click the **Corporate Sales** report in the Navigation Pane and select **Copy** from the shortcut menu that appears.
2. Right-click in a blank area in the Navigation Pane and select **Paste** from the menu. The Paste As dialog box appears.
3. In the Paste As dialog box, replace the name of the report in the Report Name field by keying **Sales by Salesperson** and clicking **OK**.
4. Open the Sales by Salesperson report in Design view. You want to remove the subform from the report and keep only the sales related to each salesperson.
5. In the Detail section, click the **Future Period Contract Projections** subform as shown in Figure 11-16. [Press **Delete**] on the keyboard to delete the subform.

Take Note Throughout this lesson you will see information that appears in black text within brackets, such as [Press **Enter**], or [**your e-mail address**]. The information contained in the brackets is intended to be directions for you rather than something you actually type word-for-word. It will instruct you to perform an action or substitute text. Do **not** type the actual text that appears within brackets.

Figure 11-16

Future Period Contract
Projections subform

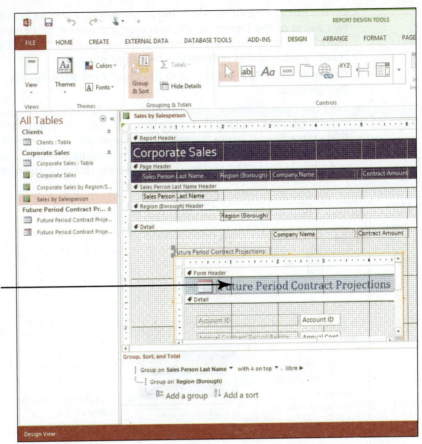

Figure 11-16

Future Period Contract
Projections subform

Future Period Contract
Projections subform

6. On the HOME tab, in the Views group, click the lower half of the **View** button and select **Print Preview** from the menu. The report is displayed in Print Preview, as shown in Figure 11-17. Notice the large area of blank space between company names in the detail section.

Figure 11-17

Report in Print Preview

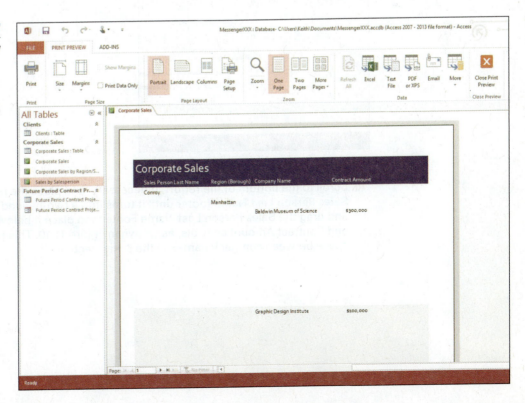

Figure 11-17

Report in Print Preview

7. On the PRINT PREVIEW tab, in the Zoom group, click the **Two Pages** button. The first two pages of the report are displayed on the screen. Notice the second page has no report data on it. You need to correct these issues in Report Design view to ensure the report print layout is appropriate before printing.

8. On the PRINT PREVIEW tab, click the **Close Print Preview** button to return to Report Design view.

9. Click the **Error Checking Options** button ![] next to the Report Header section title to view the Error Checking Options menu, as shown in Figure 11-18. Notice the menu text that states *Report width is greater than page width*. Click the **Remove Extra Report Space** menu option. The report's width is automatically adjusted; however, the issue is not entirely corrected and the Error Checking Option button still appears.

Figure 11-18

Error Checking Options
button and menu

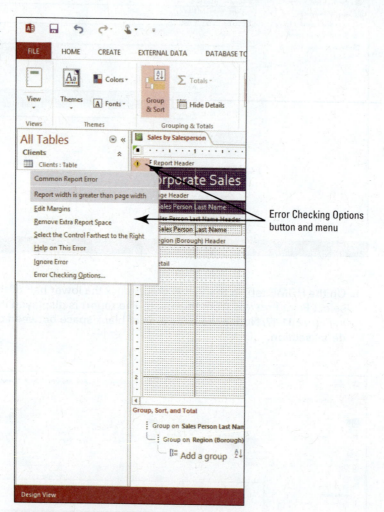

Error Checking Options
button and menu

10. Scroll to the bottom of the report, if necessary, and place the pointer over the top of the **Sales Person Last Name** footer until it turns into a two-headed vertical pointer. Click and drag the Sales Person Last Name Footer and place it below the Company Name and Contract Amount controls, as shown in Figure 11-19. This removes the excess blank space between company names in the Detail section.

Figure 11-19

Sales Person Last Name Footer

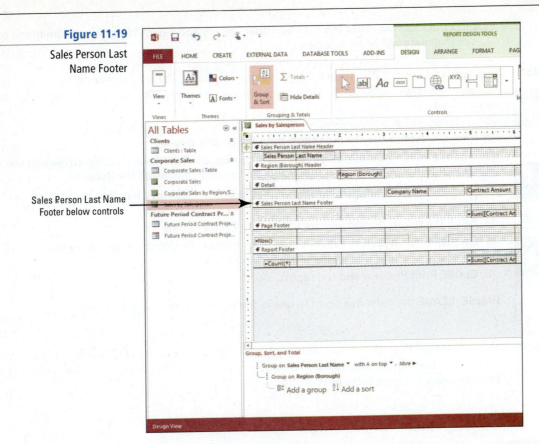

Sales Person Last Name Footer below controls

11. Switch to Print Preview. Notice the report layout still appears on two pages. The Remove Extra Report Space didn't entirely fix the issue. The page number control is exceeding the width of the page in Design view as evident by the page numbering text appearing in the footer section of the second page. On the PRINT PREVIEW tab, in the Page Layout group, click the **Landscape** button. The report is displayed in landscape orientation and the formatting appears correctly.

12. On the PRINT PREVIEW tab, in the Page Layout group, click the **Portrait** button. The report is displayed in portrait orientation again.

13. On the PRINT PREVIEW tab, in the Page Layout group, click the **Page Setup** button. The Page Setup dialog box appears, as shown in Figure 11-20. Notice it contains many of the same options that are available in the Page Layout group but also includes additional options and details that can be modified.

Another Way

You can also move and/or resize the page numbering control in the Page Footer section in Report Design view to ensure it appears within the page margin width. This is one of many different ways to create a viable print layout depending on your page size.

Figure 11-20

Page Setup dialog box

Page Setup

Print Options   Page   Columns

Margins (inches)

Top: 0.333

Bottom: 0.55

Left: 0.333

Right: 0.25

Sample

☐ Print Data Only

Split Form

○ Print Form Only

○ Print Datasheet Only

OK   Cancel

14. Click the **Page** tab. Click the **Size box** down arrow and select **Tabloid** from the menu to see if all data will fit on one page.

You may also use the Page Setup dialog box to change the left margin size to match the right margin size to prevent the layout from appearing on two pages. This will cause your report data to appear on two pages.

15. Click **OK**. Notice that all the report data fits on one page.
16. On the PRINT PREVIEW tab, in the Zoom group, click the **Zoom** button arrow and select **50%** from the menu. Notice that you have to scroll to view all the data.
17. Click the **Close Print Preview** button on the PRINT PREVIEW tab. You are back in Design view.
18. **SAVE** the report design and switch back to Print Preview.
19. On the PRINT PREVIEW tab, click the **Print** button. The Print dialog box appears. Click **OK** to print or click **Cancel** to close the dialog box.
20. **CLOSE** Print Preview and the report.

PAUSE. LEAVE the database open to use in the next exercise.

You can add the Print Preview and/or the Quick Print command to the Quick Access Toolbar by clicking the **Customize Quick Access Toolbar** down arrow at the end of the toolbar and selecting **Print Preview** or **Quick Print** from the menu.

USING THE LABEL WIZARD

You can create labels for mailing, or other purposes, using the data in your Access databases. The **Label Wizard** helps you create a label-sized report that you can use to print labels. The Label Wizard asks you a series of questions about the labels you want and then creates the labels based on your answers. You can choose from a wide variety of sizes, including sizes to fit label sheets that you purchase at the office supply store or custom-created labels.

Creating Labels Using the Label Wizard

You can create mailing labels or other types of labels from an Access table or query. Access allows you to choose the font name, font size, font weight, and text color for your labels. You can also choose to underline or italicize text in the label. The Sample box displays the choices you make. In this exercise, you use the Label Wizard to create labels.

You can select predefined label sizes that match popular manufacturer's label sheets. These are listed by Product Number in the first Label Wizard screen. If you don't know the manufacturer of your label sheets, you can choose a sheet with similar dimensions and with the correct number of labels across the sheet. If you don't see the size you need, you can customize the size and create a new label using the Customize button.

As you add fields to the Prototype label, remember to use the Spacebar to add a space between fields and press Enter to move to the next line. You can also key text directly in the Prototype label that you want to appear on each label.

You can sort the labels by one or more fields, such as zip code for bulk mailings. On the last Label Wizard screen, if you choose to see the labels as they will look when printed, they will be displayed in Print Preview. Choose Modify the label design to view the label report in Design view.

STEP BY STEP   **Use the Label Wizard**

USE the database that is open from the previous exercise.

1. Select the **Clients** table in the Navigation Pane.

2. On the CREATE tab, in the Reports group, click the **Labels** button. The first Label Wizard dialog box appears, as shown in Figure 11-21.

Figure 11-21

First Label Wizard dialog box

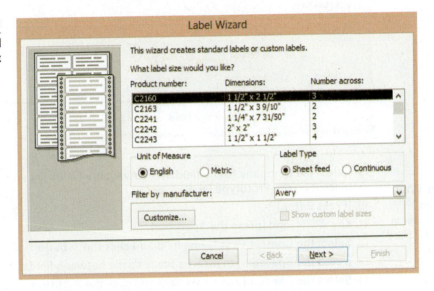

3. Scroll down in the Product Number box and select **Avery USA 5160** and click the **Next >** button. The second Label Wizard dialog box appears, as shown in Figure 11-22.

Figure 11-22

Second Label Wizard dialog box

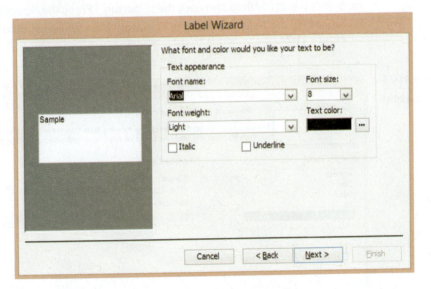

Another Way

Instead of scrolling through a menu of options, you can simply start typing the first few characters of the option you want to choose to have it automatically appear.

4. Click the **Font name: down arrow** and scroll down to select **Times New Roman**. Notice the preview sample displays the new font.

5. Click the **Font size: down arrow** and select **9**.

6. Click the **Font weight: down arrow** and select **Normal**.

7. In the *Text color* section, click the **Ellipses** button to display the Color dialog box. Notice the options available, then click **Cancel** to close it.

8. Click the **Next >** button. The third Label Wizard dialog box appears, as shown in Figure 11-23.

Figure 11-23

Third Label Wizard
dialog box

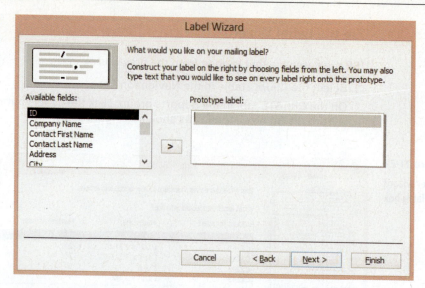

Another Way

You can also double-click each field name in the Available Fields list to place it on the Prototype label.

9. Select the **Company Name** field in the Available Fields list and click the > button to place it on the Prototype label.

10. [Press **Enter.**]

11. Key **ATTN:** and [press the **Spacebar**].

12. Select the **Contact First Name** field and click the > button.

13. [Press the **Spacebar**] to insert a blank space between fields.

14. Select the **Contact Last Name** field and click the > button.

15. [Press **Enter.**]

16. Select the **Address** field and click the > button. [Press **Enter.**]

17. Select the **City** field and click the > button. Key a **comma** and [press the **Spacebar**].

18. Select the **State** field and click the > button. [Press the **Spacebar.**]

19. Select the **Zip** field and click the > button. Your screen should look similar to Figure 11-24.

Figure 11-24

Completed Prototype label

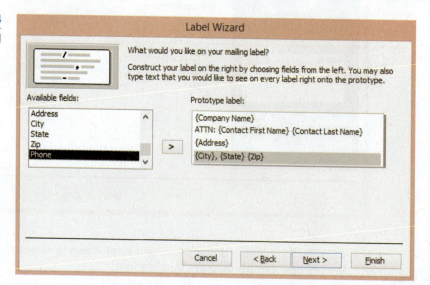

20. Click **Next** >. The fourth Label Wizard dialog box appears, as shown in Figure 11-25.

Figure 11-25

Fourth Label Wizard
dialog box

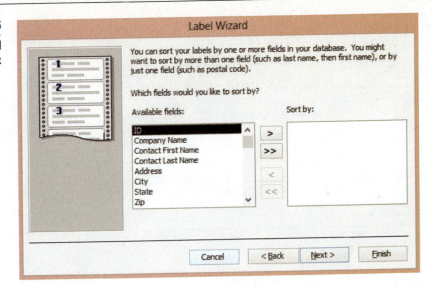

21. Select the **Zip** field and click the > button.
22. Click **Next** >. The fifth Label Wizard dialog box appears, as shown in Figure 11-26.

Figure 11-26

Fifth Label Wizard
dialog box

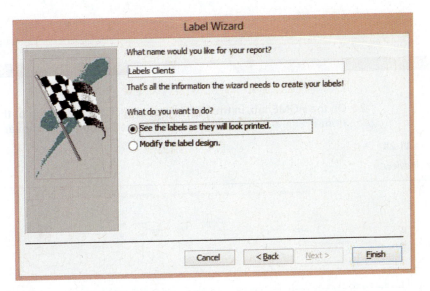

23. Click the **Modify the label design** option button and click **Finish**. Your screen should look similar to Figure 11-27.

Figure 11-27

Label report

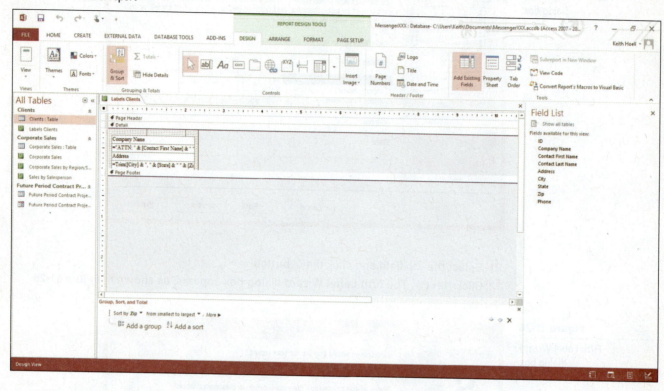

24. On the HOME tab, in the Views group, click the lower half of the **View** button and select **Print Preview** from the menu. Your screen should look similar to Figure 11-28.

Figure 11-28

Report in Print Preview

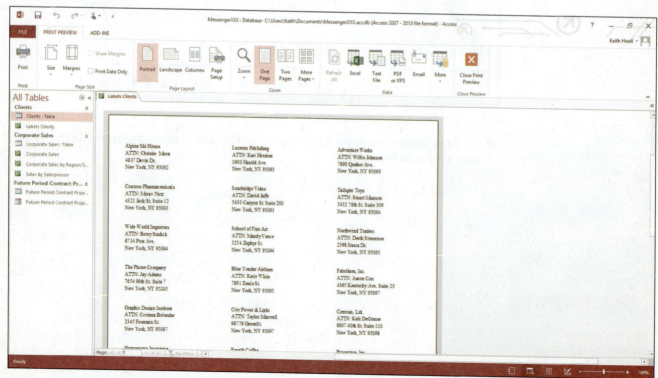

25. Click the **Print** button. The Print dialog box appears. Click **OK** to print or click **Cancel** to close the dialog box.

26. **CLOSE** Print Preview and the report.

CLOSE the database.

 **Troubleshooting** If Access displays a message warning you that some of your data may not be displayed, this means the controls on the label are too wide for the allotted space. If this happens, try reducing the size of the controls in Design view so that they fit in the space available for a single label or try reducing the page margins using Page Setup.

Take Note As an alternative to printing labels, you can print addresses directly onto envelopes. To do this, you will need to create a custom label instead of a predefined label and set the Label Type setting to Sheet Feed.

SKILL SUMMARY

In This Lesson You Learned How To:	Exam Objective	Objective Number
Define Groups	Group records	2.3.8
	Group data by fields	5.2.1
Create Aggregate Fields		
Create a Subform on a Report	Add subforms	5.2.3
Create the Print Layout	Print reports	1.5.1
	Print records	1.5.2
	Change report orientation	5.3.5
Use the Label Wizard		

Knowledge Assessment

Matching

Match the term in Column 1 to its description in Column 2.

Column 1	Column 2
1. group	a. asks you questions about the labels and data you want to display and then creates labels based on your answers
2. group header	b. field that contains an aggregate function to calculate data
3. group footer	c. a field by which data is grouped
4. Hide Details command	d. the nested arrangement of groups in a report
5. grouping field	e. a collection of records separated visually with any introductory or summary information displayed with it
6. aggregate field	f. the section of a report where the name of a grouped field is displayed and printed
7. Print Preview	g. the sample in the Label Wizard where you create the label design
8. grouping levels	h. hides the data in the Detail section of a report
9. Label Wizard	i. the section of a report where the data in a group is summarized
10. Prototype label	j. displays a report as it will look when printed

True/False

Circle T if the statement is true or F if the statement is false.

T F   1. Grouping intervals establish the way that records are grouped together.

T F   2. You cannot group data in the Report Wizard.

T F   3. Group headers take on the name of the group.

T F   4. Group footers are optional in a report.

T F   5. The arrows at the end of a Group On row determine sort order.

T F   6. Average is an aggregate function.

T F   7. The Totals command adds group footers and calculated controls for you.

T F   8. You must preview a report before you can print.

T F   9. You can modify labels in Design view.

T F   10. Labels can be printed using reports.

Competency Assessment

Project 11-1: Create Address Labels for Authors

You need to send out confidential contract information to the authors in the Business Books division. Create labels for the authors using the Author Contact Information table.

GET READY. LAUNCH Access if it is not already running.

1. **OPEN** the *Lucerne* database.
2. **SAVE** the database as *LucerneXXX* (where XXX is your initials).
3. Select the **Author Contact Information** table in the Navigation Pane.
4. On the CREATE tab, in the Reports group, click the **Labels** button.
5. Select the **C2242** label in the *Product number* box and click **Next**.
6. Select **Arial** from the *Font name* menu and select **9** from the *Font size* menu.
7. Click the **Italic** button and click **Next>**.
8. Key **CONFIDENTIAL** in all caps and [press **Enter**].
9. Key **For Addressee Only** and [press **Enter**].
10. Select the **Author First Name** field and click the > button. [Press the **Spacebar**.]
11. Select the **Author Last Name** field and click the > button. [Press **Enter**.]
12. Select the **Author Address** field and click the > button. [Press **Enter**.]
13. Select the **Author City** field and click the > button. Key a **comma** and [press the **Spacebar**].
14. Select the **Author State** field and click the > button. [Press the **Spacebar**.]
15. Select the **Author Zip** field and click the > button.
16. Click **Finish**.
17. **CLOSE** the report.

LEAVE the database open for the next project.

Project 11-2: Total and Preview the Book Sales Report

Finish the Book Sales report to show totals for Domestic and International Sales. You also need to make some adjustments in Print Preview before printing.

USE the database that is open from the previous project.

1. **OPEN** the **Book Sales** report.
2. In Layout view, select the **Domestic Sales** field header.

3. On the DESIGN tab, in the Grouping & Totals group, click the **Totals** button and select **Sum** from the menu.

4. Select the **International Sales** field header.

5. On the DESIGN tab, in the Grouping & Totals group, click the **Totals** button and select **Sum** from the menu.

6. Select the **Book Title** field header.

7. On the DESIGN tab, in the Grouping & Totals group, click the **Totals** button and select **Count Records** from the menu.

8. On the DESIGN tab, in the Views group, click the **View** menu and select **Print Preview** from the menu.

9. On the PRINT PREVIEW tab, in the Page Size group, click the **Margins** button and select **Wide** from the menu.

10. On the PRINT PREVIEW tab, in the Zoom group, click the **Zoom** button arrow and select **Fit to Window**.

11. **SAVE** the report.

12. On the PRINT PREVIEW tab, in the Print group, click the **Print** button or click **Cancel** to close the dialog box.

13. **CLOSE** the report.

CLOSE the database.

Proficiency Assessment

Project 11-3: Create a Grouped Report with Aggregate Fields

Your supervisor at Fourth Coffee asks you to create a report using the Monthly Sales by Store table.

GET READY. LAUNCH Access if it is not already running.

1. **OPEN** *Fourth Coffee* from the data files for this lesson.

2. **SAVE** the database as *Fourth CoffeeXXX* (where *XXX* is your initials).

3. Select the **Monthly Sales by Store** table.

4. Use the Report Wizard to create a report that includes the **Month**, **Store**, and **Sales** fields.

5. Group **by Store** and create a **Stepped** layout.

6. Close Print Preview and switch to Layout view to decrease the width of the Month and Sales columns.

7. Click the **Group & Sort** button to open the Group, Sort, and Total pane.

8. Click the **Add a sort** button and select **Sales** from the menu. Sort from smallest to largest.

9. Select the **Sales** column.

10. Click the **Totals** button and select **Sum** from the menu.

11. **SAVE** the report.

LEAVE the report open for use in the next project.

Project 11-4: Preview and Print the Monthly Sales by Store Report

You need to print the Monthly Sales by Store report. View the report in Print Preview to make sure the report is centered on the page before printing.

USE the *FourthCoffeeXXX* database that you saved in a previous exercise.

1. Switch to Print Preview.

2. Click the **Zoom** button arrow and select **Fit to Window**.

3. Click the **Margins** button and select **Wide** from the menu.

4. Click the **Landscape** button.

5. Click the **Page Setup** button.

6. Click the **Print Options** tab. In the Margins section, key **1** in the Top box, **1** in the Bottom box, **1.5** in the Left box, and **1.5** in the Right box.

7. Click **OK**.

8. Click the **Print** button and click **OK** to print the report or click **Cancel** to close the dialog box.

9. **SAVE** the report.

10. Click the **Close Print Preview** button.

11. **CLOSE** the report.

CLOSE the database.

Mastery Assessment

Project 11-5: Group and Total the Inventory Report

As the marketing manager at Wingtip Toys, you review inventory information regularly with other employees. Add groups and totals to the Inventory report before your meeting with the production manager.

GET READY. LAUNCH Access if it is not already running.

1. **OPEN** *Wingtip* from the data files for this lesson.

2. **SAVE** the database as *WingtipXXX* (where *XXX* is your initials).

3. Open the **Inventory** report.

4. Switch to Layout view and open the Group, Sort, and Total pane.

5. Group the report by the **In Stock** field.

6. Sort the Description column from **A to Z**.

7. **Sum** the Price field. Show a **grand total** and **subtotals** in the group footers.

8. **SAVE** and **CLOSE** the report.

CLOSE the database.

Project 11-6: Create a Subform on a Report

In your position as Administrative Assistant for Alpine Ski House, you are involved in a variety of database administration projects that involve requests from the owners. The owners want to view the reservations that customers make on the same report as customer details. Add a reservations subform to the preexisting customers report.

GET READY. LAUNCH Access if it is not already running.

1. **OPEN** *Alpine* from the data files for this lesson.

2. **SAVE** the database as *AlpineXXX* (where *XXX* is your initials).

3. Open the **Customers** report in Design view.

4. Click and drag the **Reservation Details** form object from the Navigation Pane to the Report *Detail* section under the *Customer Last, Customer First,* and *Phone Number* controls.

5. Switch to Report view to view the report and related subform.

6. **SAVE** the report and subform with the default names and close the report.

7. **CLOSE** the database.

CLOSE Access.

LESSON SKILL MATRIX

Skill	Exam Objective	Objective Number
Creating Crosstab Queries	Create crosstab queries	3.1.2
Creating a Subquery	Add new fields	3.2.2
	Remove fields	3.2.3
	Add conditional logic	3.3.2
	Use comparison operators	3.3.4
Saving a Filter as a Query		
Creating Action Queries	Create action queries	3.1.4
Understanding Advanced Query Modification	Create multi-table queries	3.1.5
	Add calculated fields	3.3.1
	Use basic operators	3.3.5
	Format fields within queries	3.2.6
	Group and summarize data	3.3.3

© GgWink/iStockphoto

KEY TERMS

- action query
- aggregate function
- append query
- calculated field
- cross join
- crosstab query
- delete query
- inner join
- join
- left outer join
- make table query
- outer join
- right outer join
- SELECT statement
- subquery
- unequal join
- update query

© GgWink/iStockphoto

World Wide Importers is a car dealership that specializes in imported luxury cars. The company has recently opened a used car division that sells vehicles acquired in trade and expands the buyer's purchasing options. As the office manager for the new division, you have started using Access to track inventory and sales. In this lesson, you learn how to create an action query, a crosstab query, and a subquery and how to save filters as a query. You also learn how to create joins, include calculated fields in a query, and create aggregated queries.

CREATING CROSSTAB QUERIES

The Bottom Line

Queries are powerful tools that can be used to retrieve exactly the data you need from your database, showing only the relevant records. Depending on the information you want to display, these advanced queries can help refine the results of your search or perform the actions you want. A **crosstab query** calculates a sum, average, count, or other type of total on records and then groups the results by two types of information: one down the left side of the datasheet and the other across the top. When you summarize data using a crosstab query, you select values from specified fields or expressions as column headings so you can view data in a more compact format than with a select query.

 Cross Ref

In Lesson 7, you learned how to create and modify several types of queries.

Creating Crosstab Queries

A crosstab query is a special type of query that displays its results in a grid similar to an Excel worksheet. Crosstab queries summarize your values and then group them by two sets of facts—a set of row headers down the side and a set of column headers across the top. A crosstab query typically includes data from more than one table and always includes three types of data: the data used as row headings, the data used as column headings, and the values that you want to sum or otherwise compute. A crosstab query does not always populate all the fields in the result set because the tables that you use in the query do not always contain values for every possible data point. In this exercise, you create a crosstab query.

The easiest way to create a crosstab query is to use the Crosstab Query Wizard. To run a crosstab query, double-click it in the Navigation Pane or click it and then press Enter. When you run a crosstab query, the results are displayed in Datasheet view.

STEP BY STEP **Create Crosstab Queries**

GET READY. Before you begin these steps, be sure to **LAUNCH** Microsoft Access.

1. **OPEN** the *Importers* database from the data files for this lesson.
2. **SAVE** the database as *ImportersXXX* (where *XXX* is your initials).

3. On the CREATE tab, in the Queries group, click the **Query Wizard** button to display the New Query dialog box, shown in Figure 12-1.

Figure 12-1

New Query dialog box

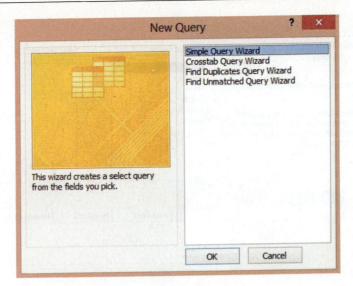

4. Click **Crosstab Query Wizard** and click **OK** to display the Crosstab Query Wizard, shown in Figure 12-2.

Figure 12-2

Crosstab Query Wizard, first screen

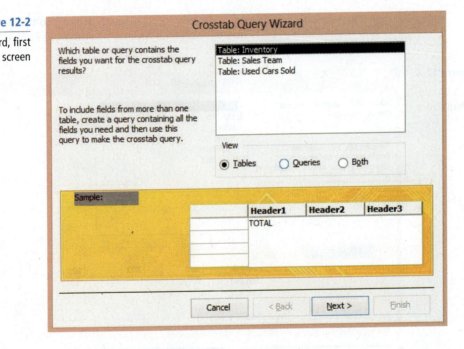

5. Click **Table: Used Cars Sold** and then click **Next >** to display the next screen, shown in Figure 12-3.

Figure 12-3

Crosstab Query Wizard,
second screen

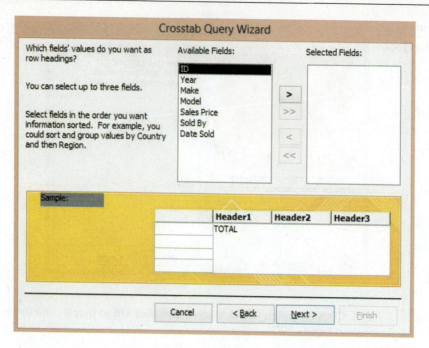

6. In the Available Fields box, double-click **Sold By** to move it to the Selected Fields box and then click **Next >**. The next screen appears, as shown in Figure 12-4.

Figure 12-4

Crosstab Query Wizard,
third screen

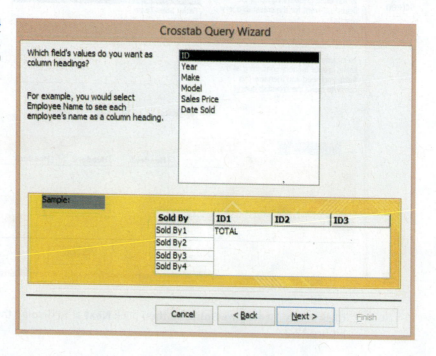

7. Click **Date Sold** and then click **Next >** to display the next screen, as shown in Figure 12-5.

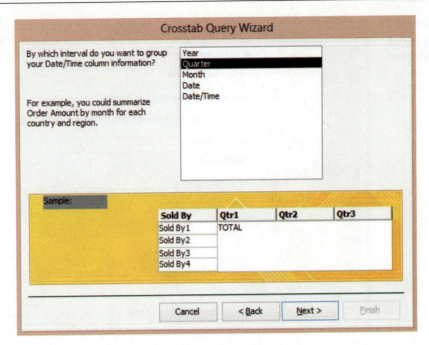

Figure 12-5

Crosstab Query Wizard,
fourth screen

8. Click **Month** and then click **Next** > to display the next screen, as shown in Figure 12-6.

Figure 12-6

Crosstab Query Wizard,
fifth screen

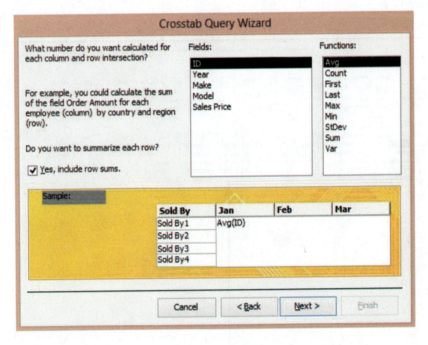

9. In the Fields box, click **Sales Price**, and in the Functions box, click **Sum**. Click **Next** > to display the final screen, as shown in Figure 12-7.

Figure 12-7

Crosstab Query Wizard,
final screen

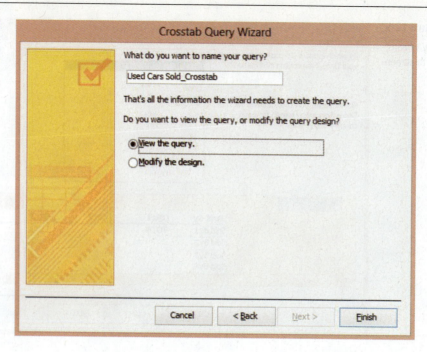

10. Click **Finish** to display the results of the crosstab query, as shown in Figure 12-8.

Figure 12-8

Crosstab query results

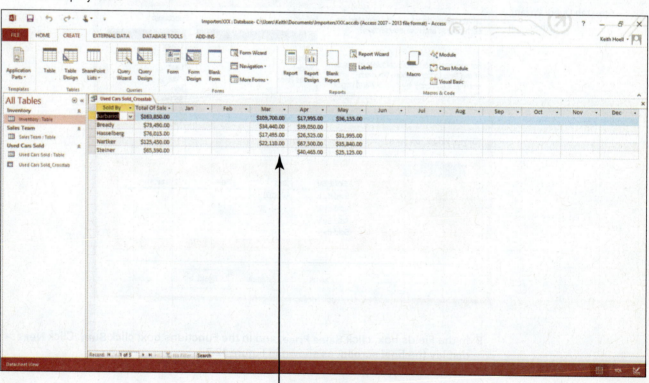

A crosstab query does not always populate all the fields in the result set because
the tables used do not always contain values for every possible data point

CERTIFICATION READY?   3.1.2

How do you create crosstab queries?

The Bottom Line

11. Click the **Close** button to close the Used Cars Sold_Crosstab query.

PAUSE. LEAVE the database open to use in the next exercise.

CREATING A SUBQUERY

You can use a subquery to limit the amount of data returned by a query. A **subquery** is a SELECT statement that is inside another select or action query. A **SELECT statement** is a Structured Query Language (SQL) command that instructs the Microsoft Access database engine to return information from the database as a set of records. This type of statement invokes conditional logic using expressions that evaluate to true or false; if true, Access returns a result that meets the condition that you have specified; if false, Access can return a different result depending on what you've specified. For example, you can use a conditional expression to create a new field that displays an adjusted salary with a 3% bonus for all employees who had annual sales revenue of $50,000 or more and display a message like "Not Bonus Eligible" for everyone else. The data that appears after the expression is evaluated can be communicated on reports to provide useful information to employees who make decisions in your organization.

At a minimum, the syntax for a SELECT statement is:

SELECT *fields* FROM *table*

An asterisk (*) can be used to select all the fields in a table. The following example selects all the fields in the Inventory table:

SELECT * FROM Inventory

Clauses such as WHERE and ORDER BY can be used in a SELECT statement to restrict and organize your returned data. Table 12-1 shows some SELECT statements and the results that are returned.

Table 12-1

Select statements with returned results

SELECT statement	Result
SELECT [FirstName], [LastName] FROM [Employees] WHERE [LastName] = "Cooper";	Displays the values in the FirstName and LastName fields for employees whose last name is Cooper.
SELECT [ProductID], [ProductName] FROM [Products] WHERE [CategoryID] = Forms. [New Products].[CategoryID];	Displays the values for ProductID and ProductName in the Products table for records in which the CategoryID value matches the CategoryID value specified in an open New Products form. Note: "Forms.[New Products].[Category ID]" references the New Products form and the CategoryID field on the form in case a New Products table and field also exist. The "." character is used to substantiate these form and field relationships.
SELECT Avg([ExtendedPrice]) AS [Average Extended Price] FROM [Order Details Extended] WHERE [ExtendedPrice] > 1000;	Displays in a field named Average Extended Price the average extended price of orders for which the value in ExtendedPrice field is more than 1,000.
SELECT [CategoryID], Count([ProductID]) AS [CountOfProductID] FROM [Products] GROUP BY [CategoryID] HAVING Count([ProductID]) > 10;	Displays in a field named CountOfProductID the total number of products for categories with more than 10 products.

A SELECT statement can be entered in a field or criteria cell in Design view. If you need more space in which to enter the SELECT statement in a field or criteria cell, press Shift+F2 and enter the statement in the Zoom box. You can see the entire SQL statement by switching to SQL view.

In a subquery, you use a SELECT statement to provide a set of one or more specific values to evaluate in the WHERE or HAVING clause expression. A subquery has three parts:

- **Comparison:** An expression and a comparison operator that compares the expression with the results of the subquery
- **Expression:** An expression for which the result set of the subquery is searched
- **Sqlstatement:** A SELECT statement, following the same format and rules as any other SELECT statement. It must be enclosed in parentheses.

Creating a Subquery

In this exercise, you create a subquery that returns only the records from the Inventory table whose asking price is equal to or greater than the average asking price. You also add, remove, and reposition fields while working within the query design grid.

Subqueries are created in Design view. Using the Show Table dialog box, you first need to select the table that contains the desired information. This will add the table window, which contains the table's field list, to Design view. You can then easily add fields from the table window to the design grid at the bottom of the screen by either double-clicking the field name or by clicking and dragging the field to the query design grid. You can remove fields from the query design grid by moving the mouse pointer above the field name you want to remove until the pointer changes to a bold down arrow, clicking, and then pressing Delete on the keyboard, or by clicking the Delete Columns button in the Query Setup group on the DESIGN tab. You can rearrange fields on the grid by moving the mouse pointer above the field you want to move until the pointer changes to a bold down arrow, then clicking and dragging the field to any position on the grid using the vertical placeholder bar that appears as a guide.

STEP BY STEP **Create a Subquery**

USE the database that is open from the previous exercise.

1. On the CREATE tab, in the Queries group, click **Query Design**. The query design grid opens, and the Show Table dialog box appears, as shown in Figure 12-9.

Figure 12-9

Show Table dialog box

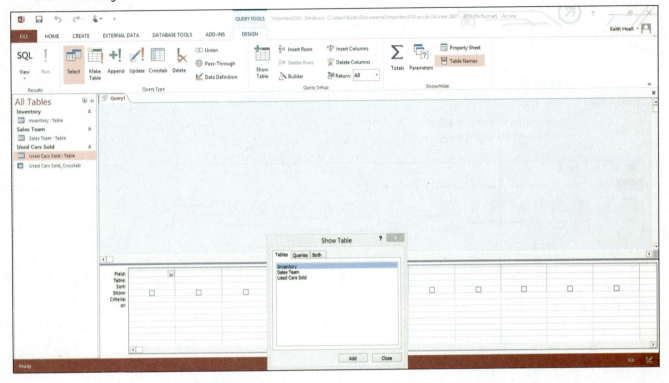

2. On the Tables tab, click **Inventory**, click **Add**, and then click **Close**. The table field list appears as a window in the upper section of the query design grid, as shown in Figure 12-10.

Figure 12-10

Query design grid

Table field list

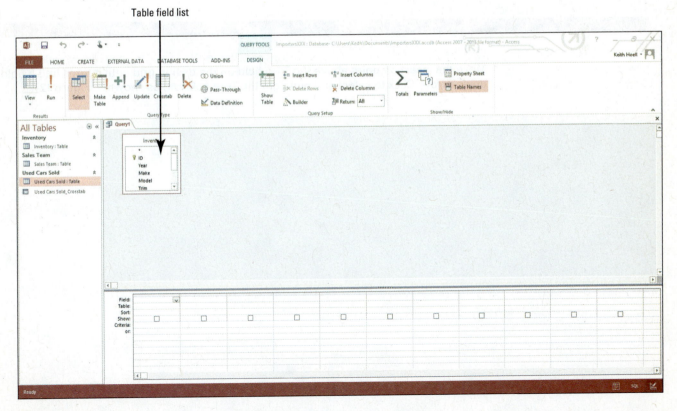

Another Way
To quickly add all the fields in a table, double-click the asterisk (*) at the top of the list of table fields.

3. In the list of table fields, double-click **Year**, **Make**, **Model**, **Trim**, and **AskingPrice** to add those fields to the design grid, as shown in Figure 12-11.

Figure 12-11

Fields added to design grid

Double-click a field name to add it to the query design grid below

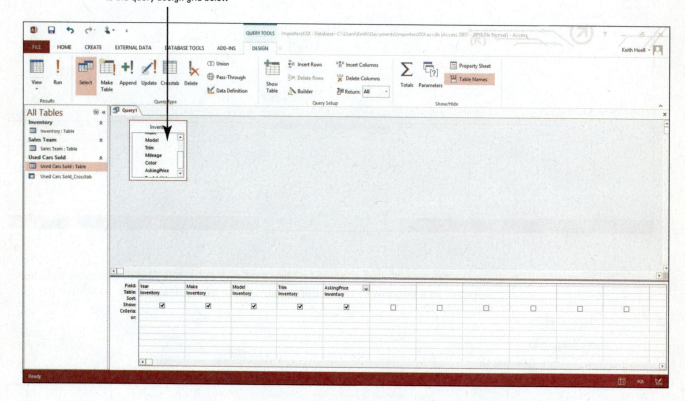

4. Move the insertion point above the Trim field on the design grid until it turns into a bold down arrow. Click to select and highlight the **Trim column**, as shown in Figure 12-12.

Figure 12-12

Column highlighted on design grid

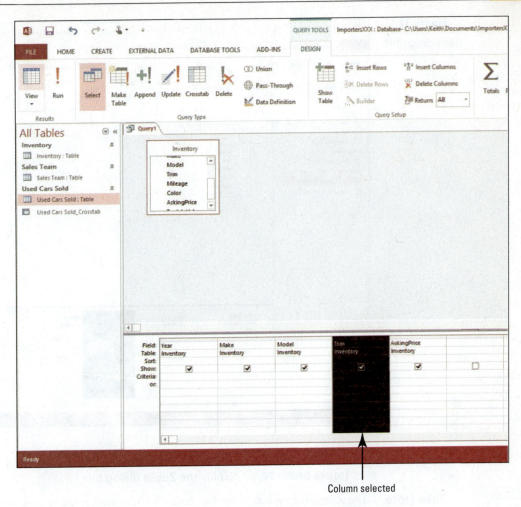

Column selected

5. [Press the **Delete** key] on the keyboard and the Trim column is deleted. The AskingPrice field moves to the left to replace the Trim column.

6. Move the insertion point above the **Model** field on the design grid until it turns into a bold down arrow. Click to select and highlight the **Model** column.

7. On the DESIGN tab, in the Query Setup group, click the **Delete Columns** button. The Model column is deleted.

8. In the table field list in the Inventory table window, double-click the **Model** field to add it back to the query design grid as the last column.

9. Move the insertion point above the Model field on the design grid until it turns into a bold down arrow. Click to select and highlight the **Model** column. Click and hold the mouse button down and drag the Model field to the left until the black vertical placeholder bar is positioned between the Make and AskingPrice fields, then release the mouse button. Your screen should resemble Figure 12-13.

Figure 12-13

Query design grid

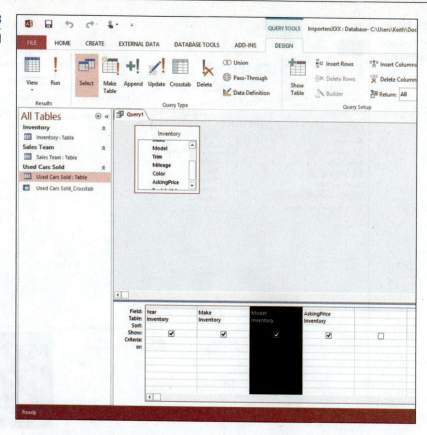

10. Place the insertion point in the Criteria row of the AskingPrice field and [press **Shift+F2**] to display the Zoom dialog box.

Take Note   The Zoom dialog box is used to create a larger workspace to help you focus on expressions and limit typing errors.

11. Key the following expression in the Zoom dialog box, as shown in Figure 12-14, to have the query eventually return all car makes that have an asking price greater or equal to the average asking price for all car makes:

    >=(SELECT Avg(AskingPrice) FROM Inventory WHERE Make = Inventory.Make)

Figure 12-14

Zoom dialog box with expression

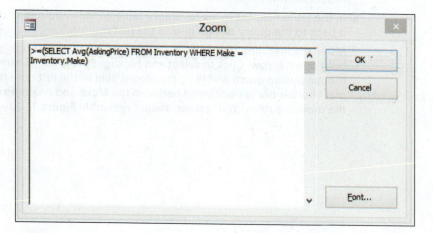

Take Note   Since you are already working inside the Inventory table, the reference in the expression to the Inventory table preceding the Make field can be omitted and the expression can also be constructed as follows: >=(SELECT Avg(AskingPrice) FROM Inventory WHERE Make = Make)

12. Click **OK** to insert the expression in the Criteria row of the **AskingPrice** field.

13. On the DESIGN tab, in the Results group, click the lower half of the **View** button and click **SQL View** to see the entire expression, as shown in Figure 12-15.

Figure 12-15

SQL View

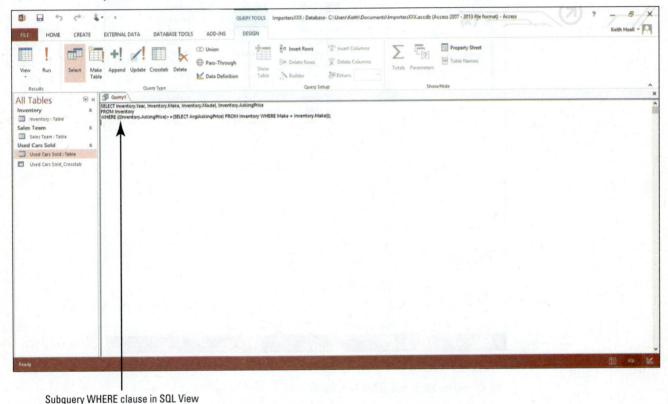

Subquery WHERE clause in SQL View

14. On the DESIGN tab, in the Results group, click **Run**. The query results are displayed, as shown in Figure 12-16.

Figure 12-16

Subquery results

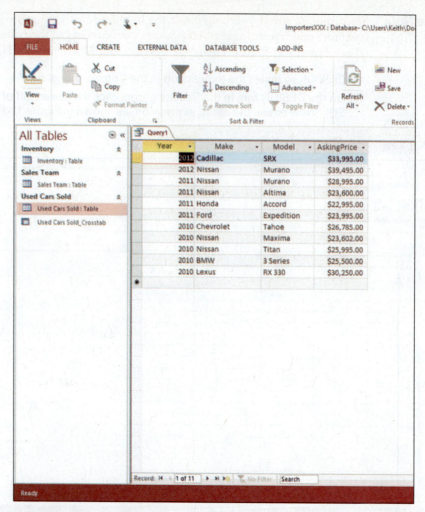

15. Click the **FILE** tab and click **Save**.
16. In the Save As dialog box, key **Subquery** as the query name and click **OK**.
17. Click the **Close** button to close the Subquery query.

PAUSE. LEAVE the database open to use in the next exercise.

CERTIFICATION READY?	3.2.2

How do you add new fields to a query?

CERTIFICATION READY?	3.2.3

How do you remove fields from a query?

CERTIFICATION READY?	3.3.2

How do you add conditional logic to a query?

CERTIFICATION READY?	3.3.4

How do you use comparison operators within a query?

SAVING A FILTER AS A QUERY

The Bottom Line

A filter can be saved as a query so it can be run again anytime you want. If you often work with certain filters, you might want to save these filters so you are not wasting time defining them each time. You cannot save more than one filter for each table, query, or form; but you can save a filter as a query and then apply the query as a filter when and where you want.

Saving a Filter as a Query

In this exercise, you create a simple select query, filter it, and then save it.

When you want to save a filter as a query, you first use the Query Wizard to create a new query using all the fields from a table or another query. You can then use the Filter by Form command to choose the data by which to filter the newly created query and then apply the filter. Next, on the HOME tab, in the Sort & Filter group, you can click the Advanced button and then click Advanced Filter/Sort. The new query design grid will appear. It will automatically include all the fields you've previously chosen to filter. On the HOME tab, in the Sort & Filter group, click the Advanced button and click Save As Query. Key a name for the query and click OK.

To apply the query as a filter, click the Advanced button and click Load from Query to display the Applicable Filter dialog box, as shown in Figure 12-17.

Figure 12-17

Applicable Filter dialog box

Only queries that are based on the same table or query as the form or datasheet will appear in the dialog box. Select the filter, click OK, and then apply the filter.

STEP BY STEP **Save a Filter as a Query**

USE the database that is open from the previous exercise.

1. On the CREATE tab, in the Queries group, click the **Query Wizard** button.
2. In the New Query dialog box, click **Simple Query Wizard** and click **OK**.
3. In the Tables/Queries drop-down list, click **Table: Used Cars Sold**.
4. Click the **>>** button to move all the fields from the Available Fields box to the Selected Fields box and then click **Next >**.
5. Click **Next >** again and then click **Finish** to display a simple select query.
6. On the HOME tab, in the Sort & Filter group, click the **Advanced** button and then click **Filter by Form**.
7. In Filter by Form view, click the **Year** field down arrow and click **2010**, as shown in Figure 12-18.

Figure 12-18

Filter by Form

Click the down arrow to select
criteria by which to filter a field

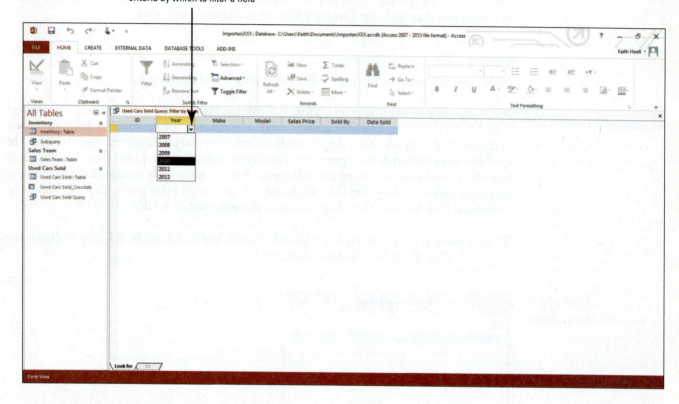

8. On the HOME tab, in the Sort & Filter group, click the **Toggle Filter** button to apply the filter. The results are displayed, as shown in Figure 12-19.

Figure 12-19

Filter by Form results

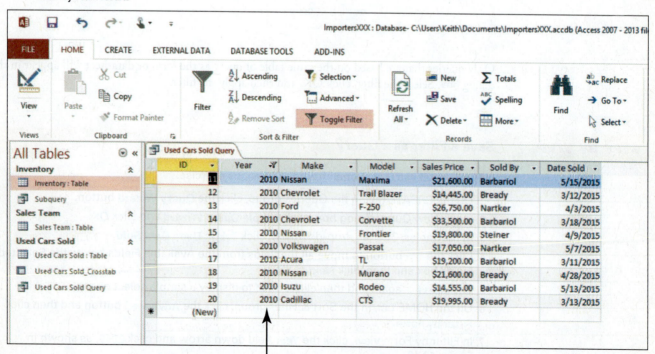

Results filtered to show only 2010 cars

9. On the HOME tab, in the Sort & Filter group, click the **Advanced** button and then click **Advanced Filter/Sort** to display the new query design grid, as shown in Figure 12-20.

Figure 12-20

New query design grid

New query filter tab

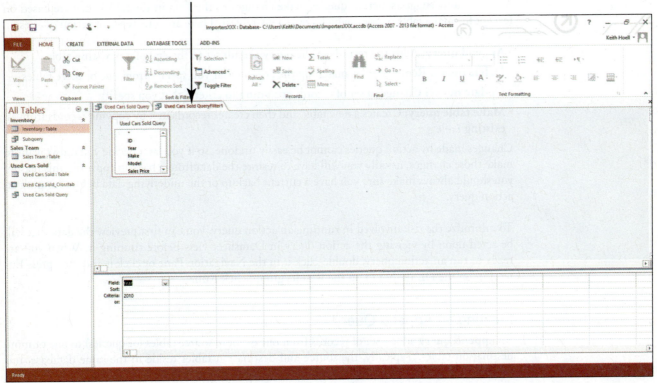

10. On the HOME tab, in the Sort & Filter group, click the **Advanced** button and then click **Save As Query**. The Save As Query dialog box appears, as shown in Figure 12-21.

Figure 12-21

Save As Query dialog box

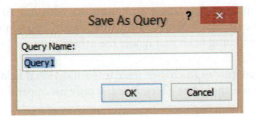

11. Key **Filter Query** in the Query Name box and click **OK**.

12. Click the **Close** button to close the Used Cars Sold QueryFilter1 query.

13. On the HOME tab, in the Sort & Filter group, click the **Toggle Filter** button to remove the filter.

14. Click the **Close** button to close the Used Cars Sold Query and save the changes when prompted. If another dialog box appears informing you that another user may have changed the data, click **Yes**.

PAUSE. LEAVE the database open to use in the next exercise.

CREATING ACTION QUERIES

The Bottom Line

An **action query** changes the data in its datasource or creates a new table. There are four types of action queries—append, delete, update, and make table—and except for the make table query, action queries make changes to the data in the tables on which they are based.

As their name suggests, action queries make changes to the data in the tables they are based on (except for make table queries, which create new tables). There are four types of action queries:

- **Append query:** Adds the records in the query's result set to the end of an existing table
- **Delete query:** Removes rows matching the criteria that you specify from one or more tables
- **Update query:** Changes a set of records according to criteria that you specify
- **Make table query:** Creates a new table and then creates records in it by copying records from an existing table

Changes made by action queries cannot be easily undone, so if you later decide you didn't want to make those changes, usually you will have to restore the data from a backup copy. For this reason, you should always make sure you have a current backup of the underlying data before running an action query.

To minimize the risk involved in running an action query, you can first preview the data that will be acted upon by viewing the action query in Datasheet view before running it. When you are ready to run an action query, double-click it in the Navigation Pane or click it and then press Enter. Or, on the DESIGN tab, in the Results group, click Run.

Creating an Append Query

An **append query** adds a set of records from one or more source tables (or queries) to one or more destination tables. Typically, the source and destination tables reside in the same database, but they don't have to. For example, suppose you acquire some new customers and a database that contains a table of information about those customers. To avoid entering that new data manually, you can append it to the appropriate table in your database. In this exercise, you practice creating an append query.

You can also use append queries to append fields that are based on criteria. For example, you might want to append only the names and addresses of customers who have outstanding orders. Or you can use append queries to append records when some of the fields in one table don't exist in the other table. For example, suppose that your Customers table has 10 fields, and the fields in the Clients table in another database match 8 of your 10 fields. You can use an append query to add only the data in the matching fields and ignore the others.

You cannot use append queries to change the data in individual fields in existing records. To do that type of task, you use an update query. You can only use append queries to add rows of data.

STEP BY STEP **Create an Append Query**

USE the database that is open from the previous exercise.

1. On the CREATE tab, in the Queries group, click the **Query Design** button.
2. In the Show Table dialog box, double-click **Inventory** to add it to the upper section of the query design grid.
3. Click **Close** to close the Show Table dialog box.
4. In the list of table fields, double-click **Year**, **Make**, **Model**, and **Asking Price** to add those fields to the design grid. Your screen should look similar to Figure 12-22.

Figure 12-22

Design grid

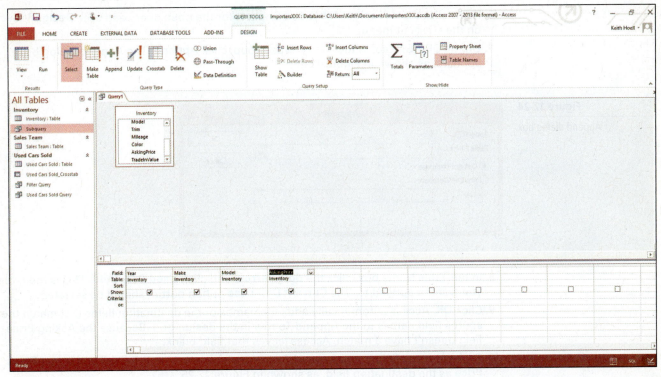

5. On the DESIGN tab, in the Results group, click **Run**. Verify that the query returned the records that you want to append, as shown in Figure 12-23.

Figure 12-23

Records to be appended

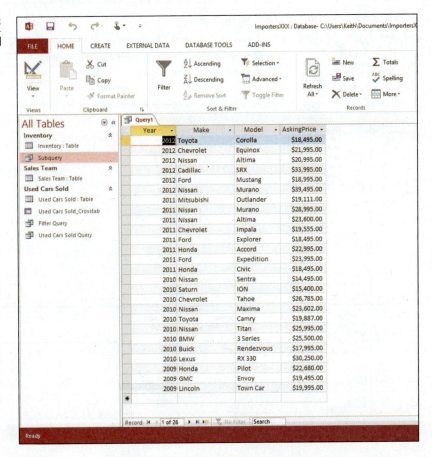

Take Note If you need to add or remove fields from the query, switch back to Design view and double-click to add fields or select the fields that you don't want and press Delete to remove them from the query.

6. Right-click the **document tab** (titled Query1) for the open query and click **Design View** on the shortcut menu.

7. On the DESIGN tab, in the Query Type group, click **Append**. The Append dialog box appears, as shown in Figure 12-24.

Figure 12-24

Append dialog box

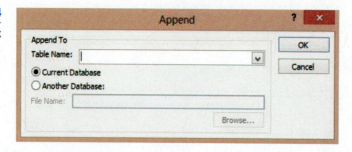

8. In the Table Name box, click the **down arrow** and click **Used Cars Sold**. This is the table you want to append to. The **Current Database** option button should be selected.

9. Click **OK**. Access automatically adds the names of the destination fields that match the source field names to the Append To row in the design grid. Because the Asking Price field doesn't have a match, Access leaves that field blank.

10. Click the blank field in the Append To row under the Asking Price cell and select **Sales Price** as the destination field, as shown in Figure 12-25.

Figure 12-25

Source and destination fields matched

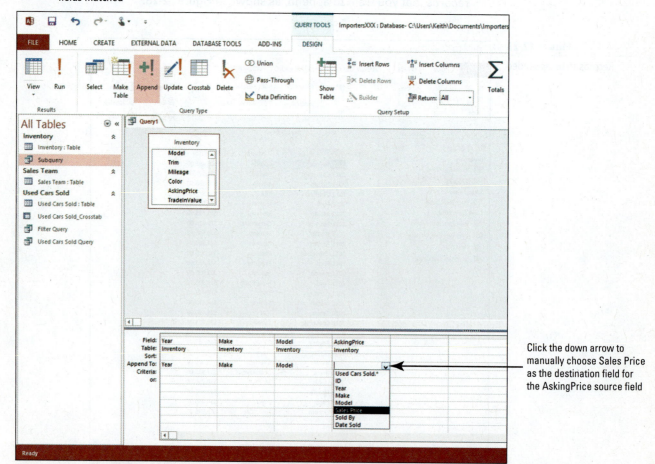

11. Right-click the **document tab** for the query, and then click **Datasheet View** to preview your changes.
12. Right-click the **document tab** for the query, and then click **Design View**.
13. On the DESIGN tab, in the Results group, click **Run**. An alert message appears, as shown in Figure 12-26.

Figure 12-26

Append alert message

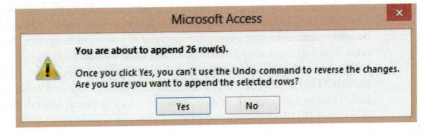

14. Click **Yes**.
15. Open the **Used Cars Sold** table and scroll down to see that the records from the Inventory table have been appended to the end, as shown in Figure 12-27.

Figure 12-27

Results of append query

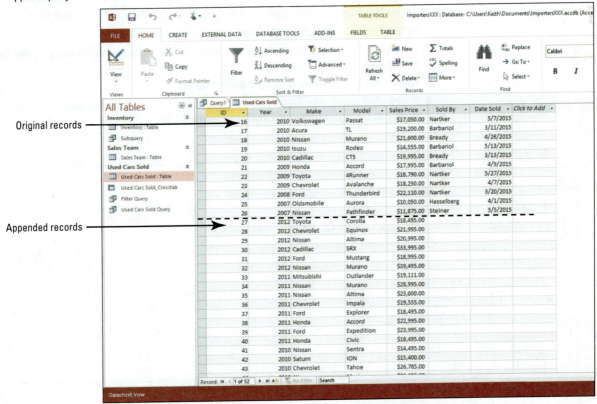

16. Click the **Close** button to close the Used Cars Sold table.
17. Click the **FILE** tab and click **Save**.
18. In the Save As dialog box, key **Append Query** as the query name and click **OK**.
19. Click the **Close** button on Append Query to close the query.

PAUSE. LEAVE Access open to use in the next exercise.

Creating a Make Table Query

A **make table query** is an action query that creates a new table and then creates records in it by copying records from an existing table. You use a make table query when you want to create a new table based on query criterion or criteria from an existing table. For example, you may work for a telecommunications provider and be provided with a table with thousands of cellphone service customers who live in various states. You may find it easier to work with a subset of customers from New York, New Jersey, and Connecticut who have had cellphone service for less than one year, since you need to contact and produce reports on only those individuals. A make table query can be advantageous in this example, especially if you want to ensure the data is stored in a separate table (i.e., you want to export the data as a table to a new database). If you run a make table query with no criterion or criteria, Access will make a duplicate of the table titled after the name you provide. This is helpful when you need to copy the data in a table or to archive data, especially before you run an append, update, or delete query in case it amends the table data in a way that you don't want. In this exercise, you practice creating a make table query to create a backup of a table.

STEP BY STEP   **Create a Make Table Query**

USE the database that is open from the previous exercise.

1. On the CREATE tab, in the Queries group, click the **Query Wizard** button.
2. In the New Query dialog box, click **Simple Query Wizard** and click **OK**.
3. In the Tables/Queries drop-down list, click **Table: Sales Team**.
4. Click the >> button to move all the fields from the Available Fields to the Selected Fields box and then click **Next >**.
5. Click **Finish** to display a simple select query.
6. Right-click the **Sales Team Query** document tab and click **Design View** to display the query in Design view, as shown in Figure 12-28.

Figure 12-28

Query in Design view

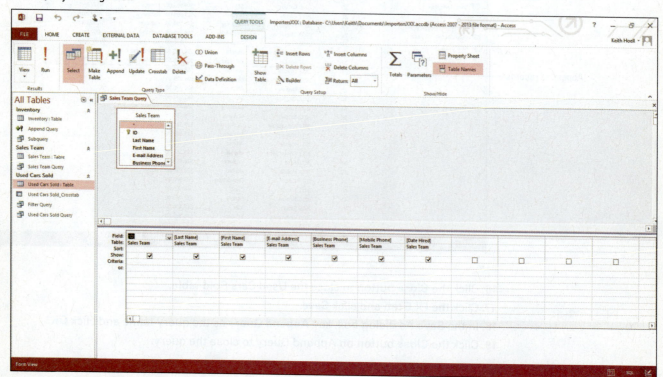

7. On the DESIGN tab, in the Query Type group, click **Make Table**. The Make Table dialog box appears, as shown in Figure 12-29.

Figure 12-29

Make Table dialog box

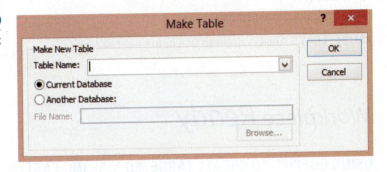

8. In the Table Name box, key **Sales Team Backup**. If it isn't already selected, click **Current Database**, and then click **OK**.

9. On the DESIGN tab, in the Results group, click **Run**. An alert message appears, as shown in Figure 12-30.

Figure 12-30

Make table alert message

10. Click **Yes**. A new table named Sales Team Backup appears in the Navigation Pane.

11. Double-click **Sales Team Backup: Table** in the Navigation Pane to open the new table, as shown in Figure 12-31.

Figure 12-31

New table

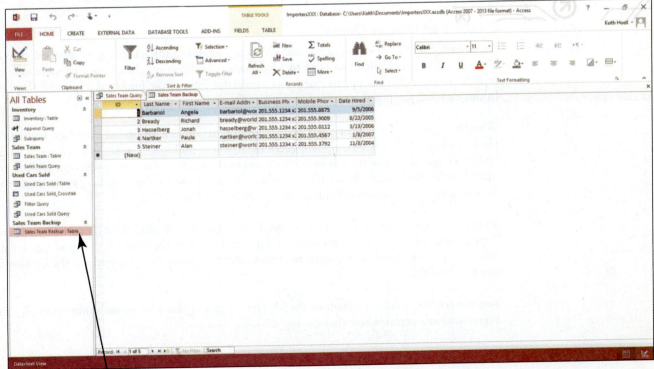

New table now available in the Navigation Pane

12. Click the **Close** button to close the Sales Team Backup table.
13. Click the **Close** button to close the Sales Team query. Save the changes when prompted.
14. **LEAVE** the database open.

PAUSE. LEAVE Access open to use in the next exercise.

Workplace *Ready*

USING QUERIES TO CREATE TARGETED MAILING LABELS

Keeping track of sales data and contacts is vital to the success of any business. Access provides the tools you need to not only keep these records available and secure, but also to generate sales and provide customer service. Whether you need to mail a single sales brochure or do a mass mailing of two thousand, you can use Access to create the labels using the records you maintain in your Access databases.

Imagine you are a partner in a start-up software firm named Proseware, Inc., that has developed specialized software for colleges and universities. You have created an Access database with tables that include information for customers as well as sales leads for professors to whom you are marketing the product.

As you saw in Lesson 11, you can use the Label Wizard to create mailing labels and sort them by zip code for bulk mailing. You can create an action query, like a make table query, that uses one or more criteria to select only certain records for labels and makes a new table to include only those records you will use for mailing. For example, you can use a make table query to create a new table that includes professors who have expertise in a certain area, or those who instruct at a certain college or university. You can then use this new table as the source for the Label Wizard. Using the Label Wizard and a make table query, you can produce labels for mailings to your targeted audience quickly and efficiently.

Creating an Update Query

An **update query** is an action query that changes a set of records according to specified criteria. Use an update query when you need to add, change, or delete the data in one or more existing records. You can think of update queries as a powerful form of the Find and Replace dialog box. In this exercise, you practice making an Update Query.

When making an update query, you enter a select criterion and an update criterion. Unlike the Find and Replace dialog box, update queries can accept multiple criteria. You can use them to update a large number of records in one pass and to change records in more than one table at one time. You can also update the data in one table with data from another—as long as the data types for the source and destination fields match or are compatible.

To create an update query, first create or open a select query. On the DESIGN tab, in the Query Type group, click Update. Access adds the Update To row in the query design grid. Locate the field that contains the data you want to change, and type your change criteria in the Update To row for that field.

You can use any valid expression in the Update To row. Table 12-2 shows some common valid expressions and explains how they change data.

Table 12-2

Expressions and how they
change data

Expression	Result
"Chicago"	In a Text field, sets a text value to Chicago.
#9/25/15#	In a Date/Time field, changes a date value to 25-Sept-15.
Yes	In a Yes/No field, changes a No value to Yes.
"PN" & [PartNumber]	In the PartNumber field, adds "PN" to the beginning of each specified part number.
[UnitPrice] * [Quantity]	Sets a Total field to the result of multiplying values in fields named UnitPrice and Quantity.
[Shipping] * 1.5	In the Shipping field, increases values by 50 percent.
DSum("[Quantity] * [UnitPrice]", "Order Details", "[ProductID] ="& [ProductID])	Where the ProductID values in the current table match the ProductID values in a table named Order Details, this expression updates sales totals when specified in the SalesTotal field by multiplying the values in a field named Quantity by the values in a field named UnitPrice. The expression uses the DSum function because it can operate against more than one table and table field.
Left([PostalCode],5)	In the PostalCode field, removes the rightmost characters in a text or numeric string and leaves the 5 leftmost characters.
IIf(IsNull([SalesPrice]), 0, [SalesPrice])	In the SalesPrice field, changes a null (unknown or undefined) value to a zero (0) value.

STEP BY STEP   **Create an Update Query**

USE the database that is open from the previous exercise.

1. On the CREATE tab, in the Queries group, click the **Query Wizard** button.
2. In the New Query dialog box, click **Simple Query Wizard** and click **OK**.
3. In the Tables/Queries drop-down list, click **Table: Inventory**.
4. Click the >> button to move all the fields from the Available Fields to the Selected Fields box.
5. Click **Trim** and then the < button to move it back to the Available Fields box. Click **Color** and then the < button to move it back to the Available Fields box. Click **Next >**.
6. Click **Next >** again and then click **Finish** to display a simple select query in Datasheet view, as shown in Figure 12-32.

Figure 12-32

Select query in Datasheet view

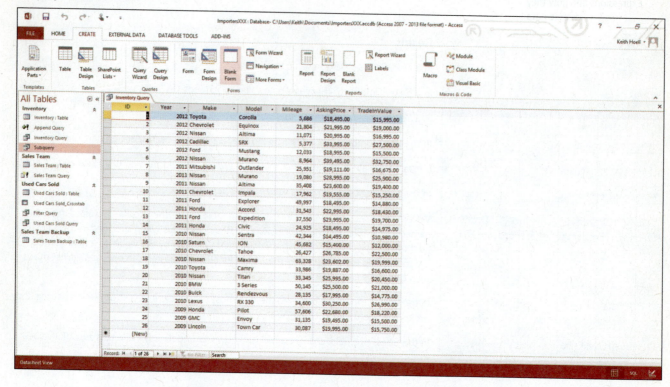

7. Right-click the **Inventory Query** document tab and click **Design View** to display the query in Design view.

8. Key **2012** in the Criteria row of the Year field.

9. On the DESIGN tab, in the Query Type group, click **Update**. Access adds the Update To row in the query design grid, as shown in Figure 12-33.

Figure 12-33

Select query in Design view

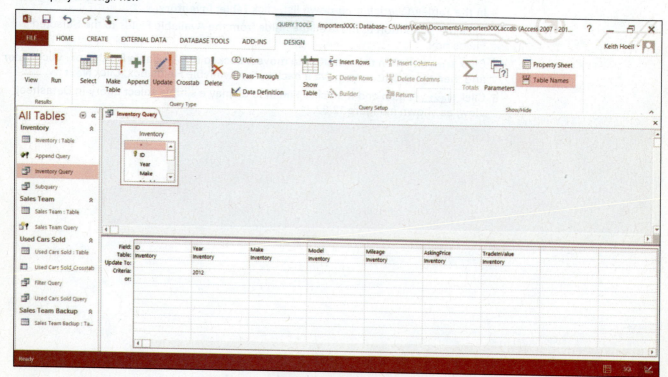

10. In the Update To row of the AskingPrice field, key [AskingPrice] + 500. The design grid should look similar to Figure 12-34.

Figure 12-34

Select and update criterion

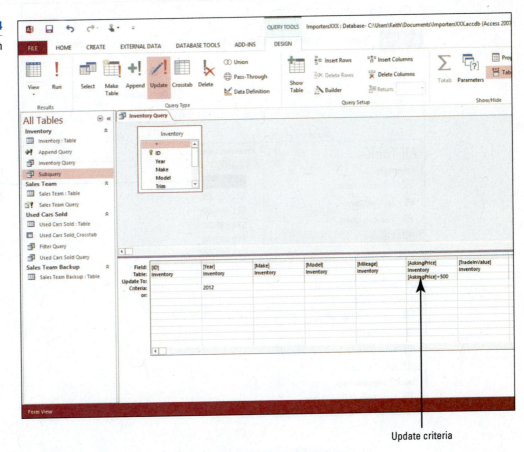

Update criteria

11. On the DESIGN tab, in the Results group, click **Run**. An alert message appears, as shown in Figure 12-35.

Figure 12-35

Update alert message

12. Click **Yes**.
13. Right-click the **Inventory Query** document tab and click **Datasheet View** to display the update query results, as shown in Figure 12-36.

Figure 12-36

Update query results

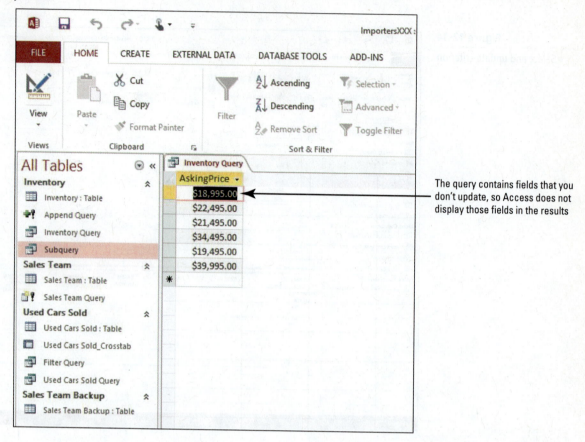

The query contains fields that you don't update, so Access does not display those fields in the results

14. Click the **Close** button to close the Inventory query. Save the changes when prompted.
15. Double-click **Inventory: Table** in the Navigation Pane to open it. Notice that the asking price for all 2012 cars has been increased by $500.
16. Click the **Close** button to close the Inventory table.
17. **LEAVE** the database open.

PAUSE. LEAVE Access open to use in the next exercise.

Creating a Delete Query

A **delete query** is an action query that removes rows matching the criteria that you specify from one or more tables. A delete query is used to delete entire records from a table, along with the key value that makes a record unique. Typically, delete queries are used only when you need to change or remove large amounts of data quickly. To remove a small number of records, open the table in Datasheet view, select the fields or rows that you want to delete, and press Delete.

To create a delete query, first create or open a select query and add criteria to return the records you want to delete. On the DESIGN tab, in the Query Type group, click Delete. Access changes the select query to a delete query, hides the Show row in the lower section of the design grid, and adds the Delete row. The word Where appears in the Delete row for all fields of the query.

When you click Run, Access prompts you to confirm the deletion. Click Yes to delete the data and then open the table to see that the records have been deleted.

| STEP BY STEP | **Create a Delete Query** |

USE the database that is open from the previous exercise.

1. On the CREATE tab, in the Queries group, click **Query Wizard**.
2. In the New Query dialog box, click **Simple Query Wizard** and click **OK**.
3. In the Tables/Queries drop-down list, click **Table: Used Cars Sold**.
4. Click the >> button to move all the fields from the Available Fields to the Selected Fields box and then click **Next >**.
5. Click **Next >** again.
6. Key **Delete Query** as the title and then click **Finish** to display the results of the simple select query.
7. Right-click the **Delete Query** document tab and click **Design View** to display the query in Design view.
8. Key <**#3/31/2015#** in the Criteria row of the Date Sold field, as shown in Figure 12-37.

Figure 12-37

Date Sold criteria

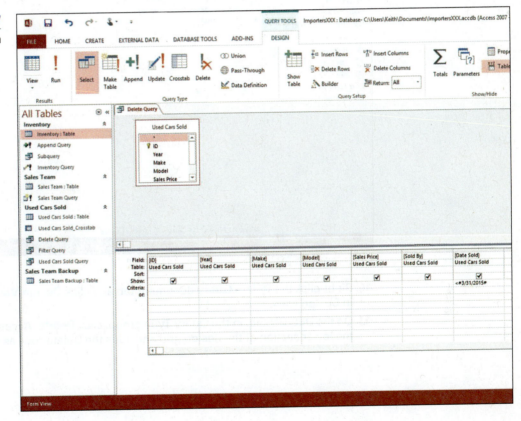

9. On the DESIGN tab, in the Results group, click **Run** to display the records to be deleted, as shown in Figure 12-38.

Figure 12-38

Records to be deleted

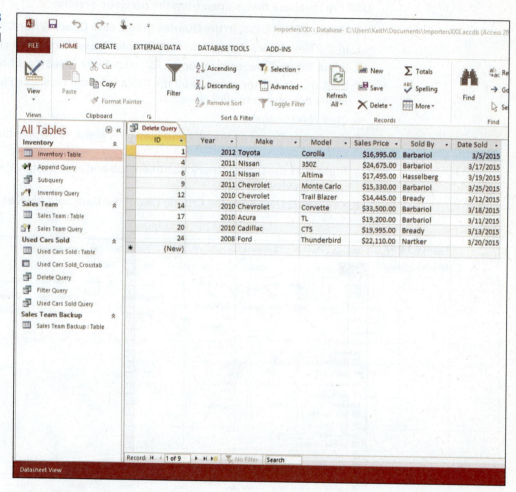

10. Right-click the **Delete Query** document tab and click **Design View** to display the query in Design view.

11. On the DESIGN tab, in the Query Type group, click **Delete**. Access hides the Show row in the lower section of the design grid and adds the Delete row, as shown in Figure 12-39.

Figure 12-39

Delete row in design grid

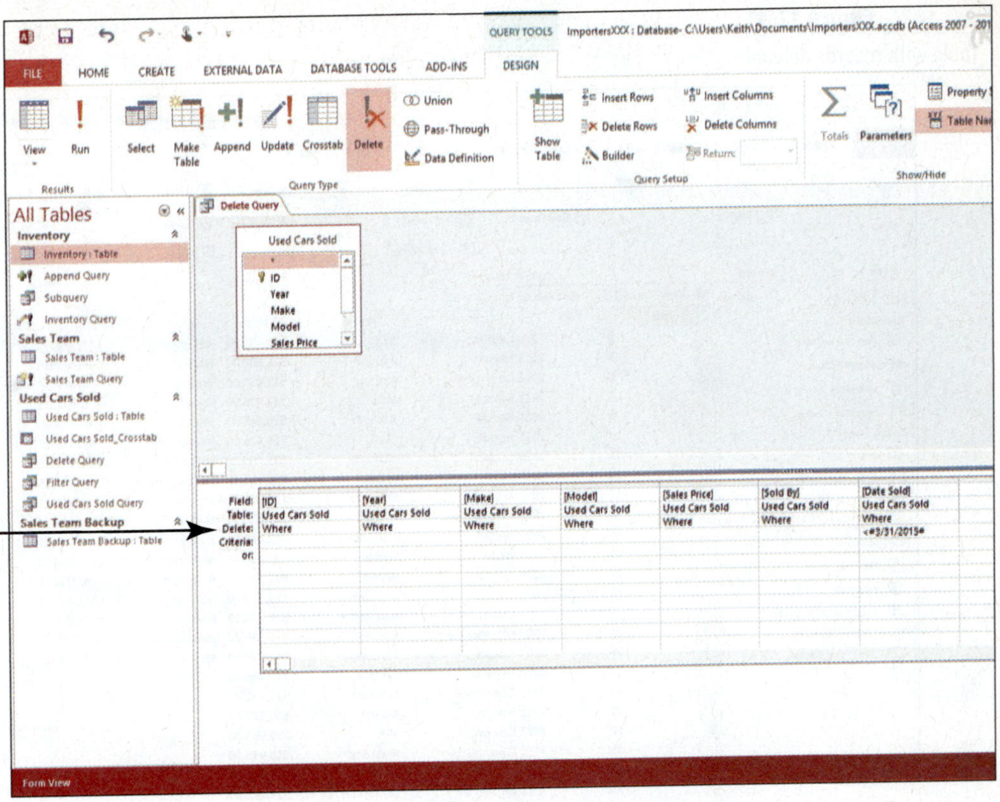

Delete row added →

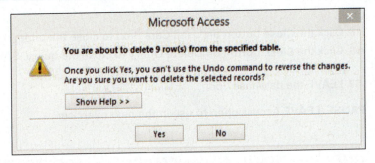

12. On the DESIGN tab, in the Results group, click **Run**. An alert message appears, as shown in Figure 12-40.

Figure 12-40

Delete alert message

> **Microsoft Access**
>
> ⚠ You are about to delete 9 row(s) from the specified table.
>
> Once you click Yes, you can't use the Undo command to reverse the changes. Are you sure you want to delete the selected records?
>
> [Show Help >>]
>
> [Yes]   [No]

13. Click **Yes**.

14. Double-click **Used Cars Sold: Table** in the Navigation Pane to open it. Notice that all the records for cars sold before March 31, 2015, have been deleted, as shown in Figure 12-41.

Figure 12-41

Table with records deleted

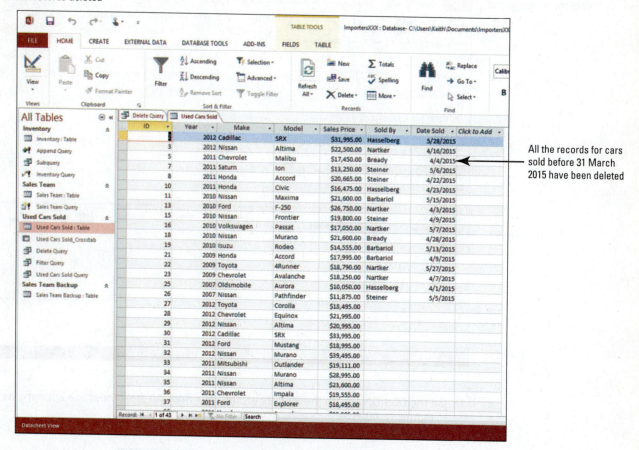

All the records for cars sold before 31 March 2015 have been deleted

15. Click the **Close** button on Used Cars Sold to close the table.

16. Click the **Close** button on Delete Query to close the query. SAVE the changes when prompted.

17. **LEAVE** the database open.

PAUSE. LEAVE Access open to use in the next exercise.

The Bottom Line

UNDERSTANDING ADVANCED QUERY MODIFICATION

After a query has been created, you can modify it in various ways to suit your purposes—by creating a join, creating calculated fields, or using aggregated functions.

Creating a Join

Relational databases consist of tables that have logical relationships to each other. You use relationships to connect tables based on fields they have in common. A relationship between identical fields in different tables is represented by a **join** in Design view. When you include multiple tables in a query, you use joins to help you get the results you want. A join helps a query return only the records from each table you want to see based on how those tables are related to other tables in the query. When you add tables to a query, Access creates joins that are based on relationships that have been defined between the tables. You can manually create joins known as ad hoc relationships in queries, even if they do not represent relationships that have already been defined. In this exercise, you create a join between tables.

Take Note   If the relationship is one-to-many, Access displays a "1" above the join line to show which table is on the "one" side and an infinity symbol (∞) to show which table is on the "many" side.

The four basic types of joins are inner joins, outer joins, cross joins, and unequal joins. An **inner join** includes rows in the query only when the joined field matches records in both tables. Inner joins are the most common type of join. Most of the time, you don't need to do anything to use an inner join. Access automatically creates inner joins if you add two tables to a query and those tables each have a field with the same name and the same or compatible data type and one of the join fields is a primary key.

An **outer join** includes all of the rows from one table in the query results and only those rows from the other table that match the join field in the first table. You create outer joins by modifying inner joins. To create an outer join, double-click the line joining the tables to display the Join Properties dialog box. In the Join Properties dialog box, Option 1 represents an inner join. Option 2 is a **left outer join**, where the query includes all of the rows from the table on the left and only those records from the table on the right that match the join field in the left table. Option 3 is a **right outer join**, where the query includes all of the rows from the table on the right and only those rows from the table on the left that match the join field in the right table.

Because some of the rows on one side of an outer join will not have corresponding rows from the other table, some of the fields returned in the query results from the other table will be empty when the rows do not correspond.

Take Note   To tell which table is the left table or the right table in a given join, double-click the join to view the Join Properties dialog box.

In a **cross join**, each row from one table is combined with each row from another table. Any time you run a query that has tables that are not explicitly joined, a cross join is produced. Cross joins are usually unintentional, but there are cases where they can be useful. A cross join can be used if you want to examine every possible combination of rows between two tables or queries.

If you want to combine the rows of two sources of data based on field values that are not equal, you use an **unequal join**. Typically, unequal joins are based on either the greater than (>), less than (<), greater than or equal to (>=), or less than or equal to (<=) comparison operators. Unequal joins are not supported in Design view. If you wish to use them, you must do so in SQL view.

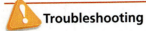 **Troubleshooting**   If you create a join by mistake, for example, a join between two fields that have dissimilar data types, you can delete it. In the query design grid, click the join you want to remove and press Delete.

STEP BY STEP   Create a Join

USE the database that is open from the previous exercise.

1. On the CREATE tab, in the Queries group, click **Query Design**.
2. In the Show Table dialog box, double-click **Sales Team** and **Used Cars Sold** to add them to the design grid.
3. Click **Close**.
4. In the Sales Team field list, double-click **E-mail Address**.
5. In the Used Cars Sold field list, double-click **Year**, **Make**, **Model**, and **Sales Price**. Your screen should look similar to Figure 12-42.

Double-click join line to open the
Join Properties dialog box

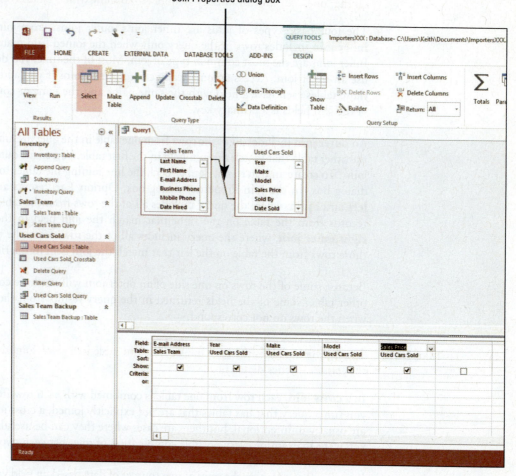

6. Double-click the join line between the tables, indicating which fields are joined. The Join Properties dialog box opens, as shown in Figure 12-43.

Figure 12-43

Join Properties dialog box

Inner join option

Left outer join option

Right outer join option

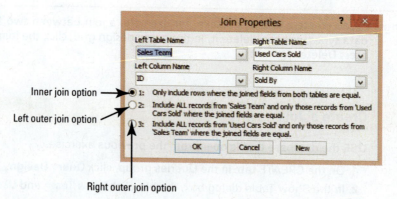

7. Click the option button for option 2: and then click OK to create a left outer join.
8. On the DESIGN tab, in the Results group, click Run.
9. The results of the query are displayed, as shown in Figure 12-44.

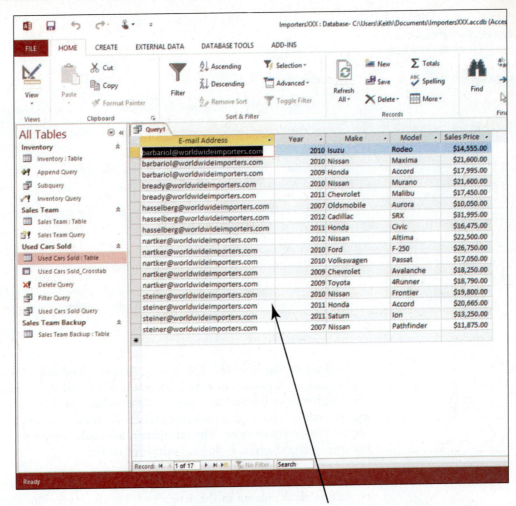

Figure 12-44

Left outer join

Results include all of the rows from the first table and only those records from the second table that match the join field in the first table

10. Save the query as **Join Query** and **CLOSE**.

11. **LEAVE** the database open.

PAUSE. LEAVE Access open to use in the next exercise.

Creating a Calculated Query Field

You can create a new field that displays the results of a calculation you define with an expression or that manipulates field values. A **calculated field** is a column in a query that results from an expression. For example, you can calculate a value; combine text values, such as first and last names; or format a portion of a date. You can also format the calculated field value by choosing an appropriate format in the Property Sheet pane. In this exercise, you use the Expression Builder to create a calculated query by subtracting two fields to determine a markup price in both U.S. dollars and Euros.

You can use expressions that perform arithmetic operations in calculated fields using basic operators (+,−,*, /) to add, subtract, multiply, and divide the values in two or more fields. You can also perform arithmetic operations on dates or use expressions that manipulate text. Table 12-3 shows examples of expressions and basic operators that can be used in calculated fields. The results can then be formatted by selecting the calculated field and then selecting a format in the Format box of the Property Sheet pane. For example, a number can be formatted in several different ways, including as Currency or Scientific values. The Property Sheet button in the Show/Hide group on the DESIGN tab displays the Property Sheet pane.

Another Way

You can also display the Property Sheet pane by right-clicking the expression and choosing Properties from the shortcut menu that appears.

Table 12-3

Expressions that can be used in calculated fields

Expression	Description
PrimeShip: [Ship] * 1.1	Creates a field called PrimeShip, and then displays shipping charges plus 10 percent in the field.
OrderAmount: [Quantity] * [Price]	Creates a field called OrderAmount, and then displays the product of the values in the Quantity and Price fields.
LeadTime: [RequiredDate] – [ShippedDate]	Creates a field called LeadTime, and then displays the difference (in number of days) between the values in the RequiredDate and ShippedDate fields.
TotalInventory: [UnitsInStock] + [UnitsOnOrder]	Creates a field called TotalInventory, and then displays the sum of the values in the UnitsInStock and UnitsOnOrder fields.
FullName: [FirstName] & " " & [LastName]	Creates a field called FullName that displays the values in the FirstName and LastName fields, separated by a space. ("&" is called the concatenation operator and is used to put strings together.)
Address2: [City] & " " & [Region] & " " & [PostalCode]	Creates a field called Address2 that displays the values in the City, Region, and PostalCode fields, separated by spaces. ("&" is called the concatenation operator and is used to put strings together.)

A well-designed database does not store simple calculated values in tables. For example, a table might store an employee's hire date, but not how long she has worked for the company. If you know both today's date and the employee's date of hire, you can always calculate her employment length, so there is no need to store that in the table. Instead, you create a query that calculates and displays the pertinent value. The calculations are made every time you run the query, so if the underlying data changes, so do your calculated results.

To create a calculated field, first open or create a query and switch to Design view. In the Field row of the first blank column in the design grid, key the expression. You can use the Zoom box to access a larger screen area to help you enter the expression or, as you learned in Lesson 8, you can use the Expression Builder to easily select the elements of the expression (fields, operators, and built-in functions) from menus. To name the field, key a name followed by a colon before the expression. If you do not supply a name, Access will use a generic name for the field, for example, EXPR1. The string following the colon is the expression that supplies the values for each record. To see the SQL code, you can switch to SQL View.

STEP BY STEP   **Create a Calculated Query Field**

USE the database that is open from the previous exercise.

1. On the CREATE tab, in the Queries group, click **Query Design**.
2. In the Show Table dialog box, double-click **Inventory** to add the table to the design grid.
3. Click **Close**.
4. In the Inventory field list, double-click **Year**, **Make**, **Model**, **AskingPrice**, and **TradeInValue**.
5. Click the **Field** cell in the first blank column (to the right of the TradeInValue field) and click the **Builder** button in the Query Setup group to open the Expression Builder dialog box.
6. In the blank area of the dialog box, key the following:

   Markup: [AskingPrice]

7. In the Expression Elements category, click **Operators**. The dialog box should resemble Figure 12-45.

Figure 12-45

Expression Builder

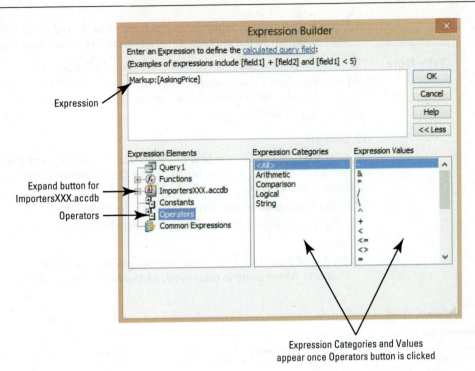

Figure 12-45

Expression Builder

Expression

Expand button for
ImportersXXX.accdb

Operators

Expression Categories and Values
appear once Operators button is clicked

8. In the Expression Values category, double-click the **minus sign (–)**. The minus sign should appear in the expression and next to the AskingPrice field.

9. In the Expression Elements category, click the **expand** button next to ImportersXXX. accdb. Tables, Queries, Forms, and Reports should appear under ImportersXXX.accdb.

10. In the Expression Elements category, click the **expand** button next to Tables to expand it. The available table names appear. Click **Inventory**. The available fields from the Inventory table should appear in the Expression Categories box. Your screen should resemble Figure 12-46.

Figure 12-46

Expression Builder with
Expression Elements expanded

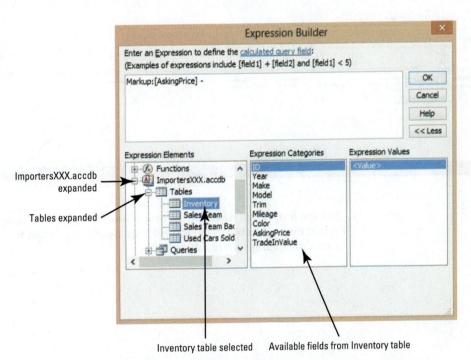

ImportersXXX.accdb
expanded

Tables expanded

Inventory table selected   Available fields from Inventory table

11. In the Expression Categories box, double-click **TradeInValue**; [Inventory]! [TradeInValue] should appear in the expression and next to the minus sign (–).

Take Note *The part of the expression that reads [Inventory]![TradeInValue] specifies that the TradeInValue field originates from the Inventory table; however, even though Access automatically formats it this way, this expression format is not required since you're already referencing the Inventory table in the Table row of the design grid.*

12. Click **OK**.

13. Click the **Field** cell in the first blank column (to the right of the newly created calculated field) and click the **Builder** button in the Query Setup group to open the Expression Builder dialog box.

14. In the blank area of the dialog box, key the following:

   Markup in Euros: ([AskingPrice] – [TradeInValue]) * .7534

15. Click **OK**.

16. On the DESIGN tab, in the Show/Hide group, click the **Property Sheet** button. The Property Sheet pane is displayed, as shown in Figure 12-47.

Figure 12-47

Property Sheet Pane

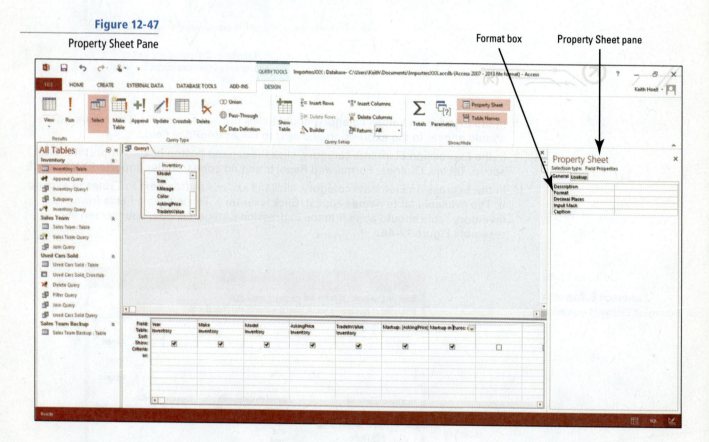

17. Click the empty cell next to the Format box, then click the **down arrow** to display the Format menu, as shown in Figure 12-48. Select **Euro** from the options that appear to format the expression result as Euro.

Figure 12-48

Format menu

Click down arrow to display format menu

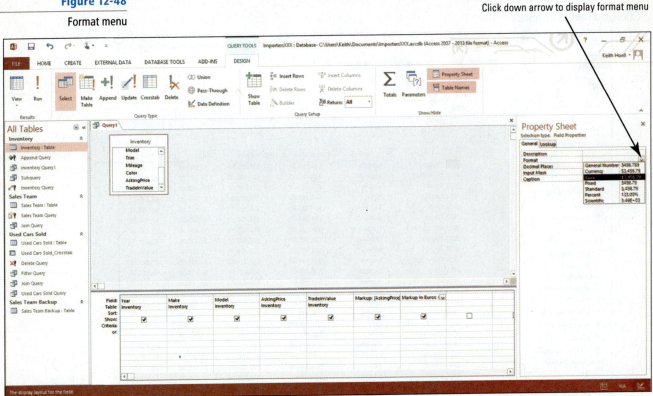

18. On the DESIGN tab, in the Results group, click **Run**. The query with the new calculated Markup and Markup in Euros fields is displayed, as shown in Figure 12-49.

Figure 12-49

Calculated field query results

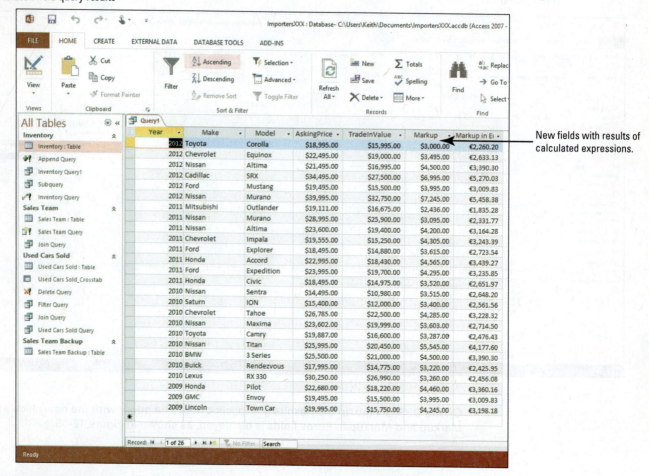

New fields with results of calculated expressions.

19. **SAVE** the query as **Calculated Query** and **CLOSE**.
20. **LEAVE** the database open.

PAUSE. LEAVE Access open to use in the next exercise.

Creating Aggregated Queries

An **aggregate function** performs a calculation on a set of values and then returns a single value. You can add, count, or calculate other aggregate values and display them in a special row, called the Total row, which appears below the asterisk (*) row in Datasheet view. You can use a different aggregate function for each column and you can also choose not to summarize a column. You can use aggregated functions to count the data returned by a query, calculate average values, and find the smallest, largest, earliest, and latest values using a feature called the Total row, which doesn't alter the design of your query. You can work with the Total row in both query Design and query Datasheet views. In this exercise, you create an aggregated query using the Total row in both query Design and query Datasheet views.

You can also apply aggregated functions in Design view where you have the ability to use the Group By function in the Total row on the design grid. The Group By function can be used in combination with other fields and aggregated functions. For example, if you're managing a human resource database, you can group by employees' gender and display the average salary per group.

CERTIFICATION READY?   3.3.1

How do you add calculated fields within queries?

CERTIFICATION READY?   3.3.5

How do you use basic operators within queries?

CERTIFICATION READY?   3.2.6

How do you format fields within queries?

The following aggregated functions are available in both Datasheet view and Design view:

- **Count:** Counts the number of items in a column
- **Sum:** Sums a column of numbers
- **Average:** Averages a column of numbers
- **Maximum:** Finds the highest value in a column
- **Minimum:** Finds the lowest value in a column
- **Standard Deviation:** Measures how widely values are dispersed from an average value (a mean) in a column
- **Variance:** Measures the statistical variance of all values in a column

The following additional aggregated functions are available in Design view:

- **First:** Finds the first value in a field
- **Last:** Finds the last value in a field
- **Expression:** Groups data based on an expression you can specify
- **Where:** Groups data based on criteria you can specify

Cross Ref   In Lesson 9, you use the Total row with tables to provide a summary of table data.

Take Note   Many of the aggregated functions work only on data fields set to specific data types. For example, if you are in a column that only displays text values, some functions—such as Sum or Average—are not relevant, and are therefore not available.

STEP BY STEP   **Create an Aggregated Query**

USE the database that is open from the previous exercise.

1. On the CREATE tab, in the Queries group, click **Query Design**.
2. In the Show Table dialog box, double-click **Inventory** to add the table's field list window to the design grid.
3. Click **Close**.
4. In the Inventory field list, double-click **Year**, **Make**, **Model**, **Mileage**, **AskingPrice**, and **TradeInValue** to add them to the design grid.
5. On the DESIGN tab, in the Results group, click **Run**.
6. On the HOME tab, in the Records group, click the **Totals** button. Scroll down, if necessary, to see the Total row at the bottom of the result set.
7. In the Total cell of the **Year** field, click the **down arrow** to display the menu and click **Count**, as shown in Figure 12-50. Notice the cell displays 26, denoting 26 values (years) in the Year column.

Figure 12-50

Total row menu options

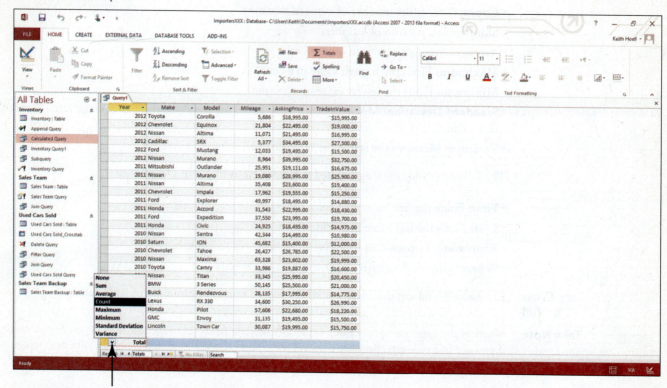

Click the down arrow in the Total row
to see aggregate function options

8. Click the down arrow in the **Total** cell of the Mileage field and click **Average**.

9. Click the down arrow in the **Total** cell of the AskingPrice field and click **Maximum**.

10. Click the down arrow in the **Total** cell of the TradeInValue field and click **Sum**. Your Total row should appear similar to Figure 12-51.

Figure 12-51

Aggregate function results

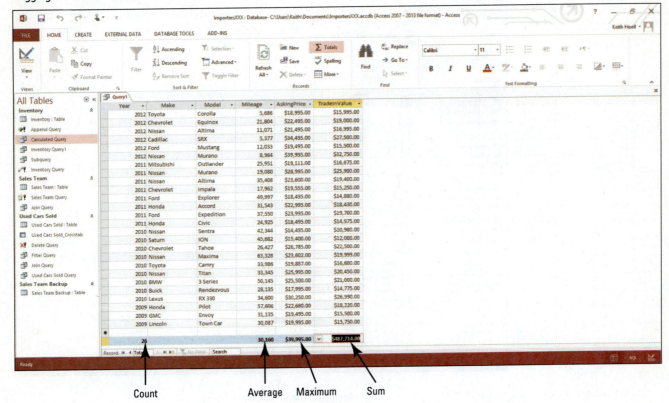

Count   Average   Maximum   Sum

11. Switch to Design view and remove the Model, Mileage, AskingPrice, and TradeInValue fields from the design grid. The Year and Make fields should be the only ones remaining on the grid.

12. On the DESIGN tab, in the Show/Hide group, click the Totals button. A new Totals row should appear below the Table row on the design grid.

13. Click the Group By cell below the Make field cell and click the down arrow to display the aggregate function menu.

14. Click the Count aggregate function to select it from the menu, as shown in Figure 12-52.

Figure 12-52

Aggregate function menu in
Design view

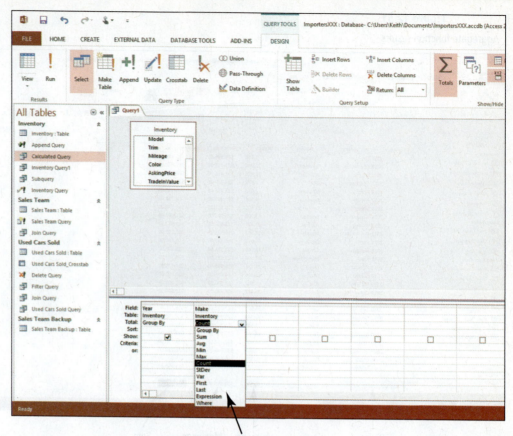

Aggregate function menu in Total row

15. Switch to Datasheet view. Your screen should resemble Figure 12-53. Notice the records in the Make field are grouped by Year and counted with the results appearing in a new column named CountOfMake. Also notice the Year field is grouped and each year remains counted as applied from the aggregate function we created previously in Datasheet view.

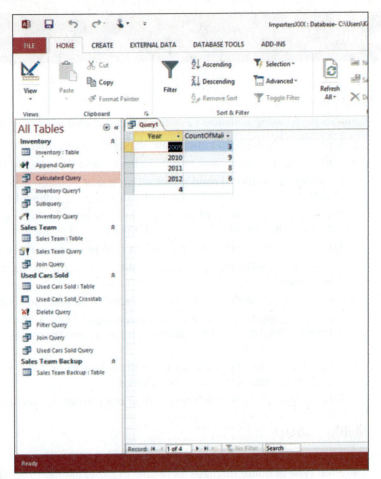

Figure 12-53

Aggregate function results

16. **SAVE** the query as **Aggregated Query** and **CLOSE** it.

17. **CLOSE** the database.

PAUSE. CLOSE Access.

SKILL SUMMARY

In This Lesson You Learned How To:	Exam Objective	Objective Number
Create crosstab queries	Create crosstab queries	3.1.2
Create a subquery	Add new fields	3.2.2
	Remove fields	3.2.3
	Add conditional logic	3.3.2
	Use comparison operators	3.3.4
Save a filter as a query		
Create action queries	Create action queries	3.1.4
Understand advanced query modification	Create multi-table queries	3.1.5
	Add calculated fields	3.3.1
	Use basic operators	3.3.5
	Format fields within queries	3.2.6
	Group and summarize data	3.3.3

Knowledge Assessment

Fill in the Blank

Complete the following sentences by writing the correct word or words in the blanks provided.

1. A(n) _____ is a SELECT statement that is inside another select or action query.
2. A(n) _____ removes rows matching the criteria you specify from one or more tables.
3. To minimize the risk of running an action query, you can first preview the data that will be acted upon by viewing the action query in _____ view before running it.
4. A(n) _____ includes all of the rows from one table in the query results and only those rows from the other table that match the join field in the first table.
5. A(n) _____ is a column in a query that results from an expression.
6. You can use the Group By function in the _____ row on the design grid in query Design view.
7. A(n) _____ performs a calculation on a set of values and then returns a single value.
8. A(n) _____ query always includes three types of data: the data used as row headings, the data used as column headings, and the values that you want to sum or otherwise compute.
9. To quickly add all the fields in a table to the design grid in Design view, double-click the _____ at the top of the list of table fields.
10. To be able to apply a filter when and where you want, save the filter as a(n) _____.

Multiple Choice

Select the best response for the following statements or questions.

1. What type of query displays its results in a grid similar to an Excel worksheet?
   a. crosstab
   b. append
   c. aggregated
   d. subquery

2. What can you use for a more intuitive interface in which to enter criteria or an expression in a field or criteria cell?
   a. Zoom box
   b. Field list pane
   c. control label
   d. Expression Builder

3. Which action query does not make changes to the data in the tables that it is based on?
   a. append
   b. make table
   c. update
   d. delete

4. Which type of query can be thought of as a powerful version of the Find and Replace dialog box?
   a. filter
   b. calculated field
   c. update
   d. crosstab

5. Which of the following is *not* a type of join?
   a. inner join
   b. exterior join
   c. cross join
   d. unequal join

6. Which of the following is not an aggregated function?
   a. Lowest
   b. Sum

    c. Average

    d. Count

7. Which of the following SELECT statements selects all the fields from the Inventory table?

    a. SELECT all fields FROM Inventory

    b. SELECT [ALL] from [INVENTORY]

    c. SELECT from INVENTORY {all fields}

    d. SELECT * FROM Inventory

8. For more space in which to enter the SELECT statement in a field or criteria cell, what do you press to display the Zoom box?

    a. Shift+F2

    b. Ctrl+2

    c. Shift+Enter

    d. Ctrl+Spacebar

9. To display the pane used to format a calculated value in query Design view, click the _____ in the Show/Hide group on the DESIGN tab of the Ribbon.

    a. Undo button

    b. Property Sheet button

    c. Datasheet View button

    d. Totals button

10. Which type of query adds the records in the query's result set to the end of an existing table?

    a. append

    b. make table

    c. update

    d. delete

Competency Assessment

Project 12-1: Create a Calculated Query Field

In your job as a travel agent at Margie's Travel, you are frequently asked the length of various trips. So that you don't have to calculate it mentally, create a calculated field that will give you this information.

GET READY. LAUNCH Access if it is not already running.

1. **OPEN** the *M Travel* database from the data files for this lesson.
2. **SAVE** the database as *M TravelXXX* (where *XXX* is your initials).
3. On the CREATE tab, in the Queries group, click **Query Design**.
4. In the Show Table dialog box, double-click **Events** to add the table to the design grid.
5. Click **Close**.
6. In the Inventory field list, double-click **Event**, **StartDate**, and **EndDate** to add the fields to the design grid.
7. Click the **Field** cell in the first blank column and [press **Shift+F2**] to open the Zoom dialog box.
8. In the Zoom dialog box, key the following expression:

    TripLength: [EndDate] – [StartDate]

9. Click **OK**.
10. On the DESIGN tab, in the Results group, click **Run**. The query is displayed, with a new **TripLength** field calculating the number of days for each trip.
11. **SAVE** the query as **Calculated Query** and **CLOSE**.
12. **CLOSE** the database.

LEAVE Access running for the next project.

Project 12-2: Save a Filter as a Query

As sales manager for Fourth Coffee, you frequently run the same filters on the database. Now that you have learned to save a filter as a query, you can save yourself some time.

GET READY. LAUNCH Access if it is not already running.

1. **OPEN** *Fourth Coffee* from the data files for this lesson.
2. **SAVE** the database as *Fourth CoffeeXXX* (where *XXX* is your initials).
3. On the CREATE tab, in the Queries group, click the Query Wizard button.
4. In the New Query dialog box, click Simple Query Wizard and click OK.
5. In the Tables/Queries drop-down list, click Table: Order Summary.
6. Click the >> button to move all the fields from the Available Fields to the Selected Fields box and then click Next >.
7. Click Next > again and then click Finish to display a simple select query.
8. On the HOME tab, in the Sort & Filter group, click the Advanced button and then click Filter by Form.
9. In the Filter by Form, click the down arrow in the Status field and click Completed.
10. On the HOME tab, in the Sort & Filter group, click the Toggle Filter button to apply the filter. The results are displayed.
11. On the HOME tab, in the Sort & Filter group, click the Advanced button and then click Advanced Filter/Sort to display the new query design grid.
12. On the HOME tab, in the Sort & Filter group, click the Advanced button and then click Save As Query. The Save As Query dialog box appears.
13. Key Filter Query in the Query Name box and click OK.
14. Click the Close button to close the Order Summary QueryFilter1 query.
15. On the HOME tab, in the Sort & Filter group, click the Toggle Filter button to remove the filter.
16. Click the Close button to close the Order Summary Query and save the changes when prompted. If presented with a message box stating the query has been changed, click Yes.
17. **LEAVE** the database open.

LEAVE Access open for the next project.

Proficiency Assessment

Project 12-3: Create a Subquery

You are interested in extracting specific information about monthly sales for all Fourth Coffee stores from the database. Create a subquery to determine which months and corresponding stores have sales that are above average.

USE the database that is open from the previous project.

1. On the CREATE tab, in the Queries group, click Query Design.
2. Use the Show Table dialog box to add the Monthly Sales by Store table to the upper section of the query design grid and then close the Show Table dialog box.
3. Add the Month, Store, and Sales fields to the design grid.
4. Place the insertion point in the Criteria row of the Sales field and display the Expression Builder.
5. Key the following expression in the Expression Builder, using the available categories and menus:

> (SELECT AVG([Sales]) FROM [Monthly Sales by Store])

6. Click OK.

7. Use the Property Sheet pane to change the calculated field format to Euro.

8. On the DESIGN tab, in the Results group, click Run to display the query results.

9. SAVE the query as Subquery and CLOSE.

10. CLOSE the database.

LEAVE Access open for the next project.

Project 12-4: Create a Make Table Query

As the manager at Southridge Video, you want to archive the current table with information about used games. Use the make table action query to create a backup table.

GET READY. LAUNCH Access if it is not already running.

1. OPEN *Games Southridge* from the data files for this lesson.

2. SAVE the database as *Games SouthridgeXXX* (where *XXX* is your initials).

3. Create a simple select query named Games Query using all the fields in the Games: Table.

4. Display the query in Design view if it is not already.

5. On the DESIGN tab, in the Query Type group, click Make Table to display the Make Table dialog box.

6. In the Table Name box, key Games Backup. If it is not already selected, click Current Database, and then click OK.

7. On the DESIGN tab, in the Results group, click Run. An alert message appears.

8. Click Yes. A new table appears in the Navigation Pane.

9. CLOSE the Games Query and save the changes when prompted.

10. CLOSE the database.

LEAVE Access open for the next project.

Mastery Assessment

Project 12-5: Create a Crosstab Query

As a regional manager for Contoso Pharmaceuticals, you are in charge of overseeing the sales reps in your division. To determine the total samples given by each rep in the first two weeks of the quarter, you decide to create a crosstab query.

GET READY. LAUNCH Access if it is not already running.

1. OPEN *Contoso Data* from the data files for this lesson.

2. SAVE the database as *Contoso DataXXX* (where *XXX* is your initials).

3. Using the Samples Given: Table and the skills you have learned in this lesson, create and save a crosstab query named Samples Given_Crosstab, as shown in Figure 12-54.

Figure 12-54

Crosstab query

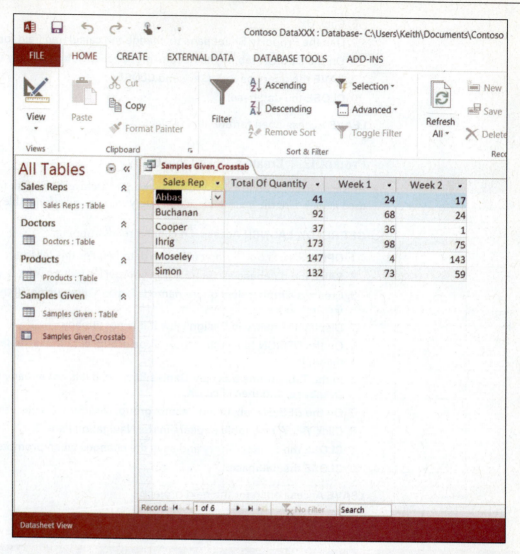

LEAVE the database open for the next project.

Project 12-6: Create an Update Query

The name of one of the hospitals in your region has recently been changed. You need to create an update query to change the name in the database.

USE the database that is open from the previous project.

1. Create a select query named **Update Query** that includes all the fields in the **Doctors: Table**.

2. Switch to Design view.

3. Use criteria to select only the records that have Community Medical Center in the Hospital field.

4. Use the skills you have learned in this lesson to create and save an update query that will change the name of Community Medical Center to Community Regional Hospital.

5. Open the **Doctors: Table** to verify that the hospital name has been changed. Then, close the table and the query.

6. **CLOSE** the database.

CLOSE Access.

LESSON SKILL MATRIX

Skill	Exam Objective	Objective Number
Creating a Chart Using the Chart Wizard	Add report controls	5.2.5
Formatting a Chart	Modify data sources	5.2.4
Changing Chart Types		
Saving a Database Object as Another File Type		
Printing a Database Object		

KEY TERMS

- chart
- chart body
- Chart Wizard
- client object
- legend
- PDF
- XPS

© dan_prat/iStockphoto

© dan_prat/iStockphoto

Blue Yonder Airlines is a small but rapidly growing regional airline. In your position as Investor Relations Specialist, you assist in building investor relations programs, creating and distributing analyst reports, maintaining and updating databases, and preparing materials for conference presentations. In this lesson, you will create, save, and print charts that will be reproduced and included in a report detailing the growth of Blue Yonder Airlines. You will also save a table as a report to help communicate data in a more effective way.

CREATING A CHART USING THE CHART WIZARD

The Bottom Line

Charts are often used in the business world to give a visual representation of numeric data. Because a picture is worth a thousand words, charts play an important role in reports and presentations. In Access 2013, you can insert a chart into a new or existing form or report using the Chart control.

Creating a Chart Using the Chart Wizard

The Chart control lets you insert a chart into a new or existing report or form using a table or query as your data source. This allows you to insert a pictorial view of the data along with the numbers. Once a chart has been inserted, the Chart Wizard asks you questions about the chart you want and then creates the chart based on your answers. In this exercise, you will insert a chart into the Page Footer section of a report because it is a one-page report and it is helpful to show the data at the bottom of the page after the columnar data.

Take Note   Charts and graphs are terms used synonymously in Microsoft Access. For example, the Chart control inserts a chart into reports or forms; however, a chart is referred to as a graph in Visual Basic for Applications (VBA) code.

A **chart** is a graphical representation of data. Although charts can contain various components used to help make data more meaningful, most are made up of two basic parts, the body and the legend. The **chart body** is the main area that displays the chart. The **legend** displays a list of the colors, shapes, or patterns used as categories in a chart.

Once a chart has been inserted into a report or form using the Chart control, the **Chart Wizard** asks you questions to quickly create a customized chart. Once you insert a chart, you may need to resize it later; you can do so by clicking and dragging the selection handles to increase or decrease the height or width.

You could also place the chart in the Detail section of the report and set the chart to change with each record by enabling this option within the Chart Wizard. You would then have a report displaying the record data and a chart for each record.

You can create 20 different charts using the Chart Wizard, including column, bar, area, line, XY scatter, pie, bubble, and doughnut charts.

To delete a chart, right-click it in Design view and select Delete from the shortcut menu.

STEP BY STEP   **Create a Chart**

GET READY. Before you begin these steps, be sure to turn on and/or log on to your computer and **LAUNCH** Access.

1. **OPEN** *Blue Yonder Airlines* from the data files for this lesson.

2. **SAVE** the database as *Blue Yonder AirlinesXXX* (where *XXX* is your initials).

3. Open the Income & Expenses report.

4. Switch to Design view.

5. On the REPORT DESIGN TOOLS DESIGN tab, in the Controls group, click the Chart button. The pointer changes to a plus sign with a chart icon.

6. Click in the upper-left corner of the Page Footer section and drag to the lower-right corner to create a rectangular placeholder where the chart will be inserted, as shown in Figure 13-1.

Figure 13-1

Report in Design view

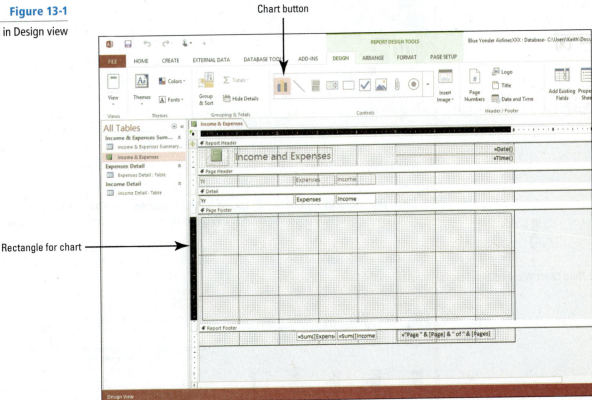

7. Release the mouse button. The first Chart Wizard dialog box appears, as shown in Figure 13-2.

Figure 13-2

First Chart Wizard dialog box

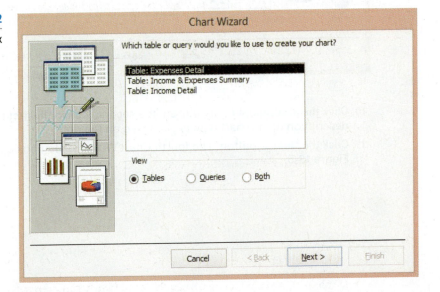

8. Select the **Income & Expenses Summary** table as your data source and click the **Next >** button. The second Chart Wizard dialog box appears, as shown in Figure 13-3.

Figure 13-3

Second Chart Wizard dialog box

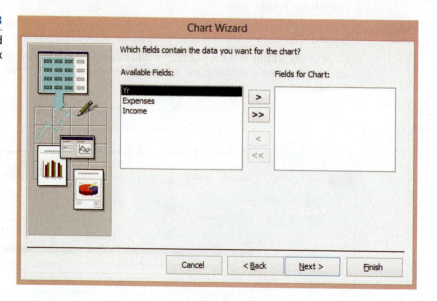

9. Click the More (**>>**) button to move all the fields to the Fields for Chart box and click the **Next >** button. The third Chart Wizard dialog box appears, as shown in Figure 13-4.

Figure 13-4

Third Chart Wizard dialog box

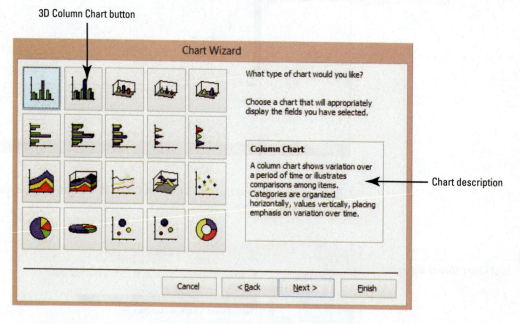

10. Click the **3D Column Chart** button, the second icon in the first row. Notice that the description of the chart type is displayed on the right.

11. Click the **Next >** button. The fourth Chart Wizard dialog box appears, as shown in Figure 13-5.

Figure 13-5

Fourth Chart Wizard dialog box

Preview Chart button

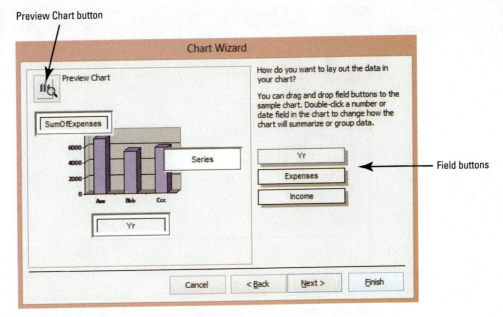

12. Click and drag the **Income field button** to the upper left of the chart and drop on the SumofExpenses data list. Both the SumofExpenses and SumofIncome fields should be listed.

13. Click the **Preview Chart** button. The Sample Preview dialog box appears, displaying a sample of your chart, as shown in Figure 13-6.

Figure 13-6

Sample Preview dialog box

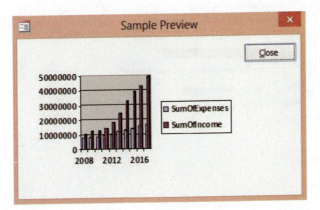

14. Click the **Close** button. The Sample Preview dialog box closes.

15. Click the **Next >** button. The fifth Chart Wizard dialog box appears, as shown in Figure 13-7.

Figure 13-7

Fifth Chart Wizard dialog box

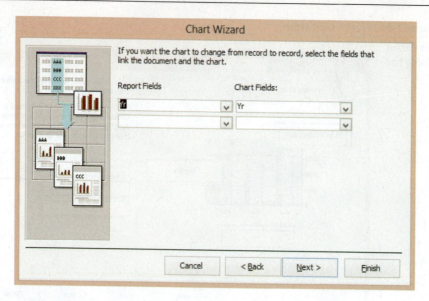

16. Click the **down arrow** in the Report Fields menu and select **<No Field>** since you don't want to display a chart for each record in the data source.

17. Click the **down arrow** in the Chart Fields: menu and select **<No Field>** again, since you don't want to display a chart for each record in the data source.

18. Click the **Next >** button. The sixth Chart Wizard dialog box appears, as shown in Figure 13-8.

Figure 13-8

Sixth Chart Wizard dialog box

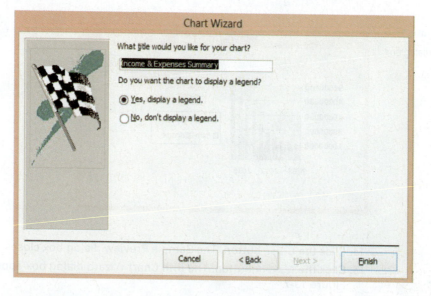

19. Key **2008-2017 Income and Expenses** in the Title box.

20. The **Yes, display a legend** button should be selected. If not, select it and click the **Finish** button. Access inserts your chart. Notice that Design view displays sample data and not the actual data from your chart.

21. Click the chart to select it.

22. On the REPORT DESIGN TOOLS DESIGN tab, in the Tools group, click the **Property Sheet** button, if necessary.

23. Click the **DATA** tab of the Property Sheet. Click the **down arrow** at the end of the Enabled cell and select **Yes**. This enables the chart to accurately display the associated table data.

24. **CLOSE** the Property Sheet.

25. Switch to Report view.

26. On the HOME tab, in the Records group, click the **Refresh All** button to ensure the chart displays the latest table data.

27. Scroll to the bottom of the report to view your chart, which should look similar to Figure 13-9.

Figure 13-9

Report with 3D bar chart

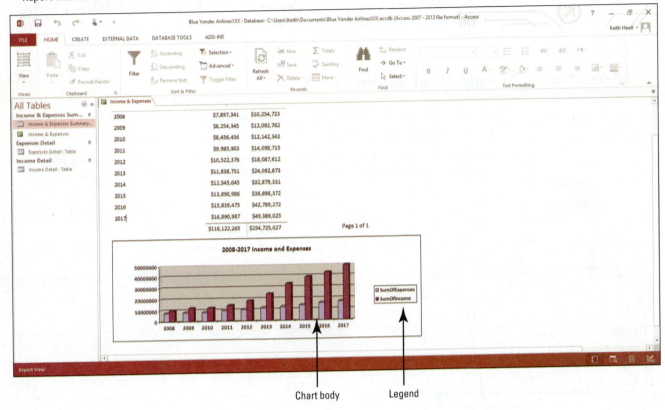

Chart body   Legend

Troubleshooting   If your chart is not displaying correctly, you probably need to increase or decrease the width and/or height of the placeholder. You do this the same way you resize any control. Switch to Design view and click the resize handles in the center of the vertical borders and drag to increase or decrease the size. Drag the resize handles on the horizontal borders to change the height. Then, return to Report view to see the results.

CERTIFICATION READY?   **5.2.5**

How do you add report controls?

28. **SAVE** the report.

PAUSE. LEAVE the report open to use in the next exercise.

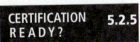

FORMATTING A CHART

You can use Microsoft Graph to change the formatting of charts created with the Chart Wizard. You can change chart options such as how the title and labels are displayed and where you want the legend located. You can also change formatting options, such as the color of the chart's background and the color and size of the data blocks in the chart.

After you create a chart using the Chart Wizard, you can edit it using Microsoft Graph, which is a component of Office 2013. To launch Microsoft Graph, double-click a chart in Design view. Microsoft Graph displays the chart and datasheet. You can choose commands from the menu bar or the toolbar.

After you make changes to the chart, it is important to save the changes using the Save command on the File menu. After you save a chart, Microsoft Graph closes and switches you back to Design view.

Changing Chart Options

The Chart Options dialog box has six tabs with options for changing the look and layout of a chart. You can access the Chart Options dialog box from the Chart menu or by right-clicking the white Chart Area and selecting Chart Options from the shortcut menu. In this exercise, you will change chart options using Microsoft Graph.

STEP BY STEP   Change Chart Options

USE the report that is open from the previous exercise.

1. Switch to Design view.
2. Double-click the chart. The Microsoft Graph software launches, displaying the chart in a view similar to Design view, as shown in Figure 13-10.

Figure 13-10

Chart displayed in Microsoft Graph

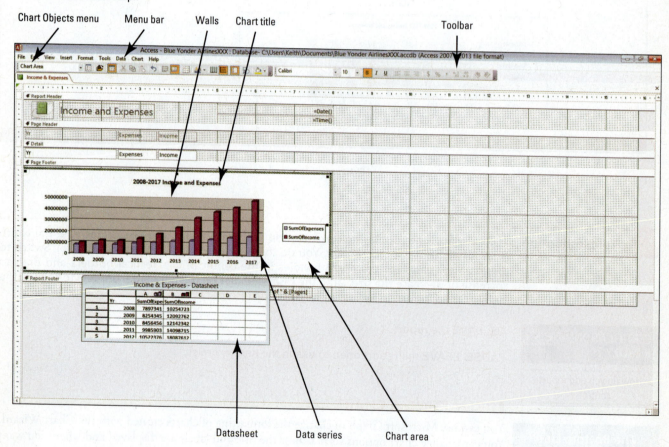

Chart Objects menu   Menu bar   Walls   Chart title   Toolbar

Datasheet   Data series   Chart area

3. Click **Chart** on the menu bar and select **Chart Options** from the menu that appears. The Chart Options dialog box appears, as shown in Figure 13-11.

Figure 13-11

Titles tab on the Chart Options dialog box

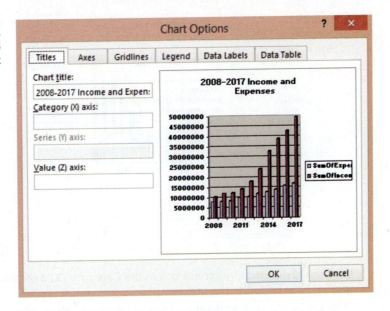

4. Click the **Axes** tab to display the options on the tab, as shown in Figure 13-12.

Figure 13-12

Axes tab of the Chart Options dialog box

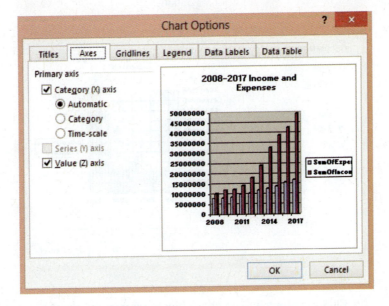

5. Click the **Value (Z) axis** check box to remove the check mark. Notice that the values on the Z axis are removed.

6. Click the **Value (Z) axis** check box again to insert the check mark.

7. Click the **Gridlines** tab to display the options on the tab, as shown in Figure 13-13.

Figure 13-13

Gridlines tab of the Chart
Options dialog box

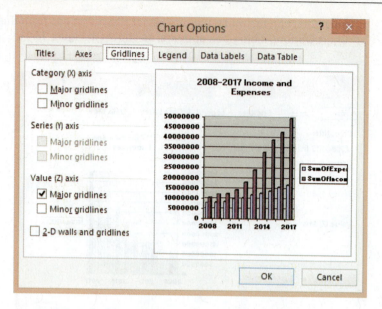

Figure 13-13

Gridlines tab of the Chart
Options dialog box

8. Click the **Major gridlines** check box in the Category (X) axis section. Notice that gridlines are added to the preview.

9. Click the **Legend** tab to display the options on the tab, as shown in Figure 13-14.

Figure 13-14

Legend tab of the Chart
Options dialog box

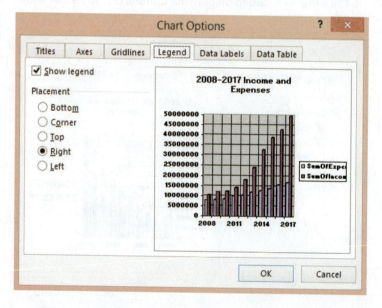

10. Click the **Show legend** check box to remove the check mark. Notice that the legend is removed from the chart.

11. Click the **Show legend** check box again to insert the check mark. The legend is displayed in the preview.

12. Click the **Bottom** option button to move the legend to the bottom of the chart.

13. Click the **Data Labels** tab to display the options on the tab, as shown in Figure 13-15.

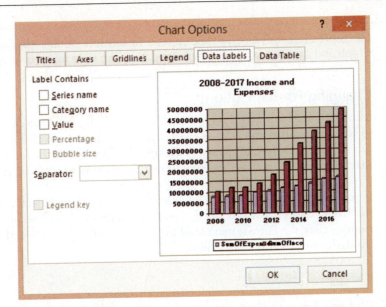

Figure 13-15

Data Labels tab of the Chart Options dialog box

14. Click the Value check box to insert a check mark. Notice that values are added to the columns in the chart.
15. Click the Value check box again to remove the check mark.
16. Click the Data Table tab to display the options on the tab, as shown in Figure 13-16.

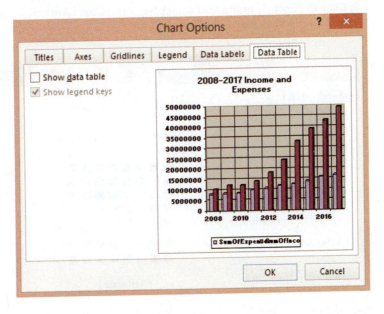

Figure 13-16

Data Table tab of the Chart Options dialog box

17. Click the Show data table check box to insert a check mark. Notice that the datasheet is added to the bottom of the chart.
18. Click the Show data table check box again to remove the check mark.
19. Click OK.
20. Click the File menu and select Save. The Microsoft Graph software closes and the report is switched back to Design view.

PAUSE. LEAVE the report open to use in the next exercise.

 **Troubleshooting** Microsoft Graph has its own Help system. To access it, double-click a chart to launch Microsoft Graph and choose Microsoft Graph Help from the Help menu or press F1.

Changing Format Options

Microsoft Graph makes it easy to format a chart. Each part of the chart is an independent object, so you can simply right-click the chart object that you want to change and choose Format [Chart Object] from the shortcut menu. A dialog box appears with the formatting choices available for that object. In this exercise, you will format the chart you have been creating.

If you prefer to use the menus, you can click on the chart object to select it or choose it from the Chart Objects list box on the toolbar. Once you have specified the object you want to change, click the Format menu and choose Selected [Chart Object] from the menu to launch the dialog box of available options.

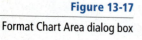 **Change Format Options**

USE the database that is open from the previous exercise.

1. Double-click the chart to open Microsoft Graph.
2. Click the **Chart Area**, the white background of the chart, to select it. The Chart Area should be displayed in the Chart Objects list box in the upper-left corner of the toolbar.
3. Click the **Format** menu and select **Selected Chart Area**. The Format Chart Area dialog box appears, as shown in Figure 13-17.

Figure 13-17

Format Chart Area dialog box

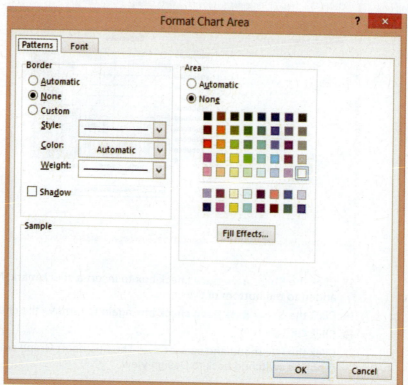

4. Click the **Fill Effects** button. The Fill Effects dialog box appears, as shown in Figure 13-18.

Figure 13-18

Fill Effects dialog box

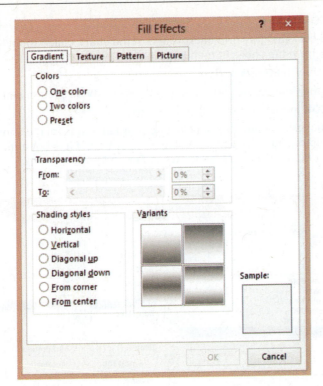

5. Click the **Horizontal** option button in the Shading styles section and click **OK**.

6. Click **OK** in the Format Chart Area dialog box. Notice the shading style of the chart background changes to your selection.

7. Right-click any of the purple Data Series columns in the chart to display the shortcut menu. Notice that Series "SumOfIncome" is displayed in the Chart Objects list box.

8. Select **Format Data Series** from the shortcut menu. The Format Data Series dialog box appears.

9. Select the **Green** color (second row, fourth from the left) as shown in Figure 13-19.

Figure 13-19

Format Data Series dialog box

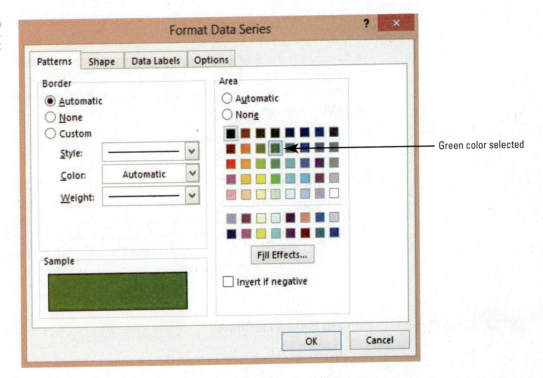

Green color selected

10. Click **OK** in the Format Data Series dialog box.

11. Right-click the gray grid background of the chart, called the Walls, and select **Format Walls** from the shortcut menu.

12. Click the **Fill Effects** button.

13. Click the **From center** button in the Shading styles section and click **OK**.

14. Click **OK** in the Format Walls dialog box.

15. Right-click the **Legend** and select **Format Legend** from the shortcut menu. The Format Legend dialog box appears. Select the **Font** tab if it is not already displayed. The Font tab menu now appears, as shown in Figure 13-20.

Figure 13-20

Font tab of the Format Legend dialog box

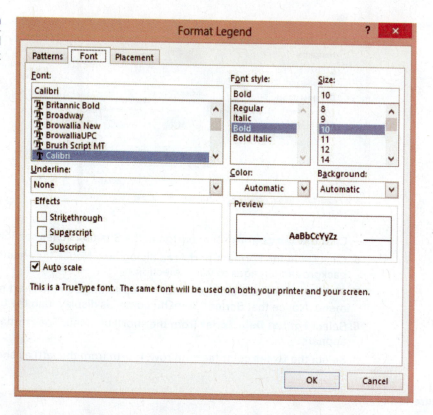

16. Select **12** in the Size: menu and click **OK**. Notice the font size of the legend text has increased.

17. Click the **File** menu and select **Save**. Switch to Report view to view your changes.

18. **SAVE** the report.

PAUSE. LEAVE the report open to use in the next exercise.

Refreshing Data in a Chart

The Refresh All button can be a useful tool when working with charts. When you make a change to the data source of a chart, be sure to save the new data in the table or query. When you switch back to the form or report containing your chart, click Refresh All to update the data in the chart with the modified data. In this exercise, you will make a change to a table record and then refresh the data in a chart to view the change.

STEP BY STEP   **Refresh Data in a Chart**

USE the database that is open from the previous exercise.

1. **OPEN** the **Income & Expenses Summary** table.

2. In the first row, in the Income column, select the data and key **9004523** and [press **Enter**].

3. **SAVE** and **CLOSE** the table.

4. Click the **Income & Expenses report** tab. Notice that the numbers in the report data and the numbers in the chart have not changed.

5. On the HOME tab, in the Records group, click the **Refresh All** button. The data in the report and in the chart are updated.

6. **SAVE** the report.

PAUSE. LEAVE the report open to use in the next exercise.

CHANGING CHART TYPES

Access provides many different chart types and variations of those chart types for you to choose from in the Chart Type dialog box. Access makes it easy to experiment with different configurations before you decide on the chart that best displays the data you want to emphasize. In this exercise, you will change the type of chart with which you have been working.

Changing Chart Types

Access 2013 has many different types of charts you can choose from. The key is to choose one that displays your data in a meaningful way. Often, you have a specific chart in mind that you want to use, but sometimes it requires experimentation, choosing and changing chart types until you get the results you want.

STEP BY STEP   **Change Chart Types**

USE the database that is open from the previous exercise.

1. Switch to Design view.

2. Double-click the chart. Microsoft Graph opens.

3. Click the **By Row** button on the toolbar, as shown in Figure 13-21. The chart is changed to show all the expenses together and all the income together.

Figure 13-21

Microsoft Graph toolbar

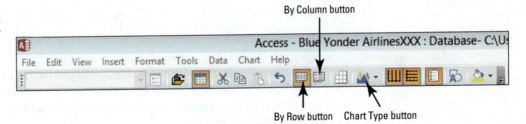

By Column button

By Row button   Chart Type button

4. Click the **By Column** button on the toolbar to change it back to the original chart.

5. Click the **Chart Type** drop-down arrow in the toolbar and select **3D Area Chart** from the menu, as shown in Figure 13-22. The chart changes to an area chart.

Figure 13-22

Chart Type button and menu

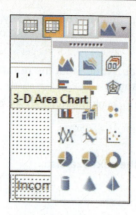

6. Click the **Chart** menu and select **Chart Type**. The Chart Type dialog box appears, as shown in Figure 13-23.

Figure 13-23

Chart Type dialog box

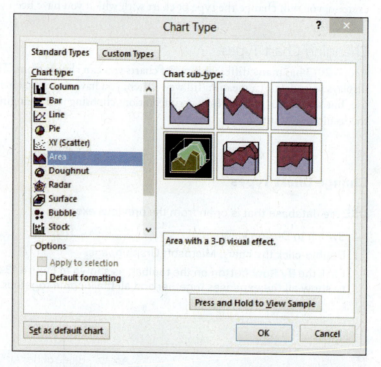

7. On the Standard Types tab, click **Pie** in the Chart type list. In the Chart sub-type section, click **Pie with a 3D visual effect**, the second icon on the first row.

8. Click and hold the **Press and Hold to View Sample** button to see a preview of the chart, as shown in Figure 13-24.

Figure 13-24

Sample pie chart

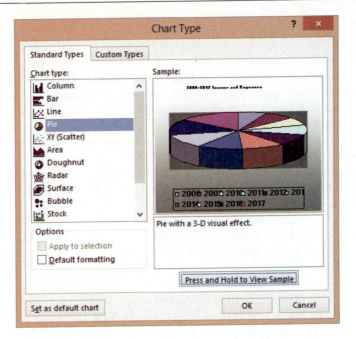

9. Click the **Custom Types** tab.
10. Click **Colored Lines** in the Chart type: list and click **OK**.
11. Click the **File** menu and select **Save**. Your screen should resemble Figure 13-25.

Figure 13-25

Chart in Report Design view

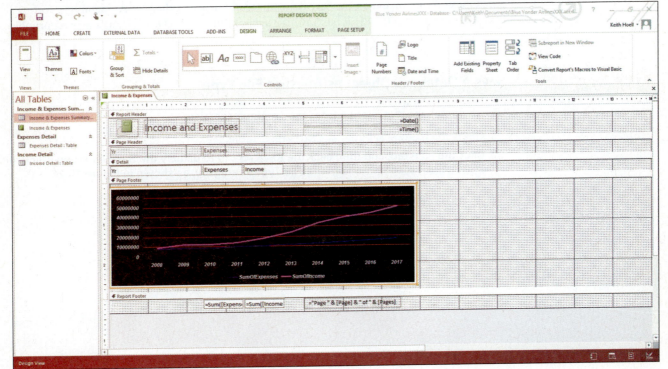

12. Switch to Report view to view your changes.
13. **SAVE** and **CLOSE** the report.

PAUSE. LEAVE the database open to use in the next exercise.

SAVING A DATABASE OBJECT AS ANOTHER FILE TYPE

The Bottom Line

Microsoft Access 2013 allows you to save database objects, such as tables, forms, and queries, as other types of objects. For example, you can save a table as a report. Although you can save tables, forms, and queries as at least one other type of database object, Access doesn't permit you to save reports as other object types; however, you can save all database objects as PDF or XPS files. Saving a database object as another file type allows you to share data with other users or repurpose the data in other ways. Since you can create Access objects to be used on the web, you can also save all web-based database objects as the same object of a different type called a client object. For example, you can save a web-based table object as a client table object type, but you cannot directly save the web-based table object as a form object until after it's saved as a client table object. A **client object** is an object that can be accessed and modified in the Access application installed on your computer.

The Save Object As command gives you the option of saving database objects such as tables, forms, and queries as other types of objects. You can also use the Save Object As command to save a database object in Portable Document Format (PDF) or XML Paper Specification (XPS) file formats. You might already be familiar with PDF files from documents you view on the Internet or share via emails. The **PDF** file format maintains the exact layout of the original file and can easily be shared. A new alternative to PDF, the **XPS** file format preserves document formatting; can be easily shared, printed, and archived; and is more secure. The Save Object As command also gives you the option of saving a database object as a client object. Saving an object as a client object is used when you want to save a web-based Access object as one that can be accessed and modified in the Access application installed on your computer.

Using the Save Object As Command

You can save objects such as tables, reports, and queries as other types of objects or files using the Save Object As command on the Save As menu. You can access the Save As menu by selecting the Save As command on the FILE tab. In this exercise, you save a table object as a new report object.

STEP BY STEP **Save a Database Object as Another File Type**

USE the database that is open from the previous exercise.

1. OPEN the Income & Expenses Summary table.
2. Click the FILE tab, and then click the Save As tab to display the Save As menu. Click the Save Object As command in the File Types category, as shown in Figure 13-26.

Figure 13-26

Save Object As command

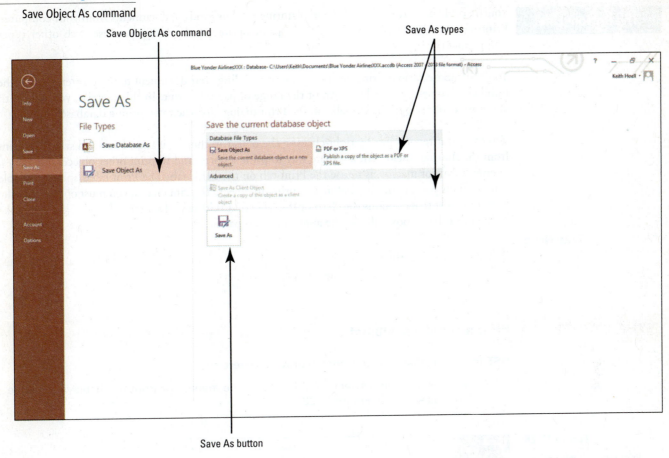

Save Object As command

Save As types

Save As button

3. Notice the Save Object As option is already highlighted in the Save the current database object category. Click the **Save As** button. The Save As dialog box appears, as shown in Figure 13-27.

Figure 13-27

Save As dialog box

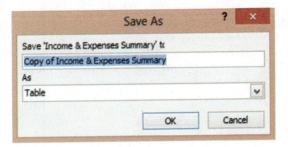

4. Key **Summary Report** in the Save box.
5. Click the **down arrow** on the As menu and select **Report**.
6. Click **OK**. The table object is saved as a report object and the new Summary Report appears in Layout view.

PAUSE. LEAVE the report open to use in the next exercise.

PRINTING A DATABASE OBJECT

The Bottom Line

You are probably already familiar with printing various kinds of documents from your computer. Printing a database object uses the same print options and settings you use with other types of documents.

You can choose various printing options before sending your document to the printer, such as the number of copies, size of the paper, or the range of pages to print. In this exercise, you will learn about some of the options available in the Print dialog box when you print a database object.

You can print reports just by right-clicking the object in the Navigation Pane and selecting Print from the shortcut menu. An alternate way to print reports, and to print other objects like tables, queries, forms or macros, is to use the Print tab on the FILE tab. The Print tab displays available print options you can modify before you print an object. To print charts, you must open either the form or report that contains the chart or the table that is its record source. Changes that you make in the Print dialog box will only be applied to that particular document.

Take Note

When printing lengthy reports, you can choose other options, such as printing a range of pages, collating the pages, or printing multiple pages per sheet.

STEP BY STEP

Print a Database Object

USE the report that is open from the previous exercise.

1. Click the **FILE** tab and select the **Print** tab on the menu. The Print tab displays available options, as shown in Figure 13-28.

Figure 13-28

Print tab available options

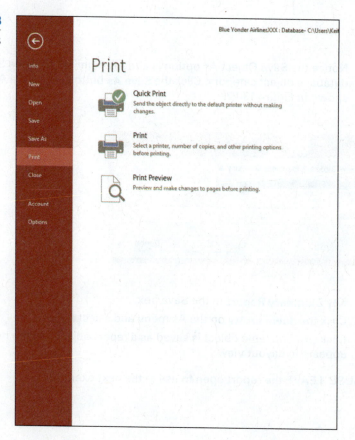

2. Click the Print button. The Print dialog box appears, as shown in Figure 13-29.

Figure 13-29

Print dialog box

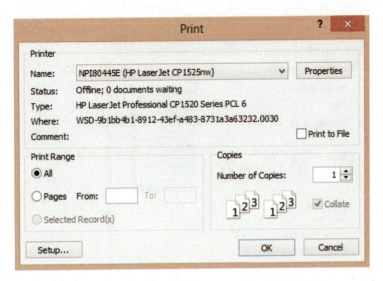

3. Click the Properties button. The Properties dialog box appears, as shown in Figure 13-30. Depending on your type of printer, the Properties dialog box could be different. You can change the quality, paper, printing, and orientation options available for your printer. Click the Cancel button.

Figure 13-30

Properties dialog box

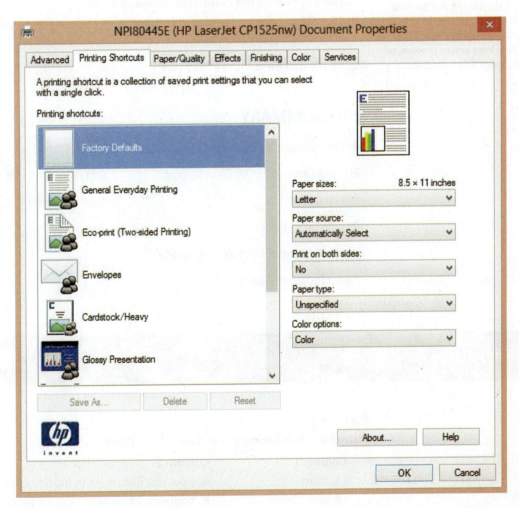

4. Click the **Setup** button. The Page Setup dialog box appears, as shown in Figure 13-31. Click the **Cancel** button.

Figure 13-31

Page Setup dialog box

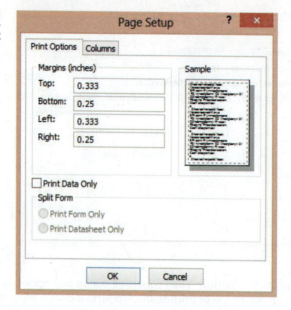

Another Way

You can also press Ctrl+P to display the Print dialog box.

Another Way

To print a document quickly, you can skip the Print dialog box and use the default print settings by clicking the Quick Print button, if added, on the Quick Access Toolbar.

5. In the Copies section of the Print dialog box, click the **up arrow** in the Number of Copies menu to change the number of copies to **2**.

6. Click **OK** to print two copies of the report, or click **Cancel** (if you choose not to Print).

7. **CLOSE** the report and table.

CLOSE the database.

SKILL SUMMARY

In This Lesson You Learned How To:	Exam Objective	Objective Number
Create a Chart Using the Chart Wizard	Add report controls	5.2.5
Format a Chart	Modify data sources	5.2.4
Change Chart Types		
Save a Database Object as Another File Type		
Print a Database Object		

Knowledge Assessment

Matching

Match the term in Column 1 to its description in Column 2.

Column 1

1. chart
2. chart body

Column 2

a. asks you questions to quickly create a customized chart.
b. contains 6 tabs with options for changing the look and layout of a chart

3. Chart Wizard	**c.** a file format that maintains the exact layout of the original file and can easily be shared
4. legend	**d.** a file format that preserves document formatting, can be easily shared, printed, and archived, and is more secure
5. PDF	**e.** a component of Access 2013 used to make changes to a chart created by the Chart Wizard
6. Chart Options dialog box	**f.** a graphical representation of data
7. XPS	**g.** allows you to save objects as other file formats like PDF and XPS
8. Refresh All button	**h.** the main area that displays the chart
9. Microsoft Graph	**i.** displays a list of the colors, shapes, or patterns used as categories in a chart
10. Save Object As command	**j.** updates the data in a chart

True/False

Circle T if the statement is true or F if the statement is false.

T F   1. You can choose from 20 different chart types in the Chart Wizard.

T F   2. The Chart Wizard is a control.

T F   3. A legend can be displayed only on the right side of a chart.

T F   4. Microsoft Graph displays the chart and the datasheet of the underlying data source.

T F   5. The Chart control can be used to insert charts in queries, forms, and reports.

T F   6. The Refresh All button updates data in a chart with data modified in the underlying data source.

T F   7. You can save a table as a report.

T F   8. You can print reports by right-clicking the object in the Navigation Pane and selecting Print from the shortcut menu.

T F   9. An Axis is a type of chart.

T F   10. After you save a chart in Microsoft Graph, Microsoft Graph closes.

Competency Assessment

Project 13-1: City Power & Light Salary Pie Chart

The City Power & Light human resources department is reviewing the salary budgets for the office. Your supervisor asks you to create a pie chart within a report to show the distribution of funds for each employee.

GET READY. LAUNCH Access if it is not already running.

1. **OPEN** the *City Power & Light* database.
2. **SAVE** the database as *City Power & LightXXX* (where *XXX* is your initials).
3. **OPEN** the Salary report in Design view.
4. Click the Chart button and draw a large rectangle in the space provided in the Page Footer section. The Chart Wizard dialog box appears.
5. Click the Next > button.
6. Move the Employee ID and Salary fields to the Fields for Chart: list and click Next >.
7. Click the Pie chart button and click Next >.
8. Drag and drop the Salary field button just below the SumofEmployee ID box Data box.
9. Drag and drop the Employee ID field button to the Series box.

10. Click the **Preview Chart** button.
11. Click **Close**.
12. Click **Finish**.
13. Click the **DATA** tab of the Property Sheet and set the Enabled property to **Yes**.
14. Switch to Report view.
15. Click the **Refresh All** button.
16. **SAVE** the Report.
17. Click the **FILE** tab and select the **Print** tab from the menu.
18. Click the **Print** button and then click **Cancel**.
19. **CLOSE** the report.

LEAVE the database open for the next project.

Project 13-2: Change the City Power & Light Chart Type

You decide to create a variation of the pie chart that will more clearly show the salary amounts in relationship to each other.

USE the database that is open from the previous exercise.

1. **OPEN** the **Salary** report in Report view.
2. Click the **FILE** tab, and select **Save As**.
3. Click the **Save Object As** button.
4. Click the **Save As** button.
5. Key **Salary Line Chart** in the "Save 'Salary' to" box and click **OK**.
6. Switch to Design view.
7. Double-click the chart to launch Microsoft Graph.
8. Click the **Chart** menu and select **Chart Type** from the menu.
9. Click **Line** in the Standard types list.
10. In the Chart subtype list, if not already selected, click the **Line with markers displayed at each data value** button.
11. Click **OK**.
12. Click the **Chart** menu and select **Chart Options** from the menu.
13. Click the **Legend** tab and click the **Bottom** option button.
14. Click **OK**.
15. **SAVE** the chart.

CLOSE the database.

Proficiency Assessment

Project 13-3: Create and Format an Expenses Chart

You created a chart representing the Income & Expenses Summary table for Blue Yonder Airlines earlier. Now you need to create a chart solely for the expenses.

GET READY. LAUNCH Access if it is not already running.

1. **OPEN** *BlueYonderAirlinesXXX* that you saved in an earlier exercise.
2. Create a chart using the Expenses Detail table as the data source.
3. Move the Amount and Yr fields to the Fields for Chart list and click **Next >**.

4. Click the Doughnut chart type button and click Next >.

5. Drag and drop the Yr field button to the Axis box and click Next >.

6. Select <No Field> in the Report Fields and Chart Fields drop-down boxes and click Next >.

7. Click Finish.

8. View the chart in Report view.

9. Switch to Design view and double-click the chart to launch Microsoft Graph.

10. Click the Chart menu and select Chart Options from the menu.

11. Click the Data Labels tab and click the Percentage check box.

12. Click OK.

13. SAVE the chart.

14. View the chart changes in Report view.

15. CLOSE the report.

CLOSE the database.

Project 13-4: Create a Chart for Lucerne Publishing

As a sales manager for Lucerne Publishing, you are constantly analyzing and sharing sales data in meetings with the sales force as well as other departments in the corporation. Create a chart for your presentation at the next sales meeting.

GET READY. LAUNCH Access if it is not already running.

1. **OPEN** *LucernePublishing* from the data files for this lesson.

2. **SAVE** the database as *LucernePublishingXXX* (where *XXX* is your initials).

3. Create a chart using the Sales table.

4. Use the Region, Gross Sales, and Net Sales fields as the fields for the chart.

5. Create a Column chart.

6. Drag and drop the Net Sales field button just below the SumOfGross Sales box and click Next >.

7. Select <No Field> in the Report Fields and Chart Fields drop-down boxes and click Finish.

8. **CLOSE** the report.

LEAVE the database open for the next project.

Mastery Assessment

Project 13-5: Format the Lucerne Publishing Chart

The chart you created worked fine for your presentation; however, you have just been asked to present the information at a meeting with your boss, so you decide to add formatting to make it look more professional.

USE the database that is open from the previous exercise.

1. Create a copy of the Sales report named Formatted Sales Chart.

2. Using Microsoft Graph, change the chart to a new Chart Type of your choice.

3. Format the Chart Area using your choice of a Fill Effect.

4. Format the data series by changing the color and format the walls of the chart (if applicable to the chart type chosen, if not applicable, this step may be skipped).

5. Format the legend of the chart by changing its font and size.
6. **SAVE**, print, and **CLOSE** the chart.

CLOSE the database.

Project 13-6: Fix the Wingtip Toys Yearly Sales Chart

You asked an assistant to create a chart for the Yearly Sales Report, but it isn't exactly what you wanted. Fix the chart.

GET READY. LAUNCH Access if it is not already running.

1. **OPEN** *WingtipToys* from the data files for this lesson.
2. **SAVE** the database as *WingtipToysXXX* (where *XXX* is your initials).
3. **OPEN** the Yearly Sales Report.
4. **LAUNCH** Microsoft Graph and remove the data table at the bottom of the chart.
5. Move the legend to the bottom of the report.
6. Change the background color and pattern of the chart area to a solid light gray.
7. **SAVE** and **CLOSE** the report.

CLOSE Access.

LESSON SKILL MATRIX

Skill	Exam Objective	Objective Number
Importing Data	Import external data into tables	2.1.2
	Append records from external data	2.3.4
	Import tables from other databases	2.1.4
	Create linked tables from external sources	2.1.3
Saving and Running Import Specifications		
Exporting Data	Export to alternate formats	1.5.6
Saving and Running Export Specifications		

KEY TERMS

- delimited file
- delimiter
- fixed-width file
- linked table
- specification

© AfricaImages/iStockphoto

© AfricaImages/iStockphoto

You are the human resources coordinator at Tailspin Insurance, a private company dedicated to offering products that provide quality protection with value pricing for rural and low-income families, as well as senior citizens on fixed incomes. Your department has just begun to use Access, but you still receive data in different formats that must be merged with your Access databases. At times, you also want to distribute information that your manager prefers to view in a different format. In this lesson, you will learn how to import data, link to an external data source, and save and run import specifications. You also learn how to export data from a table and from a query as well as how to save and run export specifications.

SOFTWARE ORIENTATION

EXTERNAL DATA Tab

The EXTERNAL DATA tab contains commands that will be used to import and export data in various formats. Use Figure 14-1 as a reference throughout this lesson as well as the rest of this book.

View and run the import operations that you previously saved

View and run the export operations you previously saved

Figure 14-1
EXTERNAL DATA tab

IMPORTING DATA

The Bottom Line

To store data from an external source in Access, you can import the data into a new or existing database. After you run an import operation, you can save the import settings for reuse. You can also link to data from an external source without actually maintaining a copy of the data in the database.

Importing Data from a Specific Source

You can import data from a variety of sources into an Access database. When you import data, Access creates a copy of the data in a new or existing table without altering the source file. Before you start the import operation, decide whether you want to store the data in a new or existing table. If you choose to store the data in a new table, Access creates a table and adds the imported data to this table. If a table with the specified name already exists, Access overwrites the contents of the table with the imported data. If you choose to add the data to an existing table, the imported data is appended to the specified Access table. In this exercise, you will import data from an Excel worksheet into a new Access table. You then import a table from another Access database into the current Access database as a new table.

You can also import data from other specific sources besides Excel, such as a SharePoint list, a Word file, another Access database, or a text file. The same general process is used for importing data, regardless of the source. On the EXTERNAL DATA tab, in the Import & Link group, click the More button to see additional formats that you can import from or link to.

Take Note You can import only one Excel worksheet at a time during an import operation. To import data from multiple worksheets, repeat the import operation for each worksheet.

Before you import, you should always review the source data and make any necessary modifications, as described in Table 14-1.

Table 14-1

Source data elements

Element	Description
Number of columns	You cannot import more than 255 source columns, because Access does not support more than 255 fields in a table.
Skipping columns and rows	It is a good practice to include only the rows and columns that you want to import in the source worksheet or named range. Note that you cannot filter or skip rows during the import operation. If you choose to add the data to an existing table, you cannot skip columns during the import operation either.
Tabular format	Ensure that the cells are in tabular format. If the worksheet or named range includes merged cells, the contents of the cell are placed in the field that corresponds to the leftmost column, and the other fields are left blank.
Blank columns, rows, and cells	Delete all unnecessary blank columns and blank rows in the worksheet or range. If the worksheet or range contains blank cells, try to add the missing data. If you are planning to append the records to an existing table, ensure that the corresponding field in the table accepts null (missing or unknown) values. A field will accept null values if its Required field property is set to No and its Validation Rule property setting does not prevent null values.
Error values	If one or more cells in the worksheet or range contain error values, such as #NUM and #DIV, correct them before you start the import operation. If a source worksheet or range contains error values, Access places a null value in the corresponding fields in the table.
Data type	To avoid errors during importing, ensure that each source column contains the same type of data in every row. It is a good practice to format each source column in Excel and assign a specific data format to each column before you start the import operation, especially if a column includes values of different data types.
First row	If the first row in the worksheet or named range contains the names of the columns, you can specify that Access treat the data in the first row as field names during the import operation. If your source worksheet or range does not include the names, it is a good idea to add them to the source before you start the import operation. Note: If you plan to append the data to an existing table, ensure that the name of each column exactly matches the name of the corresponding field. If the name of a column is different from the name of the corresponding field in the table, the import operation will fail. To see the names of the fields, open the table in Design view in Access.

 Troubleshooting The file to be imported should be closed before beginning the import operation. Keeping the source file open can result in data conversion errors.

 Troubleshooting After an import operation, you should review the contents and structure of the table to ensure that everything looks correct before you start using the table. If you see the message *An error occurred trying to import file*, the import operation failed. If the data imports and you find just a few missing values, you can add them directly to the table. However, if you find that entire columns or a large number of values are either missing or were not imported properly, use Access Help to troubleshoot the results and correct the problem in the source file. After you have corrected all known problems, repeat the import operation.

STEP BY STEP Import Data from Excel

GET READY. Before you begin these steps, be sure to **LAUNCH** Microsoft Access.

1. **OPEN** the *Tailspin* database from the data files for this lesson.
2. **SAVE** the database as *TailspinXXX* (where *XXX* is your initials).
3. On the EXTERNAL DATA tab, in the Import & Link group, click Excel. The *Get External Data – Excel Spreadsheet* dialog box appears, as shown in Figure 14-2.

Figure 14-2

Get External Data – Excel
Spreadsheet dialog box

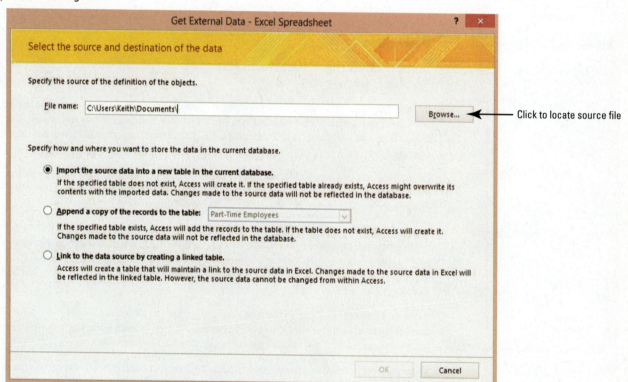

4. Click Browse to open the File Open dialog box.
5. Use the File Open dialog box to locate the New_Employees spreadsheet file and then click Open.
6. Notice the three options you have when importing data. Select the option button for **Import the source data into a new table in the current database** and click OK. The Import Spreadsheet Wizard appears, as shown in Figure 14-3.

Figure 14-3

Import Spreadsheet Wizard, first screen

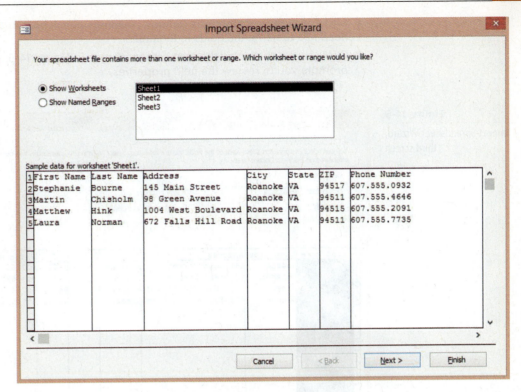

Take Note In the Get External Data – Excel Spreadsheet dialog box, Access also allows you to append a copy of the records to an existing table in the database. You can choose **Append a copy of the records to the table** and then select an available table from the drop-down list.

7. Click **Next >** to display the next screen, as shown in Figure 14-4.

Figure 14-4

Import Spreadsheet Wizard, second screen

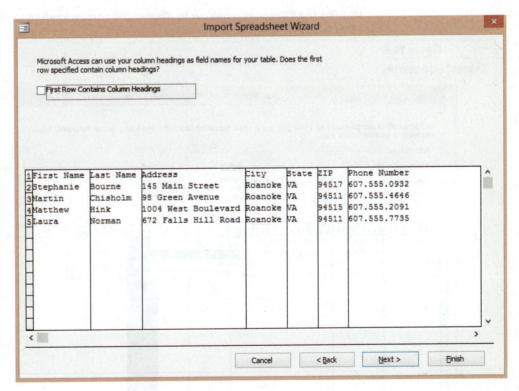

8. Click the **First Row Contains Column Headings** check box. Access uses these column headings to name the fields in the table.

9. Click **Next >** to display the next screen, shown in Figure 14-5, where the wizard prompts you to review the field properties.

Figure 14-5

Import Spreadsheet Wizard, third screen

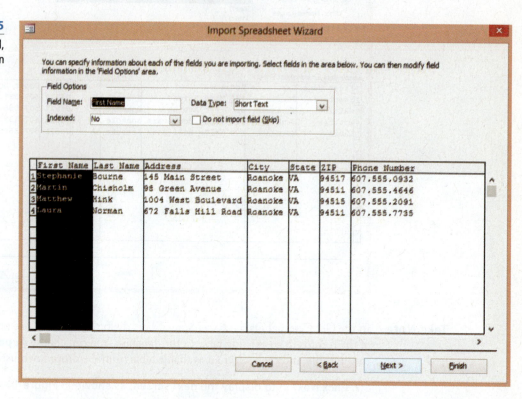

10. Click the **ZIP** column header to display the corresponding field properties.

11. Click the **Data Type:** down arrow and click **Short Text**, as shown in Figure 14-6.

Figure 14-6

Change field properties

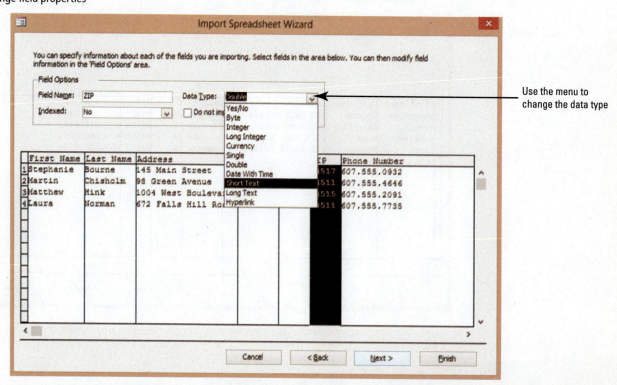

Take Note Access reviews the first eight rows in each column to suggest the data type for the corresponding field. If the column contains different types of values, the wizard suggests a data type that is compatible with all of the values in the column—usually the Short Text data type. Although you can choose a different data type, values that are not compatible with the chosen data type will be ignored or converted incorrectly during the import process.

12. Click **Next** > to display the next screen, as shown in Figure 14-7.

Figure 14-7

Define a primary key

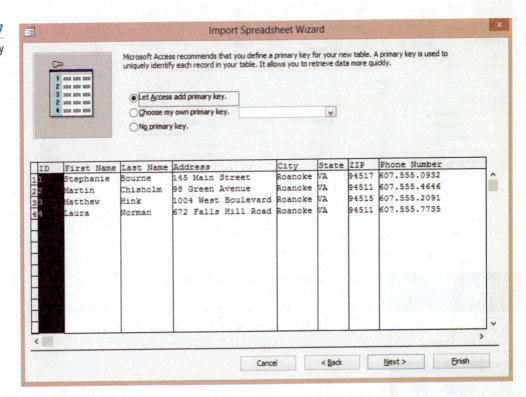

13. Click **Next** > to let Access add the primary key. The final screen appears, as shown in Figure 14-8.

Figure 14-8

Import Spreadsheet Wizard, final screen

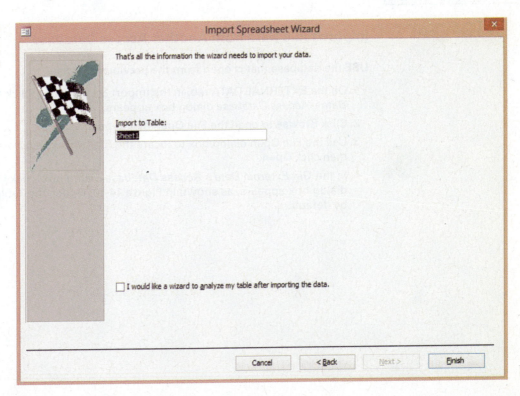

14. In the Import to Table box, key **New Employees** and then click **Finish**. When the Save Import Steps prompt appears, click **Close**.

15. In the Navigation Pane, double-click the **New Employees: Table** to open the new table with imported data, as shown in Figure 14-9.

Figure 14-9

New table with imported data

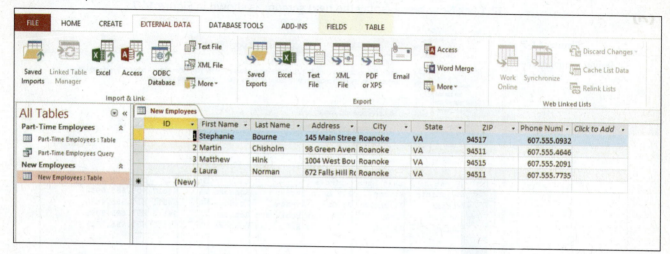

16. **CLOSE** the New Employees table.

PAUSE. LEAVE the database open to use in the next exercise.

CERTIFICATION READY?	2.1.2

How do you import external data into a table?

CERTIFICATION READY?	2.3.4

How do you append records from external data?

STEP BY STEP   Import Table Data from Another Access Database

USE the database that is open from the previous exercise.

1. On the EXTERNAL DATA tab, in the Import & Link group, click **Access**. The *Get External Data – Access Database* dialog box appears.

2. Click **Browse** to open the File Open dialog box.

3. Use the File Open dialog box to locate the **Minute Insurance** Access database file and then click **Open**.

4. In the *Get External Data – Access Database* dialog box, click **OK**. The Import Objects dialog box appears, as shown in Figure 14-10. Notice the Tables object tab is selected by default.

Figure 14-10

Import Objects dialog box

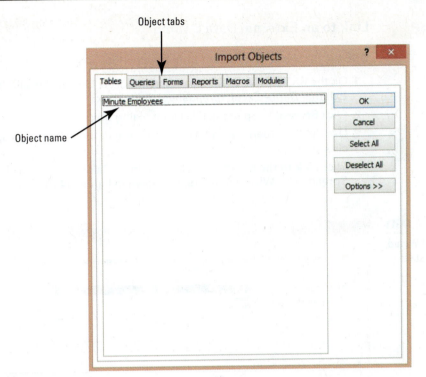

Take Note   You can import a variety of Access database objects into another Access database. Objects can be found by using the objects tabs at the top of the Import Objects dialog box.

5. In the Import Objects dialog box, click **Minute Employees** to select the table you wish to import.
6. Click **OK** to return to the *Get External Data – Access Database* dialog box and click **Close**. Notice the newly imported Minute Employees table appears in the Navigation Pane.
7. In the Navigation Pane, double-click the **Minute Employees: Table** to open the new table with imported data.
8. **CLOSE** the Minute Employees table.

PAUSE. LEAVE the database open to use in the next exercise.

Linking to an External Data Source

By linking an Access database to data in another program, you can use the querying and reporting tools that Access provides without having to maintain a copy of the external data in your database. You can also link to other external data sources, such as linking tables in another Access database (although you cannot link to queries, forms, or reports), HTML documents, or text files. In this exercise, you will link to an Excel spreadsheet.

When you link to an Excel worksheet, Access creates a new table that is linked to the source cells, called a **linked table**. The table shows the data in the source worksheet, but it does not actually store the data in the database. Any changes you make to the source cells in Excel appear in the linked table. However, you cannot edit the contents or structure of the corresponding table in Access. If you want to add, edit, or delete data, you must make the changes in the source file.

Take Note   If you don't want to link to the entire worksheet, define a range in Excel that includes only the cells to which you want to link. To create a named range, select the cells, right-click, and click Define Name. In the New Name dialog box, key a name for the range and then click OK.

After linking, you should open the linked table and review the fields and data to ensure that you see the correct data in all the fields. If you see error values or incorrect data, use Access Help to troubleshoot the source data and then try linking again.

| STEP BY STEP | Link to an External Data Source |

USE the database that is open from the previous exercise.

1. On the EXTERNAL DATA tab, in the Import & Link group, click Excel to open the *Get External Data – Excel Spreadsheet* dialog box.

2. Click Browse to open the File Open dialog box.

3. Use the File Open dialog box to locate the *Benefit_Providers* spreadsheet file and then click Open.

4. Click Link to the data source by creating a linked table and click OK. The Link Spreadsheet Wizard appears, as shown in Figure 14-11.

Figure 14-11

Link Spreadsheet Wizard, first screen

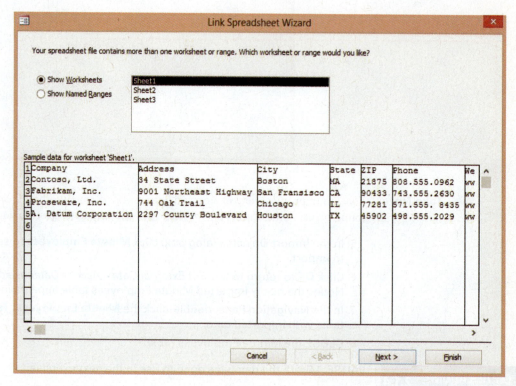

5. Click Next > to display the next screen.

6. Click the First Row Contains Column Headings check box, shown in Figure 14-12, to use the first row of data as field names in the table.

Figure 14-12

Link Spreadsheet Wizard,
second screen

Click this checkbox to use the first row as field names

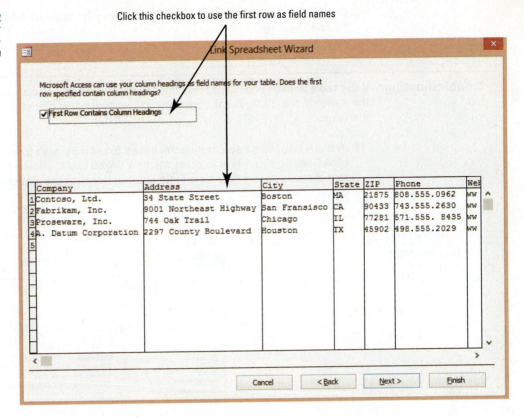

Figure 14-12

Link Spreadsheet Wizard,
second screen

7. Click **Next >** to display the next screen.

8. In the Linked Table Name box, key **Benefit_Providers**, as shown in Figure 14-13.

Figure 14-13

Link Spreadsheet Wizard,
final screen

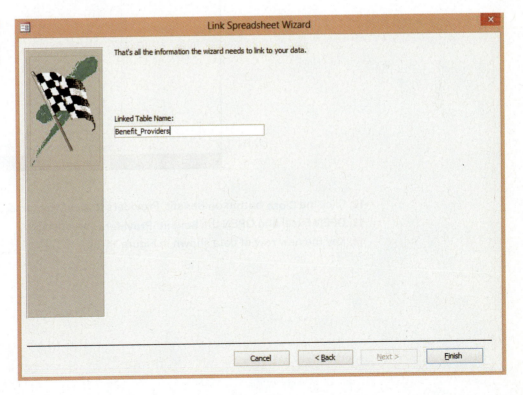

9. Click **Finish**. A Link Spreadsheet Wizard message appears informing you that Access finished linking.

10. Click **OK**.

Troubleshooting If the table with the name you specified already exists, you are asked if you want to overwrite the existing file. Click Yes if you want to overwrite the file; click No to specify a different filename.

11. In the Navigation Pane, notice the linked Excel icon next to Benefit_Providers. Double-click **Benefit_Providers** to open the new linked table, shown in Figure 14-14. Notice that there is not an Add New Field column because the structure of a linked table cannot be changed.

Figure 14-14

New linked table

Excel icon next to linked
Benefit_Providers table object →

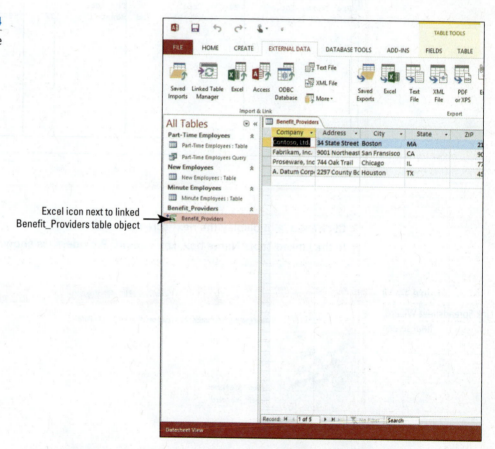

12. Click the **Close** button on Benefit_Providers to close the table.

13. **OPEN** Excel and **OPEN** the **Benefit_Providers** spreadsheet.

14. Key the new row of data shown in Figure 14-15.

Figure 14-15

New Excel data

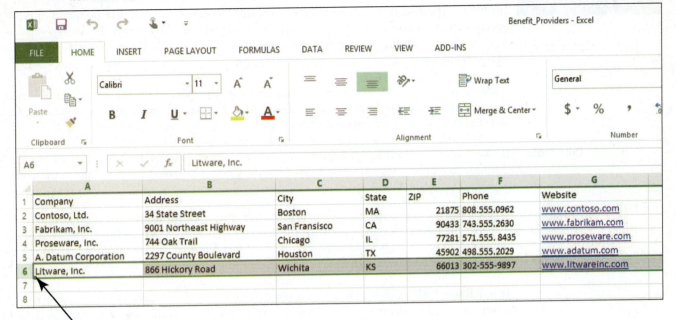

Key the new data into row
6 of the Excel worksheet

15. **SAVE** and **CLOSE** the spreadsheet.

16. **CLOSE** Excel.

17. In the Navigation Pane of Access, double-click **Benefit_Providers** to open the linked table. Notice that the new row of data has been added, as shown in Figure 14-16.

Figure 14-16

New Excel data added
to linked table

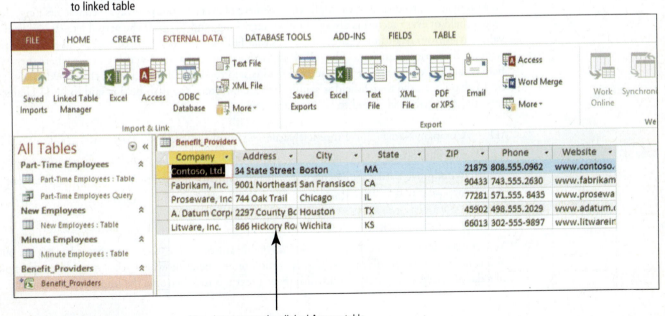

New data appears in a linked Access table

CERTIFICATION
READY?   2.1.3

How do you create linked
tables from external sources?

18. **CLOSE** the **Benefit_Providers** table.

PAUSE. LEAVE the database open to use in the next exercise.

SAVING AND RUNNING IMPORT SPECIFICATIONS

The Bottom Line

Saving the details of an import operation as a specification allows you to repeat the operation at any time. A **specification** contains all the information Access needs to repeat an import or export operation without user input. When you run an import wizard, you can save the settings you used as a specification so that you can repeat the operation at any time without having to provide any additional input.

A specification is flexible. For example, you can change the name of the source file or the destination file before you run the specification again. This way, you can use a single specification with several different source or destination files.

Take Note

If you regularly repeat this saved operation, you can create an Outlook task that reminds you when it is time to perform this operation by clicking the Create Outlook Task check box in the import wizard.

To use a text file as a source file for importing, the contents of the file must be organized in such a way that the Import Wizard can divide the contents into a set of records (rows) and each record into a collection of fields (columns). Two types of text files that are organized for importing are delimited files and fixed-width files.

In a **delimited file**, each record appears on a separate line and the fields are separated by a single character, called the delimiter. The **delimiter** can be any character that does not appear in the field values, such as a tab, semicolon, comma, space, and so on. The following is an example of a comma-delimited file:

ID, Company Name, Employee Name, Position

1, Fourth Coffee, Lauren Halian, Sales Manager

2, Woodgrove Bank, Michael Damato, Vice President

3, Wingtip Toys, Karl Vogelmann, Owner

In a **fixed-width file**, each record appears on a separate line and the width of each field remains consistent across records. For example, the first field of every record is always 9 characters long, the second field of every record is always 14 characters long, and so on. If the actual length of a field's value varies from record to record, the values that fall short of the required width must be padded with trailing space characters. The following is an example of a fixed-width text file where the first field is said to be 3 characters, the second field is said to be 15 characters, the third field is said to be 13 characters, the fourth field is said to be 12 characters, the fifth field is said to be 11 characters, and the sixth field is said to be 11 characters:

ID	CompanyName	EmpFirstName	EmpLastName	PositionF1	PositionF2
1	Fourth Coffee	Lauren	Halian	Sales	Manager
2	Woodgrove Bank	Michael	Damato	Vice	President
3	Wingtip Toys	Karl	Vogelmann	Owner	

Saving Specifications

You can save an import or export operation involving any of the file formats supported in Access, but you cannot save the details of a linking operation or an operation where you export only a portion of a datasheet. In this exercise, you will import a text file and then save the import specifications.

STEP BY STEP

Save Import Specifications

USE the database that is open from the previous exercise.

1. On the EXTERNAL DATA tab, in the Import & Link group, click **Text File** to open the *Get External Data – Text File* dialog box.
2. Click **Browse** to open the File Open dialog box.

3. Use the File Open dialog box to locate the *applicants* text file and then click **Open**.

4. Click **Import the source data into a new table in the current database** and click **OK**. The Import Text Wizard appears, as shown in Figure 14-17. Notice the Delimited option button is selected and the data preview of the file contains fields separated by commas. In this case, you will keep the delimited selection.

Figure 14-17

Import Text Wizard, first screen

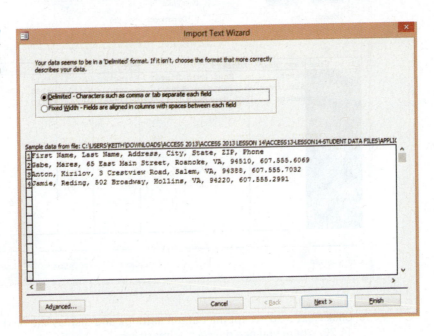

5. Click **Next >** to display the next screen, shown in Figure 14-18.

Figure 14-18

Import Text Wizard, second screen

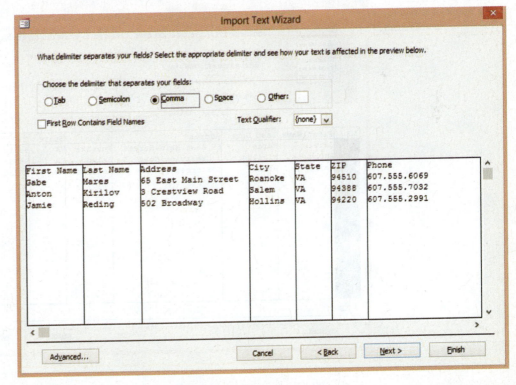

6. Comma should be selected as the delimiter. Click the **First Row Contains Field Names** check box to use the first row of data as field names in the table.

7. Click **Next >** to display the next screen, shown in Figure 14-19, where you can specify field information.

Figure 14-19

Import Text Wizard,
third screen

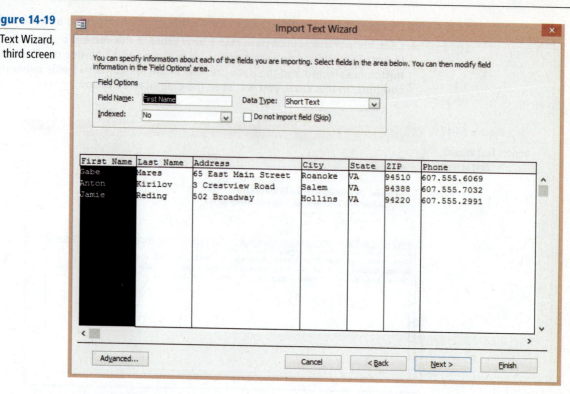

8. Click **Next >** to accept the default settings and display the next screen, shown in Figure 14-20, where you can define a primary key.

Figure 14-20

Import Text Wizard,
fourth screen

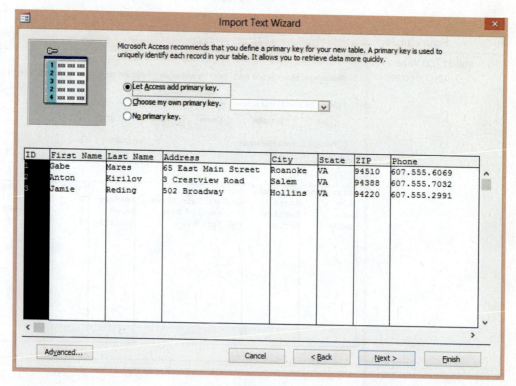

9. Click **Next >** to let Access add the primary key and to display the final screen, shown in Figure 14-21.

Figure 14-21

Import Text Wizard, final screen

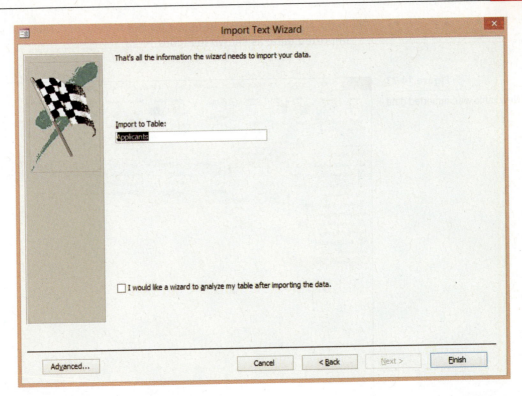

10. Click **Finish** to accept the default table name. A Save Import Steps screen appears.
11. Click the **Save import steps** check box to display the specification details, shown in Figure 14-22.

Figure 14-22

Save Import Steps screen

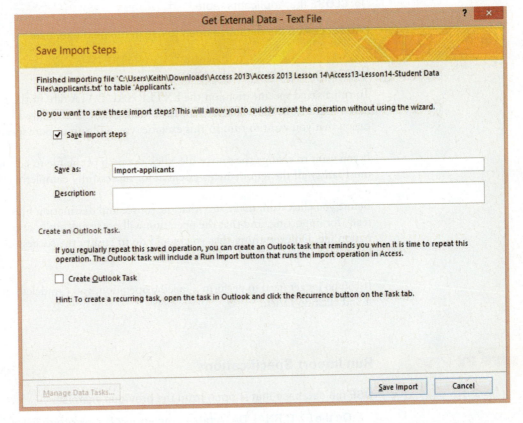

12. In the Description box, key **Import text file with job applicant contact information**.
13. Click **Save Import**.

14. In the Navigation Pane, double-click the **Applicants: Table** to open the new table with imported data, as shown in Figure 14-23.

Figure 14-23

New table with imported data

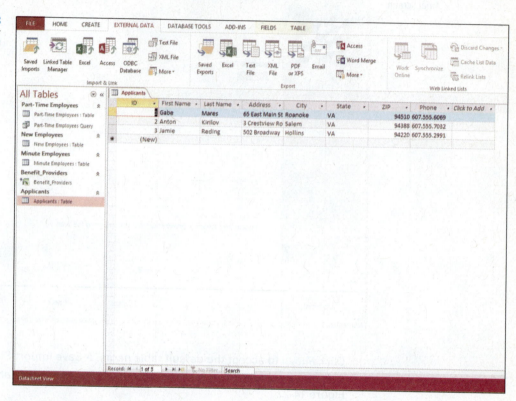

15. **CLOSE** the Applicants table.

PAUSE. LEAVE the database open to use in the next exercise.

Running Import Specifications

To run a saved specification, on the EXTERNAL DATA tab, in the Import & Link group, click Saved Imports. In the Manage Data Tasks dialog box, on the Saved Imports tab, click the specification that you want to run. In this exercise, you will run import specifications.

If you want to change the source file, click the path of the file to edit it. The new file you specify must satisfy all the requirements essential for successfully completing the operation.

Before you click Run, make sure that the source and destination files exist, that the source data is ready for importing, and that the operation will not accidentally overwrite any data in your destination file. Do everything that you would do to ensure the success of a wizard-driven operation before running any saved specification, and then click Run.

If you no longer need to perform a specific operation, you can delete the specification by selecting it and clicking Delete.

STEP BY STEP   **Run Import Specifications**

USE the database that is open from the previous exercise.

1. On the EXTERNAL DATA tab, in the Import & Link group, click **Saved Imports** to open the Manage Data Tasks dialog box, shown in Figure 14-24.

Figure 14-24

Manage Data Tasks dialog box

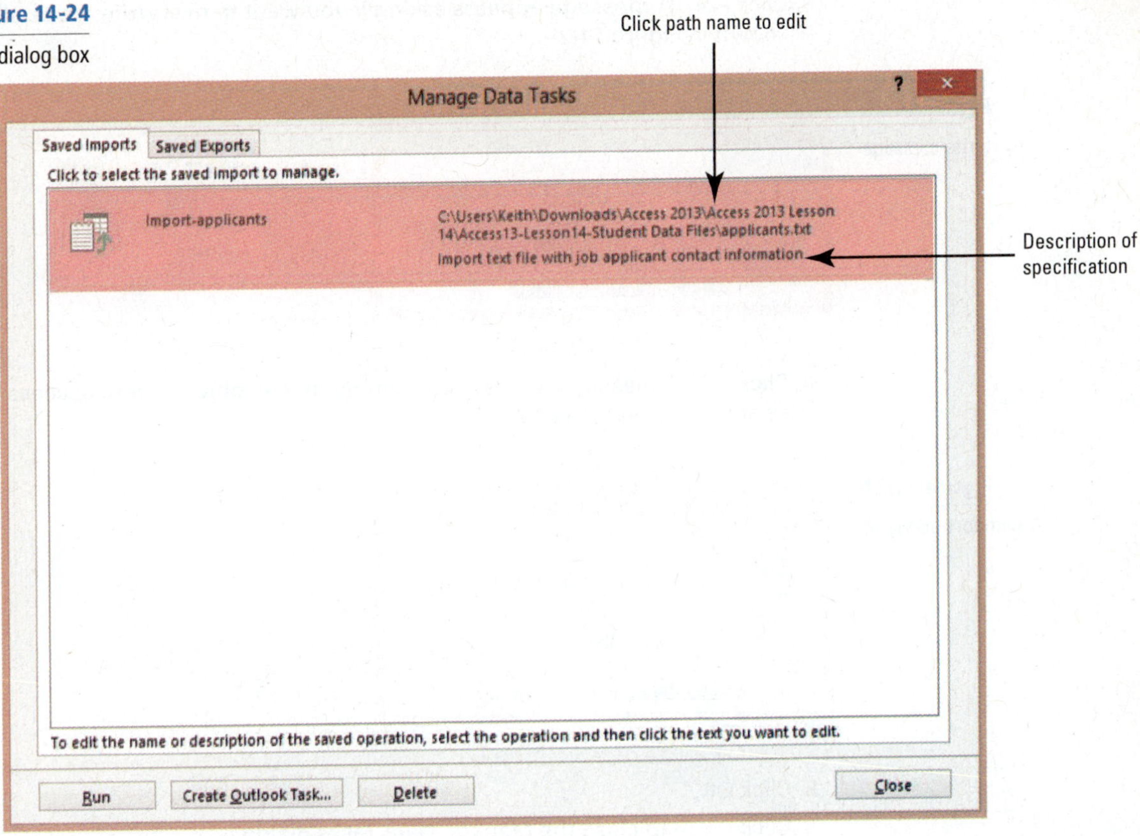

Click path name to edit

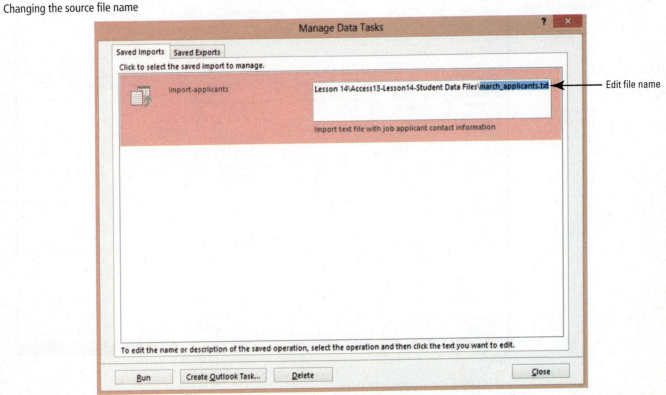

Description of specification

2. Click the file path and edit it by changing the source file name to **march_applicants.txt**, as shown in Figure 14-25.

Figure 14-25

Changing the source file name

Edit file name

3. Click **Run**. A message appears asking if you want to overwrite the existing table, as shown in Figure 14-26.

Figure 14-26

Overwrite message

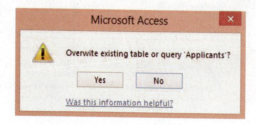

4. Click **Yes**. A message appears confirming that all objects were successfully imported, as shown in Figure 14-27.

Figure 14-27

Successful import message

5. Click **OK**.
6. Click **Close** to close the Manage Data Tasks dialog box.
7. In the Navigation Pane, double-click the **Applicants: Table** to open the table. The existing data has been replaced with new imported data, as shown in Figure 14-28.

Figure 14-28

Table with new imported data

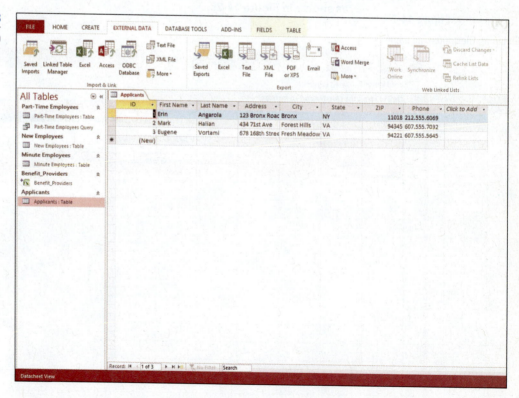

8. **CLOSE** the Applicants table.

PAUSE. LEAVE the database open to use in the next exercise.

EXPORTING DATA

To use Access data in another program, you can use the various commands in the Export group of the EXTERNAL DATA tab to export the selected object in the format you want.

Exporting from a Table to Excel

When you export data from a table to Excel, Access creates a copy of the data and then stores the copy in an Excel worksheet. In this exercise, you will export data from an Access table to an Excel worksheet.

Besides exporting to Excel, you can also export data to other destinations, such as a SharePoint list, a Rich Text Format file, another Access database, or a text file. The process for exporting data is similar, regardless of the destination. The Export group contains all the formats Access can export to. The More button on the Export group has even more exportable formats from which you can choose.

If the source object is a table or a query, decide whether you want to export the data with or without its formatting. By default, Access exports table and query objects without formatting; all fields and records in the underlying object are exported and the Format property settings are ignored during the operation. You can also choose to export a table or query object with formatting; only the fields and records displayed in the current view are exported and the Format property settings are maintained.

If the source object is a form or report, you don't have the option to export the data without its formatting since a form or report object contains, by definition, a formatted layout of fields.

Table 14-2 summarizes the options for creating or overwriting an Excel workbook.

Table 14-2

Destination workbook options

Destination Workbook	Source Object	Data Exported	Result
Does not exist	Table, query, form, or report	With (for tables, queries, forms, or reports) or without (for tables or queries) formatting	Workbook is created during the export operation.
Already exists	Table or query (Forms and reports cannot be exported without their formatting)	Without formatting	The workbook is not overwritten. A new worksheet is added to the workbook and is given the name of the object from which the data is being exported. If a worksheet having that name already exists in the workbook, Access prompts you to either replace the contents of the corresponding worksheet or specify another name for the new sheet.
Already exists	Table, query, form, or report	With formatting	The workbook is overwritten by the exported data. All existing worksheets are removed, and a new worksheet having the same name as the exported object is created. The data in the Excel worksheet inherits the format settings of the source object.

You can export a table, query, form or report to Excel. You can only export one database object in a single export operation. However, you can merge the data in multiple worksheets in Excel after completing the individual export operations. The data is always added in a new worksheet. You cannot append the data to an existing worksheet.

STEP BY STEP   **Exporting from a Table to Excel**

USE the database that is open from the previous exercise.

1. In the Navigation Pane, select the **Part-Time Employees: Table**.
2. On the EXTERNAL DATA tab, in the Export group, click **Excel**. The Export – Excel Spreadsheet dialog box appears, as shown in Figure 14-29.

Figure 14-29

Export – Excel Spreadsheet
dialog box

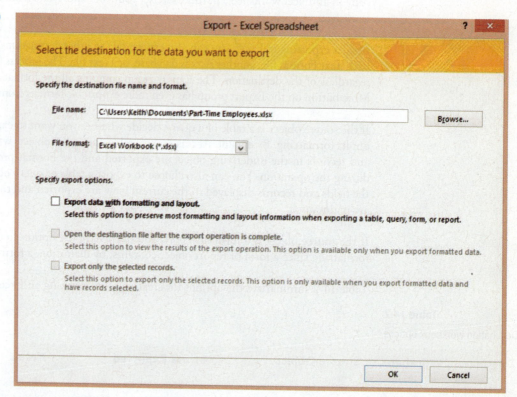

3. If you want to specify a different destination, click **Browse** to open the File Save dialog box, use the File Save dialog box to choose a folder, and then click **Save**.
4. Click the **Export data with formatting and layout** check box and then click the **Open the destination file after the export operation is complete** check box.
5. Click **OK**. Excel opens and the new worksheet with exported data is displayed, as shown in Figure 14-30.

Figure 14-30

Excel worksheet with
exported data

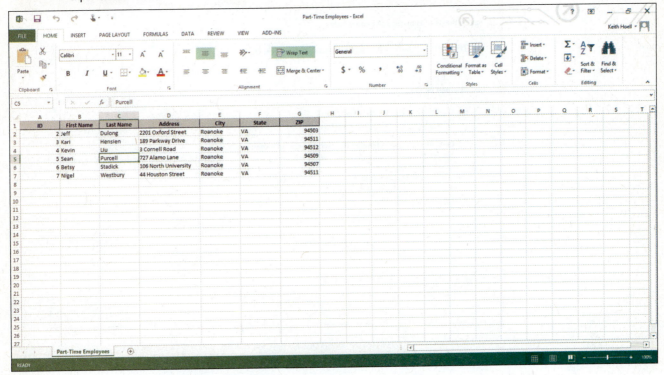

6. **CLOSE** the worksheet and **CLOSE** Excel.

7. Switch to Access.

8. On the Save Export Steps screen, click **Close**.

PAUSE. LEAVE the database open to use in the next exercise.

Exporting from a Query to Word

You can export data from an Access query to a variety of formats, just as you can export data from an Access table. In this exercise, you will export a query to Word.

You can export a table, query, form, or report to Word. When you export an object to Word, Access creates a copy of the object's data in a Microsoft Word Rich Text Format file (*.rtf), and the visible fields and records appear as a table, with the field names in the first row.

Take Note   Pictures or attachments that are part of the source data are not exported to Word. Expressions are not exported either, but the results are.

When you export from Access to a Word document, the Export Wizard always exports formatted data and the data is always exported into a new Word file. You cannot append data to an existing Word document.

STEP BY STEP   **Export from a Query to Word**

USE the database that is open from the previous exercise.

1. In the Navigation Pane, select the **Part-Time Employees Query**.

2. On the EXTERNAL DATA tab, in the Export group, click the **More** button. On the menu that appears, click **Word**. The Export – RTF File dialog box appears, as shown in Figure 14-31.

Figure 14-31

Export – RTF File dialog box

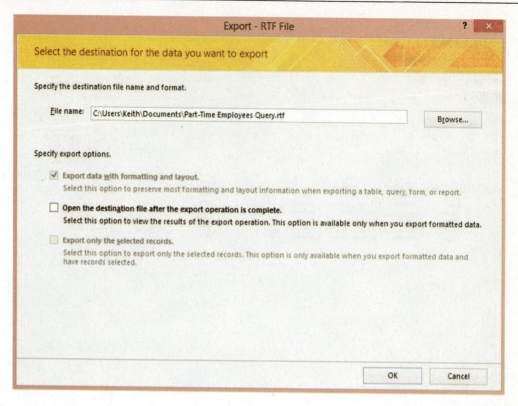

3. If you want to specify a different destination, click **Browse** to open the File Save dialog box, use the File Save dialog box to choose a folder, and then click **Save**.

4. Click the **Open the destination file after the export operation is complete** check box.

5. Click **OK**. Word opens and the new document with exported data is displayed, as shown in Figure 14-32.

Figure 14-32

Word document with exported data

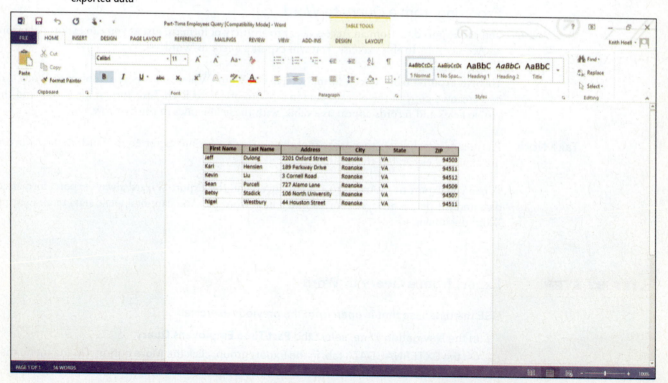

CERTIFICATION   1.5.6
READY?

How do you export to
alternate formats?

6. **CLOSE** the document and **CLOSE** Word.

7. Switch to Access.

8. On the Save Export Steps screen, click **Close**.

PAUSE. LEAVE the database open to use in the next exercise.

SAVING AND RUNNING EXPORT SPECIFICATIONS

The Bottom Line

In the Export Wizard Save as box, type a name for the export specification. Optionally, type a description in the Description box. If you want to perform the operation at fixed intervals, such as weekly or monthly, select the Create Outlook Task check box. Doing this creates an Outlook task that lets you run the specification by clicking a button.

Once these details are saved, you can use the Saved Exports command in the Export group on the EXTERNAL DATA tab on the Ribbon to repeat the operation. Once clicked, the Manage Data Tasks dialog box appears.

In the Manage Data Tasks dialog box, you can change the name of the specification, its description, and the path and file name of the destination file by clicking and making changes in the text box and then pressing Enter. Repeat an operation by clicking the specification and then clicking Run. If you are exporting data with formatting and layout, you are asked to choose the encoding to be used for saving the file. When the operation is complete, you will see a message that communicates the status of the operation.

Although you can export Access data in various formats, sometimes you might need to export data to a program that uses a file format that Access does not support. In that case, if the destination program can use text (*.txt) files, you can export your data as a text file and open the resulting file with the second program. When you export the contents of a table or query to a text file with formatting and layout, hyphens (-) and pipe characters (|) are used to organize the content in a grid in the text file. The records appear as rows, fields appear as columns, and field names appear in the first row.

When exporting without formatting or layout, the Export Wizard gives you the option of creating a delimited file or a fixed-width file, as shown in Figure 14-33.

Figure 14-33

Export Text Wizard file options

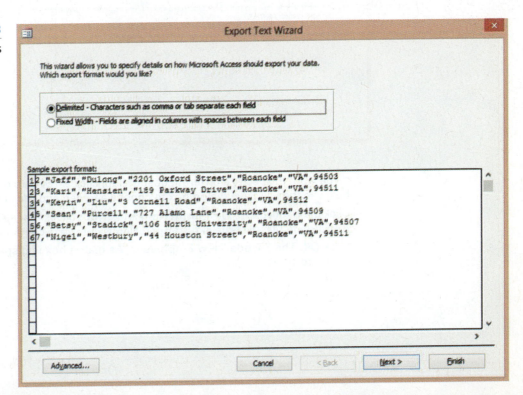

The choice you make usually depends on the system that works with the exported files. If users need to look at the data, a fixed-width file can be much easier to read than a delimited file.

Saving Export Specifications

After you have performed an export operation, you are given the opportunity to save it for future use. Saving the details helps you repeat the same export operation in the future without having to step through the wizard each time. In this exercise, you will export data from Access to a text file and then save the export specification.

STEP BY STEP   **Save Export Specifications**

USE the database that is open from the previous exercise.

1. In the Navigation Pane, select the **New Employees: Table**.
2. On the EXTERNAL DATA tab, in the Export group, click **Text File**. The Export – Text File dialog box appears, as shown in Figure 14-34.

Figure 14-34

Export – Text File dialog box

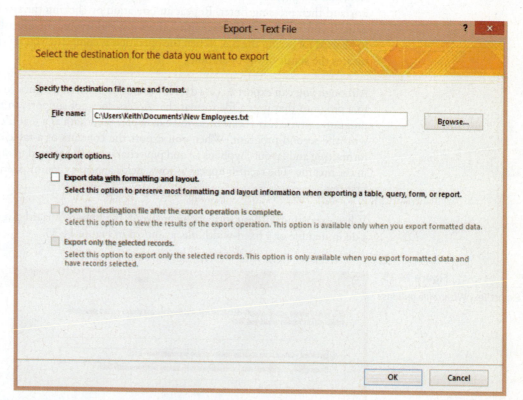

3. If you want to specify a different destination, click **Browse** to open the File Save dialog box, use the File Save dialog box to choose a folder, and then click **Save**.
4. Click the **Export data with formatting and layout** check box and then click the **Open the destination file after the export operation is complete** check box.
5. Click **OK**. The Encode 'New Employees' As dialog box is displayed, as shown in Figure 14-35.

Figure 14-35

Encode 'New Employees' As dialog box

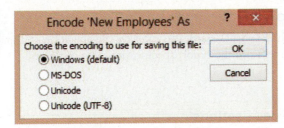

6. Windows (default) should be selected. Click **OK**. Notepad opens and the new file with exported data is displayed, as shown in Figure 14-36.

Figure 14-36

Notepad with exported data

ID	First Name	Last Name	Address	City	State	ZIP	Phone Number
1	Stephanie	Bourne	145 Main Street	Roanoke	VA	94517	607.555.0932
2	Martin	Chisholm	98 Green Avenue	Roanoke	VA	94511	607.555.4646
3	Matthew	Hink	1004 West	Roanoke	VA	94515	607.555.2091
4	Laura	Norman	672 Falls Hill	Roanoke	VA	94511	607.555.7735

7. **CLOSE** Notepad.

8. Switch to Access.

9. On the Save Export Steps screen, click the **Save export steps** check box to display the specification details, as shown in Figure 14-37.

Figure 14-37

Save Export Steps screen

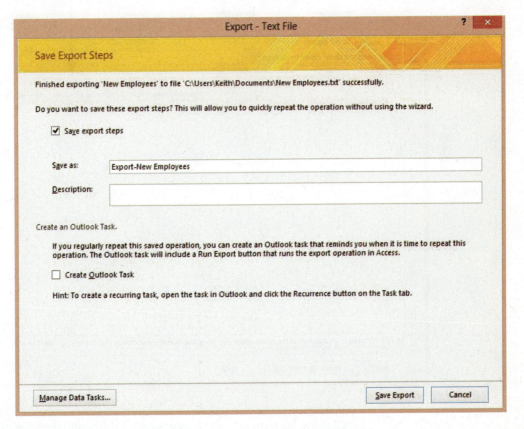

10. In the Description box, key **Export new employee information to a text file**.

11. Click **Save Export**.

PAUSE. LEAVE the database open to use in the next exercise.

Running Export Specifications

When you run the Export Wizard, you can save the operation as a specification for future use. In this exercise, you will run the export specifications you just saved.

STEP BY STEP **Run Export Specifications**

USE the database that is open from the previous exercise.

1. In the Navigation Pane, double-click the **New Employees: Table** to open it, if necessary.
2. Add another record with the following information:
   First Name: **Rachel**
   Last Name: **Valdez**
   Address: **39 Vista Drive**
   City: **Roanoke**
   State: **VA**
   ZIP: **94510**
   Phone Number: **607.555.1218**
3. Click the **Close 'New Employees'** button to close the table.
4. On the EXTERNAL DATA tab, in the Export group, click **Saved Exports** to open the Manage Data Tasks dialog box, as shown in Figure 14-38.

Figure 14-38

Manage Data Tasks dialog box

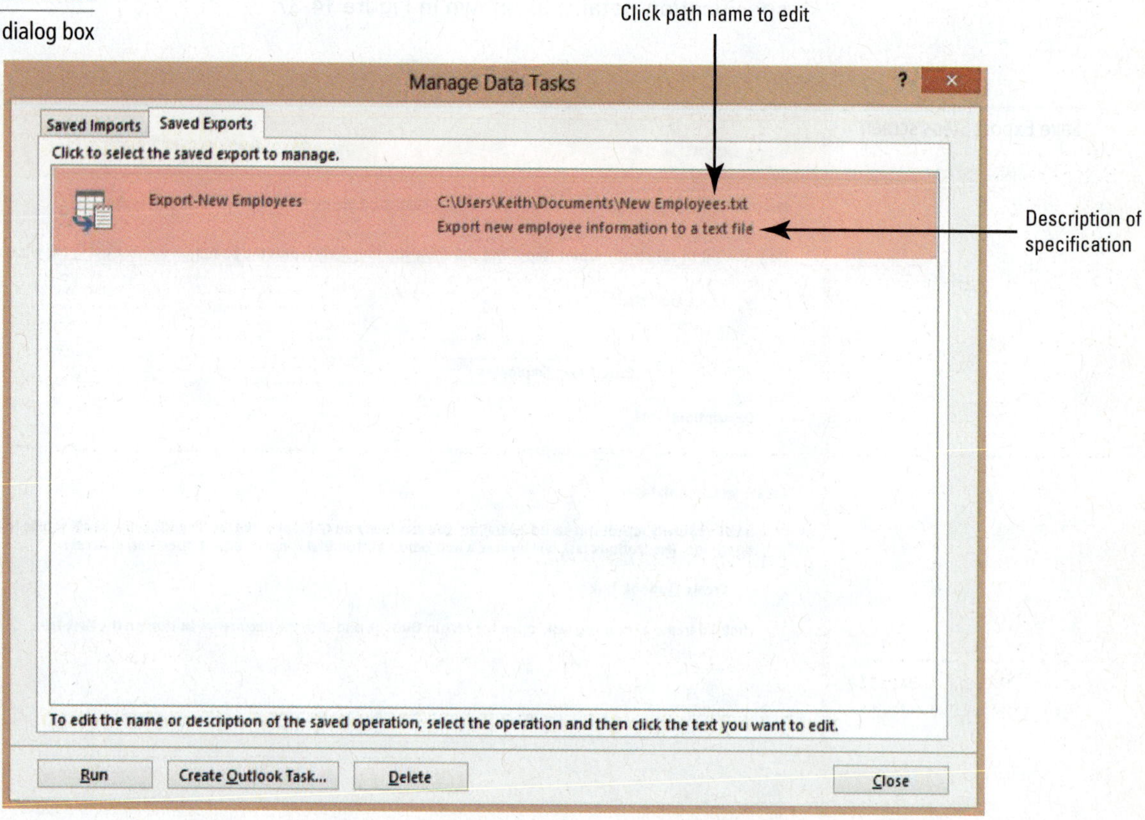

5. Click the file path and edit it by changing the destination file name to **New Employees2. txt**, as shown in Figure 14-39.

Figure 14-39

Edit destination file

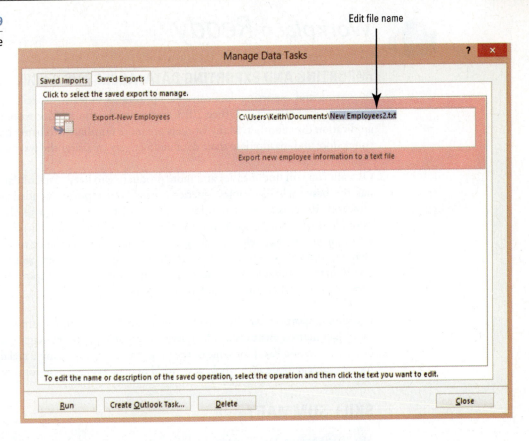

6. Click **Run**. Notepad opens and the new file with exported data is displayed, as shown in Figure 14-40.

Figure 14-40

Notepad with exported data

7. Switch to Access. A message confirms that the export operation was successful, as shown in Figure 14-41.

Figure 14-41

Successful export operation message

Microsoft Access

ⓘ Finished exporting 'New Employees' to file 'C:\Users\Keith\Documents\New Employees2.txt' successfully.

OK

Was this information helpful?

8. Click **OK** and then click **Close** to close the Manage Data Tasks dialog box.

9. **CLOSE** Notepad.

10. **CLOSE** the database.

PAUSE. LEAVE Access open to use in the projects.

Workplace *Ready*

IMPORTING AND EXPORTING DATA: ACCESS VS. EXCEL

Importing and exporting data can be helpful tasks to learn, especially when you're working with the other applications in Office 2013. For example, some office workers prefer to work with one application over another. Many workers are more familiar with using Excel than Access and sometimes store and manipulate their data ineffectively by using the wrong application.

Overall, you will find it easier and more productive to keep track of data using Access since Access has the best tools like tables, queries, forms, and reports intended to manage and track data. However, Excel is a better tool for analyzing data and using it to create charts and graphs. For example, Excel can be used to create PivotTables and PivotCharts, which are tables and corresponding charts that help you analyze data more effectively since rows and columns can be interchanged and data can be aggregated to help you gain a new perspective of it. The ability to create PivotCharts from tables was discontinued in Access 2013, so exporting Access data to Excel is an important step when analyzing data in this way.

Likewise, importing data from Excel tables into Access is an important step when you need to perform data management tasks, like querying, reporting, and managing data in various ways. Many office workers use Excel for some of the wrong reasons; importing Excel data into Access and exploring its tools can open up a whole new world of data management for those who primarily use Excel.

SKILL SUMMARY

In This Lesson You Learned How To:	Exam Objective	Objective Number
Import Data	Import external data into tables	2.1.2
	Append records from external data	2.3.4
	Import tables from other databases	2.1.4
	Create linked tables from external sources	2.1.3
Save and Run Import Specifications		
Export Data	Export to alternate formats	1.5.6
Save and Run Export Specifications		

Knowledge Assessment

Fill in the Blank

Complete the following sentences by writing the correct word or words in the blanks provided.

1. When you import data, Access creates a(n) _____ of the data in a new or existing table without altering the source file.

2. When you link to an Excel worksheet, Access creates a new table, called a(n) _____ , that is linked to the source cells.

3. A(n) _____ contains all the information Access needs to repeat an import or export operation without user input.

4. In a(n) _____ file, each record appears on a separate line and the fields are separated by a single character.

5. A(n) _____ is any character that separates fields and does not appear in the field values, such as a tab, semicolon, comma, or space.

6. In a(n) _____ file, each record appears on a separate line and the width of each field remains consistent across records.

7. You can schedule an import or export operation to run automatically at specified intervals by creating a(n) _____ task.

8. When you export the content of a table or query to a text file with _____ and _____ , hyphens (-) and pipe characters (|) are used to organize the content in a grid.

9. When exporting to Excel, the data is always added in a new _____ .

10. To repeat an import or export operation, click the specification and then click _____ .

Multiple Choice

Select the best response for the following statements or questions.

1. Which tab contains options for importing or exporting data?
   a. Manage Data
   b. Database Tools
   c. External Data
   d. Create

2. Before beginning an import operation, the source file should be
   a. open.
   b. closed.
   c. copied.
   d. backed up.

3. If you want to add, edit, or delete data in a linked table, you must make the changes in the
   a. first row of data.
   b. Access object.
   c. field headers.
   d. source file.

4. You can save an import or export operation involving any of the file formats supported in Access, but you cannot save the details of a
   a. linking operation.
   b. text file import operation.
   c. query export operation.
   d. fixed-width file.

5. The following is an example of what kind of text?

   1, Fourth Coffee, Dana, Burnell, Sales Manager
   a. HTML
   b. linked
   c. fixed-width
   d. comma-delimited

6. How many database objects can you export in a single export operation?
   a. one
   b. two
   c. three
   d. unlimited

7. When you export an object to Word, Access creates what type of file?
   a. MS-DOS Text
   b. Rich Text Format
   c. HTML
   d. linked

8. If you choose to store imported data in a new table, Access
   a. links the new table to an existing table.
   b. overwrites the data in the existing table.
   c. creates a table and adds the imported data to this table.
   d. gives you an error message.

9. What is an advantage of linking an Access database to data in another program?
   a. maintaining a copy of the external data in Access
   b. being able to use Access querying and reporting tools

c. being able to edit the linked table in Access

d. easily being able to change the structure of the Access table

10. Which dialog box allows you to manage saved import and export specifications?
    a. External Data
    b. Saved Specifications
    c. Import/Export Tasks
    d. Manage Data Tasks

Competency Assessment

Project 14-1: Import Data from Excel

You are the purchasing manager for Fourth Coffee, and an associate has provided some information about exotic coffees that are being considered for the monthly coffee club. The data is in an Excel worksheet and will need to be imported into the database.

GET READY. LAUNCH Access if it is not already running.

1. **OPEN** the *Fourth Coffee* database from the data files for this lesson.
2. **SAVE** the database as *Fourth CoffeeXXX* (where *XXX* is your initials).
3. On the EXTERNAL DATA tab, in the Import & Link group, click **Excel** to display the *Get External Data – Excel Spreadsheet* dialog box.
4. Click **Browse** to open the File Open dialog box.

5. Use the File Open dialog box to locate the *Coffee_Exotic* spreadsheet file and then click **Open**.
6. Click **Import the source data into a new table in the current database** and click **OK**. The Import Spreadsheet Wizard appears.
7. Click **Next >** to display the next screen.
8. Click the **First Row Contains Column Headings** check box if it is not already selected.
9. Click **Next >** to display the next screen where the wizard prompts you to review the field properties.
10. Click the column headings to display the corresponding field properties.
11. Click **Next >** to display the next screen.
12. Click **Next >** to let Access add the primary key. The final screen appears.
13. In the Import to Table box, key **Coffee_Exotic** and then click **Finish**. When the Save Import Steps screen appears, click **Close**.
14. In the Navigation Pane, double-click the **Coffee_Exotic: Table** to open the new table with imported data.
15. **CLOSE** the Coffee_Exotic table.
16. **LEAVE** the database open for the next project.

LEAVE Access open for the next project.

Project 14-2: Export Data to Word

Your supervisor at Fourth Coffee wants a list of customer information in a Word file. Use the Customers table in the Access database to export the data to a Rich Text Format file.

USE the database that is open from the previous project.

1. In the Navigation Pane, select the **Customers: Table**.
2. On the EXTERNAL DATA tab, in the Export group, click the **More** button. On the menu that appears, click **Word** to display the Export – RTF File dialog box.

3. If you want to specify a different destination, click **Browse** to open the File Save dialog box, use the File Save dialog box to choose a folder, and then click **Save**.

4. Click the **Open the destination file after the export operation is complete** check box.

5. Click **OK**. Word opens and the new file with exported data is displayed.

6. **CLOSE** the file and **CLOSE** Word.

7. Switch to Access.

8. On the Save Export Steps screen, click **Close**.

9. **CLOSE** the database.

LEAVE Access open for the next project.

Proficiency Assessment

Project 14-3: Save Export Specifications

As a travel agent at Margie's Travel, a client asks you to e-mail information about the dates for available travel packages. Because you don't know what program the client will use to open it, you export the data to a text file. Because you do this frequently, you decide to save the export operation as a specification that can be used later.

GET READY. LAUNCH Access if it is not already running.

1. **OPEN** the *Trip Events* database from the data files for this lesson.

2. **SAVE** the database as *Trip EventsXXX* (where *XXX* is your initials).

3. In the Navigation Pane, select the **2015 Events: Table**.

4. On the EXTERNAL DATA tab, in the Export group, click **Text File** to display the Export – Text File dialog box.

5. Specify the location where you want to store the file.

6. Click the **Export data with formatting and layout** check box and then click the **Open the destination file after the export operation is complete** check box.

7. Click **OK**. The Encode '2015 Events' As dialog box is displayed.

8. Windows (default) should be selected. Click **OK**. Notepad opens and the new file with exported data is displayed.

9. **CLOSE** Notepad.

10. Switch to Access.

11. On the Save Export Steps screen, click the **Save export steps** check box.

12. In the Description box, key **Export event information to a text file**.

13. Click **Save Export**.

LEAVE the database open for the next project.

Project 14-4: Run Export Specifications

One of the trip packages is no longer available. Delete the information from the table and run the export specification to create a new text file with the updated information.

USE the database that is open from the previous project.

1. **OPEN** the **2015 Events: Table**.

2. Delete the **World Series** record from the table.

3. **CLOSE** the 2015 Events table.

4. On the EXTERNAL DATA tab, in the Export group, click **Saved Exports**.

5. Click the file path and change the destination file name to **2015 Events updated.txt**.
6. Click **Run**. Notepad opens and the new file with exported data is displayed.
7. Switch to Access. A message confirms that the export operation was successful.
8. Click **OK** and then click **Close** to close the Manage Data Tasks dialog box.
9. **CLOSE** Notepad.
10. **CLOSE** the database.

LEAVE Access open for the next project.

Mastery Assessment

Project 14-5: Export Data to a New Database

You are the manager at Southridge Video. You have created a new database to store information about new video games. You want to export the Games table to the new database. You have exported an Access table to other destinations, but not to another Access database. Use Access Help if you need more information.

GET READY. LAUNCH Access if it is not already running.

1. Create a new database called **New GamesXXX** (where *XXX* is your initials).
2. **CLOSE** the New Games database.

3. **OPEN** *Sale Games* from the data files for this lesson.
4. **SAVE** the database as **Sale GamesXXX** (where *XXX* is your initials).
5. Use the export skills you have learned in this lesson to export the definition and data of the Games table to the **New GamesXXX** database.
6. Do not save the export steps.
7. **OPEN** the **New GamesXXX** database to be sure the Games table was successfully exported.
8. **CLOSE** both databases.

LEAVE Access open for the next project.

Project 14-6: Appending Data to a Table

You are the human resource manager for Contoso, Inc. You have received information about new employees that needs to be imported into the employee database. You already have a table with information about sales reps, so you want to append the information instead of creating a new table. Because you have never appended data before, use Access Help if you need additional information.

GET READY. LAUNCH Access if it is not already running.

1. **OPEN** the *Contoso Employees* database from the data files for this lesson.
2. **SAVE** the database as *Contoso EmployeesXXX* (where *XXX* is your initials).
3. Choose to import from Excel using the *New_Contoso* spreadsheet file.
4. Choose the options necessary to append the spreadsheet data to the Sales Reps table.
5. Do not save the import steps.
6. **OPEN** the **Sales Reps: Table**. The data from the Excel spreadsheet should be appended to the table, as shown in Figure 14-42.

Figure 14-42

Appended data

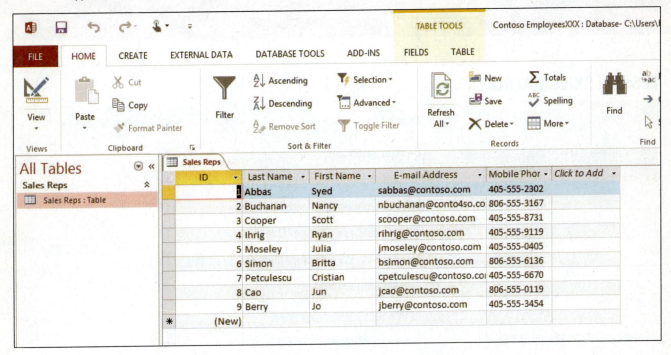

7. **CLOSE** the Sales Reps table.

8. **CLOSE** the database.

CLOSE Access.

15 Database Tools

LESSON SKILL MATRIX

Skill	Exam Objective	Objective Number
Maintaining a Database	Backup databases	1.4.3
	Recover data from backups	1.4.7
	Save databases to external locations	1.5.5
	Create databases in older formats	1.1.3
	Maintain backward compatibility	1.5.3
	Compact databases	1.4.1
	Repair databases	1.4.2
Saving a Database as a Template	Save databases as templates	1.5.4
Merging Databases	Merge databases	1.4.6
Setting Database Properties		
Encrypting a Database	Encrypt databases with a password	1.4.5
Configuring Database Options	Set a form as the startup option	1.3.2
Using Database Tools	Split databases	1.4.4

KEY TERMS

- back-end file
- backup
- Database Documenter
- database properties
- Database Splitter
- database template
- decrypting
- encrypting
- front-end file
- object dependencies

© JanMika/iStockphoto

450

© JanMika/iStockphoto

Fabrikam, Inc., is a furniture manufacturer that supplies new lines, or collections, of furniture and wall hanging art to showrooms each season. Fabrikam also recently acquired two new companies to help diversify its business, Alpine Ski House and Northwind Traders. It has decided to combine the operations of Northwind Traders, a product distributor, with Alpine Ski House, a ski resort. Its intent is to include a large store that mimics a trading post within the ski house. As an intern in the office, you help maintain the records related to the furniture and art collections and the showrooms that sell them for your company. You're also responsible for the data of the two recently acquired companies. Your supervisor is concerned about the maintenance, security, and overall integrity of the database files, so your assignment is to safeguard these files. In this lesson, you learn to back up a database, compact and repair a database, merge databases, set database properties, save a database as a template, and save a database in a previous version of the software. You also learn to use database tools to configure database options, encrypt a database, identify object dependencies, document a database, refresh linked tables, and split a database.

MAINTAINING A DATABASE

The Bottom Line

You can perform some important database maintenance tasks by using the commands on the Info menu and Save As menu on the FILE tab. Though the commands available on these menus might not seem as important as the actual data in your database, these commands allow you to provide protection for all the data in the file, and that is important. By using the options on the Info menu, you can compact and repair your database, set database properties, and protect your database by using encryption. The options on the Save As menu let you save your database in another file format and back up your database.

 Cross Ref

You explored some of the commands on the Save As menu in Lessons 13 and 14.

Backing Up a Database

After all the work you have put into a database, you start to depend on being able to access and update the data and the information in it on a regular basis. To protect your work, it is a good idea to back up a database. A **backup** is a copy of a file. It is a good idea to create backup files of all your databases and continue to back them up on a regular basis. Essentially, you are making another copy of the database that you can store on your computer, on a network drive, or in another safe location to prevent the loss of your data. In this exercise, you back up a database.

You can store a backup copy in the same place as your original file, such as on your computer. However, if something happened to your computer, both files would be affected. A better solution is to save a backup copy to a network drive or removable media that is stored in a different physical location. For example, some companies that maintain sensitive client data have elaborate processes in place to store backup copies on computers or other media in another part of the city or in another part of the country. If an entire office building is destroyed by fire or a city is involved in a natural disaster, the backup files containing client data are safe in another location. It is a good idea to consider the appropriate precautions needed for even a small company's data.

When backing up a database, Access automatically adds the date to the filename. You can keep this filename as an identifier for the backup file or change the filename to something else. Just keep in mind that you need a new name or location so that you aren't just overwriting your original file. In the Save In box, choose the location where you want to save the file.

STEP BY STEP   **Back Up a Database**

GET READY. Before you begin these steps, be sure to turn on and/or log on to your computer and **LAUNCH** Access.

1. **OPEN** *Fabrikam* from the data files for this lesson.
2. Save the database as *FabrikamXXX* (where *XXX* is your initials).
3. Click the **FILE** tab and then click **Save As**. The Save As menu appears, as shown in Figure 15-1.

Figure 15-1

Save As menu

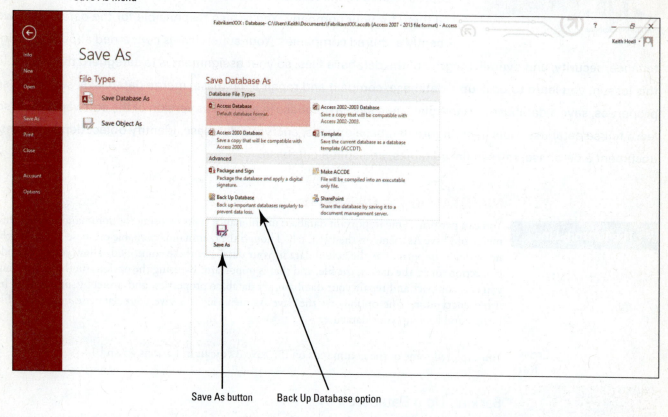

Save As button   Back Up Database option

4. In the Advanced category, click **Back Up Database** and then click the **Save As** button. The Save As dialog box appears, as shown in Figure 15-2. Notice that Access automatically adds the current date to the end of the filename.

Figure 15-2

Save As dialog box

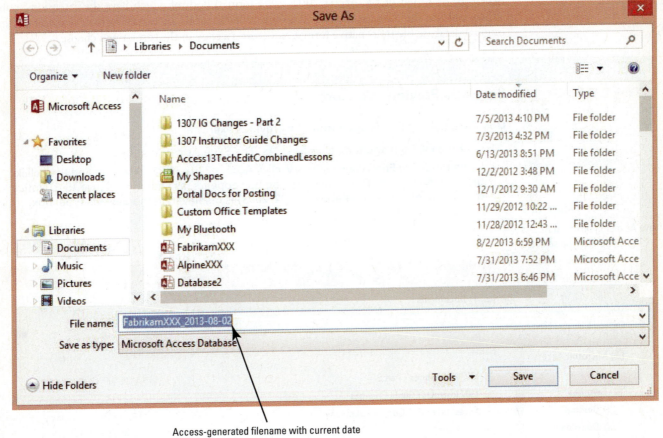

Access-generated filename with current date

5. Click the **Save** button to accept the generated filename and save location. You could also navigate to an external drive to save the database to an external location to increase its physical security. Data can be recovered simply by opening the database backup file you just created.

PAUSE. LEAVE the database open to use in the next exercise.

CERTIFICATION READY? 1.4.3

How do you backup databases?

CERTIFICATION READY? 1.4.7

How do you recover data from backups?

CERTIFICATION READY? 1.5.5

How do you save databases to external locations?

Saving as a Previous Version

Access 2013 allows you to save a database in a previous Access file format so that those using earlier versions of the software can use the database. When you're able to save a database file—or any computer file—in an earlier file format, it means you're maintaining backward compatibility. However, some features of Access 2013 cannot be converted into a file format prior to Access 2007. Access will alert you when this is the case, and you can always remove that feature in order to save the database as a previous version. Before you can save a database in a previous file format, you should open the database but make sure all objects are closed. In this exercise, you save an Access 2013 database as a previous version so a user who has an earlier version of Access can open your document without any difficulty.

When you save a new, blank database in Microsoft Access 2013, you are prompted to give it a filename. Although you may have created the database in Access 2013, it is saved in the Access 2007–2013 file format by default, which gives it the .accdb extension. The Access 2007–2013 format is not readable by earlier versions of Access. If you need to share a database with others using earlier versions of the software, the Save As command allows you to save the database in the Access 2000 format or the Access 2002–2003 format, both of which have the extension .mdb. When you use the Save As command to save a database in an earlier format, it preserves the original database file in its native format and creates a copy in the format you choose.

STEP BY STEP **Save as a Previous Version**

USE the database that is open from the previous exercise.

1. Click the **FILE** tab and then click **Save As**. The Save As menu appears.
2. In the Database File Types category, click **Access 2002–2003 Database** and then click the **Save As** button. The Save As dialog box appears, as shown in Figure 15-3. Notice that Microsoft Access Database (2002–2003) is displayed in the Save as type: box.

Figure 15-3

Save As dialog box with Access 2002–2003 file type selected

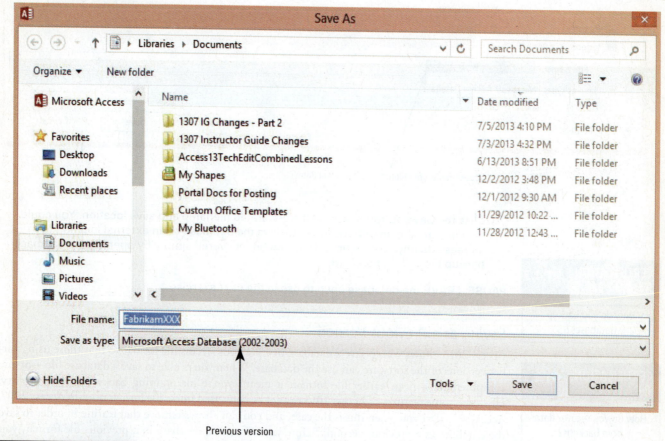

Previous version

3. Key **Fabrikam2002–2003** in the file name box.
4. Click the **Save** button. Notice the filename and format change is displayed in the title bar, as shown in Figure 15-4.

Figure 15-4

Database saved in Access
2002–2003 format

File format displayed in the title bar

[Screenshot of Access application window showing the title bar: Fabrikam2002-2003 : Database- C:\Users\Keith\Documents\Fabrikam2002-2003.mdb (Access 2002 - 2003 file format) - Access. The ribbon shows FILE, HOME, CREATE, EXTERNAL DATA, DATABASE TOOLS, ADD-INS tabs. The Tables navigation pane lists: Atlanta, Charleston, Collections, Finishes, Lexington, Montgomery, Product Placements, Showroom Contact, Upholstery.]

Take Note   After a database is saved in another format, the Navigation Pane view may need to be modified to display all database objects in the new file format.

PAUSE. LEAVE the database open to use in the next exercise.

Take Note   If an Access 2013 database file contains complex data, offline data, or attachments created in Access 2013, you will not be able to save it in a format earlier than Access 2007.

Compacting and Repairing a Database

The Compact and Repair command on the Info menu on the FILE tab optimizes files and fixes minor problems in the file structure that may result from normal, everyday use of a database file. In this exercise, you compact and repair a database.

As records or objects in a database are deleted, the empty space within the file might not be replaced right away, leaving the file fragmented or with large empty spaces within the file structure. In databases with many records and objects, these issues can affect the database's performance over time. In the same way, minor errors can occur in any file, especially when it is shared by many different users on a network drive. Using the Compact and Repair command on a regular basis will help optimize the file and repair minor problems before they become major ones.

Take Note   Before you use this command on a shared file, make sure no one else has the file open.

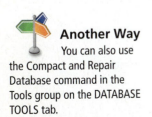

Another Way
You can also use the Compact and Repair Database command in the Tools group on the DATABASE TOOLS tab.

STEP BY STEP **Compact and Repair a Database**

USE the database that is open from the previous exercise.

1. Click the **FILE** tab and then click **Info** (if the Info menu doesn't already appear). Select **Compact & Repair Database** on the Info menu that appears, as shown in Figure 15-5. Access compacts and repairs the database.

Figure 15-5

Info menu

Compact & Repair Database command

View and edit database properties link

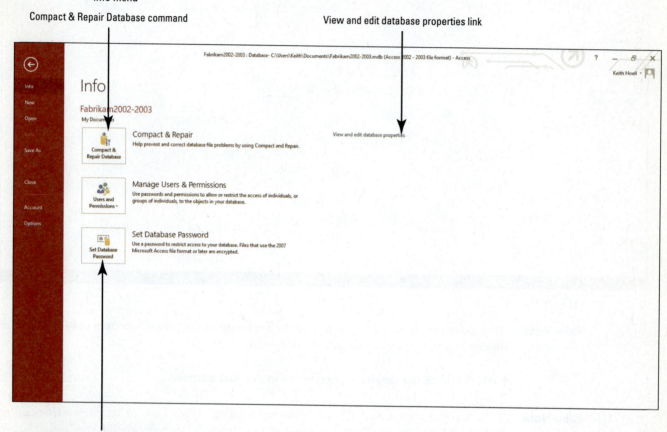

Set Database Password command

How do you compact a database?

2. **CLOSE** the database.

PAUSE. LEAVE Access open to use in the next exercise.

How do you repair a database?

 Another Way
You can set Access to compact a database every time you close it. On the FILE tab, click Options and select Current Database in the Access Options dialog box. Click the Compact on Close check box and click OK.

SAVING A DATABASE AS A TEMPLATE

The Bottom Line

You may find it useful to reuse a database you or others have spent a lot of time creating. For example, you may have created the structure of a database, including relevant tables, queries, forms, and reports—with or without sample data—and may want to save this underlying structure to reuse or to share with others. In this exercise, you create a database as a template.

Access allows you to create a **database template**, a file (extension type *. accdt) that can be used to create a new, prefabricated database. You can even share database templates with the Access community or with your colleagues—simply provide them with the file Access creates after you save the template. Besides saving databases as templates, you can also save and reuse predesigned applications parts and pre-constructed tables, forms, and other objects. These predesigned objects can then be directly inserted into a pre-existing database. You can also create data type templates, which are elements you can use to create new fields or field combinations. Application parts and data type templates can also be shared with others.

You can save a database as a database template or create a new application part by using the commands on the Save As menu. You can access the Save As menu by selecting Save As on the FILE tab. The Database File Types category includes the option to save the database as a template. Once this option is chosen and you click the Save As button, the Create New Template from This Database dialog box appears with the options described in Table 15-1.

Take Note   Data type templates can be created when a table is open by using the *Save Selection as New Data Type* command located on the More Fields menu in the Add & Delete group on the TABLE TOOLS FIELDS tab. You first need to select a field or combination of fields from the open table to execute this command.

Take Note   Database templates, applications parts, and data type template files that you create are saved to the following folder in both Windows 7 and Windows 8: C:\Users\<username>\AppData\Roaming\Microsoft\Templates\Access\. Others can share these files with you and you can put them in this folder to use them from within Access. Similarly, you can share your template files with others by providing them with copies from this folder.

Table 15-1

Create New Template from This Database options

Option	Description
Name	Required text that identifies the template or application part being saved.
Description	Text that describes the contents or purpose of the template or application part.
Category	Used for application parts. Defaults to the User Templates category which has the application part show up under User Templates on the Ribbon.
Icon	Optional. The icon displayed on the appropriate Access menu for the template or application part.
Preview	Optional. The preview image that shows when you click on the database template on the Access menu.
Primary Table	Used for application parts. The table used by default to relate the application part to other tables in a database to which the part is added. A wizard is started when the application part is first used, and this table is the first that is presented to the user to relate to other objects in the database.
Instantiation Form	Form that opens as a startup form when databases made by this template are first opened.
Application Part	Used to select database as an application part. When not selected, database is used as a template.
Include Data in Template	Used to include sample data in the database as part of the template to share with users who create new databases from this template.

Take Note   To use a newly created database template from within Access, click the *Personal* link on the New menu after clicking New on the FILE tab. The newly created application part can be accessed on the Application Parts menu in the Templates group on the CREATE tab on the Ribbon. The data type template can be accessed by opening the table in which you want to create the field and clicking the newly created data type template on the More Fields menu in the Add & Delete group on the TABLE TOOLS FIELDS tab on the Ribbon.

STEP BY STEP   **Save a Database as a Template**

GET READY. LAUNCH Access if it is not already running.

1. **OPEN** the *Graphic Art* database from the data files for this lesson.
2. Click the **FILE** tab.
3. Click **Save As** to display the Save As menu. Click the **Template** option in the Database File Types category, as shown in Figure 15-6.

Figure 15-6

Template option

Template option on Save As menu

Graphic Art : Database- C:\Users\Keith\Downloads\Access 2013\Access 2013 - Lesson 15\Access13-Lesson15-Student Data Files\Lesson15-Files\Graphic Art.a (

Save As

Info
New
Open
Save
Save As
Print
Close
Account
Options

File Types

- Save Database As
- Save Object As

Save Database As

Database File Types

Access Database Default database format.	**Access 2002-2003 Database** Save a copy that will be compatible with Access 2002-2003.
Access 2000 Database Save a copy that will be compatible with Access 2000.	**Template** Save the current database as a database template (ACCDT).

Advanced

Package and Sign Package the database and apply a digital signature.	**Make ACCDE** File will be compiled into an executable only file.
Back Up Database Back up important databases regularly to prevent data loss.	**SharePoint** Share the database by saving it to a document management server.

Save As

4. Click the **Save As** button. The *Create New Template from This Database* dialog box appears, as shown in Figure 15-7.

Figure 15-7

Create New Template from
This Database dialog box

Name box →

Description box →

5. Key **Photo Exhibit** in the Name box.
6. Key **This template contains a standard photo exhibit table with standardized fields and a related form** in the Description box. Review the other boxes and options in the *Create New Template from This Database* dialog box.
7. Click **OK**.
8. Notice the file path and name of the saved template in the message box that appears, as shown in Figure 15-8. Click **OK** to close the message box.

Figure 15-8

Template Saved message box

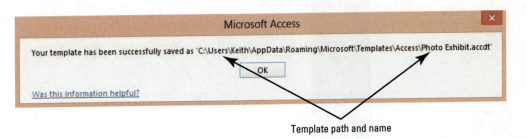

Template path and name

9. Click the **FILE** tab, and then click **New** to display the New menu. Click the **Personal** link, as shown in Figure 15-9. The newly created Photo Exhibit database template appears, as shown in Figure 15-10.

Figure 15-9

Personal link

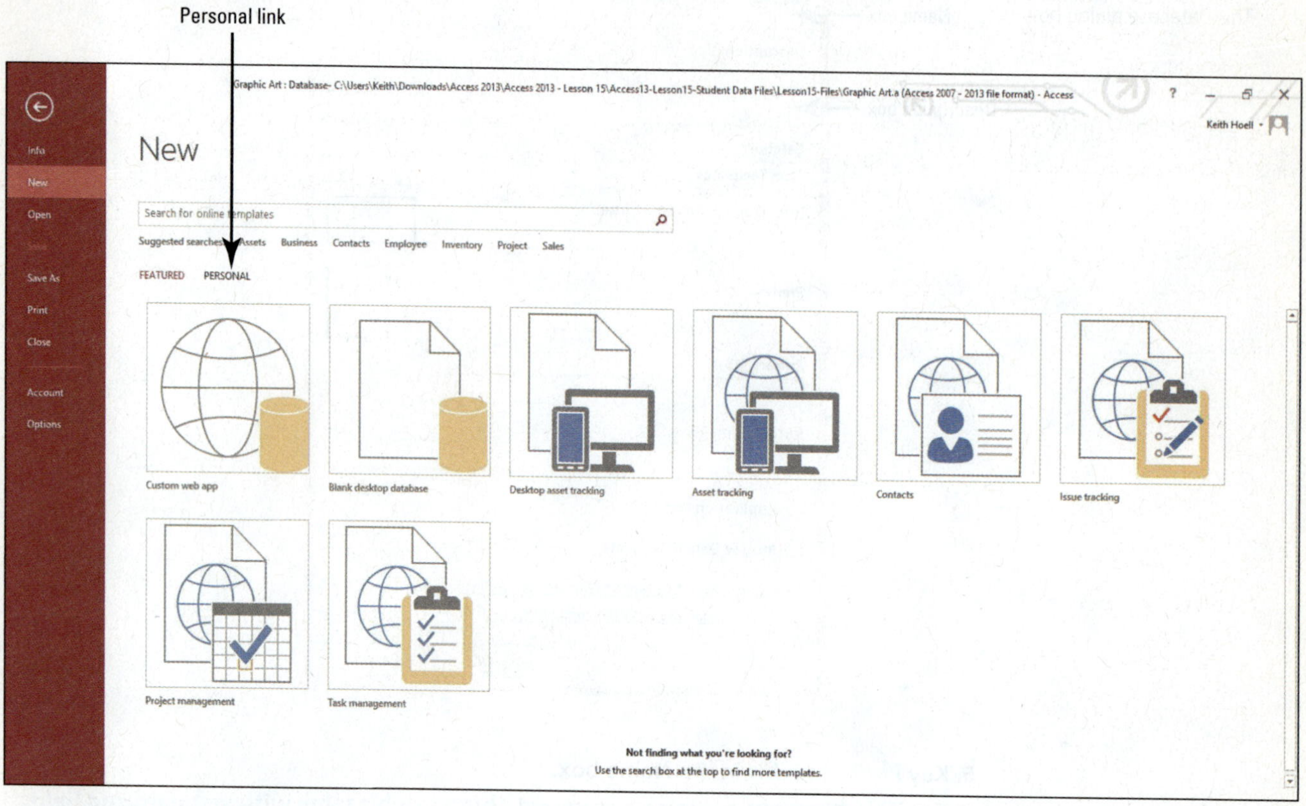

Personal link

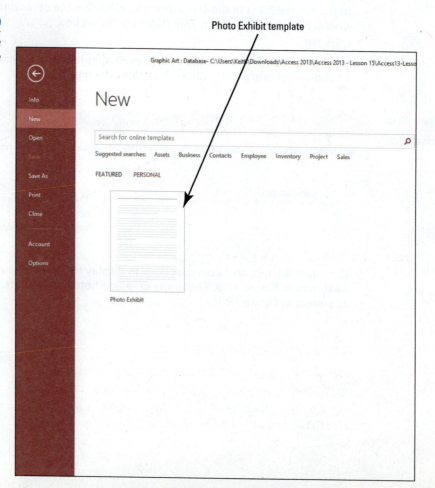

Figure 15-10

Photo Exhibit database
template

Photo Exhibit template

CERTIFICATION
READY?   1.5.4

How do you save databases
as templates?

The Bottom Line

10. CLOSE the database.

PAUSE. LEAVE Access open to use in the next exercise.

MERGING DATABASES

Sometimes you will have a situation where you need to merge the data from several databases into one. In this case, you will need to import several Access database objects—or an entire database—into another database. In this exercise, you import several objects from one Access database in to another.

You may experience a situation in business where each department maintains their own employee records in separate databases stored in separate tables using separate queries, forms, and reports. Using the Access button in the Import & Link group on the EXTERNAL DATA tab on the Ribbon, you can import tables, queries, forms, and reports into the current database. The Import Objects dialog box, which appears before the import process, allows you to choose all or some of the objects you'd like to import. You can also choose to import object relationships, table definitions and actual data (or just table definitions), and other tools, as shown in Figure 15-11.

Figure 15-11

Import Objects dialog box

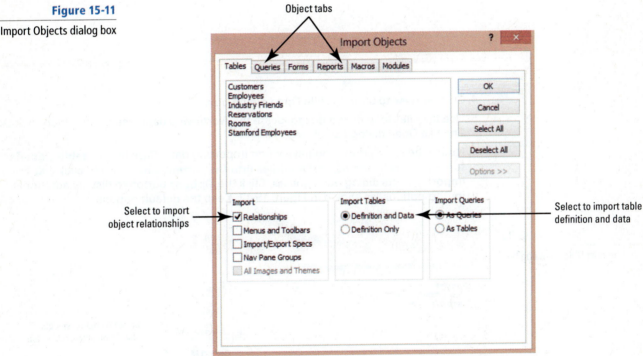

Cross
Ref

You learned about importing and exporting data in Lesson 14.

STEP BY STEP   **Merge Databases**

GET READY. LAUNCH Access if it is not already running.

1. **OPEN** the *Alpine* database from the data files for this lesson.
2. **SAVE** the database as *AlpineXXX* (where *XXX* is your initials).
3. On the EXTERNAL DATA tab, in the Import & Link group, click the **Access** button. The *Get External Data – Access Database* dialog box appears, as shown in Figure 15-12.

Figure 15-12

Get External Data – Access
Database dialog box

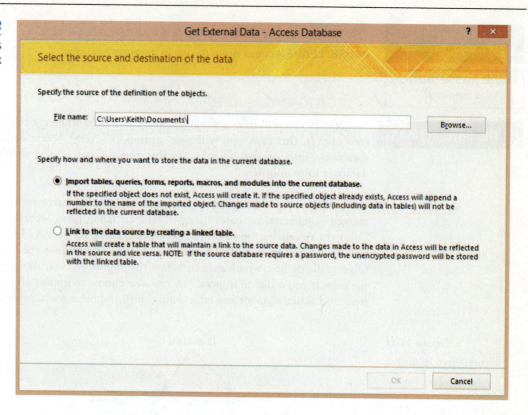

4. Click **Browse** to open the File Open dialog box.

5. Use the File Open dialog box to locate the *Northwind* database file and then click **Open**. The File Open dialog box closes.

6. Notice the two options you have when importing data. Click **Import tables, queries, forms, reports, macros, and modules into the current database** and click **OK**. The Import Objects dialog box appears. Click the **Options** button to display additional import options, as shown in Figure 15-13. Keep the default options.

Figure 15-13

Import Objects dialog box

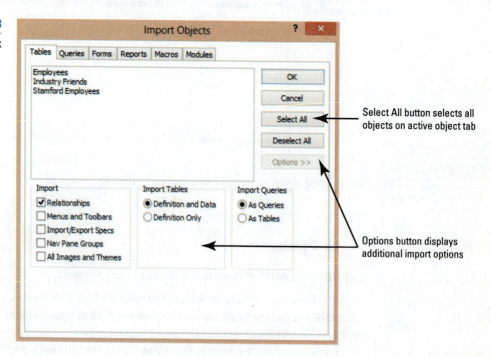

7. Click the **Select All** button.

8. Click each **object tab** for tables, queries, forms, and reports, and click the **Select All** button as the contents for each tab are displayed to select all the objects in the Northwind database.

9. Click **OK**.

10. When the Save Import Steps screen appears, click **Close**.

11. Notice the Navigation Pane now includes objects imported from the Northwind database, as shown in Figure 15-14. Both databases have now been merged.

Figure 15-14

Navigation Pane

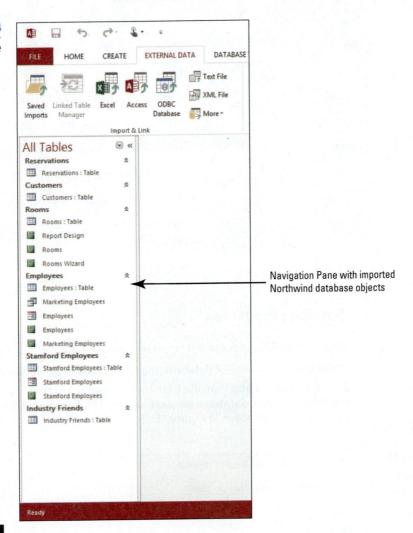

Navigation Pane with imported Northwind database objects

CERTIFICATION READY? 1.4.6

How do you merge databases?

12. **CLOSE** the database.

PAUSE. LEAVE Access open to use in the next exercise.

SETTING DATABASE PROPERTIES

The Bottom Line

Database properties are details about a file that describe or identify it. Using database properties makes it easier to organize and identify databases later. Some properties can be specified by you and some are automatically updated by Access. You can search to find files that contain certain properties, such as keywords, file size, or creation date. Standard properties are those such as author, title, and subject that are associated with a document by default. In this exercise, you set database properties that will help you identify and organize it later.

Table 15-2 describes each Standard property on the Summary tab of the Properties dialog box. These properties can all be changed by the user; however, some properties on the General, Statistics, and Contents tabs—such as the file size and date the document was created or updated—are automatically updated properties that are updated by Access and cannot be changed. On the Custom tab, you can define Custom properties by assigning text, time, numeric, or yes/no values to custom properties.

Table 15-2

Standard Database Properties

Property Name	Description
Title	Title of the database
Subject	Topic of the contents in the database
Author	Name of the individual who has authored the database
Manager	Name of the manager who is responsible for the database
Company	Name of the company that owns the database
Category	Category in which the database can be classified
Keywords	A word or set of words that describes the database
Comments	Summary or abstract of the contents of the database
Hyperlink base	Path to the destination of the file; the path may point to a location on your hard drive, a network drive, or the Internet

STEP BY STEP   **Set Database Properties**

GET READY. LAUNCH Access if it is not already running.

1. **OPEN** the *FabrikamXXX* database that you saved in an earlier exercise.
2. Click the **FILE** tab and then click **Info**, if necessary. On the Info menu that appears, click the **View and edit database properties** link. The FabrikamXXX.accdb Properties dialog box appears, as shown in Figure 15-15.

Figure 15-15

Summary Tab of the FabrikamXXX.accdb Properties dialog box

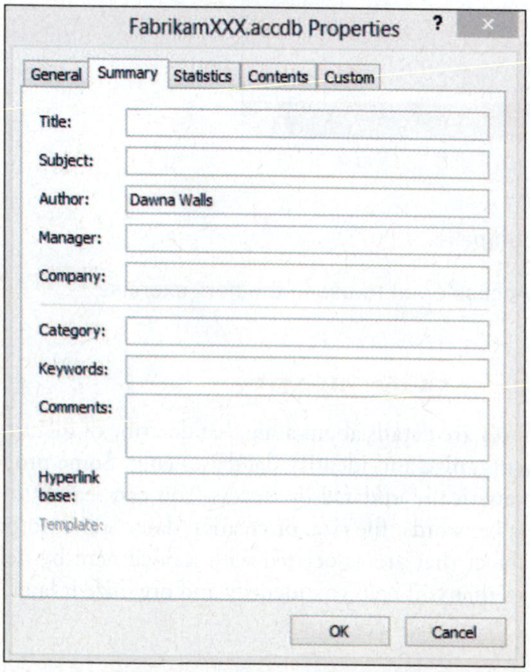

3. Key **Fall Collection** in the Title box.

4. Key **preview** in the Subject box.

5. Select the text in the Author box and key [**Your Name**].

6. Key **Britta Simon** in the Manager box.

7. Key **Fabrikam, Inc.** in the Company box

8. Click the **General** tab. Notice that this tab displays the file type, location, and size as well as the dates the file was created, modified, and accessed.

9. Click the **Contents** tab to view a list of the types of objects within the database file.

10. Click **OK**.

PAUSE. LEAVE the database open to use in the next exercise.

ENCRYPTING A DATABASE

The Bottom Line

Encrypting a database means to scramble the data in a way that can only be reconverted by an authorized user who has the password. When you use a database password to encrypt a database, you make all data unreadable by other tools and you force users to enter a password to use the database. Encrypting a database can provide security for sensitive data. You can use the Decrypt Database command to change the password on a regular basis or to remove it.

Take Note   Use strong passwords that combine uppercase and lowercase letters, numbers, and symbols. Weak passwords do not mix these elements. Strong password: W5!dk8@R. Weak password: CAR381. Passwords should be 8 or more characters in length. A pass phrase that uses 14 or more characters is better.

When you open an encrypted database, the Password Required dialog box appears where you key the password. Passwords are case sensitive, meaning you can use uppercase and lowercase letters as well as numbers and symbols, but you must enter them exactly as they were entered when the password was set in order for there to be a match. It is very important for you to remember your password, because if you forget it Microsoft cannot retrieve it for you. Write down the password and store it in a safe location.

Encrypting and Decrypting a Database

To encrypt a database, you first need to open it in Exclusive mode. **Decrypting** a database is removing the password from a file that has been encrypted. In this exercise, you help secure a database by encrypting it and then unsecure it by decrypting it.

If you want to remove a password, open the database in Exclusive mode, then click the Decrypt Database button from the Database Tools group and key the password in the Unset Database Password dialog box exactly as it was entered to encrypt the database.

STEP BY STEP   **Encrypt and Decrypt a Database**

USE the database that is open from the previous exercise.

1. Click the **FILE** tab and then click **Info**, if necessary. On the Info menu that appears, click the **Encrypt with Password** button. A Microsoft Office Access message box appears saying you must open the database in Exclusive mode, as shown in Figure 15-16.

Figure 15-16

Exclusive Mode message box

2. Click **OK**.

3. **CLOSE** the database but don't close Access.

4. Click **Open** on the FILE tab. The Open menu appears.

5. Navigate to the data files for this lesson and select *FabrikamXXX*.

6. Click the **down arrow** on the Open button and select **Open Exclusive** from the menu, as shown in Figure 15-17. The *FabrikamXXX* database file opens in exclusive mode.

Figure 15-17

Open menu

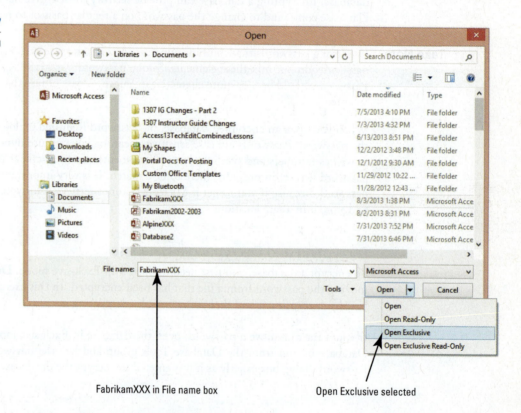

FabrikamXXX in File name box

Open Exclusive selected

7. On the FILE tab, on the Info menu, click the **Encrypt with Password** button. The Set Database Password dialog box appears, as shown in Figure 15-18.

Figure 15-18

Set Database Password dialog box

8. Key **$Fabrikam09fc** in the Password box.

 **Troubleshooting** Be careful to key the passwords exactly as printed throughout this exercise to avoid error messages.

9. Key **$Fabrikam09fc** in the Verify box.

10. Click **OK**. If you get another message box informing you that an option will be ignored, click **OK**. The database is now encrypted with a password.

11. **CLOSE** the database.

12. **OPEN** the database in Exclusive mode again. The Password Required dialog box appears, as shown in Figure 15-19.

Figure 15-19

Password Required dialog box

Take Note You only need to open the database in Exclusive mode if you are going to set or unset a password. The database will be protected with the password in any mode.

13. Key **$Fabrikam09fc** and click **OK**. The database opens.

14. On the FILE tab, on the Info menu, click the **Decrypt Database** button. (If you hadn't opened the database in Exclusive mode, you would get a message prompting you to do so.) The Unset Database Password dialog box appears.

15. Key **$Fabrikam09fc** and click **OK**. The database is not decrypted.

16. **CLOSE** the database.

17. **OPEN** the database in regular mode. Notice that a password is no longer required to open the file.

18. **CLOSE** the database.

CERTIFICATION READY? 1.4.5

How do you encrypt databases with a password?

PAUSE. LEAVE Access open to use in the next exercise.

Workplace *Ready*

PROTECTING AN ORGANIZATION'S DATA

Data stored in an organization's database is often sensitive and confidential. For example, think of the data a human resources department stores on its employees like social security numbers and salary information, both forms of private data. In fact, an entire employee's record should be kept at the highest level of confidentiality; however, many organizations are careless when it comes to following database security best practices.

As you learned in this lesson, encrypting, regularly backing up, and merging databases are effective ways to manage data. It's easy to see how encrypting a database helps keep data safe from prying eyes since it requires others to input a password to access the database, thus helping protect the confidentiality of the data. But how do the other two methods, regularly backing up and merging databases, become effective tools to help prevent others from accessing confidential data?

Regularly backing up a database is like archiving data. When you archive data, you can confidently remove the data that's been archived from the database to keep older data out of the entire dataset while only keeping the newest data readily available. If you're regularly backing up your database and the database is ever compromised or damaged, others will only be able to see the most current data; likewise, if the database is ever damaged, only the current data would be affected and not the entire dataset. Backing up should occur at regular intervals, perhaps every quarter or more often, depending on the nature of the data.

You may want to back up a database then delete table records to provide others with just the table structure and supporting database objects. In an organization, technical staff who may not have database access privileges to view data may be responsible for creating complex queries, forms, or reports you need to extract fields and data from tables. You can provide a database without record data to technical staff so objects can be created and modified without the staff's access to sensitive data. Once the technical staff has performed its work, you can merge your table data into the database with the newly created objects.

Most people take safety for granted, but whether it's ensuring personal security or database security, an ounce of prevention is worth a pound of cure.

CONFIGURING DATABASE OPTIONS

The Bottom Line

The Access Options dialog box provides many ways to customize your copy of Access by allowing you to change popular options to other unique options. Through the Access Options dialog box, you can enable error checking, show/hide the Navigation Pane, and select a startup display form.

If you want a form to be displayed automatically when you open a database, the Display Form menu lets you choose from available forms in the database. You can choose none if you do not wish to display a form.

The Display Navigation Pane option is turned on by default, but if you don't want the Navigation Pane to be displayed when you open your database, click the Display Navigation Pane check box to remove the check mark. You must close and reopen the current database for these settings to take effect.

Enable Error Checking, located in the Object Designers options, is another feature you can change. Error checking is on by default, but you can clear the check box to disable all types of error checking in forms and reports. For example, Access places error indicators in controls that encounter one or more types of errors. The indicators appear as triangles in the upper-left or upper-right corner of the control, depending on text direction. The default indicator color is green, but you can change that to another color if you choose.

Configuring Database Options

The Access Options dialog box lets you customize certain aspects of Access and your databases. The Access Options dialog box has 11 sections of customizable options, including General, Current Database, Datasheet, Object Designers, Proofing, and Language. In this exercise, you use the Access Options dialog box to display a form and hide the Navigation Pane.

STEP BY STEP   **Configure Database Options**

OPEN *Fabrikam Inc* from the data files for this lesson.

1. SAVE the database as *Fabrikam IncXXX* (where *XXX* is your initials).
2. Click the **FILE** tab and click **Options**. The Access Options dialog box appears.
3. Click the **Current Database** button on the left to display the Current Database menu of the Access Options dialog box, as shown in Figure 15-20.

Figure 15-20

Access Options dialog box,
Current Database menu

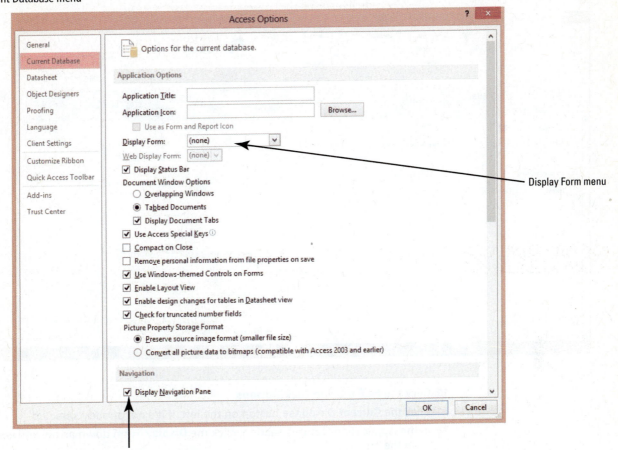

Display Form menu

Display Navigation Pane checkbox

4. In the Application Options section, click the **Display Form** down arrow and select **Showroom Contact Form** from the menu.

5. In the Navigation section, notice that the **Display Navigation Pane** is turned on by default.

6. Click the **Display Navigation Pane** check box to remove the check mark and click **OK**. A Microsoft Access message box appears, as shown in Figure 15-21, saying you need to close and reopen the database for the changes to take effect.

Figure 15-21

Close and reopen message box

7. Click **OK**.

8. **CLOSE** the database.

9. OPEN the *Fabrikam IncXXX* database. Notice that the Navigation Pane is not visible and the Showroom Contact Form is displayed, as shown in Figure 15-22.

Figure 15-22

Showroom Contact form

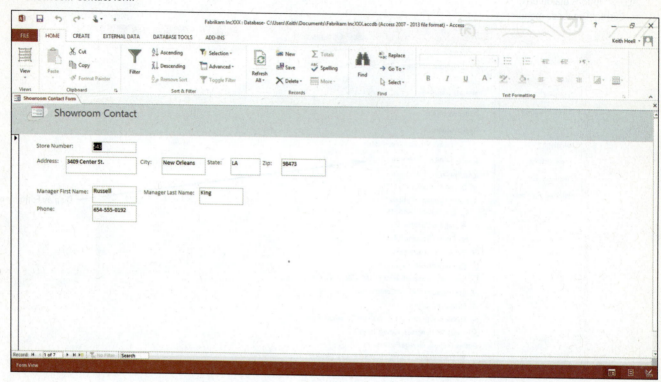

10. Click the **FILE** tab and click **Options**.

11. Click the **Current Database** button on the left, if it's not already selected.

12. In the Application Options section, click the **Display Form** down arrow and select **None** from the menu.

13. In the Navigation section, click the **Display Navigation Pane** check box to insert a check mark.

14. In the Navigation section, click the **Navigation Options** button. The Navigation Options dialog box appears. Notice the grouping and display options that are available and click **Cancel**.

15. Click the **Object Designers** button on the left.

16. Scroll to the bottom of the window to see the Error checking section. The Enable Error Checking options are turned on by default.

17. Click **OK**. The Microsoft Access dialog box appears again.

18. Click **OK**.

19. **CLOSE** the database.

20. **OPEN** the *Fabrikam IncXXX* database. Notice the Navigation Pane is displayed and the form is not.

PAUSE. LEAVE the database open to use in the next exercise.

CERTIFICATION READY?   1.3.2

How do you set a form as the startup option?

SOFTWARE ORIENTATION

DATABASE TOOLS Tab

The DATABASE TOOLS tab on the Ribbon contains advanced commands for maintaining documents. Use Figure 15-23 as a reference throughout this lesson.

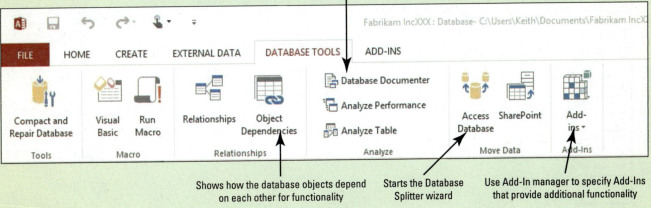

Figure 15-23
DATABASE TOOLS tab

USING DATABASE TOOLS

The Bottom Line

The DATABASE TOOLS tab has advanced commands for maintaining databases. Using this tab, you can do such things as identify object dependencies, create object reports with the Database Documenter, and split a database.

Identifying Object Dependencies

Object dependencies describe how objects in a database rely on other components to function properly. The Object Dependencies task pane helps you manage a database by displaying how all its components interact. This can be helpful if you want to delete a table or form. You will be able to see which other objects may also need to be changed so they will still function without the deleted table. In this exercise, you identify object dependencies.

The Object Dependencies task pane displays how database objects, such as tables or forms, use other objects. This process helps keep databases running smoothly by preventing errors that could result when changes or deletions are made to objects in a database. The Object Dependencies task pane works only for tables, forms, queries, and reports in an Access database.

STEP BY STEP   **Identify Object Dependencies**

USE the database that is open from the previous exercise.

1. Click the **Product Placements: Table** in the Navigation Pane to select it.
2. On the DATABASE TOOLS tab, in the Relationships group, click the **Object Dependencies** button. The **Object Dependencies task pane** displays dependency information for the selected table, as shown in Figure 15-24. Notice that the *Objects that depend on me* option button is selected.

Figure 15-24

Object Dependencies
task pane

Object Dependencies task pane

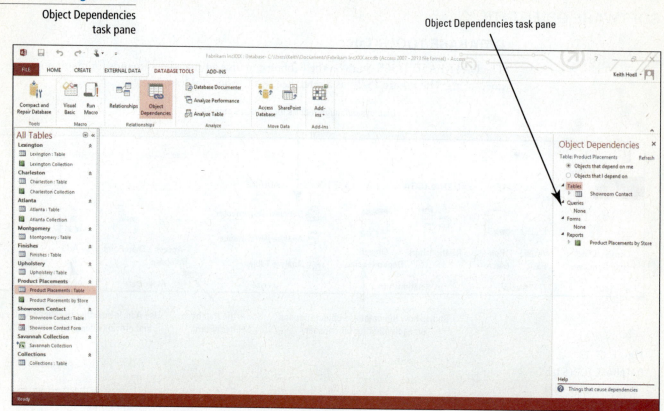

3. Click the **Objects that I depend on** option button. Notice the changes in the Reports section.

4. Click the **Objects that depend on me** option button. Click the **right-pointing triangle** beside the Showroom Contact table to see the tables and forms that depend on the Showroom Contact table.

5. Click the **Showroom Contact** link to display it in Design view where you could make any necessary changes

6. **CLOSE** the Showroom Contact table.

7. **CLOSE** the Object Dependencies task pane.

PAUSE. LEAVE the database open to use in the next exercise.

Using the Database Documenter

The **Database Documenter** provides detailed information about a database and presents it as a report that can be printed. Use the Database Documenter when you need to have a printed record of this information, such as for record-keeping purposes or as insurance in case you have to re-create the database or object. In this exercise, you use the Database Documenter to create a report about the objects included in the database.

The Database Documenter creates a report that shows details, or definitions, about a selected object and opens it in Print Preview. You can view the properties for a form as well as properties for each section of the form and each label, button, or control on the form. The Documenter dialog box contains tabs for each type of object as well as a tab that displays all objects. Select the object whose definitions you want to view or print. The Options button lets you further specify the features of the object for which you want to view the definitions.

STEP BY STEP   **Use the Database Documenter**

USE the database that is open from the previous exercise.

1. On the DATABASE TOOLS tab, in the Analyze group, click the **Database Documenter** button. The Documenter dialog box appears, as shown in Figure 15-25.

Figure 15-25

Documenter dialog box

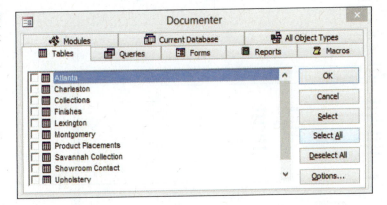

2. Click the **All Object Types** tab.
3. Click the **Tables** tab.
4. Click the **Showroom Contact** check box in the Tables list.
5. Click the **Options** button. The Print Table Definition dialog box appears, as shown in Figure 15-26.

Figure 15-26

Print Table Definition
dialog box

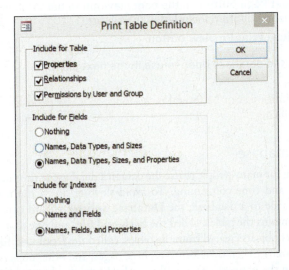

6. Click **OK** to close the Print Table Definition dialog box.
7. Click **OK** to close the Documenter dialog box. The Object Definition report appears in Print Preview.
8. Click the **Zoom** button in the Zoom group to view the report, as shown in Figure 15-27. At this point, you could print the report or make any changes to the layout and then print it.

Figure 15-27

Object Definition report

Zoom button

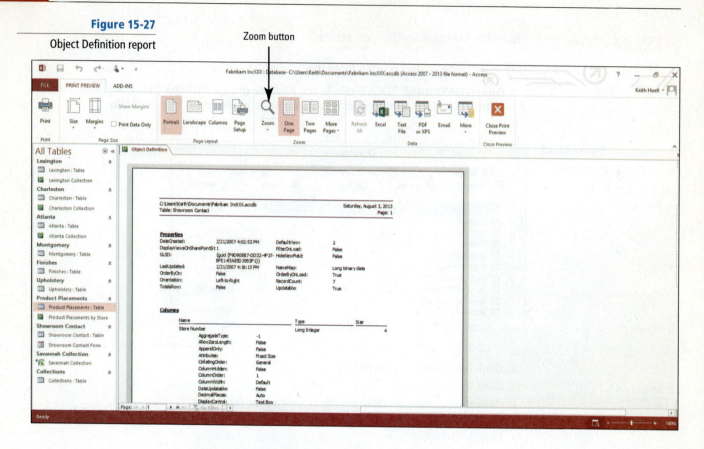

9. Click the **Next Page** button on the page navigation bar until you reach page 4. Notice the relationship diagram included in the report.

10. Click the **Close Print Preview** button.

PAUSE. LEAVE the database open to use in the next exercise.

Take Note   Some object definitions can be several pages long, so it is a good idea to check the length of the report before printing.

Splitting a Database

It can be difficult for many people to use the data in a database at the same time. Synchronizing data can be difficult and time consuming. To avoid slowing down the network because of constant changes being made to a database, the **Database Splitter** wizard can split the database into two files: one that contains the tables, called the **back-end file**; and one that contains the queries, forms, reports, and other objects created from the tables, called the **front-end file.** Users who need to access the data can customize their own forms, reports, pages, and other objects while maintaining a single source of data on the network. Essentially, the back-end database tables are dynamically linked to the front-end database tables, so a change of record data in one table will automatically change the same data in the corresponding table in the other database. It is a good idea to back up the database before splitting it. In this exercise, you use the Database Splitter wizard to split a database.

STEP BY STEP   **Split a Database**

USE the database that is open from the previous exercise.

1. On the DATABASE TOOLS tab, in the Move Data group, click the **Access Database** button. The Database Splitter Wizard appears, as shown in Figure 15-28.

Figure 15-28

Database Splitter Wizard

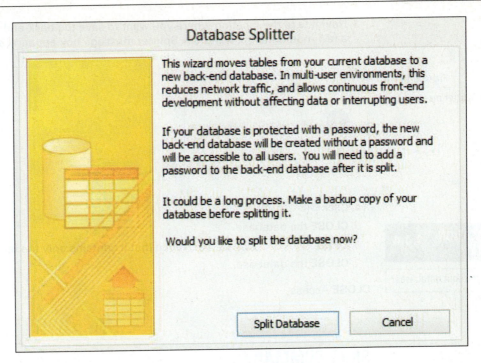

2. Click the **Split Database** button. The Create Back-end Database dialog box appears, as shown in Figure 15-29.

Figure 15-29

Create Back-end Database dialog box

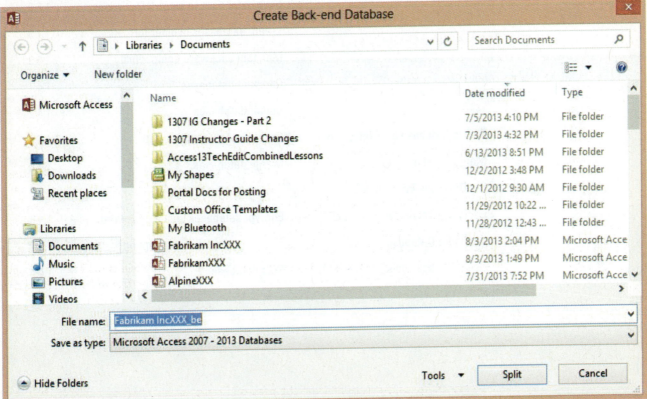

3. Navigate to the location where you want to save the back-end file and click **Split**. After a few moments, the Database Splitter message box appears, as shown in Figure 15-30.

Figure 15-30

Database Splitter message box

4. Click **OK**.
5. **CLOSE** the database.
6. **OPEN** *FabrikamIncXXX_be*. Notice that it contains only the tables for the database.
7. **CLOSE** the database.

CLOSE Access.

CERTIFICATION READY? 1.4.4

How do you split databases?

SKILL SUMMARY

In This Lesson You Learned How To:	Exam Objective	Objective Number
Maintain a Database	Backup databases	1.4.3
	Recover data from backups	1.4.7
	Save databases to external locations	1.5.5
	Create databases in older formats	1.1.3
	Maintain backward compatibility	1.5.3
	Compact databases	1.4.1
	Repair databases	1.4.2
Save a Database as a Template	Save databases as templates	1.5.4
Merge Databases	Merge databases	1.4.6
Set Database Properties		
Encrypt a Database	Encrypt databases with a password	1.4.5
Configure Database Options	Set a form as the startup option	1.3.2
Use Database Tools	Split databases	1.4.4

Knowledge Assessment

Matching

Match the term in Column 1 to its description in Column 2.

Column 1	Column 2
1. backup	a. in a split database, the file that contains the queries, forms, reports, and other objects created from the tables
2. back-end file	b. details about a file that describe or identify it
3. front-end file	c. optimizes files and fixes minor problems in the file structure of a database
4. database properties	d. to scramble data in a way that can only be reconverted by an authorized user who has the correct password
5. Database Splitter	e. removing the password from an encrypted file
6. Compact and Repair command	f. describe how objects in a database are dependent on or rely on other components to function properly
7. encrypting	g. creates a report that shows details, or definitions, about a selected object database and opens it in Print Preview
8. object dependencies	h. a copy of a database file
9. Database Documenter	i. the file that contains the tables in a split database
10. decrypting	j. a wizard that splits a database for you

True/False

Circle T if the statement is true or F if the statement is false.

T F 1. Backing up files on a regular basis is really not necessary.

T F 2. When you back up a database, Access automatically adds the date to the filename.

T F 3. Compacting and repairing a database leaves the file fragmented.

T F 4. Some database properties are updated by Access and cannot be changed.

T F 5. The .accdb extension is for the Access 2002–2003 file format.

T F 6. Access Options allow you to customize Access.

T F 7. If you forget a password for a database, Microsoft can retrieve it for you.

T F 8. You can print a report from the Database Documenter.

T F 9. The Compact and Repair command allows you to find missing table links.

T F 10. It is a good idea to back up a database before splitting it.

Competency Assessment

Project 15-1: Set Database Properties and Compact and Repair the Blue Yonder Database

As an investor relations specialist for Blue Yonder Airlines, you need to maintain and safeguard the databases that you use. Set the database properties and compact and repair the Income and Expenses database.

GET READY. LAUNCH Access if it is not already running.

1. **OPEN** the *BlueYonder* database from the data files for this lesson.
2. **SAVE** the database as *BlueYonderXXX* (where *XXX* is your initials).
3. Click the **FILE** tab, and then click **Info**, if necessary, and select the **View and edit database properties** link.
4. Key **Income and Expenses** in the Subject box.
5. Key **[Your Name]** in the Author box.
6. Key **Andrew Lan** in the Manager box.
7. Key **BlueYonder Airlines** in the Company box.
8. Click **OK**.
9. Select **Compact & Repair Database**.

CLOSE the database.

Project 15-2: Merge, Back Up and Split the WingTip Database

As part of your maintenance of database files at WingTip Toys, you decide to merge a database with another database with similar data to consolidate the two databases. You also decide to create a backup of a database and split it so that others in the company can create their own forms and reports using the data in the tables.

GET READY. LAUNCH Access if it is not already running.

1. **OPEN** the *Wingtip* database from the data files for this lesson.
2. **SAVE** the database as *WingtipXXX* (where *XXX* is your initials).
3. On the **EXTERNAL DATA** tab, in the Import & Link group, click the **Access** button.
4. Click **Browse** to open the File Open dialog box.

5. Locate the *Toys* database file and the click **Open**.
6. Import all objects into the current database.
7. When the Save Import Steps screen appears, click **Close**.
8. Click the **FILE** tab, and then click **Save As**, and then select **Back Up Database**.
9. Click the **Save As** button and then, using the generated file name with the date, click **Save**.
10. On the **DATABASE TOOLS** tab, in the Move Data group, click the **Access Database** button.
11. Click the **Split Database** button.
12. Accept the *WingtipXXX_be* file name and click **Split**.
13. Click **OK**.

CLOSE the database.

Proficiency Assessment

Project 15-3: Encrypt the Blue Yonder Database

Create a password to protect the data in the Income and Expenses database.

USE the *BlueYonderXXX* database that you saved in a previous exercise.

1. **OPEN** the *BlueYonderXXX* database in Exclusive mode.
2. Click the **FILE** tab, and on the Info menu click the **Encrypt with Password** button.
3. Key **#1BlueYonder$87** in the Password box.
4. Key **#1BlueYonder$87** in the Verify box.

5. Click **OK**.

6. **CLOSE** the database.

7. **OPEN** the database.

8. Key **#1BlueYonder$87** in the Enter database password box and click **OK**.

9. Open the **Database Documenter**.

10. Select the **Income & Expenses Summary** table and click **OK** to view the report.

11. Print the report.

12. Close Print Preview.

CLOSE the database.

Project 15-4: Save the Lucerne Database as a Template and in a Previous File Format

1. **OPEN** the *Lucerne* database from the data files for this lesson.

2. On the FILE tab, in the Save As menu, click the **Template** option.

3. Click the **Save As** button. In the *Create New Template from This Database* dialog box, key **Lucerne Structure** in the Name box.

4. Key **This template contains standard book, sales, and author objects** in the Description box.

5. **SAVE** the template.

6. **SAVE** the Lucerne database in the Access 2002–2003 Database file format with the name *Lucerne2002–2003*.

CLOSE the database.

Mastery Assessment

Project 15-5: Decrypt and Back Up the Blue Yonder Database

Password protection for the Blue Yonder Income and Expenses database is no longer necessary. Remove the encryption.

USE the *BlueYonderXXX* database that you saved in a previous exercise.

1. Remove the encryption from the Blue Yonder database by entering the correct password when prompted.

2. Create a backup file for the database using the generated file name. **SAVE** it in the same location as the original version.

CLOSE the database.

Project 15-6: View Object Dependencies in the Tailspin Database

An assistant at Tailspin Insurance needs to perform some maintenance on a database and wants to review whether a particular table can be deleted while still maintaining functionality of all other existing database objects. Use the Object Dependencies task pane to display dependency information about a particular table.

OPEN *TailspinInsurance* from the data files for this lesson.

1. **SAVE** the database as *TailspinInsuranceXXX* (where *XXX* is your initials).

2. View the Object Dependencies information for the *Part-time Employees* table.

3. **SAVE** the database.

CLOSE Microsoft Access.

Circling Back

As Woodgrove Real Estate grows, you continue to learn more about Access and use the database for more advanced tasks.

Project 1: Create a Grouped Report

You want to see the houses that have been sold each month. Use the Report Wizard to create a report that groups the data according to the closing date. Then create an aggregate field that will sum the total amount of sales for each month.

GET READY. Launch Access if it is not already running.

1. **OPEN** the *Woodgrove Real Estate* database from the data files for this lesson.
2. **SAVE** the database as *Woodgrove Real EstateXXX* (where XXX is your initials).
3. **OPEN** the Houses Sold table.
4. On the CREATE tab, in the Reports group, click the Report Wizard button to display the first screen in the Report Wizard.
5. Select the Listing Agent field and click the single right arrow to move the field to the Selected Fields list.
6. Using the same method, move the Address, Selling Price, and Closing Date fields from the Available Fields list to the Selected Fields list.
7. Click the Next > button to display the second screen in the Report Wizard.
8. Select the Closing Date field and click the single right arrow to move it to the grouping levels box.
9. Click the Next > button to display the third screen in the Report Wizard.
10. Click the down arrow on the Sort menu and select Closing Date.
11. Click the Next > button to display the fourth screen in the Report Wizard.
12. In the Layout section, the Stepped option button should be selected and in the Orientation section Portrait should be selected.
13. Click the Next > button to display the fifth screen in the Report Wizard.
14. Click the Finish button to accept the settings and create the report.
15. **CLOSE** Print Preview.
16. Switch to Layout view.
17. Right-click the first cell under the Selling Price header to display the shortcut menu.
18. Click Total Selling Price and then click Sum. The totals for each month are displayed. Resize the controls, if necessary, so all the labels and data can be read. Your report should look similar to Figure 1.

Figure 1

Sales report grouped by month

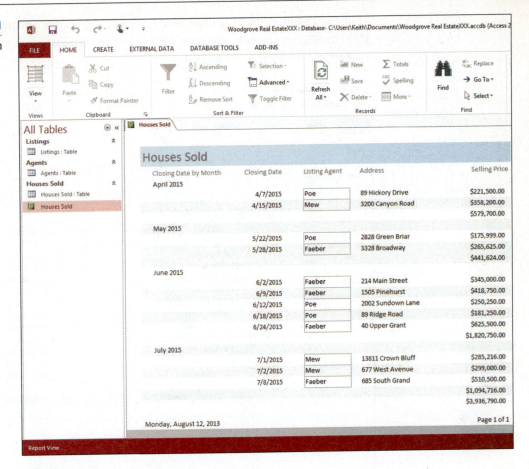

19. **SAVE** and **CLOSE** the report.

PAUSE. LEAVE the database open to use in the next project.

Project 2: Create a Calculated Query Field

You are interested in knowing the difference between each house's asking price and selling price. Create a query with a calculated field that will give you this information. Then add a Total row so you can find the average asking price, selling price, and difference.

USE the database that is open from the previous project.

1. On the CREATE tab, in the Queries group, click **Query Design**.
2. In the Show Table dialog box, double-click **Houses Sold** to add the table to the design grid.
3. Select the **Houses Sold** table in the Navigation Pane.
4. In the Houses Sold field list, double-click **Address**, **Bedrooms**, **Bathrooms**, **Asking Price**, and **Selling Price**.
5. Click the Field cell in the first blank column and press **Shift + F2** to open the Zoom dialog box.
6. In the Zoom dialog box, key the following expression:

   Difference: [Asking Price] - [Selling Price]

7. Click **OK**.
8. On the DESIGN tab, in the Results group, click **Run** to create a query with the new calculated Difference field.
9. On the HOME tab, in the Records group, click the **Totals** button. Notice the Total row at the bottom of the result set.
10. In the Asking Price field, click the **Total** cell down arrow to display the menu and click **Average**.

11. In the Selling Price field, click the **Total row** down arrow and click **Average**.

12. In the Difference field, click the **Total row** down arrow and click **Average**. Your query should look similar to Figure 2.

Figure 2

Query results

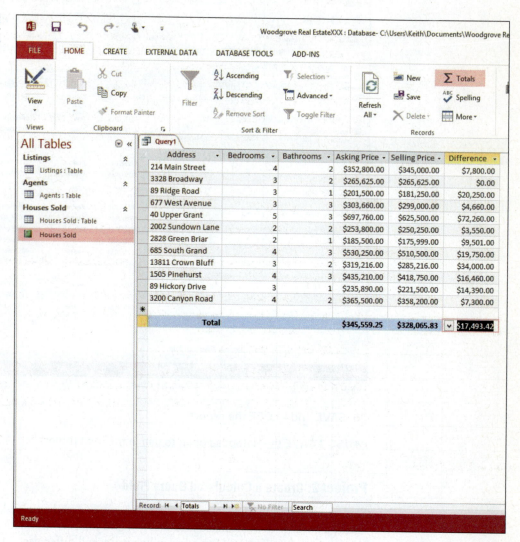

13. **SAVE** the query as **Price Difference Query** and close the query.

PAUSE. LEAVE the database open for the next project.

Project 3: Create a Chart

In the report you created, you want to have a pictorial view of the data along with the numbers. Use the Chart Wizard to insert a 3-D column chart into your existing report.

USE the database that is open from the previous project.

1. **OPEN** the **Houses Sold** report.

2. Switch to Design view.

3. On the DESIGN tab, in the Controls group, click the **Chart** button. The pointer changes to a plus sign with a chart icon.

4. Click in the upper-left corner of the **Page Footer section** and drag to the lower-right corner to create a rectangular placeholder where the chart will be inserted.

5. Release the mouse button. The first Chart Wizard dialog box appears.

6. Select the **Houses Sold** table as your data source and click the **Next >** button. The second Chart Wizard dialog box appears.

7. Double-click the **Asking Price**, **Selling Price**, and **Closing Date** fields to move them to the Fields for Chart box and click the **Next >** button. The third Chart Wizard dialog box appears.

8. Click the **3-D Column Chart** button, the second icon in the first row.

9. Click the **Next >** button. The fourth Chart Wizard dialog box appears.

10. Click and drag the **Selling Price** field button to the upper-left of the chart and drop it just below the **SumofAskingPrice** data list. Both the **SumofAskingPrice** and **SumofSellingPrice** fields should be listed.

11. Click the **Preview Chart** button. The Sample Preview dialog box appears, displaying a sample of your chart.

12. Click the **Close** button. The Sample Preview dialog box closes.

13. Click the **Next >** button. The fifth Chart Wizard dialog box appears.

14. Click the **Report Fields** down arrow and in the menu select **<No Field>**.

15. Click the **Chart Fields** down arrow and in the menu select **<No Field>**.

16. Click the **Next >** button. The sixth Chart Wizard dialog box appears.

17. Key **Summer 2015** in the Title box.

18. The *Yes, display a legend* button should be selected. If not, select it and click the **Finish** button. Access inserts your chart.

19. Click the chart to select it and resize it appropriately. Move the Date and Page # controls below the chart, if necessary.

20. On the **DESIGN** tab, in the Tools group, click the **Property Sheet** button.

21. Click the **DATA** tab of the Property Sheet. Click the down arrow at the end of the **Enabled** line and select **Yes**.

22. **CLOSE** the Property Sheet.

23. Switch to Report view.

24. On the HOME tab, in the Records group, click the **Refresh All** button.

25. Scroll to the bottom of the report to view your chart, which should look similar to Figure 3.

Figure 3

Report with 3-D Column Chart

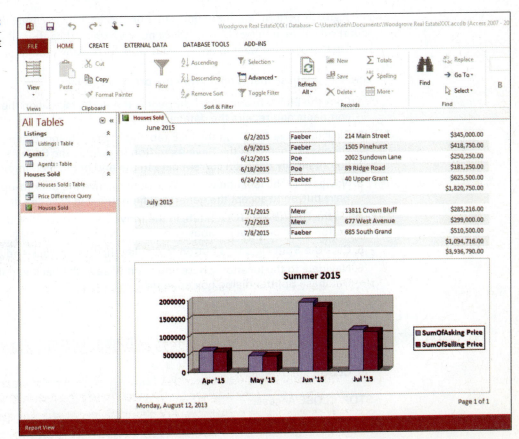

26. **SAVE** and **CLOSE** the report.

PAUSE. LEAVE the database open for the next project.

Project 4: Export Data and Save Specification

You need to provide listing information to the agents in your office in another format, so you export the data to Excel. Because you will perform this export operation on a regular basis, you save the specification for future use.

USE the database that is open from the previous project.

1. In the Navigation Pane, select the **Listings: Table**.
2. On the EXTERNAL DATA tab, in the Export group, click **Excel**. The Export - Excel Spreadsheet dialog box appears.
3. If you want to specify a different destination for the data you want to export, click **Browse** to open the File Save dialog box, choose a folder, and then click **Save**.
4. Click the **Export data with formatting and layout** checkbox and then click the **Open the destination file after the export operation is complete** checkbox.
5. Click **OK**. Excel opens and the new worksheet with exported data is displayed.
6. **CLOSE** the worksheet and **CLOSE** Excel.
7. Switch to Access.
8. On the Save Export Steps screen, click the **Save export steps** checkbox to display the specification details.
9. In the Description box, key **Export listing information to Excel**. Click **Save Export**.

PAUSE. LEAVE the database open for the next project.

Project 5: Maintain, Back Up, and Split a Database

You regularly perform routine maintenance on the database to ensure data integrity. You decide to split the database into two files to reduce network traffic, but after all the work you have put into the database you first want to protect your work by backing it up to prevent data loss.

USE the database that is open from the previous project.

1. Click the **FILE** tab, and click **Compact & Repair Database** on the Info menu. Access compacts and repairs the database.
2. Click the **Save As** tab on the FILE tab and in the Advanced category, click **Back Up Database,** then click the **Save As** button to display the Save As dialog box. Access automatically adds the current date to the end of the filename.
3. Navigate to the location where you want to save the backed-up database then click the **Save** button to accept the generated filename and save the database.
4. On the DATABASE TOOLS tab, in the Move Data group, click the **Access Database** button to display the Database Splitter Wizard.
5. Click the **Split Database** button to display the Create Back-end Database dialog box.
6. Navigate to the location where you want to save the back-end file and click **Split**. The Database Splitter dialog box appears.
7. Click **OK**.
8. **CLOSE** the database.

9. **OPEN** *Woodgrove Real EstateXXX_be*. Notice that it contains only the tables for the database.
10. **CLOSE** the database.

STOP. CLOSE Access.

Matrix Skill	Objective Number	Lesson Number
Create and Manage a Database	**1**	
Create a New Database	1.1	
Create new databases	1.1.1	2
Create databases using templates	1.1.2	2
Create databases in older formats	1.1.3	15
Create databases using wizards	1.1.4	5
Manage Relationships and Keys	1.2	
Edit references between tables	1.2.1	3
Create and modify relationships	1.2.2	3
Set primary key fields	1.2.3	3
Enforce referential integrity	1.2.4	3
Set foreign keys	1.2.5	3
View relationships	1.2.6	3
Navigate through a Database	1.3	
Navigate to specific records	1.3.1	3
Set a form as the startup option	1.3.2	15
Use navigation forms	1.3.3	10
Set navigation options	1.3.4	1
Change views	1.3.5	1
Protect and Maintain a Database	1.4	
Compact databases	1.4.1	15
Repair databases	1.4.2	15
Backup databases	1.4.3	15
Split databases	1.4.4	15
Encrypt databases with a password	1.4.5	15
Merge databases	1.4.6	15
Recover data from backups	1.4.7	15

Matrix Skill	Objective Number	Lesson Number
Print and Export a Database	1.5	
Print reports	1.5.1	11
Print records	1.5.2	11
Maintain backward compatibility	1.5.3	15
Save databases as templates	1.5.4	15
Save databases to external locations	1.5.5	15
Export to alternate formats	1.5.6	14
Build Tables	**2.0**	
Create a Table	2.1	
Create new tables	2.1.1	2, 9
Import external data into tables	2.1.2	14
Create linked tables from external sources	2.1.3	14
Import tables from other databases	2.1.4	14
Create tables from templates and application parts	2.1.5	2
Format a Table	2.2	
Hide fields in tables	2.2.1	3
Change data formats	2.2.2	9
Add total rows	2.2.3	9
Add table descriptions	2.2.4	4
Rename tables	2.2.5	4
Manage Records	2.3	
Update records	2.3.1	3
Add new records	2.3.2	3
Delete records	2.3.3	3
Append records from external data	2.3.4	14
Find and replace data	2.3.5	3
Sort records	2.3.6	3
Filter records	2.3.7	3
Group records	2.3.8	11
Create and Modify Fields	2.4	
Add fields to tables	2.4.1	4
Add validation rules to fields	2.4.2	4
Change field captions	2.4.3	4

Matrix Skill	Objective Number	Lesson Number
Change field sizes	2.4.4	4
Change field data types	2.4.5	1
Configure fields to auto-increment	2.4.6	9
Set default values	2.4.7	4
Use input masks	2.4.8	4
Delete fields	2.4.9	4
Create Queries	**3.0**	
Create a Query	3.1	
Run queries	3.1.1	7
Create crosstab queries	3.1.2	12
Create parameter queries	3.1.3	7
Create action queries	3.1.4	12
Create multi-table queries	3.1.5	7, 12
Save queries	3.1.6	7
Delete queries	3.1.7	7
Modify a Query	3.2	
Rename queries	3.2.1	7
Add new fields	3.2.2	12
Remove fields	3.2.3	12
Hide fields	3.2.4	7
Sort data within queries	3.2.5	7
Format fields within queries	3.2.6	12
Utilize Calculated Fields and Grouping within a Query	3.3	
Add calculated fields	3.3.1	12
Add conditional logic	3.3.2	12
Group and summarize data	3.3.3	12
Use comparison operators	3.3.4	12
Use basic operators	3.3.5	12
Create Forms	**4.0**	
Create a Form	4.1	
Create new forms	4.1.1	5
Create forms with application parts	4.1.2	10
Save forms	4.1.3	5
Delete forms	4.1.4	5

Matrix Skill	Objective Number	Lesson Number
Set Form Controls	4.2	
Move form controls	4.2.1	8
Add form controls	4.2.2	8
Modify data sources	4.2.3	8
Remove form controls	4.2.4	8
Set form control properties	4.2.5	8
Manage labels	4.2.6	8
Format a Form	4.3	
Modify Tab order in forms	4.3.1	8
Format print layouts	4.3.2	8
Sort records	4.3.3	5
Apply themes	4.3.4	5
Change margins	4.3.5	8
Insert backgrounds	4.3.6	8
Auto-order forms	4.3.7	8
Insert headers and footers	4.3.8	8
Insert images	4.3.9	8
Modify existing forms	4.3.10	8
Create Reports	**5.0**	
Create a Report	5.1	
Create new reports	5.1.1	6
Create reports with application parts	5.1.2	2
Delete reports	5.1.3	6
Set Report Controls	5.2	
Group data by fields	5.2.1	11
Sort data	5.2.2	6
Add sub-forms	5.2.3	11
Modify data sources	5.2.4	13
Add report controls	5.2.5	8, 13
Manage labels	5.2.6	8
Format a Report	5.3	
Format reports into multiple columns	5.3.1	8
Add calculated fields	5.3.2	8
Set margins	5.3.3	8

Matrix Skill	Objective Number	Lesson Number
Add backgrounds	5.3.4	8
Change report orientation	5.3.5	11
Change sort order	5.3.6	6
Insert headers and footers	5.3.7	8
Insert images	5.3.8	8
Insert page numbers	5.3.9	8
Apply themes	5.3.10	6
Modify existing reports	5.3.11	8

Glossary

action query changes the data in its datasource or creates a new table.

aggregate functions functions that calculate values across a range of data, such as in a column.

append query type of action query that adds the records in the query's result set to the end of an existing table.

Application Parts predefined templates that you can add to an existing database to help extend its functionality.

ascending order that sorts data from beginning to end, such as from A to Z.

B

back-end file in a split database, the database that contains the tables.

Backstage view a menu of options and commands that allows you to access various screens to perform common tasks with your database files.

backup a copy of a file.

badges small square labels where KeyTips are located.

Blank Forms category that contains a collection of 10 form parts that allow you to add predefined forms to a database.

Blank Form tool creates a new form in Layout view.

bound control a control that uses a field in a table or query as the data source.

C

calculated control a control that displays the result of a calculation or expression.

calculated field a column in a query that results from an expression.

Change Help Location menu lets you choose between the help topics that are available online and the help topics installed in your computer offline.

chart a graphical representation of data.

chart body the main area that displays the chart.

Chart Wizard asks you questions to quickly create a customized chart.

common filters popular filters available as context menu commands, depending on the type and values of the field.

composite key two or more primary keys in a table.

conditional formatting changes the appearance of a control or the value in a control when certain conditions are met.

control an object that displays data, performs actions, and lets you improve the look and usability of a form or report.

control layouts align controls horizontally and vertically to give reports or forms a uniform appearance.

control tab order refers to the order in which the selection, or focus, moves from field to field in a form or report.

Control Wizard helps you create controls such as command buttons, list boxes, combo boxes, and option groups.

cross join a join in which each row from one table is combined with each row from another table.

crosstab query calculates a sum, average, count, or other type of total on records and then groups the results by two types of information: one down the left side of the datasheet and the other across the top.

D

database a tool for collecting and organizing information.

Database Documenter provides detailed information about a database and presents it as a report that can be printed.

database management system (DBMS) enables you to easily collect large volumes of data organized into categories of related information. This type of database allows you to store, organize, and manage your data, no matter how complex it is, and then retrieve and present it in various formats and reports.

database properties details about a file that describe or identify it.

Database Splitter wizard that can split the database into two files: one that contains the tables, and one that contains the queries, forms, reports, and other objects created from the tables.

database template a file (extension type *.accdt) that can be used to create a new, prefabricated database.

datasheet the visual representation of the data contained in a table or of the results returned by a query.

data type controls the type of data a field will contain—whether it is text, number, date/time, or some other type of data.

decrypting removing the password from a file that has been encrypted.

delete query type of action query that removes rows matching the criteria that you specify from one or more tables.

delimited file a text file where each record appears on a separate line and the fields are separated by a single character.

delimiter any character that does not appear in the field values, such as a tab, semicolon, comma, space, and so on.

descending order that sorts data from the end to the beginning, such as from Z to A.

dialog box launcher a small arrow in the lower-right corner of the group that you click to launch a dialog box that displays additional options or information.

E

encrypting scrambling data in a way that can only be reconverted by an authorized user who has the password.

Expression Builder a feature that provides names of the fields and controls in a database, lists the operators available, and has built-in functions to help you create an expression.

F

field each column in a table.

field list a window that lists all the fields in the underlying record source or database object.

File tab accesses the Backstage view.

filter a set of rules for determining which records will be displayed.

filter by form allows users to filter several fields in a form or find a specific record.

fixed-width file a text file where each record appears on a separate line and the width of each field remains consistent across records.

foreign key a primary key from one table that is used in another table.

Form Design button a tool that creates a new blank form in Design view.

Form tool creates a form with a single mouse-click.

Form Wizard a form building tool that allows you to select the fields that will appear on the form, choose the form layout, and choose a predefined style, if desired.

forms database objects that control data entry and data views and provide visual cues that make data easier to work with.

front-end file a database that contains the queries, forms, reports, and other objects created from the tables.

G

group footer the section of the report where the data in the group is summarized.

group header the section of a report where the name of a grouped field is displayed and printed.

grouping field a field by which data is grouped.

grouping intervals establish the way that records are groupedtogether.

grouping levels the nested arrangement of the groups in a report.

groups common commands arranged by tabs.

H

hierarchical forms form/subform combinations, also called mater/detail forms or parent/child forms.

I

inner join type of join which includes rows in the query only when the joined field matches records in both tables.

innermost field a secondary sort field in a multifield sort.

input mask placeholder characters that require users to enter dates in a specific format, for example, DD-MM-YYYY.

J

join a relationship between identical fields in different tables.

K

KeyTips small letters and numbers on the Ribbon that execute commands when used with the ALT key. Every command on the Ribbon has a KeyTip.

L

Label Wizard helps you create a label-sized report that you can use to print labels.

left outer join a join where the query includes all of the rows from the table on the left and only those records from the table on the right that match the join field in the left table.

legend displays a list of the colors, shapes, or patterns used as categories in a chart.

linked table a new table created when a database is linked to an Excel worksheet.

Long text data type that can display up to 64,000 characters on the screen, but can store about one gigabyte of text.

M

main form the primary form in a form/subform combination.

make table query type of action query that creates a new table and then creates records in it by copying records from an existing table.

Multiple Items tool creates a customizable form that displays multiple records.

multivalued lookup field a field that lets you select more than one choice from a list, without having to create a more advanced database design.

N

Navigation form includes a set of navigation tabs that you can click to display forms and reports.

normal forms standards and guidelines that can be used to determine if your database is structured correctly.

normalization he process of applying rules to your database design to ensure that you have divided your information items into the appropriate tables.

null value a marker that a value does not exist for a field and is differentiated from a value that has been missed being entered by a user.

O

object dependencies describe how objects in a database rely on other components to function properly.

objects elements in a database, such as forms, queries, tables, and reports.

outer join type of join that includes all of the rows from one table in the query results and only those rows from the other table that match the join field in the first table.

outermost field the primary sort field in a multifield sort.

P

parameter query query in which the user interactively specifies one or more criteria values.

PDF a file format that maintains the exact layout of the original file and can easily be shared.

primary key a column that uniquely identifies each row, such as Student ID Number.

Print Preview displays a report as it will look when printed.

properties controls the appearance or behavior characteristics for objects and related parts like fields and controls.

Q

queries database objects that enable stored data to be searched and retrieved.

query criterion a rule that identifies the records you want to include in the query result.

Quick Access Toolbar contains the commands that you use most often, such as Save, Undo, and Redo.

Quick Start category of templates that contains a collection of predefined objects arranged by parts for tracking things such as comments, contacts, and issues.

Quick Start field a predefined set of characteristics and properties that describes a field, including a field name, a data type, and a number of other field properties.

R

record   a row in a database table.

record source   the table or query that provides the data used to generate a report.

redundant data   duplicate information.

referential integrity   an option that you can select in the Edit Relationships dialog box to prevent orphan records.

relational database   stores information in separate tables and these tables are connected or linked by a defined relationship that ties the data together.

reports   database objects that present your information in ways that are most useful to you.

Ribbon   a graphic band located across the top of the screen that contains tabs and groups of commands.

right outer join   type of join where the query includes all of the rows from the table on the right and only those rows from the table on the left that match the join field in the right table.

S

Short text   data type used to store up to 255 characters of data in a field and is a good data type for a field that stores small amounts of text, such as names, cities, and states.

select query   query that creates subsets of data that you can use to answer specific questions or to supply data to other database objects such as forms and reports.

SELECT statement   a Structured Query Language (SQL) command that instructs the Microsoft Access database engine to return information from the database as a set of records.

sort   to arrange data alphabetically, numerically, or chronologically.

specification   contains all the information Access needs to repeat an import or export operation without user input.

split form   gives you two views of your data at the same time—in both Form view and Datasheet view.

stacked layout   layout where controls arranged vertically with a label on the left and the control on the right.

subform   a form that is inserted into another form.

subquery   a SELECT statement that is inside another select or action query.

T

tab   an area of activity on the Ribbon.

table   the most basic database object; stores data in categories

Table Analyzer   a wizard that performs the normalization process for you by examining a table design and suggesting a way to divide the table for maximum efficiency.

tabular layout   layout where controls are arranged in rows and columns like a spreadsheet, with labels across the top.

templates   ready-to-use databases that contain all of the tables, queries, forms, and reports needed for performing specific tasks.

Themes   command that applies a predefined color and font scheme to a form or report.

Total Row   a row inserted at the bottom of a table that provides a menu of functions for each column in the row.

U

unequal join   a type of join that is not based on the equivalence of the joined fields.

unbound control   a control that displays information such as lines, shapes, or pictures; it is not bound to a field.

update query   type of action query that changes a set of records according to criteria that you specify.

V

validation rule   an expression that limits the values that can be entered in the field.

validation text   specifies the text in the error message that appears when a user violates a validation rule.

W

wildcard   characters used to find words or phrases that contain specific letters or combinations of letters.

X

XPS   file format that preserves document formatting, can be easily shared, printed, and archived, and is more secure.

Z

zero-length string   a string that contains no characters; you use the string to indicate that you know no value exists for a particular field.

Index

A

Access Help dialog box, 25f, 26f
Access Options dialog box, 21f, 468, 469f
Action query, 356–359, 357f, 358f, 359f
  append query, 356
  delete query, 356
  make table query, 356
  update query, 356
Adobe Portable Document Format, 51
Aggregate fields, 322, 323f
Aggregate functions, 275, 278t, 378–383, 380f, 381f, 382f, 383f. *See also* Queries, advanced
  in Design view, 382f
  results, 381f, 383f
Alignment of control, 249
Anchoring, controls, 246–249, 246f, 247f, 248f
Anchor menu, 248f
Append query, 356–359, 357f, 358f, 359f
Applicable Filter dialog box, 353f
Application Parts Blank Forms, 295
Application Parts button and menu, 284f
Application Parts gallery, 46–47, 46f, 47f
ARRANGE tab, 240f
Ascending, 72
Assets template database, 42f
Asset templates, 40f
Attachment data type, 69–71
Attachments dialog box, 70f

B

Back-end Database dialog box, 475f
Back-end file, 474
Backstage view, 22, 22f, 23, 24f. *See also* Database
Backup, 451–453, 452f, 453f. *See also* Database tools
Badges, 21
Blank database, 43–45, 44f, 51f
Blank desktop database screen, 44f
Blank forms, 295–299, 296f, 297f, 298f
  in Design view, 129f
  in Form view, 296f
  in Layout view and Field List pane, 297f
Blank Form tool, 132
Blank report in Design view, 165f
Blank table in Design view, 265f

Bound controls, 216–221, 221f
Button controls using wizard, 227–231, 228f, 229f, 230f

C

Calculated controls, 221–224, 222f, 223f
Calculated query field, 373–378, 374t, 375f, 376f, 377f, 378f
Caption property field, 108
Change Help Collection Menu, 24–27, 25f, 26f. *See also* Database
Change page orientation, 252–255. *See also* Controls in reports/ forms
Chart
  defined, 390
  in Report Design view, 405f
  types, changing, 403–405, 404f, 405f
Chart body, 390
Chart control, 390
Chart formatting, 395–396
  chart options, changing, 396–399, 396f–399f
  format options, changing, 400–403, 400f, 401f, 402f
Chart Options dialog box, 396, 397f
Chart Type button and menu, 404f
Chart Type dialog box, 404f
Chart with Chart Wizard, 390, 391f–395f
Chart Wizard, 390
Chart Wizard dialog box, 391f, 392f, 393f, 394f
Client object, 406
Combo Box Wizard, 226f, 227f
Comments table, 47f
Common filters, 141
Compact and Repair command, 455–456, 456f
Competency assessment
  controls in reports/forms, 257–259
  data, displaying/sharing, 411–412
  data, exporting/importing, 446–447
  database tables, 55
  database tools, 477–478
  forms, 147–148
  forms, advanced, 303–304
  queries, advanced, 385–386
  query, 208
  reports, 175–176
  tables, advanced, 279–280

tables and database records, 89–90
tables and fields, 121–122
Composite keys, 66, 67
Conditional formatting on controls, 238, 239f
Conditional Formatting Rules Manager dialog box, 238
Configuring of database, 468–470, 469f, 470f. *See also* Database tools
Control, defined, 213
Control Formatting group, 234
Control label and control, 216
Control layout, 240–243, 241f, 242f
  stacked, 240
  tabular, 240
Control Padding button, 245f
Controls in reports/forms
  add/move/remove, 243–246, 244f, 245f
  alignment/size/position of controls, 249–251, 250f, 251f
  arranging/anchoring, 246–249, 246f, 247f, 248f
  bound controls, 216–221, 221f
  Button controls using wizard, 227–231, 228f, 229f, 230f
  calculated controls, 221–224, 222f, 223f
  change page orientation, 252–255
  competency assessment, 257–259
  conditional formatting on, 238, 239f
  control layout, 240–243, 241f, 242f
  control tab order, 231–233, 232f, 233f
  Control Wizard, 224–227, 225f, 226f, 227f
  formatting controls on form, 236–238, 236f, 237f
  formatting controls on report, 234–236, 234f
  knowledge assessment, 256–257
  mastery assessment, 261–262
  page margins, 252–255
  proficiency assessment, 259–261
  unbound controls, 213–216, 220f
Control tab order, 231–233, 232f, 233f
Control Wizard, 224–227, 225f, 226f, 227f
Criteria, adding to query, 195–200, 196f, 197f, 198f, 199f, 199t–200t
Cross joins, 371. *See also* Joins
Crosstab query, 340–345, 341f–344f

Crosstab Query Wizard, 341f, 342f
Custom filter dialog box, 75f, 141f, 142f, 205f
Customize Quick Access Toolbar menu, 20f, 21
Custom table
  creating, 264–267, 265f, 266f
  in Design view, 267f
  inserting/deleting rows, 268, 268f

D

Data, exporting/importing
  competency assessment, 446–447
  exporting
    from query to Word, 437–439, 438f
    from table to Excel, 435–437, 435t, 436f, 437f
    export specifications, 439–440, 439f
    running, 442–443, 442f, 443f
    saving, 440–441
  importing
    external data source, 423–427, 424f–427f
    from specific source, 416–423, 417t, 418f–423f
    import specifications
    running, 432–434
    saving, 428–432, 429f–432f
  knowledge assessment, 444–446
  mastery assessment, 448–449
  proficiency assessment, 447–448
Data, finding and replacing, 67–69, 68f
Database
  Access 2013, starting, 3–5
    in Windows 7, 5, 5f
    in Windows 8, 3–4, 4f
  Access 2013 Window, working in, 8–18
    Navigation Pane, using, 9–14, 10f, 11f, 12f, 13f, 14f
    object tabs, using, 14, 15f, 16f
    view, changing, 16–18, 17f, 18f
  Backstage view, 23, 24f
  competency assessment, 34–35
  creating
    blank database, 43–45, 44f
    template, use of, 39–43, 39f, 40f, 41f, 42f, 43f
  data needs/types
    database fields, reviewing, 27–28, 28f
    database tables, defining, 31–33, 32f
    data types for fields, 28, 29f, 30f, 31t

Database (*continued*)
defined, 3
existing database, opening, 5–8, 6f, 7f, 8f
knowledge assessment, 33–34
mastery assessment, 36
Microsoft Access Help button
Change Help Collection Menu, 24–27, 25f, 26f
on-screen tools
Quick Access Toolbar, 20–22, 20f, 21f, 22f
Ribbon, using, 18, 19f
proficiency assessment, 35–36
Database Documenter, 472–474, 473f, 474f
Database fields, reviewing, 27–28, 28f
Database management system (DBMS), 3
Database object
printing, 408–410, 408f, 409f, 410f
table, saving, 51–53, 51f, 52f
Database object as file type
Save Object As command, 406–407, 407f
Database object menu, 48f, 49f
Database properties, 463–465, 464t
Database splitter, 474–476, 475f
Database tables
competency assessment, 55
database creation
blank database, 43–45, 44f
template, use of, 39–43, 40f–43f
database object, saving
table, saving, 51–53, 51f, 52f
defining, 31–33, 32f
knowledge assessment, 53–54
mastery assessment, 56–57
proficiency assessment, 56
table, creating
from another table, 48–50, 48f, 49f, 50f
Application Parts gallery and Quick Start, 46–47, 46f, 47f
Database template, 457, 458f, 459f
Database tools
backup, 451–453, 452f, 453f
compacting/repairing database, 455–456, 456f
competency assessment, 477–478
configuring database options, 468–470, 469f, 470f
Database Documenter, 472–474, 473f, 474f
database properties, 463–465, 464t
encrypting/decrypting, 465–467, 466f
knowledge assessment, 477
mastery assessment, 479
merging databases, 461–463, 461f, 462f, 463f
Object Dependencies, 471–472, 472f
previous version, saving, 453–455, 454f, 455f
proficiency assessment, 478–479
splitting database, 474–476, 475f

template, database as, 457–460, 457t, 458f, 459f, 460f
DATABASE TOOLS tab, 471f
Data Labels tab, 399f
Datasheet, 16
Datasheet form, 136, 136f
Datasheet Formatting dialog box, 19f
Datasheet view, 18f, 59, 100
Data Type menu in Design view, 266f
Data types for fields, 28, 29f, 30f, 31t
Data validation rules, 106–108, 107f, 108f. *See also* Fields
Date and Time dialog box, 214f
Decrypting, 465
Default Value property, 100
Delete Field command, 114f
Delete field confirmation message, 115f
Delete field message, 114f
Delete query, 356, 366–370, 367f, 368f, 369f, 370f
Delete table confirmation message, 98f
Deleting
of field, 113–115, 114f, 115f
of records, 62, 64f
of report, 158–160
of rows, 268
of table, 98, 98f
Delimited file, 428
Delimiter, 428
Descending, 72
Description field control, 247f
Design Custom filter dialog boxiew
report in, 164–167, 164t, 165f, 166f
Design View, 17f, 100
fields inserted in, 131f
forms in, 128–132, 129f, 130f, 131f, 132f
Desktop faculty template preview screen, 40f
Desktop home inventory template preview screen, 39f
Destination workbook options, 435t
Detachment of documents, 69–71
Dialog box launcher, 18, 19f
Doctors form with subform, 294f
Documents, attaching and detaching, 69–71, 70f, 71f
Duplicate information, 32
Duplicates for Industry Friends query, 186f

E

Edit/Delete shortcut menu, 85
Edit destination file, 443f
Editing of data, 62
Edit Relationships dialog box, 84f
Encrypting, 465
Entering of records, 62, 63f
Error checking, 468
Error Checking Options button, 328f
Excel, data import from, 418, 418f
Excel data, 427f
Excel worksheet, 437f
Export–Excel Spreadsheet dialog box, 436f

Export of data
from query to Word, 437–439, 438f
from table to Excel, 435–437, 435t, 436f, 437f
Export operation message, 443f
Export – RTF File dialog box, 438f
Export specifications, 439–440, 439f. *See also* Data, exporting/importing
running, 442–443, 442f, 443f
saving, 440–441
Export Text Wizard file options, 439f
Expression Builder, 222, 223f, 375f
Expression Builder button, 107f
External data source, 423–427, 424f–427f. *See also* Import of data
EXTERNAL DATA tab, 432, 435, 461

F

Field, 27
Field list, 194
Field List pane, 129, 129f, 130f, 165f, 218f
Field Name in Design view, 265f
Field Properties in Design view, 267f
Fields
captions, entering, 108
creating, 99–100, 109–113, 111f, 112f, 113f
data validation rules, 106–108, 107f, 108f
deleting, 113–115, 114f, 115f
freezing/unfreezing/hiding/unhiding, 79–81, 80f, 81f
input masks, defining, 102, 102f, 103f, 104f
multivalued lookup fields, 115, 116f, 117f, 118f, 119f
properties, setting, 100–102, 100t–101t, 101f
zero-length strings in, 105, 106f
Field view options, 71
File Name box and folder icon, 41f
File New Database dialog box, 41f
FILE tab, 23
Fill Effects dialog box, 401f
Filter, 74, 138
by form, 143–146, 144f, 145f, 146f, 354f
as query, saving, 353–355, 353f, 354f, 355f
removing, 78–79, 78f
Filtered query, 206f
Filter Indicator, 60
Filtering, 71
data within forms, 141, 141f, 142f, 143f
data within query, 204–206, 205f, 206f
data within report, 171–173, 172f, 173f
of data within table, 74–78, 75f, 76f, 77f
Filter menu, 75f, 77f
Final Table Analyzer Wizard dialog box, 274f

Find and Replace dialog box, 67, 68, 68f
Find command, 173–174
Find dialog box, 175f
Find Duplicates Query, 183–186, 184f, 185f, 186f
Finding data within report, 173–174, 174f
Finding of data, 67–69, 68f
Find Unmatched query, 189–192, 189f–192f. *See also* Query
First Normal Form (1NF), 33
Fixed-width file, 428
Fonts menu, 168f
Foreign key, 65
Format Chart Area dialog box, 400f
Format Data Series dialog box, 401f
Format options, changing, 400–403, 400f, 401f, 402f. *See also* Chart formatting
Format Painter button, 234
FORMAT tab in Report Design Tools, 233f
Formatting, chart. *See* Chart formatting
Formatting of controls
on form, 236–238, 236f, 237f
on report, 234–236, 234f
Form Design button, 128
Form Design view
with controls, 250f
with right-aligned controls, 251f
Form filter, 144f, 146f
Form filter field options, 145f
Form in Layout view, 138
FORM LAYOUT TOOLS DESIGN contextual tab, 213f
Form print layout, 254f
Forms, 9. *See also* Forms, advanced
creating, 126–127
deleting, 127
in Design view, 128–132, 129f, 130f, 131f, 132f
filter by, 143–146, 144f, 145f, 146f
filtering data within, 141, 141f, 142f, 143f
Form Wizard, using, 134–136, 135f, 136f
in Layout view, 132–134, 133f, 134f
simple form, creating, 127, 127f
sorting data within, 138–140, 139f, 140f
theme application, 136, 137f, 138f
Forms, advanced
blank forms, 295–299, 296f, 297f, 298f
competency assessment, 303–304
knowledge assessment, 302–303
mastery assessment, 305–306
multi-item form, 286–287, 286f
navigation forms, 299–301, 300f, 301f
proficiency assessment, 304–305
split form, 287, 287f, 288f, 289f, 290f, 291t
subform, 291–295, 292f, 293f, 294f

Forms group, 126, 126f
Form tool, 127
Form view, 132f
Form with background image, 237f
Form Wizard, 134–136, 135, 135f, 136f, 292f, 293f
Freezing, fields, 79
Front-end file, 474

G

Gridlines tab, 398f
Group, 11f, 14, 18
   defined, 313
Group, Sort, and Total pane, 170f, 171f
Group footer, 317, 318f
Group header, 317, 319f
Grouping field, 313
Grouping intervals, 313
Grouping Intervals dialog box, 315f
Grouping levels, 313
Grouping options, 319–321, 320f, 321f
Grouping Options button, 313

H

Help button, 24–27
Hidden fields, 79, 81f
Hierarchical form, 291
Hyperlink and Insert Image buttons, 217

I

Identifiers, 221
Import message, successful, 434f
Import Objects dialog box, 423f, 461f, 462f
Import of data
   external data source, 423–427, 424f–427f
   from specific source, 416–423, 417t, 418f–423f
Import specifications. See also Data, exporting/importing
   running, 432–434
   saving, 428–432, 429f–432f
Import Spreadsheet Wizard, 419f, 420f
Import Text Wizard, 429f, 430f
Inner join, 371. See also Join
Innermost field, 73
Input masks
   defining, 102, 102f, 103f, 104f
   to standardize business data, 105
Input Mask Wizard, 102f, 103f, 104f
Inserting of rows, 268, 275
Inventory Form in Design view, 230f

J

Join. See also Queries, advanced
   cross, 371
   defined, 370
   inner, 371
   Join Properties dialog box, 372f
   outer
      left, 371, 373f
      outer join
         right, 371
   unequal, 371

K

Keyboard, use of, 59, 60f. See also Record navigation
Keyboard Commands for navigating records, 60f
KeyTips, 21, 22f
Knowledge assessment
   controls in reports/forms, 256–257
   data, displaying/sharing, 410–411
   data, exporting/importing, 444–446
   database essentials, 33–34
   database tables, 53–54
   database tools, 477
   forms, 147
   forms, advanced, 302–303
   queries, advanced, 384–385
   query, 206–208
   reports, 175
   tables, advanced, 278–279
   tables and database records, 88–89
   tables and fields, 120–121

L

Label Wizard, 330–335, 331f, 332f, 333f, 334f
   dialog box, 331f, 332f, 333f
   label report, 334f
   prototype label, 332f
Layout view, form in, 132–134, 133f, 134f
Left outer join, 371. See also Joins
Legend, 390
Legend tab, 398f
Linked table, 423, 426f
Link Spreadsheet Wizard, 424f, 425f
Long Text data type, 29
Lookup Wizard, 116f, 117f, 118f

M

Main form, 291
Main report, 324
Make table query, 356, 360–362, 360f, 361f
Master/detail form, 291
Mastery assessment, 281–282
   controls in reports/forms, 261–262
   data, displaying/sharing, 413–414
   data, exporting/importing, 448–449
   database essentials, 36
   database tables, 56–57
   database tools, 479
   forms, 150–151
   forms, advanced, 305–306
   queries, advanced, 387–388
   query, 209
   reports, 178
   tables and database records, 91–92
   tables and fields, 123–124
Media field text filters, 141
Merging of databases, 461–463, 461f, 462f, 463f
Microsoft Access 2013, 453, 455f
   starting, 3–5
      in Windows 7, 5, 5f
      in Windows 8, 3–4, 4f
      tile, 4f

Microsoft Access Help, 24–27, 25f, 26f
Microsoft Access startup screen, 4f
Microsoft Graph toolbar, 403f
Microsoft Office Specialist (MOS) skills for Access 2013, 485–489
Microsoft Visual Basic, 230f
Multiple Items form, 286–287, 286f
Multiple tables, query from, 186–189, 186f, 187f, 188f
Multivalued lookup fields, 115, 116f, 117f, 118f, 119f. See also Fields

N

Name & Caption property, 100
Navigation button, 60–61, 61f, 285f. See also Record navigation
Navigation forms, 299–301
   displaying Doctors form, 300f
   displaying Doctors report, 301f
   in Layout view, 300f
Navigation Pane, 9–14, 10f–14f
   collapsed, 14f
   menu, 11f
   shortcut menu, 12f
Normal forms, 32–33
   First Normal Form (1NF), 33
   Second Normal Form (2NF), 33
   Third Normal Form (3NF), 33
Normalization, 32
Notepad with exported data, 443f
Null value, 199t

O

Object Definition report, 474f
Object Dependencies, 471–472, 472f. See also Database tools
Objects, 9, 12, 14, 16
Object tabs, 14, 15f, 16f
On-screen tools
   Quick Access Toolbar, 20–22, 20f, 21f, 22f
   Ribbon, using, 18, 19f
On-screen tools. See also Database
Open button menu, 8, 8f
Open dialog box, 6f
Operators, 221
Outer join. See also Join
   left, 371, 373f
   right, 371
Outermost field, 73
Overwrite message, 434f

P

Page header/footer, 164t
Page margins, 252–255
Page Numbers dialog box, 215f
Page Setup dialog box, 329f, 410f
Page Size group, 252
Parameter query, 195
Parameter query criteria, 198f
Parent/child form, 291
Password Required dialog box, 467f
Pie chart, 405f
Portable Document Format (PDF), 51, 406

Position of control, 249
Preview pane, 42f
Previous version, saving, 453–455, 454f, 455f. See also Database tools
Price field number filters, 142f
Price field shortcut menu, 139
Primary form, 291
Primary key, 27, 421
   defined, 65, 65f
   multifield, 66–67, 66f
Primary report, 324
Print dialog box, 409f
Print layout, 326–330, 327f, 328f, 329f
Print menu, 253f
Print Preview, 326
   report in, 334f
PRINT PREVIEW tab, 252f, 325, 326
Print Table Definition dialog box, 473f
Proficiency assessment, 280–281
   controls in reports/forms, 259–261
   data, displaying/sharing, 412–413
   data, exporting/importing, 447–448
   database essentials, 35–36
   database tables, 56
   database tools, 478–479
   forms, 149
   forms, advanced, 304–305
   queries, advanced, 386–387
   query, 209
   reports, 176, 177f
   tables and database records, 90–91
   tables and fields, 122–123
Properties, 94
   field, 99f, 100–102, 100t–101t, 101f
   table, 94–96, 95f
Properties dialog box, 409f
Property sheet, 217, 289f
Property Sheet Pane, 220f, 376f

Q

Queries group, 180, 180f
Query, 9
   competency assessment, 208
   creating, from table, 181–183, 181f, 182f, 183f
   criteria examples, 199t–200t
   defined, 180
   deleting, 181–183
   in Design view, 193
   filtering data within, 204–206, 205f, 206f
   Find Duplicates Query, 183–186, 184f, 185f, 186f
   knowledge assessment, 206–208
   mastery assessment, 210
   modifying
      adding criteria to, 195–200, 196f, 197f, 198f, 199f, 199t–200t
      adding table to, 193–194, 193f, 194f
      removing table from, 194–195

Query (*continued*)
from multiple tables, 186–189, 186f, 187f, 188f
proficiency assessment, 209
sorting data within, 200–204, 201f, 202f, 203f, 204f
unmatched records, 189–192, 189f, 190f, 191f, 192f
Query, advanced
action query, 356–359, 357f, 358f, 359f
competency assessment, 385–386
crosstab query, 340–345, 341f, 342f, 343f, 344f
delete query, 366–370, 367f, 368f, 369f, 370f
filter as query, saving, 353–355, 353f, 354f, 355f
knowledge assessment, 384–385
make table query, 360–362, 360f, 361f
mastery assessment, 387–388
modification
aggregate queries, 378–383, 380f, 381f, 382f, 383f
calculated field, 373–378, 374t, 375f, 376f, 377f, 378f
join, 370–373, 372f, 373f
proficiency assessment, 386–387
subquery, 345–352, 345t, 347f, 348f, 349f, 350f, 351f, 352f
update query, 362–366, 363t, 364f, 365f, 366f
Query criterion, 195, 196f
Query design grid, 347f
Query dialog box, 341f
QUERY TOOLS DESIGN tab, 192f, 193
Quick Access Toolbar, 20–22, 20f, 21f, 22f. *See also* On-screen tools
Quick Print command, 326
Quick Start, 46–47, 109
Quick Style gallery, 236f

R

Record, 27
Record navigation
deleting, 62, 64f
editing, 62
entering, 62, 63f
keyboard, use of, 59, 60f
navigation buttons, 60–61, 61f
Record Selector Box, 62f
Records Group, 62f
Record Shortcut Menu, 62f
Record source, 159
Redundant data, 32, 269
Referential integrity, 85
Relational database, 31
Remove Layout button, 243
Renaming of table, 96, 97f, 98f
Replacing of data, 67–69, 68f
Report and subform, 325f
REPORT DESIGN TOOLS
DESIGN contextual tab, 212, 212f

Report Design view, 244f
Report header, 164t, 215f
Reports, 9
competency assessment, 175–176
defined, 158
deleting, 158–160
in Design view, 164–167, 164t, 165f, 166f
filtering data within, 171–173, 172f, 173f
finding data within, 173–174, 174f
knowledge assessment, 175
mastery assessment, 178
proficiency assessment, 176, 177f
Report Wizard, 160–163, 161f, 162f, 163f
simple report, creating, 158–160, 159f
sorting data within, 169–171, 170f, 171f
theme, applying, 167–169, 168f
Reports, advanced
aggregate fields, creating, 322, 323f
group headers/footers, 317–319, 318f, 319f
grouping options, 319–321, 320f, 321f
groups, defining, 313
Label Wizard, 330–335, 331f, 332f, 333f, 334f
print layout, print preview for, 326–330, 327f, 328f, 329f
Report Wizard, 313–317, 313f, 314f, 315f, 316f, 317f
subform on, 324–325, 325f
Report Wizard, 160–163, 161f, 162f, 163f, 313–317, 313f, 314f, 315f, 316f, 317f
Report Wizard dialog box, 314f, 315f, 316f
Ribbon, 18, 19f, 240. *See also* On-screen tools
Right outer join, 371. *See also* Joins

S

Sample Preview dialog box, 393f
Save As dialog box, 52f, 128f, 453f
Save As Query dialog box, 355f
Save Object As command, 406–407, 407f
Second Normal Form (2NF), 33
Select query, 180, 183f
in Datasheet view, 364f
in Design view, 364f
SELECT statement, 345, 345t
Shortcut menu, 52f, 170f, 172f, 173f
Short Text data type, 29
Show Table button and dialog box, 83f
Show Table dialog box, 194f
Simple form, creating, 127, 127f
Simple Query Wizard, 182f, 183f

Simple report, creating/deleting, 158–160, 159f. *See also* Reports
Size of control, 249
Sizing & Ordering group, 249
Sort data, 72
Sorted query, 201f, 204f
Sort & Filter Group, 72f
Sorting, 71
data within forms, 138–140, 139f, 140f
data within query, 200–204, 201f, 202f, 203f, 204f
data within report, 169–171, 170f, 171f
of data within table, 72–74, 72f, 73f, 74f
Source data elements, 417t
Source object, 435, 435t
Specification, defined, 428
Split form, 286, 287, 287f, 288f, 289f, 290f, 291t
with datasheet, 290f
editing, 288f
properties related to, 291t
Splitter, database, 474–476, 475f
Stacked layout, 240, 242f. *See also* Control layout
Status field drop-down box options, 113f
Structured Query Language (SQL), 345, 351f
Student Details dialog box, 28f
Subform, 286, 291–295, 292f, 293f, 294f, 324
Subquery, 345–352, 345t, 347f, 348f, 349f, 350f, 351f, 352f
comparison, 346
expression, 346
results, 352f
Sqlstatement, 346
Subreport Wizard, 324
Summarizing of table data, 275–278, 276f, 277f, 278t

T

Table, 9
adding, to query, 193–194, 193f, 194f
creating (*See also* Database tables)
from another table, 48–50, 48f, 49f, 50f
Application Parts gallery and Quick Start, 46–47, 46f, 47f
deleting, 98, 98f
properties, modifying, 94–96, 95f
removing, from query, 194–195
renaming of table, 96, 97f, 98f
saving, 51–53, 51f, 52f
Table Analyzer, 268–274, 269f–274f
Table data, summarizing, 275–278, 276f, 277f, 278t
Table open in Access work area, 10f
Table relationships

defining, 82–84, 83f, 84f
modifying, 84–86, 85f
printing, 86, 87f
Tab Order dialog box, 232f, 233f
Tab shortcut menu, 16f
Tabular layout, 240, 242f. *See also* Control layout
Templates, 39
database as, 457–460, 457t, 458f, 459f, 460f
use of, 39–43, 39f, 40f, 41f, 42f, 43f
Text Align property, 100
Text box control, 222f
Text files, 439
Themes, 136, 137f, 138f, 167–169, 168f. *See also* Forms
Themes gallery, 137f, 168f
Third Normal Form (3NF), 33
Toggle Filter button, 171
Total row, 275, 276f, 277f
Total row menu options, 380f
Totals command, 322, 323f
Touch/Mouse Mode command, 20

U

Unbound controls, 213–216, 220f
Unequal joins, 371. *See also* Joins
Unfreezing, fields, 79
Unhiding, fields, 79, 81f
Unmatched records, finding, 189–192, 189f, 190f, 191f, 192f. *See also* Query
Update alert message, 365f
Update query, 356, 362–366, 363t, 364f, 365f, 366f

V

Validation field properties, modified, 108f
Validation rule
data types, 106
field properties, 106
field sizes, 106
table properties, 106
Validation text, 106
View Code button, 230f
View Menu, 16–18, 17f, 18f
Visual Basic for Applications (VBA), 227, 275, 295

W

Wildcard characters, 68
Windows 7, Access 2013 in, 5, 5f
Windows 8, Access 2013 in, 3–4, 4f
Windows 8 Start screen, 4f

X

XML Paper Specification (XPS), 51, 406

Z

Zero-length strings, 105, 106f. *See also* Fields
Zoom dialog box, 95f